Advertising

fourth edition

MAURICE I. MANDELL

Prentice-Hall, Inc., Englewood Cliffs, New Jersey 07632

Library of Congress Cataloging in Publication Data

MANDELL, MAURICE I.
  Advertising.

  Bibliography: p.
  Includes index.
  1. Advertising. I. Title.
HF5823.M219 1984   659.1   83-26911
ISBN 0-13-014499-1

Editorial/production supervision by Pamela Wilder
Interior and cover design by Jayne Conte
Manufacturing buyer: Ed O'Dougherty

Quotations on pages 63, 67, 145 from John O'Toole, *The Trouble with Advertising . . .*, copyright © 1981. By permission: Chelsea House, New York. Quotations on pages 130, 184, 255, 433, 464 from Wm. A. Marsteller, *Creative Management*, copyright © 1981. By permission: Crain Books, Chicago. Quotations on pages 6, 13, 17, 30, 34, 48, 50, 51, 56, 73, 80, 89, 91, 96, 117, 147, 148, 162, 166, 171, 179, 181, 188, 193, 208, 209, 212, 224, 228, 229, 249, 257, 266, 273, 282, 285, 288, 313, 318, 320, 324, 331, 340, 341, 346, 348, 354, 355, 357, 359, 380, 389, 401, 404, 432, 441, 442, 463, 490, 492, 496, 501, 506, 511, 535, 541, 544, 562, 563, 565, 588, 611 from *Lasting Ideas, Some Expressions on the Art of Persuasion Wise and Witty Enough to Endure*, copyright © 1969. By permission: The Reader's Digest Association, Pleasantville, N. Y. Quotations on pages 15, 32, 53, 55, 65, 88, 95, 122, 127, 128, 146, 163, 164, 167, 185, 203, 225, 251, 271, 287, 315, 316, 339, 356, 399, 403, 436, 450, 468, 493, 515, 516, 531, 559, 561, 567 from various issues of *Time*. Copyright © 1950, 1951, 1952, 1953, 1954, 1957, 1958, 1959, by Time Inc. All rights reserved. Reprinted by permission from TIME. The quotations on pages 481 and 618 from a speech by William Bernbach at the Doyle Dane Bernbach International Seminar, New York, April 1982. By permission: Doyle Dane Bernbach Inc. Quotation on page 592 is the title of the book of Jacques Séguéla published by Flammarion, 1979, France.

Printed in the United States of America
10 9 8 7 6 5 4 3 2 1

ISBN 0-13-014499-1

Prentice-Hall International, Inc., *London*
Prentice-Hall of Australia Pty. Limited, *Sydney*
Editora Prentice-Hall do Brasil, Ltda., *Rio de Janeiro*
Prentice-Hall Canada Inc., *Toronto*
Prentice-Hall of India Private Limited, *New Delhi*
Prentice-Hall of Japan, Inc., *Tokyo*
Prentice-Hall of Southeast Asia Pte. Ltd., *Singapore*
Whitehall Books Limited, Wellington, *New Zealand*

to dear Natalie . . . and David and Lisa

About the Author

Before entering an academic career, Maurice I. Mandell worked in the advertising business in New York City, including the advertising departments of a retailer, a manufacturer, and an advertising medium, and also in several advertising agencies. He holds degrees from New York, Syracuse, and Indiana Universities, receiving his doctorate in marketing (advertising) and journalism.

Dr. Mandell founded and served as the first chairperson of the Department of Marketing at Bowling Green State University, after having taught previously at several other schools. He has also taught and lectured in such countries as Finland, Norway, Sweden, Bangladesh, Colombia, and Brazil. In addition, he has been active as an advertising and marketing consultant and writer both here and abroad. He is co-author of *Marketing,* 2nd edition (Prentice-Hall), as well as author of a variety of journal articles.

In 1981, Dr. Mandell moved to Sarasota, Florida, where he continues to write, consult, and serve as a visiting professor at a number of universities, while returning to Bowling Green State to teach each summer term.

Over the years, Dr. Mandell has combined the practice of advertising with its teaching, not only through consulting but also through fellowships with major advertisers and advertising agencies in Chicago and New York. Awards include those for scholarship, service, and outstanding teaching. He has also been active in the American Academy of Advertising and the American Marketing Association.

CONTENTS

v

ADVERTISING MANAGEMENT

7

8

9

10

Contents

vii

ADVERTISING MEDIA PLANNING AND SELECTION PART THREE

Contents

ix

ADVERTISING CREATIVITY

PART FOUR

Contents

xi

PART
FIVE **SOME OTHER VIEWS OF ADVERTISING**

Contents
xiii

PREFACE

Advertising today is an instrument of major proportions, both as an economic tool and as a social phenomenon. Virtually every organization in the business community makes use of advertising. And the public can well attest to this extensive use of advertising, for surely no one has escaped exposure to this highly effective tool of communication and persuasion. As a result, there is an ever-growing interest in learning more about advertising.

This book has been designed as an introductory overview of advertising. It is intended not only for those who are interested in careers in advertising but also for those who are interested in such diverse activities as the many other facets of business, the mass communications media, and the management of eleemosynary organizations. As advertising increases in importance as a communication and persuasion tool, it behooves all such persons to understand it and evaluate its potential contribution to the success of all these enterprises.

To all those who will affect and be affected by advertising, this text aims to provide a solid foundation of understanding of why and how advertising works. To be sure, we all have *some* knowledge of advertising, because as consumers we are the target of at least some advertising efforts. Unfortunately, such a limited knowledge tends to give many people a distorted view of advertising, and it is hoped that the reader can come away from this book with a more balanced insight on the subject.

It must be noted, however, that the more I examine the field of advertising, the more I realize that it is a most dynamic subject—ever changing, ever evolving. Therefore, I have consciously avoided making too many hard-and-fast statements. I recognize that advertising is, after all, an art as well as a science. Sometimes all I can do is raise questions, for there are times when there simply are no absolute answers.

Each new edition reflects the changing world of advertising, and in this edition I also reflect my own changing perspectives, which come from experiences—academic, business, and writing. Thus, in addition to the updating of all subject materials, there has been some reorganization and overhauling of chapters. Advertising organization has been included in Part I as a component of the background of the advertising business. Because of requests by so many adopters, the chapters on retail, business, and international advertising, which were integrated into the main body of the text in the previous edition, have been reinstated as separate chapters. Creative examples have been placed at the ends of appropriate chapters instead of being combined in a single chapter.

Data and illustrations for this edition represent the most recently attainable, commensurate with the production time lag of a book of this size and nature. I hope these are not just ornamental, but rather that they make the text matter both clearer and more stimulating. As in previous editions, I have tried to reduce the aura of mystery by minimizing the jargon of both "Madison Avenue" and academia. In short, I have borrowed from the lessons I learned as a practitioner of advertising: to write to the audience in a manner that I hope is clear, comprehensible, and interesting.

ORGANIZATION OF THE TEXT

Because so many people approach a first course in advertising with preconceived ideas about its economic and social implications, I feel these topics must be considered first. Thus, Part I of the text addresses these topics, as well as the control of advertising and its historical roots.

Part II of the book considers the management of advertising. We explore the advertising planning process, the advertising opportunity, the interrelation of advertising to other aspects of marketing, how many dollars to spend, understanding consumers, gathering information, and evaluating effectiveness.

This leads naturally in Part III to the planning and selection of media to carry our messages, for most of the dollars spent in advertising are spent here. Following media is Part IV of the text, dealing with the message. We will look at the creative process and techniques for developing effective advertisements and commercials.

Although retail, business, international, and noncommercial advertising are discussed at various points in the book, the next section, Part V, examines these other views of advertising in greater detail.

Finally, Part VI contains four useful supplemental aids for students, in the form of appendices on careers, media data, a glossary, and a bibliography.

KEY FEATURES

The following pedagogical aids and features have been incorporated into the text to make it an effective teaching tool:

1. *Objectives*: Each chapter begins with a list of objectives that serve as a guide for what a student should have learned after reading it.
2. *Illustrations*: Print and broadcast advertisements, charts, and tables appear throughout the book to provide examples and clarify the topics discussed in the text.
3. *Quips and Quotes*: Significant comments on advertising by noted persons from all fields of endeavor and bits of humor in advertising are sprinkled throughout the text to add interest and amusement.
4. *Summaries*: Each chapter ends with a summary covering the main points discussed.

5. *Questions and Problems*: Chapter-ending questions provide a test of comprehension of the material covered and an opportunity for discussion. Also included are problems that can provide students with hands-on experiences.
6. *Case Examples*: Extensive examples of a marketing plan, a media plan, and three creative strategies offer built-in applications of text material.
7. *Appendices*: Four valuable appendices supplement student knowledge:
   a. Career advice on advertising
   b. An appendix crammed full of media rates and data
   c. A glossary of advertising terms, cross-referenced for easier use
   d. A bibliography of current and classic further readings in advertising and related topics
8. *Indexes*: Combined subject-name index, plus a special index of advertisers whose advertisements appear in the text

SUPPLEMENTS

The *Advertising Resource Book*, a teacher's manual, contains suggestions on adapting the text to different course lengths, class projects, transparency masters; teaching aids, mini-lectures and chapter outlines; and a test bank of objective questions.

Also available as a package, or in individual components, are multimedia teaching aids, including a video tape of television commercials, slides of print advertisements, and an audio tape of radio commercials.

ACKNOWLEDGMENTS

Every opportunity to learn more about what is currently happening in the advertising business helps when writing a textbook on the subject. Therefore, I was extremely fortunate to have the opportunity to participate in three events in recent years that provided me with valuable learning experiences, and more significantly, with friends who have been so helpful in so many ways. A special note of appreciation is therefore due to:

Jarlath J. Graham for inviting me to be the guest of Crain Communications Inc., at the Advertising Age Workshop
William A. Marsteller and Richard C. Christian for asking me to be a participant in the Marsteller Inc., Educator Seminar
Louis T. Hagopian and Edward J. Rogers for arranging for me to spend a sabbatical term at N W Ayer Incorporated

As in past editions, I have sought assistance, advice, and suggestions from a whole host of generous practitioners, academicians, and students. It is not possible to acknowledge everyone who answered questions or supplied materials and illustrations, but some persons made such major contributions in reading manuscript and providing case example material that I want to recognize them here as a small token of my appreciation. Without them I could not have written this book. I do hope I have not omitted anyone to whom I am so indebted. Among the practitioners are:

Charles F. Adams, Executive Vice-President, American Association of Advertising Agencies Inc.
Herbert A. Ahlgren, Vice-President, Association of National Advertisers, Inc.

Thomas E. Berry, Assistant Media Analyst, Campbell-Ewald Company

Ted Bird, Vice-President/Director of Broadcast Services, Doyle Dane Bernbach Inc.

Kate Black, Chief Staff Assistant/Washington Office, American Association of Advertising Agencies Inc.

Jim Conaghan, Media Information, Newspaper Advertising Bureau, Inc.

Kenneth J. Costa, Vice-President/Marketing Information, Radio Advertising Bureau, Inc.

David DuSina, Senior Clerk, Campbell-Ewald Company

Richard G. Ebel, Vice-President, Specialty Advertising Association International

Kate Ferris, formerly Staff Executive, American Association of Advertising Agencies Inc.

Steven E Forsyth, Manager, Public Relations/Lite, Miller Brewing Company

Evelyn French, Director/Information Services, American Business Press Inc.

Larry Frerk, Promotion Director, A.C. Nielsen Company

Thomas J. Glynn, Executive Vice-President, Campbell-Ewald Company

Robert M. Grebe, Vice-President/Communications, Television Bureau of Advertising

Benjamin S. Greenberg, Director of Public Affairs, The Advertising Council Inc.

Lyle Greenfield, Senior Vice-President, Compton Advertising, Inc.

Marvin M. Gropp, Vice-President/Research, Magazine Publishers Association

Bernard Guggenheim, Senior Vice-President/Media Information Services, Campbell-Ewald Company

Helen B. Johnston, Vice-President/Director of Media Analysis, Grey Advertising Inc.

John M. Kawula, Vice-President, Point-of-Purchase Advertising Institute

James H. Liberatore, President, SalesCom, A unit of Carr Liggett Inc.

Irma Nicholson, Vice-President/Sales Promotion, Jacobson Stores

John E. O'Toole, Chairman of the Board, Foote, Cone & Belding Communications, Inc.

Joseph Palastak, former Executive Director, Transit Advertising Association, Inc.

Harry Paster, Executive Vice-President, American Association of Advertising Agencies Inc.

Joe Plummer, Executive Vice-President, Young & Rubicam Inc.

Jan Reeves, University Information Coordinator, Arbitron Ratings Company

Klaus F. Schmidt, Senior Vice-President, Young & Rubicam Inc.

Andrew J. Schmitt, Vice-President, Young & Rubicam Inc.

Suzanne Shawn, Network Media Buyer, Campbell-Ewald Company

Frank Stanton, President, Simmons Market Research Bureau, Inc.

Ellis Veech, Vice-President/Media Group Supervisor, Campbell-Ewald Company

William N. Wilkins, President, Institute of Outdoor Advertising

Those colleagues in academia whom I especially want to thank for reading manuscript and offering invaluable suggestions are:

Isabella C.M. Cunningham, University of Texas

Charles H. Patti, University of Denver

Joseph R. Pisani, University of Florida
Terrence H. Witkowski, California State University, Long Beach

It helps to have a great publisher with a professional team, and I want to acknowledge with appreciation the work of the following people: Elizabeth Classon, Pam Wilder, Jayne Conte, and Rita DeVries.

Families are terribly important to an author, for they are understanding, encouraging, and so proud that the task seems easier for their support. In my case, they also made some very real contributions. Son David Gould and daughter Lisa Rose, now both working in business management, have taken the time to make important technical suggestions and design charts, and to seek out illustrative materials. My dear wife Natalie typed into the wee hours and proofread so very many galleys and page proofs.

And finally, to those many students whose enthusiasm toward advertising provided the inspiration to write the book in the first place, and to all the others mentioned above, I say thank you for making it all possible.

Maurice I. Mandell
Sarasota, Florida

1

A Framework
of Advertising

After completing this chapter, you should be able to:
1. Define what advertising is and is not
2. See advertising's relationship to overall business strategy
3. Understand some of the basic terms used in the advertising business
4. Describe how advertising functions in a model of communications theory

Of all business activities, probably none is better known, more widely discussed, or more highly criticized by the American public than advertising. One reason for this is that advertising has become the spokesperson for American business. Each year, business directs myriad messages to the public through advertising in magazines, newspapers, posters, television, radio, car cards, direct mail, and many other media, from skywriting to calendars. It is no wonder that, as the source of this constant barrage, the advertising industry has assumed such importance in our society. Yet advertising is grossly misunderstood. Critics frequently exaggerate its effectiveness or oversimplify its complexity. Indeed, the value of advertising as a tool of business has so often been distorted by the public that many businesspeople have been led to share some of the popular misconceptions about the value and place of advertising in business strategy.

Advertising is an integral part of our social and economic system. To criticize it is to be critical of the society of which it is a part; and in recent years, many people have done just that as traditional social values have been scrutinized and criticized. There is no doubt that advertising deserves some criticism, and a basic premise of our social order is that criticism is permitted and, indeed, welcome. But it is important to have all the necessary facts at hand to be critical intelligently. This book is an attempt to explain not only the effective use of advertising but also the role of advertising in our society.

Because we are all consumers, we are exposed to advertising. We should recognize that although there is room for criticism of advertising, it is also an effective communications tool used even by its critics. In the chapters that follow, the benefits to the consumer will be shown. Likewise, advertising's weaknesses and abuses will be recognized and discussed. *No attempt is made to whitewash advertising*. Rather, the advertising story is presented in what is hoped is a fair and reasonable manner. Then it is up to each of us to draw our own conclusions.

The prime purpose of this discussion of advertising is to consider its use as a tool of business to assist in the promotion of both goods and services. Whether or not businesspeople are involved directly with advertising, they should be at least familiar enough with it to know its potentialities and its limitations, for it directly and indirectly pervades the whole business scene. Because this is so, a knowledge of advertising gives business managers additional breadth so that they can make business decisions more effectively.

Before proceeding with a detailed consideration of advertising, we need to establish some working definitions. The nature of advertising is such that definitions and classifications are arguable. Still, if a discussion of advertising is to proceed in a systematic way, working terminology, even if somewhat arbitrary, must be established. The remainder of this chapter, for the most part, will provide the necessary framework for what follows through the rest of the book.

ADVERTISING DEFINED The Definitions Committee of the American Marketing Association defines advertising as "any paid form of nonpersonal presentation and promotion of ideas, goods, or services by an identified sponsor."[1] The key words here are "paid," "nonpersonal," and "identified." Advertising differs from the related activity of *publicity,* a tool of public relations, primarily in that advertising is paid for directly and its sponsorship is almost always clearly identified. The term *publicity* refers generally to significant news about a product, service, institution, or person that is not paid for by the sponsor. Advertising can be distinguished from *personal selling* because it is a nonpersonal presentation. That is, the message may appear to be directed toward individuals, but it is not made in person by the seller in the presence of the prospect, as is most personal selling.

Frequently, the terms *advertising* and *sales promotion* are confused. Used in a broad sense, the term *sales promotion* (or, more simply, *promotion,* as we shall use it here) includes advertising, personal selling, and other selling activities. More often, however, the term *sales promotion* is used in a narrower sense to refer to those other selling activities that supplement advertising and personal selling, such as exhibitions, displays, demonstrations, premiums, samples, sweepstakes, price incentives, and other nonrecurrent selling activities. Difficulty arises in distinguishing between advertising and sales promotion because business firms vary in their methods of classifying their own activities.

Although one frequently hears talk about something called "word-of-mouth advertising," in fact there is no such form of advertising, as the term advertising is defined above. So-called word-of-mouth advertising is a person-to-person communication that is perceived as being noncommercial, concerning goods or services; it is face-to-face product-related communications between and among friends, relatives, and others. Because it is noncommercial, it is usually seen as being an unbiased source of information. As such, it is important to the advertiser for several reasons. It can work against the advertiser's promotional efforts in favor of another firm's goods or services, or it can work for the advertiser by serving as an extension of the advertising efforts, in that the communicator's attitudes are formulated in terms of the producer's advertising message. Certainly, the effects of word-of-mouth advertising should be considered in the overall promotional efforts of the firm.

CLASSIFICATIONS OF ADVERTISING

For our purposes, advertising can be classified in several broad categories that are not necessarily mutually exclusive: (1) product reputation and corporate advertising; (2) commercial and noncommercial advertising; and (3) primary- and selective-demand advertising.

PRODUCT REPUTATION VERSUS CORPORATE ADVERTISING Notice that in our definition of advertising, we refer to the "presentation and promotion of *ideas, goods, or services.*" Thus advertising is not limited to selling goods and services (although the bulk of advertising is used for these purposes) but also can be used effectively to sell ideas. Firms that produce or distribute goods generally devote the major portion of their advertising efforts to selling them. Similarly, firms that provide a service use advertising primarily to sell that service. This ad-

FIGURE 1-1

A product reputation advertisement. Like most advertisements its purpose is to sell the product directly on the basis of its merits. (Original in color) *By permission: Hanes Hosiery.*

Gentlemen prefer Hanes®

Sensuously smooth. Luxuriously sheer. Unmistakably Hanes.

vertising is referred to as *product reputation advertising*, the word *product* being used in the broad sense to include services as well as goods. Occasionally, however, such firms have other objectives for their advertising—they may want to sell ideas. This is called *corporate advertising* (or *institutional advertising*), to distinguish it from product reputation advertising. Corporate advertising takes three forms: *patronage, public relations,* and *public service.*

PATRONAGE ADVERTISING Patronage advertising is used to sell the idea of patronizing a producer or retailer for reasons other than specific product merits. For example, an advertisement that uses the slogan, "At Ford, quality is job 1," is designed to build patronage for the manufac-

FIGURE 1-2

A patronage advertisement by a manufacturer. Note that rather than sell any particular car model, it sells the firm. (Original in color) *By permission: Ford Motor Company.*

turer's brands. Similarly, when a retail advertisement describes the store, its services, or its wide selections and does not mention specific merchandise, the retailer is attempting to build patronage for the store. Patronage advertising is designed to increase profits by increasing the prestige of an institution through means other than selling the merits of its products.

PUBLIC RELATIONS ADVERTISING As the name suggests, public relations advertising is designed to improve the firm's image or reputation by means of advertising. For example, when a firm wishes to remedy ill will that some segment of the public feels toward it (whether or not this segment represents customers), or when a firm wants to *forestall* public ill will, it can engage in public relations advertising. Such advertising might present management's side of a labor dispute, counter government accusation that the company is violating antitrust laws, or show the benefits of privately owned public utilities. It is certainly an adjunct of the overall public relations program of the firm. Public relations advertising, when used to present a position on a controversial public issue, is also called *advocacy* advertising.

PUBLIC SERVICE ADVERTISING This is a means of using advertising to promote *noncontroversial* causes in the interest of the public. Especially since the establishment of The Advertising Council during World War II, many firms use a portion of their advertising appropriations to promote highway safety, better schools, religion in American life, forest fire prevention, an understanding of the American economic system, and so on. The motive for such advertising is in some cases altruistic, in others to build good public relations in a subtle way. In the latter case, the advertising is perhaps just another form of public relations advertising.

COMMERCIAL ADVERTISING Advertising can be divided into commercial and noncommercial categories. Because analysis of expenditures will show that advertising is used most extensively for commercial purposes, the major emphasis in this book will be on the advertising of goods, services, and ideas by business.

CONSUMER ADVERTISING Commercial advertising may be divided into consumer advertising and business advertising. Consumer advertising may be subdivided into *national* and *retail* advertising. Generally, advertising media have different rate structures for national and retail advertising. Rates for national advertisers are usually called *general* advertising rates by media. These terms cause some confusion, because national advertising does not have to be national in scope. Actually, many producers may advertise only regionally or locally; but the advertising is still referred to as national to distinguish it from advertising by retailers. Likewise, some retailers advertise nationally (such as department stores that advertise in the women's fashion magazines), but such advertising is still referred to as retail advertising. Thus, national advertising refers to any advertising by a producer of goods or services,

ADVERTISING
BACKGROUND, SOCIAL
IMPLICATIONS, AND
ORGANIZATION

FIGURE 1-3

A public relations advertisement. This one offers reprints of a series of advertisements directed at college students to improve their reading and writing skills. See Figure 23-2 for an example of one of these advertisements. *Reprinted by permission of International Paper
Company.*

FIGURE 1-4

A public service advertisement by The Advertising Council and the newspapers that carry it. *By permission: The Advertising Council Inc.*

whereas retail advertising refers to any advertising by a retailer, in both instances without regard to the geographical scope of the advertising.

BUSINESS ADVERTISING This advertising may be divided into several categories. It includes industrial advertising, directed at industrial producers; trade advertising, directed at the various types of intermediaries (such as wholesalers and retailers); and professional advertising, directed at groups such as doctors, lawyers, certified public accountants, and clergymen.

NONCOMMERCIAL ADVERTISING Every year we see and hear advertising by federal, state, and local governments, by charitable institutions, by religious organizations, or by political groups. Such advertis-

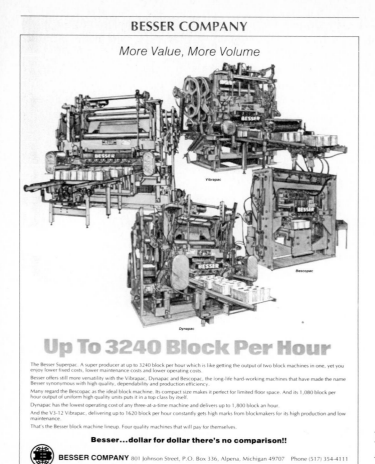

FIGURE 1-5

An example of an advertisement to business. (Original in color) *By permission: Besser Company.*

ing may have many purposes, such as support of civic ventures, solicitation of donations and contributions, support of candidates for political office, and so on. The methods used in the preparation of such advertising are basically the same as those used in commercial advertising. It should be made clear, however, that some of the groups mentioned above may also engage in advertising programs for commercial purposes—just as businesses sometimes use noncommercial advertising. For example, the government may advertise to dispose of surplus goods, and a university's press may advertise to sell the books it has published. Despite the major emphasis in this book on commercial advertising, noncommercial advertising is so very important today that the last chapter looks at this subject in greater detail.

PRIMARY- AND SELECTIVE-DEMAND ADVERTISING   Commercial advertising is designed to stimulate demand for the goods or services of the advertiser. There are two kinds of demand: *primary demand* and *selective demand*. Primary demand means demand for the generic product of an entire industry. For example, the demand for television receivers is primary demand. Selective demand is the demand for a particular brand produced by a particular firm—for instance, demand for a television receiver made by RCA.

Advertising is used to stimulate primary demand for a new type of product. It is also used at times for established products when the advertiser is important in the industry and reasons that the advertiser's brand will get the largest share of any increase in the demand for the

FIGURE 1-6

A television commercial by an association aimed at stimulating primary demand. *By permission: American Dairy Association.*

american dairy association®
Milk- "Waking Up" :30

SING (VO): THE MORNING SUN

GETS ME OUT OF BED

I WAKE UP TO THE TASTE OF MILK

I'VE GOT A TASTE FOR SOMETHING FRESH

I'VE GOT A TASTE FOR THE TASTE OF MILK.

ANNC (VO): Milk, the fresher refresher.

With the taste that gets you up and going.

Wouldn't a cold,

smooth glass of milk taste good right now?

SING (VO): I'VE GOT A TASTE FOR A FRESHER TASTE

I'VE GOT A TASTE FOR THE TASTE OF MILK.

ANNC (VO): Mmmmmm milk. The fresher refresher.

FIND ANOTHER DISHWASHER WITH ALL THESE QUALITY FEATURES, AND KITCHENAID WILL BUY IT FOR YOU.

It's no gimmick. Check these features against any other dishwasher brand. If you find one with all of these dishscrubbing and long lasting features found in the KitchenAid KD-20 dishwashers, we'll buy it for you. Nothing truly compares to a KitchenAid.
Offer expires December 31, 1982.

Extra-Clean Dishscrubbing Features.

☐ **High Pressure Multi-Level Wash System.**
KitchenAid dishscrubbing power is greater than all major dishwasher brands because our wash system delivers more water under greater pressure.

☐ **100% Usable Large Capacity Racks with ChinaGuard.**

No lost loading space because there are no cutouts in the lower rack. Exclusive ChinaGuard protects dishes against chipping.

☐ **Sure-Temp Water Heating.**
Insures sanitized cleaning every time. Automatically heats water to approximately 150°F in every complete cycle.

☐ **Built-In Soft Food Disposer.**
Assures sparkling clean dishes without pre-rinsing. Grinds soft foods during drain.

☐ **Gentle Forced Air Drying.**
It's safe. With no hot spots on dishes, pots or pans. Unlike other dishwashers, there's no exposed heating element in the KitchenAid dishwasher.

Long-Life Durability Features.

☐ **Porcelain and Steel Construction.**
To protect from scratches, stains, and odors, KitchenAid uses a full steel wash tank with two coats of tough, chip-resistant TriDura® porcelain plus an overglaze.

☐ **Heavy Duty ½ Horsepower Motor.**
Most others use a ⅓ horsepower or less. Since a stronger motor strains less, it's a lot less likely to wear out.

☐ **Reversible Front Panels.**
You can change panels with the stainless steel trim kit with four decorator colors provided. Choose from six optional solid and edged colors for unmatched flexibility.

☐ **Overflow Protection Twin Fill Valve.**
You don't have to worry about overflowing water. If one valve fails, the other continues to operate and normal dishwasher operation is maintained.

☐ **Triple Protection Warranty.**
A 1-Year parts and labor Full Warranty on the complete dishwasher. A 5-Year Limited Warranty on the motor. And a 10-Year Limited Warranty on the porcelain tank and inner door.

TRIPLE PROTECTION WARRANTY

KitchenAid. Don't settle for less.

Hobart Corporation, Troy, Ohio 45374   KitchenAid and TriDura are registered trademarks of Hobart Corporation

FIGURE 1-7

This advertisement attempts to stimulate selective demand. It suggests brand benefits rather than generic product benefits. (Original in color) *By permission: KitchenAid Division, Hobart Corporation.*

generic product. When associations, such as the American Meat Institute, the Small Brewers Association, and the Bituminous Coal Institute, advertise goods or services, they attempt to stimulate primary demand because they represent more than one member of the industry. Association advertising is also known as *horizontal cooperative* advertising.

Selective-demand advertising is always used by individual firms. Generally, it is employed to stimulate demand for established brands. It assumes that there is a primary demand for the generic product and it emphasizes the reasons for buying a specific brand. It is also used as reminder advertising when the firm wants to maintain its established position.

ADVERTISING'S RELATION TO OVERALL BUSINESS STRATEGY

Advertising has a large voice, but it is only a small factor in overall business strategy. It would be foolish indeed to expect advertising to solve all the problems of business by itself. Advertising is a tool of promotion, and promotion is a function of marketing. Although promotion is essential to the successful conduct of any business, advertising is not, for there are other promotional tools, such as personal selling, sales promotion, and public relations, that might be more valuable in a given situation. Therefore, some firms use advertising and others do not. And some firms use advertising extensively while others use it sparingly. When used, advertising can be of maximum effectiveness only when all other aspects of a business are considered. When advertising plans are made, the product, the package, the brand name, personal selling strategy, sales promotion activity, public relations plans, production, and the firm's financial situation must all be taken into account.

IMPORTANCE OF ADVERTISING IN THE ECONOMY

Some may question the social value of advertising, but it is undeniably of considerable importance in the economy. It is estimated that in 1982 about $66.5 billion was spent on advertising in this country. This represents 2.18 percent of the gross national product for that year—a sizable percentage for just one factor in the economy. Measuring the total advertising investment in another way, for every man, woman, and child in the United States in 1982, $285 was spent on advertising.

Advertising revenue represents a substantial part of the income of mass communications media such as newspapers, magazines, radio, and television. Without such revenue, these media would be forced to seek other sources of revenue, most likely from consumers.

There is no doubt that advertising has been a significant factor in the economic success of many American businesses. Although it is true that an *exact* measure of advertising's effectiveness is difficult if not impossible to obtain, there is sufficient evidence to show that advertising has been the ingredient that has made many firms profitable. To eliminate advertising would result in a decrease in profits and, in many cases, an actual loss for the firm. Even though advertising costs increase total expenses for the firm, well-planned and well-executed advertising can increase sales and, hence, profits. Advertising thus contributes to the health of the whole economy.

If I were starting life over again, I am inclined to think that I would go into the advertising business in preference to almost any other. This is because advertising has come to cover the whole range of human needs and also because it combines real imagination with a deep study of human psychology. Because it brings to the greatest number of people actual knowledge concerning useful things, it is essentially a form of education. . . . It has risen with ever-growing rapidity to the dignity of an art. It is constantly paving new paths. . . . The general raising of the standards of modern civilization among all groups of people during the past half century would have been impossible without the spreading of the knowledge of higher standards by means of advertising.

FRANKLIN D. ROOSEVELT (1882–1945), Statesman

READER'S DIGEST

WHO WORKS WITH ADVERTISING?

Advertising activity is carried on by a number of different groups. Among them are the advertising departments of producers and retailers, advertising agencies, and the media that carry the advertising. We mention these at this point to introduce basic terms, but Chapter 6 will describe their activities in detail.

PRODUCER AND RETAILER ADVERTISING FUNCTION The advertising function of a producer sometimes includes the direct preparation of advertisements. In most instances, however, the advertiser's chief functions are to determine policy, to supervise the advertising program, and to act as liaison between the producer and the advertising agency. The retail company's advertising department, on the other hand, is usually responsible for the complete advertising program and the actual preparation of the advertisements.

ADVERTISING AGENCIES Although advertising agencies are increasingly preparing advertising for retailers, for the most part their work consists of preparing advertising for producers. In recent years, they have expanded their activities so that in addition to providing advertisements for their clients, many offer a considerable amount of counseling assistance, such as marketing research, public relations counsel, and assistance in merchandising and sales promotion activities. Most of the compensation they receive comes from commissions paid by the media in which they place their clients' advertisements.

ADVERTISING MEDIA Advertising media themselves have advertising departments that perform several functions. First of all, there is an advertising department concerned with selling space or time to advertisers. The activity being performed is really personal selling instead of advertising, although the "product" sold is advertising space or time. In addition, media maintain advertising departments much the same as that of an advertiser, to promote the medium to potential advertisers and to increase circulation or listeners. Finally, many media maintain advertising *service* departments that offer advice and assistance in the preparation of advertisements for those advertisers desiring such help.

A Framework of Advertising

13

COMMUNICATIONS THEORY

Looking back on what has been said about what advertising is and how it operates, we see that advertising is a form of communications. To understand what happens when advertising communication takes place, we should examine the communications system in general and the advertising communications system in particular.

INTERPERSONAL COMMUNICATIONS   In its most simple form, communication is one person sending a message to another. This may involve an idea, thought, attitude, opinion, or the like. In order to communicate, the *sender* or source makes use of an *encoding* process. That is, the concept to be communicated is put in message form by making use of *symbols.* Typically, in the case of interpersonal one-on-one communications, the symbols used are oral sounds in the form of words. Additionally, the sender may use other symbols, such as gestures and facial expressions. If the communications are written instead of spoken, the symbols will probably still include words, this time expressed through a series of arrangements of letters of the alphabet. However, these may be enhanced with other symbols, in the form of pictures and diagrams.

The encoded message is directed by the sender to a *receiver* or destination through an appropriate *channel.* In one-on-one communications, these channels are simple. In oral face-to-face communications, the channel is simply the air that carries the sound. In other instances, the channels might be telephones or CB radios, or in the case of written messages, they might be the mails. In order to comprehend the message, the receiver must *decode* that message. For proper decoding of the message, the sender and receiver must share some degree of common experience. Obviously, when the sender and receiver speak different languages, the sender will not encode spoken or written words that the receiver will be able to decode or comprehend. This may even be true when both speak the same language. An English tourist pulls into an American service station and requests the attendant to "top it up with petrol, wash the windscreen, check under the bonnet, and see if the tyres need air, including the spare in the boot." What the tourist needs

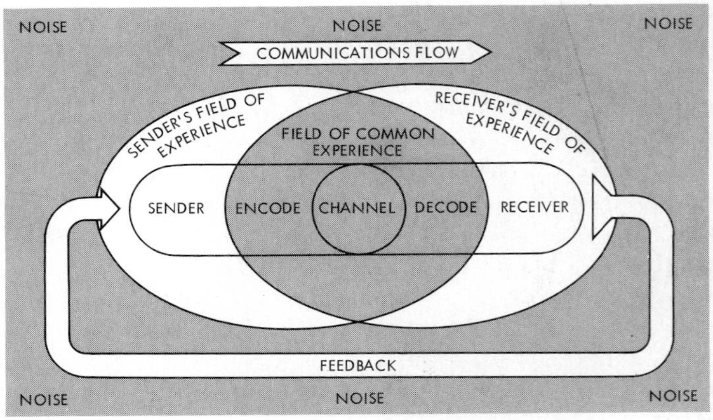

FIGURE 1-8

A model of the interpersonal communications process.

to say, of course, if the attendant is to decode readily, is, "Fill the tank with gas, wash the windshield, check under the hood, and see if the tires need air, including the spare in the trunk." There are, to be sure, also encoding and decoding problems between people of different generations, occupations, ethnic origins, geographic areas, and the like. Although words used orally may be readily decoded by the receiver, when those same words are communicated in written form to a 5-year-old, the decoding may again break down, this time because of the child's inability to read. In both cases, however, symbols other than the spoken or printed word, such as pictures, might better communicate the meaning if the illustrations are part of a field of common experience.

The sender, of course, is anxious to know if the communications were effective. To ascertain this, the sender must look to the receiver for a response, or *feedback.* In one-on-one interpersonal communications, the feedback is usually immediate, and it is frequently in the form of further communications, with the receiver now becoming the sender and the sender acting as receiver. If the sender was not clear in the original message, the feedback should indicate this, and additional clarifying messages may be sent.

Finally, it is possible that certain interferences—or *noise,* as it is frequently referred to—may affect the ability of the receiver to decode the message. This noise may be *internal;* for example, a hoarse voice of the sender, or in the case of written communications, a poor handwriting. Or the receiver, preoccupied with other thoughts, may block out the message. *External* noise comes from an almost infinite variety of sources. Other people may be sending messages simultaneously, or the stereo volume may be up too high, or the receiver may be absorbed in a magazine article or watching a television show.

This process of interpersonal communications is presented graphically as shown in the model in Figure 1-8.

ADVERTISING COMMUNICATIONS   Advertising communications basically follows the same model as that for interpersonal communications, except that here one is dealing with *mass* communications. And the advertising communications model tends to be more complex. Although the originator of the advertisement may be an individual, as in the case of someone running a classified advertisement, more often the source or sender is a commercial entity and is a collective group. This source or sender is called the *advertiser.* To advertise, the advertiser makes use of the encoding process to prepare the *message.* This usually involves the talents of professional advertising people, such as members of the advertising department of the advertiser and, in most cases, advertising agency personnel such as, among others, copywriters and art directors, who make use of such symbols as copy, artwork, typography, sound effects, music, and the like.

Perhaps the most significant difference between one-on-one interpersonal communications and advertising is the channels. For advertising, the message must be delivered to a large number of people, referred to as the *audience.* These audiences are reached through a variety of

Varnish Off. *Near Santa Rosa, Calif., a sign by the Redwood Highway says: "We buy junk—sell antiques."*

TIME

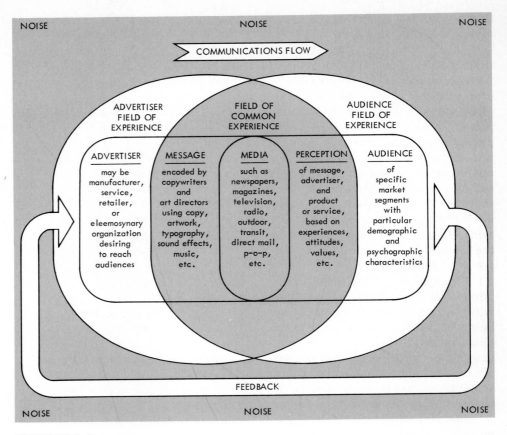

FIGURE 1-9

A model of the advertising communications process.

channels, referred to as mass *media*. Media must be chosen that will reach the audience with which the advertiser wants to communicate. In the case of commercial advertisers, these audiences will be specific market segments that can be described by particular demographic characteristics or geographic locations, or some combination of the two. The medium chosen will affect the way the message is created. For example, the broadcast media permit the use of music symbols, but print media do not. The medium will also affect the way the advertisement will be decoded or *perceived* by the audience. An audience responds differently to advertisements in *Playboy* and in *U.S. News & World Report* because the environment of the medium connotes certain values and attitudes.

The way an audience perceives the generic product or service being advertised will affect the perception of the advertised brand. In fact, the sum total of the experiences of the audience affects its perceptions of advertisements. Thus, for example, the perceptions of an audience that remembers World War II are likely to be quite different from those of one that can remember only Vietnam.

Audiences also react to advertisements in terms of their perceptions of the advertiser. For example, if the audience perceives the advertiser as a credible source, it is more inclined to believe the contents of the message. Thus, the well-established firm with a good product reputation will find it easier to communicate product advantages for a new product than will a new, unknown firm or an established firm with a poorer reputation. Not only does the advertiser thus become a symbol, but the product itself also creates an image as a symbol. Therefore, the advertiser must be concerned not only with messages containing salient selling points and product benefits, but also with advertising in ways that are compatible with the image of the advertiser. As a result, many advertisers engage in institutional advertising and various public relations programs in order to improve their images and thereby improve the perceptions of the audiences for their product- or service-related advertising messages.

Advertisers, then, must use research capabilities that will determine who the audiences are (market segments) for their messages and what the audiences' perceptions are of the generic products or services being advertised, as well as their perceptions of the advertiser. Advertisers must also learn as much as they can about their audiences' values and attitudes in general in order to be able to appeal to them most effectively. Similarly, advertisers must engage in careful planning and selection of media to choose those vehicles that will most effectively carry their messages to their chosen audiences.

Noise is a significant problem for the advertiser, because most advertising represents an intrusion upon other communications being delivered by many of the media carrying the advertising messages. Newspaper and magazine advertisements vie for attention with articles in these media. Radio and television commercials intrude on program content. Media for advertising that do not involve articles or programs, such as direct mail, outdoor posters, and point-of-purchase displays, must also contend with noise—for example, letters and other mail in the case of direct mail, other posters and traffic in the case of outdoor advertising, and other displays and the store merchandise itself in the case of point-of-purchase advertising. Additionally, all the noise factors described for interpersonal communications are also applicable to advertising. Thus, the advertiser must develop skills in preparing messages so that they will come through the noise and reach the audiences. This involves making use of creative talent who can write copy and design advertisements that will stand out.

Because there is such a wide chasm between the advertiser and the audience, it is difficult to appraise the effect of the advertising on the audience. Thus, feedback is vital if one is to appraise the effectiveness of the advertising. But advertising practitioners have devised numerous methods of evaluating advertising effectiveness not only after the fact but also in pretesting advertisements.

The cynic's definition:
ADVERTISING: The art of making people think they've always wanted something they've never even heard of before.

READER'S DIGEST

A model for the advertising communications process might be as depicted in Figure 1-9. It should be noted that this advertising communications model is also applicable to advertising by eleemosynary (charitable or nonprofit) organizations.

DEMARKETING

Although advertising by business is used for the most part to sell goods and services, in recent years some advertisers have used it in an antithetical way. With short-run and long-run shortages of energy sources, many energy firms such as oil, gas, and electricity companies have employed advertising to urge users to consume less and thereby alleviate the effects of overdemand. This demarketing activity by such advertisers is vital to their own interests so that they have enough of their products to prevent hardships by users. It also serves the best interests of the public and, in so doing, enhances the public relations image of the advertisers. Advertising as a means of demarketing will undoubtedly be used by more firms in years to come as they face similar kinds of problems.

ADVERTISING: AN ART OR A SCIENCE?

As you read the literature of the advertising field, you find many references to advertising as an art and as a science. Is advertising an art? Is it a science? Can it be both? If we distinguish a science—a systematized body of knowledge—from an art, which may be defined as knowledge made efficient by skill, we can see that advertising is to some degree a science, inasmuch as there has evolved over the years a generally agreed-upon body of knowledge. That is, there are certain principles that people should know if they are to engage in advertising. Indeed, if this were not the case, there would be little justification for textbooks on advertising.

But advertising is also an art, for creativity plays a considerable role in advertising, and it is also essential for you to know when and how to use advertising principles for greatest effectiveness. You may study the science of advertising, but beyond this, you must develop through practice and experience the art of using it.

TO SUM UP

Advertising is an integral part of our social and economic system. Advertising is a paid form of nonpersonal promotion by a sponsor. It has a distinct meaning and should be differentiated from other forms of promotion, such as personal selling, sales promotion, and public relations.

There are a number of ways to classify advertising. Product reputation advertising sells specific goods and services. Corporate advertising sells ideas to build patronage, improve public relations, or promote causes in the interest of the public. Most advertising is done by business for commercial purposes and may be directed toward consumers or other businesses. But there is also noncommercial advertising by government, charities, religious organizations, and political groups. Advertising may be used to stimulate demand for a generic product (primary demand) or for a specific brand (selective demand).

Advertising is a tool of promotion, as are personal selling, sales promotion, and public relations. They may be used together or separately. All of these represent one function of marketing. When advertising is being planned, all the other areas of marketing must be taken into account.

The work of advertising is carried on by advertising departments of producers and retailers, advertising agencies, and the media that carry the advertising.

The model for advertising communications follows that of interpersonal communication, except that we are dealing with *mass* communications. The *sender* of advertising is called the *advertiser*. Advertising people *encode* their communications to produce a *message*. This message is carried to the *receiver* or *audience* by means of mass *media*. The audience *decodes* the message according to its *perception* of the message, the advertiser, and the product or service. Advertisers seek *feedback* from audiences to indicate whether the message was properly perceived. And they must always be aware of the various kinds of *noise* that may interfere with or distract the audience from the message.

---

1. As you approach the study of advertising, what are your personal attitudes and opinions of advertising as a social and business force?
2. Distinguish between advertising on the one hand and personal selling, publicity, and sales promotion on the other. Give examples of each.
3. What is word-of-mouth advertising? Why is it not considered advertising as that term is described in the text?
4. From a current magazine, select advertisements that are examples of (a) product reputation advertising, (b) patronage advertising, (c) public relations advertising, and (d) public service advertising.
5. Distinguish between primary-demand and selective-demand advertising. Give examples of each.
6. "It would be foolish indeed to expect advertising to solve all the problems of business by itself." Do you agree or disagree? Support your position.
7. What are the three different groups who work with advertising? What role does each play?
8. Take an advertisement from a current magazine or newspaper and hypothesize on how its message would go through the advertising communications model.
9. What is the purpose of *feedback* in the advertising communications model? Why is it important?
10. How does business use advertising for *demarketing*? Why is this unusual when compared to most advertising?

---

[1] "Report of the Definitions Committee," *Journal of Marketing*, XII, No. 2 (October 1948), 202.

History of Advertising

After completing this chapter, you should be able to:

1. Explain how advertising has evolved over time
2. Appreciate the role of advertising in the United States' economic and social development
3. Understand the problems of advertising's reputation
4. See how advertising arrived where it is today

Perhaps because it is so much a part of the present social scene, we may think of advertising primarily as a modern development.

Actually, commercial advertising dates back several hundred years, although it is largely within this century that it has become so important in the economic scheme of things. Even so, earlier advertising, its use probably confined by the limited economic development and the limited advertising media of the past, was an important tool in its own time.

If, when we look back at these early advertisements, we find them amusing and naive and rather archaic, we should look again. We would find that many of our "modern" concepts of advertising are not modern at all, but are old ideas in new dress. Certainly, the purpose of advertising has not changed. The language has changed; new media have appeared; scientific research and planning of advertisements have been highly developed; but advertising is still used for the dissemination of information and for persuasion through commercial messages in visual and oral form. No doubt, in the decades that follow, people will look back upon today's advertising as we now look on that which came before.

By looking back at the development of advertising, we not only learn about the past but can better understand the present. In fact, we may even be able to see into the future. Why is advertising as it is today? As advertising has evolved, yesterday's new ideas have become the accepted axioms of today. This chapter explores the history of advertising, so that its present—and future—may be better understood.

But quite aside from our looking at its history as insight into advertising, it also provides us with an understanding of many of the values and attitudes of the public at any given time. Leonard Lanfranco says:

Advertising . . . is an excellent indicator of the societal echo, and the historian may search for clues he needs to reconstruct past life by what products or services that advertiser offers, and how he offers them. . . . The advertisement, then, is as accurate as a history book itself in depicting the life and times of a people, and "ad-less newspapers" would deprive society of the most flawless mirror of itself, both present and past, and the historian of one of the most unimpeachable [sources] of evidence at his command.[1]

ANCIENT ADVERTISING

Just when advertising began depends on how one wishes to define the term. In his *History of Advertising*, published in 1875, Henry Sampson says of the beginnings of advertising:

> . . . There is little doubt that the desire among tradesmen and merchants to make good their wares has had an existence almost as long as the customs of buying and selling, and it is but natural to suppose that advertisements in some shape or form have existed not only from time immemorial, but almost for all time.[2]

Because oral skills developed before reading and writing did, it is only natural that the earliest advertising medium was the spoken word. There is evidence that criers and hawkers were shouting their wares as far back as the days of the early Greeks, Romans, and Phoenicians. This primitive advertising, refined over the centuries, has carried down to the present day. Although hawkers do not often roam the streets with their cries, they have entered the home to make their pleas on radio and television.

Before long, competition and the need for identification necessitated signs. Signs used for identifying shops, with such appropriate illustrations as a goat (for a dairy) or a mule driving a mill (for a baker), were unearthed in the ruins of Pompeii. (At the door of a schoolmaster there was a sign depicting a boy receiving a whipping!)[3] There is also evidence of announcements painted on walls during this period. These included notices for theatrical performances, sports and gladiatorial ex-

FIGURE 2-1

"Signs" found on walls in excavations at Pompeii. *By permission: Frank Presbrey*, The History and Development of Advertising, *Garden City, N.Y.: Doubleday & Co., Inc., 1929.*

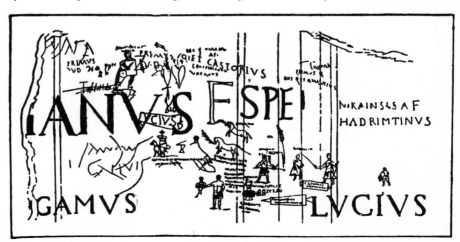

hibitions, advertisements of houses for rent, and appeals to tourists to visit the local taverns.[4] Perhaps the first written advertisement, however, was this three-thousand-year-old one inscribed on papyrus and found by an archaeologist in the ruins of Thebes:

> The man-slave, Shem, having run away from his good master, Hapu the Weaver, all good citizens of Thebes are enjoined to help return him. He is Hittite, 5′2″ tall, of ruddy complexion and brown eyes. For news of his whereabouts, half a gold coin is offered. And for his return to the shop of Hapu the Weaver, where the best cloth is woven to your desires, a whole gold coin is offered.[5]

There is no doubt that advertising flourished in this period, but with the fall of the Roman Empire and the onset of the Dark Ages, advertising temporarily declined in importance to Western civilization.

Perhaps the oldest relic of advertising among English-speaking people is family names referring to the various specialized crafts. The earliest of these designations was Smith. Names like Miller, Weaver, Wright, Tailor, and Carpenter were the earliest means of product identification— the forerunner of the brand name so essential to modern advertising.

As in Roman times, criers and signs were the chief advertising media in England for a long time. Until the seventh century, England was almost completely agrarian. Domestic trade was virtually nonexistent. At about this time, the "chapman," an itinerant pack-peddler, appeared on the scene. Although the importance of marketing grew quite slowly, periodic markets began to appear and, under the influence of the Church, the fair was established, ultimately becoming a marketing institution. From 1200 to 1700, the guild system flourished in England. Although guilds disapproved of sales or advertising efforts by individual members, they did advertise as groups—for example, in pageants during festivals. Each group acted an episode in a Biblical story that was frequently chosen for its appropriateness:

> . . . Thus the shipbuilders presented Noah's Ark, and the butchers the Crucifixion. Occasionally some sales talk was inserted in the dialogue, as when the thatchers presented the story of the Nativity, the character of Joseph introduced a long harangue on the leaky condition of the stable roof.[6]

FROM *SIQUIS* TO ADVERTISEMENT Advertising in England through the fifteenth century was not much different from that of ancient Rome. Indeed, in many ways it was not as advanced. The principal medium of advertising remained the public crier, supplemented by processions, pageants, and signs. By the close of that century, however, tack-up, handwritten advertisements began to appear. These were known as *siquis,* from the Latin *si quis,* meaning "if anybody." Initially, these were announcements posted on church doors by members of the clergy seeking vicarages. Because of widespread illiteracy, their use was severely restricted, but eventually they came to be used by professional men. A flourishing business soon grew up for scribes who would hand letter these "want ads," and before long they were being used to secure servants and by servants to secure positions.

By 1640, the term *advices* began to supplant *siquis*. *Advertisement* had been used earlier in the century, in the King James Bible, to mean notification or warning, and in 1655, book publishers began heading their announcements with the word *advertisement*. The term had come into popular usage several years earlier, when newspapers used it to indicate news of special attention value. By 1660, it was generally used as a heading for commercial announcements.

BEGINNING OF PRINTED ADVERTISEMENTS   One of the most significant events in the development of advertising was the invention of a system of casting movable type by the German, Johann Gutenberg,

FIGURE 2-2

Posting bills in Old England. *By permission: Henry Sampson*, A History of Advertising, *London: Chatto and Windus Ltd., 1875.*

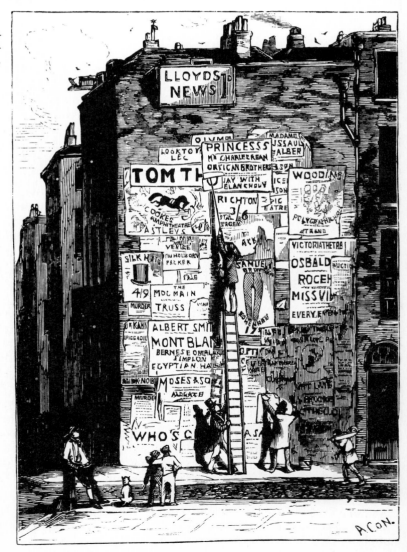

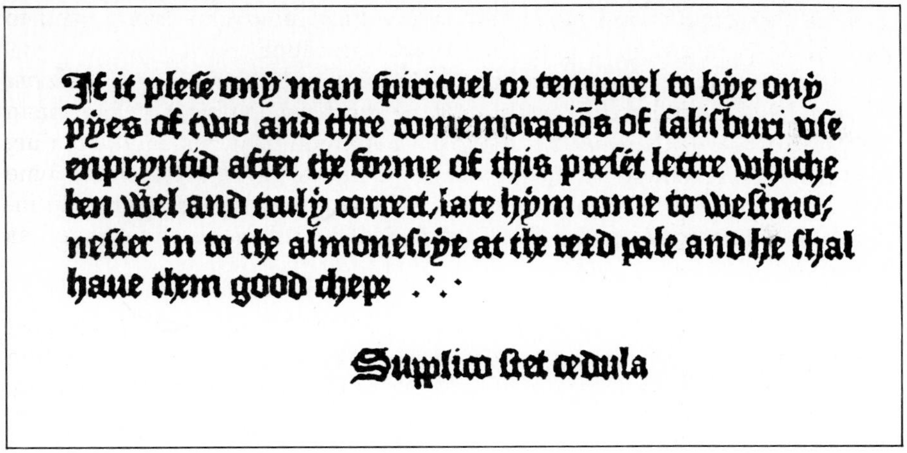
If it plese ony man spirituel or temporel to bye ony pyes of two and thre comemoracios of salisburi use enpryntid after the forme of this preset lettre whiche ben wel and truly correct, late hym come to westmo-nester in to the almonestrye at the reed pale and he shal haue them good chepe

Supplico stet cedula

FIGURE 2-3

First known printed English advertisement. *By permission: Frank Presbrey,* The History and Development of Advertising, *Garden City, N.Y.: Doubleday & Co., Inc., 1929.*

in 1438. Paper had been invented more than a thousand years earlier by the Chinese and was introduced to Europe by the Turks in the twelfth century. Now all the necessary components were available for mass printing. At the same time, literacy was increasing. William Caxton, an early English printer, made advertising history in 1478 when he printed a handbill now regarded as the first known *printed* English advertisement. It advertised a book he had printed, the *Salisburi Pye,* rules for the clergy at Easter. The advertisement read:

> If it please ony man spirituel or temporel to bye ony pyes of two and thre comemoracios of Salisburi use enpryntid after the forme of this preset lettre whiche ben wel and truly correct, late hym come to Westmonester in to the almonestrye at the reed pale and he shal have them good chepe.
>
> *Supplico stet cedula*

The Latin phrase at the end translates, "Let this notice stand."

FIRST NEWSPAPER ADVERTISING By this time, advertising media included criers, signs, tack-ups, handbills, and tradesmen's cards. News was first hand-lettered in *newsletters* and subsequently printed in the newsbook, forerunner of the newspaper. The first newsbook advertisement in English appeared in "Mercurius Britanicus" on February 1, 1625:

> Here is this present day published an excellent Discourse concerning the Match betweene our most Gracious and Mightie Prince Charles, Prince of Wales, and the lady Henrette Maria, daughter to Henry the fourth, late King of France, etc., sister to Lewis the Thirteenth, now King of those Dominions: Manifesting the Royall Ancestors of both these famous Princes, and truly explaining the severall interchanges of Marriages which hath beene betweene France and England: with the lively Picture of the Prince and the Lady cut in Brasse.

It was some twenty years before the next newsbook advertisement appeared, but subsequently such advertising caught on and grew rapidly. Along with the development of newsbooks and their transition to newspapers was the introduction of periodicals containing no news—only advertising. On May 26, 1657, the first food advertisement—an advertisement for coffee, which reads more like a patent medicine advertisement, in that it depicts coffee as something other than today's beverage—appeared in the *Public Adviser,* one of these advertising periodicals:

> In Bartholomew Lane, on the back side of the Old Exchange, the drink called coffee, which is a very wholesome and physical drink, have many excellent virtues, closes the orifices of the stomach, fortifies the heat within, helpeth digestion, quickeneth the spirits, maketh the heart lightsum, is good against eye-sores, coughs, or colds, rhumes, consumptions, head ache, dropsie, gout, scurvy, King's evil, and many others; is to be sold both in the morning and at three of the clock in the afternoon.

If the old adage that success invites imitation is true, this advertisement must have been eminently successful, for on June 22, 1657, the following advertisement appeared:

> An advertisement [i.e., notice of special importance]. In Bishopsgate Street in Queens's Head Alley, at a Frenchman's house, is an excellent West India drink, called chocolate, to be sold, where you may have it ready made at any time and also unmade at reasonable rates.

A year later still another drink was advertised:

> That Excellent, and by all Physicians approved, China drink, called by the Chinese Tcha, by other nations Tay alias Tee, is sold at the Sultaness Head Cophee-House, in Sweeting's Rents, by the Royal Exchange.

NEWSPAPER ADVERTISING WELL ESTABLISHED   By the beginning of the eighteenth century, newspaper advertising was well established in England, as evidenced by this comment by Joseph Addison in the *Tatler* in 1710. He pointed out that the use of newspaper advertising:

> . . . is to inform the world, where they may be furnished with almost everything that is necessary for life. If a Man has pains in his head, cholic in his bowels, or spots in his clothes, he may here meet with proper cures and remedies. If a man would recover a wife or a horse that is stolen or strayed; if he wants new sermons, electuaries, asses milk, or anything else either for his body or his mind, this is the place to look for them in.

THE ENGLISH NEWSPAPER TAX   Because even in the eighteenth century only a small part of the population of England could read, criers and pictorial signs were still the most widely used forms of advertising. Furthermore, the growth of newspaper advertising was slowed in 1712 when the government imposed a periodical tax and an additional tax on periodical advertisements. This tax was not imposed as a means of raising revenue, but rather to silence the press, which

FIGURE 2-4

Advertising the last lottery in England in 1826. This "traveling display" represents a distinctive form of advertising medium. *By permission: Henry Sampson*, A History of Advertising, *London: Chatto and Windus Ltd., 1875*.

was in the main hostile to the Tory party in power. Its purpose was almost immediately achieved, and the tax remained in effect for almost a century and a half. However, the value of newspapers and newspaper advertising had already been proven, and it was not too many years before they were flourishing again, despite the burden of the tax.

The American colonists brought with them their English heritage, so it was only natural that they should soon be using many of the advertising techniques of the mother country. (In fact, America's leadership in advertising technique is largely a twentieth-century development.) In the earliest days of the colonies, commercialism was not as far advanced as in England, and there was relatively little advertising until 1704, when the first successful newspaper, with advertising, was launched.

BENJAMIN FRANKLIN'S CONTRIBUTION TO THE DEVELOPMENT OF ADVERTISING Twenty-five years later, periodical advertising really received its great impetus—from the great American patriot to whom so many other achievements have been credited. One need hardly be surprised to find that the father of American advertising was Benjamin Franklin. In addition to publishing periodicals in which he welcomed and solicited advertising, Franklin was a considerable user of advertising to promote his own numerous ideas and enterprises, including a stove that still bears his name and is still promoted today.

FIGURE 2-5

"Modern Advertising: A Railway Station in 1874." This was the caption for this illustration at the time. Notice that even though this is an English scene, there is an advertisement for an American watch (upper left). *By permission: Henry Sampson*, A History of Advertising, *London: Chatto and Windus Ltd., 1875.*

He showed new imagination in advertising display, with better use of typography and illustration. Records show that other historical figures of the day likewise made use of advertising, including Paul Revere, who sold false teeth, and George Washington, who promoted real estate. Much of the advertising of this period consisted of "personals": requests for the return of lost or stolen merchandise, runaway slaves, and indentured servants; real estate; and consumer goods. The manufacturer had not yet become important enough and had not yet found the means or need for much advertising.

THE STAMP TAX AND OTHER OBSTACLES TO ADVERTISING By 1765, newspapers were thriving in the colonies, and their number had increased to twenty-five. In that same year, the stamp tax on various documents, newspapers, and advertising that had been levied in England about a half a century earlier was extended to the colonies. Presbrey writes of this incident, "The intense excitement caused in America by the attempt of the British Parliament to tax people who were not represented in that body grew in a decade to rebellion against the mother country and resulted in independence for the colonies."[7] From Presbrey's comment, it might be conjectured that advertising and advertisers played an important role in the Revolution. The immediate effect of the act was that some newspapers closed down at once, but the majority continued to publish and carry advertising, simply ignoring the tax. Shortly afterward, Benjamin Franklin went to England to testify before the House of Commons, and his appeal helped to bring about the repeal of the act in 1766.

Probably a factor of greater detriment to the development of the American press and consequently to advertising was the shortage of paper. Most printing paper was imported, and frequently it was scarce enough to force newspapers to restrict operations temporarily. Several paper manufacturing plants were subsequently established in America, but they suffered from a shortage of the rags needed in production. The problem was solved through advertisements making patriotic appeals to the citizenry to supply rags and help establish domestic manufacturing.

INDUSTRIAL DEVELOPMENT AND NATIONAL ADVERTISING

The Revolution was fought and won, and the republic was established. But change in the economy was slow. The new nation was still largely agrarian, and what it lacked for self-sufficiency it imported. By 1807, however, the Industrial Revolution slowly began to affect the United States. Frontiers moved westward, markets expanded, and sellers could not depend upon potential customers knowing their wares. The most significant developments of this period were probably the tariffs of 1816 and the encouragements of home industry, because as manufacturers grew, they began to need advertising to sell what they produced.

And now, behold, I go unto my people; come therefore and I will advertise thee what this people shall do to thy people in the latter days.

NUMBERS XXIV, 14

Nevertheless, progress was slow, and it was not until the second half of the nineteenth century that manufacturing became an important element in the economy. The victory of the North in the Civil War meant that tariffs were enforced and the manufacturing interest, which was strongest in the North, was emphasized. The result was, of course, a need to develop larger markets—national markets. This movement gave birth to national advertising, but not without some important assistance.

BRANDING AND TRADEMARKS Archaeologists have found vessels bearing the mark of the maker among prehistoric ruins. In thirteenth-century England, Parliament required artisans to place their mark on their products in order to protect the consumer and punish the producer of faulty goods. Producers considered this requirement a liability. Through time, consumers found that such marks, when they appeared on good products, provided a guide for future purchases, and eventually the trademark became an asset for the manufacturer. Specifically, trademarks made national advertising by manufacturers feasible by allowing the consumer to identify the advertised goods at the point of purchase.

MAGAZINE ADVERTISING Prior to the Civil War, media had been largely local. As national magazines began to develop after the war, they first resisted advertising but finally succumbed to manufacturers, who then had a means of disseminating their advertising messages nationally through a single publication.

History of Advertising

With the use of magazines as an advertising medium and with the development of national branding, national advertising grew by leaps and bounds. The adage at the turn of the century was that "it pays to advertise." Magazines grew fat, with heavy advertising sections on either side of the editorial matter.

> *Advertising is the genie which is transforming America into a place of comfort, luxury and ease for millions. . . . . Advertising is the Archimedean lever that is moving the world. If things were done in another and elder age that advertising is doing now, a whole mythology would gather about it, and we should witness the birth of a young god—powerful, restless, indomitable and wise, dominating. He would flash in the sylvan glades of the want advertisements and disport himself in the sunny whiteness of the department stores' wide species. But what a god he would be! How beneficent, how omnipresent, how powerful!*
>
> *WILLIAM ALLEN WHITE (1868–1944), Journalist*
>
> READER'S DIGEST

DEVELOPMENT OF ADVERTISING AGENCIES

The advertising agent first appeared on the scene in England in 1610, when James I appointed two knights as advertising agents for the kingdom. Their activity consisted of running a register of advertisements, accepting those they saw fit. The idea was apparently successful, for soon they had competition. This activity, however, was so far removed from that of the present-day American advertising agency that it can hardly be said to be the foundation of today's agency.

PALMER: FIRST AMERICAN ADVERTISING AGENT The first American advertising agent is said to have set up shop in Philadelphia in 1841. Wood begins his discussion of this topic startlingly: "The first advertising agent in the United States went mad. After operating in Boston, New York, and Philadelphia through the middle years of the nineteeth century, Volney B. Palmer grew violently insane, and Horace Greeley hired a man to look after him."[8] (Although the hectic activity and physical and mental strain of agency work have probably resulted in many physical ills, it is unfair to say that this progenitor of advertising agents went mad because of his work and thus established the basis for the behavior of agents who followed!)

Palmer offered none of the services associated with today's agencies. He was ostensibly a newspaper agent, with newspapers as his principals. From them he collected a 25 percent commission on space that he sold to advertisers. That someone should come along at this time and establish himself as an advertising agent is not surprising, for by 1840 there were 1,400 newspapers in the United States, and soliciting advertising was becoming an increasingly difficult and competitive affair. Some newspapers were already employing people to call on advertisers to sell space. Advertisers, too, were facing problems. They needed to know which newspapers were most advantageous for their advertisements and how best to word and set up these advertisements.

Acting as an agent, a person could represent many newspapers at once, making the person's time more profitable and offering greater service to the advertisers.

PERIOD OF TRANSITION   As new agents entered the field, they changed practices somewhat. Agents sold space to advertisers and then bought space from newspapers to fill the orders. Later, they contracted with newspapers for large segments of space at reduced rates, which they then sold in small amounts to various advertisers at much higher rates. When S.M. Pettingill, an employee of Palmer, decided to go into business for himself, he added a new service: preparing copy for clients.

George P. Rowell, most famous of these pioneer advertising agents, made still other contributions. In 1869, he published his first *American Newspaper Directory,* listing all the papers in this country with accurate circulation figures. He also founded *Printers' Ink,* an advertising periodical, in 1888.

Another kind of advertising agent appeared in the 1890s who did not deal in space but confined activities to copywriting, layout, and planning for advertisers and for space agencies that did not offer these services. Some agencies already were moving in the direction of today's agencies. By 1879, N.W. Ayer & Son had made its first formal market survey.[9] In 1892, the same agency employed its first full-time copywriter, and in 1898 its first artist. By this time, its services had also expanded to include magazines and outdoor advertising as well as newspapers.

Thus, by the turn of the century, the advertising agent had changed from newspaper agent to space broker to wholesaler and was becoming a counselor for the advertiser in the preparation and placing of advertisements.

What were advertisements like in the nineteenth century? Like any youngsters, they were suffering from growing pains. They were at times reserved, at times boisterous. They were crude, they were cunning, they were ludicrous, they were pathetic. They were feeling their way, finding their place. They had their gains and their setbacks. There were moments of glory and moments of shame. The young business did not grow to maturity until the twentieth century.

THE EARLY YEARS   If advertising had made any advances in physical form in the eighteenth century, these were lost around 1800. Restricted to agate type size with no illustrations, they looked like the legal notices in today's newspapers. These restrictions were caused by paper shortages, mechanical limitations that kept newspaper size down, and the publishers' idea that a large number of advertisements (even if this meant they were limited in display and length of copy) was necessary for prestige. Little attention was given to advertisements except insofar as they provided necessary revenue for the newspapers. Advertisements sold at a fixed price of $30 per year, and the copy was seldom changed. On rare occasions, a small cut (illustration) would get into an advertisement.

INCREASING ADVERTISING REVENUE As new newspapers appeared during the early nineteenth century, it was common practice for them to copy advertisements from other newspapers and run them without cost to the advertiser as a means of establishing themselves as advertising media. They would then sell these advertisements to the advertisers or seek new advertisers to replace the old ones. By the middle of the century, with the problems of paper and printing overcome, an estimated 11 million advertisements appeared yearly in some 2,000 newspapers. Newspapers prospered, and advertising contributed to this prosperity not only by providing needed advertising revenue but because readers bought newspapers as much to read the advertising as to read the news.

USE OF ADVERTISING Advertising for this period was largely for retailers and wholesalers, patent medicines, situations wanted, transportation, lost merchandise, and lotteries. These included Harvard and Yale universities as lottery sponsors. Many buildings on their campuses were financed in this manner. The return of runaway apprentices was also advertised. In June 1824, this advertisement appeared for a young man destined to be president of the United States:

Ten Dollars Reward.

Ran away from the Subscriber, on the night of the 15th instant, two apprentice boys, legally bound, named William and Andrew Johnson. The former is of dark complexion, black hair, eyes, and habits. They are much of a height, about 5 feet 4 or 5 inches. The latter is very fleshy freckled face, light hair, and fair complexion. They went off with two other apprentices, advertised by Messrs. Wm. & Chas. Fowler. When they went away, they were well clad—blue cloth coats, light colored homespun coats, and new hats, the maker's name in the crown of the hats, is Theodore Clark. I will pay the above Reward to any person who will deliver said apprentices to me in Raleigh, or I will give the above Reward for Andrew Johnson alone.

All persons are cautioned against harboring or employing said apprentices, on pain of being prosecuted.

JAMES J. SELBY, Tailor.

Raleigh, N.C. June 24, 1824

THE LIVELY YEARS

P.T. BARNUM, MASTER SHOWMAN If early nineteenth-century advertising was rather dull, it was not to stay so under the genius of Phineas Taylor Barnum. Although this great showman did not invent the superlative, he used it in advertising and publicity to an extent never known before.

He was the master of the advertising gimmick. Instead of saying, "Now Showing," he said, "Wonderful and Most Astonishing Exhibition." He hired a man to lay down bricks on each street corner as he headed for Barnum's American Museum, and when the man entered the exhibition, the curious onlookers who had followed him entered also.

When the crowds got too thick, he posted a sign "To the Egress," and those who went through the door to see this wonder found themselves out on the street. (Although not commonly used, *egress* is defined in the dictionary as an exit.) His promotional techniques skyrocketed to fame such personalities as General Tom Thumb and Jenny Lind. He advised merchants, "Advertise, or the chances are the sheriff will do it for you." Although we would frown upon his activities in our day, they were relished in his.

CIRCUMVENTING THE AGATE RULE Barnum's promotional success was primarily in posters, handbills, parades, and street stunts. He made the most of newspaper advertising but was restricted by the agate-only and single-column limititations. Display advertising was, at midcentury, still almost unheard of in the popular newspapers, but American ingenuity would not be stymied by publishers' restrictions. The American public wanted advertising, and publishers, realizing its value for increasing circulation, sought to have the copy changed every day. The New York *Herald* even ran a display line on top of each page: "Advertisements Renewed Every Day." Some advertisers circumvented restrictions by using agate type to provide the copy but arranging it to form illustrations such as pyramids or the numerals of a business address. In 1856, Robert Bonner, publisher of a literary periodical called the *New York Ledger,* hit upon an idea—inspired by English advertisers—to run ninety-three identical advertisements one under the other to fill a single column in the New York *Herald*. The advertisement was:

> ORION, THE GOLD BEATER is the title of Cobb's
> sensational story in the New York Ledger.

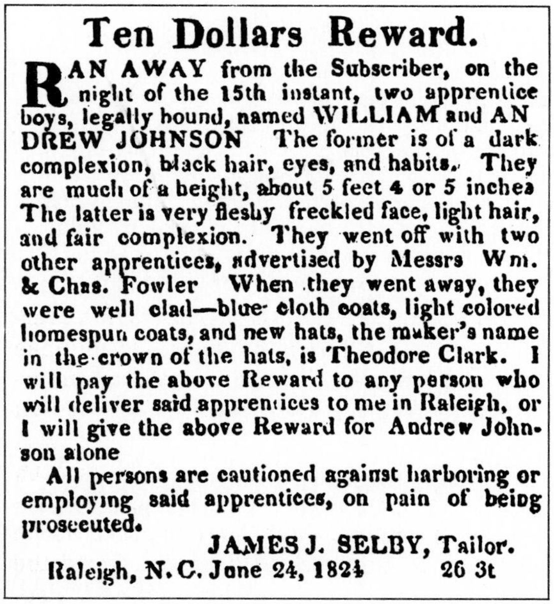

Ten Dollars Reward.

R AN AWAY from the Subscriber, on the night of the 15th instant, two apprentice boys, legally bound, named WILLIAM and AN DREW JOHNSON The former is of a dark complexion, black hair, eyes, and habits. They are much of a height, about 5 feet 4 or 5 inches The latter is very fleshy freckled face, light hair, and fair complexion. They went off with two other apprentices, advertised by Messrs Wm. & Chas. Fowler When they went away, they were well clad—blue cloth coats, light colored homespun coats, and new hats, the maker's name in the crown of the hats, is Theodore Clark. I will pay the above Reward to any person who will deliver said apprentices to me in Raleigh, or I will give the above Reward for Andrew Johnson alone

All persons are cautioned against harboring or employing said apprentices, on pain of being prosecuted.
JAMES J. SELBY, Tailor.
Raleigh, N. C. June 24, 1824   26 3t

FIGURE 2-6

Advertising for the return of runaways. One of these apprentices later became the President of the United States. *By permission: Frank Presbrey*. The History and Development of Advertising, *Garden City, N.Y.: Doubleday & Co., Inc., 1929.*

After that he used the same technique using full pages. If he did not in fact break the "no-display" rule, he demoralized it. He was, of course, eminently successful. By the late 1860s and early 1870s, display advertising became a reality through the advertising of Lord & Taylor and R.H. Macy.

NOSTRUMS AND PERSONALS Although patent medicine advertising dates back many years, it hit its peak just after the Civil War. It was the most flamboyant, most unethical advertising of its time—and the biggest in volume. Being timely, it was not then looked upon with the contempt it meets today. Medical science had not made such great strides, and the ignorant populace, eager to grab at any straw to relieve its maladies, looked to those nostrums for a cure and peace of mind. The industry was highly competitive; only the strong survived. One means of strength was advertising, and the ingenuity of the patent medicine advertiser is not to be belittled. Names like Dr. H.T. Helmbold's Buchu, Radway's Ready Relief, and Ayer's Cherry Pectoral became household words.

One well-known remedy was Drake's Plantation Bitters. Its advertising used the mysterious inscription "S. T. 1860 X." The meaning of this inscription became the subject of so much curiosity that the remedy sold largely as a result of this cryptogram. Rowell recalls this success story and others:

> A conspicuous feature of the Plantation Bitters advertising was a mysterious combination of the letters and figures which read "S. T. 1860 X." and which was displayed everywhere, and puzzled everybody. There were many inquiries "What do they mean?" and as many explanations. One most commonly given was, "Started trade in 1860 with ten dollars' capital." Mr. Drake and his partner, Mr. William P. Ward, the present head of the Lyon Manufacturing Company, owners of the old trademarks, Lyon's Kathairon, Hagan's Balm and Mustang Liniment, always asserted that there was really no meaning attached to the combination. It was said to be simply an advertising scheme to make people ask questions; but when I knew that Santa Cruz rum was the basis of the Bitters, and noted that if the figures 1860 were substituted for the letters c-r-o-i-, in the word St. Croix, I have thought that those facts and conditions might be a partial elucidation of the riddle; still Mr. Drake always insisted that it meant positively nothing. Such combinations do come to have an advertising value, as is evidenced by the three R's of Radway's Ready Relief, the three S's of Swift's Syphilitic Specific, the double B of Burdock Bitters, the P.P.P. of a certain kidney remedy, the C.C.C. of Cascarets Candy Cathartic, and dozens of others that might be mentioned.

> It is sometimes said that the sale of a proprietary article, after being once established, never entirely ceases. Hostetter's Bitters, introduced about the same time, are said to sell now about as well as ever, and to have been the most profitable "medicine" ever put on the market. Col. Hostetter, when he died, left a fortune of eighteen million dollars, which nearly or quite equaled that left by Dr. J. C. Ayer of Lowell, Mass., who began business earlier, owned many preparations and advertised ten times as much.[10]

Lotteries, many of which were fraudulent, also flourished during this period. And the ethics of the "personals" columns often left something to be desired.

A sweet dainty little passion flower from a land where there is no snow in April, dire distressed, will marry non-hard-times man. Address POOR CHILD, 208 Herald Main Office.

IMPERIAL HOTEL, 1 A.M.—Will lady with white trimmings on cape who took cab with gentleman and lady friend correspond with IMPERIAL HOTEL, 184 Herald Main Office?

LADY 23d St. Hargreaves, photographer—The party who saw you entering would like to meet you. Address L., box 225, Herald 23d Branch.

THE "IVORY" is a Laundry Soap, with all the fine qualities of a choice Toilet Soap, and is 99 44-100 per cent. pure.

Ladies will find this Soap especially adapted for washing laces, infants' clothing, silk hose, cleaning gloves and all articles of fine texture and delicate color, and for the varied uses about the house that daily arise, requiring the use of soap that is above the ordinary in quality.

For the Bath, Toilet, or Nursery it is preferred to most of the Soaps sold for toilet use, being purer and much more pleasant and effective and possessing all the desirable properties of the finest unadultered White Castile Soap. The Ivory Soap will "float."

The cakes are so shaped that they may be used entire for general purposes or divided with a stout thread (as illustrated) into two perfectly formed cakes, of convenient size for toilet use.

The price, compared to the quality and the size of the cakes, makes it the cheapest Soap for everybody for every want. TRY IT.

SOLD EVERYWHERE.

FIGURE 2-7

The first advertisement for Ivory Soap, published in 1880. *By permission: The Procter & Gamble Company.*

WILL pretty blonde with lady companion, left "L" train 6th Av. 42d St., 3:20/PM Tuesday, please address admirer who sat opposite? Mention occurrence. CAESAR, box 168 Herald 23d St. Branch.

116th ST "L" station, Tuesday, 12:30/am; blonde in black noticed dark gentleman. SLEEPY, Herald Downtown Branch.

BEAUTIFUL young maiden, abundant means, would marry: reason for advertising, am stranger here. LORRAINE, 263 Herald Main Office.

DEVELOPMENT OF ELOQUENT COPY In the closing years of the nineteenth century, advertising had become a natural part of the marketing plans of retailers and manufacturers. Placed in this new position, it naturally took new forms. Literary freelancers turned to writing eloquent copy, with this kind of result:

> We state with great confidence that ladies attired in our styles for Fall and Winter goods will find the effect so rejuvenating that all the cares incident to domestic life will be as blithesome as kissing the dew from the roses of beauty that bloom in perennial fragrance in the fields of ecstatic love.

SLOGANS, JINGLES, AND TRADE CHARACTERS This was the era of the catchy phrase—the advertising slogan. Some from that time have remained with us to this day:

> It floats (Ivory soap)
> 99-44/100 per cent pure (Ivory soap)
> The Prudential has the strength of Gibraltar
> The Beer that made Milwaukee famous (Schlitz)
> All the news that's fit to print (the *New York Times*)
> Children cry for it (Fletcher's Castoria)

FIGURE 2-8

From a famous series of posters. The jingles and the trade character were well known. *By permission: Erie-Lackawanna Railroad Co.*

And there were jingles. To be sure, they had been used before, but never, before or since, in such volume. Typical of the advertising jingles was this one:

> *Isabel! Oh, Isabel*
> *How is it you dress so well?*
> *Your summer suits cannot be new—*
> *You've worn them all the season through.*
> *Why is it then they do not fade*
> *When washed, but keep their full rich shade;*
> *And e'en the coarser, cheaper prints*
> *Preserve their delicate fair tints?*
> *Isabel, sweet Isabel*
> *Prithee me your secret tell.*
> *Would you know, said Isabel*
> *Why my dresses look so well,*
> *For like perfection all can hope*
> *By simply using IVORY SOAP!*
> *In hottest water, make the suds;*
> *But not till lukewarm, wash your "duds";*
> *They will not fade—and this is why—*
> *There is not too much Alkali*
> *In IVORY SOAP, said Isabel;*
> *That's why I always look so swell.*

This was also the time of the trade character, as advertisers sought to identify their products with figures such as the man on the Quaker Oats box, the Baker Cocoa woman carrying a tray, the dog listening to "His Master's Voice" (RCA Victor), the Cream of Wheat chef, and Aunt Jemima.

The nineteenth century made its mark in advertising history. If it left something wanting, it also had its positive side. Advertising was firmly established and had proved to be an invaluable asset in an economy becoming ever more complex.

ADVERTISING IN THE TWENTIETH CENTURY

THE FIGHT FOR TRUTH IN ADVERTISING At the close of the century, the story was told of an advertising man whose employer, a great retail merchant, asked him to supply something new in advertising. "Let's try honesty," he replied. Although this story may be apocryphal, John E. Powers nonetheless had the spirit of the thought. In 1919, Charles Austin Bates, who followed Powers' philosophy, said:

The grasp of the true inwardness of advertising which he had was what influenced our work and what has made the profession of advertising the respectable thing it is today. By and large, I think I may safely say that Powers' influence is responsible for honesty in advertising—not because we are inherently virtuous but because we have found that it pays. Powers did not fail to consider fully the ultimate consumer; and there is where he founded the profession of advertising, as it likes to think itself today. All of us who are interested in advertising must give thanks to two men— to John E. Powers for the infusion of the fundamental factor of brutal honesty, which not only has had its effect on advertising but which has indirectly made manufacturing and merchandising cleaner—and to George P. Rowell, who brought system and order to a new and as yet undeveloped business. The millennium has not come. There is still a lot of advertising that is plain "bunk." But the Powers idea constantly gains ground.[11]

In the opening years of the twentieth century, the millennium certainly had not come. American business was experiencing its most dynamic period of growth and was riding roughshod over the interests of the citizenry. The spirit of the day seemed to be expansion at all costs, and the price was dear. It was inevitable that such activity made American business vulnerable to attack. The attack was made by so-called "muckrakers," who soon filled the magazines of the day with shocking exposés of American business.

It was only natural that advertising, with its own sins, likewise came under attack. The criticism was directed at patent medicine and financial advertising. It was sharp and it was painful. But most advertisers had already seen the shortsightedness of false and misleading advertising, and the industry prepared to clean house. Forces were joined in the Associated Clubs of the World (now the American Advertising Federation), and vigilance committees were established to police advertising. Out of these grew the Better Business Bureaus. *Printers' Ink* drew up a model state law penalizing false and misleading advertising. Media began to adopt codes of advertising that excluded advertising thought not to be in the best interest of their readers. There is no doubt that there was considerable housecleaning, although the job was by no means complete.

ASSAULT DURING THE 1930s With the depression of the 1930s came a new, stronger assault on business. Someone had to take the blame for the economic collapse and the human misery it caused. Because advertising had become the spokesperson of business, it was only natural that much of the abuse should be directed toward it. The attack on advertising was two-pronged—from the consumer and from the government.

The consumer movement had started back in 1916, but the field was much more fertile for attack now. Soon there was a flood of books denouncing advertising. As a result of this movement, two consumer organizations, Consumers' Research and Consumers Union, were established. Their periodicals made recommendations based on tests of consumer goods. Ironically, these groups used many of the promotional techniques that they sought to supplant through their consumer buying guides.

Of perhaps more significance was government activity. Although the New Deal administration of President Franklin D. Roosevelt urged advertisers to help prime the pump of consumer spending and itself made considerable use of advertising, the "Brain Trust," a group of academic advisors to the President, were openly hostile to advertising. They saw it as one more obstacle to the planned economy they advocated. Largely through their efforts, a considerable amount of restrictive

FIGURE 2-9

An early automobile advertisement. This advertisement is considered by many to be one of the greatest of all time. It appeared in the *Saturday Evening Post* on January 2, 1915. Ironically, the man who wrote it, Theodore F. McManus, never learned to drive an automobile. *By permission: Cadillac Motor Car Division, General Motors Corporation.*

legislation affecting advertising was passed. Among these laws were the Federal Food, Drug, and Cosmetic Act; the Wheeler-Lea Amendment to the Federal Trade Commission Act; and laws vesting control of advertising in the Securities and Exchange Commission, the Post Office, and the Alcohol and Tobacco Tax Division of the Internal Revenue Service.

Although the extremely restrictive legislation proposed by the Brain Trust did not materialize, restrictions nevertheless were imposed, and advertising continues to face government control, with new legislation passed almost every year at the federal and state levels.

SALESMANSHIP IN PRINT All through the early years of the twentieth century, changes in advertising were taking place. Some of the most significant of these came out of a Chicago advertising agency, Lord and Thomas, headed by the amazingly successful Albert Lasker. (Lasker estimated that he made between $40 and $60 million from the advertising agency business.) He hired two copywriters who had a tremendous influence on advertising content. The first of these, John E. Kennedy, expounded an axiom that advertising is *salesmanship in print*

History of Advertising

and that it must therefore state the reason *why* one should buy. Thus, he started replacing the catchy slogans of older advertisements with hard-sell copy giving reasons why people should want the products being advertised. When Kennedy left the agency, Lasker hired Claude C. Hopkins, who for seventeen years with the agency wrote very hard-sell copy and was responsible for many outstanding advertising success stories by making *copy* the main advertising ingredient and *copywriting* the main function of the advertising agency.

RADIO AND TELEVISION ADVERTISING Probably the most significant change in advertising in the United States during this period was in media. In 1922, the most ancient of all advertising techniques, the crier, again shouted messages across the land; but this time he entered the homes of America through radio. For over two decades, this new medium grew by leaps and bounds. Soon the great names of the entertainment world, and later, great names born of radio itself, were helping to sell everything from automobiles to watches. Finally, in 1948, radio advertising was struck hard by television, but when television took over the kind of job radio had been doing for advertisers, radio found a new role for itself as an advertising medium. This development will be described later in this text.

SCIENTIFIC ADVERTISING Advertising was the great panacea for businesspeople. If you wanted to make your fortune, you advertised. Advertising had grown up with the American economy, and, since it was accepted as an integral part of the American success story, its effectiveness was seldom questioned. With the Great Depression, however, businesspeople began to ask questions. Was advertising worthwhile for them? If it was, how could they spend their scarce dollars most advantageously? What media should they use? What appeals were best? Who composed the market, and how could they be persuaded? In an effort to find the answers to these and other questions, advertising turned to a new tool—scientific research. Again, a new advertising era was born. No longer was the advertising tune played by ear. Advertisers wanted a guide to the best results.

TO SUM UP

By studying the history of advertising, we can better understand the advertising of today. Such a study also provides us with an understanding of the public's values and attitudes at various times.

It is difficult to say when advertising first began, but there is evidence that it existed among the early Greeks, Romans, and Phoenicians. In England, advertising first appeared with criers and signs, and later by guilds in pageants during festivals. The development of printing saw advertisements move from hand-written notices to announcements in newspapers.

In the United States, the first newspaper advertising appeared in 1704. However, the stamp tax imposed by the British on the newspapers published in the colonies resulted in a decline in advertising. But after the American Revolution, and with growing industrialization, advertising grew in importance. Advertising agencies began appearing in the mid-nineteenth century. As advertising

Somewhere West of Laramie

SOMEWHERE west of Laramie there's a broncho-busting, steer-roping girl who knows what I'm talking about. She can tell what a sassy pony, that's a cross between greased lightning and the place where it hits, can do with eleven hundred pounds of steel and action when he's going high, wide and handsome.

The truth is—the Playboy was built for her.

Built for the lass whose face is brown with the sun when the day is done of revel and romp and race.

She loves the cross of the wild and the tame.

There's a savor of links about that car—of laughter and lilt and light—a hint of old loves—and saddle and quirt. It's a brawny thing—yet a graceful thing for the sweep o' the Avenue.

Step into the Playboy when the hour grows dull with things gone dead and stale.

Then start for the land of real living with the spirit of the lass who rides, lean and rangy, into the red horizon of a Wyoming twilight.

FIGURE 2-10

Another famous automobile advertisement. This one was written by the manufacturer, Edward S. Jordan, and appeared in the June 23, 1923 issue of the *Saturday Evening Post*. The advertisement broke with tradition. There was no mention of product features, materials, mileage, or the like. Instead, a strong appeal was made to the emotions through copy that was thoroughly romantic and poetic in its lilt. That it was successful is evident from the fact that in the first year Jordan made a net profit of a million dollars on the Playboy. In virtually every list of great advertisements, this one appears.

volume grew, so did the amount of socially questionable advertising. This was the heyday of patent-medicine advertising and other frauds. Toward the close of the nineteenth century, copy turned eloquent, and slogans, jingles, and trade characters were popularized.

The twentieth century brought with it a movement for truth in advertising. During the depression of the 1930s, consumer groups and government questioned advertising practices and sought reform. Advertising began to change. *Reason why* copy with a hard sell became popular. Broadcasting opened new opportunities to reach consumers through commercials.

QUESTIONS AND PROBLEMS

1. How does the history of advertising help us to understand the advertising of today and tomorrow?
2. What similarities and what differences can you see between early advertising and today's advertising?
3. Visit a library and examine some magazines covering a period of years to see how the advertising for a commodity has changed over time. Prepare a report discussing the evolution of the advertising by decades.
4. What famous Americans had connections with early advertising?
5. What were the reasons for the growth of national advertising in the United States?
6. How did branding, magazines, and the development of advertising agencies contribute to the growth of national advertising?
7. Explain Barnum's adage, "Advertise, or chances are the sheriff will do it for you."
8. How do you explain the tremendous use of patent medicine advertising during the last century?
9. Explain what is meant by the axiom that advertising is salesmanship in print.
10. Assume that it is fifty years from now. How would you describe the advertising of the 1980s?

ENDNOTES

[1] Leonard W. Lanfranco, "Advertising as a Tool of Historical Research: A Beginning," in *Making Advertising Relevant* (Columbia, S.C.: American Academy of Advertising, 1975), p. 124.
[2] Henry Sampson, *History of Advertising* (London: Chatto & Windus, Ltd., 1875), p. 19.
[3] Jacob Larwood and John Camden Hotten, *English Inn Signs* (London: Chatto & Windus, Ltd., 1951), p. 1.
[4] Frank Presbrey, *The History and Development of Advertising* (Garden City, N.Y.: Doubleday & Company, Inc., 1929), pp. 5–9.
[5] James Playsted Wood, *The Story of Advertising.* Copyright © 1958 The Ronald Press Company (New York: The Ronald Press Company, 1958), p. 27.
[6] George Burton Hotchkiss, *Milestones of Marketing* (New York: The Macmillan Company, 1938), p. 43.
[7] Presbrey, *The History and Development of Advertising*, p. 150.
[8] Wood, *The Story of Advertising*, pp. 136–37.
[9] Ralph M. Hower, *The History of an Advertising Agency*, rev. ed. (Cambridge, Mass.: Harvard University Press, 1949), p. xxiii.
[10] George P. Rowell, *Forty Years an Advertising Agent* (New York: Franklin Publishing Company, 1926), pp. 389–90.
[11] Presbrey, *The History and Development of Advertising*, p. 310.

Advertising and the Economy

After completing this chapter, you should be able to:

1. Understand the effect of advertising on demand
2. Evaluate the utility of advertising
3. Describe how advertising may help a weak economy
4. Appraise the effects of advertising on costs, price, and freedom of entry

Early economic theory found little if any place for advertising. Economic models were drawn on the basis of pure competition, and there was no need for advertising to promote sales. As theories of imperfect and monopolistic competition developed, the role of advertising (selling costs) was recognized, but economists believed that it was one of the very ills that their theories sought to identify and remedy. The Great Depression stimulated a careful scrutiny of our economic system and the various tools it employed, including advertising. As the ideas of the welfare economists and those advocating social control of the economic sytem grew in popularity, advertising came to be regarded as a detriment to economic well-being and was placed under close observation.

There is an old adage that if you build a better mousetrap, the world will beat a path to your door. Without belittling the importance of the product—for a good product is essential to the effective use of advertising—we should nevertheless recognize that it would be naïve to suppose that in an economic society such as ours, with all its complexities and frictions, the world would even *know* of a better mousetrap, let alone beat a path to it if it was not advertised. Thus, if we are to devise economic models that reflect the real world, they must take into account selling tools, including advertising.

This chapter explains advertising's relation to economics. In doing so, it attempts to show the economic justification of advertising. It is perhaps ironic that the many economists who criticized advertising and found no place for it in their models seldom ignored its existence, for it is a very real phenomenon in the real world. There is no denying that it plays a role in our economy—a role that is, some contend, vital to the success of our economic system.

Unfortunately, many students of advertising have been introduced to the idea that advertising is an economic waste from having been exposed to the subject in basic economics textbooks.

In the simplified treatment of economics found in elementary textbooks, students learn that there would be no advertising outlays in a world of perfect competition! In such a world an individual firm can sell as much as it likes at the going price. If this is so, then obviously advertising is unnecessary. Since we see advertising in the real world, the conclusion seems obvious. In the real world competition is imperfect.[1]

Even though there is some evidence that economists in basic textbooks have moved away from considering advertising solely in the context of the theoretical perfect competition, value judgments by these economists about advertising tend to be mainly negative.[2]

Although the neoclassical economist Alfred Marshall found no place for advertising is his economic theory, he did recognize its existence in his institutional work, *Industry and Trade*.[3] There he distinguished between "constructive" advertisements that are used for giving information and "combative" advertisements that try to supplant competitors. Advertisements that are mainly combative, he contended, are socially wasteful.

Similarly, A.C. Pigou divided advertising into "informative" and "competitive," the latter producing economic waste. In suggesting a remedy for competitive advertising, he said:

> . . . The evil might be attacked by the State through taxation or prohibition of competitive advertisements—if these could be distinguished from advertisements which are not strictly competitive.[4]

And so the economists have generally divided advertising into two broad classifications—constructive or informative on the one hand, and combative, competitive, stimulative, manipulative, superfluous, misleading, puffing, or product-differentiating on the other. Almost universally, these latter types of advertising have been considered an economic waste.

PRIMARY- AND SELECTIVE-DEMAND ADVERTISING In Chapter 1, advertising was classified as either primary-demand advertising or selective-demand advertising. These terms, probably less emotionally charged than those used above, relate to informative and competitive advertising respectively. When we speak of advertising falling into either category, we are talking theoretically. In actual practice, there is often an element of primary demand in a selective-demand advertisement and vice versa. It is only by determining the relative degree of either primary or selective demand in an advertisement that we can categorize it. Because no two advertisements are exactly alike, there is no scientific yardstick to aid in this classification.

Let us suppose, for the sake of a workable theory, that advertisements can be classified precisely. Many economists would contend that primary-demand advertising, because it is informative, is good (or acceptable, or at least tolerable), whereas selective-demand advertising, because it is competitive, is wasteful and hence should be eliminated. The fallacy in this thinking lies in the fact that *all* advertising is com-

FIGURE 3-1

An association stresses the value of competition. It would seem obvious that advertising as a form of competition encourages innovation. The general result is to give the consumer products that offer greater satisfaction. *By permission: Brand Names Foundation, Incorporated.*

petitive, whether it be primary or selective demand. Using the latter, the advertiser is competing within the industry for a greater share of the market for the advertiser's brand; using primary-demand advertising, the advertiser is competing with all producers, including those outside the industry, for a share of the consumers' dollars. A shift in demand from one *industry* to another as the result of primary-demand advertising *may* or *may not* contribute to greater consumer satisfaction, compared with the shift in demand from one *firm* to another within the same industry. In order to evaluate properly whether one category of advertising is better than the other, we must determine which gives the consumer the greatest satisfaction. Selective-demand advertising, stressing brand differentiation, may provide greater consumer satisfaction than primary-demand advertising for a generic product. It appears, therefore, that no generalization as to the relative merits of the categories can be made. Each advertisement must be examined individually in appraising the economic effects of advertising.[5]

ADVERTISING AND MONOPOLISTIC COMPETITION   In the economic theories of monopolistic, imperfect, or nonprice competition, attempts have been made to integrate advertising into economic models by depicting it as a nonprice competitive factor influencing demand. Joan Robinson has said:

> Advertising has never been very well digested into the body of economic analysis. It cannot be fitted into a theory of demand in which consumers with "given tastes" are depicted equalizing marginal satisfaction or climbing to the optimum position on an indifference surface.[6]

Consumers do not have given tastes, nor do they have perfect knowledge. A theory of demand that assumes that they do has no need to consider advertising, but it does not reflect the real world. Business firms attempt to stimulate demand for their goods. *They make their markets*. One means of stimulating demand is advertising.

But J.M. Clark raises the question, "And what comfort is to be derived from the thought that demand is the governor of production, when demand is the plaything of the arts of advertising hypnotism?"[7] Perhaps his language is somewhat harsh. Is Clark possibly giving advertising more credit than it is due? There is no question that advertising influences demand, but this does not mean that demand is merely "the plaything of the arts of advertising hypnotism." We cannot really sell refrigerators to Eskimos through advertising hypnotism. Clark begs the question by assuming the very point that is in doubt: the *extent* to which advertising influences demand.

Even in his famous work, *The Theory of Monopolistic Competition*, Edward H. Chamberlin finds it difficult to generalize about the influence of advertising on demand: "The effect of advertising in any particular case depends upon the facts of the case."[8] K.W. Rothschild points out that:

> . . . it is extremely difficult to get an idea of the quantitative effects of advertising. We know that it is very difficult for a single entrepreneur to trace the effects of an advertising campaign on the demand for his commodity, and this in spite of the advanced stage of cost accounting. If he is only able to get a vague idea of these effects I think it is hopeless to try a quantitative estimate of the effects of total advertising on total consumption. All we can say is that the habit of advertising must be responsible for a considerable increase in the propensity to consume.[9]

CREATE VS. STIMULATE   Advertising influences demand, but there are many instances when demand has been influenced without advertising. Even when there is influence from advertising, the degree of influence varies with each product and with every advertisement. The important factor to note, however, is that advertising does not *create* demand. It is not so powerful as Clark would lead us to believe. All that advertising can do is *stimulate* demand that is already there—latent, perhaps, but there. Other factors, of course, act similarly to produce the same result. Thus, advertising has little effect if the trend underlying the primary demand is not favorable. At best, we can say that advertising will stimulate demand effectively when the various environmental influences (such as society, technology, human behavior, the economy, and the political-legal climate) that *create* demand are favorable. As J.J. Lambin comments, "The *economic power of advertising* 'per se' has been overstated by advertising critics and apologists. Socioeconomic forces are more important, and advertising has a limited capacity to stimulate total market growth."[10] There is no valid formula that X number of advertising dollars will produce Y sales. It is not possible to use advertising effectively to build a demand for a product that provides no satisfaction to the consumer. If it were, how simple the problem would be for the firm!

EMPIRICAL ANALYSIS OF DEMAND   Can empirical analysis get us any further? Neil H. Borden's monumental work, *The Economic Effects of Advertising*, is devoted in large part to such analysis.[11] Borden warns his readers, however, that the quantitative effects of the advertising studied are not precise. "The number of variables concomitant with demand is large, it is often difficult even to determine just what variables are present, and frequently it is impossible to get data by which to measure those that are known."[12] He sums up the effect of advertising upon demand: "Advertising can and does increase the demand for many individual companies, but the extent to which it does so varies widely and depends upon the circumstances under which the enterprises operate."[13]

> The pre-eminence of America in industry, which has constantly brought about a reduction in costs, has come very largely through mass production. Mass production is only possible where there is demand. Mass demand has been created almost entirely through the development of advertising.
>
> *CALVIN COOLIDGE (1872–1933), Statesman*
>
> READER'S DIGEST

ADVERTISING AND UTILITY

One of the major criticisms of advertising made by economists is that advertising is wasteful because it does not add real utility to goods and services and, in fact, frequently makes for dissatisfaction. (Some writers have referred to utility as the "value added" theory.) Let us consider this criticism. At the outset it is essential to recognize that utility is subjective, depending upon the individual concerned and the object considered. In his *Principles of Economics*, Alfred Marshall writes:

> Man cannot create material things . . . when he is said to produce material things he really only produces utilities; or in other words, his efforts and sacrifices result in changing the form or arrangement of matter to adapt it better for the satisfaction of wants.[14]

Economists in general have regarded these wants as being fixed and known, and the entrepreneur is considered to create utilities by "changing the form or arrangement of matter" in relation to wants.[15]

Advertising is one of several stimuli that affect the wants of the consumer audience; consumer wants are the result of reactions to stimuli. It provides time utility by indicating to the consumer that goods are accessible when they are wanted—for example, an advertisement in June for swimsuits. It provides place utility by indicating that goods are accessible where they are wanted—for example, an advertisement by a retailer announcing that the summer selection of swimsuits is now in stock. It provides possession utility by enhancing the goods in the consumer's mind so that greater satisfaction results from owning them —for example, an advertisement that expresses a consumer's satisfaction with a national-brand product the consumer owns. It provides form utility by satisfying the human desire for something new—for example, an advertisement that stresses the styling of a new model of automobile.

Returning to Marshall's statement, we see that he indicates that utilities are created by "changing the form or arrangement of matter." But such change can also create *dis*utility. Baking an apple changes the form or arrangement of matter. Therefore, for some people, it is an improvement that offers greater satisfaction than a raw apple does. But for those who like a crisp, raw apple, baking has made it less desirable. Certainly, changes as such do not offer satisfaction unless consumers in their own minds believe they do. This is part of what advertising is about, for advertising appeals to consumers' purchases of products in terms of satisfying life-styles, moods, and values. Thus, advertising is a real creator of utilities for consumers by "moving and arranging minds."[16] The utility for most products comes into being only as a result of the given or changing attitudes and values of consumers, and advertising is one effective tool that producers and distributors have to appeal to consumers in an attempt to get them to perceive sufficient utilities so they will buy their products. Advertising, which appeals to the mind, therefore creates utilities just as physical changes in a product do, for utility is subjective. There is no difference between elements in the physical form of a commodity that make no difference in its efficiency, on the one hand, and advertising on the other; for advertising makes a difference in the mind of a consumer as much as the physical elements of the products do.

Keynesian economics, a rather influential school of economic thought in recent decades, suggests that when there is less than full employment, savings must be offset by investment to maximize employment. This theory, in contrast to older theories, would appear to justify advertising as a productive rather than a wasteful enterprise.

In a period of less than full employment, advertising can be used in several ways to alleviate the situation. First, if people can be persuaded to increase the propensity to consume, it follows that there will be greater employment of resources. Advertising has as a major objective persuading people to buy. Increased demand results in increased production and more jobs. Second, advertising can be used to inform people and stimulate a desire for new inventions. The result is not only increased demand but new investment that leads to increased employment, increased income, and generally greater well-being. Third, proponents of this theory hold that no economic resources should be left unused, for unused resources are lost. It is argued, therefore, that even resources that are relatively unproductive should be put to work, for they produce income that helps the economy. Thus advertising could be justified, if for no other reason than it makes use of resources. Of course, in all these instances, it is assumed that the advertising is ethically sound and not fraudulent.

Whereas advertising may thus be economically justified in a period of less than full employment, what of advertising during full employment? It might be and has been argued that in such a period, when there is scarcity of resources, with demand exceeding supply, any resources that are being used unproductively should be reallocated to try to equate supply and demand. Thus, advertising, which serves to stimulate demand, should be dispensed with and the resources that formerly went into it should be redirected to increasing supply. During World War II, our economy was in such a position, and many people advocated the elimination of advertising for the duration. This, however, was in all probability a shortsighted point of view, for advertising has a cumulative effect, and in the long run, it is to be expected that the economy will return to a condition of less than full employment. There is ample evidence to indicate what happens to demand for the firms when they stop their aggressive promotion. Thus, preparing for future potential even in periods of full employment, firms must continue to advertise in order not to lose the cumulative effect of past advertising and to safeguard demand for the future. To be sure, such advertising must be planned with considerable discretion, lest its effect be to increase an already excessive demand. But with careful planning and judicious curtailment, advertising undoubtedly should continue during a period of full employment as an investment in future economic security.

Advertising is vital to the American economy. The fruits of industrial progress, scientific discovery and business innovations could not be fully understood by society without entrepreneurial promotion through advertising. The social wastes supposedly inherent in competitive advertising are small indeed when compared with the social losses caused by alternative means for achieving consumer choice.

HERMAN B WELLS, Educator

READER'S DIGEST

OTHER ASPECTS OF ADVERTISING AND ECONOMICS

There are many other areas of economics that can be explored in terms of the effects of advertising. What is the effect of advertising on distribution costs? What effect does advertising have on production costs? Is advertising monopolistic? Does advertising affect price competition? What is the effect of advertising on the business cycle? What effect does advertising have on quality and variety of merchandise? Does advertising affect media prices to the consumer? These are some of the areas that will be touched upon briefly here.[17]

ADVERTISING AND DISTRIBUTION COSTS   Advertising has frequently been criticized as an unnecessary expense and a waste in the distribution process, although sufficient empirical data are not available to generalize as to the effect of advertising on distribution costs. These costs, including advertising, have risen continually with the growth of our industrial economy. This should not be surprising, for with the division of labor and specialization of production, the size of markets grew. With their growth came the complexities of marketing goods. Still, the aggregate cost of advertising in the United States is only a small part of total distribution costs.

An increase in advertising cost, it is sometimes argued, results in a decrease in other distribution costs because of the greater efficiency of advertising compared to, say, personal selling. Although this can be true in some cases, there is little doubt that in other cases, such expenditures do not decrease overall distribution costs, but rather increase them. It is interesting to note that although higher distribution costs resulting from aggressive advertising may be reflected in higher selling prices, this has not dissuaded the consumer from buying such products instead of less-advertised or unadvertised products at lower prices.

In industries that follow different promotional strategies, with some firms advertising aggressively while others do not, the firms that do not advertise may enjoy considerable demand. This would appear to indicate that advertising is wasteful. However, although there is no evidence to support the contention, it seems reasonable to speculate that the selective-demand advertising of the aggressive firm serves in part to stimulate demand for the generic product, thus increasing demand for the nonadvertising firm's product. It is also possible that high advertising costs to the producer may reduce distribution costs to the retailer, inasmuch as the product is presold. In such cases, the retailer's margin is usually reduced, so that the price paid by the ultimate consumer is not as high as it would be if traditional margins were left in effect.

ADVERTISING AND PRODUCTION COSTS   One of the arguments businesspeople use most often to justify advertising is that it results in lower production costs. As a result of his study, Borden found that the effects of advertising on production costs are indeterminate.[18] Nevertheless, certain conclusions and judgments seem reasonable. If it is agreed that advertising can stimulate demand, then if the production nature of a firm is such that economies of scale can be achieved, production costs will be lowered to the extent that advertising can provide the necessary demand. As Jules Backman states, "To the extent advertising is successful, total sales volume expands and may result in reductions in unit costs for production and overhead."[19] Of course, the necessary demand may be created by other means—for example, personal selling, price, quality, or the nature of the product itself. Furthermore, it does not always follow that large-scale production results in

Advertising is to business what steam is to machinery—the great propelling power.

THOMAS BABINGTON
MACAULEY
(1800–1859), Historian

READER'S DIGEST

FIGURE 3-2

An association in the advertising business speaks out for advertising and its role in the economy. *By permission: American Association of Advertising Agencies.*

economies, for often the product—such as high-fashion clothing—is such as to make small-scale production necessary.

One other aspect of advertising's effect on production costs should be noted. It may be possible for advertising to lower overhead costs by spreading demand. Thus, through advertising, a firm with a high seasonal demand may be able to extend that demand over a broader time period, effecting economies by reducing storage or reducing the size of plant that might have been necessary with a highly peaked demand.

Assuming that advertising does in some instances result in lower production costs, what happens to the savings? Businesspeople, in their eagerness to make a point, too often say that savings are passed on to the consumer in the form of lower prices. Actually, when consumer prices are lowered, business usually expects demand to be increased sufficiently so that while unit profits are less, total profits are greater. In other instances, the production cost savings may go directly toward profit to be reinvested. Regardless of where the savings go, however, they end up as a contribution to the economy, for they result in either increased consumption or increased investment.

ADVERTISING AND FREEDOM OF ENTRY   Yale Brozen, in considering the question "Is advertising a barrier to entry?" says:

> To anyone who has noticed the use of advertising by any business to woo the customers of other firms, it must seem a bit surrealistic to be considering the evidence for and against the view that advertising is a means of monopolizing. To any casual observer, it would seem that advertising is a means of competing. Most important, advertising is much more a means of entry than a barrier to entry.[20]

There is insufficient evidence to substantiate any claim that advertising limits entry to an industry. It is probably true that advertising in individual cases has built so strong a demand for a brand as to tend toward concentration in an industry. But aggressive advertising by many firms in the drug and cosmetic industries, for example, has not limited freedom of entry. Indeed, there are other firms in these industries that use little or no advertising and survive and also flourish. Philip Nelson points out:

> Contrary to the critics, advertising probably . . . reduces barriers to entry. . . . A new brand entering the market can capture its share of the new customers who are guided by advertising, but it cannot get any customers who are guided by past sales. Advertising makes entry easier rather than more difficult. It is no wonder that the scraps of evidence that we have show that entry occurs more easily for highly advertised goods.[21]

Whereas Joe Bain claims that advertising represents a substantial barrier to entry,[22] Richard Schmalensee concludes rather emphatically, "There is no evidence to suggest that advertising outlays have permitted some firms to create barriers to entry."[23]

It should be noted that there is little if any causal relationship between the *size* of an advertising appropriation and its effect on demand. Size can be important only when the *quality* of the advertising is held constant among competitors, which is not readily feasible. Indeed, there are many instances of small advertisers upsetting the position of the giants because of the quality of the small advertiser's advertising. In industries with apparently limited entry, such as the automobile industry, factors like capital investment offer much greater entry limitations than does advertising. In industries in which an innovator has successfully built a strong brand demand through advertising, such success frequently attracts competition ready to take advantage of an established market, appealing for a share through price competition or design modifications. Ironically, although advertising stands accused of fomenting monopoly (barriers to entry) on the one hand, it is charged with causing brand proliferation on the other!

ADVERTISING AND PRICE COMPETITION   It has been generally believed that advertising tends to make for price rigidity. This is because firms using extensive advertising believe demand for their products to be inelastic. Private branders and price-competitive firms, however, have shown that they can cut into the demand of advertised

Schuylkill Passport. In Philadelphia an ad on the wall of Don's Sunoco station says: "Foreign cars washed only in imported water."

TIME

Advertising and the Economy

Give me one good reason for advertising in 1984!

1985!

A message to American business from Crain Communications Inc., publishers of Advertising Age, American Trade Magazines, Automotive News, AutoWeek, Business Insurance, Crain's Chicago Business, Crain's Cleveland Business, Crain's Illinois Business, Crain's Special Events Report, Electronic Media, Humm's Guide to the Florida Keys, Industrial Marketing, Modern Healthcare, Pensions & Investment Age, Rubber & Plastics News.

FIGURE 3-3

A famous advertisement suggests an important economic reason for advertising. *By permission: Crain Communications Inc.*

brands. Several recent studies have also provided some significant new insights into the effect of advertising on price. For example, in states where advertising of prescription drugs and eyeglasses is permitted, consumer prices are lower than in states where advertising of these commodities is prohibited.[24] In an extensive study by Robert Steiner for the toy business, Steiner constructed productivity indexes in the pretelevision and posttelevision advertising eras.[25] The second index "rose significantly despite the sizable advance in manufacturers' marketing costs, principally because the heavy advertising weights, by increasing the efficiency of distribution, led to lower trade markups and retail prices and to higher consumption and output."[26]

Advertising, like other forms of nonprice competition, may act to lessen the sensitivity of demand to price. However, its effectiveness appears to be strongly related to industry and economic conditions. In the drug and cosmetics industries, in which price is considerably less important than brand appeal because of the emotionalism involved in purchases, advertising undoubtedly impedes quick-acting price competition. But when the consumer is indifferent to brand because of the nature of the product (for example, sugar), the commodity is so sensitive to price that there is insufficient margin to permit much use of advertising, and it is questionable whether advertising would effectively stimulate brand demand anyway. In any case, there is evidence to show that during a depression, for example, price competition asserts itself even for those products that have made strong use of advertising. As indicated before, there are, in every industry, firms that prefer price competition to nonprice competition; in such an industry, the firm that relies upon advertising rather than price may be able to maintain its demand for a while, but ultimately its demand will suffer as the gap widens between its selling prices and those of firms resorting to price competition. Ultimately, such a firm may find it necessary to lower prices.

ADVERTISING AND BUSINESS CYCLES Although advertising, like many other factors, has some effect on business cycles, the effect cannot be considered very important. Certainly, fluctuations existed long before advertising assumed its present importance. Generally, advertising has followed such fluctuations and has thus tended to accentuate them somewhat. Advertising increases in the aggregate when demand is high and decreases when it is low. During past downward cyclical fluctuations, there have been notable exceptions in a few industries, which have attempted, with gratifying results, to increase sales by means of aggressive advertising.

Some have suggested that advertising might be used in counteracting recession, and this thought certainly has merit. If the consumer could be induced to spend rather than save, this money would surely pump new life into the economy. There would appear to be some evidence to support this possibility in the research of Taylor and Weiserbs, who found that, "Based on an analysis of advertising expenditures in the aggregate, our results suggest that advertising does in fact tend to increase consumption at the expense of saving.[27] Yet there are certain problems with this recommendation. Individual firms and even industries might elect to advertise, and although the result undoubtedly would be beneficial to these firms, the effect on the total economy would be negligible. The difficulty in getting all industry to participate is the lack of necessary funds, although more firms are saving funds for such purposes as well as for capital expansion during recessions. Then, too, the advertising task admittedly becomes more difficult at such times, and the amount of advertising dollars necessary to stimulate a given demand would probably be greater than during an economic peak. This difficulty might be overcome to some extent by holding constant product improvement, innovation, and so forth for such periods. It is interesting to note that cooperative institutional campaigns through The Advertising Council have been used during recent recessions in an attempt to restore faith in the economy, but the effect is difficult, if not impossible, to measure.

ADVERTISING, QUALITY, AND THE MERCHANDISE VARIETY Advertising has had a profound, although necessarily indirect, effect on the quality and variety of merchandise available to the American consumer. Although advertising has been criticized for stressing

Love for Sale. *In Jonesboro, Ark., Floyd Bailey, 22, took an advertisement in the* Sun *offering matrimony to any girl with enough money to help him get out of jail.*

TIME

product differences, this practice generally has resulted in improving products. To build demand effectively, advertising must have something to talk about. It is true that this is sometimes imaginary, but only because the producer has been unable to make it real. Obviously, the more important the product differences are, the more effective the advertising is likely to be in building demand. Thus, advertising has provided strong impetus to producers to find competitive advantages for their products, and the results have been a constant improvement of their goods. When price competition firms in the same industry imitate these improvements, the aggressive advertising producer seeks new improvements.

Because advertising makes possible a high volume of demand in a relatively short time, it encourages research and innovation. A firm is more willing to invest in developing a new product when it has some assurance that the cost of development will be recovered quickly through demand built by advertising. Then, too, the large initial demand that advertising can build for a new product may make possible sufficient economy of scale for the producer to be able to price the product initially at a reasonable level.

As has been mentioned before, advertising frequently builds enough demand to encourage competition. Thus it stimulates variety. Some critics contend that variety, especially when the difference between brands is negligible, is economically wasteful. However, consumers find that even brand differences that critics consider negligible permit them to enjoy greater satisfaction by finding brands of products that more nearly meet their personal preferences.

Quality has also been raised through advertising. In order to safeguard the reputation of an advertised brand, quality must be consistent. Therefore, quality control is more likely to be instituted for an advertised than an unadvertised brand. Also, the degree of quality becomes a competitively differentiating factor that can be effectively used in advertising; thus, many firms make improvements in quality in order to have this important competitive advantage.

ADVERTISING AND MEDIA PRICES   There is no question that the consumer pays less for magazines and newspapers and enjoys radio and television without charge because of the advertising revenue that these media enjoy. But to say that the consumer does not pay for these may be naïve, for the consumer pays indirectly in the price paid for advertised products. The direct price charged for newspapers, for example, is substantially lowered by the advertising revenue, but other factors also determine price. As the *New York Times* has a considerably higher advertising linage and revenue than the *Daily News*, the lower price of the latter undoubtedly results from its substantially higher circulation and the resulting production economies.

Some critics say that the lower price a consumer pays as a result of advertising is indeed a dear price to pay for advertising control of media. As we shall see in Chapter 4 with regard to the media, this criticism has no validity. In some nations, radio and television are paid for

He who whispers down a well
About the goods he has to sell
Will never reap the golden dollars
Like him who shows them round and hollers.

Anonymous
READER'S DIGEST

directly by the consumer in the form of taxes or license fees; such a system in this country, critics say, would vastly improve the quality of program offerings. This argument, however, fails to recognize an important economic principle. Advertisers want to maximize their profits and, to accomplish this end, they try constantly to find programs that meet the demand of the largest part of the consumer audience. To do otherwise would be to discourage audiences for their advertising messages. There may be some merit in presenting not what the public wants but what it should have, but the arguments here center on the merits of democratic determination vs. autocratic authoritarianism. Advertisers, with their profit motives, give considerable assurance of serving the public demand.

SOME CONCLUSIONS

Advertising has considerable effects on our economic system. Just what these effects are, however, is difficult, if not impossible, to explain. The economic effects of advertising involve too many intangibles to be included in an economic theory that accurately depicts the real world. "The generalizations made about the economic implications of advertising are often controversial, and there is no strong theoretical ground on which to relate conclusions drawn from empirical tests."[28]

Yet advertising is an integral part of the modern American economic system. Like any other part, it has its weaknesses and it presents certain problems to the smooth workings of the economy. Without it, however, the economy would perhaps suffer greater problems.

TO SUM UP

Advertising is a very real part of our economy and plays a vital role in it. In theoretical perfect competition, there is no need for advertising, but our system is one of imperfect competition, and advertising is used by firms to stimulate demand. Demand, however, must be there—latently, perhaps—for advertising to be effective. Demand is the result of various environmental influences, and only when these are present will advertising effectively stimulate sales.

Advertising may be said to add utility by "moving and arranging minds." Thus, if a consumer believes there is greater satisfaction in owning an advertised brand, this is as much utility creation as a change in the form or arrangement of matter in the production of that brand.

During periods of less-than-full employment, advertising can result in priming the economic pump by encouraging people to buy. Because the economy fluctuates and advertising has a cumulative effect, even in a period of full employment, advertising should be continued in anticipation of a period of less-than-full employment.

There is no conclusive evidence that advertising raises distribution costs. Through resulting economies of scale, advertising may contribute to decreasing production costs. It probably does not result in restraining freedom of entry in an industry and, in fact, may encourage new entries. Advertising may act to lessen the sensitivity of demand to price, but this varies with industries, and for certain classes of goods, price elasticity is strong.

Unfortunately the economic implications of advertising are still not sufficiently proven through research to enable us to explain exactly the effects of advertising on the economy.

QUESTIONS AND PROBLEMS

1. Why did economic theory find little if any place for advertising?
2. The economist J.M. Clark refers to demand as the "plaything of the arts of advertising hypnotism." Is this a valid explanation of advertising and its effect on demand? Explain your position.
3. "Advertising creates utilities by moving and arranging minds." Do you agree or disagree? Support your position.
4. On what basis might advertising be justified in a period of full employment?
5. Advertising has frequently been criticized as an unnecessary expense and a waste in the distribution process. Do you agree or disagree? Support your position.
6. Does advertising result in lowering production costs? Explain.
7. Is advertising a barrier to entry? Explain.
8. Does advertising tend to make for price rigidity? Explain.
9. How might advertising be used in a recession to help stimulate the economy?
10. Would the economy be better off without advertising? Explain.

ENDNOTES

[1] Lester G. Telser, "Advertising and the Consumer," in Yale Brozen, ed., *Advertising and Society* (New York: New York University Press, 1974), p. 26.

[2] Michael V. Laric and Lewis R. Tucker, "The Issue of Fairness: How Do Economists Treat Advertising?" *Journal of Advertising*, VI, No. 4 (Fall 1977), 29.

[3] Alfred Marshall, *Industry and Trade*, 3d ed. (London: Macmillan & Co. Ltd., 1927), pp. 304–7.

[4] A.C. Pigou, *The Economics of Welfare*, 4th ed. (London: Macmillan & Co. Ltd., 1950), p. 199.

[5] For two other approaches to this topic, see Shelby D. Hunt, "Informational vs. Persuasive Advertising: An Appraisal," *Journal of Advertising*, V, No. 3 (Summer 1976), 5–8; and Phillip Nelson, "The Economic Value of Advertising," in Yale Brozen, ed., *Advertising and Society* (New York: New York University Press, 1974), pp. 43–52.

[6] Joan Robinson, "Book Review," *Economica*, IX (new series), No. 35 (August 1942), 294.

[7] J.M. Clark, *Social Control of Business*, 2nd ed. (New York: McGraw-Hill Book Company, 1939), p. 41.

[8] Edward H. Chamberlin, *The Theory of Monopolistic Competition*, 7th ed. (Cambridge, Mass.: Harvard University Press, 1948), p. 167.

[9] K.W. Rothschild, "A Note on Advertising," *Economic Journal*, LII, No. 205 (April 1942), 116.

[10] Jean Jacques Lambin, *Advertising, Competition and Market Conduct in Oligopoly over Time* (Amsterdam: North-Holland Publishing Company, 1976), p. 167.

[11] Neil H. Borden, *The Economic Effects of Advertising* (Homewood, Ill.: Richard D. Irwin, Inc., 1942).

[12] *Ibid.*, p. 193.

[13] *Ibid.*, p. 433.

[14] Alfred Marshall, *Principles of Economics*, 8th ed. (London: Macmillan & Co. Ltd., 1920), p. 63.

[15] E.A. Lever, *Advertising and Economic Theory* (London: Oxford University Press, 1947), pp. 48–50.

[16] *Ibid.*, p. 49.

[17] For a more extensive treatment of the subject, see Borden, *The Economic Effects of Advertising,* Chap. 6 and 28; Michael Pearce, Scott M. Cunningham, and Aron Miller, *Appraising the Economic and Social Effects of Advertising* (Cambridge, Mass.: Marketing Science Institute, 1971); John Schleede, "A Review of the Literature Pertinent to the Economics of Advertising," in Gordon E. Miracle, ed., *Sharing for Understanding* (East Lansing, Mich.: American Academy of Advertising, 1977), pp. 14–23; and Mark S. Albion and Paul W. Farris, *The Advertising Controversy* (Boston: Auburn House Publishing Company, 1981).

[18] Borden, *The Economic Effects of Advertising,* p. 854.

[19] Jules Backman, *Advertising and Competition* (New York: New York University Press, 1967), p. 143.

[20] Yale Brozen, "Is Advertising a Barrier to Entry?" in Yale Brozen, ed., *Advertising and Society* (New York: New York University Press, 1974), p. 79.

[21] Nelson, "The Economic Value of Advertising," p. 54.

[22] Joe S. Bain, *Industrial Organization,* 2nd ed. (New York: John Wiley & Sons, Inc., 1968), p. 282.

[23] Richard Schmalensee, *The Economics of Advertising* (Amsterdam: North-Holland Publishing Company, 1975), p. 244.

[24] John F. Cady, *Drugs on the Market: The Impact of Public Policy on the Retail Market for Prescription Drugs* (Lexington, Mass.: D.C. Heath & Company, Lexington Books, 1975); and Lee Benham, "The Effect of Advertising on the Price of Eyeglasses," *Journal of Law and Economics,* XV, No. 2 (October 1972), 337–52.

[25] Robert L. Steiner, "Economic Theory and the Idea of Marketing Productivity," working paper (Cambridge, Mass.: Marketing Science Institute, 1974). See also Robert L. Steiner, "Does Advertising Lower Consumer Prices?" *Journal of Marketing,* XXXVII, No. 4 (October 1973), 19–26.

[26] Robert L. Steiner, "The Prejudice Against Marketing," *Journal of Marketing,* XL, No. 3 (July 1976), 4–5.

[27] Lester D. Taylor and Daniel Weiserbs, "Advertising and the Aggregate Consumption Function," *The American Economic Review,* LXII, No. 4 (September 1972), 642.

[28] Albion and Farris, *The Advertising Controversy,* p. x.

Advertising and Society

After completing this chapter, you should be able to:
1. Enumerate the various criticisms of advertising
2. Understand why the public is so often critical of advertising
3. Explain advertising and taste, emotion, and fraud
4. Appraise the effect of advertising on stereotypes

Criticism of advertising is almost as old as advertising itself. In 1759, with printed advertising still in its infancy, Dr. Samuel Johnson wrote an essay on the "Art of Advertising" in which he spoke its praise, but with reservations:

> The trade of advertising is now so near to perfection, that it is not easy to propose any improvement. But as every art ought to be exercised in due subordination to the publick good, I cannot but propose it as a moral question to these masters of the publick ear. Whether they do not sometimes play too wantonly with our passions, as when the registrar of lottery-tickets invites us to his shop by an account of the prize which he sold last year; and whether the advertising controvertists do not indulge asperity of language without any adequate provocation; as in the dispute about *straps for razors*, now happily subsided, and in the altercation which at present subsists concerning *eau de luce*?[1]

That advertising should be the target of so much criticism is not surprising. By its very nature it is highly visible, and this very visibility makes it an easy target for critics to shoot at. As Walter Taplin so aptly states:

> Advertising, because it is ubiquitous and obstructive, is a subject on which everyone tends to form strong opinions. This is an encouragement to the serious investigator of the nature of the phenomenon and at the same time it is something of a barrier in his path. It means that everyone is interested in the subject, but nobody is quite disinterested. Investigation itself, the search for the truth, soon begins to turn up ideas and facts, but these are at once seized upon by partisans who regard them as potential evidence to support their preconceived opinions.[2]

The persistent criticism of advertising need hardly be surprising. After all, the major use of advertising through the years has been for commercial purposes, and even the most steadfast advocate of business enterprise will admit that business has not always had the best of reputations. The doctrine of *caveat emptor* ("let the buyer beware") has carried down from earliest times to at least the beginning of this century, implying that selling was a dirty game. By the rules of the day, buyers were to consider themselves duly warned, and sellers were more or less permitted to engage in every form of trickery, chicanery, and deceit. Advertising, as one of the tools of the seller, was used to accomplish the seller's ends without moral considerations. Thus, much of the criticism was well founded, and the only defense advertising could make was that, insofar as *caveat emptor* was the motto of the time, buyers accepted the challenge, put themselves on guard, and did not take advertising at face value.

ADVERTISING CRITICISM TODAY

As we saw in Chapter 2, the twentieth century brought a new series of attacks on advertising. At the same time, government regulations and internal business actions were bringing reforms to the business community. The attacks leveled against advertising by social critics seemed to diminish with World War II, and the prosperity that followed the war brought with it a lull in the battle on advertising. By the late 1950s, however, in the wake of scandals involving the rigging of television quiz shows, criticism was becoming stronger. The critics were primarily educators, social reformers, and government officials, for the general public was for the most part either in favor of advertising or disinterested. As late as 1967, an extensive study showed public attitudes to be largely favorable.[3]

The 1960s saw the development of a series of significant events that had the effect of controlling advertising and raising questions about it. Government agencies were taking actions against what they considered business excesses, and many of these related to advertising. The attacks were joined by educators, social reformers, and the press, all of whom, as usual, claimed to act in the name of the consumer. But this time a new force entered the battle—the consuming public itself. By the end of the decade, American citizens were awakening to the social revolution stirring in the land. In a period marked by growing concern with race relations, poverty, crime, social justice, American involvement in southeast Asia, equality for women, ecology, and the like, it was only natural that there should also be concern with malpractice in the marketplace. The consumer advocacy of Ralph Nader, who was at first shrugged off as a meddlesome do-gooder, has found support from large segments of the general public. The consuming public itself soon joined the battle, led initially by youthful advocates. Most surprising is the fact that many businesspeople have also become critical of advertising—at least in areas where it is abusive.

The decade of the 1970s continued to foster skepticism of advertising by many citizens, as a result of shortages of natural resources such as petroleum while automobile manufacturers continued to advertise cars with relatively low fuel efficiency; the lack of credibility during the Nixon presidency, which resulted in questioning the credibility of advertising ("if you cannot trust the president of the United States, what can you trust?"); the growing concerns that advertising has been unfairly manipulative of children. No longer is American society willing to accept the doctrine of *caveat emptor*, "let the buyer beware." The new cry is *caveat venditor*, "let the seller beware." It will not settle for anything less than reform in the marketplace.

And so the criticism of advertising continues into the 1980s. Not too long ago, Robert Heilbroner wrote:

> If I were asked to name the deadliest subversive force within capitalism—the single greatest source of its waning morality—I should without hesitation name advertising. How else should one identify a force that debases language, drains thought, and undoes dignity? If the barrage of advertising, unchanged in its tone and texture, were devoted to some other purpose—say the exaltation of the public sector—it would be recognized in a moment for the corrosive element that it is. But as the voice of the private sector it escapes this startled notice.[4]

This is far from the last attack on advertising. Let us, therefore, take a look at some of the criticisms of advertising and of how it affects society as these criticisms are seen today.

ADVERTISING IS A TOOL

Used correctly, a hammer will drive home a nail. Used incorrectly, it will mash a thumb. Advertising, like a hammer, is inanimate. It is a tool for communications. Used correctly, it can be effective and beneficial. Unfortunately, advertising can be—and in some instances is—used incorrectly from a social point of view. However, incorrect use cannot diminish the potential value of the tool for doing an effective job of communicating. We do not dispose of the hammer when we hit our thumb. It would be just as foolish to dispose of advertising when we find a socially poor advertisement.

If we are to make relevant criticisms of advertising, we must turn our attention from the tool itself to those animate creatures who use it. There are four such groups: the advertising practitioners, the users of advertising, the carriers or media of advertising, and the advertising audience. Each must share in the social responsibility for advertising. Each does—and still there are abuses. These may be minimized, but it is too much to hope that they will be completely eliminated, for in a free society, the price for freedom is the individual's right of nonconformity.

Advertising is an inescapable part of almost everyone's life in America. Thus, almost everyone has an attitude about the subject. And the attitudes, as expressed, seem extremely negative, in terms of both the product and those who produce it.

JOHN O'TOOLE, Advertising Agent

AREAS OF CRITICISM

Many of the most common criticisms directed against advertising are based on emotion rather than reason. Frequently the critics of advertising launch their attacks without examining the issue dispassionately. In the pages that follow, many of the current criticisms will be considered from the advertising viewpoint. We do not mean to imply by this procedure that advertising today is beyond reproach. Such an implication would be hopelessly naïve. But we do mean to make clear that there are two sides to every argument. As you examine the arguments, *you* must decide on the validity of the criticisms and the defenses.

Criticisms of advertising have been so often repeated that there is almost a "standard" list. These include advertising as an economic waste, which was discussed in Chapter 3, and the following:

Advertising is too much with us.
Advertising stresses materialism.
Advertising creates false needs.
Advertising is in poor taste.
Advertising appeals to the masses.
Advertising appeals to emotion.
Advertising is misleading or fraudulent.
Advertising supports stereotypes.
Advertising manipulates children.

ADVERTISING IS TOO MUCH WITH US As Blake Clark said, ". . . the average man lives with the advertising man's work more hours a day than with his family, and is certainly more familiar with advertising slogans than with the proverbs in his Bible."[5] And it is still true today. Perhaps we are so heavily and continuously barraged by advertising that we resent it. Unfortunately, we can't avoid advertising as we could a disagreeable person. Like the weather, it becomes a common topic of conversation, and we react to it accordingly, saying little as long as it is pleasant. We look forward to the advertisements announcing the new automobiles much as we look forward to the first snowfall. But when the competition sharpens, amid a blizzard of claims, counterclaims, and reasons for buying one brand rather than another—especially when we have already made our purchase or cannot make one—we react as we do to the pile-up of winter snow. The major difference is that we have little control over the weather and accept it as inevitable. But advertising is a product of people. Shouldn't we be able to do something about it? Thus, the sheer volume of advertising becomes an irritant. This, however, is a natural concomitant of a prosperous economy in which the consumer has the resources for so much discretionary spending. This has been a nation of plenty. To be critical of the amount of advertising to which we are exposed without being critical at the same time of the amount of mass communications media, the number of choices in products available to us, and the vast amounts of everything else is to be inconsistent. For the firm to survive in this economy of plenty, it is necessary to shout to be heard, and the firm does this through advertising.

ADVERTISING STRESSES MATERIALISM Commenting on the work of advertising people, Vance Packard wrote:

The real needs of most of us were satisfied long ago. About 40 percent of the things we buy today are unnecessary in terms of any real need. Even our wants are pretty well satisfied. It has become a question of creating in our minds new, unrealized wants and needs.[6]

Thus, so the argument goes, advertising stresses material gratification and a false set of values with the apparent aim of making us dissatisfied so that we may strive to realize new wants and needs. As Canadian Member of Parliament Murdo Martin said, "You are buying things you don't need with money you haven't got, trying to impress people you don't like."

There is no doubt that material acquisition should be a means to an end and not an end in itself. The ends of life are determined by the individual and should be guided not by an advertising pitch but by the great philosophic systems. It is true that people do not live by bread alone, but it is just as true that without bread people would not live at all. And the acquisition of material things in most instances provides the time for people to pursue the nonmaterial. Regardless of this, however, in a democracy, people determine for themselves their ends and the means of achieving them.

Ray Hutchinson makes an interesting point when he says:

> Moaning that advertising reflects a "materialist vision" of America as a collection of money-hungry slobs is hopelessly naïve. It is like condemning railroads for showing American cities to their patrons as oases of junkyards, rusty sidings, ding-dong crossing signals, freight yards, and the iterative arcs of little red lanterns. As it happens, railroad rights-of-way happen to go through that portion of the cityscape. And as it happens, advertising of its nature happens to dote on manufactured goods. If we should demand that the railroad fly high above the material world, all the junkyards would of course disappear—but so would the railroad. The same thing is true of advertising. Ads are paeans to material objects, but economies deal in the production of material objects. I have not lately seen an advertisement that offers the reader "summer bargains on the four cardinal virtues, individually packaged, with any one of the three theological virtues thrown in free to the first fifty readers who answer the ad." Courage, nobility, patriotism, insight, self-sacrifice, and love of God are not advertised on television, or anywhere else.[7]

Today's materialism is clearly not an invention of modern advertising but the result of an economic condition (of which advertising has been a part) that for the first time permits the masses of society to obtain material things. Does this mean that the ends of people must become more base, or is it possible that people can now achieve more noble ends with the material means at their disposal?

ADVERTISING CREATES FALSE NEEDS   Some critics feel that advertising tends to create false needs. On the subject of "need," Fairfax Cone says:

> The terms of real need are something I cannot argue. I am certain that few women I know *need* a home permanent wave or five colors of lipstick or an automatic dishwasher or a rotisserie. Few men I know *need* an electric shaver or a power lawn mower or a wardrobe that includes twelve

The Wild West. *In Portales, N. Mex., the* Daily News *ran an advertisement for the Bud & Cliff Wrecking Yard: "We do wench*

TIME

Advertising and Society

65

nerve-jarring sport shirts. Few families I know *need* a 21-inch television set to replace an electronically satisfactory 14-inch television set, or need to belong to a book club.[8]

The question is, what is "need"? We need only those things necessary for survival. Such a list would indeed be quite small. If our civilization wants to do more than survive, then we have additional needs. Furthermore, if we go back to the turn of the century, our civilization of that time did not *need* automobiles and electric refrigerators and wash-and-wear clothing. But what is a luxury to one generation may well be a necessity to the next.

Advertising, however, does not create these needs—indeed, advertising cannot *create* any needs. When we speak of advertising's role, all we can say is that it *stimulates* wants or needs, but these are already there—latent perhaps, but there. We need or want anything that will provide satisfaction, make life more pleasant, enable us to do things we would otherwise not be able to do. However, when we blame advertising for making us want things we do not need, we are passing the buck. We are rationalizing to save face. We blame advertising because of our puritanical attitudes about materialism; we excuse ourselves by saying we are the victims of that devious plot called advertising. Thus, having salved our consciences, we can enjoy those things we buy and really "do not need."

ADVERTISING IS IN POOR TASTE   Lester G. Telser comments:

> The critics of advertising . . . deplore the vulgarity, the shrillness, and the selfish appeals in advertising. The content of advertising is a reflection of the audience to which it is directed. If we were all philosophers or poets, the content of advertising would change accordingly.[9]

If advertising is to be successful—and the critics of advertising are quick to admit that it is, which is one of their complaints—then it must appeal to the audience it is trying to persuade. It follows then that the advertiser must present advertisements that are perceived to be in good taste by the segment of the market the advertiser is trying to reach. Who then is complaining about bad taste? It is the individual who cannot empathize with the values of the market to whom the advertising is addressed. Thus, "philosophers" and "poets" find advertising that is directed to mass markets to be generally tasteless. But taste, after all, is subjective, and what is in good or bad taste is a matter of individual preference. In extreme cases, where there can be general agreement, the problem is quickly solved, but in many cases, advertising taste is controversial—just as it is in theater, literature, home furnishings, and personal dress. If the taste of others differs from ours, we call it poor. As Stephen Greyser so aptly states:

> . . . in an increasingly diverse society, common acceptable standards on matters of taste are ever more unlikely. In short, one man's fantasy is another's annoyance, one man's bad taste is another's amusement, one

man's threshold of intolerance for a particular theme or ad is another's threshold of awareness.[10]

PRODUCT VS. ADVERTISEMENT Frequently, people who hold advertising to be in bad taste confuse the advertisements with the product being advertised. For example, if some people contend that liquor, cigarettes, or cosmetics are not in the best interest of the public, they would contend that advertisements for such products are in bad taste. However, even though it might be in bad taste to advertise questionable products, the advertisements themselves may be tastefully executed. It is important to distinguish here between the appropriateness of the product being advertised and the advertisements, which are too often judged guilty by association.

OTHER CRITICISMS OF ADVERTISING TASTE There are people who consider certain advertisements in poor taste because of the advertising technique used. They object to scare or fear copy. They dislike both advertisements that appear to be editorial matter and advertisements that aggressively shout their wares. They criticize the constant repetition in some advertisements. They rebel at advertisements that they feel insult the intelligence. They abhor advertisements that use circuslike techniques to gain attention—the singing commercials, the raucous sound effects, the stunts. They feel the testimonial technique is terribly abused. They contend that advertisements encourage snobbishness and class consciousness. They oppose advertisements with sexual overtones and advertisements for adult products that appear in media available to children. And they object to high pressure and emotionalism directed at children for children's products. They disapprove of certain types of programs (for example, those depicting crime and violence) sponsored on radio and television by advertisers. They view with disfavor advertising billboards obliterating the view on the nation's highways, and mailboxes stuffed with "junk" mail. And they decry the number of minutes of every hour on radio and television and the number of pages in each issue of the nation's newspapers and magazines devoted to advertising.

These are the views not just of the "professional" critics, but of the general consuming public. Indeed, many advertisers are themselves critical of bad taste in advertising. Unfortunately, one cannot legislate or regulate taste in most instances, so little can be done. Still, some measures have been taken to deal with the problem. Media regulate copy. Laws have been enacted limiting placement of billboards. Codes have been established by the trade associations. Some "bad taste" advertising, nonetheless, will continue to appear. This is part of the price to be paid for freedom of opinion in a democracy.

ADVERTISING APPEALS TO THE MASSES

Personal selling has much the same objective as advertising—to make sales. Yet there is not as much complaint against personal selling, partly because the personal selling effort is tailored to appeal to the individual prospective

> *The critics . . . don't understand that advertising isn't witchcraft, that it cannot wash the brain or coerce someone to buy what he doesn't want.*
>
> *JOHN O'TOOLE,*
> *Advertising Agent*

consumer, whereas advertising must appeal to a mass of people. To be sure, advertising can be directed to small subgroups of ultimate consumers, but it cannot be tailored to specific individuals without hindering its *raison d'etre*. When scholars say that advertising is a "torrent of mendacity, imbecility, and bilge," they are not altogether incorrect from their point of view, yet they fail to recognize that the fault is largely with them and not with the advertising, in that their own superior intellect makes them atypical. The largest market for the sale of the largest number of goods and services is the great mass of consumers whose intellect is not on a par with that of scholars. Advertising is in large measure directed toward the average consumer, as are most motion pictures, newspapers, magazines, and other mass media with which scholars also find fault. Perhaps if we all had the intellect and education of these scholars, toothpaste and automobiles would be sold with

FIGURE 4-1

An advertising agency presents a position on the social effects of advertising. *By permission: Foote, Cone & Belding Communications, Inc.*

"I hate Advertising, but I like the ads."

To hear the pollsters, advertising is roundly disliked. More than half of American consumers consider TV advertising, for example, to be "uninformative, exaggerated, seriously misleading."

Who in their right mind would act on such suspect information?

Millions do. Millions more make buying decisions on the basis of advertisements in newspapers and magazines, on billboards and radio.

The reason is simple. The pollsters, to keep their research within bounds, ask their questions broadly. They ask about advertising in general.

Consumers, on the other hand, respond to advertisements in particular. They're quick to suspend preconceived notions when they come face to face with ads that talk to them about something they want in a language they understand.

It all comes down to communication.

Where agencies fit in business

The role advertising agencies play in American business today is very clearly defined.

Advertising agencies are communicators. They are entrusted to speak in favor of products on behalf of the companies who offer these products for sale.

How they speak is all important. It is all important to the consumer, who may find in the product an opportunity to enrich his or her life.

It is all important to the product itself, which may stand or fall on how it is presented.

It is all important to the company, whose image, for better or worse, is mirrored in its communications.

Full-service advertising agencies are superbly prepared to make these communications. They have the tools—research, marketing, management, media selection, creative services, and production. They have the imponderables—a high degree of specialization, objectivity, independence, experience with many products and markets, and the rare ability to make their clients' interests their own.

Advertising agencies are, indeed, the avowed experts in economic communications.

It is a beautiful thing to see a professional, full-service agency set to work on a new project. Skills and talents swarm together. The place buzzes like a hive of bees as the staff begins to acquire new knowledge.

Knowledge about the company they're working for. Knowledge about the goods and services they are entrusted to sell. And knowledge about the consumer—the ultimate factor—they must sell to.

The ultimate factor

Although economic communications involve millions of people and trillions of dollars in goods and services, they still are at their most telling when they are made person-to-person, one-to-one.

Some years ago our Fairfax Cone wrote, "Good advertising is always written from one person to another. When it is aimed at millions, it rarely moves anyone."

At FCB we have been making person-to-person communications for 106 years. Today we are making them for over 900 clients in 17 countries.

We are cheered to know that these communications have made both sales and friends for many fine companies.

And we are cheered to know—because we take polls ourselves—that consumers really like the ads and commercials we do.

Even if they hate advertising.

Foote, Cone & Belding
People listen to us. Because we listen to them.

This space provided by The Chicago Tribune.   © 1979 Foote, Cone & Belding, Inc.

advertisements like those now used for scholarly books and technical research equipment. But we do not live in such a world, and advertising must reflect the realities it finds. No thinking person should belittle the scholars' dissatisfaction with much of modern advertising, not even the businesspeople responsible for it. But the opinion of scholars is far from being the only one that counts.

ADVERTISING APPEALS TO EMOTION A large portion of all consumer advertising appeals to the emotions rather than to reason. This playing on the emotions is frequently regarded as foul play. We resent buying things "against our better judgment." We likewise resent knowing that appeals are being made to our emotions, because we are brought up to control our feelings. To admit that we succumb to emotional appeals is deflating to our egos. Thus, Steuart Henderson Britt explained the public's distaste for advertising, saying:

> The basic reason so many people are against advertising is emotional. All forms of advertising and sales promotion are trying to get people to react —to do something they might not do just on their own. In a sense advertising must be "upsetting" to be effective . . . and we hate to be upset.
>
> What is more, advertising tries to get us to *spend* money, whereas most of us from our earliest childhood have heard that it is better to save than to spend. It is considered more moral. So most advertising is asking us continually to do things we may feel emotionally are not quite right . . . and at a profit to the advertiser.[11]

There is good reason to believe, however, that most of our everyday actions are the result of our emotions, not our reason. Is it any wonder that the advertiser, recognizing us as we are rather than as we would like to be, appeals to the real person by appealing to the emotions? The politician, the novelist, the playwright, the lover, and the next-door neighbor all appeal to emotion. It is only logical that the advertiser does the same. This is not a justification, merely an explanation for the use of emotional appeal in advertising.

THE "HIDDEN PERSUADERS" Undoubtedly one of the strongest indictments against advertising in recent times has been the conception of advertising people as "hidden persuaders." At the outset, it should be made clear that no advertising people would deny that they are engaged in persuasion. There is, they feel, no immoral or unethical implication in this description of their role. Surely, every consumer must be aware of this objective of advertising. Although there is some criticism of the art of persuasion, however, most of the criticism today is directed toward the tools used in developing persuasive advertisements. Vance Packard, whose book, *The Hidden Persuaders,* helped rekindle the advertising controversy in the late 1950s, said that advertising persuasion is an aspect of

> . . . the large-scale efforts being made, often with impressive success, to channel our unthinking habits, our purchasing decisions, and our thought

processes by the use of insights gleaned from psychiatry and the social sciences. Typically these efforts take place beneath our level of awareness; so that the appeals which move us are often, in a sense, "hidden." The result is that many of us are being influenced and manipulated, far more than we realize, in the patterns of our everyday lives.

Some of the manipulating being attempted is simply amusing. Some of it is disquieting, particularly when viewed as a portent of what may be ahead on a more intensive and effective scale for all of us. Cooperative scientists have come along providentially to furnish some awesome tools. . . .

This depth approach to influencing our behavior is being made in many fields and is employing a variety of ingenious techniques. It is being used most extensively to affect our daily acts of consumption. The sale to us of billions of dollars' worth of United States products is being significantly affected, if not revolutionized by this approach, which is still only barely out of its infancy. Two-thirds of America's hundred largest advertisers have geared campaigns to this depth approach by using strategies inspired by what marketers call "motivation analysis." . . .

What the probers are looking for, of course, are the *whys* of our behavior, so that they can more effectively manipulate our habits and choices in their favor. This has led them to probe why we are afraid of banks; why we love those big fat cars; why we really buy homes; why men smoke cigars; why the kind of car we draw reveals the brand of gasoline we will buy; why housewives typically fall into a hypnoidal trance when they get into a supermarket; why men are drawn into showrooms by convertibles

FIGURE 4-2

An advertising association presents a position on the value of advertising. *By permission: American Advertising Federation.*

Garage Sale!
Everything's going.
Are you coming?

When your neighbors decide to unload their white elephants at your expense, you hear about it through advertising. That's what advertising is all about—advertising communicates. About where to find a bargain elephant (but not where to put it). **Without advertising, you wouldn't know.**

American Advertising Federation

but end up buying sedans; why junior loves cereal that pops, snaps, and crackles.

We move from the genial world of James Thurber into the chilling world of George Orwell and his Big Brother, however, as we explore some of the extreme attempts at probing and manipulating now going on.[12]

The criticism here is not of advertising per se, but rather of the techniques used to find out why the consumer buys—information used as the basis for advertising. As Packard describes these techniques, they indeed appear ominous, forbidding, and in the poorest of taste. But advertising people are simply trying to do a better job of communicating by better understanding why people behave as they do. Educators try to understand their students. Politicians try to understand their constituents. Clergy try to understand their congregations. Isn't it reasonable to expect advertisers to try to understand their consumers? Does there have to be suspicion of underhandedness, manipulation, or other devious intent? Could it not simply be that the better we know our market, the more efficient will be our advertising efforts? Certainly, there is no empirical evidence that advertising is capable of *making* people buy, either consciously or subconsciously.

ADVERTISING IS MISLEADING AND FRAUDULENT

DELIBERATE DECEPTION There is no question that some advertisements are misleading and fraudulent. There have always been some such advertisements, and despite all efforts there probably always will be. Two classic cases make excellent illustrations. An advertisement offered a steel engraved etching of the Father of Our Country together with instructions for framing. The unsuspecting victim received a current postage stamp picturing George Washington. Another advertisement offered a bug killer guaranteed to kill all insects. The recipient in this case received two blocks of wood with instructions to place the bug on one block and stamp down on it with the other! Ludicrous as these cases might seem, they are hardly a laughing matter to their victims, and practices such as these give a black eye to the advertising industry. These incidents can be and are controlled through law, the industry, and media, but there are always some advertisers who succumb to the temptation for the dishonest dollar. Although the vast majority of advertising practitioners abhor such advertising and themselves encourage punitive action, there is little that can be done *before the fact.*

ADVERTISING AND EXAGGERATION Advertising that is intentionally designed to mislead and deceive is inexcusable and must be dealt with harshly. However, in a society of the superlative, many persons have come to expect advertisers to voice their conviction of the absolute superiority of their product. The argument is made that it is doubtful that anyone is really disturbed when two or more competitive firms make equal and irreconcilable exaggerated claims for their products. The Federal Trade Commission, watchdog of national advertising, has in the past admitted to this position and called such advertising claims "trade puffing." Recently, however, there has been an increased questioning of trade puffery. Ivan Preston says:

> Puffery lies to you and deceives you, but the law says it doesn't. You can't always be "sure if its Westinghouse," but the law says such statements are permissible. State Farm isn't "all you need to know about insurance," but State Farm may claim so without fear of prosecution. . . . Blatz may not be "Milwaukee's finest beer," Nestle's may not make "the very best chocolate," and Ford may not give you "better ideas."[13]

When all the false and misleading advertising is added up, it still represents only a very small percentage of advertising. This does not excuse false and misleading advertising, but it is mentioned to help set the record straight and offset the considerably exaggerated claims of critics.

ADVERTISING SUPPORTS STEREOTYPES In the last two decades, a new criticism of advertising has developed. The claim is made that advertising supports or reinforces demeaning stereotypical characterizations of various segments of the population in the manner in which these segments are portrayed in advertisements. The earliest major complaint was a natural concomitant of the black civil rights movement. Blacks either had generally been omitted from advertisements completely (except in the black media) or were depicted in subservient roles. Advertisers were at first reluctant to succumb to civil rights pressures, not because of any lack of a sense of social justice, but because they feared a white backlash, which they thought would result in decreasing sales. But experimentation allayed these fears, and blacks have been substantially integrated into advertisements, with the result that there has been virtually no effect on sales to whites and very salutary results among blacks.

As the whole social reform movement has grown in this country, other population segments have reacted to advertisements that show them in an unfavorable light. This has included Chicanos, American Indians, Italian-Americans, and the like. Most recently, advertisers have seen reactions from fat people being portrayed as unhappy and the elderly objecting to old people being depicted as senile and childlike. Certainly advertisers recognize that alienation of any segment may be likely to result in brand boycott, and so they are increasingly careful to avoid negative stereotyping in their advertisements.

Perhaps the major controversy in stereotype advertisements involves women. The women's movement strongly opposes women being depicted in advertisements as sex objects and as "homemakers." If women feel strongly about this, then shouldn't advertisers change their ways? But many advertisers will argue that up until now, there has not been a clear mandate by all women on this subject. Many women, perhaps even most, are either neutral or negative on the woman's role and still believe "a woman's place is in the home." Since they are primarily homemakers, some advertisers feel it would be antagonistic to depict women in their advertisements contrary to their beliefs. Thus, advertisements aimed at liberated women reflect their image and those directed toward the old conception continue to reflect the old stereotypes. But time is on the side of change, and as the role of women in our society continues to move toward equality, so advertising will change to reflect the times. ✕

ADVERTISING MANIPULATES CHILDREN Because they are thought to be so vulnerable, children have been considered by social critics as "unfair game" for advertising. The major criticism has been directed toward television programming and commercials specifically directed toward youngsters. This is really a doubleheaded criticism—one being the nature of the programs and their effect on the behavior of children, and the other the accompanying advertising that supposedly manipulates their values. However, there is little concrete evidence to support the idea that children are so pliable in the hands of advertisers. Although their value systems are typically at odds with those of adults, this is not the result of exposure to commercials, and they seem to be more discriminating in dealing with information processing than adults would credit them with being. Certainly, there is need for more study on the subject. And many advertisers are very cautious about what they include in such commercials, because of their own social responsibility and because of the practicality of avoiding restrictive legislation.

I believe that advertising itself is the greatest safeguard a consumer has today against inferior and worthless products, for no inferior product will stand up under a national advertising campaign.

FRANK A. BLAIR, *Manufacturer*

READER'S DIGEST

ADVERTISING AND THE MEDIA

Any discussion of advertising and society would be incomplete without a consideration of the effects of advertising on the mass communications media of the United States. One often-quoted justification of advertising is that without the revenue it provides, American mass media would be considerably curtailed. Although this is undoubtedly true to some extent, there is some question as to how dependent the printed media are upon advertising. Because the press in America generally has come to depend upon advertising revenue, a sudden stoppage or curtailment of it would have an immediate effect but would not necessarily present an insurmountable problem. There is too much evidence, both here and abroad, that operating magazines, newspapers, radio, and television is feasible without advertising revenue. To be sure, someone must pay the bill. The alternatives to advertising—government, political parties, the public—raise the question, Which is the least of the evils? History shows that advertising freed the press from political domination by providing advertising revenue to replace political subsidy.

What advantage, you may ask, has been gained by replacing political pressure with advertising pressure? What influence has the advertiser on the freedom of the media? To say "none" would be untrue, but an examination would reveal many instances in which the "threats" of an advertiser to influence the media backfire. When an advertiser uses the threat of canceling advertising if the media present bad publicity, the advertiser will generally have to back away from it, because the advertising is not placed in the medium to get favorable publicity but rather to sell goods or services. To discontinue such advertising is to invite a decline in sales.

Most intelligent business executives today realize that the way to be heard by the media is through their reporters and not their advertising managers. In many instances in which it may appear that pressure had gained an advertiser favorable publicity in the media, it is likely that the advertiser had received this favor because of the sympathetic position of the management who, as businesspeople, have much in common with the advertiser. Thus, a newspaper might side with a business in a labor dispute because the management of the newspaper is in sympathy with the management of the business. Then, too, the advertiser's publicity may have genuine newsworthiness. The media may carry the news not because of the advertising pressure but despite it. After all, the fact that the business executive places advertising is no reason to deny the executive publicity when it is news just to avoid the cry of pressure and influence. And publicity that advertisers receive is not always what they would like. You have only to recall some of the segments of CBS's "Sixty Minutes," or the consumer reports of the various morning news shows, to see that advertising and editorial content are quite separate.

If a business executive has determined correctly that a particular medium is the best one to carry the firm's advertising message, then the executive really has no weapon of pressure. To withdraw one's advertising to exert pressure would be to bite off one's nose to spite one's face. What is more, the media do business with many advertisers. They are either quite heterogeneous or highly competitive. If a medium acquiesces to the pressures of one advertiser, there is a good possibility that it would antagonize another. The medium's best defense is a complete separation of its editorial and business aspects.

SOME CONCLUSIONS

In this chapter as in the previous chapter, it can be seen that a good part of the criticism of advertising comes from the fact that advertising is given more credit than is due. Advertising is envisaged as capable of *creating* demand, making people act against their own better judgment. If all advertising were as powerful as the critics deem it, the solution to marketing problems would indeed be simple. But even advertising that would make use of all the devious methods and devices suggested by its critics must face its reckoning with the consumer. Although it might be possible to fool a consumer once, most advertisers are dependent upon repeat sales if they are to recoup their advertising investments and make a profit. And the old adage, "Once bitten, twice shy," would indicate that a deceived consumer will not be back a second time. Stephen Greyser comments:

> Underlying a substantial amount of the criticism of advertising's persuasive powers is an assumption that advertising is extremely powerful. Indeed, attitude surveys show that both the public and private sectors attribute considerable power to advertising in affecting consumer needs and wants. Many an advertiser, as he viewed the wreckage of a product failure which had heavy advertising support, has wished that this were so. The myth of the defenseless consumer is one of the most enduring outputs of the social critics of advertising.[14]

The inanimate tool we call advertising cannot be blamed for the way it is used. If there are faults—and few people would say there are none—they lie with those who use the advertising tool. Indeed, the advertising tool is so useful that it has been employed to rally support for consumer groups, and for those seeking election to political office on a platform that includes reform in the marketplace. Obviously, such a tool cannot be used without some control. This is the subject of the chapter that follows.

Criticisms of advertising are not new. In recent times, there has been a renewed interest by the consuming public in reform in the marketplace.

Advertising is an inanimate tool, and as such, its use is dependent on those animate persons who use it. Many of the criticisms of advertising involve more emotion than reason. It is difficult to avoid contact with advertising, and its sheer volume alone can be an irritant.

Even though advertising stresses materialism, this need not be at the expense of other values. Advertising does not *create* needs. And each individual's needs are unique. Similarly, different people have different tastes, and advertising that may be considered tasteful to one group may be distasteful to another.

It seems reasonable that advertising appeals to the emotions, for our behavior is largely emotional rather than rational. There is no room in business for deliberate deception through advertising, and most firms avoid such practice. Exaggeration, on the other hand, can be expected in a society of the superlative.

As advertisers have become more aware that demeaning stereotypes of various segments in the society reinforce the wrong ideas, businesses have sought to avoid such advertising. Critics are concerned that advertising to children manipulates their values, but the evidence is not there.

The media separate their editorial and advertising operations. Thus, it is not reasonable to assume that advertisers influence the kind of publicity they receive from the media.

---

1. Take a current issue of a magazine or newspaper and examine each advertisement, indicating which might be criticized according to the kinds of criticisms discussed in the text. Label each of these advertisements with the specific criticism.

2. Almost everyone has been critical of advertising or of specific advertisements at one time or another. What have been your criticisms?

3. Why is it that advertising is probably more highly criticized than any other aspect of business?

4. Is it possible for advertising that stresses materialism to be socially acceptable? Why, or why not?

5. Why is judgment of advertising taste so difficult to determine?

6. Is advertising that is based on the study of consumer behavior socially undesirable? Explain.

7. Is trade puffery an unfair tactic in advertising? Explain.

8. Does stereotyping of groups of people in advertising tend to perpetuate the characterization depicted in the stereotype?

9. Does advertising control the American media?

10. Why would the firm using socially undesirable advertising be the loser in the long run?

ENDNOTES

1 *The Works of Samuel Johnson, L.L.D.*, IV (Oxford: Talboys and Wheeler, 1825), 269.

2 Walter Taplin, *Advertising: A New Approach* (Boston: Little, Brown & Co., 1963), p. 3.

3 Raymond A. Bauer and Stephen A. Greyser, *Advertising in America: The Consumer View* (Boston: Division of Research, Graduate School of Business Administration, Harvard University, 1968).

4 Robert Heilbroner, "The Demand for the Supply Side," *The New York Review of Books* (June 11, 1981), p. 40. Reprinted with permission from *The New York Review of Books.* Copyright © 1981, Nyrev, Inc.

5 Blake Clark, *The Advertising Smokescreen* (New York: Harper & Row, Publishers, Inc., 1944), pp. 1–2.

6 Vance Packard, "The Growing Power of Admen," *The Atlantic,* CC, No. 3 (Sept. 1957), 55. Copyright © 1957 by the Atlantic Monthly Company, Boston, Massachusetts 02116. Reprinted with permission.

7 Ray Hutchinson, *The Gospel According to Madison Avenue* (New York: The Bruce Publishing Company, 1969), pp. 157–58.

8 Fairfax M. Cone, "Advertising Is Not a Plot," *The Atlantic,* CCI, No. 1 (Jan. 1958), 71. Copyright © by the Atlantic Monthly Company, Boston, Massachusetts, 02116. Reprinted with permission.

9 Lester G. Telser, "Advertising and the Consumer," in Yale Brozen, ed., *Advertising and Society* (New York: New York University Press, 1974), p. 41.

10 Stephen A. Greyser, "Advertising: Attacks and Counters," *Harvard Business Review,* L, No. 2 (March–April 1972), p. 144.

11 Steuart Henderson Britt, *The Spenders* (New York: McGraw-Hill Company, 1960), p. 147.

12 Vance Packard, *The Hidden Persuaders* (New York: David McKay Company, 1957), pp. 3–5.

13 Ivan L. Preston, *The Great American Blow-Up* (Madison, Wis.: The University of Wisconsin Press, 1975), pp. 3–4.

14 Greyser, "Advertising: Attacks and Counters," p. 24.

Control
of Advertising

After completing this chapter, you should be able to:
1. Point out how practitioners deal with advertising abuses
2. Appreciate how media regulate advertising standards
3. Understand the consumer movement and its effect on advertising practice
4. Describe how government exercises advertising control

There have been major attacks on advertising before, but never to the extent of and for so long a time as the current one. For the first time, advertising is being challenged not only in the name of the consumer but also *by* the consumer. This new grass-roots movement has more potency than any previous movement, because both the media and the politicians have responded to the demands of the consumer.

Any advertising people who slough off this latest attack with the idea that "this too shall pass" are not reading the signs correctly. In the last decade, substantial restrictive legislation and rulings were set in motion. And although there has been some cooling off by government, at least temporarily, as a degree of conservatism has moved into political power, agitation for more and more legislation to control advertising remains in the offing. Still, those who advocate advertising reform continue to push for it with fervor. Such reform includes restrictions on what may be advertised and to whom and through which media (including advertising to children), proposals to tax advertising, and requirements to disclose product disadvantages in advertisements, to mention just a few. In fact, there are those who would legislate advertising out of existence. Such efforts may have been thwarted temporarily, but there is little question that critics will pursue their aims over the long run.

Control does not just happen. There must be cause. Sometimes the cause can be traced to ignorance of the facts or devious plotting to undermine the very foundation of the economic system. But to some extent also, the source of attempts at control can be found in actual abuses that have not been remedied internally and that therefore seem to require the interposition of outside forces to effect reform.

And business is aware of the growing concerns of consumers. Their attitudes were measured by Greyser and Diamond, who conclude:

> From the responses to the comprehensive . . . questionnaire, we see a picture of broad recognition and acceptance of consumerism by managers as a permanent part of the business landscape. Although some of this acceptance is grudging, a strong majority of executives consider consumerism a positive force in the marketplace.

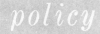

policy 3104

ADVERTISING

Distinctive, coordinated advertising, designed to command
favorable attention, tell the Company's story convincingly,
and reflect the Company's merchandising character, will
be utilized to build consumer awareness and acceptance of
the Company and its offerings. Advertising will be tasteful
and honest, supply needed consumer buying information, and
comply with all laws and regulations. Optimum coordination
with the Company's other sales promotion efforts will be
assured.

   .01   Character of Advertising

        The Company will seek to maintain a distinctive
        advertising style which is most effective in
        producing store traffic and profitable sales and
        is worthy of consumer attention. Advertising
        will be designed to meet both overall Company
        objectives and the requirements of selling units.
        Advertising will be oriented to the presentation
        of merchandise and services but, at the same
        time, also will convey the desired image statement
        about the Company in every feasible way. All
        advertising will be based on the actual
        characteristics of the Company and its offerings.

        Freshness, creativity, excitement, honesty, and
        proof of value, as well as the other factors
        which interest consumers, will be emphasized in
        Company advertising. Art, layout, headlines,
        copy, and all physical characteristics will be
        designed to support the effectiveness of
        advertising in producing sales and reinforcing
        the Company's merchandising character. The
        importance of continuity will be recognized
        fully.

        Copy for advertising will be clear and factual
        and will supply information needed by consumers
        to support a buying decision as well as all
        information required by law. (See 0901:
        Compliance With the Law; 2100: Merchandising
        Character; 3101: Character of Sales Promotion)

Sales Promotion   *William R. Johnson*   1 of 7   11/1/71

FIGURE 5-1

This first page of an advertising policy statement from a major retailer provides guidelines
not only for the business of advertising but also its social aspects (see the last paragraph). *By
permission: J. C. Penney Co., Inc.*

. . . There is surprising sympathy for some of the more restrictive ideas
about advertising that have been put forward by consumerists. . . . Executives agree that "consumerism will lead to major modifications in advertising content."[1]

    In Chapter 4 it was pointed out that four groups involved in the
use of advertising must assume the responsibility for advertising. They
are the advertising practitioners, the users of advertising, the media or

carriers of advertising, and the advertising audience. Such responsibility implies control. Although control seems offensive to some champions of free enterprise, it is probably unrealistic to assume that an institution of such importance can be given a completely free reign in our complex society. We live in a society of controls. The extent to which advertising is and should be controlled is determined by its importance and influence. The question of who shall control is and shall be determined by the extent to which those who use and create advertising meet the responsibilities their roles thrust upon them.

Advertising people are also consumers, and as citizens they are responsive to the social values of the times. Thus, it should not be surprising that one of the most rational statements on regulation of advertising comes from a top advertising agent:

> Regulation itself should not be a harsh word. We approve of regulations that set speed limits and realistic standards of automotive safety. We are not apt to quarrel with regulations about the drinking age of minors or safe and sane levels of jet noise over our neighborhoods, or ways to preserve our national parks. But to many of us in the agency business, the word regulation seems to have a fairly sinister connotation: Something or somebody outside our industry who tells us what we can and cannot do in exercising our legitimate powers of persuasion on behalf of our clients' products and services. Something which is unnecessarily restrictive and unreasonably harsh. Something which is limiting our effectiveness and invading our right to free speech and expression. I, too, believe that some regulations are bad. They would hurt us and our clients immediately and the public in the not so long run. While I will join in the hue and cry at some specific regulations that I believe are ill-conceived and can be harmful, I will not condemn and indeed I will accept in principle the idea of regulation in advertising.[2]

It is not sufficiently recognized—especially by the critics of advertising—that romance in its broad sense is the most wanted product in the world. So many people lead lives of "quiet desperation" that any advertising which offers them escape, and any product which offers them utility plus color, performs a profound service.

JAMES WEBB YOUNG, *Advertising Agent*

READER'S DIGEST

CONTROL BY ADVERTISING PRACTITIONERS

Because advertising practitioners create commercial advertising, it should be relatively simple for them to exercise control over a large portion of all advertising through self-imposed rules and codes. However, this sounds simpler than it is. Although many people refer to advertising practitioners as professionals, the background and training of advertising men and women are varied, and many have never had any formal advertising study. Hence, there is little opportunity to expose them to a formal code of ethics. Indeed, this is true for businesspeople generally. Furthermore, unlike medical doctors or lawyers, they do not have to be licensed or certified and cannot be kept from practicing; any code they follow can only be voluntary.

CREATIVE CODE

American Association of Advertising Agencies

The members of the American Association of Advertising Agencies recognize:

1. That advertising bears a dual responsibility in the American economic system and way of life.

To the public it is a primary way of knowing about the goods and services which are the products of American free enterprise, goods and services which can be freely chosen to suit the desires and needs of the individual. The public is entitled to expect that advertising will be reliable in content and honest in presentation.

To the advertiser it is a primary way of persuading people to buy his goods or services, within the framework of a highly competitive economic system. He is entitled to regard advertising as a dynamic means of building his business and his profits.

2. That advertising enjoys a particularly intimate relationship to the American family. It enters the home as an integral part of television and radio programs, to speak to the individual and often to the entire family. It shares the pages of favorite newspapers and magazines. It presents itself to travelers and to readers of the daily mails. In all these forms, it bears a special responsibility to respect the tastes and self-interest of the public.

3. That advertising is directed to sizable groups or to the public at large, which is made up of many interests and many tastes. As is the case with all public enterprises, ranging from sports to education and even to religion, it is almost impossible to speak without finding someone in disagreement. Nonetheless, advertising people recognize their obligation to operate within the traditional American limitations: to serve the interests of the majority and to respect the rights of the minority.

Therefore we, the members of the American Association of Advertising Agencies, in addition to supporting and obeying the laws and legal regulations pertaining to advertising, undertake to extend and broaden the application of high ethical standards. Specifically, we will not knowingly produce advertising which contains:

a. False or misleading statements or exaggerations, visual or verbal.

b. Testimonials which do not reflect the real choice of a competent witness.

c. Price claims which are misleading.

d. Comparisons which unfairly disparage a competitive product or service.

e. Claims insufficiently supported, or which distort the true meaning or practicable application of statements made by professional or scientific authority.

f. Statements, suggestions or pictures offensive to public decency.

We recognize that there are areas which are subject to honestly different interpretations and judgment. Taste is subjective and may even vary from time to time as well as from individual to individual. Frequency of seeing or hearing advertising messages will necessarily vary greatly from person to person.

However, we agree not to recommend to an advertiser and to discourage the use of advertising which is in poor or questionable taste or which is deliberately irritating through content, presentation or excessive repetition.

Clear and willful violations of this Code shall be referred to the Board of Directors of the American Association of Advertising Agencies for appropriate action, including possible annulment of membership as provided in Article IV, Section 5, of the Constitution and By-Laws.

Conscientious adherence to the letter and the spirit of this Code will strengthen advertising and the free enterprise system of which it is part.   *Adopted April 26, 1962*

Endorsed by

Advertising Association of the West, Advertising Federation of America, Agricultural Publishers Association, Associated Business Publications, Association of Industrial Advertisers, Association of National Advertisers, Magazine Publishers Association, National Business Publications, Newspaper Advertising Executives Association, Radio Code Review Board (National Association of Broadcasters), Station Representatives Association, TV Code Review Board (NAB)

FIGURE 5-2

One effort for the control of advertising by advertising agencies. *By permission: American Association of Advertising Agencies, Inc.*

Certainly, the practitioners of advertising would have little trouble controlling it if the users of advertising (business management) took it upon themselves to curb any abuses. The vast majority of business firms sponsor advertising that falls within the scope of reasonableness. Yet, unfortunately, there are exceptions. To make matters worse, these exceptions are not always fly-by-night firms but are frequently major business concerns that ought to know better. Of course, not everyone agrees that a given practice is malpractice. In such cases, control is virtually impossible unless it is arbitrary. Furthermore, it is not unreasonable to grant that advertisers, spurred on by competition and their own enthusiasm, may be oblivious to any malpractice in their advertising.

But business has not been blind to its advertising excesses and abuses. Indeed, it has taken the initiative in correcting such abuses, if not alone for altruistic motives, then because advertising malpractice could hurt business in the long run, and because increased outside controls might be imposed if business does not put its own house in order. Some individual firms have established their own working codes for advertising. And from time to time business has organized collectively to clean up advertising.

BETTER BUSINESS BUREAUS   One of the first organized efforts by advertisers and practitioners to clean up advertising started in 1911 under the auspices of the Associated Advertising Clubs of America, precursor of the American Advertising Federation. Resulting from the national convention that year was the theme, "Truth in Advertising," and shortly afterward the National Vigilance Committee was organized, together with local committees, to "act against false and misleading statements in advertising by moral suasion."[3] In 1916 the committee became the Better Business Bureau. Today there are 150 local bureaus operating in major cities across the country, besides the Council of Better Business Bureaus. Although these organizations cooperate with government agencies, they are completely private, receiving all their financial support from business. They still devote considerable attention to truthful advertising, but their activities have expanded to include all business practices. They make continual examinations of advertising on their own and also act on complaints of any individual. When malpractice is found, they suggest that the guilty firm cease the activity in question. Although this is usually sufficient to alleviate the problem, they may initiate legal action or turn the evidence over to the appropriate state or federal agency if the firm does not respond. Unfortunately, this action is after the fact, and frequently the damage has already been done.

THE ADVERTISING CODES   There are several advertising organizations that have prepared codes to regulate advertising internally. These include the creative code of the American Association of Advertising Agencies, which is shown in Figure 5-2, and "The Advertising Code of American Business," developed by the American Advertising

Federation and the Association of Better Business Bureaus International, which is shown in Figure 5-3.

Although the creators of these codes have the best of intentions, the fact remains that the codes are difficult, if not impossible, to enforce. In fact, there are no real penalties for violation except, perhaps, withdrawal from the organizations themselves. Furthermore, not all practitioners are members of any of the organizations, and although many nonmembers follow the practices of the organizations, there are some who ignore them. If the codes were adhered to by members of these organizations, much of the criticism of advertising would be eliminated. However, one has only to glance through a recent issue of a major magazine to find violations of the codes by some of the largest national advertisers employing the talents of some of the largest advertising agencies. Why do advertising practitioners ignore their own codes? Perhaps it is because of the pressure of competition. Maybe it is the enthusiasm of the creators of advertisements, or a feeling that they must satisfy the advertisers in order not to lose business. Certainly practitioners know right from wrong. Although most advertising meets the stipulations of the

THE ADVERTISING CODE
OF AMERICAN BUSINESS

1~ *TRUTH*... Advertising shall tell the truth, and shall reveal significant facts, the concealment of which would mislead the public. 2 ~ *RESPONSIBILITY*... Advertising agencies and advertisers shall be willing to provide substantiation of claims made. 3~ *TASTE AND DECENCY*... Advertising shall be free of statements, illustrations or implications which are offensive to good taste or public decency. 4~ *DISPARAGEMENT*... Advertising shall offer merchandise or service on its merits, and refrain from attacking competitors unfairly or disparaging their products, services or methods of doing business. 5~ *BAIT ADVERTISING*... Advertising shall offer only merchandise or services which are readily available for purchase at the advertised price. 6 ~ *GUARANTEES AND WARRANTIES*... Advertising of guarantees and warranties shall be explicit. Advertising of any guarantee or warranty shall clearly and conspicuously disclose its nature and extent, the manner in which the guarantor or warrantor will perform and the identity of the guarantor or warrantor. 7 ~ *PRICE CLAIMS*... Advertising shall avoid price or savings claims which are false or misleading, or which do not offer provable bargains or savings. 8 ~ *UNPROVABLE CLAIMS*... Advertising shall avoid the use of exaggerated or unprovable claims. 9 ~ *TESTIMONIALS*... Advertising containing testimonials shall be limited to those of competent witnesses who are reflecting a real and honest choice.

CREATED, DEVELOPED AND DISTRIBUTED BY THE
American Advertising Federation
and the
Association of Better Business Bureaus International

FIGURE 5-3

Another effort for the control of advertising by business. *By permission: Joint Committee for the Advertising Code of American Business.*

Control of Advertising

code, some practitioners, for whatever reasons, fail to live up to standards of good practice, and further controls are then necessary.

THE NATIONAL ADVERTISING REVIEW BOARD As a result of the increased threat of government control, the advertising industry in 1971 established a new mechanism for internal regulation, called the National Advertising Review Board (NARB). Its sponsors include the Council of Better Business Bureaus (CBBB), the American Advertising Federation (AAF), the American Association of Advertising Agencies (AAAA), and the Association of National Advertisers (ANA).

These sponsors have organized an administrative corporation called the National Advertising Review Council, Inc. (NARC). The organization operates through two arms: the National Advertising Division of the Council of Better Business Bureaus (NAD), and the National Advertising Review Board.

The NAD operates on a full-time basis, staffed by people with backgrounds in advertising and employed by the CBBB. It receives all complaints relating to the truthfulness of national advertising. Where it finds the complaints valid, it consults with the advertiser and urges modification or withdrawal of the advertising in question. If satisfactory resolution cannot be obtained, the case is submitted to the NARB.

The NARB is composed of thirty representatives of national advertisers, ten representatives of agencies, and ten people with no connections with the industry, plus a chairperson. These people serve for two years and may be called upon to serve on five-member panels that hear complaints submitted by the NAD. The NARB panel may override or modify the decision of the NAD; if the decision is upheld, however, the NARB panel joins in trying to persuade the advertiser to take corrective action. If the advertiser does not take action, the NARB reports the deceptive action to the appropriate government agency and publicizes the action.

False and deceptive advertising complaints are the major concern of both the NAD and NARB. However, the NARB will also consider other complaints. In such cases, it will issue reports to the industry or the general public regarding positions on advertising practice without making mention of the particular case in question. Thus, its enforcement powers are limited to cases involving truthfulness in advertising, but it also serves in an educational and persuasive role regarding other facets of advertising.

Since their inception, the NAD and the NARB have had an impressive record of action.[4] To be sure, there are many consumer advocates who will argue that the NARB has not been as effective as it should have been, but an objective evaluation of its performance has to give it high marks.

CONTROL BY ADVERTISING MEDIA

It has been suggested that media have a responsibility to control advertising in order to serve the public interest. Magazines and newspapers accept this responsibility partly in order to preserve the special privilege of second-class postal rates; television and radio accept it in order

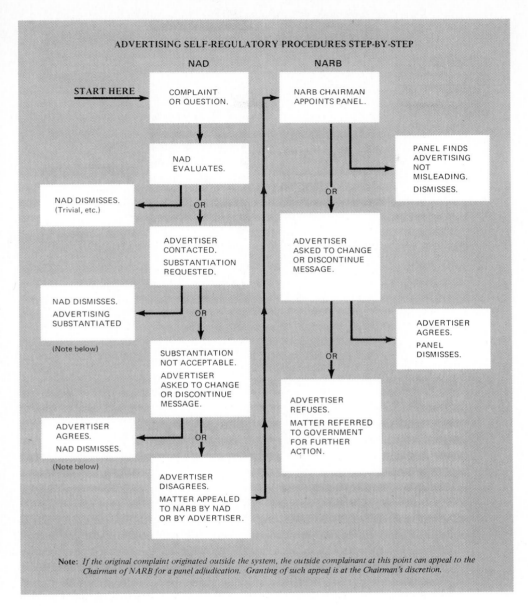

ADVERTISING SELF-REGULATORY PROCEDURES STEP-BY-STEP

Note: *If the original complaint originated outside the system, the outside complainant at this point can appeal to the Chairman of NARB for a panel adjudication. Granting of such appeal is at the Chairman's discretion.*

FIGURE 5-4

Flow chart of procedures of NAD/NARB. *By permission: National Advertising Review Board.*

to keep their licenses. They may be motivated, too, by a fear of offending their audiences or injuring their reputation, or by other considerations. As a result, media have exercised varying degrees of control over the advertising they accept. They do this in two ways: by excluding advertising for certain products, and by censoring advertising, requiring that it meet certain specifications if it is to be accepted.

Encouraged in the 1950s to put their house in order lest the government impose its own restrictions, the broadcast media, through the Na-

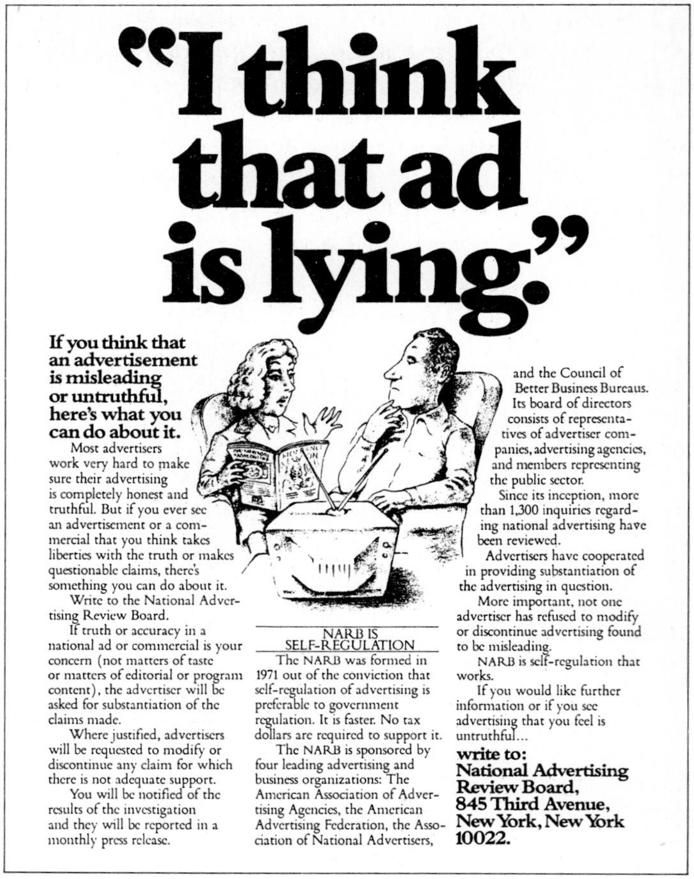

FIGURE 5-5

This advertisement by NARB urges consumers to write to the Board about advertisements thought to be false or misleading. *By permission: National Advertising Review Board.*

tional Association of Broadcasters (NAB), established the Code Authority, with codes for both television and radio station members governing program standards and advertising standards, including commercial time standards. Even though not all stations were members of the NAB, most followed the Code rules. But in 1982, the rights of the Code Authority were challenged on antitrust grounds. As a result, the Codes were suspended. At this point it remains to be seen what the future of the Code Authority, if any, will be. Also unknown is whether this deregulation will result in lowering advertising standards and increasing the amount of commercial time. One of the areas that had been given considerable coverage in the Code related to advertising to children. The void left by the judicial decision against the Code has been picked up, in part at least, by the National Advertising Division of the Council of Better Business Bureaus.

To be sure, there is still control by the media. The individual broadcast networks continue to control advertising standards, as do individual stations. And, of course, magazines and newspapers also have regulations regarding advertising acceptability.

Media standards for advertising should provide effective controls, but in practice they are not as effective as desired. For one thing, media depend on advertising revenue for profits, and at times some have bent standards to gain needed revenue. For another, their standards vary, and what one medium finds objectionable another finds acceptable. Still, media can provide effective control over their advertising if they are sufficiently committed to the goal.

The public to whom advertising is directed obviously has an important responsibility toward advertising and its control, for much of the socially questionable advertising undoubtedly has existed because of public indifference. Fortunately for the consumer, there has been a small but vociferous group of public-spirited advertising critics who have been responsible for initiating some control. Unfortunately, some of these critics, who are generally sincere and well meaning, have on occasion been so fanatical that they have lost their sense of objectivity and have been guilty of the same sins they have attributed to advertising. Undoubtedly, much of the control of advertising would be unnecessary if the consuming public were more sophisticated. But consumer education has been rather weak, and thus the unethical advertiser has found a large unknowing and gullible audience.

The leading consumer advocate today is Ralph Nader, who since 1964 has captured the imagination of the consuming public in his crusade for consumer protection. As he and other consumer advocates have appealed to the general public for support in correcting abuses, they have helped to change the generally apathetic state of public opinion. This new consumerism not only has wide-based consumer support, but has also brought about a substantial reform in the marketplace.

Today's consumerism is three-pronged, directed at consumer education, consumer information, and consumer remedies. Most of the progress in these areas has been through government action, which is discussed in the next section of this chapter.

THE CONSUMER MOVEMENT   By the turn of the century, there was sufficient dissatisfaction with business practices to spur consumer groups into organizing to bring about legislation for reforms. The press took up the consumer challenge and the era of the "muckrakers"—journalists who revealed in print some big business practices that were posing hazards to the health and well-being of the public—was born. Some of them wrote books as well, such as Upton Sinclair, who exposed the meat-packing industry in Chicago in his book, *The Jungle*. This book and other such writing led to the passage of the first pure food and drug law.

As business became aware of public dissatisfaction, one of the results was the formation of the Better Business Bureau, mentioned above. But perhaps the strongest impetus for action came in 1927 when Stuart Chase and F.J. Schlink wrote *Your Money's Worth*. The book urged the establishment of independent testing agencies and staple-goods standards. The success of this book was followed by a host of exposés during the 1930s, including *100,000,000 Guinea Pigs* by Arthur Kallet and F.J. Schlink, *Skin Deep* by M.C. Phillips, *The American Chamber of Horrors* by Ruth De Forest Lamb, and *Poisons, Potions and Profits* by Peter Morell, to mention but a few.

A year after publication of *Your Money's Worth*, F.J. Schlink founded the first consumer testing agency. The concern with economic matters that came with the depression of the 1930s apparently provided the foundation upon which consumer organizations could be firmly established, and they remain important factors in the control of advertising.

THE CONSUMER ORGANIZATIONS Consumers' Research, Inc., founded in 1928, is an independent, nonprofit organization financed wholly by subscriber-members. It publishes the monthly *Consumer Bulletin* and an *Annual*. Its purpose has been to collect and provide consumer information to protect the consumer from misleading advertising and high-pressure selling. This purpose is accomplished by means of testing products and reporting results, together with articles on sound consumer practices. In 1935, Consumers' Research had labor trouble with its employees; as a result, a group of employees broke away from the organization and founded Consumers Union of the United States. Consumers Union operates ostensibly in the same manner as the older organization, and it publishes *Consumer Reports* and the *Buying Guide*.

There is no doubt that both organizations serve a useful purpose in providing information for the consumer. However, this information probably does not supplant the efforts of the advertiser, partly because the information is disseminated to only a small part of the consuming public. Because these are likely to be the more informed consumers, it remains true that those who need the help most do not get it. In addition, the testing sometimes leaves something to be desired; there have been instances when the two organizations, testing the same product, have come up with different recommendations. Finally, they have been highly critical of advertising but have themselves used advertising to gain new membership (subscribers).

Philip Nelson suggests that advertising is not threatened by *Consumer Reports* when he states:

> The distaste for advertising of its critics is only matched by their love of *Consumer Reports*. Indeed, some advocate replacing advertising by one giant consumer union heavily subsidized by the government. The obvious basis for that position is the problem of authentication. One can place a lot more faith in *Consumer Reports* saying that "Zenith is the best television set" than Zenith making the same claim. There is, indeed, evidence that consumers do regard the information they get from the recommendations of relatives and friends and consumer magazines as better information than the information they get from advertising.

> In our present market system, however, consumers are free to choose whether they will be guided in their purchases by *Consumer Reports* or advertising or some combination of the two. That advertising has been

Buyer, Beware! *In Detroit, Car Dealer Ray Whyte quickly repaired his mammoth "Whyte Oldsmobile" sign after the last two letters of his name burned out.*

TIME

ADVERTISING
BACKGROUND, SOCIAL
IMPLICATIONS, AND
ORGANIZATION

88

able to survive in the face of competition from *Consumer Reports* suggests strongly that advertising has something going for it that *Consumer Reports* does not have.[5]

In addition to these organizations, there are other groups that have planned consumer programs. These include the American Association of University Women, The General Federation of Women's Clubs, and the National League of Women Voters, along with many lesser-known organizations that have had an interest in consumerism for many years. In 1967 the Consumer Federation of America was organized. This activist federation is composed of approximately 200 national, state, and local consumer organizations, labor unions, cooperatives, and other organizations. And there are similar organizations in virtually every developed country in the free world.

Every time an advertising agent overpromises, he gives a black eye to advertising. Advertising should be sold for what it is—just a tool, just one of the ingredients of a business success.

JOSEPH KATZ, Advertising Agent

READER'S DIGEST

CONTROL BY GOVERNMENT

In 1962, President John F. Kennedy defined four basic consumer rights: the right to be informed, the right to safety, the right to choose, and the right to be heard, President Lyndon B. Johnson appointed the first Special Assistant to the President for Consumer Affairs, and each president since Kennedy has requested consumer legislation—until President Ronald Reagan; today, a new conservatism in government has resulted in halting, at least temporarily, any further government action.

Although there have always been consumer advocates among legislators, in the past several years they have supported substantial amounts of consumer protection legislation. In addition to federal legislative action, there has also been an increasing amount of state and local government activity.

In a democracy, the government represents the public. Thus, government control of advertising can be justified as a means of protecting the consuming public. Some government control has come about through the direct action of the public. Some has been created by consumer-advocate legislators who took the initiative, recognizing that they were acting in the public interest. It is apparent that industry self-control and consumer control of advertising, although desirable, have not been completely effective; therefore, federal, state, and local governments have intervened.

FEDERAL CONTROLS

Controls of advertising are to be found in numerous and sometimes strange areas of the federal government. They include the Federal Trade Commission, the Federal Communications Commission, the Postal Service, the Bureau of Alcohol, Tobacco and Firearms of the Treasury Department, and the Food and Drug Administration, to mention the more important ones. Ironically, much of the early control of advertising by the federal government came largely from the constitutional right of Congress to regulate interstate commerce, which has led to legislation to regulate competition or competitors. Any protection afforded the consumer in most instances was only incidental to protection of firms from unfair competitive practices. Of course, this is changing as consumerism has become a potent force.

THE FEDERAL TRADE COMMISSION Of all the numerous administrative bodies of the federal government concerned with advertising, the Federal Trade Commission is the most important; for although the others deal only with certain media or certain products, the FTC is concerned with *all* advertising, even if it does not have authority over all advertising.

The Federal Trade Commission Act of 1914 was a result of efforts to curb monopoly in this country. For many years, action against advertising abuses was not considered within its scope. It was not until 1922, when the Supreme Court made its decision in the *Winsted Hosiery Company* case, that the Commission gained the power to control unfair methods of competition involving false labeling and advertising. However, the Commission had to wait until 1938 when the Wheeler-Lea Act was passed and then again until 1975 when the Magnuson-Moss Act was passed to get the broad powers of control of advertising that it now has. Even now, much of the FTC's power comes not from legislation but from precedent developed out of specific court decisions.

WHEELER-LEA AMENDMENTS Until the Wheeler-Lea amendments, the FTC could take action against abusive advertising only when there was evidence that such advertising was injurious to competition. The amendments gave the FTC authority to act on acts or practices unfair or deceptive to the *public,* aside from their effects upon competition. The Commission was also given statutory authority to control false advertising of food, drugs, cosmetics, and "devices."

The Wheeler-Lea amendments also strengthened the FTC's enforcement ability by making the Commission's order final and enforceable sixty days after service on the advertiser, unless the advertiser seeks a court review. If the FTC's orders are ignored, it can bring suit against the advertiser. It also can get a preliminary injunction against the continued use of false advertising that may be injurious to the public health. The injunction can be continued in force until a cease-and-desist order is entered or the courts set it aside on review.

OTHER ENABLING ACTS STRENGTHENING THE FEDERAL TRADE COMMISSION In 1939, the Wool Products Labeling Act was passed, to be administered and enforced by the Federal Trade Commission. Its purpose is to protect producers, manufacturers, and the public from adulteration or mislabeling of wool products. Similarly, the Fur Products Labeling Act was passed in 1951 to protect consumers from misnamed and falsely advertised furs. In 1953 the Flammable Fabrics Act (amended and strengthened in 1967) was passed. In 1958 Congress passed the Textile Fiber Products Identification Act. By 1965 the Cigarette Labeling and Advertising Act was passed requiring each cigarette package to bear the imprint, "Caution: Cigarette Smoking May Be Hazardous to Your Health."[6] The Fair Packaging and Labeling Act of 1966 provides for regulation of packaging and labeling of consumer goods.

MAGNUSON-MOSS ACT[7] When this legislation was signed into law in 1975, it provided for two significant changes in the law controlling advertising. One aspect deals with the necessity of providing minimum standards for disclosure with regard to written consumer product warranties.

The more important aspect of the legislation involves the section that affects the authority of the FTC. Under this law, the FTC's power was broadened to regulating advertising *affecting* commerce rather than just that involved in interstate commerce. Thus, since it is reasonable to assume that all commerce affects interstate commerce, it is now all under FTC jurisdiction.

The Magnuson-Moss Warranty Federal Trade Commission Improvement Act also permits the FTC to establish Trade Regulation Rules (TRRs) applicable to an entire product category or an industry. Such rules have the force of law with fines of up to $10,000 a day, "so the FTC now has the clout to get advertisers to pay attention."[8] Now, instead of the FTC's having to deal with one deceptive advertisement at a time, the FTC can issue TRRs that control an abuse for all advertisers of the same type or industry.

NEW LEGAL DOCTRINES In recent years, the FTC has developed several doctrines to strengthen its actions in countering deceptive advertising. In 1971 a program of substantiation of advertisements was instituted. It was later modified and operates as follows. The Commission screens advertising claims and when it has some question as to the validity of such claims, it requires the advertiser to substantiate the claim with a technical report and with a report in lay language. This action has shifted the burden of proof from the FTC (which heretofore had to show proof that the advertisement was deceptive) to the advertiser (who must now prove the claims made are true).

Whereas heretofore the advertiser alone has been liable for deceptive advertisements, the FTC has now also brought action against advertising agencies that prepare such advertisements for advertisers.

Through the affirmative disclosure of information doctrine, the FTC has stipulated that consumers shall have sufficient information by requiring specific advertisers, for example, to state in their advertisements the inherent dangers in using the product.

The Commission has stopped the use of trick mock-ups in television advertising unless the advertisers make it known in the commercials that tricks have been employed in the mock-ups.

Good advertising is salesmanship with a sense of social responsibility.

THOMAS D'ARCY BROPHY,
Advertising Agent

READER'S DIGEST

Control of Advertising

Altogether, the FTC over the years has become a much more potent force in controlling advertising deception. Still, it has had some recent setbacks. Toward the close of the 1970s, Congress showed increasing irritability with the extent to which the FTC was hampering business activity. Thus, for a period of two years, it refused to approve a formal budget for the Commission. In 1980, Congress passed the FTC Improvement Act, which, in addition to providing a budget, established a procedure for congressional review of FTC actions. Further, a moratorium was placed on writing Trade Regulation Rules resulting from principles of the unfairness doctrine described below.

PROCEDURES OF THE FTC Cases handled by the FTC may originate from a complaint by a consumer or a competitor, from other government agencies, or as a result of observation by the Commission itself. An investigation will generally start with a request for information from the advertiser. A decision is then made to either drop the case or issue a complaint.

The FTC has a number of ways of dealing with advertisers involved in deceptive advertising. A simple procedure without formal complaints and hearings is to obtain a letter of voluntary compliance from an advertiser stating that the advertising in question will be discontinued. After a formal complaint has been issued by the Commission, a consent order may be issued in which the advertiser agrees to stop the particular practice without any admission of guilt. If, through formal hearings, the FTC finds the advertiser guilty of deception, the FTC may issue an order to cease and desist from such practice. The Commission also publicizes the complaints and cease and desist orders it issues. This adverse publicity for the advertiser proves to be an important weapon for the FTC.

When dealing with alleged deception in advertising, the FTC considers a number of questions.[9] At each point, a decision is made to either drop the matter or proceed to another decision point until the matter is finally settled. The first and most important decision point is whether, in fact, the advertisement is deceptive. For many years, deception was regarded as an act of the advertiser or sender of the message in the wording or visual depicting of the advertisement, but today the FTC has broadened the meaning to include deception in the mind of the receiver of the advertising message. This is known as the *unfairness doctrine*. The following definition by David Gardner might best indicate this attempted new direction of the FTC:

> If an advertisement (or advertising campaign) leaves the average consumer within some reasonable market segment with an impression(s) and/or belief(s) different from what would normally be expected if the average consumer within that market segment had reasonable knowledge and that impression(s) and/or belief(s) is factually untrue or potentially misleading, then deception is said to exist.[10]

After initially moving aggressively with the unfairness doctrine, the FTC has had to back away from it as a result of congressional action, and, indeed, it may become a dead issue altogether. Of course, advertisements that are deceptive in word or visual representation continue to be prosecuted by the FTC.

On this first decision point, if the respondent can show that there are no erroneous beliefs or that such beliefs are not the result of the advertisement(s) in question, the matter must be dropped. (See Figure 5-6.) If the FTC staff can maintain its position that the erroneous beliefs really exist because of the advertisement in question, then a series of additional decision steps are considered.

If the advertisement is still running, the second decision point involves whether an injunction should be obtained to stop it. (Although injunction power has long been implicitly claimed for the FTC, it has only been through the explicit authorization of the Magnuson-Moss Act that it has at last been used.)

The third decision point is to consider if the erroneous beliefs caused by the advertisement still exist. This point generally involves the amount of time that has elapsed from when the advertisement appeared and when this point is up for decision. When there is a substantial time lag, the erroneous-belief effects of the advertisement may have

FIGURE 5-6

From H. Keith Hunt, "Decision Points in FTC Deceptive Advertising Matters," Journal of Advertising, *VI, No. 2 (Spring 1977), 29.*

	ISSUE	POSSIBLE ACTIONS	WHAT SHOULD BE DONE	ACTION
STEP 1	Did the ad create erroneous beliefs?			
STEP 2	Is the ad running now? $\longrightarrow$		Should an injunction be obtained? $\rightarrow$	Obtain injunction.
STEP 3	Do the erroneous beliefs still exist? $\rightarrow$	How can the erroneous beliefs be corrected? $\rightarrow$	Should the erroneous beliefs be corrected? $\rightarrow$	Design the corrective action.
STEP 4	Might this company use this deceptive practice again? $\longrightarrow$			Obtain cease and desist order.
STEP 5	Is the problem common to the industry? $\rightarrow$	What industrywide action can be taken? $\rightarrow$ 1. Advertise substantiation 2. Trade regulation rule 3. Generalized cease and desist	Should industrywide actions be taken? $\rightarrow$	Initiate appropriate industrywide actions.

been completely forgotten. If not, consideration is given to whether or not these erroneous beliefs should be corrected. In serious question is, of course, how the FTC staff measures erroneous beliefs and determines their cause. If it is assumed that some adequate measures are possible, then how are such beliefs to be corrected? Is the remedy of a cease and desist order sufficient, or is a corrective advertisement necessary? Corrective advertising has grown out of court cases, and it now is possible for the Commission to require that a portion of future advertising be used to correct erroneous beliefs by disclaiming these beliefs in the advertisements.

The fourth decision step raises the question of whether or not the advertiser or the advertising agency involved might resort to the same deceptive practice again. Since the possibility does exist, in most instances a cease and desist order is obtained.

The fifth and final decision step is to determine if the problem is common to the industry or just an isolated incident. If it is the latter, this ends the decision steps. If it is common to the industry, however, the FTC must decide how to respond to the practice. First, the FTC staff could conduct an advertising substantiation round for the industry, requesting that advertisers substantiate any advertisement claims for which the staff has concerns. Another approach is to issue a Trade Regulation Rule (severely hampered by the moratorium mentioned above) on the matter. The newest approach is to say that any cease and desist order is binding on the advertisements of the rest of the firms in the industry.

FEDERAL COMMUNICATIONS COMMISSION Because the airwaves are limited and in the public domain, the Federal Communications Commission was established in 1934 to regulate radio (and later television) by granting and revoking licenses. The FCC's guiding rule is that radio and television must operate in the public interest, convenience, and necessity. On this basis it indirectly exercises some control over advertising. Specifically, it concerns itself with the quality of advertising and seeks to prevent obscene, profane, fraudulent, and deceptive advertising, all of which are obviously not in the public interest, convenience, or necessity. For the same reason, it also concerns itself with the quantity of time devoted to advertising.

The FCC may suspend the license of any radio or television station that is transmitting profane or obscene words. This severe threat largely eliminates any violation of this sort, but it should be noted that profanity and obscenity are constantly subject to redefinition as social mores change. Fraudulent and deceptive radio and television advertising, on the other hand, is generally handled by the Federal Trade Commission's taking action against the advertiser. When the FCC receives complaints against advertising, it notifies the station, and the station usually sees that the advertiser corrects the situation. If the station ignores the complaint, the FCC takes this fact into consideration when the license comes up for renewal.

One of the most frequently heard criticisms of radio and television commercials is that there are too many of them. The FCC maintains the right to regulate the amount of time devoted to advertising. However, doing so is somewhat complicated, for advertising revenue is necessary if a station is to broadcast at all. Nevertheless, the FCC considers the quantity of advertising in reviewing a station's license for renewal.

In 1967, as a result of a petition, the FCC ruled that stations carrying cigarette advertising would have to carry without charge public service messages on the health dangers from smoking cigarettes. The precedent for this action was the Fairness Doctrine, which was originally conceived with the idea that since the airwaves are limited, a reasonable amount of time should be devoted to public issues, and that the opportunity for conflicting points of view should be present. In 1971 cigarette advertising was banned from the broadcast media by legislation, but there were then requests from various citizen groups to counter advertising claims for a number of other socially controversial products with free time for messages of rebuttal. The FCC objected, citing the cigarette case as a special one. The Court, however, ruled against the Commission, although it indicated that opposing points of view to advertised products could be satisfactorily presented in programs in which the editorial content presented such views. In reviewing its position on the extension of the Fairness Doctrine in 1974, the FCC indicated that although it would continue the practice for editorial advertising of important public issues, it would no longer be applied to product advertising even for controversial products. When the Federal Trade Commission suggested a broadcast policy of counter advertising to permit time for those who challenged the claims of advertisers, the FCC refused, suggesting that this was a clear danger to the economic well-being of broadcasters and that other remedies for deceptive advertising should be used. Thus, the Fairness Doctrine as it pertains to product advertising has, for the present, been set aside.

Invitation. *In Memphis, the* Commercial Appeal *carried this classified ad: "Café must be sacrificed. . . . Owner has ulcerated stomach. Must sell at once. . . ."*

TIME

THE POSTAL SERVICE Over the years, the Postal Service has been granted powers that directly and indirectly control certain advertising. A law enacted in 1912 made it mandatory for publishers of newspapers and magazines using second-class mail privileges to mark plainly as "advertisement" all editorial or other reading matter for which they receive payment. In this way, any attempt to disguise advertisements as editorial matter was thwarted. Second-class mailing privileges are so important economically to the publisher that most adhere to this and other postal regulations rigidly.

Through both statutory regulation and legal precedents, the second-class mailing privilege may also be withheld from publications containing obscene, scurrilous, or otherwise offensive materials. Some materials are obviously offensive; others are less clearly objectionable. In most instances, when the Postal Service has brought charges, the offender has discontinued the practice complained of. Other cases have gone to court, with various results.

MAIL FRAUD Perhaps the most important postal regulation of advertising concerns the use of the mails to defraud. Advertisements frequently contain free offers, money-back guarantees, and contests—techniques that, from time to time, have been used for fraudulent purposes.

The Postal Service controls mail fraud by issuing a fraud order that denies the offender the right to receive mail or money orders. Although this is not designed as punitive action, it nevertheless generally results in a cessation of such fraudulent actions, because the mail is so important to the continuation of business operations and because the Postmaster may revoke the order when satisfied that corrective action has been taken.

Unlike the Federal Trade Commission, which has considerable control over advertising but which generally has to go through long and involved legal procedures, the Postal Service can act quickly and very effectively. Aside from being able to prosecute under criminal statutes, it has the very powerful weapon of being able to discontinue mail delivery and to revoke mail privileges.

BUREAU OF ALCOHOL, TOBACCO AND FIREARMS No other advertising is so closely controlled as that pertaining to alcoholic beverages. Because of considerable public disapproval of liquor, much legislation has been enacted to control its advertising. In addition to federal control, there are laws governing the advertising of alcoholic beverages in all the states. In the case of federal control, the authority is vested in the Bureau of Alcohol, Tobacco and Firearms of the Treasury Department.

The Bureau makes the following information mandatory in all such advertising: the name and address of the advertiser, the class and type of beverage, and its alcoholic content. All these statements must be printed in a type size that is "conspicuous and readily legible."

In addition, a number of statements are specifically prohibited in alcoholic-beverage advertising. These include false and misleading statements; disparagement of competition; obscenity; misleading references to tests; misleading guarantees; inconsistency with label; misuse of the term "bonded"; promise of curative and therapeutic effect; confusion of brands; flags, seals, coats of arms, and other insignia; and misleading information about age and origin.

The Bureau accepts the submission of proposed advertisements for its approval or disapproval. Approval, however, does not prevent the Bureau from subsequently taking action against the advertising. The strength of this body lies in its licensing authority, for a producer must have a license before engaging in the sale of the product. Should an advertiser fail to correct a point of dissatisfaction in its advertising, the Bureau can revoke the license and perhaps force the firm out of business. The firm is invited to show cause why its license should not be revoked, and if it does not wish to accede to the wishes of the Bureau regarding its advertising, the testimony becomes a matter of public record and can cause considerable adverse publicity. Because of these powers, the Bureau's authority to control alcoholic-beverages advertising has never been challenged in the courts. The future of this Bureau is currently uncertain, as there has been legislation proposed to move alcohol and tobacco to the Customs Department.

THE FOOD AND DRUG ADMINISTRATION   The Federal Food, Drug and Cosmetic Act of 1938 provides for the principal control over manufacturing, branding, and labeling of commodities falling in the categories described in the title of the act. The act created the Food and Drug Administration, whose control in the areas of branding and labeling indirectly affects advertising.

Both the Food and Drug Administration and the Federal Trade Commission are concerned with preventing deception of the public through misrepresentation of food, drugs, and cosmetics. In order to avoid duplication of effort, the two organizations have an agreement whereby the FDA concerns itself with false labeling and misrepresentation in branding and the FTC is directly concerned with false advertising.

As the FDA interprets "labeling," it includes not only the physical label but any printed material accompanying the product, even though the advertising practitioner might more correctly refer to much of this material as advertising.

Under the enabling act, the party guilty of misbranding or false labeling is guilty of a misdemeanor and subject to fine, imprisonment, or both, and the products involved are subject to confiscation.

ADVERTISING AND THE FIRST AMENDMENT   Apparently the framers of the Constitution failed to mention advertising, so that over the years, advertising has failed to have the First Amendment protection of free speech and free press accorded to others. This position was substantiated in a Supreme Court decision in 1942, and it remained until 1976, when a new decision modified the doctrine significantly. This decision, upholding the First Amendment right to advertise abortions, was followed in 1976 with another that struck down a law banning the advertising of prices of prescription drugs. Finally, in 1977, the Supreme Court held that banning advertising of legal services violated constitutional rights to lawyers' commercial speech.

What the full implications of this reversal mean are difficult to predict. Dorothy Cohen points out:

> In some areas, there is likely to be no change. Advertising control is based on trade regulation law, and such laws will no doubt continue to prohibit advertisements that are false, deceptive, and misleading. The recent Supreme Court cases clearly imply that First Amendment protection to commercial speech does not grant the acceptability of false advertisements.[11]

It is important to note that consumerism has been a substantial force behind these decisions that advocate the right to commercial information so that the consumer may make intelligent buying decisions. Thus, advertising is recognized as a positive force that is indispensable to the operation of free enterprise, and commercial speech protection by the Constitution assures that it will be possible to perform such adver-

FIGURE 5-7

As a result of a decision of the U.S. Supreme Court, the legal profession may now use advertising. This is a pioneering effort by one law firm. *By permission: Legal Centers of Neller & Dettelbach Co.*

tising activity. To date, the decisions have dealt with specific situations, and it remains to be seen how these decisions will affect other cases. It is fairly clear, however, that bans on advertising by the professions will probably be ended primarily as a result of First Amendment decisions of the Supreme Court. This may improve public attitudes toward advertising in general if it results in greater efficiency and lower prices by professionals. Of course, if prices become higher and if professionals engage in deceptive advertising, then the whole image of advertising will suffer.[12]

STATE AND LOCAL GOVERNMENT CONTROLS

All the state and many local governments have legislation controlling advertising. Because advertising must be involved in or affect interstate commerce for the federal agencies other than the FTC to have jurisdiction, government control of intrastate commerce must come from state and local legislation. Unfortunately, there is a wide variation in legislation among the several states, which makes for a good deal of confusion for the advertiser cutting across state lines. At the local level, it is frequently difficult even to determine what legislation exists.

PRINTERS' INK MODEL STATUTE   The most uniform state legislation has been the adoption directly or with some variation by almost every state of a model statute, relating to false and deceptive advertising, drawn up by *Printers' Ink*, an advertising periodical, in 1911 and revised in 1945. (This statute has been used in a modified form by seventeen other states.)

> Any person, firm, corporation or association or agent or employee thereof, who, with intent to sell, purchase or in any wise dispose of, or to contract with reference to merchandise, real estate, service, employment, or anything offered by such person, firm, corporation or association, or agent or employee thereof, directly or indirectly, to the public for sale, purchase, distribution, or the hire of personal services, or with intent to increase the consumption of or to contract with reference to any merchandise, real estate, securities, service, or employment, or to induce the public in any manner to enter into any obligation relating thereto, or to acquire title thereto, or interest therein, or to make any loan, makes, publishes, disseminates, circulates, or places before the public, or causes, directly or indirectly, to be made, published, disseminated, circulated, or placed before the public, in this state, in a newspaper, magazine, or other publication, or in the form of a book, notice, circular, pamphlet, letter, handbill, poster, bill, sign, placard, card, label, or over any radio or television station or other medium of wireless communication, or in any other way similar or dissimilar to the foregoing, an advertisement, announcement, or statement of any sort regarding merchandise, securities, service, employment, or anything so offered for use, purchase or sale, or the interest, terms or conditions upon which such loan will be made to the public, which advertisement contains any assertion, representation or statement of fact which is untrue, deceptive, or misleading, shall be guilty of a misdemeanor.[13]

Unfortunately, it is generally felt that these statutes have been ineffective, because state legal officers have many other statutes to deal with that appear to be more pressing—as those dealing with violent crime.

OTHER AREAS OF STATE CONTROL   In addition, various state laws control advertising of certain commodities, outdoor advertising, professional advertising, and political advertising. Much of this legislation is quite specifically related to special problems peculiar to the state. Frequently states have used prohibitive licensing fees or taxes as a device to control advertising in an indirect manner.

In an effort to control fraudulent advertising practices at the state level where there was not adequate existing legislation, the American Advertising Federation in 1969 drew up the Model Deceptive Practices Act. This proposal goes much further than the *Printers' Ink* Model Statute. The new proposal was presented at consumer protection hearings of the Federal Trade Commission, where it was well received. Portions of it were later incorporated by the Commission into its own recommended "Little FTC Act" for states and has now been adopted by most of them.

SOME CONCLUSIONS

There is no question but that consumerism is here to stay. Unlike past attempts at social reform, this latest effort has so strong a base of support that it cannot and will not be ignored. It is a part of the social reform movement that has hit all facets of contemporary American society. That the advertising industry has not exercised sufficient internal control to eliminate the necessity for government control is unfortunate but not surprising. To be sure, there were many advertising people who advocated more stringent self-regulation in the past, but without outside pressure for reform, there could be little reasonable expectation for effective self-regulation in a vigorous, free marketplace.

It must also be recognized that there has been in the last several years a significant change of attitudes about the rules of the marketplace. What may have been acceptable, or at least tacitly approved, in the past is not acceptable today. Those who fear that increased control will erode the whole economic system are probably unnecessarily alarmed. If we examine advertising from a historic perspective, we see that it has changed with changing social mores before, and the changes called for today will undoubtedly result in advertising's becoming a more vital tool than ever. How many times have the prophets of doom forecast the Armageddon for advertising in the past? Yet advertising has survived, because it is a useful and valuable tool for communication.

Although the current political climate is moving toward deregulation of business, more government control of advertising practices of business are in the long run probably inevitable. The reform of the marketplace is far from over. If advertising people want to minimize the amount of restrictive legislation, they must take the initiative to set their house in order so as to reflect the thinking of contemporary society. Some positive steps have already been taken, such as the formation of the NARB. But beyond industrywide self-regulation, there is a need for a change in individual advertiser behavior.

As Neal O'Connor states:

> We should know by now that consumerists and the government will register complaints and respond with regulations when advertising violates the precepts of honesty, completeness, clarity, candor and accuracy—the precepts that we must use in this business. Knowing that, can we not realize that future regulation of our business isn't really up to them? It is indeed our choice. Morality in business really is not a choice. It is a requisite. It is the only way to do business, and no business faces the public more regularly than advertising. No business is more open to examination. No business is in a better position to demonstrate to the American people that the truth succeeds, and whether we like it or not, we are the vanguard and the opportunity for leadership is ours.[14]

This chapter has endeavored to consider all kinds of control—by the industry, by consumers, and by government. It was not practical to present all aspects of the government regulations that were discussed or, indeed, all the regulations imposed on advertising by government.

Certainly it should be clear that with the vast amount of government control of advertising, the advertiser is well advised to seek competent legal counsel. To be sure, this discussion was not designed to give you any legal competence. Rather, it is hoped that it will dissuade you from the folly of do-it-yourself law.

One final point. Legal control of advertising has probably never been so volatile—probably as a result of all the pressures being applied from so many different directions. As George and Peter Rosden explain:

> The law of advertising is in a period of turmoil as a consequence of pressures exerted from many sides. These pressures come from groups of behavioral scientists as well as from jurists. One group tends to stress self-regulations. Others want to use action against deception in advertising for the purpose of eliminating advertising completely, alleging that advertising constitutes a complete waste. Still others want to inhibit advertising in a paternalistic attempt to prevent the individual from spending improvidently. Some opponents of regulations produce scientific evidence according to which advertising has no influence upon the consumer. And there are proponents of strict regulations according to which the consumer is defenselessly prone to the advertiser's wiles.
>
> It is a gigantic task for Congress, courts, and the regulatory agencies to find a path through this labyrinth of conflicting evidence. They will have to eliminate first the arguments of those who are really opposing the system of free enterprise under the banner of fighting deceptive practices in advertising. They will have to be conscious of the fact that every regulatory step in effect reduces the freedoms a little more. On the other hand, they must balance the scales by rooting out deception as effectively and as speedily as it can be detected.[15]

The challenge has been handed to the advertisers. Either they set their houses in order or others will do it for them.

It should be noted that the attack is not on advertising per se, but on the way it has been used by business. The advertising tool is still an effective one—as we can see from the fact that it has been used most effectively by those who seek reform in the marketplace.

Attacks on advertising in recent years have resulted in substantial restrictive legislation and rulings. Although there has been some cooling off by a conservative government, critics continue to push for reform.

Within business, there have been many attempts toward self-regulation of advertising through the Better Business Bureaus, advertising codes, and the National Advertising Review Board. Because there is little enforcement power behind these efforts, they have not been as effective as might be desired.

Media also attempt to control advertising excesses through codes and censorship, but individual standards vary, and the lure of advertising revenue sometimes outweighs the enforcement of codes.

Consumer organizations offer an alternative to advertising information through their buying guides. But most consumers pay little attention to them and rely instead on advertising.

Control of Advertising

The government provides the greatest control of advertising. The major force is the Federal Trade Commission, which over time has become a potent force in the policing of advertising practice. Recent court decisions have virtually ended any prohibitions of professional advertising by such groups as doctors and lawyers.

QUESTIONS AND PROBLEMS

1. What are the four groups that must share the responsibility for advertising?
2. What is the major shortcoming of control of advertising by its practitioners?
3. Select an advertisement that you believe to be unsubstantiated and run it through the review procedure of NAD/NARB. Prepare appropriate reports, assuming the case is not resolved.
4. Should advertising media have the right to refuse certain advertising? Justify your answer.
5. "That advertising has been able to survive in the face of competition from Consumer Reports suggests that advertising has something going for it that Consumer Reports does not have." What might this "something" be?
6. How has the Magnuson-Moss Act broadened the power of the Federal Trade Commission?
7. The FTC has recently adopted a policy known as the unfairness doctrine. What is it? Why might it be difficult for an advertiser to have advertisements comply with this doctrine?
8. Select an advertisement that you believe to be deceptive and run it through the five steps of the FTC decision points. Explain the actions that might be taken in each instance.
9. What are the effects of recent Supreme Court decisions on advertising and the First Amendment?
10. If you could pick and choose, what controls over advertising would you eliminate because you consider them unfair, and what controls would you add because you think there are voids?

ENDNOTES

1 Stephen A. Greyser and Steven L. Diamond, "Business Is Adapting to Consumerism," *Harvard Business Review*, LII, No. 5 (September–October 1974), 38, 52.

2 Neal W. O'Connor, "Regulation—Creative Friend or Foe?" Paper from the 1975 Western Region Convention of the American Association of Advertising Agencies, p. 1.

3 H.J. Kenner, *The Fight for Truth in Advertising* (New York: Round Table Press, Inc., 1936), p. 36.

4 *A Review and Perspective on Advertising Industry Self-Regulation* (New York: National Advertising Review Board, 1978), pp. 7, 14.

5 Phillip Nelson, "The Economic Value of Advertising," in Yale Brozen, ed., *Advertising and Society* (New York: New York University Press, 1974), p. 63.

6 In 1970 this was changed effective 1971 to read, "The Surgeon General Has Determined That Cigarette Smoking Is Dangerous to Your Health."

7 For more detail, see Harold L. Nelson and Dwight L. Teeter, Jr., *Law of Mass Communication*, 3rd ed. (Mineola, N.Y.: The Foundation Press, Inc., 1978), pp. 508–9.

8 *Ibid.*, p. 509.

9 This section is based on H. Keith Hunt, "Decision Points in FTC Deceptive Advertising Matters," *Journal of Advertising*, VI, No. 2 (Spring 1977), 28–31.

[10] David M. Gardner, "Deception in Advertising: A Receiver Oriented Approach to Understanding," *Journal of Advertising*, V, No. 4 (Fall 1976), 7.

[11] Dorothy Cohen, "Advertising and the First Amendment," *Journal of Marketing*, XLII, No. 3 (July 1978), 63.

[12] Paul N. Bloom, "Advertising in the Professions: The Critical Issues," *Journal of Marketing*, XLI, No. 3 (July 1977), 103.

[13] Copyright 1959 by *Printers' Ink* Publishing Corporation.

[14] O'Connor, "Regulation—Creative Friend or Foe?" p. 6.

[15] George Eric Rosden and Peter Eric Rosden, *The Law of Advertising* (New York: Matthew Bender, 1978), p. vii

6

The Organization of Advertising

After completing this chapter, you should be able to:

1. Understand the evolution of the advertising function in the producer's organization
2. Define product management and marketing services
3. Explain the differences between producer and retail advertising organizations
4. Describe the various components of an advertising agency
5. Identify the various ways an agency is compensated
6. Discuss why an agency should be used and the best way to select one

There are three major components involved in developing advertising: advertisers, advertising agencies, and advertising media. In this chapter we will examine the organization of the advertising function. For advertisers, we will consider organization for producers of goods and services separately from that of their distributors or retailers because of the substantial differences that exist. Next, we will examine the organization of one of the major facilitators of advertising, the advertising agency. The other facilitating institutions, such as advertising media, research suppliers, commercial broadcast production houses, art studios, photographers, typographers, printers, and other graphic arts suppliers, and the like, are considered elsewhere in the text, for even though they are of significant importance to the performance of the advertising function, the structure of their internal business organizations is not.

The organization of the advertising function for producers varies substantially from firm to firm, depending upon the kind of business each is in, the complexity of that business, and the importance of advertising to that business' success. As management science has evolved, so too has the philosophy of organization structure in general and the organization of the advertising function in particular. Small new firms most often start their organizations in a very functional manner. As they grow, they reorganize to more efficiently meet their goals.

THE PLACE OF ADVERTISING IN THE PRODUCER'S ORGANIZATION How the producer will treat the advertising function within the organization depends upon the importance of advertising to the overall promotional strategy of the firm. Historically, if advertising was extremely important, the advertising department might have reported directly to the president. (See Figure 6-1.) If, on the other hand, advertising was of minor importance, the advertising department might have reported to the sales manager. (See Figure 6-2.) Such an advertising department operated in a staff capacity, with responsibility for ad-

PRODUCERS' ORGANIZATION[1]

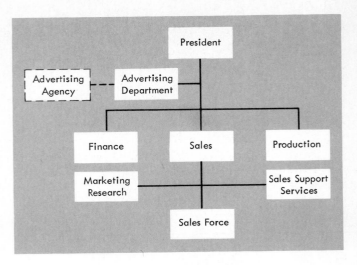

FIGURE 6-1

An early functional organization in which advertising was of great importance. Such organizations are still used by some firms.

vertising planning, budgeting, and evaluation, usually working with an advertising agency and acting as liaison between that agency and its own management to whom it reported.

As firms became more marketing-oriented, with greater focus on marketing functions to maximize their profits, the functional areas of advertising, sales, new-product development, and marketing research required a catalyst that would integrate all these efforts and provide for better marketing planning. This took the form of the *marketing manager,* and eventually all the various marketing functions reported to this chief marketing officer—usually a vice-president for marketing. (See Figure 6-3.)

PRODUCT MANAGEMENT   Many firms still handle advertising in the functional manner described above, but as corporations have grown, especially among consumer packaged-goods companies, the organization of the advertising function has changed. In part, this reflects

FIGURE 6-2

An early functional organization in which advertising was of minor importance. Such organizations are still used by some firms.

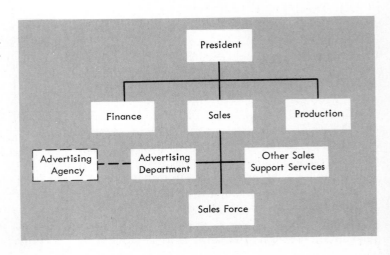

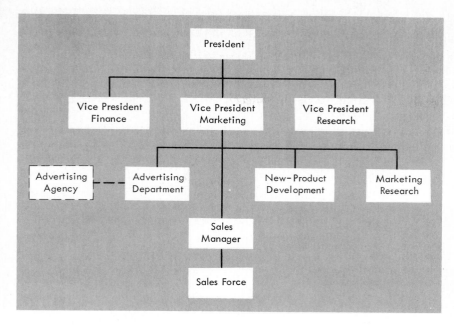

FIGURE 6-3

A contemporary functional organization with a centralization of marketing activity.

the problems and complexities of size, but it is also a response to a recognition of the need for ever-closer integration of advertising with the total marketing activity of the firm, as will be seen more clearly in Part II of the book.

As these packaged-goods companies expanded, they took on more and more product lines. Some brands, in fact, competed with other brands of the same producer (like General Foods' Sanka and Brim, or Procter & Gamble's Charmin and White Cloud). The traditional functional organizations no longer worked effectively. Then a new concept of organization was developed, called *product* or *brand management.*

The idea of product management was to put each product or product group under the direction of a separate manager (or management group). The product manager, then, essentially became the marketing manager for a single product or service or a small group of them. Early on, although the product managers were responsible for the success of the brand, they usually had little authority over the functions that were responsible for that success. Advertising, for example, remained the responsibility of the advertising department. But for consumer packaged goods especially, this was a less-than-satisfactory arrangement, because even though advertising was usually the chief ingredient in the marketing success of such products, the person responsible for that success—the product manager—did not make the advertising decisions. Therefore, the trend has been to increase the authority of the product manager to make advertising decisions.

But this product management system, although it has been widely adopted, has had its problems when the advertising functions have been turned over to the product managers. Critics of product management argue that advertising decisions are now made by advertising amateurs rather than professionals. The older position of advertising manager was filled by someone educated and experienced in advertising practice, but product managers have been largely recruited from the ranks of master of business administration graduates, who are highly trained in areas of financial and analytical skills but who have little background in advertising—especially the creative side. This, it is argued, results in advertising conservatism, an overconcern with copy testing, and a lack of empathy for advertising creativity. Thus, although product managers now more often have greater control over the advertising function and therefore should be able to improve their brand's performance, their lack of advertising training and experience may negate the advantage of their increased authority. But this problem is not inherent in the system or in MBAs, and care in the recruiting and selection process for people with greater sensibility toward advertising should minimize the difficulty.

There are, of course, other kinds of businesses besides consumer packaged-goods producers. These include consumer hard goods, such as appliances and furniture; consumer soft goods, like clothing; consumer services, including airlines and life insurance companies; commercial services, such as brokerage houses and air freight; and industrial goods, like machinery and operating supplies. Many of these producers of goods and services also use product management organizations as their size and needs warrant. However, in some instances, their attention is focused not on the proliferation of different brands within the firm, but on different markets. In such cases, the business may be organized around *markets,* with a *market manager* responsible for the profitability for the firm's or division's products within each particular market. Otherwise, the job responsibilities of market manager and product manager organizations are quite similar.

MARKETING SERVICES As business organizations have embraced product management and market management systems, the advertising department as it used to be has all but faded from the scene in such firms. In its place is the *marketing services department,* also sometimes called the advertising services department or the communications services department. Such departments, which generally report to the top marketing executive, assume varying degrees of responsibility for advertising and other marketing services (with the exception of personal selling, which remains a separate function in virtually all cases), depending upon the amount of advertising and other marketing responsibilities vested in the product managers. (See Figure 6-4.)

DUTIES OF THE MARKETING SERVICES DEPARTMENT Most often, the marketing services department is responsible for media planning and coordination of media buying, which is especially important for multiproduct companies using more than one advertising agency in order to control media costs through quantity discounts and by scheduling the most effective selection of time and space.

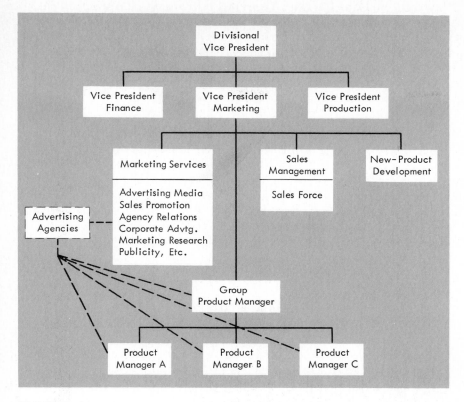

FIGURE 6-4

A contemporary product management organization with a centralized marketing services department.

In many instances, these marketing services also handle the sales promotion function, in the belief that the planning, designing, buying, and distribution of sales promotional material can be done better internally than through advertising agencies. (Sales promotion is so vitally linked to advertising as a promotional tool that it is explored in depth in Chapter 10.)

Marketing services also frequently handles advertising agency relations with regard to selecting agencies, compensation negotiations, and agency performance reviews.

Finally, marketing services departments in some instances handle corporate (institutional) advertising, marketing research, advertising design (art) and photography, printing operations, and publicity activities for the various products or brands.

ORGANIZATION PRACTICES   The actual organization structure of advertising within any individual firm will vary with the special circumstances of that firm. Thus, there are almost as many different organizational variations as there are companies. To determine the best advertising organization for a particular firm, you must consider the scope of product/brand proliferation, complexity of markets, size of advertising investment in terms of sales, importance of advertising to profitability, and so forth. It is not unusual for a business to reorganize the advertising, and indeed the whole marketing function, periodically as it grows and changes directions and objectives.

RETAIL ORGANIZATION

Virtually all retailers advertise. Their strategies and techniques may differ, but their objectives are essentially the same. Retail advertising, although generally local in nature, can also be "national." That is, some larger retailers, such as chains and large department stores, use media that are national in scope in order to reach a national market or to build prestige. However, the great bulk of retail advertising is local, with the result that the retailer is very close to the market and, perhaps, has a better day-to-day working knowledge of it than a producer would. At any rate, because of the nature of their market and advertising task, retailers employ a type of advertising organization somewhat different from that of producers.

RETAIL AND NATIONAL ADVERTISING DIFFERENCES Retail and national advertising are essentially similar in many ways. Most of the advertising principles applicable to national advertising are applicable to retail advertising as well. Much of the difference is only apparent, resulting from a different frame of reference. The principles suggested for national advertisers will, in most cases, be applicable to retail advertising as well if you will make a simple adjustment in your frame of reference. Notwithstanding the essential similarity, however, certain aspects of retail advertising warrant special consideration. Certain differences are real, and some similarities need special attention from the retail point of view. These are spelled out in detail in Chapter 27.

LARGE-RETAILER ADVERTISING ORGANIZATION Because large retailers do a substantial volume of advertising, they generally maintain extensive advertising organizations. Many small retailers, however, cannot afford this and frequently turn to other means, which are discussed below.

Unlike most large producers, most large retailers, like department stores, make little or no use of advertising agencies. They handle most of their advertising themselves. One reason for this is the rate structure of advertising media. For most media, commissions are paid to advertising agencies for advertising placed at the "national" or "general" advertising rate. But most media also offer considerably lower "local" or "retail" advertising rates, and these are not commissionable, thus negating the economic advantage of using an advertising agency. This, however, would be an insufficient reason for not using an advertising agency if the agency could do a better job than the retailer, for if that were the case, it might well be more economical to pay the agency the commission it would normally get from the media.

What, then, are the other reasons for these retailers' handling the advertising themselves? First, there is the time factor. The nature of retail advertising is such that advertisements are prepared on relatively short order. An advertising agency is generally geared to producing an advertisement over several months, but the retail advertisement must usually be prepared in no more than several weeks and not infrequently in as little as two or three days. Obviously, the necessary communication between advertiser and advertising agencies lengthens preparation time. Second, by maintaining an operating advertising department, the retailer can bring the specialist close to the market—the customers. Because each retailer has a unique character that attracts a particular type of customer, the retail advertising department can be close to the customer and know the customer's buying and use habits. This knowledge helps the retailer appear most effectively to the customer through advertising. Third, the large retailer has a wide assortment of merchandise, running to tens of thousands of items. In order to get the salient selling points for advertising these items, the advertising specialist must be close to the merchandise and the personnel who can provide the necessary data.

Finally, the retailer advertising department works with a great many different people in the store organization and in a sense is an "advertising agency" with the different store divisions acting as "clients." To add an advertising agency to such a structure would serve little purpose except to duplicate efforts and make the advertising task more complex. Advertising agencies are sometimes used by department stores, as will be seen later, but generally they have a different relationship to the retailer than they do to the producer. It should be noted, however, that one of the fastest-growing types of retailers, franchise fast-food restaurants, is a heavy user of advertising agencies. These businesses have rather limited lines of things for sale, which are generally standardized in many retail outlets all over the regions or country. Obviously, for such businesses, it may well pay the advertiser to use an advertising agency in much the same way and for the same reasons that producers do.

DEPARTMENT STORE ADVERTISING ORGANIZATION Department store advertising organizations differ, but there is enough similarity between them to permit us a description of a typical operation. Department stores generally have several divisions, one of which is the merchandising division, responsible for buying and selling. Included as a part of this division is the sales promotion department (sometimes known as the publicity department), although in some instances this is a separate division on an equal basis with merchandising. The functions of the sales promotion department include advertising, display, special events, press releases, and signs. The sales promotion department of such retailers is concerned with all the nonpersonal areas of promotion.

The various functions of the sales promotion department are generally handled as separate departments whose interrelation and need for coordination are obvious. The display department is responsible for interior displays, window displays, and special displays and exhibits (the latter usually in connection with the special events department). The special events department is concerned with such generally noncontinuous activities as demonstrations, special classes, fashion shows, parades, visiting celebrities, contests, and other special activities like flower shows and foreign-merchandise fairs. The press release department, as the name suggests, is concerned with the release of news stories that are published or broadcast without space or time costs. The sign shop is responsible for printing signs for window, interior, and miscellaneous use. In addition to these functions, comparison shopping, fashion coordination, home economics, and other activities are sometimes included as a part of the duties of the sales promotion department.

THE RETAIL ADVERTISING DEPARTMENT The retail advertising department, as a part of sales promotion, is concerned with the preparation of institutional and merchandise advertisements for media as well as direct advertising such as envelope stuffers, catalogs, and broadsides. It is headed by the advertising manager, and the organization under this executive is generally subdivided by activity: copy, art, and production, for example. The advertising manager formulates advertising plans and supervises their implementation and is also responsible for initiating the advertising budget. Finally, the advertising manager coordinates the advertising effort with other areas of sales promotion and

FIGURE 6-5

A typical organization chart of the sales promotion operation for a department store.

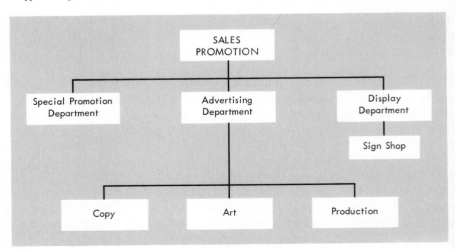

with merchandising and works with personnel in all other areas of the store to secure the necessary cooperation to maximize the effectiveness of the advertising. The manager's secretary usually keeps a file of all advertisements run and secures reports from buyers on the sales results of the advertisements. The department comptroller checks invoices, charges against budget the advertising expenses for each department, and keeps running records of planned and actual expenditures for each department.

As the title suggests, the *assistant advertising manager* assists the advertising manager in carrying out all the manager's duties, but the chief responsibility is implementation of the actual advertisements. This person usually coordinates the buyer's advertising requests and supervises the preparation of the first rough layouts; initiates the writing of copy and preparation of layouts; and sees to it that production schedules are met and that work is released to the media on time.

The *copy chief* supervises the work of copywriters, making sure that they write copy consistent with the advertising style of the store. There are usually several copywriters in the department, each of whom is assigned to a group of merchandise departments. They work closely with buyers and assistant buyers to develop the most effective selling points for the products being advertised.

The *art director* is responsible for layouts and artwork (including photography). Under the art director's supervision, layout artists prepare finished layouts. Other artists prepare the finished artwork for the advertisements. The artists are generally highly specialized, with, for example, one doing women's fashion figures and another working in appliance and housewares still lifes. In the smaller departments and for special art in large departments, much of the artwork comes from outside freelance artists. The larger departments also have their own photographers when photographs are used frequently.

The *production manager* and staff are responsible for production of the advertisements, including specifying and frequently setting type, preparing camera-ready mechanicals, and giving other technical instructions. Under this same manager is the proofreader, who checks all proofs for errors, gets the buyer's approval, and releases corrected and approved advertisements.

DEPARTMENT STORE USE OF ADVERTISING AGENCIES As indicated above, department stores generally prepare their own advertising instead of using the services of advertising agencies. Still, agencies play a role in department store advertising. Some stores retain the services of an advertising agency as a consultant on a fee basis. The agency offers advice to the advertising department on campaign approach and format. More frequently, the store will employ an advertising agency to handle its corporate store patronage advertising or advertising in media other than newspapers (especially if the advertising department has not had sufficient experience in these other media). An agency may also be used for special advertising promotions when a fresh slant is sought or if the department staff is not in a position to take on the promotion in addition to its regular workload. Some few stores use no merchandise advertising, but devote their complete budget to patronage advertising. Under such circumstances, it becomes practical to use an advertising agency for the preparation of all advertisements.

CHAIN STORE ADVERTISING DEPARTMENT ORGANIZA-TION Chain stores such as food, variety, department store chains (but excluding department store ownership groups in which each member store operates virtually autonomously), and fast-food franchises differ considerably in their organization of the advertising department. Its structure will depend upon such factors as the degree of centralization or decentralization, the size of the chain, and the place of promotional strategy in the firm's policy.

Usually, however, there is a central advertising department headed by an advertising manager who may hold a position as high as vice-president. This department may plan actual advertisements, or it may function largely in a staff capacity and as a policymaker. The personnel of this department is similar to that of the department store advertising department. Each geographical region or division generally has an advertising manager and staff responsible for advertising in that area. In the highly centralized organization, the central department prepares advertisements for all divisions, leaving some degree of leeway at the divisional level for changes and additions. When the organization is decentralized, individual divisional advertising managers prepare their own advertisements, working with the central office regarding policy, copy style, and format.

Generally, advertising agencies are employed to handle the chain's advertising in national media and to offer counsel to the central advertising department. For this latter activity they are usually paid a retainer fee.

SMALL RETAILER ADVERTISING ORGANIZATON Some small retailers do a large enough volume of advertising to warrant having their own advertising departments. When this is the case, they generally follow an organization similar to that of the department store. However, the staff may be considerably smaller, with several of the subfunctions described above combined under one person. Indeed, the whole department may be a one-person operation. On the other hand, many small retailers find it economically impractical to maintain an advertising department and have no employee who possesses the necessary skill to prepare the advertising. Nevertheless, they recognize the need for advertising. In such instances, they must turn to other means to carry on the advertising function.

ADVERTISING SPECIALISTS The freelance advertising specialist is available to the small retail firm not having its own advertising staff. The freelancer will function on a part-time basis as the "advertising department" for a number of small retailers in the same town or in nearby communities. This specialist may either operate alone or maintain a small staff of advertising personnel. In addition, there are other specialists such as artists, photographers, and copywriters who can be similarly employed on a freelance basis.

ADVERTISING AGENCIES Many smaller advertising agencies welcome small retail accounts and will take over the entire advertising function for the store. Because retail advertising rates are not commissionable, the agencies either place the store's advertising at the commissionable national advertising rate or use the retail rate and add 15 percent or 17.65 percent, or sometimes more.

ADVERTISING SERVICE COMPANIES Advertising service companies offering a wide variety of services to retailers may be used effectively by the small retailer. One kind of company sells an "idea service" to retailers. Periodically, sets of proofs of complete retail advertisements in various sizes and proofs of components of advertisements, such as merchandise artwork and display lines, are mailed to subscribers. The retailer selects what is wanted from the proofs and sends these to the newspaper, which makes plates from them. There is sufficient flexibility in these proofs to permit changes in copy, price, artwork, and display lines so that the advertiser can tailor the advertisements to the firm's own particular needs.

Some advertising service companies provide similar retailers in different trading areas with a "syndicated" advertising service for newspapers, broadsides, and catalogs. These firms send proofs of advertisements to retail subscribers and get corrections from them, which are paid for by the retailer. These corrections are then incorporated in the advertisements for that particular retailer. In the case of direct advertising, the advertising service company prints the advertisements and supplies the retailer with the number of copies ordered. In this manner, the retailer can obtain "tailor-made" advertisements with a professional look at a reasonable cost, because the original creative and production costs are proportionately allocated to all subscribers of the service.

The advertising service companies also provide useful advertising suggestions to subscribers, such as tie-in promotions with holidays, and will send copies of unusual and highly successful retail advertisements of other retailers.

VOLUNTARY CHAINS Small, independent retailers who are members of voluntary chains have the chain's central offices handle their advertising. One of the advantages of voluntary chain membership is the fact that all members use the same store name and can, therefore, run collective advertisements featuring that name. Aside from the obvious sharing of the cost burden, the member store has the advantage of larger and more frequent advertisements (which the individual store might

FIGURE 6-6

A reproduction proof of an "idea service" advertisement. When the retailer has the advertisement reproduced, prices and the store name will be inserted. *By permission: Metro Associated Services, Inc.*

not be able to afford alone), plus the skills of professional advertising personnel employed by the wholesaler who sponsors the voluntary chain.

PRODUCERS' ADVERTISING DEPARTMENTS Manufacturers are obviously anxious to have retailers advertise to promote the sale of their products. For this reason, they supply retailers with point-of-purchase advertising materials and frequently participate in dealer cooperative advertising programs. In addition, manufacturers frequently supply dealers with proofs and artwork for use in the retailers' advertisements. Some will even prepare copy and layouts for retailers who request them.

ADVERTISING MEDIA In an effort to encourage advertising by retailers that lack facilities or skills for the preparation of advertising, many media (especially newspapers, radio, and television stations) maintain facilities to assist the retailer in the preparation of advertising. These copy service departments, as they are generally known, subscribe to idea services that they make available to their retail advertisers; in some cases, they even maintain copywriters and artists to assist the retailer. Broadcast stations also provide technical assistance in the preparation of commercials.

When people think of the advertising business, they think of the advertising agency. Although the agency is but a part of advertising organization, it is, nevertheless, a vital part, and advertising is its *raison d'être*. Unfortunately, novels and motion pictures have created the impression that the advertising agency is a rather parasitic glamourboy of American business. To be sure, in one way the advertising agency is glamorous. It is creative; it deals with writing and art and radio and television. But the image of plush offices, the gray flannel suit, the smooth operator, the firm handshake, and the glib talk with nothing to back it up is highly exaggerated. Agencies are people, quite normal people of all sorts who put in a full workweek and frequently something extra, who have desks and telephones and typewriters, and who, if they are fortunate, have offices of their own. Still, although advertising agency glamour has been exaggerated out of all proportion, working in an agency can be an immensely satisfying experience. As a service business meeting the needs of its clients, it can be terribly frustrating because of the unpredictability of creative work and the tightness of time schedules. But when an individual advertisement or television commercial, or an advertising campaign, has been completed and run and proven successful for the client, there is naturally a great feeling of accomplishment.

WHAT AN ADVERTISING AGENCY IS In the United States, there are approximately 4,000 advertising agency offices, including branches. (It is interesting to note, however, that more than 7,000 firms classified themselves as "advertising agencies" in the Census of Service Industries of the U.S. Department of Commerce.) In addition, many of the larger advertising agencies maintain offices in principal cities throughout the world. And, of course, there are many other advertising agencies in foreign countries. Agencies vary in size and organizational structure. They are to be found in cities all over the country, with the major concentration, as might be expected, in large metropolitan areas. But regardless of their size, organization, or location, all advertising agencies serve essentially the same purpose. That is, they are independent firms composed of creative talent and businesspeople who, on the basis of marketing objectives, develop, prepare, and place advertising in advertising media for sellers seeking to find customers for their goods and services. Beyond this, advertising agencies may do work in public relations, sales promotion, packaging, marketing strategy, and so on; but to qualify as advertising agencies, they must meet only the minimum definition given above.

It should be recognized that advertising cannot be created in a vacuum—that it is a part of the whole marketing strategy. Thus, before an advertising agency can create advertisements, the whole marketing plan must be developed. Advertising agencies, therefore, must be involved in planning the whole marketing strategy, not just advertisements.

In order to create advertising to sell a client's goods or services or both, an agency will be involved in the following kinds of activities:

1. A study of the client's product or service in order to determine the advantages and disadvantages inherent in the product itself, and in its relation to competition.
2. An analysis of the present and potential market to which the product or service is adapted:
   a. As to location
   b. As to extent of possible sale
   c. As to season

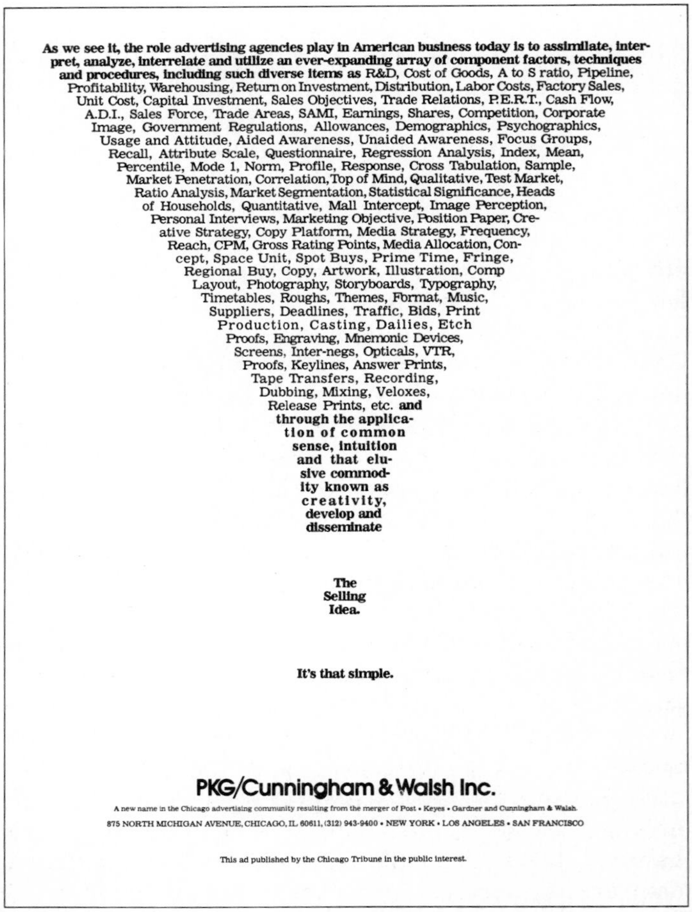

FIGURE 6-7

In this advertisement, the agency states some of the broad range of activities of the full-service agency. *By permission: PKG/Cunningham & Walsh Inc.*

As we see it, the role advertising agencies play in American business today is to assimilate, interpret, analyze, interrelate and utilize an ever-expanding array of component factors, techniques and procedures, including such diverse items as R&D, Cost of Goods, A to S ratio, Pipeline, Profitability, Warehousing, Return on Investment, Distribution, Labor Costs, Factory Sales, Unit Cost, Capital Investment, Sales Objectives, Trade Relations, P.E.R.T., Cash Flow, A.D.I., Sales Force, Trade Areas, SAMI, Earnings, Shares, Competition, Corporate Image, Government Regulations, Allowances, Demographics, Psychographics, Usage and Attitude, Aided Awareness, Unaided Awareness, Focus Groups, Recall, Attribute Scale, Questionnaire, Regression Analysis, Index, Mean, Percentile, Mode 1, Norm, Profile, Response, Cross Tabulation, Sample, Market Penetration, Correlation, Top of Mind, Qualitative, Test Market, Ratio Analysis, Market Segmentation, Statistical Significance, Heads of Households, Quantitative, Mall Intercept, Image Perception, Personal Interviews, Marketing Objective, Position Paper, Creative Strategy, Copy Platform, Media Strategy, Frequency, Reach, CPM, Gross Rating Points, Media Allocation, Concept, Space Unit, Spot Buys, Prime Time, Fringe, Regional Buy, Copy, Artwork, Illustration, Comp Layout, Photography, Storyboards, Typography, Timetables, Roughs, Themes, Format, Music, Suppliers, Deadlines, Traffic, Bids, Print Production, Casting, Dailies, Etch Proofs, Engraving, Mnemonic Devices, Screens, Inter-negs, Opticals, VTR, Proofs, Keylines, Answer Prints, Tape Transfers, Recording, Dubbing, Mixing, Veloxes, Release Prints, etc. and through the application of common sense, intuition and that elusive commodity known as creativity, develop and disseminate

The Selling Idea.

It's that simple.

PKG/Cunningham & Walsh Inc.

A new name in the Chicago advertising community resulting from the merger of Post • Keyes • Gardner and Cunningham & Walsh. 875 NORTH MICHIGAN AVENUE, CHICAGO, IL 60611, (312) 943-9400 • NEW YORK • LOS ANGELES • SAN FRANCISCO

This ad published by the Chicago Tribune in the public interest.

d. As to trade and economic conditions

e. As to nature and amount of competition

3. A knowledge of the factors of distribution and sales and their methods of operation.

4. A knowledge of all the available media and means that can profitably be used to carry the interpretation of the product or service to consumer, wholesaler, dealer, contractor, or other factor. This knowledge covers:

a. Character

b. Influence

c. Circulation:

    Quantity

    Quality

    Location

d. Physical requirements

e. Costs

Acting on the study, analysis, and knowledge as explained in the preceding paragraphs, recommendations are made and the following procedure ensues:

5. Formulation of a definite plan and presentation of this plan to the client.

6. Execution of this plan:

a. Writing, designing, illustrating of advertisements, or other appropriate forms of the message

b. Contracting for the space, time, or other means of advertising

c. The proper incorporation of the message in mechanical form and forwarding of it with proper instructions for the fulfillment of the contract

d. Checking and verifying of insertions, display, or other means used

e. The auditing and billing for the service, space, and preparation

7. Cooperation with the client's sales work, to ensure the greatest effect from advertising.[2]

SERVICE AREAS OF ADVERTISING AGENCIES   Each advertising agency performs a number of services. It is in the large advertising agency that these functions are probably most clearly delineated, because each of them is the responsibility of one individual or group. In the small agency, however, one individual may be responsible for several of these functions. Besides those service areas that are essential to the minimum needs of an advertising agency, some of the services that have been added as agencies have increased the scope of their operations will also be discussed. These may not be found in all advertising agencies. There are four basic service areas: account services, marketing services, creative services, and management and financial services.

ACCOUNT SERVICES   The liaison between the advertising agency and clients is the *account managers* or *account executives*. They work in two directions. On the one hand, it is their job to be sufficiently aware of the clients' needs and desires that they can instruct the agency's personnel properly. On the other hand, they represent the agency to clients and are responsible for "selling" the agency's recommendations to clients and securing their approval. In their capacity as liaison, they must naturally have some creative ability and marketing knowledge, but seldom are they expert in all these areas. Therefore, they work closely

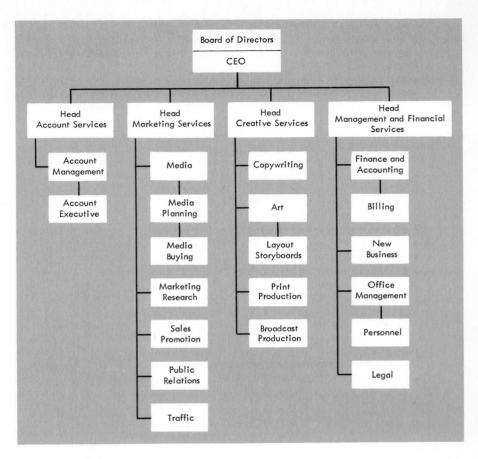

FIGURE 6-8

Schematic of advertising agency components.

with the specialists in each field, having them assist in making client presentations as appropriate.

MARKETING SERVICES The herculean task of determining which *media* to use starts with the development of the media plan. This plan is drawn from the marketing strategy and, of course, considers the creative strategy. A media strategy is then developed to implement this plan, and a schedule spells out the times and places in which the advertisements are to appear. Obviously, there is a tremendous amount of analytical work involved, and the computer is an invaluable tool for determining which vehicles are best for delivering the advertising message at the lowest costs consistent with the greatest efficiencies.

Responsibility for the operation of the media department is delegated to the media director, whose department in a larger agency includes planning groups who are responsible for the plans and strategies; a local broadcast buying group; a network broadcast buying group; a print media buying group (these last three groups are responsible for buying and scheduling media); and a media research group, which is responsible for evaluating available media data for the other groups. In smaller agencies, these same activities are carried on by fewer people.

Although *research* is a relative newcomer to the advertising agency, it is today indispensable to the successful operation of the agency. Before any effective advertising can be prepared, information must be gathered. The job of the research department primarily involves gathering the facts necessary to provide the basis on which to build effective advertising strategy. This involves not only advertising research but also more basic marketing research, of which the former is a part. The agency research department not only must determine what information is needed and how the answers may be obtained, but must also be responsible for interpreting the data and drawing conclusions that will help formulate the marketing strategy.

Such a department is usually headed by a director of marketing research and consists of assistants and statisticians. The agency research department may design the research project, but it has to rely on outside suppliers for the necessary fieldwork and tabulation. In many instances, the research department will make use of the many independent specialized research services it can buy to provide needed data.

As an advertising agency grows in size, there is an increasing need for coordinating the activities of the various departments and centering the responsibility for meeting schedules and closing dates (deadlines for submitting advertisements and commercials to media). This is the task of the *traffic department*. Traffic is the nerve center of the advertising agency, and its role is to get the work out.

CREATIVE SERVICES Today there is a tendency to merge some of the creative service areas into one creative department, on the assumption that creativity is a total process frequently stemming from the collective thinking of people in several of these areas. Such creative departments are headed by a creative director.

Where separate *copy departments* exist, they are headed by the *copy director,* and working under the director are *copy chiefs*. They, in turn, have *copywriters* working for them. The copy chiefs and copywriters are usually assigned to a particular account or group of accounts and are responsible for writing the display lines (headlines and subheads) and body copy (text). Because creative activity is not narrowly confined, the copywriter may prepare a rough or visual layout of the advertisement in addition to writing the copy, just as the art director may develop copy ideas. In any case, the copywriter functions as part of a team effort and seldom works alone.

The art department is responsible for the creation of the pictorial element in the advertisement (artwork) and for the design of the whole advertisement, which is called a layout. In the case of a television commercial, the layout is known as a storyboard. In general, the art director and assistant artists are responsible for the visualization of artwork, the execution of layouts and storyboards, the preparation of mechanicals (guides for the production of advertisements), and specification of type. Because little finished artwork is produced in an agency, it must be purchased from freelance artists and photographers. Consequently, the art department has an art buyer, who is responsible for locating suitable artists and photographers and purchasing finished artwork from them.

After the copy and layout have been approved, the artwork completed, and the mechanicals prepared, advertisements for print media must be put into production. Because the physical production of advertisements is not done by the agency, the production department acts as a sort of purchasing department, responsible for making all specifications. For this reason, the production department must have a thorough knowledge of the graphic arts. Production people also assist copywriters and artists by delineating the limitations of the various graphic arts techniques, so that what they prepare will be practical for reproduction in the various media.

In the early years of television, advertising agencies not only prepared the commercials but frequently originated the format of programs and prepared their content. Today, this latter activity has been taken over almost entirely by the networks and individual stations and by independent specialists known as package producers, leaving the radio and television production departments of advertising agencies responsible in most instances only for the production of the commercials. Using the storyboard as a guide or script, the agency department will cast the commercial, secure the necessary props, and usually have the commercial filmed or taped by an outside studio under its supervision. In the case of a radio commercial, a tape will be made. In the increasingly rare cases of live commercials, of course, there is no filming or recording, and the agency's television and radio production department simply supervises the commercial portion of the program.

MANAGEMENT AND FINANCIAL SERVICES Because the advertising agency deals with numerous media and suppliers on behalf of its clients, there is a considerable amount of billing work involved. This is the task of the *accounting* department, whose work involving agency compensation and billing will be discussed later in this chapter.

The lifeblood of an advertising agency is, of course, its clients. For an agency to grow, it must secure *new business.* In some instances, the agency is approached by an advertiser; in other instances, the agency takes the initiative in soliciting new business. This activity is handled in a variety of ways by different advertising agencies. In some, the task is left to the top executive personnel; in others, it is done by account managers. Some agencies have special "new business" departments as part of their management and financial services whose sole task it is to secure new clients.

A large source of new business for agencies comes from new products. Some agencies have, therefore, set up new-product task forces for new-product growth from existing clients. Other agencies develop this area within the existing organization structure. In either case, a large

Package Deal. *In Atlanta, the Jack Salmon (Realty) Co. advertised in the* Constitution: *"Beautiful Estate. . . . Astounding Value, including two wonderful maids and other interesting features . . . can be seen any time. . . ."*

TIME

source of new business and, hence, new revenue is derived from taking a new product into national expansion.

OTHER FUNCTIONS   All the functions described in the preceding sections will be found in some manner in all advertising agencies. Over the years, however, some advertising agencies have expanded their activities beyond the realm of advertising per se in order to serve the needs of their clients. One of these areas involves sales promotion. In an effort to improve their advertising, many agencies have established sales promotion departments, staffed by personnel who are well versed in sales management. They generally have had a considerable amount of experience in the particular industry of some client and understand the problems of sales and distribution. They, in turn, impart their knowledge of the trade to the account manager and creative people, and they help in the determination of advertising strategy. In addition to this, they work on allied activities such as dealer cooperative advertising, point-of-purchase display, direct-mail advertising, dealer promotion, and contests and premiums.

As businesses have become more interested in formal public relations, a number of advertising agencies have established public relations departments. These departments generally make their services available on a fee basis to clients who want this service.

Some advertising agencies doing a sizable volume of business with consumer-goods accounts have established home economics departments. These departments test consumer products and offer advice on advertising strategy and the creation of advertisements. In some instances, they maintain test kitchens where recipes can be tried and new recipes developed.

Advertising agencies may also offer assistance in the preparation of packages for their clients. They may retain the services of economists to make long-range economic forecasts for the benefit of clients. Finally, with the growth of competition, various legislative restrictions, and the desire to keep advertising on a high moral and ethical plane, many agencies today maintain legal departments whose job it is to approve all advertising in terms of possible legal liabilities.

ADVERTISING AGENCY ORGANIZATION   There are probably as many possible organizational structures as there are agencies. The organization depends upon such factors as the size of the agency, the functions it performs, the clients it serves, and the managerial planning of its executives. Still, among larger agencies there are two broad, general kinds of organizational structure: by group and by department. With some variation, most agencies will fit one of these patterns.

In the group agencies, each product or related line of products is dealt with by its own group of personnel. This group might include an account executive, a copywriter, an art director, a media person, a traffic person, and so on. These people work together to plan the advertising strategy and create the advertisements for a product. Individual members of the product group may, if they have the time, serve in several such groups; an art director's time, for example, might be divided between a food account group and a typewriter account group. When large agencies use the group system, they operate as a sort of federation of small agencies. Each group becomes an agency within the agency. Perhaps the only difference between such groups in a large agency and a small agency, which because of its size is more or less equivalent to a group, is the amount of resources the large agency has to back up its groups.

A second type of advertising agency structure is the departmentalized arrangement, in which the organization is completely departmentalized by function. With the exception of the account executives, who serve only their own accounts, each department serves all clients. The account executive calls upon the copy chief for copywriting, who in turn assigns a copywriter for that particular job. Likewise, the art director might be asked to assign an artist for a layout. In the final analysis, agencies follow almost all variations of the group or departmental organizations.

PLANS BOARD As a part of either departmental or group organization, there may be a plans board, made up of the chief executives of the agency. When the advertising strategy has been worked up for the account, this plan is presented to the plans board for its critical evaluation and approval, after which the plan will be presented to the client. This assures top management control over work coming out of the agency and also permits advertising plans to have a trial run before presentation to the client so that the kinks can be worked out.

TYPES OF ADVERTISING AGENCIES   Advertising agencies may be classified according to the kinds of accounts they handle as well as by their form of organization. These include consumer-goods, industrial-goods, financial, and international advertising agencies.

CONSUMER-GOODS AGENCIES The most common type of advertising agency is the consumer-goods or general account agency. Although most of their clients are producers of consumer goods, these agencies will generally take on any kind of account. This type of advertising agency will place the bulk of its advertising in commissionable advertising media and will derive most of its income from commissions received from the media. Because this type of agency accounts for the major portion of agency business, except where otherwise noted, it will be the one discussed throughout the text.

INDUSTRIAL-GOODS ADVERTISING AGENCIES Some advertising agencies specialize in industrial-goods accounts, although they may also include some consumer-goods advertising. They differ from consumer-goods agencies because of the difference in advertising strategy for industrial goods. First of all, the bulk of industrial-goods advertising appears in business publications and such noncommissionable media as catalogs, manuals, and direct mail. Because of the relatively low space costs of business publications as compared to consumer media, the media commissions are quite small, although the cost of preparing the advertising may be as large as that for consumer media. Consequently, the gross income from media commissions is insufficient to make the agency operation profitable with the type of compensation plan enjoyed by consumer-goods agencies. For this reason, industrial agencies frequently charge clients a monthly or yearly fee and may then apply commissions earned as a credit against these fees, or may use one of the other variations in the compensation plans discussed below. Second, the advertising tends to be highly specialized and technical and requires agency personnel with the necessary technical product knowledge and experience to analyze the market and create advertising that will sell.

FINANCIAL ADVERTISING AGENCIES Few advertising agencies have the highly specialized knowledge necessary to deal mostly with financial accounts. These agencies include among their accounts commercial and savings banks and investment banking houses. Because they are surrounded by legal restrictions, their work is quite technical and must be extremely accurate. The nature of the business of financial institutions means that great speed is frequently necessary in getting the advertising to the public, because fluctuations in money markets occur frequently, rapidly, and sometimes without advance notice. The increased emphasis by commercial banks and savings and loan companies in recent years in marketing activity has led many of them to seek general agencies instead of financial agencies.

INTERNATIONAL ADVERTISING AGENCIES Many American businesses sell their products abroad as well as in the United States and consequently wish to advertise abroad. Advertising agencies with only domestic offices may handle foreign advertising in several ways. They may place it directly with foreign media; they may use the facilities of foreign advertising agencies by maintaining some sort of affiliation with these agencies; or they may use the services of export agencies. The latter specialize in placing advertising abroad, acting as a sort of export division for the domestic agency. The export agency may also have its own accounts through which it handles the foreign advertising for clients who have placed their domestic advertising with a domestic agency. A number of the larger advertising agencies in this country might be termed multinational advertising agencies, for they have their own offices abroad and handle their foreign advertising through them. In addition, their foreign branches frequently handle the advertising for local business firms located in these foreign countries.

Of course, just as American agencies have international arrangements, so do foreign agencies. At the multinational level, agencies from

France, England, Germany, and Japan, for example, have offices in New York, although they are nowhere near as prolific as U.S. agencies abroad.

ADVERTISING AGENCY NETWORKS The larger advertising agencies generally have branches located in principal cities throughout the United States, in addition to their main offices. This arrangement facilitates their operation and permits them to better serve the needs of their clients. The smaller advertising agencies are not in a position to maintain branch operations, although they may have similar need for them. Their solution to this problem has been to establish advertising agency networks. The first of these was established in 1928, and today there are ten agency networks with over 300 member agencies.[3] These networks are composed of a number of noncompetitive advertising agencies located in different parts of the country. They provide members with an interchange of services, information, and resources.

OTHER CLASSIFICATIONS Although, as a rule, advertising agencies do not handle competitive accounts (for example, two automobile accounts or two soft-drink accounts), some few agencies are exceptions; thus, there are advertising agencies specializing in women's fashions, others specializing in children's wear, and so on. Generally, an advertiser uses such an agency when it needs special agency skills but is too small to make it practical for a general agency to provide these skills. The specialist agency, unlike the general agency, can spread the cost of such skills over a number of accounts.

Some small advertising agencies will handle virtually no national advertising, but instead will take on a number of small retail advertiser accounts. Because retail advertising is generally not commissionable by media, these agencies either work on a fee basis or place retail advertising at the national rate, which is commissionable.

It should also be noted that many retail operations, especially chains and franchise businesses like fast-food restaurants, have become very large advertisers, especially in the broadcast media. Because this advertising is conducive to the use of agencies and because agencies find it highly profitable, many large agencies have started retail advertising divisions.

AGENCY OF RECORD   As noted earlier in the chapter, many large advertisers, because of the diversity or competitive nature of their products, employ more than one advertising agency. Because of the discount structure of the media and because the advertiser may choose to advertise several products handled by different agencies in the same medium, coordination and billing may be a problem. In such instances, the advertiser appoints one advertising agency to serve as *agency of record.* This agency is in charge of the insertion orders, with full responsibility for handling all details. The advertisements are prepared by this agency for the product accounts it handles, while *participating agencies* prepare advertisements for their product accounts to be used in the medium or media in question. For its efforts, the agency of record receives the 15 percent commission on its share of the charges and 15 percent of the commissions of participating agencies. Thus, the participating agency receives 12.75 percent commission on its portion of the advertising handled by the agency of record, and the latter receives 2.25 percent commission for its efforts.

AGENCY COMPENSATION   Advertising agencies receive compensation for their work from several different sources. There is some variation in the way that different agencies handle their compensation, and within individual agencies the method of payment by clients may differ according to the nature of the work performed. Still, certain generalizations can be made regarding compensation, and these will be the subject matter of this section.

COMMISSION Much of the advertising agency's compensation comes in the form of commissions, not from the client, but rather from the advertising media in which the advertisements appear. These media bill the advertising agency according to their national rates, less a 15 percent commission (in the case of outdoor media, the allowable commission is 16$^2/_3$ percent). This commission is retained by the advertising agency, and it in turn bills the client at the national or gross rate. Thus, for example, if the rate for one page in a magazine were $10,000, the agency would be billed by that magazine for $10,000 less $1,500 (15 percent), for a net amount of $8,500. The agency in turn would bill the client for $10,000 and pay out to the magazine $8,500, thus retaining $1,500 as its gross income. Most media also offer cash discounts, usually 2 percent, and these are applied to the *net* amount of the bill. Thus, in the example given above, a 2 percent cash discount would be $170 (2 percent of $8,500) or a net after cash discount of $8,330. The agency will usually pass this cash discount on to the client, provided the client meets the discount terms. Thus, provided the client takes advantage of the cash discount period, the client would pay $10,000 less $170, or $9,830.

AGENCY SERVICES COMPENSATION Some advertising agencies make no charge for writing copy and preparing layouts in connection with commissionable advertising. Others do, however, and there are also many other expenses incurred by the agency in the preparation of advertisements and commercials. These are generally charged to the client at cost plus a percentage—17.65 percent, usually, with some few agencies charging 15 percent and others charging a higher percentage. In the example above, if the cost of the mechanical, typography, photostats, films, and artwork for the magazine advertisement came to $3,000, the agency would bill the client $3,000 plus 17.65 percent, or a total of $3,529.50.

The Company He Keeps. In Utica, N.Y., Figaro, pet cat at the Moser & Cotins advertising agency, began to look sick, was found to be suffering from ulcers.

TIME

Thus, from the compensation from media commissions and the 17.65 percent added to out-of-pocket expenses, the agency will perform such services as the planning, preparing, and placing of advertising in such media as newspapers, magazines, television, radio, and outdoor advertising; and, when the advertising agency has the facilities, the rendering of sales, promotion, marketing, and research services wherever and whenever they are deemed advisable in the interest of the client's advertising.

In addition to the methods of agency services compensation described above, there are a number of other compensation arrangements used. These include billing the client for net out-of-pocket cost with no markup, an hourly rate based on direct time costs, an hourly rate including overhead but not profit, an hourly rate including overhead and profit, project fees, negotiated fees, and a flat rate.

Clients frequently request agencies to do other work in addition to preparing advertising for commissionable media. This *collateral* work may include the creation and production of point-of-purchase material, leaflets, recipe folders, catalogs, dealer films, training films, sales manuals, and other similar material. For such work, an hourly charge is generally made for creative time, and out-of-pocket expenses are generally billed to the client at cost plus a percentage, although any of the above-mentioned might be used.

Public relations counsel, when provided by an agency, is sometimes given without charge, but generally it is paid for by a negotiated fee. Special research projects when not without charge are most often paid for by a negotiated fee, but almost all other arrangements are used as well.

It should be noted that the compensation elements described represent gross income, from which the agency has to deduct its expenses; the remainder, a considerably smaller amount, represents net profit.

TRENDS IN AGENCY COMPENSATION Advertising agency compensation has been hotly debated for many years. The traditional system of compensation has been commissions paid by media. But with the ever-increasing costs of doing business, commissions alone have not given some agencies a profit. Conversely, some advertisers who ran very large media appropriations had provided their agencies with billings for which the media commissions were, they felt, greater than the cost of preparing the advertising. Thus, in recent years some firms have moved away from the commission system. Media still allow the usual 15 percent commission to agencies, but in such cases, commissions are combined with other provisions for compensation, or they are not used as a basis for compensation. These systems vary from agency to agency and from client to client.

For many years, the government was concerned with what it believed was a restraint of trade in the advertising industry, claiming that the American Association of Advertising Agencies and the various media associations were engaged in fixing charges through the commission system. Virtually all agencies used commissions and out-of-pocket charges plus a markup because the Association recommended it. The argument for maintaining uniform compensation systems was that agencies should sell quality and not price. The government, however, prevailed, and in 1956 the Association signed a consent decree prohibiting it from advising or requiring agencies to follow any single compensation arrangement.

The decree was applicable only to the Association and in no way bound individual agencies, publishers, and advertisers. Most clients and their advertising agencies continued to use their established compensation systems, which were based on commissions. But the decree provided a renewed interest in the subject of agency compensation, and some agencies and clients have arranged alternative compensation plans. While still using commissions, some compensation plans involve reduced commissions (rebates to clients), increased commissions (percentage added to media charges to client in addition to commissions), combination of hourly rates and commissions, volume rebates, minimum guarantees, and efficiency incentive compensation plans.

Other arrangements for compensation are without consideration of commissions and are categorized under a general heading of a fee system (not to be confused with negotiated fees and project fees, mentioned above). These arrangements include cost plus profit; fixed fee (flat fee, fixed compensation); flat fees plus direct costs; and supplemental fees (project fees). And, of course, there are numerous other compensation systems arranged by agencies and their clients to suit a particular situation.

After the signing of the consent decree, there was a substantial flurry of activity to arrange nontraditional compensation systems, but then the situation seemed to stabilize. Approximately 57 percent of the arrangements remain commission plus markup on out-of-pocket costs, commissions and fees account for 18 percent, and strictly fees for 25 percent.[4]

CHANGES IN AGENCY BUSINESS In recent years, there have been some significant changes in the advertising agency business. The discussion thus far has been on what are called full-service agencies— those providing all the advertising services expected from an agency. But because of the development of some new kinds of businesses to provide advertising services, and certain dissatisfactions with full-service agencies, such as compensation, media buying, and creativity, there are now alternatives to using the independent full-service advertising agency.

CREATIVE BOUTIQUES In the late 1960s, the direction of advertising was heavily toward creativity, with clients demanding highly creative advertisements. With the ensuing high demand for creative talent, some bright and talented creative people set up a type of limited-service advertising agency that sold only creative work. These are known as *cre-*

ative boutiques. The advertiser using these boutiques must still seek other sources for the other advertising services that are needed.

In addition to the creative boutiques, there are freelance copywriters and moonlighting copywriters, artists, and television producers. In the quest for highly creative advertisements, there was a demand for the services of all these, but this demand has lost its appeal in the last few years.

MEDIA BUYING SERVICES Some years ago, because of the selling practices of individual television stations, a new kind of agent appeared on the media buying scene—the independent time buyer who could negotiate for spot television time at low prices and pass on the savings to advertisers buying television. Independent time buyers sold their services to both clients and agencies. Their success led them to expand their services to include buying all media. Thus a new kind of organization was born—the *independent media buying service.* The major selling point of these organizations has been the claim that they can save money for advertisers because of their volume purchases. In fact, some guarantee it. Medium and small agencies might use a buying service because it could save them departmental administrative and overhead costs. Some of these organizations have been redefined as media companies and offer media planning as well as buying. Big agencies dispute the claim that these buying services can save money for their clients, because these major agencies themselves deal in high-volume buying and have personnel in place to do the job.

IN-HOUSE AGENCIES Some advertisers have established *in-house agencies* that operate as company departments or as wholly owned subsidiaries. These organizations either function in all service areas— buying media directly, creating and producing advertisements—or carry on only limited services, using boutiques, media buying services, independent research firms, and/or limited or à la carte services of independent full-service agencies.[5] These options are possible, of course, because media that traditionally would offer commissions only to independent agencies will pay these commissions to in-house agencies because of the availability of boutiques and media buying services.

In-house agencies appear to be most attractive and practical for large producers of consumer packaged goods, and in actuality such arrangements represent only a small portion of advertisers. The motivation for such an organization is cost savings and perceived performance benefits.

The agency that serves its clients best is the one with the principles and courage to be sure that the promotion it prepares and places is honest, in good taste, representative of its best abilities, and is the kind of advertising it would run if it were held fully liable for the success or failure of the plan.

WILLIAM A. MARSTELLER, Advertising Agent

Other than some kinds of retailers, most firms that are advertisers of any consequence use full-service advertising agencies, but apparently some do not, and others probably need not. In any case, it is probably valuable for the advertiser to ask from time to time, Why use an advertising agency? The answer should help in determining whether or not the advertising should be handled in-house, whether to employ the independent services available, or what agency will do the best job for the firm.

There are several reasons why an advertiser uses the services of an advertising agency. For one thing, it may cost less to use an agency than to bypass it. The agency receives a large part of its compensation in the form of commissions from the media (15 percent), whereas the national advertiser does not get this commission if the advertisements are placed directly. It is increasingly possible, however, for the advertiser to place advertising with media and still earn the commission or a substantial part of it. One of the motives for buying advertising services piecemeal is economy, but there is the real question of whether purchasing piecemeal is really more economical than using a full-service agency. Besides, economy should not be the major motive, for if it were,

THE CONSUMER CONNECTION

—by Paul C. Harper, Jr.
Chairman of the Board
Needham, Harper & Steers, Inc.

With the gradual decline of personal salesmanship in our complex society, advertising has become the principal contact between business and the public.

And advertising agencies have become responsible for keeping the conversation going between clients and consumers.

Fortunately, most agencies have kept up on their homework. So today, as we peer into the murky Eighties, *advertising agencies possess an unparalleled body of knowledge of what works and what doesn't in the influencing of human behavior.*

Agencies are the only business organizations that work with clients: In every sector of the social and economic structure. On a continuing basis. In every medium of communications. Within an accountable framework where work must show results.

They provide American business with an exclusive source of sound communication strategy, coupled with an enormous pool of widely talented people on hand to carry it out.

So, while advertising agencies are primarily concerned with writing and placing ads so they are heard, believed, and acted upon, it goes a good deal deeper than that.

They must also make sure that what business *says* is what the public *hears*, and that what the public hears is *true* and in the interest of both the consumer and business alike.

Agencies must make certain that the consumer connection is never broken.

FIGURE 6-9

The case for using an advertising agency is aptly stated to the business community in this advertisement. *By permission: Needham, Harper & Steers, Inc.*

then no advertising would be the most economical move of all. Money spent on advertising is spent to *maximize profits,* not to minimize advertising cost. Bypassing the advertising agency may be the most economical means of advertising, but will it be the most profitable? Of course, other things being equal, the most economical means of advertising becomes good business practice. The question then becomes one of evaluating the use of an advertising agency in terms of profit maximization.

It is also contended that an agency can do a more effective job because its independence provides for greater objectivity and because the constant threat of losing the account keeps the agency on its toes. A full-service agency is involved in all aspects of advertising. Thus, it will consider all of them without bias, whereas the specialized services are likely to be biased in favor of the particular services they offer.

But all those advantages would be offset if the agency did not produce more effective advertising than the client could. Moreover, the greater objectivity could be lost if advertiser–agency relations persisted for a long period of time (and the tendency in recent years has been an increased longevity of such relations). It is easy to fire an inefficient agency, but it is just as easy to fire inefficient employees. Yet evidence indicates that in most instances, agencies are used. The underlying reason is that an advertising agency can generally prepare advertising that is more productive and makes a greater contribution to profit. Why? What sets the advertising agency apart so that it is difficult, if not impossible, for the advertiser to do as good a job without it? The answer lies in the milieu in which the advertising agency exists. Creativity does not take place by chance. To flourish, it must be nurtured by the proper setting. Just as it is not by accident that people in the arts gravitate to such cities as Paris, so the advertising agency is the "Paris" of creativity for advertising people. Within the agency, there is the opportunity for interchange of ideas from the agency's diversified accounts. By the same token, a boutique or freelancer or moonlighter does not enjoy the interaction of creativity with media, research, merchandising, and the like, the way the creative department of an agency does. Furthermore, an agency enjoys a certain freedom in relation to a producer that an employee does not. There is a flavor—a character—to the advertising agency, intangible perhaps, that cannot be reproduced by the advertising department of the client. So the independent full-service advertising agency flourishes, and the in-house agency cannot apparently offer serious competition to it.

GUIDES TO SELECTING AN AGENCY

Selecting an advertising agency is at best a calculated guess. There is no simple formula, for the advertiser is buying an unknown quantity. True, one can judge past performance, but the services bought are not yesterday's but tomorrow's. Some advertisers have met with considerable frustration in trying to make an intelligent selection. At least one has suggested placing some names in a hat and drawing one out. Although in the final analysis executive judgment will be the basis for the decision, certainly there must be some guides to selection.

SPECULATIVE PRESENTATIONS It would appear that a natural way to evaluate the effectiveness of an advertising agency would be to have it prepare a suggested advertising campaign for the firm. Such a procedure is known as a speculative presentation. In fact, many advertisers demand such presentations when selecting a new agency. These speculative assignments can take several forms, such as working up advertising concepts, specific problem solving, and hypothetical cases. When several agencies are invited to compete for the advertiser's business like this, sufficient time must be provided if the agencies are to do the work properly. It is also not unusual for the advertiser to pay the participating agencies for their efforts whether they win or lose.

Some agencies will not be involved in speculative presentations, claiming that they cannot do justice to the assignment without having more insights into the marketing objectives and strategy of the advertiser and that although speculative advertisements may look good on the surface, the real test of their effectiveness can be measured only after they are run. Also, there is always the possibility that an unscrupulous client may "appropriate" an idea developed by an agency in a speculative presentation even though that agency does not get the account.

THE ADVERTISING TASK Perhaps the first step in selecting an agency is to determine the scope of the advertising task by taking a self-inventory in the form of a job description. What is the role of advertising in the overall promotional strategy of the firm? What is the philosophy of the firm with regard to the advertising function? What are the firm's policies regarding advertising? What job should the advertising or marketing services department be performing in the light of the firm's promotional strategy, advertising philosophy, and advertising policies? What job has the advertising or marketing services department been performing? With these questions answered, thinking can now be directed toward the agency. If the firm has had an agency, what job has that agency been performing? Regardless of whether the firm has had an agency in the past, what job should the new advertising agency be performing in view of the advertising or marketing services department's role and the firm's promotional strategy, advertising philosophy, and advertising policies?

Now the advertising or marketing services department can begin to screen advertising agencies by taking this job description and from it formulating the job qualifications that the agencies being considered should fulfill. The job qualifications will obviously differ for each company, but they will undoubtedly take into consideration a number of points that are discussed below.

EXPERIENCE WITH THE SAME TYPE OF ACCOUNT One way of measuring the experience of a prospective advertising agency is to examine its record with similar or related products. As a rule, agencies do not handle competitive accounts, but they may have or have had clients whose products are similar or related. For example, a dairy-product firm looking for an agency would be interested in other food

J. WALTER SUNSHINE

This little boy eats mustard sandwiches. Sings "You Are My Sunshine." And sells more mustard than anybody around.

He's one of the kids in the Sunshine Mustard commercials created by J. Walter Thompson USA for French's.

No cast of thousands. No budget-busting cost in either media or production.

Nothing big, except response.

An independent research company, Video Storyboard Tests, surveyed 22,000

consumers to find America's best remembered, best liked TV campaigns.

Right up in the select circle of winners was the Sunshine Mustard campaign.

It also helped win an impressive gain in French's market share.

That's response for you.

J. Walter Response.

Call Burt Manning at (212) 210-7250. He'll tell you more about it.

J. WALTER USA
J. WALTER THOMPSON USA   Atlanta · Chicago · Detroit
Los Angeles · New York   San Francisco · Washington

FIGURE 6-10

Agencies use *house advertising* to sell their services to other advertisers. In this advertisement the agency cites a successful campaign for one of its clients. *By permission: J. Walter Thompson USA.*

and beverage accounts the agency has. Obviously, an agency with such accounts would have greater insight into and knowledge of the problems of the food industry. It would have had the opportunity to develop some skills for handling such advertising. And it would have a record of effectiveness for such advertising.

AGENCY SIZE   Would the advertiser be better off with a large or a small advertising agency? There are arguments in favor of both, and there is no general agreement on an answer to this question. In some instances, the problem of size resolves itself, because most large agencies set a minimum appropriation for new clients and, conversely, some client appropriations are so large that a small agency would not be equipped to handle them. Thus, large accounts tend toward large agencies and small accounts toward small agencies. But some large advertisers prefer to be the most important client of a smaller agency, whereas some small advertisers seek out the big agencies, hoping to benefit from the work done for larger clients. At any rate, the size of an agency does not necessarily relate to its ability. In fact, many large agencies are organized in the product-group manner to simulate the small agency. In the final analysis, the agency need only be as large as is necessary to handle the task assigned it by the client.

AGENCY FACILITIES Somewhat related to the size problem is the question of facilities. Generally, the large agency will have greater facilities available to the client. But here again, what is required will depend upon the task assigned to the agency by the client. Some clients want to assign the jobs of merchandising, marketing research, and public relations to an agency equipped to handle them. On the other hand, if the client looks to the agency primarily for the preparation of advertisements, the client may wish to avoid agencies that have extra facilities, because these facilities would tend to increase the overhead costs of the agency and result in additional and unnecessary expenses for the advertiser. Many agencies today, however, will negotiate different compensation rates for clients who wish to buy only certain services.

It should be noted, however, that advertising agencies are becoming increasingly important to many advertisers in areas peripheral to advertising, such as sales promotion and public relations. As a result, agencies continue to expand their scope of operations and facilities.

AGENCY ORGANIZATION AND PERSONNEL In trying to choose the right advertising agency, the advertiser should examine the organization structure with an eye to finding an agency whose organization is similar to that of the manufacturer's own advertising or marketing services department. Likewise, the advertiser should pay close attention to the personnel in the agency's organization. Ultimately, the organizational structure will be only as good as the people in the organization. More than anything else, the advertiser is buying the talents of *people.* At the higher levels, the personnel have established reputations of skill, achievement, and talent. The advertiser should determine to what extent these talents are needed. Key agency people who would work on the account should be interviewed.

AGENCY CHARACTER, PHILOSOPHY, AND POLICIES Aside from its personnel and organizational structure, what really sets one advertising agency apart from another is its character, philosophy, and policies. Thus, some agencies have a character of reserve, whereas others are innovators; some agencies emphasize copy, and others emphasize visualization. Similarly, agencies vary in their advertising philosophies; some, for example, subordinate advertising to a role in the marketing mix, whereas others look upon advertising as being rather independent of other marketing activities. Agencies differ in their philosophies regarding copy, art, and media. Of course, each agency will have its own policies with regard to both its internal operation and client relations. These policies should be examined carefully to determine whether they will be compatible with the policies of the advertiser.

OTHER AGENCY QUALIFICATIONS If an advertising agency is fully recognized (that is, recognized by all media), it will receive commissions from all media, and therefore there will be little question of its objectivity in selecting media for its client. However, many smaller agencies are recognized by only certain media or classes of media. When this is the case, the only concern is whether or not the advertiser is apt to use certain types of media for which the agency does not have recognition, for the agency may tend to avoid recommending them. On the other hand, if the advertiser's media needs are limited (for example, an industrial advertiser may use only business publications and newspapers), then it is only necessary that the agency chosen has recognition by these media.

Other things being equal, it might be wise for the advertiser to shop around to determine what is available for the money from various agencies. Although commissions received by agencies from media are uniform, the amount of work an agency will provide for the client for these commissions will vary with the agency. In addition, agencies vary their charges to clients for other work performed.

Three out of four advertisers maintain some kind of written agreements with agencies.[6] When these are used, care should be taken to see that the advertiser's interests are protected. The other agencies and clients rely instead on goodwill and mutual respect in the agency-and-client relationship.

ADVERTISER AND AGENCY RELATIONS

Unfortunately, advertisers and agencies tend to be fickle, and their marriages are sometimes short-lived, despite the fact that the increasing complexity of the marketing task makes it costly to change agencies frequently, for an agency must carry on relations with an advertiser for a long time before it can have sufficient knowledge to do the most effective job. Thus, many practitioners today are concerned with how to make the marriage last.

One of the best ways of building a lasting relationship is to take the necessary time and effort to select the right agency in the first place. Having made a careful choice of agency, the advertiser should be prepared to take the agency into its confidence. If the client fails to disclose all the facts of its operation to the agency, it cannot expect the agency to do the best possible job. Because the advertising task is but a part of the overall marketing plan, the agency must be concerned with marketing in formulating advertising plans and should also be encouraged to contribute to the firm's marketing strategy.

The advertiser should recognize that one of the main values of the advertising agency is its creativity and independent point of view. Thus, the client should encourage the agency to be uninhibited in presenting its views. This does not mean that the client should be required to accept all agency recommendations, but the advertiser's attitude should encourage freedom of expression on the part of the agency and recognize that, after all, the agency's counsel is likely to be of value.

On the other hand, the agency must remember that it is working *for* the client, who, therefore, has the right to the last word. Although

Thanks, Ayer

Twenty Million Voices

American Telephone & Telegraph Company

April 1908

Seventy-five years ago this month, NW Ayer produced and placed the Bell System's first national ad.

We've been together ever since.

When that first ad was printed, Teddy Roosevelt was president. Telephones were shaped like candlesticks. And even the biggest ad agencies had only a handful of people.

One of Ayer's handful wrote in a 1908 call report: "The word 'advertising' to the Telephone Company means something different than it does to the ordinary advertiser of commercial products. The Telephone Company...wants to please the public really more than some smaller corporations would ever think of doing."

The telephone system was comparatively small in 1908. But even then it was looked upon as a big business, with all the advantages and problems of such a position. The idea of keeping the public informed about the conduct of its affairs, an entirely new idea at the time—and not too common even today—was unquestionably an important decision by the management.

A selected few of the ads of the past 75 years are shown here. Something of the course of the country, in different business eras, and in peace and war, is reflected in their text and timing.

All are chapters in the story of a great and growing business. And all reflect the enduring partnership between agency and client that has spanned much of the history of our business.

Seventy-five years is a very long time for any relationship. For a client and an ad agency, it's rare indeed.

So thanks, Ayer.

We're glad you still have our number.

AT&T

...and Associated Companies of the Bell System

FIGURE 6-11

Good advertiser-agency relations can result in long marriages. This advertisement in the business press was created as a surprise by the client, using another agency to prepare it, to show its appreciation for 75 years of working together. *By permission: American Telephone & Telegraph Company.*

the agency should not subjugate itself to the whims of the client, it should acquiesce to the wishes of the client even if these are not in agreement with its own ideas. The agency should not, of course, submit to client wishes where they violate the agency's own moral and ethical standards.

To serve the interests of its clients best, the advertising agency must not show any partiality toward any single advertising medium or group of media. A bona fide agency should not have any undisclosed interest in an advertising medium, for it must be free to choose objectively those media that will do the best job in selling the client's product.

The advertising agency generally assumes liability for, and makes payment to media for, space or time contracted in behalf of a client. This is true whether or not the client pays the agency. The advertising medium for its part agrees to publish its rates, to contract with the

ADVERTISING
AGENCY AND
MEDIA
RELATIONS

137

agency at the lowest rate charged for that particular space or time, and not to discriminate against any agency. The advertising medium maintains the right to approve the content of the advertising prepared by the agency, but it may not make any changes without the agency's approval.

ADVERTISING ASSOCIATIONS

The leading advertising organization of manufacturers is the Association of National Advertisers, Inc., which was founded in 1910. It has a membership of about 600 companies, and, although this represents a small number of the total producers using advertising, its members' appropriations make up a large part of the total advertising investment in this country. According to the ANA, it provides a clearinghouse of impartial, useful, and timely information not available from any other source; conducts workshops and seminars for the training and development of member company personnel; and expresses advertisers' practices, attitudes, and legitimate interests to agencies, media, and other suppliers of services, as well as to the public and government.

In addition to the ANA, a great many general trade associations for individual industries concern themselves with the advertising activities of their members through special advertising divisions. They may conduct studies of advertising practices in the industry, establish advertising codes of ethics, and assist members in establishing advertising programs. In many instances, these associations also engage in industrywide advertising campaigns to stimulate primary demand for the industry's products.

The American Association of Advertising Agencies, or AAAA, (referred to orally as the "Four As") is the national trade association for the advertising agency business. It was organized in 1917 at the suggestion of advertising media. Although there are only about 550 AAAA agencies, they place about three-fourths of all advertising handled by agencies in the United States; therefore, the AAAA is an important voice in the advertising world. Its three major objectives are as follows:

1. To foster, strengthen, and improve the advertising agency business
2. To advance the cause of advertising as a whole
3. To give service to members; to do things for them which they cannot do for themselves[7]

INFORMATION ON ADVERTISERS AND AGENCIES

A publication providing pertinent information about advertising agencies is the *Standard Directory of Advertising Agencies*. This publication lists most of the advertising agencies in the United States, and their addresses, telephone numbers, and branches. Association affiliations are given, as well as a listing of those media associations recognizing the agency. The major personnel and their titles and the current accounts that the agency is serving are also listed. In the front of the directory is a geographical index of agencies by states and cities.

A companion publication, *The Standard Directory of Advertisers*, lists some 16,000 advertiser companies and their executives. In most instances, the listings include the advertising agencies handling the accounts and such information as the amount of the advertising appropriation and the media used.

The three major components in advertising development are advertisers, advertising agencies, and advertising media. Their organization of the advertising function varies considerably from firm to firm. Producers traditionally organized advertising functionally as a department reporting to the president or sales manager. Today such a department reports to a marketing vice-president. As firms have grown in size and complexity, new organization structures have developed—especially for consumer packaged goods. Responsibility for individual brands has been given to product managers, including responsibility for advertising planning. The advertising departments have been incorporated, in such instances, in marketing services departments reporting to central marketing management and including in their responsibilities such possible activities as advertising media planning and buying, sales promotion, advertising agency relations, corporate advertising, and marketing research, among other duties.

Retailers organize the advertising function in advertising departments. In the case of large department stores, these are a part of a sales promotion department, which includes, besides the advertising department, those for special promotions and for display. Small retailers who cannot afford their own advertising departments can make use of a variety of outside services to assist them in advertising.

Most producers and an increasing number of retailers make use of advertising agencies. These agencies are typically made up of four component service areas: account services, marketing services, creative services, and management and financial services. The major source of agency compensation is commissions allowed by advertising media. Additionally, there are markups on out-of-pocket expenses incurred for clients, and fees charged for certain other activities.

From time to time, advertisers seek to find alternatives to full-service advertising agencies, but ultimately most come back to them because they afford the most effective means of carrying on the advertising function. Periodically, a client must choose a new agency, and there are a number of important criteria to consider, including the task to be performed, agency experience, size, facilities, organization, character, philosophy, and policies.

QUESTIONS AND PROBLEMS

1. Assume that you are a large producer of diversified lines of consumer packaged goods. Advertising plays an important role in the company's promotional strategy. Suggest the type of organization you would use to handle the advertising function. Qualify your answer by making the necessary assumptions about the nature of your firm.

2. Explain the difference between a product manager and a market manager.

3. Describe the five main functions of a producer's marketing services department.

4. Describe the typical organization of a department store advertising department.

5. What resources are available to small retailers who cannot operate their own advertising departments economically?

6. Choose some product to be advertised and explain how each service area of an advertising agency would contribute to its advertising and promotion.

7. Explain what is meant by media commissions and agency services compensation as elements of agency compensation.

The Organization of Advertising

139

8. An advertising agency using the commission system of compensation prepares an advertisement for a client. The gross charge by the medium for the space is $14,000. Out-of-pocket expenses include artwork, $500; separation films, $300; typography, $150; and miscellaneous other expenses, $50. Assume that the agency and client take all available discounts. What would the agency pay the medium? What would the agency bill the client? (Media charges and out-of-pocket expenses are generally billed separately.) What would be the gross margin for the agency?

9. Why should an advertiser use an advertising agency?

10. Assume that you are an advertiser who must select an advertising agency. What questions would you ask of each agency you are considering?

ENDNOTES

[1] This discussion is based in part on Victor P. Buell, *Organizing for Marketing/Advertising Success* (New York: Association of National Advertisers, Inc., 1982).

[2] Frederic R. Gamble, *What Advertising Agencies Are—What They Do and How They Do It*, 7th ed. (New York: American Association of Advertising Agencies, Inc., 1970), pp. 6–7.

[3] Benjamin J. Katz, "Growth Effects in Agency Network Functions," *Making Advertising Relevant* (Columbia, S.C.: American Academy of Advertising, 1975), p. 121.

[4] Association of National Advertisers, *Current Advertiser Practices in Compensating Their Advertising Agencies* (New York: Association of National Advertisers, Inc., 1979), p. 1.

[5] Edward C. Bursk and Baljit Singh Sethi, "The In-House Agency," *Journal of Advertising*, Vol. 5, No. 1 (Winter 1976), p. 24.

[6] Association of National Advertisers, *Current Advertiser Practices*, p. 3.

[7] Gamble, *What Advertising Agencies Are*, pp. 29–30.

Advertising and Marketing Planning

After completing this chapter, you should be able to:

1. Understand how advertising is a part of marketing
2. Identify the various elements in the marketing mix
3. Explain the marketing concept
4. Define the different kinds of market segmentation
5. Appreciate the importance of marketing planning
6. Describe the basic elements of the marketing plan

Advertising is not an end in itself. It is a means to an end—or, more correctly, to several ends. In business, advertising is used as a means of maximizing profits. This is its long-range objective. The short-range objectives may be more narrowly defined in terms of selling a particular quantity of a product, gaining public acceptance for a product, or building a particular image for a product.

Experience with advertising as a business tool will quickly show that there is little if anything that advertising can accomplish by itself. Business operation is a matter of teamwork, and advertising is a member of the team. The whole team must pull together to win. Each member makes a contribution but always bears in mind the efforts of all the other members. The result is the accomplishment of objectives.

ADVERTISING: THE TOOL OF MARKETING

Business may be divided into three broad areas: production, finance, and marketing (sometimes referred to as distribution). Production is concerned with the manufacture of goods. Finance is concerned with providing the funds necessary for the operation of the business. Marketing is concerned with all the activities that occur from the point of production to the point of consumption.

Marketing involves two spheres of activity—internal and external. The internal activities, which are used to move goods from production to consumption, can be lumped into four major elements—product, price, distribution, and promotion. Product activity includes developing the right product or product line, packaging, and branding. Price deals with setting the selling price so as to maximize the profits of the firm. Distribution involves determination of the right channels for moving the product to the consumer or user, including transportation, storage, wholesaling, and retailing. Promotion is concerned with communications and persuasion, making use of advertising, sales promotion, personal selling and public relations.

All these four activities are essential to marketing, although the way they are employed will vary with the situation and the strategy employed by the marketing decision makers within the firm. Thus, there

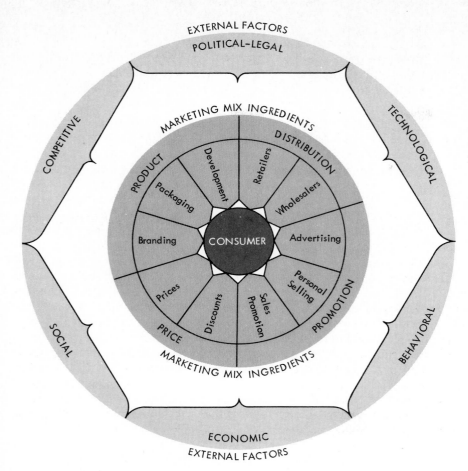

FIGURE 7-1

The consumer as a target, showing the internal marketing activities and the external factors that influence the consumer.

is a need for promotion, but it may take the form of advertising, sales promotion, personal selling, public relations, all of these, or some combination.

To a considerable extent, the marketing activity of the firm will be influenced by its financial and production activity. Certainly, marketing activity decisions cannot be made in a vacuum, and top management must coordinate its decisions in this area with finance and production factors.

Nor can marketing decisions be made intelligently or effectively unless the external forces in the marketing environment that affect them are taken into consideration. Even though marketing management cannot control these external forces, it cannot afford to ignore them. They include the competitive situation, economic conditions, the political climate, legislative action, technology, social phenomena, and human behavior.

All marketing activity revolves around the consumer or user, who therefore becomes the target of marketing efforts. This section of the text considers advertising as a part of marketing. Therefore it will examine the interrelationship between marketing activities, especially as they relate to advertising, and the market target—the consumer or user.

THE MARKETING MIX

The teamwork of marketing can be called the *marketing mix*. That is, the marketing mix involves a blending of the various marketing activities in the proper manner and proportion to produce the most effective marketing effort in order to maximize the profits of the firm. Advertising can be, and frequently is, one of the ingredients in this mix. The idea of the marketing mix can be explained by an analogy to baking a cake. In order for the result to be successful, you must combine a number of ingredients, carefully measured in different amounts. You do not always use the same ingredients, however. If it is to be a chocolate cake, chocolate or cocoa must be used. If it is a white cake, neither will be used. The selected, measured ingredients are not just tossed together. They must be carefully combined in a logical order and then blended to form the batter. At the outset, you have to make an important decision—the kind of cake you want. With your objective determined, you will probably consult a cookbook that prescribes several methods of meeting your objective with slight variations. You choose one and, following the proper procedure, achieve the desired results, much to the joy of the stockholders—your family or friends. It should be noted, however, that although you controlled the ingredients going into the cake, you had little or no control over certain forces affecting the outcome. For example, the altitude or humidity might affect the cake, so you must adjust the ingredients accordingly.

The marketing mix follows essentially the same procedure, but with one notable omission. For the marketing manager, there are no cookbooks or recipes. In recent years, however, there has been increasing interest in the collection of marketing case histories, which afford businesspeople an opportunity to examine methods others have used to accomplish their objectives. Although this technique can provide some small measure of help, the dynamic nature of marketing makes each new situation sufficiently different so that it requires a new method.

Because no two marketing situations are ever really the same, marketing managers have to prepare their own method or "recipe." This is known as the marketing plan and is discussed in detail later in the chapter. They then determine what ingredients go into the mix and in what amounts. These may include advertising, personal selling, sales promotion, packaging, branding, pricing, product design and development, distribution channels, and publicity, for example. They must then determine how and in what proportion to use them. If they have chosen the right ingredients and put them together properly, they will meet their objectives. Marketers, too, are faced with certain forces over which they have little if any control. Thus, the marketing environment must be considered. Their marketing mix must be adjusted to meet the effects of this environment. The political climate and legislation have been discussed in an earlier chapter. The effect of the other influences will be considered in later chapters.

Strategy is the key to success for an advertising campaign. It is not possible to succeed with a brilliant idea and superb execution of the wrong strategy, but it is possible to attain some success with no idea and a dull execution of the right strategy. This becomes painfully apparent almost every time you turn on your television set.

JOHN O'TOOLE, *Advertising Agent*

THE MARKETING CONCEPT

Historically, business developed around production. A person found the money to produce a product and then looked for people to buy it. To be sure, such production-oriented business made profits for the firm. But it became evident that consumers were not going to buy just because goods were produced. Rather, consumers are more receptive to those products that are designed and marketed to meet their tastes and desires.

In recent years, therefore, there has been a switch in emphasis from production orientation to marketing orientation. This new emphasis is called the marketing concept; it may be defined as a state of mind of the firm that says that the entire firm looks to the consumer or user for its direction and responds through an integrated and coordinated marketing function, which is in turn melded with all of the other functions of the firm in an effort to maximize long-range profits.

Thus, through the emphasis on marketing, the firm looks to the consumers and users for its direction—its objectives. Their points of view pervade the whole business enterprise. Consumers tell the firm their wants and desires, and this information is translated into product, package, brand, price, channels of distribution, and promotion. It is, therefore, immediately obvious that advertising, as a promotional activity, is not an end in itself, but rather a part of the whole that is marketing.

MARKET SEGMENTATION   Advertisers soon learn that their messages are not perceived in the same way by all those they reach. Furthermore, the use of their specific brands or the generic products that their brands represent will be greater among some consumers than others. So most advertisers market their products on the basis of identifying certain subsets of consumers, which we refer to as *market segmentation*. That is, they identify those portions of the market with the greatest potential and then direct their promotional efforts toward them by selecting the most suitable copy approaches and media to reach them.

Thus, advertisers can identify, through market segmentation, one or more *target markets* on which they can concentrate their efforts. They may find that different market segments prefer different varieties of the same generic product; therefore, they may produce and market several varieties of the same product, each to a different market segment. An example would be Anheuser-Busch and its major brands, Budweiser, Michelob, and Busch Light. Or, again, they may find that different market segments buy the same brand for different reasons. In these instances, advertisers can use different advertising strategies to most effectively reach each market segment. For example, pickup trucks are advertised differently to farmers, businesses, and young adults who are buying them as noncommercial, recreational vehicles.

There are three major ways to segment markets in an attempt to identify target markets for the advertiser. These are geographic, demographic, and psychographic market segmentations. Each of these is considered below.

GEOGRAPHIC SEGMENTATION Consumers in different geographic regions may have different buying behavior. One of the earliest forms of market segmentation was to recognize geographic differences. Automobile manufacturers found, for example, that certain colors and styles—two-door and four-door sedans, station wagons, and convertibles—were more popular in some regions than in others. Then, some very obvious geographic differences exist between nations. In this country, black is worn as a symbol of mourning, but in the Orient, white is worn for that purpose. Here a bride traditionally wears white; in Japan, she wears red! A firm that sells its product nationwide may see special sales opportunities in specific geographic areas. For example, a manufacturer of flaked coconut found that the greatest demand for the product was in the Southeast and New England, so national advertising was supplemented with special regional campaigns in these areas.

DEMOGRAPHIC SEGMENTATION Most advertisers today make use of demographic data in segmenting their markets. Demographic classifications can include age, sex, education, occupation, income, marital status, family size, religion, race, and the like. It is easy to see that such information collected in terms of product usage can help advertisers identify who their most promising customers are; they can then direct their advertising messages to them through the media that will most efficiently reach them. Therefore, if demographic analysis shows that the heaviest usage for our product is by women who are married and under 35 years of age, with two or more children under eight and a blue-collar occupation by the head of household, then we know who our market is. And from this we can determine what appeals in our advertising will be most effective. Finally, we can find those advertising media with similar demographics to reach our market most effectively with our message.

SOURCES OF DEMOGRAPHIC DATA Advertisers and advertising agencies collect demographic data on their own or from secondary sources. Producer and retailer sales and credit records often yield such data. Census data can also be valuable. And, of course, consumer research studies can be undertaken to get demographic profiles of the market.

There are also syndicated research services that compile such data, and although there are certain methodological and coverage differences among them, they provide essentially similar demographic profiles of heavy, medium, and light users of a wide variety of generic products and sole users, primary users, secondary users, and nonusers of each brand of the generic product. Similar information is obtained for various media vehicles, so that advertisers can ascertain the demographic characteristics not only of product users but also of media audiences. These services can tell an advertiser who are the heavy users of, say, coffee, and what specific magazines they read.

STUDY OF MEDIA AND MARKETS One of the syndicated research services is the *Study of Media and Markets,* published by Simmons Market Research Bureau, Inc. SMRB collects information from 19,000 adults each year. From this it provides marketing data on product and service usage in over 750 categories and subcategories for thousands of different brands. It also provides qualitative and quantitative media data on audiences of magazines, newspapers, television, radio, and outdoor. Simmons breaks down all its data by sex, age, census region, marketing region, county size, locality type, education, employment status, occupation, household income, race, marital status, household size, presence of children, market value of residence, parents, and top areas of dominant influence. In addition, in its demographic volumes it provides the following data: residence ownership, type of dwelling, respondent's company size, individual employment income, head-of-house employment status, market value of residence, mothers, Spanish-speaking, respondent's type of business, head-of-household education, head-of-household occupation, head-of-household age, and head-of-household index of social position.

PSYCHOGRAPHIC SEGMENTATION For some purposes, geographic and demographic market segmentation may leave something to be desired. For example, age is a commonly used demographic classification. From it, advertisers have defined the "youth market." However, the youth market may need a new definition. Is it really an age group, or is it a state of mind? The youth market overflows the traditional age brackets and today can be defined more meaningfully in terms of those who think young in any age bracket—that is, in terms of youthfulness, not youth. Even among youth within the demographic age bracket there is a wide range of differences. Consider, for example, the polar positions of the "preppy" and the "street-smart" youth. It can be seen, therefore, that differentiation could be based on values as well as demographics. Thus, there is an increasing interest by advertisers in using this new dimension to define market targets in terms of attitudes and activities. Such research is called *psychographics.*

Advertising and
Marketing Planning

147

> *Advertising has induced progress in the use of manufacturers of new materials, new tools, and new processes of manufacture by calling their attention to economies which could be achieved and to the new uses to which they could be put. Without such advertising, information of this kind would take years to reach all of those who might benefit by it and progress would be delayed.*
>
> *HARRY S. TRUMAN (1884–1973), Statesman*
>
> READER'S DIGEST

THE MARKETING PLAN

As we have seen, advertising does not just happen. The general objective of commercial advertising is to maximize the profits of the firm, but the day-to-day purpose of advertising is conceived in terms of more specific objectives that will ultimately lead to the same end. First, the marketing plan must define these objectives. Then strategies must be developed for advertising that will accomplish them. Obviously, all advertising by all advertisers involves planning. Unfortunately, much of what passes for planning is inept waste motion, for many advertisers confuse the marketing plan with a "bull session" preceding the preparation of each advertisement.

The importance of planning has been mentioned several times now. The kind of planning we are talking about is specific. It is the marketing plan. The marketing plan is a written document, prepared annually, that contains the basic objectives and strategies for a given product or brand for the coming fiscal year.

The marketing plan serves two purposes: First, it is designed to provide top management with a marketing statement for a brand that contains sufficient information so that management can make a ready decision. Second, it is a working document for guiding marketing people in the implementation of the plan and as a yardstick to measure the brand's performance.

For many years, advertising agencies prepared *advertising plans* for their clients. These were primarily copy platforms or policies, together with rationales for the platforms, and media plans. But as it has become increasingly obvious that advertising is only a part of the whole and that whole is marketing, advertising plans have been replaced with *marketing plans*.

With the increasing importance of the advertising tool, the necessity for serious planning becomes obvious. Whereas in the past, many firms planned their marketing and advertising on a month-to-month basis, today the trend is toward plans for one year or even more. Intuitive judgment as a basis for advertising has given way to advertising strategy based on carefully researched facts. At present, the size of the advertising investment represents a very large share of total expenses for an increasing number of businesses. In order to evaluate advertising effectiveness, it is necessary to know what to measure. The objectives set forth in the plan provide this measure. Furthermore, because advertising is a part of an integrated effort by the whole firm, there must be a carefully delineated plan so that the advertising effort can be coordinated with the efforts of other segments of the business.

BASIC ELEMENTS OF THE MARKETING PLAN Marketing plans will vary tremendously from firm to firm, with no two alike. Nevertheless, there are certain items that should be included in all marketing plans if they are to be effective. Logically, a marketing plan should have a precise delineation of the marketing objectives; background information on the market and the brand, including significant facts about the competition; a statement of opportunities and problems; strategies to meet the marketing objectives through marketing, advertising copy platform, media plan and schedule, and sales promotion; and testing and research.[1] The responsibility for putting the marketing plan together will vary also with the particular firm. It may be the singular responsibility of the company's marketing manager, advertising manager, or product or market manager, or it may fall to the advertising agency. Frequently it is a joint responsibility of several or all of these people.

The format for a typical marketing plan is presented in Figure 7-2. Obviously, it cannot apply to every situation. This particular format is adapted from one prepared by the Association of National Advertisers for product managers of consumer-goods firms and is designed for ongoing brands. Additional inputs would be necessary for new-brand marketing plans.

FIGURE 7-2

Format for the Annual Marketing Plan   Brand Name   19—— Marketing Plan

Adapted from F. Beaven Ennis, Effective Marketing Management (New York: Association of National Advertisers, Inc., 1973), pp. 13-20.

OUTLINE	DESCRIPTION
I. CURRENT-YEAR PERFORMANCE	One or two short paragraphs summarizing how the brand performed this year relative to sales share and budget objectives; the reasons for significant variations from plan; the major events that occurred affecting the market, if any; etc.
II. RECOMMENDATION	Two or three sentences stating the brand's objectives in total shipping units and in sales value, the total expenditures to support the brand, and the share objective.
III. P & L EFFECT OF THE RECOMMENDATION	Summarize in a brief table the basic profit and loss differences between recent performance and the new fiscal year, showing the ratio of each figure to sales, as follows:

	Last Year	Current Year	New Year
Volume (value)	$—	$—	$—
(units)	—	—	—
(% increase decrease)	—%	—%	

(continued)

FIGURE 7-2 *(continued)*

OUTLINE	DESCRIPTION		
Share	—%	—%	—%
Cost of Goods	$—(%)	$—(%)	$—(%)
Adv. Prom.	$—(%)	$—(%)	$—(%)
Other Costs	$—(%)	$—(%)	$—(%)
Pre-tax Profit	$—(%)	$—(%)	$—(%)

IV. BACKGROUND

1. Market

- **Size**   Two or three short paragraphs on the size of the market in units and/or volume, plus its growth rate. Competitive brands and share position versus the company brand should be shown. If the list of competitive brands is extensive, mention only the major brands.

- **Consumer**   One or two short paragraphs describing the consumer profile (age, income, etc.) and indicating what the total comsumption of this product category is by major geographic areas.

- **Pricing**   A brief table, preferably without comment, showing competitive and company retail price structures, by unit size. If appropriate, cost per ounce/unit may also be shown.

- **Competitive Spending**   A table breaking out the previous year's competitive media and promotional expenditures by six-month periods—e.g., January–June vs. July–December—plus competitive volume consumed during these two periods if available. Estimates of promotion costs should include only regional and national promotions, and not tests. This table should be arranged as follows:

	Vol.	1st 6 Months Med.	Prom.	Total	Vol.	2nd 6 Months Med.	Prom.	Total
Brand A	—	$—	$—	$—	—	$—	$—	$—
Brand B	—	$—	$—	$—	—	$—	$—	$—

   Following this table brief comments may be made on any significant changes from the pattern above that may be taking place currently.

- **Other**   State any other facts or statistics about the market that would be helpful to management in reaching a decision on this proposal.

2. Brand

- **Product**   One or two sentences on the general makeup of the product's formula, points of uniqueness, a table on the sizes/variety it is sold in, and the profit margin by size.

- **Manufacturing**   A short paragraph on existing plant capacity, next year's capital investment requirements if known, and any production or purchasing problems encountered to date. This is an optional section and is primarily concerned with new products.

- **Product Research**   A brief summary of the major pieces of research relating to the brand and its performance. Emphasis should be placed on actual research scores obtained rather than on editorial comments.

FIGURE 7-2 *(continued)*

OUTLINE	DESCRIPTION
• Market Research	This encompasses all other significant research studies performed on the brand to include items such as the major scores obtained from the latest advertising research, test market shares, name and packaging research, etc., if appropriate.
• Other	State any other facts or statistics about the brand that would be helpful to management in reaching a decision on this proposal.
V. OPPORTUNITIES AND PROBLEMS	
1. Opportunities	In support of this recommendation, list the key areas of opportunity from which the brand expects to obtain its growth or sales objectives in the coming year.
2. Problems	Similarly, outline the major factors that might jeopardize the brand's ability to meet its objectives, explaining what steps have been taken to minimize these risks.
IV. STRATEGIES	
1. Marketing	A concise, well-defined paragraph or two on the brand's basic objective and marketing strategy. The length of this section will vary according to individual brand needs, but should be limited to approximately a half page.
2. Spending	This section is optional and is primarily intended for brands with heavy advertising expenditures that may vary significantly according to sales areas or marketing opportunities.
3. Advertising	This should consist of three brief statements: the first devoted to the primary advertising objective, the second to the strategy to achieve this objective, and the third to the brand's TV print pool or rotation policy. As a guide, this entire section should be about a half page in length.
4. Media	As with Advertising, this section should consist of three elements. The first is a statement of objective and the second the strategy to achieve the objective. Every effort should be made to make these two statements as specific as possible, particularly in terms of coverage, frequency of commercial exposure, flight advertising, etc.
	The third element of this section should be a table showing sales volume versus media expenditures by major sales areas, the current year compared to the new year, arranged as follows:

	Current Year			New Year		
Area	Vol.	Med.	Exp'd Unit	Vol.	Med.	Exp'd Unit
1	—	$—	$—/cs	—	$—	$—/cs
2	—	$—	$—/cs	—	$—	$—/cs
etc.						

FIGURE 7-2 *(continued)*

OUTLINE	DESCRIPTION
	Significant changes in expenditures per unit in any sales area, from one year to the next, should be explained briefly beneath this table. Depending upon the number of sales areas used, the entire Media section should probably not exceed three-quarters of a page. Brands with little or short-term media should eliminate the table above entirely.
5. Sales Promotion	Similarly, the three elements of this section should consist of a sales promotion objective, a well-defined strategy statement, and a table showing the differences in expenditure and deal-pack volume, by major sales areas, from one year to the next as follows:

Expend/Unit	Area 1	Area 2	Area 3	Etc.
Current Year	$—	$—	$—	
New Year	—	—	—	
% Vol. in Trade Deals				
Current Year	—%	—%	—%	
New Year	—%	—%	—%	

OUTLINE	DESCRIPTION
	As a guide, the Sales Promotion section should probably be no longer than one page.
VII. TESTS/RESEARCH	This is a brief statement on what major tests and/or research the brand will conduct in the coming year—e.g., media or promotion tests, product tests, package research, etc. Simply give the nature, purpose, and cost of each activity. The entire section should not exceed a half-page.

This concludes the written portion of the Annual Marketing Plan, to which the four recommended financial marketing exhibits should be attached.

EXHIBIT 1

Brand Name   Price and Profit Structure   19—— Budget

	SMALL	MEDIUM	LARGE	AVERAGE PER STATISTICAL CASE*
Packed:	24's	12's	6's	
Ounces/Unit:	—oz.	—oz.	—oz.	
Unit Retail Price	—	—	—	
Retail Price/Shipping Case:	—	—	—	—
Manufacturer's Price/Case:	—	—	—	—
% Trade Margin:	—%	—%	—%	—%

*A statistical case represents the conversion of all the different size units shipped into a single, standard-size case to facilitate management's understanding of the total volume moved and upon which cost relationships can be based.

FIGURE 7-2, EXHIBIT 1 *(continued)*

Brand Name   Price and Profit Structure   19—— Budget

	SMALL	MEDIUM	LARGE	AVERAGE PER STATISTICAL CASE*
Cost per Shipping Case:	—	—	—	—
Gross Margin/Case:	—	—	—	—
% of Manufacturer's Price/Case	—%	—%	—%	—%
Estimated Case Shipments (000)	—	—	—	—
Total Sales Value:	—	—	—	—
Total Profit Margin:	—	—	—	—
% of Total Sales Value:	—%	—%	—%	—%

EXHIBIT 2

Brand Name   Profit and Loss Statement   19—— Budget

	PREVIOUS YEAR	(PERCENT SALES)	CURRENT YEAR	(PERCENT SALES)	NEW YEAR	(PERCENT SALES)
1. Total Market:						
• Value	—		—		—	
• Unit Volume	—		—		—	
• Percent Increase/Decrease	—%		—%		—%	
2. Brand Share	—%		—%		—%	
3. Brand Shipments:						
• Value	—	(100%)	—	(100%)	—	(100%)
• Unit Volume	—		—		—	—%
• Percent Increase/Decrease	—%		—%		—%	
4. Cost of Goods:						
• Fixed Costs	—	(%)	—	(%)	—	(%)
• Variable Costs	—	(%)	—	(%)	—	(%)
• Total Costs	—	(%)	—	(%)	—	(%)
5. Gross Margin	—	(%)	—	(%)	—	(%)
6. Marketing Expenses:						
• Media/Production	—	(%)	—	(%)	—	(%)
• Advertising Reserve	—	(%)	—	(%)	—	(%)
• Sampling/Couponing	—	(%)	—	(%)	—	(%)
• Trade Allowances	—	(%)	—	(%)	—	(%)
• Other Promotion	—	(%)	—	(%)	—	(%)
• Total Marketing Expenses	—	(%)	—	(%)	—	(%)
7. Other Expenses:						
• Marketing Research	—	(%)	—	(%)	—	(%)
• Sales Force Cost	—	(%)	—	(%)	—	(%)
• Distribution Cost	—	(%)	—	(%)	—	(%)
• Administration	—	(%)	—	(%)	—	(%)
• Miscellaneous Income and Expense	—	(%)	—	(%)	—	(%)
• Total Other Expenses	—	(%)	—	(%)	—	(%)
8. Profit Contribution:	—	(%)	—	(%)	—	(%)
• Increase/Decrease	—%		—%		—%	

FIGURE 7-2 *(continued)*, EXHIBIT 3

Brand Name　　Media Allocation Schedule　　19—— Budget

	CURRENT YEAR		NEW YEAR		DIFFERENCE
I. National Expenditures					
Television	(000)	%	(000)	%	=(000)
• Network TV	$ —	—%	$ —	—%	$ —
• Spot TV	—	—	—	—	—
• Production	—	—	—	—	—
Total TV	—	—%	$ —	—%	$ —
Print					
• Magazines	$ —	—%	$ —	—%	$ —
• Newspapers	—	—	—	—	—
• Supplements	—	—	—	—	—
• Preparation	—	—	—	—	—
Total Print	—	—%	$ —	—%	$ —
Other Media					
• Itemize	$ —	—%	$ —	—%	$ —
Total Other	$ —	—%	$ —	—%	$ —
TOTAL MEDIA EXPENDITURES	$ —	100%	$ —	100%	$ —

II. Quarterly Expenditures	1st Qtr.	2nd Qtr.	3rd Qtr.	4th Qtr.	Total
• Television	$ —	$ —	$ —	$ —	$ —
• Print	—	—	—	—	—
• Other	—	—	—	—	—
• Total Working Media	$ —	$ —	$ —	$ —	$ —
% of Year	—%	—%	—%	—%	100%
• Planned Shipments (000)	—	—	—	—	—
% of Year	—%	—%	—%	—%	100%

PUTTING THE MARKETING PLAN INTO ACTION　　Once the marketing plan has been written, it must be approved by management. In presenting the plan to management, it is a good idea to dramatize it by means of charts, tables, slides, or, indeed, any audiovisual devices that will help to communicate the plan clearly and convincingly.

When the plan is approved, it must be put into action. The plan should not become a historical document to be ignored, but a working guide for the marketing team. The plan should be presented to all who will play a role in carrying it out, and they should be provided with copies for day-to-day reference. Periodically, the plan should be reviewed to check progress on its implementation and effectiveness. Finally, no plan should be so rigid as not to allow for revision. Because of the dynamic character of marketing, plans can quickly become outmoded. Barring the need for plan revision because of changes in the marketing picture, a plan should still be rewritten once a year in the light of what has passed and what is on the horizon.

FIGURE 7-2 *(continued)*, EXHIBIT 4

Brand Name ____ Sales Promotion Spread Sheet ____ 19—— Budget

	JAN.	FEB.	MAR.	1ST QTR.	APR.	MAY	JUNE	2ND QTR.	1ST HALF	JULY	AUG.	SEPT.	3RD QTR.	OCT.	NOV.	DEC.	4TH QTR.	TOTAL YEAR
Area 1																		
Shipments	—	—	—	—	—	—	—	—	—	—	—	—	—	—	—	—	—	—
Type promotion		Nat'l.			Area					Nat'l.				Test				
Promotion cost		$—		$—	$—			$—	$—	$—			$—	$—			$—	$—
Area 2																		
Shipments	—	—	—	—	—	—	—	—	—	—	—	—	—	—	—	—	—	—
Type promotion*		Nat'l					Area			Nat'l				Area				
Promotion cost		$—		$—			$—	$—	$—	$—			$—	$—			$—	$—
Area 3																		
Etc.	—	—	—	—	—	—	—	—	—	—	—	—	—	—	—	—	—	—
Total shipments				—%				—%	—%				—%				—%	100%
% of year		$—		$—	$—		$—	$—	$—	$—			$—	$—			$—	$—
Total costs		—%		—%				—%	—%				—%				—%	100%
% of year		$—			$—		$—	$—		$—			$—	$—			$—	$—
Cost per shipping unit																		

*Outline nature of sales promotion—e.g., 50¢ solidus cs. allowance; sweepstakes; premium offer; etc.

Business may be divided into three broad areas: production, finance, and marketing. Marketing is affected by such elements in the environment as the economy, society, behavior, technology, and the political climate. Internally, marketing is influenced by factors of the product, the price, channels of distribution, and promotion. How these are combined to maximize the marketing effort is referred to as the *marketing mix.*

The *marketing concept* is a business philosophy suggesting that the business look to the consumer for its direction. Most firms market their products by targeting their markets as specific segments. These may be geographic, demographic, or psychographic *segmentations.*

To spell out a strategy for effectively meeting marketing objectives, the firm needs a *marketing plan.* Such plans are usually drawn up for a year and become the blueprints for marketing activities to be employed—including advertising.

QUESTIONS AND PROBLEMS

1. What are the major external forces that affect marketing? Give examples of how they affect it.
2. What is the marketing mix? What position does advertising occupy in it?
3. Why are the various elements of the marketing mix important to advertising?
4. What is the marketing concept?
5. What are the three major ways of segmenting a market, and how do they differ?
6. What is the marketing plan, and what purposes does it serve?
7. Why is marketing planning so important to the success of advertising?
8. State and explain the basic elements of a marketing plan.
9. Why should a good marketing plan provide an opportunity for revision?
10. Who is involved in the preparation of the retail advertising plan?

ENDNOTE

[1] This section is based on F. Beaven Ennis, *Effective Marketing Management* (New York: Association of National Advertisers, Inc., 1973).

The Opportunity
for Advertising

After completing this chapter, you should be able to:
1. Differentiate between primary- and selective-demand advertising
2. Appraise the opportunity for advertising different products and services
3. Evaluate the appraisal criteria

As we have indicated repeatedly, advertising is a promotion tool. As one of several promotion tools—advertising, personal selling, sales promotion, and public relations—it can be used either with the others, alone, or not at all. Whether or not advertising is or should be used depends upon the overall marketing objectives and strategy. Obviously, in many cases, especially in the consumer-goods field, advertising is used and used extensively. However, the decision to use advertising cannot be made automatically. First, careful consideration must be given to marketing objectives and strategy, and the likelihood that advertising will succeed in meeting these objectives must be carefully appraised.

APPRAISING THE ADVERTISING OPPORTUNITY

Charles Patti suggests that "the first task facing advertising management should be to determine the extent to which advertising can be used to help accomplish the marketing goals of the firm."[1] In preparing a marketing plan such as the one suggested in the preceding chapter, it is necessary to estimate the degree to which advertising will help meet the marketing goal before determining the advertising budget, the creative strategy, or the media plan. This concept is presented schematically in Figure 8-1. The last step, measuring advertising results, will provide feedback to assist management in reassessing the opportunity for advertising for the next plan period.

PRIMARY AND SELECTIVE DEMAND

Before appraising the likelihood of using advertising successfully, one must determine whether the objective is to stimulate demand for the generic product (primary demand) or for a particular brand (selective demand).

PRIMARY-DEMAND ADVERTISING Before a demand for a brand can be stimulated, there must be a demand for the generic product. That is, for example, before wanting an RCA television set, the consumer must first want a television set. Primary-demand stimulation, therefore, may be concerned with the choices involved in the progress

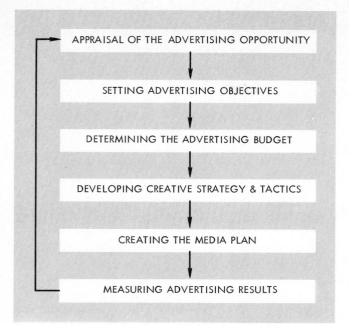

FIGURE 8-1

Advertising management sequence of decisions. Notice it starts with an appraisal of the advertising opportunity. *From Charles H. Patti, "Evaluating the Role of Advertising."* Journal of Advertising, *VI, No. 4 (Fall 1977), 31.*

of the individual or family unit toward a buying decision. Because disposable income is limited, all generic products compete for a share of the consumers' dollars. Even when selective-demand decision making has replaced primary-demand decision making for some part of the market, there are other consumers who have not yet decided upon generic product preferences and are not ready to consider appeals to brand. Thus, the problems of primary demand precede those of selective demand.

As long as a manufacturer of a new generic product is the only producer of the product, there need not be any concern with selective demand, for in such circumstances, it is synonymous with primary demand. As the firm becomes successful in building a substantial primary demand, however, its success will generally invite competition. Normally, the firm then switches to selective-demand advertising to protect its share of the market. Withdrawal from primary-demand stimulation, however, may leave the market in a static condition, so that any increase in the selective demand for its brand must mean that its competitors lose sales. Assuming that competition fights to retain its share of the market, increasing sales through selective-demand advertising may prove very expensive and unprofitable. The answer might lie in returning to a primary-demand advertising strategy to increase the size of the market and thus increase the demand proportionately or more than proportionately for the firm's brand. Such action by an individual firm may or may not be economically sound. If the firm has, for example, a two-thirds share of the market, and if it can reasonably be expected that the firm's position will remain the same or improve with the increase in primary demand, then it may be wise for the firm to follow such a strategy

FIGURE 8-2

An example of a primary demand advertisement by an association. (Original in color) *By permission: The Potato Board.*

even though the sales of its competitors will also increase. This, of course, presumes that the increase in sales is great enough to cover the increase in advertising funds and add to the profit. If, for example, the firm has a 10 percent share of the market, it is not likely that primary-demand advertising would be profitable.

There is, however, an alternative course of action. When an industry needs to increase primary demand, the primary-demand advertising task is frequently handled cooperatively by an association of industry members. For example, the meatpackers have encouraged the American Meat Institute to engage in horizontal cooperative advertising to increase the consumption of meat. Cooperating members contribute funds according to their sales, and the individual members continue their selective-demand advertising, each trying to get the greatest share of the increase in the demand for the generic product.

WAYS OF INCREASING PRIMARY DEMAND Primary-demand advertising, whether by an individual firm or an association, can be used in an effort to increase demand in three ways. First, it can attempt to get current users of the generic product to use more. For example, for many years the Florida Department of Citrus' advertising suggested the health merits of drinking a full eight-ounce glass of orange juice for breakfast in place of the customary four ounces. Second, it can attempt to get new users for the generic product. Thus, a generic product used only by women might be advertised to encourage men to use it. Permanent-wave advertising, for example, was addressed to men for the first time a few years ago. Finally, primary-demand advertising can promote new uses for the product in an attempt to increase consumption. The producer of Scotch Tape has continued to find and develop new uses for cellulose tape and to promote these in its advertising.

This last example illustrates the general fact that advertisements containing primary-demand appeals also tend to have an element of selectivity in them as well. Thus, the makers of Scotch Tape hoped that the promotion of new uses would increase consumption of the generic product, but because of the very high degree of competition in the field, brand advantages were also stressed.

PRICE AND NONPRICE COMPETITION There are two methods of increasing demand. One is based on *price* competition, the other on *nonprice* competition. In the case of price competition, the demand curve remains fixed but, depending upon the degree of elasticity, a change in price is reflected in an increase or decrease in the quantity demanded [see Figure 8-3(a)]. Advertising, as well as product differentiation, fashion, and quality, act as nonprice forces upon demand. Thus, as a result of successful primary-demand advertising, demand at all prices is increased, for the advertising results in moving the demand curve to the right [see Figure 8-3(b)]. The object of primary-demand advertising is to expand demand, but it is not always possible to do so. In many cases, advertising and price reductions may take place simultaneously, with the result that demand will grow and the quantity consumed will be greater than the expansion of demand through adver-

FIGURE 8-3

(a) In price competition, a change in price (A to A') may result in a change in quantity (C to C'). (b) In nonprice competition, advertising may move the demand curve to the right. Thus, for price A, quantity may change from C to C'. (c) With both a change in price (A to A') and advertising moving the demand curve (DD to D'D'), quantity may increase substantially (C to C').

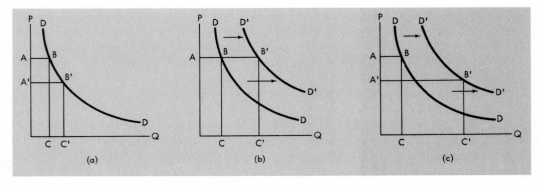

tising alone because quantity will be determined by the new position of price on the new demand curve [see Figure 8-3(c)].

SELECTIVE-DEMAND ADVERTISING As indicated above, a firm with a new generic product that has no competition may start promotional activities with primary-demand advertising. However, as competition enters the field, the firm may be forced to change its strategy to selective-demand advertising in order to maintain its share of the market. A new firm entering an established industry, on the other hand, wants a share of the existing market immediately and thus can be expected to start its promotional effort with selective-demand advertising. Typically, selective-demand advertising will stress brand benefits. When these are relatively weak, the firm may still use such advertising, stressing institutional appeals. To be sure, the cumulative effect of all selective-demand advertising by an industry has some effect on primary-demand stimulation as a result of consumer awareness.

As in the case of primary-demand advertising, the selective-demand advertiser must first decide whether increased profits will outweigh the increased expense of advertising. The advertising opportunity must be considered in terms of the whole marketing strategy.

No amount of expenditure on advertising will enable anything, which the customers can fairly test for themselves by experience to get a permanent hold on the people, unless it is fairly good relatively to its price. The chief influence of such advertisement is exerted, not through the reason, but through the blind force of habit: people in general are, for good and for evil, inclined to prefer that which is familiar to that which is not.

ALFRED MARSHALL, Economist

READER'S DIGEST

CRITERIA FOR PRIMARY-DEMAND ADVERTISING

Some circumstances affecting the firm's decision to use primary-demand advertising have already been considered briefly in this chapter. The following discussion will examine other important criteria in greater detail. Experience has shown that there are certain factors that, when considered and weighed, may help the firm in arriving at the right decision on whether or not to use primary-demand advertising. It goes without saying that each firm and each product is unique, and a firm may find that factors other than those discussed here are as important as those included in our discussion. Furthermore, some of the criteria included here may not be applicable to the particular problem faced by a particular firm or industry, and one criterion may be more or less important than another. In trying to reach a conclusion, it is necessary to weigh these criteria according to their importance for the particular situation.

Giving these precautions their due weight, the fact remains that the criteria examined here can prove helpful by removing guesswork from decision making and suggesting a technique of factor analysis in its place. Sound business decision making requires judgment in the light of sound information.

PRODUCT ADVANTAGES The first criterion, although not necessarily in the order of importance, is whether or not the generic product gives important advantages to the consumer that other products do not. There is at least one generic product for virtually every consumer want. A new generic product should obviously have distinct and apparent advantages over existing products if it is to succeed. Even when considering primary-demand advertising for an established product, it is necessary to consider its advantages over other generic products used similarly. For example, aluminum siding must be promoted in the face of other long-established products like wood siding and brick. Its advantages include the fact that, unlike wood, it will not rot and does not need to be painted for many years. Compared to brick, it has equal lasting powers and also provides variety in finish (wood effect as against brick) and lower cost.

In order to ascertain the importance of these advantages, the advertiser must consider the consumer's buying and use habits. Product advantages must always be considered from the consumer's point of view, not from the seller's. It is easy to see that the stronger and more basic the consumer wants, the more primary-demand advertising will be likely to succeed if it stresses these advantages.

BUYING MOTIVES The second criterion, related to the last point, is whether or not there are opportunities to use strong appeals to buying motives, given the nature of the generic product. Obviously, the stronger the appeals, the greater the chance of their success, provided, of course, that they are appropriate to the product. If so, basic and insistent buying motives can be appealed to through strong emotionalism. Techniques for the study of consumer behavior are continually providing greater understandings of why people buy. After such study has been made, the product must be analyzed to see if strong appeals to the motives revealed can be identified with it.

SOCIAL, ECONOMIC, AND TECHNICAL TRENDS The third consideration is what effect social, economic, and technical trends might have on the demand for the generic product. These are forces, favorable or unfavorable, over which the advertiser has little, if any, control. Consider the trends toward casual living and informality. What are the various external social, psychological, and technological influences that have brought about changes in living habits, fashion, eating habits, and the like? What effect do these trends have on demand for various generic products?

For example, in a middle-class American home 75 years ago, guests might have arrived at the front door and been ushered into the parlor. The dress for the occasion was formal, or at least the men wore dark suits and white shirts with stiff collars. The host and hostess engaged the guests in small talk until the maid announced that dinner was

Split Seconds. In Halifax, Nova Scotia, Eaton's department store advertised 400-day clocks, "covered by our one-year guarantee."

TIME

ready. They proceeded to the dining room, where a large table was formally arranged with a damask linen tablecloth and napkins, fine china and crystal, and sterling silver tableware. As the hostess rang the little bell, the maid started serving the full-course dinner, rich with sauces, gravies, and dressings. Families prided themselves on their ability to entertain in this manner and on the acquisition of the material things mentioned above, for these were the standards by which one's social position was judged. The trend toward formal and graceful living was strong, and there was a good opportunity to stimulate demand for the products that were a part of it.

In the intervening years, however, the trend has changed, and the middle-class American home today looks very different. Our hostess answers the door and leads the guests through the house onto the patio or into the back yard. There the host, clad in a loud sport shirt and shorts or cut-offs, is bending over the charcoal grill. (After millennia of struggling to tame fire and bring it into the home, it has been returned to its primitive setting!) Dinner is served on plastic plates with stainless steel tableware and paper napkins. The meal consists of lean steak and a tossed salad made with a low-calorie dressing. Half the people skip dessert and drink black, sugarless coffee. The conversation centers around the hosts' forthcoming trip abroad. Things certainly have changed! Both examples, of course, are oversimplified, yet they illustrate the changes in consumers and the forces that influence their wants.

It is not easy to explain these changes, for trends in behavior are affected by a host of sociopsychological influences. Nevertheless, one can attempt an oversimplified explanation of the trend toward informal and casual living. First of all, there are economic ramifications. Although society is today enjoying its highest standard of living in history despite an economic recession, one result of this prosperity is a labor shortage for certain kinds of work; as a result, the family maid is scarce indeed. This leaves nobody but the host and hostess to do the serving, wash the dishes, iron the napkins, and polish the silver. Affluence has also resulted in a shorter workweek, and changing mores have broken down taboos about men doing household chores, so that our host has the time and inclination to try his hand as a chef. Technological developments have led to the emancipation of the couple from the kitchen; they use plastic dishes that are less likely to be damaged in the automatic dishwasher. Our host is quite correctly attired in his sport shirt and shorts, because changes in fashion over the years are concomitant with all the other trends. Because of technological advances and the new status of women, these clothes are likely to be made of synthetics and can be tossed into an automatic washer and drier and be ready to wear again. Even the menu is a reflection of trends in dietary habits, with the emphasis on low-calorie foods that preserve one's figure. Informal entertaining is socially acceptable, and other activities now indicate social position and prestige: Funds that would have gone toward the purchase of the silver service are diverted to the trip abroad.

Due Caution. *In Dansville, N.Y., a classified advertisement appeared in the* Dansville *Breeze: "Wanted—Farmer, age 38, wishes to meet woman around 30 who owns a tractor. Please enclose picture of tractor."*

TIME

Notice that advertising has had little place in setting these trends. They were the result of external social and psychological influences and technological developments. The Irish and Scottish Linen Damask Guild would be hard put to overcome this informality through advertising to promote linen damask tablecloths. The trends are bigger than the generic product or the advertising forces behind it. As was pointed out in an earlier chapter, advertising does not *create* demand, it only *stimulates* it. The demand must be there—latent, perhaps, but there. When there is an adverse trend, there is little primary-demand advertisements can do, except perhaps slow down the rate of decline. On the other hand, if the trend is favorable, there is a real opportunity to use such advertising, for although demand for the generic product might increase without the advertising efforts of producers, advertising may be used effectively to speed up the trend or to bring demand to a higher point than it would reach unaided.

PRICE AND PRODUCT DESIGN The fourth consideration involves the effects of price and product design that may present obstacles to successful primary-demand advertising. Sale of a generic product may encounter resistance from the consumer because the price may be too high relative to the consumer's satisfaction. For example, when pocket calculators were first introduced to the market, they were priced so high that many consumers could not afford them. In a relatively short time, however, there were considerable price reductions, and price no longer represented a serious obstacle to purchase.

Although the generic product may offer distinct advantages to the consumer, product design may act as a force limiting demand. For example, there were many underlying causes for the decline in piano sales over which the industry had no control. When the trend started moving positively again, the demand for pianos increased, largely because the industry had redesigned the product to make it more acceptable. That is, in smaller homes with lower ceilings, the old upright piano and the grand piano encountered sales resistance because of size. The industry, however, revived the spinet piano, an old design originally developed around 1500, and had a product that fit modern living habits. (Both price and product design considerations will be discussed in more detail in the next chapter.)

PROFITABILITY The fifth and concluding criterion relates to the whole problem of the profitability and, hence, the effectiveness of advertising used to stimulate primary demand. Assuming that an appraisal of the other criteria indicates that the advertising opportunity is favorable, attention still must be given to profitability, for advertising cannot be justified if it does not make a contribution to profits, either immediately or in the long run.

To begin with, the cost of an adequate advertising campaign must be estimated. Ordinarily, the estimate would be for one year, unless results could not be expected for several years. (A detailed discussion of determining the advertising budget appears in Chapter 11.) Next, the sales expected as a result of the advertising must be considered. In the case of the individual firm using primary-demand advertising, additional attention must be given to the advertiser's share of the sales increase for the generic product. From all these calculations it is necessary to determine whether the sales increase will provide a gross profit large enough to cover the additional advertising expense and still make a contribution to net profits. In so doing, it is essential to estimate the effect of the advertising on increasing the sales; if there is an unsolicited increase in demand that does not result from advertising, it might be more profitable not to incur the advertising expense.

Now all the "hot air," and "bunk" and the "hooey" in the world won't make Mr. Consumer buy the second time if he is not satisfied with the first purchase. So the wise advertiser must speak truthfully of the merit of his product.

GEORGE WASHINGTON HILL, *Manufacturer*

READER'S DIGEST

CRITERIA FOR SELECTIVE-DEMAND ADVERTISING

More often, the firm is concerned with estimating the advertising opportunity for stimulating selective demand. Again, not all the criteria considered here are relevant to all situations, nor are they necessarily the only considerations to be taken into account. Each situation must be dealt with individually.

PRIMARY-DEMAND TRENDS Before there is an opportunity to sell a particular brand of a product, there must be a demand for the generic product. Thus, the first and perhaps foremost criterion for determining the suitability of selective-demand advertising is whether or not there is a favorable primary-demand trend. A favorable trend supports the use of selective-demand advertising. If the trend is unfavorable, the firm can advertise to get more and more of less and less until it has all of nothing. Of course, it should be noted that the same forces responsible for a decline in the primary-demand trend may reverse themselves of their own accord and establish a favorable trend. Thus, for example, convertible automobiles, once quite popular, all but disappeared as a result of air conditioning and high-speed roads. But in the last few years there has been a resurgence of their popularity, and demand is expected to grow.

DIFFERENTIATING CHARACTERISTICS The second criterion involves the unique characteristics of the brand. The more it differs from its competitors, the greater the selective-demand advertising opportunity, for the consumer must have a reason for choosing one brand over another. Brand benefits that offer the consumer more satisfaction than the consumer could get from another brand are stressed.

Salt is a classic example. For many years, salt was salt and it made no difference to the consumer whose salt it was. Moisture made all salt stick. Then the Morton Salt Company developed a process of dusting each grain of salt so that it would not stick because of dampness. Morton then had something to shout about. Its product was different and offered real advantages to the consumer. An advertising campaign was launched around the theme line, "When it rains, it pours," and the firm was eminently successful. When other firms also came out with free-flowing salt, Morton looked to other means of product differentiation. It developed a package closure that permitted easy filling of salt shakers. It later developed an iodized salt. Still later, it developed a low-sodium salt for people on restricted diets.

On the other hand, sugar remained sugar. Although cane sugar refineries developed different varieties of sugar, so did their competitors, and no sufficient differentiation of the product could be developed that afforded a good advertising opportunity. There was, however, one exception—the Imperial Sugar Refinery of Sugarland, Texas. This company's sugar was no different from other sugars, but it was the only sugar refined in the state of Texas. This was only a psychological difference, but a very important one in a state with considerable local pride. The firm, therefore, advertised Imperial sugar as the only sugar refined in Texas by Texans. This was enough to do the trick, and the firm was very successful.

Thus, there is a greater advertising opportunity when the brand can be differentiated from competing brands, either physically or psychologically.

HIDDEN QUALITIES   The third criterion is whether the product has hidden qualities of importance to the consumer or whether the consumer can judge the product at the time of purchase. The more the product has to be purchased and used before it can be judged—that is, the more its qualities are hidden—the greater the selective-demand advertising opportunity. For example, take lettuce. Here, there are essentially no important hidden qualities. When you buy lettuce, you go to the produce department of a store. You look at the various heads of lettuce for greenness and a lack of rust spots. You examine the heads to find one that is crisp, not wilted. You may then heft several in your hand to find one that is solid. Finally you choose the head of lettuce you want. To be sure, lettuce contains hidden qualities, such as nutritional value, but these are the same in all lettuce, regardless of the producer. If lettuce were branded and promoted, what could be said for it? If brand A and brand B were displayed in the store side by side, the consumer would still choose by the method described above.

On the other hand, a headache remedy can be judged only through usage. Each brand on the market has certain features that offer relief but that cannot be seen. Advertising is the major means of promoting these hidden qualities. And if they are important and the advertising convincing, the advertising will lead the consumer to purchase the brand.

FIGURE 8-4
This advertisement stresses the generic product. *By permission: DeBeers.*

BUYING AND USE HABITS   The fourth criterion involves consumer buying and use habits. Products with low unit value, bought only once or very infrequently, do not lend themselves as well to selective-demand advertising as do those purchased frequently, because the advertising cost is usually not recouped until several repeat purchases are made. For some types of products, the consumer is brand-conscious; for others, the consumer is not.

Consumer goods are frequently divided into convenience goods, shopping goods, and specialty goods. Convenience goods are usually items of low unit value and frequent purchase that the consumer purchases with a minimum of effort through the most accessible outlet. Shopping goods are generally items of higher unit value for which the consumer *shops,* considering features like quality, price, and fashion. Specialty goods are brands that are sufficiently distinctive for the consumer to make a deliberate purchasing effort and for which the consumer will not readily accept a substitute.

Each of these types of goods presents a different problem in ap-

Careful, your love is showing.

Your love shows in everything you do.
It's written in your smile, revealed by the warm glow
that surrounds you wherever you go. You're more alive
than ever before. Your Keepsake diamond engagement ring
reflects your joy in radiant lustre. With a diamond so
brilliant in color, so flawless in clarity, so exquisite
in cut it's guaranteed perfect by Keepsake.

Keepsake
Registered Diamond Rings

HOW TO PLAN YOUR ENGAGEMENT AND WEDDING
Everything about planning your engagement and wedding in
a beautiful 20 page booklet. Also valuable information about
diamonds and styling. Gift offer saves you 50% on a 44 page
Keepsake Bride's Book. Send 25¢ for postage and handling.

Name
Address
City _____ State _____ Zip
Keepsake Diamond Rings, Box 90, Syracuse, New York 13201
Find your Keepsake dealer under Jewelers in the Yellow Pages
or call toll free* 800-243-6000. In Connecticut 800-882-6500.
*Except from Hawaii and Alaska.

Keepsake What a perfect way to show your love when it's for keeps.

FIGURE 8-5

In contrast to Figure 8-4, this advertisement stresses selective demand. Note how the copy stresses brand preference. (Original in color) *By permission: A. H. Pond Co., Inc.*

praising the advertising opportunity. For many years, for example, R.J. Reynolds used the theme line, "I'd walk a mile for a Camel." But cigarettes are convenience goods, and despite all the advertising, if the brand is not conveniently available in all normal retail outlets, most people, even if they have a preference for the brand, are apt to accept a substitute. Advertising of convenience goods may achieve brand acceptance, and even brand preference, but it is not apt to achieve brand insistence. Specialty goods, on the other hand, offer an advertising opportunity to build brand insistence and may therefore permit a policy of selected distribution through a limited number of retailers. Which classification the product falls under must be determined. The effective use of advertising must then be weighed in the light of the strengths and weaknesses of the buying habits in this classification. Classification of industrial goods is considered in Chapter 28.

Another facet of consumer buying and use habits concerns the motivation behind these habits. After getting some understanding of consumer behavior (see Chapter 12), the firm should appraise the

The Opportunity for
Advertising

169

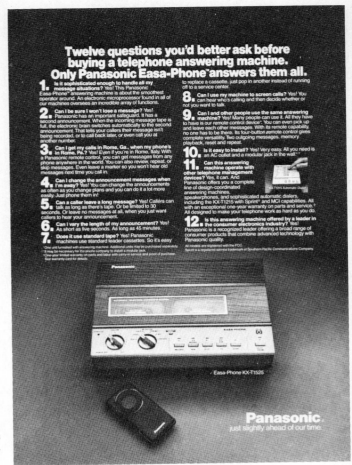

FIGURE 8-6

Differentiating characteristics of the brand improves the opportunity for effective selective demand advertising. *By permission: Panasonic.*

strength of appeals that can be associated with the generic product and, especially, with the brand. Strong appeals afford a greater advertising opportunity.

MARKETING MIX The fifth criterion involves the strength of the other ingredients in the marketing mix. No appraisal of the advertising opportunity can omit a consideration of product design, branding, packaging, distribution, and price. Although advertising may be ineffective despite a good marketing mix, it is unlikely that it will ever be effective with a bad mix.

Product design becomes important not only to distinguish the brand from others, but for styling, desirability, and quality. A brand name that does not follow sound branding practices can be a distinct liability to advertising. A good package may provide for brand differentiation and also carry the advertising message to the point of purchase. Advertising is used in some instances as a means of obtaining distribution, although generally it is essential that the firm have adequate distribution before advertising. If the consumer cannot buy the advertised brand because the store does not carry it, the consumer will probably buy another brand. Finally, price affects the advertising opportunity. A price that is higher or lower than average may prove detrimental—or a boon. All these marketing mix ingredients are discussed in greater detail in Chapter 9.

PROFITABILITY The sixth and final criterion is profitability. Like primary-demand advertising, selective-demand advertising can be undertaken only when there is a promise of increased profits, either immediately or in the long run.

The first consideration here is the cost of an adequate campaign. In cost determination, the firm must take into account what funds are available for advertising. Next, it must consider the total demand for the generic product and what share of the market the brand can expect as a result of the advertising effort. Finally, the firm must answer the question whether the advertising will increase sales sufficiently to provide a gross profit that will cover the cost of advertising and contribute to net profits. This final question must be answered in terms of a period long enough to provide for a fair test of the worth of the advertising; in some instances, the profitability may be evident in the course of several months, but in others it may take several years.

Rules, though unavoidable, always have weaknesses. Particularly so in advertising, where originality is a part of its primary force, and where a violation of "what others do" is often the way to success.

RAYMOND RUBICAM, *Advertising Agent*

READER'S DIGEST

Charles Patti suggests a useful tool for evaluating the criteria discussed in this chapter and for weighing their importance.[2] The form shown in Figure 8-7 is adapted from his model and may be used in evaluating the opportunity to use advertising to stimulate selective demand. (By substituting the criteria, this form can be used for primary-demand stimulation as well.)

First, each of the six criteria are assigned *scores* between 1.0 and 0.0. The stronger the criterion favors using advertising, the higher the score. Second, each of these criteria is given a *weight*, which reflects the importance of the criteria in the particular situation. An *advertising opportunity score* may then be calculated by multiplying each score by its weight, taking the sum of these six *weighted scores* and dividing by the sum of the six weights. This overall advertising opportunity score may be interpreted in the same way as an individual score, as indicated in the footnote to Figure 8-7.

Of course, it must be emphasized that these particular criteria may not be the most appropriate for each situation. It is suggested only as an approach, to be modified as you see fit in evaluating the advertising opportunity.

EVALUATION OF APPRAISAL CRITERIA

The Opportunity for
Advertising

FIGURE 8-7

A form for appraising the opportunity for expanding brand demand through advertising

CRITERIA	(a) SCORE*	×	(b) WEIGHT	=	(a)(b) WEIGHTED SCORE
1. Primary-demand trends	_____		_____		_____
2. Differentiating characteristics	_____		_____		_____
3. Hidden qualities	_____		_____		_____
4. Buying and use habits	_____		_____		_____
5. Marketing mix	_____		_____		_____
6. Profitability	_____		_____		_____
Total					

$$\text{Advertising opportunity score} = \frac{\sum_{i=1}^{6}(a_i b_i)}{\sum_{i=1}^{6}(b_i)}$$

*Factor scores range from 1.0 to 0.0. Assessments fall on the following continuum; 1.0–.90 = extraordinary; .89–.80 = excellent; .79–.70 = very good; .69–.60 = good; .59–.50 = average; .49–.40 = poor; .39–.30 = very poor; .29–.20 = weak; .19–.10 = extremely weak; and .09–.00 = a negative consideration.

Adapted from Charles H. Patti, "Evaluating the Role of Advertising," Journal of Advertising, VI, No. 4 (Fall 1977), 34.

TO SUM UP

The decision to advertise cannot be made automatically. Advertising can be used to stimulate primary or selective demand. Primary-demand stimulation may be used by individual firms or by industry associations to get present users to consume more, to develop new uses, and to get new users. Most advertising, however, is to build selective demand by stressing brand benefits.

Certain criteria can be helpful in appraising the advertising opportunity. In the case of primary demand, these include generic product advantages; strengths of buying motives; social, economic, and technical trends; price and product design; and profitability.

For evaluating selective-demand advertising, criteria include primary-demand trends, differentiating characteristics, hidden qualities, buying and use habits, strength of other marketing-mix elements, and profitability.

QUESTIONS AND PROBLEMS

1. How would you explain the logic of the advertising management sequence of decisions in Figure 8-1?
2. In most advertising, is the emphasis on building primary demand or selective demand? Why?
3. Why must there be a primary demand before there can be a selective demand?
4. What are the three ways of increasing primary demand through advertising?
5. How may social, economic, and technical trends affect the demand for a generic product?

6. Why would there be an unfavorable opportunity to effectively use advertising to stimulate the primary demand for buggy whips?
7. How do differentiating characteristics of the product affect the opportunity to build selective demand through advertising?
8. Select three examples each of convenience goods, shopping goods, and specialty goods and explain why each fits in the particular classification.
9. How do consumer buying and use habits affect the opportunity for selective demand advertising?
10. Select a new product or a hypothetical one and evaluate its opportunity for advertising according to the criteria in this chapter.

ENDNOTES

[1] Charles H. Patti, "Evaluating the Role of Advertising." *Journal of Advertising*, VI, No. 4 (Fall 1977), 30.
[2] Patti, "Evaluating the Role of Advertising," p. 34.

Advertising and the Marketing Mix

After completing this chapter, you should be able to:

1. See the relationship between advertising and other areas of marketing activity
2. Explain how new products are developed
3. Identify the requisites of a good brand
4. Describe how packaging is important to effective advertising
5. Relate the other tools of promotion to advertising

A lion met a tiger
As they drew beside a pool;
Said the tiger:
"Tell me, big boy,
Why you're roaring like a fool."
"That's not foolish,"
Said the lion
With a twinkle in his eyes.
"They call me king of beasts
Because I advertise."
A rabbit heard them talking
And ran home like a streak;
He thought he'd try the lion's plan
But his roar was just a squeak.
A fox came to investigate
And had luncheon in the woods.
MORAL: When you advertise,
My friends,
BE SURE YOU'VE GOT THE GOODS!
Author Unknown

Advertising, to be successful, needs the strong backing of the various ingredients in the marketing mix. Advertising does not just happen. To be effective, it needs a good product, the right brand, a good package, the right price, and the right kind of distribution, among other things. But even though advertising depends upon these other ingredients for its success, it also makes its contribution to *their* success. Advertising practitioners, both for producers and for advertising agencies, are continually concerned with these other ingredients, not only because they affect advertising but also because the advertising practitioners are frequently called upon to use their special talents in problems concerning other aspects of marketing. Frequently they can make significant recommendations regarding them.

Whole books could be written on each marketing factor, for all of them are important. Here, however, they will be considered in terms of their direct relation to advertising. Therefore, some will be analyzed in greater detail than others.

PRODUCT DEVELOPMENT

For advertising to be successful, there must be something to advertise. Because the product or service provides the *raison d'être* for all business activity of firms, business is constantly concerned not only with improvement of existing products but also with the development of new ones.

To be more specific, firms are involved in new-product and new-service development for several definite reasons. Because in many cases the demand for a firm's existing products diminishes over time, it becomes necessary to innovate just to stay competitively in the same position. As marginal products are dropped, they need to be replaced to maintain the same volume. New products can utilize excess marketing or production capacity. Seasonal fluctuation inefficiencies of sales or production can be offset by new products that will smooth out the variations. Risk can be reduced by increasing the number of products of the firm, thereby spreading the risk over a greater number of products. Byproducts from existing product manufacturing can become a basis for new products instead of being waste. New-product opportunities become apparent, and a firm may seize upon those because of their potential profitability, or to preclude their being lost to competition, or because they help to sell existing products.[1]

CONSUMER-USER-ORIENTED PRODUCTS The firm must produce what it can *sell* or it will not sell what it produces. Producing a salable product should be fairly easy with modern research techniques, but even highly successful firms have made terrible blunders.

Products with proper consumer or user orientations have been eminently successful. The spinet piano mentioned in the preceding chapter is a case in point. So are portable typewriters, portable transistor radios, citizens' band radios, garbage disposers, and electric steam irons for consumers, and forklift trucks, computers, and lasers for industrial users. The secret is that the product must be designed with the consumer or user in mind. The old idea of making a product and then finding a market is too expensive and too risky. Too often the attempt fails, not because the product is no good from a technical or engineering point of view, but because the consumer or user does not want it or is not ready for it. The new technique is to go to the market first, find out what the market wants, and design a product that fits the market's wants. An extreme example of this procedure is a firm that is reported to start with consumer research on what product the consumer wants, then to determine if there is an advertising strategy that will sell such a product effectively, and finally, to design the product. More often, the firm consults the consumer on products that are in the initial stages of development and then, using the findings from its research, refines the product to meet consumer wants.

Determining consumer wants, however, is no small task. The consumers themselves may not know what they want in products to be produced next year and the year after that. Thus, it is necessary to *project* these wants. Because there are forces at work over which the firm has no control, even the best-laid plans sometimes go awry.

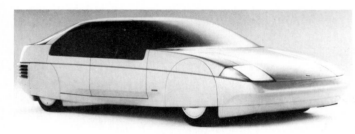

FIGURE 9-1

Changes in product design can be seen in these photographs of Ford automobiles of the past, present, and future. The first Ford is shown top left. The Model T is top right. The new Ford Tempo appears in the center. At the bottom is a future design, the Ford Probe IV. Change in design over the years has not been radical but evolved over the years to reflect changing taste and technology. *By permission: Ford Motor Company.*

APPRAISING PRODUCT IDEAS   Ideas for new products can come from a variety of sources: from those whose job it is to initiate new-product ideas (research and development and/or new-product departments), and from just about anyone inside or outside the firm. Before the development of a new-product idea is allowed to proceed very far, certain factors are commonly considered in evaluating it.

It should be noted that any list of factors for evaluation should be modified and adapted to the needs of different firms; and with changes, such a list may be useful for services as well as products. There are three basic areas that must be considered to be consistent with the marketing concept—marketing, production, and finance.

Marketing evaluation factors include determination of product need; market size, including growth trends and prospective market share; comparisons with competitive brands and prices; relation of channel needs of product and channels of distribution employed by the firm; relation of existing sales force and sales force needs; proposed advertising strategy and cost; packaging requirements and size and quantities of likely orders; pricing and terms of sale; servicing requirements that will be necessary; branding; patenting; and size of necessary inventories.

tcudorp.

The first job of an ad agency is to look at your product in every imaginable way: frontwards, backwards, sideways, upside down, inside out. Because somewhere, *right there in the product itself*, lies the drama that will sell it to people who want it.

There may be 10,000 ways to bring that inherent drama to the stage. And given a world in which "me-too" products multiply like mayflies, the drama may seem that much harder to find.

It is.

But every good product has it.

And every good agency finds it.

Please note: The "t" in tcudorp is silent.

Leo Burnett Co., Inc.
33 offices in 23 countries

FIGURE 9-2

This advertisement by an advertising agency explains the importance of product development and design to advertising. *By permission: Leo Burnett Co., Inc.*

Production considerations include internal production versus subcontracting; utilization of present production facilities; demands on production time and facilities; availability of raw materials; time frame for getting the product into production; size of any capital investment; and estimated production costs.

Financial facets to be evaluated include inventory costs; amounts of accounts receivable; costs including general and administrative costs; necessary profit margins; and anticipated return on investment.[2]

THE ROLE OF ADVERTISING IN PRODUCT DEVELOPMENT

In order to advertise effectively, the advertising practitioner must find some unique difference in a brand and offer a strong appeal to consumer motivation. Advertising research and creative imagination have been put to work at this task. Frequently, the answer is found in some existing feature of an existing product. But sometimes the advertising practitioner may recommend, as a result of doing research and thinking on the subject, product improvements or new products. Many new products have been born from the idea of a copywriter or the results of advertising research. In fact, product managers and advertising agencies today are major developers of new-product ideas.

Aside from this, any new product in the developmental stage or any proposed improvement of existing products must take into account its promotion through advertising. Frequently, some slight modification at this point will result in a product far more apt to be successfully advertised.

PRODUCT CONCEPT TO NATIONAL LAUNCH Developing a new-product concept and carrying it through to a national launching of the product should be carefully researched at a number of places along the way so as to increase the likelihood of success.[3] The first step is concept testing, in which consumer reaction to the product *concept* is studied to determine whether or not the concept should be continued, modified, or abandoned. When the product is actually producible on a limited basis, product testing should take place. This involves giving actual product samples to consumers (frequently together with competitive brands) in order to study their reactions to product use. This may result in developing a copy strategy for promotion through advertising. At this point in testing, of course, the products are presented without brand identification (brand X) or advertising.

The next step is to subject the product, with any improvements that may have been made as a result of prior research, to strategy testing. This will provide an opportunity to develop sound branding, packaging, advertising, and sales promotion, all of which are essential to the success of the new-product launch in addition to success of the product itself. Alternative strategies for each of these marketing-mix ingredients will be evaluated to find those that will most enhance the image desired for the position for which the product concept was established.

Before going national, it is sensible to minimize the risks by simulating the national marketing effort on a limited scale through the technique of test marketing. A pilot plant may now be necessary to produce a sufficient quantity of the product to be marketed in a limited geographic (test) market where advertising and other promotional efforts will be tried simulating a national promotional effort. From this experience, which may last for many months, consumer buying behavior as it relates to the product and its promotion can be evaluated and then necessary marketing strategies can be sharpened, or, if for some reason the test should prove a disaster despite all the prior research saying "go," the firm may abandon the product without the magnitude of loss that would result from waiting until the product was launched nationally.

PRODUCT POSITIONING A relatively new approach to product innovation is to develop products, their packages, and brands by ascertaining market receptivity to the generic product and its various brands. John Holmes defines a product's position as:

What you've got to do is discover what makes this product the white pea in the pod.

STANLEY RESOR,
Advertising Agent

READER'S DIGEST

. . . the perceived image consumers have of one product in relation to their perceived images of (1) similar products marketed by competing firms, and (2) kindred brands which might be offered by the innovating firm. And profitable positioning is a strategy for creating a unique product image which increases *total* profits.[4]

In this approach to product development, research would be conducted to determine consumer perceptions of the generic product in terms of factors considered in the purchasing decision. Existing brands would then be measured by a sample of consumers against the list of factors that had been determined. The new brand will then be positioned as advantageously as possible against existing brands in such a manner as to present the product more appealingly to customers. Of course, the product positioning technique can be used to *reposition* existing brands.

If, for example, one wants to get a share of the antiperspirant market by using the positioning concept, it might be discovered that existing brands have as their weakest point their wetness. Thus, Gillette's personal care division came up with a new brand entry—Dry Idea—that emphasizes dryness. As *The Wall Street Journal* comments, "The company concedes that Dry Idea won't stop perspiration any better than at least five products on the market for some time, but no matter. For Gillette says its product 'goes on dry,' feels better—and thus leads the user to feel that it is more effective."[5] Research had indicated that users found existing brands of roll-ons good but inconvenient because they went on wet and users had to wait until they were dry before dressing. Thus, a new *product concept* was born—Dry Idea.

PRODUCT LIFE CYCLE After a product or service has been developed, it starts its *life cycle*. This may be described as having four stages—market development, rapid growth, plateau or maturation, and decline. (See Figure 9-3.) Although all products have life cycles, the length and shape of the curve will vary with each product. "Fads" may

FIGURE 9-3
The product life cycle.

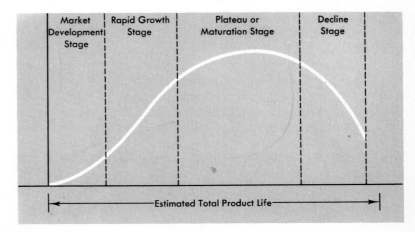

last only a few months, but the life cycle of certain goods may span several decades or more.

Advertising may play a role during the development period when a product is sent into test markets. With the full market launch, advertising, especially for consumer goods, frequently plays an important part both in the development of the life cycle and in its length. In the initial stages (market development), advertising may serve to create an awareness of the product and its benefits.

If the product shows significant potential, it will invite some limited competition, signaling the onset of the second stage of the cycle, rapid growth. This is the period in which advertising has its greatest potential for building strong brand preference and securing a substantial consumer franchise. Toward the end of this stage, the amount of competition will usually increase substantially, bringing with it the onset of the plateau or maturation stage. At this stage, the advertising campaign is generally directed toward the best customer groups for the brand. Finally, for any number of reasons, the product will move into a stage of decline and, theoretically, at least, ultimate abandonment. In this stage, advertising will usually decline, being used only to sustain sales in a declining market.

Advertising has induced progress in the use of manufacturers of new materials, new tools, and new processes of manufacture by calling their attention to economics which could be achieved and to the new uses to which they could be put. Without such advertising, information of this kind would take years to reach all of those who might benefit by it and progress would be delayed.

HARRY S. TRUMAN (1884–1973), Statesman

READER'S DIGEST

BRAND POLICY

Selective-demand advertising, which represents the majority of modern advertising, depends upon identification of the product being advertised. This identification comes primarily from the *brand*. Without brands, it is unlikely that such advertising could exist. Brands have assumed such importance in modern American business that the legal counsel for Coca-Cola has said:

> The production plants and inventories of the Coca-Cola Company could go up in flames one night, yet on the following morning there is not a bank in Atlanta, New York or anywhere else that would not lend this company the funds necessary for rebuilding, accepting as security only the good will of its trademarks.[6]

Clearly, branding looms large in modern business, although the practice is as ancient as civilization itself.[7] Although problems of branding involve the entire firm, it is above all a problem of marketing. The two segments of the firm most intimately involved in branding matters are the marketing management and the legal counsel. Both product management and the advertising agency are heavily involved in branding, because a brand name is so important to advertising and because they are the ones who usually select the brand name. Because brands are such valuable properties and because they can be protected under law, legal counsel also plays an important role here.

Not all firms use or need brands. Some producers manufacture goods for others—either wholesalers and retailers, or other producers who apply their own brands—and hence do not need brands of their own. In other instances, producers manufacture highly standardized products or raw materials for which there is little opportunity to build a selective demand. If there is no selective-demand advertising opportunity, branding is unnecessary.

DEFINITION OF TERMS A good deal of confusion may result from branding terminology. Before we proceed further, it will be helpful to have a definition of terms. It should be noted, however, that the definitions used here are not universally used in business practice. Care must be taken to be certain of the context in which a term is being used.

BRAND NAME AND TRADEMARK The American Marketing Association defines a *brand* as "a name, term, symbol, or design, or a combination of them that identifies the goods or services of one seller or group of sellers and distinguishes them from those of competitors."[8] The Trademark Act of 1946, popularly known as the Lanham Act, which became effective in 1947, defines a *trademark* as "any word, name, symbol, or device, or any combination thereof adopted and used by a manufacturer or merchant to identify his goods and distinguish them from those manufactured or sold by others."[9] Obviously, the definitions are so close as to make brand and trademark synonymous. But the AMA goes on to say that a brand *name* is that part of the brand that can be vocalized, whereas the term *trademark* generally indicates something that can be visualized. Thus, one could contend that *a brand name is the oral form of branding and the trademark is the pictorial form of branding.* This is how these terms will be used here; *brand* and *branding* will be used to describe the whole function of which these are a part. It is possible for a single brand element to be both the brand name and the trademark, if the distinctive lettering of the brand name constitutes the trademark. In other instances, the brand is made up of two distinct elements, a brand name and some design or symbol as a trademark. Finally, some firms have either a brand name or a trademark, but not both. From a strictly legal point of view, *brand* and *branding* have no significance, and the term *trademark* is used to refer to both the name and the mark. However, in marketing, *branding* and *brand* do have significance, and these terms are more generally used.

TRADE NAME A trade name is the name of a company. It is not a brand, although sometimes the brand name and trade name are synonymous, as in the case of Johnson & Johnson. More typically, a trade

16th Century housewives trusted this mark

This is the mark of a salt processor in 1545. It not only reflected the quality of his merchandise but, as a personal symbol, it meant he stood behind the quality of the goods he sold. Today's manufacturers use a modern symbol: Brand Names. It tells the customer that the manufacturer's reputation is behind the product. He "goes on record" with his advertising. He sets a standard that he must live up to (or his sales will suffer). Because he knows he can deliver what he says he can, he identifies himself with his products. Depend on Brand Names; they are the "mark of 20th century confidence" in things you buy. When you buy Leadership Brands, you know you are getting your money's worth. *BRAND NAMES FOUNDATION, INC., 292 Madison Avenue, N. Y. 17, N. Y.*

FIGURE 9-4

This advertisement points out the importance of brands. *By permission: Brand Names Foundations, Incorporated.*

name might be one like Warner-Lambert Pharmaceutical Company, one of whose brands is Listerine. Many firms today, however, are changing their trade names to make them similar to the brand so as to take full advantage of the brand's goodwill. An example is the Ohio Oil Company, which sold under the Marathon brand and changed its name to the Marathon Oil Company.

NATIONAL AND PRIVATE BRANDS Like the terms *national* and *retail* advertising, defined earlier, the terms *national* and *private* brands are somewhat misleading. *National brands* refer to brands of producers. They may be nationally promoted and sold, or they may be regionally or locally promoted and sold. *Private brands* are the brands of wholesalers or retailers who contract with producers to manufacture goods specifically for resale by them under their own brands. They too may be locally or nationally promoted and sold.

Private brands have become increasingly important in recent years and have been promoted extensively, not only in local retail advertisements but in national advertising media as well. Sears' *Silvertone,* A&P's *Ann Page,* and *Atlas* tires, batteries, and accessories are all private brand names and all are advertised. In some cases, this advertising is national in scope.

SELECTING A BRAND NAME   There are many stories of the inspirational or intuitive ways that brands have been named. Harley Procter got his inspiration for Ivory Soap while listening to a minister quote from the Forty-fifth Psalm: "Out of ivory palaces." A hotel owner was supposed to have seen a bus flashing by in the night and likening it to a greyhound. And R.E. Olds named his car for himself, as the Smith brothers named their cough drop for themselves. *Edsel* honored the memory of Henry Ford II's father, even though it did little to improve the sale of that marketing disaster. But inspiration is not enough. The right brand name is vital to the success of the advertising and the whole marketing effort. *Smucker's* as a brand has done little to enhance the sale of that outstanding product line. To minimize its becoming the basis for jokes and derisive comments, an advertising theme line was finally developed that states, "With a name like that, it has to be good."

In the Gillette antiperspirant product concept mentioned earlier, the task of selecting a brand name was assigned to the product manager and the advertising agency. More than a dozen names were tested on consumers. Some of those rejected included Dynamite, because it sounded too much like a drain cleaner; Feel Free some of the researched consumers thought might be a tampon; and Omni and Horizon subsequently turned up as names of cars. The winner was Dry Idea.[10]

In selection of a brand name, there are many factors to consider. First and foremost, the name should be strong, distinctive, and uniquely related to the firm's product. Names like *National, Premium, Star,* and *Ideal* are commonplace. How many different products and services can you identify that incorporate these names? It should also be easy to pronounce, spell, recognize, remember, and reproduce. Pronunciation is important for several reasons. If consumers cannot pronounce a brand name, they may be fearful of embarrassment in using the wrong pronunciation, and they may well ask for a brand whose name they can pronounce. *Baume Bengué* is a good example of a hard-to-pronounce name, for it requires a knowledge of French. The producer finally simplified matters by adopting a new spelling, *Ben-Gay.* Generally, foreign names and words are poor choices for this reason; for example, *Sitroux.* However, there are exceptions to this; the foreign connotation of perfume names helps to create a favorable image of the product. The name should also be pronounceable in only one way. On which syllable does the emphasis go in Socony, Conoco, and Amoco? The American Tobacco Company for many years has insisted on pronouncing *Pall Mall* as the British do, "Pell Mell," but the consumer just as insistently says, "Pawl Mawl." Since radio, television, and personal selling make use of brand names orally, it is important that the name be such that its pronunciation is clearly communicated and not confused with other names or words. Difficult spelling leads not only to errors in writing the name but also to mispronunciation.

Recognition is especially important for the trademark. When the design or symbol is related to the product, such as the Shell Oil shell, identity is quick. But if the design or symbol is too general or abstract, recognition may suffer. A good brand is one that will be remembered. Memory involves simplicity—think of *Lux, Crisco,* and *Tide*—and appropriateness, as in *Lestoil, Kool,* and *Sunkist.* Trademarks should be easy to reproduce graphically in many forms, for a colored trademark may have to appear in black and white and an intricate one may have to be reproduced in very small size. Applying a trademark to the physical product may also present difficult problems if care was not taken in its design.

A good brand should stand the test of time, be appropriate to widening of product lines, have good connotations, and be suitable in foreign trade. Times change, and with them fashions, including fashions in brands. This is especially true in the case of trademarks. White Rock's Psyche and the emblem for United States Steel had to be redrawn a number of times, as has Aunt Jemima (and it still suffers the image of black servitude). Names that suggest a quality of a product (but that are not descriptive) are good, such as *Zerone, Dentyne,* and *Thunderbird.* Compare these to the *Electrolux* gas refrigerator or *Griesedich* beer. Because so many firms today are in foreign trade or expect to be, consideration must be given to the reaction of different languages and customs to the brand. With a little care, these problems can be minimized.

Finally—and of vital importance in choosing a brand—are the legal implications. Much time and effort can be lost if attention is not paid to the legal requirements of branding. These are discussed in detail below.

Thanatopsis. In Waverly, Iowa, the H. H. Cleveland Funeral Service advertised: "Those we have served will testify as to our ability."

TIME

SOURCES OF BRAND NAMES AND TRADEMARKS A most obvious source of brand names is the dictionary, and many famous brands originated there, such as *Arrow, Camel, Prudential, Carnation, Lucky Strike,* and *Life Savers.* Coined words provide an almost limitless source of brand names. One of the most famous is *Kodak.* George Eastman liked the strength of the letter *K,* so he decided to start and finish his brand name with it and then looked for a likely combination to fill in. Other names, like *Raytheon* and *Yuban,* are likewise meaningless. Some coined names have been chosen because of their favorable suggestiveness, such as *Kleenex, Certo,* and *Fluffo.* In other cases, names are coined by misspelling dictionary words—*Arrid, Renuzit,* and *Duz.* Some firms coin brand names from initials or parts of words in the trade name, like *Nabisco* (National Biscuit Company) or *Alcoa* (Aluminum Company of America). Names of people, real or mythical, also provide a source: *Elizabeth Arden, Venus,* and *John Hancock.* There are, however, various legal restrictions that must be considered (see below). Geographical locations are another source that is likewise legally restricted, but names like *Elgin* watches, *Paris* garters, and *Pittsburgh*

FIGURE 9-5
Trademark design is of sufficient importance that many firms seek assistance from industrial designers. Here is a group of designs from a leading industrial designer and marketing consultant. *By permission: Lippincott & Margulies, Inc.*

paints have been used. Initials and numbers have also been used; for example *IBM, 57,* and *A-1.*

Trademarks can run the gamut from highly abstract designs to human figures. They can be simply typographical designs of brand names or illustrations completely unrelated to the brand name. They can make use of color, photographs, or drawings. They can be modern or traditional, abstract or pictorial, masculine or feminine, simple or complex, animate or inanimate. The possibilities are endless. For a variety of trademarks, see Figure 9-5.

Whatever the source of the brand name or trademark, it should pass the test of strength and distinctiveness, it should rank high in a check against the factors discussed above, and it should meet the legal requirements.

TRADE CHARACTERS Many firms have found it advantageous to choose a *trade character* as a trademark or a supplementary trademark. General Mills' *Betty Crocker,* Borden's *Elsie,* Chesapeake and Ohio's *Chessie,* the *Campbell Kids,* and Starkist's *Charlie the Tuna* are but a few of the many successful trade characters. They offer an opportunity not only for product identification but also for promotion. Elsie has been the central figure in many Borden advertisements. She has also made personal appearances at fairs and shows. Charlie provides a touch of humor on the television screen. Betty Crocker has been looked to by generations of women as a helpful, if imaginary, home economist. Human trade characters do date, however, and it has been necesary to modernize them from time to time.

LEGAL ASPECTS OF BRANDING Brands are very valuable assets to the firm, and for their protection they are generally registered with the U.S. Patent Office and frequently with its counterpart at the

FIGURE 9-6

The famous General Mills trade character, Betty Crocker, as she has changed over the years. The first painting, by Neysa McMein, is the first official portrait done in 1936. The second illustration represents the painting by Hilda Taylor that was used from 1954 to 1965. The third painting is by J. Bowler and represents the version used until 1968, when the fourth Betty Crocker was introduced. Because of changes in clothing and hair fashions, the fifth version was introduced in 1972. The last illustration was painted in 1980. *By permission: General Mills, Inc.*

state level. Actually, brand rights are recognized by common law, but registration affords additional protection. It shifts the burden to the other party in a dispute by forcing the other party to prove the registration invalid if the other party is to succeed in defeating an infringement claim.

THE LANHAM ACT OF 1946 The Lanham Act specifies the procedure for registering brand names and trademarks. It specifically excludes four types of names and marks: first, names and marks that so resemble other existing ones for the same generic product as to be likely to confuse or mislead consumers; second, anything that is merely descriptive, geographically descriptive, or deceptively misdescriptive; third, those that are merely surnames, because other people having the same name are entitled to use them. (Combinations of given names and surnames are registerable, but they are difficult to protect.) The fourth type excluded is anything contrary to good taste or public policy: immoral, deceptive, or scandalous matter; anything that disparages persons, beliefs, institutions, and so forth; flags or other insignia of the United States or any state, municipality, or foreign nation; or the name, portrait, or signature of any person now living unless that person gives written consent.[11]

A brand must be in use in interstate commerce before it can be registered. A certificate of registration is issued for twenty years. It may be renewed for additional twenty-year periods indefinitely, provided it is not abandoned or does not become public domain. There are two registers, the Principal Register and the Supplemental Register. The Principal Register is the more desirable, because it affords greater protection by giving "constructive notice" of ownership, which precludes others from using the name or mark. Second, it provides incontestability after five years on the register. Those names and marks that cannot be registered on the Principal Register may be registerable on the Supplemental Register; for example, descriptive words, surnames, and geographical names after they have been used for a year. The law holds that such brands assume a secondary meaning when they have come to be generally recognized as identifying and distinguishing products from a particular source (usually after a period of use of five years). These names with secondary meaning are then registerable on the Principal Register.

"IN CONFLICT" PROBLEMS With the great number of registered brands, the problem continually arises of two brands being so similar as to be in conflict. Sometimes inadvertently, and sometimes purposely in the hope of getting a "free ride" from a well-established brand, conflicting brands are submitted for registration or used without registration. These problems of conflict are decided in the courts or by the Patent Office. Because they are a matter of judgment, rulings do not always seem consistent. Conflicts occur in three areas. For identical products, *Lemon-Up* was held to sound too much like *Seven-Up,* but *Milk-O-Seltzer* and *Alka-Seltzer* or *Canadian Crown* and *Canadian Club* were allowed. For the same class of goods, *Jantina* shoes was held to be in

conflict with *Jantzen* sportswear and *Comet* floor wax with *Comet* cleanser; but *Rose Hall* and *Robert Hall,* both clothing, were allowed. For unrelated products, it is difficult to prevent the use of a conflicting brand; for instance, *Lucky Strike* has been used for tire patches as well as cigarettes. Yet *Kodak* was refused registration for bicycles and *Johnny Walker* for cigars.

GENERIC NAMES The greatest jeopardy to the sanctity of a brand name is a court ruling that the brand has become a generic name—that is, the dictionary name for the product. One of the brands to meet this fate recently was *Thermos.* The brand name had become so entrenched in consumers' minds that it has been continually substituted for the generic name—vacuum bottle. Finally, the courts held that *thermos* is a generic word. This follows a long history of other brands that have gone the same way—linoleum, saltines, kerosene, aspirin, cellophane, nylon, to mention just a few. And others are threatened even now and must constantly guard against losing their brand rights. These include Coca-Cola, Xerox, Dacron, Scotch Tape, and Sanka. It is ironic that the main reasons these brands have been threatened are that they are either such good products or names or have been so effectively advertised.[12]

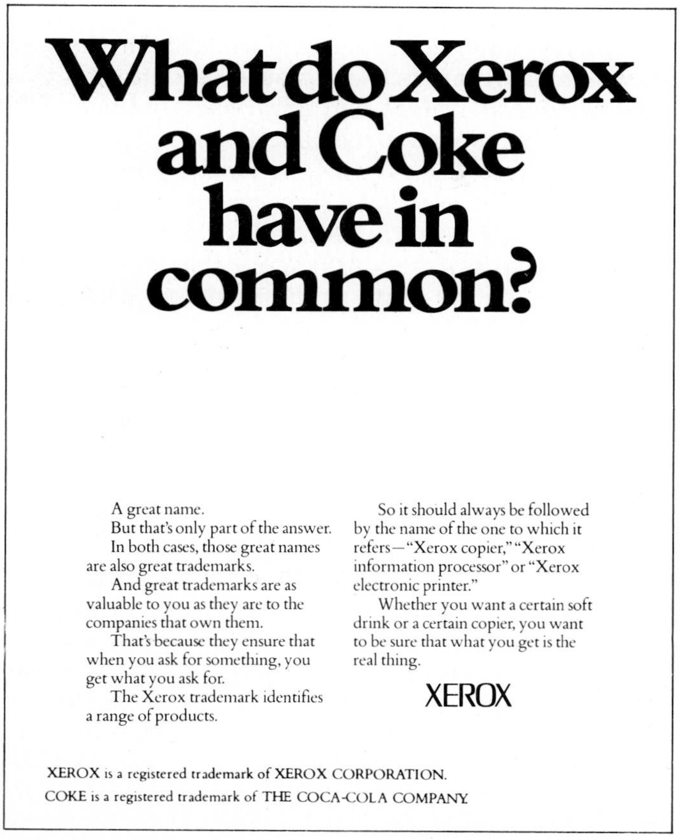

What do Xerox and Coke have in common?

A great name.
But that's only part of the answer.
In both cases, those great names are also great trademarks.
And great trademarks are as valuable to you as they are to the companies that own them.
That's because they ensure that when you ask for something, you get what you ask for.
The Xerox trademark identifies a range of products.

So it should always be followed by the name of the one to which it refers—"Xerox copier," "Xerox information processor" or "Xerox electronic printer."
Whether you want a certain soft drink or a certain copier, you want to be sure that what you get is the real thing.

XEROX

XEROX is a registered trademark of XEROX CORPORATION.
COKE is a registered trademark of THE COCA-COLA COMPANY.

FIGURE 9-7
A company uses advertising in an effort to protect its brand name. *By permission: Xerox Corporation.*

To prevent this fate for the brand, certain precautions should be taken. The main principle is to identify the brand as such whenever it appears. One means is to use the generic name together with the brand name—for example, *Q-Tips* Cotton Swabs. Second, the brand name should be so designated by actual notice. If it is registered in the U.S. Patent Office, identification can be made by means of the ®, Registered in U.S. Patent Office, or Reg. U.S. Pat. Off. Third, the name should be displayed in some special typographical manner to set it apart from other text matter. Fourth, the brand name should not be used in the wrong grammatical form. It should not be used as a common noun, in the plural, as a verb, or in the possessive. Such usage suggests that the brand is the generic name for the product. Fifth, it should not be abbreviated or added to. If the public develops an abbreviation, such as *Coke* for *Coca-Cola,* it should be registered as a separate and additional brand name. Sixth, using the brand for a line of products (when this is feasible) minimizes the likelihood of its being used as a generic name. Seventh, proper protection requires educating all concerned—company personnel, distributors, industrial users, and consumers—to the fact that the name is a brand. Because of the many complex legal requirements of branding, it is always advisable to seek legal counsel when branding problems occur.

BRANDING FABRICATED PARTS   In recent years, branding of fabricated parts that can be identified in finished products has become increasingly popular with manufacturers. Names such as *Dacron, Talon, S.K.F., Botany, Alcoa, Forstmann, Monel,* and *Ethyl* have become well-known brands used for fabricated-parts manufacturers. The object of such branding is to build recognition and prestige for the parts through advertising to the consumer in the hope that the consumer will seek out these brands in the finished product, or at least recognize that they enhance the finished product. The producer of the fabricated part thus has a sales proposition when selling the parts to the producers of the finished products.

PACKAGING POLICY

U.S. industry is spending approximately $46 billion dollars a year on packaging its goods. About two-thirds of this amount is spent for packaging products for the ultimate consumer. Packaging has come a long way from the cracker barrel and is now big business with a great effect on modern American marketing. Packaging has been an important concomitant of national advertising, for, like branding, it has made possible the identification of the advertised product at the point of purchase.

Without packaging, there is little likelihood that self-service operation would be possible. As a result of self-service, packaging has increased in importance, for it must assume a large portion of the selling effort. Modern packaging techniques have made the package a "second product," for which consumers are frequently willing to pay extra and that, in extreme cases, becomes as valuable as or even more valuable than its contents.

FIGURE 9-8

Special gift packaging. This advertisement promotes a quality product in a special decanter of fine French crystal. *By permission: W. A. Taylor & Co.*

RESPONSIBILITY FOR PACKAGING Many people in the firm have a stake in packaging. Production's interest is functional and highly important. Beyond that, packaging is an important marketing factor, and marketing people have strong interest in its development. However, because of its very close relationship to advertising and the similarity of the techniques used in advertising and packaging, the product manager and the advertising agency probably play the most important role in package development when this job is not assigned to an outside packaging specialist. Packaging problems have become so complex in recent years that these packaging specialists are increasingly being used in addition to advertising practitioners.

PHYSICAL FACTORS Generally, a solution to the packaging problem begins with physical considerations. A package's main function is to contain the product. Consideration must be given to such problems as spoilage, leakage, trasportability, protection from the elements and vermin, storage, and physical damage. Therefore, such factors as construction, closure, and material must be taken into account.

PROMOTIONAL FACTORS Beyond the physical demands of the package, there are important promotional factors to consider. The package must be consumer-oriented to meet the buyer's social, psychological, and economic needs. These needs are taken into account in package design just as they are in product development. Questions must be decided concerning the size, shape, color, and copy. Even such physical aspects as construction, closure, and material are important to promotion.

Market needs may determine size. Larger families and less frequent shopping mean larger packages. Large size also provides an opportunity for economy appeals. On the other hand, the number of single and small households demanding small packages is increasing. In either instance, package size must relate to physical problems of pantry shelf space and retailer shelf space.

The shape of the package allows promotional focus on consumer convenience. Does the package tip? Is it easy to hold? Does it fit into cupboards and refrigerators? Dealer considerations are similar. Package shape can also appeal to the emotional satisfaction of the consumer. The woman's girdle packaged in a thin, long tube suggests a quality of the product. The *Mrs. Butterworth* syrup bottle, molded in the shape of the trade character, offers eye appeal and delights children.

Color in a package provides a strong psychological stimulus. Certain colors suggest warmth or coolness, others have appetite appeal, and so forth. Color also must be considered in terms of the use of the package in advertising, at the point of purchase, and also in magazine, television, and outdoor advertising in color.

Copy considerations in packaging are extremely important, for many times they provide a last opportunity to deliver a selling message. Included in the message are such factors as brand name and trademark, trade character, copy appeals to buying, instructions for use, deals, promotion of other products of the producer, and legal notice of weight and compliance with regulations. These elements must be combined in such a manner that their layout constitutes good design, so that the individual package is appealing, lends itself to mass display, and holds up well against competitive packages.

In addition to meeting production requirements, package construction offers promotional opportunities to appeal to the consumer's desire for durability and convenience. The individual packages of Saltines within the outer package, for example, have been heavily promoted in Nabisco advertising as an important brand benefit to insure crispness. Package construction that permits reuse of the package—for example, decanter-type bottles and plastic bags—have provided strong promotional appeals.

Besides protecting the product, closures can offer great convenience to the consumer and therefore generate considerable selling power. Cans with aluminum tabs for easy opening without can openers are a case in point.

Packaging materials themselves offer many opportunities for promotional appeals. For example, there are no-deposit, no-return bottles; disposable milk containers; and plastics, which have eliminated breakage, provided new convenience (for example, squeeze bottles), and cut costs. Today, of course, there are ecological considerations to be kept in mind in using such materials.

PACKAGE CHANGES   With the tremendous promotional opportunities packages offer, firms should continually give consideration to updating their packages. On the other hand, too-frequent changes in packaging may result in a loss of brand loyalty, so that consumers switch brands with the same frequency. A package is an important part of the brand image, and it is important to preserve that image to the extent that it keeps present customers. Another consideration is cost— both the cost of making a package change and the cost of the packaging. Before undertaking a change, the firm must consider whether the costs will be offset by additional sales and profits.

Walter Margulies describes the evolution of packaging change for Ivory Soap:

> Let's start with Ivory Soap, first manufactured in 1879. The marketing genius that was Harley Procter gave it its name and such memorable slogans as, "99 and 44/100% pure," and "It floats." Whether or not Procter had anything to do with the design of the package is not known, but considering his preoccupation with all aspects of product communication, he probably did.
>
> For its time, it was an excellent package. Even today, in this era of reminiscence, it would probably function better than most in the marketplace. Its graphics displayed the strength necessary for a laundry soap and, at the same time, a feeling of gentleness that would encourage the lady of that day to use it in her toilet care.
>
> But what is really remarkable is the subtlety of packaging changes over the years, each causing absolutely no disruption of the communicative

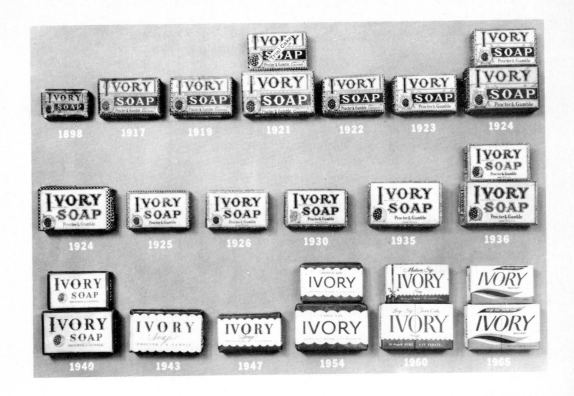

FIGURE 9-9

The evolution of a package. Not only must the product be up to date, the package must be also. Note how Ivory soap has changed its image in the wrapper through the years. At right is the current package. Notice the treatment of the different sizes and the multiple unit package. *By permission: The Procter & Gamble Company.*

stance but still moving the graphics forward to a more contemporary feel. As one can see . . . the most recent Ivory package . . . is considerably different than the original but the changes made each step of the way are so skillfully contrived that the transition is hardly noticeable.[13]

There has truly been a packaging revolution in the last several years because of technological advances. All indications are that it will continue for many years to come. To talk about recent innovations and developments is difficult; they are so soon old. Still some of the major directions in packaging deserve some mention. Plastic squeeze bottles have had wide application. Plastic bags, holding frozen foods, that are dropped in boiling water to heat are also increasing in popularity. Another popular innovation has been the blister package, whose transparent plastic bubble holds the product in place against a paperboard backing and provides excellent display of goods. Still another innovation with considerable promotional potential is the serving package, which permits cooking in the package and serving directly from it. One of the most popular developments has been the aerosol container, which has been adapted to everything from whipped cream to lubricating oil. When used for toothpaste, it was an apparent failure, however, and ecological problems have caused this packaging a severe setback, at least temporarily. For example, Dry Idea was developed by Gillette to some extent because the fluorocarbon uproar had put a big dent into sales of its highly successful aerosol packaged brand. Roll-ons were again taking the lead, and their major shortcoming—wetness—was to be the way this new product was to be positioned. This involved developing a roll-on package that could deliver the package and the product promise. Several early attempts failed, until the right product formulation and an oversized ball on the roll-on (the product is so dry that people did not think the regular-sized applicator was working) supplied large enough quantities so that it was felt.[14]

The multiple package, for many years used almost exclusively for beer and carbonated soft drinks, has now been recognized as a valuable merchandising tool to sell greater quantities of an individual product or to sell combinations of related products. Packaging of meats has become fairly universal, and now produce seems headed in the same direction. Curiously, there appear to be opportunities for premium packages and economy packages as well. On the one hand, the consumer with a high disposable income who is looking for greater convenience and novelty is willing to pay the price for expensive packaging. At the same time, high packaging costs provide an opportunity to appeal to the consumer to save by buying products in economy packages. We all like to feel we have made a good buy.

PRICING POLICIES

Price of the product may present a formidable barrier to the success of advertising. Theoretically, price is determined by adding expenses and a margin of profit to cost, but in practice, the process is much more complex. In modern American business practice, price is more likely to be determined in part on a psychological basis. What the consumer *thinks* the product should sell for is more important than what the firm *knows* it should sell for. The right price is determined by such factors as competitors' prices, product characteristics, brand image, and the segment of the market to be appealed to. In addition, there are special price problems in advertising. Should price be included in the advertisement? If so, what degree of importance should it assume? Should advertisements appeal to price or nonprice factors?

CHANNELS OF DISTRIBUTION

The channels of distribution used may vary markedly from firm to firm, and the particular channels of distribution used by a firm will affect its advertising strategy. Generally, the greater the distance between producer and consumer, the greater the advertising opportunity. With the trend toward self-service retailing and automated purchasing by retailers, there is a greater need for advertising to pull the product through the retailer by appealing directly to the consumer. Mass distribution and selective distribution suggest different advertising strategies. And, of course, spotty (that is, not national) distribution will likewise alter the advertising strategy. The recent rapid growth of direct marketing has also affected advertising plans.

PERSONAL SELLING

Personal selling is still the primary promotion tool, yet in some firms (especially consumer packaged goods), its role is subservient to that of advertising. In any case, there is a need for very careful coordination of the two and assignment of specific objectives to each. When each is allowed to go its own way, there is obvious waste. Advertising may open the door for the salesperson. In turn, the salesperson can be an important factor in merchandising the advertising.

SALES PROMOTION

Another element in the marketing mix, selling activities that are neither personal selling nor advertising, make up sales promotion. Sales promotion features include such activities as trade shows, exhibitions, salesperson's aids, and certain dealer aids. A sales promotion activity that has grown to huge proportions in recent years is the offering of "deals" to the trade and the consumer. These deals include such devices as price incentives, premiums, and combination offers. They have an intricate relation with advertising, and today many advertising agencies employ specialized personnel to work in this whole promotional area under the titles of sales promotion, merchandising, or trade personnel. This topic is discussed in detail in the next chapter.

PUBLIC RELATIONS

Until rather recently, business did not look at public relations as part of the marketing mix. But this is rapidly changing. Although there is some reasonable argument that corporate public relations advertising is not part of marketing promotion except peripherally, public relations directly related to the producer's brands and services can be as important to their success as any of the other promotion tools. Good product PR can be an inexpensive promotion with a high degree of credibility, because the audience perceives it not as communication from the firm, but rather as from the medium reporting it. And indirectly, public relations can have an important effect on perceptions of advertising, sales promotion, and personal selling, for how the audience reacts to the firm has a direct bearing on its reactions to that firm's promotional activities.

To be successful, advertising needs to be backed up by strong inputs from the other marketing-mix ingredients. The first consideration is a good product or service, designed with the customer in mind. Product characteristics can provide the main direction for advertising copy. Products may be positioned developing a product image that appeals to a particular market segment, and advertising helps to present this position to the market.

Brands are a virtual necessity for selective-demand advertising. The brand name chosen should be strong, distinctive, and uniquely related to the product. It should be easy to say, spell, recognize, and pronounce. Recognition is a key factor in designing a trademark. Brand protection is afforded by the Lanham Act.

Packaging has been important to the successful use of advertising in identifying the brand at the point of purchase. Next to the product itself, packaging provides important substance for advertising copy.

Advertising decisions must be made relative to the price of goods and services, since price helps to create the product image. The channels of distribution used likewise affect advertising in situations like self-selection retailing, mass versus selective distribution, and spotty distribution.

Personal selling is still the primary promotion tool, although for consumer packaged goods, advertising is generally more important. Sales promotion is intricately related to advertising. Public relations is another, perhaps less appreciated, tool of promotion.

1. Why do firms engage in new-product and new-service development?
2. Invent a new-product concept or choose one that has just hit the market and describe what steps should be taken in bringing it from concept stage to national launch.
3. How does product positioning relate to advertising?
4. Choose some product or service and show how its advertising might change with each stage of the product life cycle.
5. Why is branding so important to effective advertising?
6. Explain the differences between a brand name, a trademark, and a trade name.
7. Take a generic product and choose a brand name for it. Explain why this is a good choice.
8. What are the ways an advertiser can prevent a brand from becoming a generic name?
9. Why is packaging important to advertising?
10. What promotional factors should be considered when designing a package?

ENDNOTES

[1] Richard T. Hise, *Product/Service Strategy* (New York: Petrocelli/Charter, 1977), pp. 136–39.

[2] See James A. R. Stauff, *How to Plan and Develop New Products That Sell* (Chicago: The Dartnell Corporation, 1974), pp. 341–46; 382–86.

[3] See Eberhard E. Scheuing, *New Product Management* (Hinsdale, Ill.: The Dryden Press, 1974), Chapter 5.

[4] John H. Holmes, "Profitable Product Positioning," *MSU Business Topics,* 21, No. 2 (Spring 1973), 28.

[5] *The Wall Street Journal,* November 17, 1978, p. 1.

[6] *Trademarks: Orientation for Advertising People* (New York: American Association of Advertising Agencies, Inc., 1971), p. 1.

[7] See Chapter 2.

[8] Report of the Definition Committee, *Journal of Marketing,* XII, No. 2 (October 1948), 205.

[9] Public Law 489, Seventy-ninth Congress, Chapter 540, 60 Sta. 427, section 45.

[10] *The Wall Street Journal,* p. 16.

[11] Much of this material is based on *Trademarks: Orientation for Advertising People.*

[12] For more details, see Sidney A. Diamond, *Trademark Problems and How to Avoid Them* (Chicago: Crain Communications, Inc., 1973), Chap. 18.

[13] Walter P. Margulies, "Subtle Packaging Changes Can Help a Marketer Stay on Target," *Advertising Age,* XXXXIII, No. 7 (February 14, 1972), 41–42.

[14] *The Wall Street Journal,* pp. 1, 16.

10

Sales Promotion

After completing this chapter, you should be able to:

1. Explain how sales promotions and advertising work with each other
2. Suggest various ways the producer can effectively use sales promotion with dealers
3. Evaluate the different forcing methods to induce consumers to buy
4. Discuss the value of merchandising the advertising

As indicated in previous chapters, advertising, to be successful, must be coordinated with the other elements in the marketing mix. Although all the ingredients of the mix are important to advertising, certain of them are more closely akin to advertising than others. We will now consider a group of closely related promotional activities that are frequently used together with advertising as part of the *promotion mix*. These include point-of-purchase display, dealer cooperative advertising, dealer aids, contests, premiums, combination offers, price incentives, and the like.

Because of the practical limitations of space and the overall nature of this book, these activities, generally referred to collectively as *sales promotion*, will not be considered in depth. Further, they will be examined from an advertising orientation. Thus, many types of sales promotion activities are not considered. The emphasis here is for the consumer market. It should be noted, however, that there is a great amount of sales promotion activity in the industrial market as well. In many instances, however, what is said of sales promotion to consumers and retailers is also applicable to industrial markets.

SALES PROMOTION ORGANIZATION

Just who is responsible for these activities within the marketing organization of the producer depends upon the company. Many of them will be handled by a sales promotion department, if one exists. Otherwise they will fall within the province of the marketing services department. Even with a sales promotion department, some of the activities may be handled by product and sales managers. Those responsible for sales promotion may initiate and implement programs and techniques, or they may look to outside specialists who can provide various "packages," such as contests and premiums. Of growing importance in recent years is a special kind of business called a sales promotion agency. According to the Council of Sales Promotion Agencies, "A sales promotion agency is a company whose prime purpose is to develop and execute, on behalf of a client, a sales promotion without prior commitment to any medium, technique or product."

Because advertisers recognize the interrelationship of advertising and these activities, they are looking increasingly to their advertising agencies to provide them with advice and to help coordinate these activities with national advertising as they develop plans for it. The result has been the establishment of special departments in many agencies to handle this work. These departments are known as *sales promotion, merchandising,* or *marketing* departments. Their personnel are generally experienced in promotional work and calling on the trade, many having been salespeople for producers of national brands. The work done by these departments is generally referred to as *collateral.* Agency compensation for such work may come from media commissions from advertising placed for the client, or it may be paid on a cost-plus or fee basis, or some combination. Depending upon the agency, this department may actually do the complete job from planning to execution, or it may only plan sales promotional strategies, leaving execution to others. In small agencies, these activities may be assumed by one person in addition to that person's other responsibilities, and there may or may not be any charge for this time.

Perhaps there are no more confusing terms in marketing than *merchandising* and *sales promotion.* Academically speaking, *merchandising* may be defined as, "The planning to offer the right merchandise or service at the right place, at the right time, in the right quantities, and at the right price."[1] *Sales promotion* may be defined as, "Those sales activities that belong neither to personal selling nor to advertising but are necessary in coordinating them and making them effective, such as displays, shows and expositions, demonstrations, and other nonrecurrent selling efforts not in the ordinary routine."[2]

The Sales Promotion Executives Association (SPEA) defines sales promotion as "any activity which increases or speeds up the flow of goods and services from the manufacturer to the final sale." It includes the following categories in its definition: direct mail; sampling; coupons; catalogs and price lists; house organs; annual reports (other than pure financial ones); contests and incentive programs, including sales contests, exhibits, and special events (open house, tours, anniversaries, etc.); packaging; signs and displays; premiums, gifts, and specialties; product publicity; sales aids and presentations, including audiovisuals; sales meetings; and sales training.[3] The definitions of sales promotion are almost infinite. In the business community, different industries and, indeed, different firms within an industry will have their own definitions. But regardless of the terminology or organization used, the tasks need to be done. Advertising success depends upon all possible promotional efforts to elicit the full cooperation of the retailer through *dealer* promotional efforts by the producer. Likewise, the producer must employ all promotional efforts to stimulate the *consumer* to action.

Rather than trying to resolve the terminology problem, this chapter will use the term *sales promotion,* including in our definition special activities between the producer and dealer for the purpose of stimulating dealer sales, as well as special activities between the producer and consumer for the purpose of stimulating demand.

Compared to the multimillion-dollar national advertising campaigns in glamorous media, sales promotion may appear unimportant, but this is far from the case. Many manufacturers are spending huge sums on it that match or surpass the funds they devote to advertising. In fact, estimates place current sales promotion expenditures at roughly one-third more than the collective expenditures for advertising.

It is important to note that sales promotion and advertising are not competitive; instead, they are rather complementary. Advertising is frequently used to make sales promotion activities such as contests, sweepstakes, premium offers, and price incentives known to the consumer. Thus, the sales promotion activities become part of the advertising strategy. In some instances, it is difficult to determine whether the activity being considered is after all advertising or sales promotion, as, for example, point-of-purchase display. One thing is certain. Sales promotion has truly come into its own; it is recognized today as an indispensable facet of marketing.

DEALER PROMOTION

The success of producers is very much dependent upon the success of their dealers. If they do not move the merchandise the producers manufacture, these producers are locked in. After the sale is made to the dealer, the merchandise must be sold to the consumer if there are to be reorders. Therefore, it is incumbent upon producers to help retailers sell the merchandise bought from these producers. Thus, while producers frequently use their national advertising to *pull* products through retailers by directing it at consumers and hoping to build consumer demand, they also use sales promotion to *push* products through dealers by making dealer selling efforts more effective.

Because producers are usually larger enterprises than are retailers, they frequently possess the talents and expertise to make selling the merchandise to consumers easier and more effective. Furthermore, producers are "specialists" when it comes to their product or limited line of products as compared to the relatively wide assortments of products sold by retailers. Finally, since the producers have developed promotional strategies for their brands, it is a relatively easy step to adapt these to promotion at the retail level.

There are a number of broad areas in which producers can aid dealers. These include, first, assistance in the organization and management of the business. Because dealers are often small businesses, they do not have the resources of specialists to aid in the planning of store layout, selection of store location, stock control, price policy, or financing. Second, producers can help in the training and motivating of dealers' sales forces. This may include in-store training and factory training and motivational devices such as gifts, PMs (commissions paid directly to retail sales clerks by producers), and sales contests. Other aids include point-of-purchase display, dealer advertising, and store traffic stimulation. All these are valuable and useful, but only those that most closely relate to the advertising effort will be considered here in any detail.

POINT-OF-PURCHASE DISPLAY Wouldn't it be nice if producers could make one more "pitch" for their brands as consumers ponder over a purchase in the retail store? Well, they can, and the technique is called *point-of-purchase display* (P-O-P). This technique affords the producer an opportunity to sell by reminder and by impulse at the point at which the sale is consummated. It can be an important reiteration of messages previously delivered by all kinds of advertising media. It can also make an appeal independently. In either case, it can ask for the order at a critical point, the close of the sale.

Probably the greatest impetus to the increasing importance of P-O-P has been the trend to self-service retailing. In so many cases, there is no longer a retail salesperson available to help close the sale. Even when sales personnel are available in the retail store, however, a good display can assist them in making a sale. And since, in most instances, the producer's brand must be sold in competition with other brands, the display offers some assurance that the producer's brand will have some chance of being represented and receiving attention at the point of purchase.

There is a great variety of P-O-P display. Certainly the most basic form of display is the package, whose value should not be minimized, even though it is not a form of P-O-P. Beyond that, there are *shelf-talkers* (cards hung from shelves), *counter cards, wall signs, posters*, and the like, whose life is generally short. Then there are *decals* and displays made of wood, plastic, metal, or other materials, which are designed to be used for long periods of time. Another group consists of such items as clocks and thermometers; these are referred to as *service* displays. There are also *three-dimensional* displays, which may be still or animated, showing cross sections of the product or the product in use, for example. Still another variety of display is the dispensing rack, such as that used for flashlight batteries or shoe polish. And there are eye-catchers, from balloons and banners to elaborate scientific displays and mechanical curiosities, which may not have a particular relation to the products being promoted but can draw attention to them. The variety of P-O-P displays is only as limited as human ingenuity.

Dealers look to producers for P-O-P display materials and use them effectively, recognizing their value in moving merchandise. But at the same time, producers sometimes find that P-O-P displays remain unused or ill used by the dealer. This has become a problem of major concern to the producer, not only because of the increasingly higher costs of producing such materials but also because of the steady rise in shipping costs. There are several reasons why retailers may neglect P-O-P displays. One is competition: Because most producers prepare P-O-P display materials, the retailer may not have sufficient room to accommodate them all. Moreover, some dealers, usually the larger ones, have policies against using display materials supplied by producers, preferring to prepare their own to fit the store personality. Finally, other deal-

Not Particular. *In Cheboygan, Mich., a classified advertisement in the* Tribune *read: "For sale: police dog. Will eat anything. Very fond of children."*

TIME

ers, frequently smaller ones, are just not sufficiently conscious of sales promotion to see the value in using the materials.

Several steps can be taken to assure better use of P-O-P display. First of all, display materials should be appropriate, timely, and designed with the dealers' points of view in mind. Next, the better the quality of a display, the more favorable will be its reception by dealers. Finally, the manner in which display materials are distributed will affect their acceptance and use. Many firms employ "missionary" salespeople or special display people to install the displays in order to encourage use of them. Some firms pay the dealer for installation, either in cash or in case allowances. Much display material is supplied free of charge, but some producers, when producing high-unit-cost display material, believe that if dealers have financial investments in the materials, they will use them to better advantage. Therefore, they charge dealers for materials on a token basis or at cost.

Point-of-purchase display is discussed further in Chapter 21.

DEALER ADVERTISING Even though most dealers appreciate the value of using advertising, dealer advertising has several shortcomings from the producer's point of view. For one thing, many small dealers have neither the expertise to use their advertising funds most effectively nor anyone to advise them. Second, such advertising tends to give greater emphasis to store patronage than to the producer's brand. Then, too, the advertising efforts of the dealer may not be coordinated with the national advertising of the producer.

Therefore, the producer may undertake a program of assistance to the dealer's advertising efforts. Several different programs can be undertaken, including dealer cooperative advertising, assistance in the preparation of dealer advertising, supplying of advertising materials such as ready-made advertisement and artwork, and supplying of direct advertising materials.

DEALER COOPERATIVE ADVERTISING One of the major forms of advertising assistance by producers is *dealer cooperative advertising*, also known as vertical cooperative advertising. It may be described as a sharing of advertising expenses between manufacturer and distributor (wholesaler, retailer, or both) for the producer's products featured in the distributor's advertisements. This should not be confused with horizontal cooperative advertising (association advertising), which involves joint advertising efforts by producers or retailers in an industry to stimulate primary demand for the generic product.

The objectives of dealer cooperative advertising are several. One is to identify the retail source of supply for the producer brands by encouraging advertising at that level. This is especially important for the producer engaged in selected distribution. Furthermore, some producers with limited advertising budgets feel that they can get more "mileage" from their investment if they can share the cost of advertising. On the other hand, some producers with small advertising budgets who sell to a large number of retailers with large budgets (for example, furniture

FIGURE 10-1

Manufacturers frequently provide their dealers with aids for advertising, such as this reproduction proof for a newspaper advertisement. These advertisements are often part of a dealer cooperative advertising program in which the manufacturer pays a part of the media cost. *By permission: Bigelow-Sanford Inc.*

producers) feel that they cannot go into such a program because the cooperative funds necessary would exceed their funds for all advertising.

Producers with mass distribution policies, however, frequently engage in dealer cooperative advertising, although they usually use this form as another means of offering a price discount and generally refer to it as an advertising allowance. Thus, it is more of a bargaining tool for personal selling than a bona fide advertising effort, and the advertising benefits become something of a byproduct. Even when the source of supply is important, as in selected distribution, there is evidence attesting to the value of using such a cooperative advertising program for encouraging sales to dealers.

Producers have mixed feelings about the value of dealer cooperative advertising. Some believe that real advertising benefits result from such a program; others feel that such programs dissipate advertising

Sales Promotion

funds that could be used more effectively in national advertising. Nevertheless, they feel forced to participate in dealer cooperative advertising because of competitive pressures. If one producer in an industry engages in cooperative advertising, the others must do likewise or face the problem of permitting the participating producer a competitive edge.

To avoid being discriminatory as defined under the Robinson-Patman Act, the producer must offer the cooperative advertising pro-

FIGURE 10-2

An example of a television commercial prepared by the manufacturer for dealer use. *By permission: Bigelow-Sanford Inc.*

Bigelow

30-second commercial
Blue Ribbon Carpet Sale

LOCAL ANNOUNCER: Dealer message

Dealer message

VOICEOVER: The BIGELOW BLUE RIBBON CARPET SALE brings you

sensational savings on Bigelow's best-selling broadloom carpets.

Beautiful colors and textures,

with Scotchgard Carpet Protector

and Bigelow top quality at amazingly low sale prices.

But hurry, Bigelow Carpets at these prices are too good to miss.

LOCAL ANNOUNCER: Dealer Message

gram to all dealers on terms proportionate to their purchases. The most usual financial arrangement is for the producer to enter into a contract with the retailer to share the cost of advertising the producer's brand on a fifty-fifty basis. There are variations to this arrangement, however, with the producer sometimes paying 25 percent, the wholesaler 25 percent, and the retailer 50 percent. Other splits are also employed. The producer usually stipulates certain regulations for the program. These may spell out acceptable classes of media; require the use of producer-prepared mats or dealer-prepared advertisements subject to prior approval by the producer; request proof that the advertisement was submitted, in the form of tear sheets of the advertisements; and demand duplicate invoices to prove advertising rates charged by the media.

The use of dealer cooperative advertising presents several problems to the producer. For one thing, there is a lack of effective control over the execution of the advertising and its coordination with national advertising efforts of the manufacturer. One of the benefits of dealer cooperative advertising used to be that such advertising was placed at the lower retail advertising rates, but many media today insist on billing dealer cooperative advertising at the national advertising rate. Another problem, despite the aforementioned controls, is the considerable amount of "cheating" by retailers on rates, insertions, and so forth, so that the manufacturer is not getting a return on the investment. Finally, it is frequently the small dealers who will take advantage of the producer's program, and the small dealer's small advertising efforts may dissipate the dealer cooperative advertising funds.

A well-formulated dealer cooperative advertising program with a well-written contract and careful supervision can overcome many such problems and prove a valuable aid in promotional efforts.

ASSISTANCE IN PREPARATION OF DEALER ADVERTISING Many dealers simply do not have the expertise to prepare effective retail advertising. Producers, because of their size and the staff specialists they employ, are much more knowledgeable and can therefore help dealers have more effective advertising. Some firms prepare advertising manuals for use by their dealers. Others offer assistance in the planning and execution of advertising campaigns. In many instances, producers' salespeople are trained to offer advertising counsel to the dealer. The greatest obstacle to effective assistance to dealers is that producers often fail to realize that the dealers are usually interested in overall store promotion of all lines, not just the particular producer's brand. Producers who help dealers with their overall advertising problems will find greater dealer receptivity to their offers of help.

SUPPLYING ADVERTISING MATERIALS In connection with assisting dealers in their advertising, many producers provide dealers with proofs (copies of finished advertisement material that can be reproduced by the local newspaper) of complete advertisements and of components. They also supply photographs of artwork. These materials can effectively aid dealers in their advertising and at the same time help assure greater dealer promotion of the producer's brand. The producer should be careful to provide usable materials. Proofs for full-page promotion of the producer's brand, for example, will be wasted if the dealer's sales volume does not warrant so much space.

SUPPLYING DIRECT ADVERTISING MATERIAL Dealers can advertise through direct mail and handouts as well as in mass media. Frequently, they look to producers to supply direct advertising materials. In direct mail advertising, the dealer may use special mailings to promote producers' brands or may make use of envelope stuffers (mailing pieces to be included with monthly statements sent to charge account customers). In-store handouts may include leaflets, brochures, broadsides, catalogs, and the like prepared by the producer. Generally, all the direct advertising materials supplied by the producer are imprinted with the name and address of the dealer. Such materials are often supplied free of charge, but to avoid misuse or neglect of the materials by the dealer, some producers will make a token charge or bill at cost, or for the cost of the imprint, for such materials.

STORE TRAFFIC STIMULATION   Increasing store traffic is obviously the concern of the dealers, but at the same time, producers recognize its importance in moving their brands. Therefore, producers supplement dealers' efforts to build store traffic through programs usually offered at no charge. An infinite number of techniques can be employed; the discussion here will cover only the more popular ones—free offers, demonstrations, merchandise counseling, lectures, and special events. All these programs must be promoted, usually through advertising, to make them known to consumers.

FREE OFFERS Everyone likes something for nothing; therefore, many producers provide dealers with gift items to induce customers to come into the store for a demonstration or simply to see merchandise for sale. Because the free offer (premium) may be fairly expensive, the dealer frequently pays at least a part of the cost. One producer offered a free bath towel to anyone who would visit a dealer to see a demonstration of its washing machine. Ford has offered a choice of gifts to customers who would visit dealer showrooms. It is important that the offer appeal to the particular segment of the market you want to reach. Also, care must be taken not to *give away* merchandise that the dealer normally sells. When free offers are made nationally, it is possible to promote them not only through retail advertising but through national advertising by the producer as well.

DEMONSTRATIONS Show business has a universal appeal, and the store demonstration is a kind of showmanship in business. Claims may be made in advertisements, but "seeing is believing." Demonstrations also add a certain glamour to the store. Therefore, many producers have demonstrators who travel from store to store. Hoover, for example, shows its cleaning equipment in operation on the salesfloor. People watching the demonstration can ask questions that can be answered by an expert and may be able to try the product themselves. The key to good live demonstrations is effective demonstrators with both an expert knowledge of the product and a flair for the dramatic. In lieu of live demonstrators, some manufacturers use tape machines and slide projectors or movies to demonstrate their products. There are also mechanical displays capable of demonstrating the product in action. One, for example, dipped a running watch in a tank of water and then hit the watch with a hammer to show that it was waterproof and shockproof.

MERCHANDISE COUNSELING Consumers seek counsel in selecting many kinds of products. Therefore, manufacturers of such goods frequently provide stores with experts to assist customers in making selections. Revlon, for example, provides makeup consultants to advise women on the proper kinds and shades of cosmetics to use. Sometimes such counselors are supplied on a permanent basis. In addition to counseling, they may also give demonstrations and lectures and train salesclerks in the store in how to counsel customers.

LECTURES Because of the complexity of certain product lines, producers have found it helpful to encourage sales by offering instruction in how to use their products. The lectures are held on the dealer's premises and, because they are promoted through advertising, they tend to build store traffic. Producers of sewing machines offer instruction in the use of the machines; carpet producers often offer lectures on interior decorating.

SPECIAL EVENTS Finally, producers may help build store traffic by helping produce special events. Some producers—for example, dress houses and milliners—make special showings available to dealers for a limited time. These may include a complete assortment of merchandise in greater variety than that usually stocked by the store. Carpet producers may bring trailers with a complete assortment of designs and colors. Generally, these showings are accompanied by experts to counsel customers. Producers may also supply special exhibits, perhaps showing the historical development of the product. Another alternative is to provide celebrities to make guest appearances and promote the product. This practice is especially popular with book publishers. Fashion shows are another popular special event.

This is what makes good advertising—
1. Reaching the greatest possible number of prospects . . .
2. At the lowest possible cost . . .
3. With the best possible selling message.

SIGURD S. LARMON, Advertising Agent

READER'S DIGEST

In an ever-increasing attempt by producers to control their markets, they try to presell consumers rather than to rely upon dealers to make the sales. For this purpose, they spend great sums on national advertising. However, such problems as strong competition, brand differentiation that cannot readily be made evident through advertisements, and consumer inertia make the advertising task difficult. Furthermore, producers may find that advertising alone will not move the consumer as quickly as they would like. Therefore, advertisers frequently supplement product-reputation advertising with strong sales promotion stimuli to induce quick buying action on the part of the consumer. These techniques are sometimes referred to as *forcing methods*, or *trial inducers* as they are called in the jargon. Among the more popular of these methods are contests and sweepstakes, premiums, combination offers, sampling, and price incentives. Which of these methods will be most appropriate will depend upon the nature of the product and the marketing objectives.

Forcing methods are also used to get distribution for the producer and to stimulate dealers to aid in product promotion because retailers see opportunities for ready sales without the need for aggressive methods on their part.

CONTESTS AND SWEEPSTAKES Contests and sweepstakes have an almost universal appeal, and their use as a sales promotion technique has proven to be quite popular over the years. Because a condition of entry in a contest is generally some proof of purchase of the manufacturer's product—a label, boxtop, or some other part of the package—the consumer is forced to sample the product. For expensive products such as automobiles and washing machines, purchase as a condition of entry is impractical, but the consumer in such cases must visit the dealer to obtain an application blank for the contest and is then exposed to the product and usually to a demonstration. In appropriate circumstances, sweepstakes may be used. The essential difference between contests and sweepstakes is that although they are both competitions for prizes, in contests the prizes are awarded on the basis of skill in the performance of a stated service, whereas in sweepstakes the prizes are awarded on a chance drawing, lucky number, or some similar chance. To avoid being an illegal lottery, a sweepstakes may not require proof of purchase; at most, such proof must be optional. Great care should be taken to be sure that all legal and ethical considerations have been met, especially because of the considerable scrutiny of such activity by consumer advocates.

Contests and sweepstakes may be used as an effective stimulus to sample new or established products. They may also be used as a means of building store traffic and stimulating distribution; leveling out variations in seasonal sales; introducing package and product changes; and placing the brand before the public in an exciting way that stimulates publicity.

PLANNING Probably the first consideration in planning is to find an interesting vehicle. The sweepstakes are quite simple. An automobile pro-

FIGURE 10-3

An advertisement to business makes some interesting points about running a sweepstakes. *By permission: D. L. Blair Corporation.*

ducer has advertised sweepstakes through magazines and direct mail containing sweepstakes numbers that can be identified from a winners' list at dealers' showrooms. This affords an opportunity for the dealer to make a sales presentation, and it also encourages dealers to use display materials.

A simple contest may involve the completion of a sentence or a jingle. A sentence starting "I like _____ because" encourages the consumer to concentrate on the merits of the brand.

Still another type of contest involves submitting names for new products or trade characters, for example, or new uses for products or recipes. To avoid the problems of more than one entry's suggesting the same name, entrants are frequently asked also to submit a letter, which is used by the judges to break ties. Suggesting new uses or recipes for the product encourages contestants to try the product in different ways and may supply the manufacturer with valuable promotional ideas to

Sales Promotion

use in advertising. Pillsbury's Grand National Bake-Off has provided recipes to feature in advertising, for example. Finally, there are skill contests with puzzles and problems to solve. These are entertaining and therefore can generate considerable interest among consumers.

Any contest should be kept simple so as not to discourage entries and not to confuse the contestant. Rules must be written and explicit. (Generally, rules prohibit the sponsor's employees and their families from entering.)

After the type of contest is selected, the time period for running it must be determined. If it is too short, the full promotional value may not be achieved. If it is too long, interest may wane.

Prizes—cash, merchandise, or vacation trips—must be decided upon. Merchandise or vacations must be chosen to appeal to potential entrants. Cash is always welcome, but *money*, except in large amounts, usually does not stimulate desire as much as *things* do. Ideally, the greatest goodwill could be created if everyone were a winner. It is sometimes possible to have consolation prizes for everyone, such as autographed pictures of a television celebrity sponsored by the company, but this is not always economically feasible. The use of one large single prize may dampen the enthusiasm of many would-be contestants. Perhaps the best feasible arrangement is to offer one grand prize and a sizable series of smaller prizes for runners-up.

JUDGING Judging a contest can be an awesome task, for there may be a large number of entries. Therefore, machinery must be established for handling and judging entries. There are commercial houses that specialize in this work and can take over all the routine tasks. To add to the credibility of the judging, some firms use name personalities as judges.

PROMOTING A contest cannot be more effective than its promotion. Therefore, careful plans must be made to encourage entrants. The prime promotional effort will be advertising. In addition, the contest can be promoted at the point of sale through dealer cooperation. As a stimulus to dealer cooperation, some contests require the entrant to state the name of the dealer, so that the dealer can win prizes too.

PROBLEMS There are legal regulations that govern the running of contests and sweepstakes. In addition to the restrictions mentioned earlier regarding purchases to enter a sweepstakes, the Federal Trade Commission in 1969 issued additional rules covering contests and sweepstakes in certain industries. These state that when such promotions are used, the following information must be disclosed in a clear and conspicuous manner:

1. The exact number of prizes available in each category and the odds of winning each such prize. If the prizes are worth $25 or more, this information must be revised each week after the game has been running 30 days.
2. The geographic area covered by the game.
3. The total number of retail outlets participating in the game.
4. The scheduled termination date of the game.[4]

FIGURE 10-4

This advertisement promotes a sweepstakes and makes everyone a "winner" by also including a cents-off coupon. (Original in color) *By permission: Florida Department of Citrus.*

Besides federal laws governing contests and sweepstakes, most states have their own regulations, which should be examined carefully before undertaking these forms of promotion.

Although there are many case histories of successful use of consumer contests and sweepstakes, not everyone agrees that they are valuable as a sales promotional device. One major criticism is that gains in sales touched off by the contest or sweepstakes are only temporary, followed by normal or below-normal sales. To be sure, if they are used for purposes other than to get people to try the product so that they will buy more of it, the effect on sales is likely to be temporary. This problem, however, is inherent in any promotional efforts among consumers already using the brand. Except when increased purchasing results in increased consumption, the result of promotional efforts among present users is of little long-range value. Unfortunately, all the sales promotion stimulants have severe competition; brand A's contest is followed by brand B's premium offer, which is followed in turn by brand C's five-cents-off deal. Many consumers have no brand loyalty, but shift from brand to brand depending upon who is making the offer.

Contests and sweepstakes create other problems as well. Some consumers are "professional contestants," actually earning all or most of their livelihood by entering contests. They are a nuisance, but there are so few of them that they do not really affect the success of the contest—that is, the vast majority of consumers are not deterred from entering the contest because they feel there is a handicap. Perhaps more serious is the ill will that a contest can generate. Everyone who enters expects to win. When a contest to pick a name for a new brand is held, for example, many losers will feel that their suggestion was superior to the winning entry. However, a well-planned contest following some of the considerations given above can help to minimize ill will. Contests and sweepstakes may also be an end in themselves. Thus, many who buy the product to enter the contest or sweepstakes may not actually use it, especially when it is inexpensive. Second, to be successful, they must be aggressively promoted—usually through advertising—which dissipates funds that could be used to promote the product rather than the contest. Finally, the size of the contest or sweepstakes may be a problem, especially in terms of prizes. Because of the degree of competition, contests and sweepstakes over the years have grown so in size that one firm contemplated offering as a prize a pair of round-trip tickets on the first commercial space ship to the moon, with a million-dollar insurance coverage (or $25,000 in cash)! It almost behooves the firm considering a contest or sweepstakes either to offer it on a grand scale or forget it. Firms reaching small, specific markets with special interest groups, however, are an exception to this generalization.

PREMIUMS Premium offers have been increasing in importance as a sales promotional device ever since 1851, when B.T. Babbitt offered color lithographs for 25 soap wrappers. A *premium* may be defined as an article of merchandise offered as an incentive to buy or examine other goods or services. Today, premium offers take many different forms, the most important being direct premiums, self-liquidating premiums, coupon premiums, and traffic-builder premiums.

Although premiums have been used to introduce new products, they seem to be more successful in getting consumers to purchase already accepted products. Thus, a premium may be quite successful in inducing a consumer to switch from one brand to another, especially when there is little brand loyalty and brands can easily be substituted for one another, as is the case with convenience goods. At the same time, certain kinds of premium offers, such as coupons and trading stamps, have been most effective in building brand loyalty (or store loyalty) by requiring repurchase over a long period of time in order for the shopper to accumulate enough coupons or stamps for the premium.

Perhaps the most frequent criticisms of premium offers are that they attract the buyer to the premium instead of the product, which does not lead to repurchase, and that premiums are expensive. However, evidence has shown that if the product has merit, many consumers *will* repurchase. Frequently the fault lies not in the technique but in the indifference of consumers to brands, especially when product differentiation is slight and there is keen competition in premium offers and other sales promotion techniques. Some premium plans are expensive, but others, like self-liquidating premiums, are not.

After deciding that the premium technique fits marketing objectives, the producer must determine the appropriate premium merchandise. Guidelines are not infallible, but they can at least point the way to successful choice of premiums. Where feasible and appropriate, the premium that is related to the merchandise being sold is especially appealing. A book of recipes is appropriate to flour; a set of hair rollers is appropriate to hair spray. The premium should also be unusual. When the same merchandise is easily obtainable through retailers, it loses much of its appeal as a premium. The premium should be worth more than the price paid for it, in the case of a self-liquidating premium. It should be easy to handle by mail or at the point of purchase. Finally, premiums should lend themselves to interesting advertising.

DIRECT PREMIUMS Premiums given at the time of purchase without any additional charge are known as *direct premiums*. There are four types of direct premiums: one given by the retailer at the time of purchase (a separate item that can be picked up from the dealer or is displayed for self-selection pickup by customers when they purchase the product is referred to as a *near-pack premium*), one enclosed in the package (*in-pack premium*), one attached to the product (known as an *on-pack* or *banded premium*), and one that holds the product (a reusable package called a *container premium*). The two main considerations in selecting direct premiums are cost, inasmuch as the manufacturers absorb the complete cost, and size, because the premium must be handled along with the product.

FIGURE 10-5
A display for a near-pack premium offer. *By permission: Point-of-Purchase Advertising Institute, Inc.*

With the trend to self-service, especially in food and drugs, the separate premium had lost favor, because it was inconvenient to distribute through checkout counters. However, it still remains popular whenever there is personal selling (of appliances, for example) at the retail level. In self-service stores, this problem has been solved in some instances with *near-pack premiums*. Here, the merchandise and premiums are separate, but they may be placed in a special P-O-P display where, for example, cartons of cigarettes are displayed below and Christmas carol records are displayed above, together with a sign explaining the offer. Package enclosures are popular in the grocery field, especially for such items as ready-to-eat cereals, in which toys for children are easily included and whose package is a means of display advertising. Such premium promotions eliminate pilferage and any special shelving problems. A detergent producer has used this means of distributing dishes and towels, with the added value of encouraging repurchase to complete the sets. Banded premiums have the advantage of eye appeal, but they encourage pilferage and are hard to stock on shelves. Perhaps the greatest advantage of banded premiums over package enclosure premiums is that they permit the premium to be included with products that cannot hold a premium—bottles and canned goods, for example. Container premiums, which promote sales and also act as the package, serve a dual purpose and therefore, generally, reduce the cost of the premium. Examples include Kraft cheese spreads packed in attractive juice tumblers and six cakes of Ivory soap packed in a plastic refrigerator storage box.

SELF-LIQUIDATING PREMIUMS When the producer requires a payment for the premium, it is called a *self-liquidating premium*. Such a premium offer has the advantage that the only direct expense to the producer is in promoting the offer. The appeal to consumers who send in boxtops or labels plus cash is that they get a more valuable premium. Because the producer purchases a large quantity of premiums, merchandise can be offered that is worth several times the charge to consumers. The disadvantage to consumers is that they must write for it and then wait for it. Handling the mail is another problem for the producer. There are firms, however, that specialize in handling this operation for the producer.

Producers and retailers sometimes offer *continuity premiums*, which are sets of related items offered over a period of time, usually an additional item each week. Popular items include encyclopedias, cookbooks, dishes, and cooking pans. Such incentives usually bring the customer back each week in order to complete the set. These premiums are generally self-liquidating.

COUPON PREMIUMS A premium that requires a consumer to save coupons packed with the product is known as a *coupon premium*. Its value is that it provides incentives for continuity and brand loyalty.

Thus, coupon premiums seem well suited to holding customers instead of getting new users. They may be used for a single premium, such as a silverware pattern, or in connection with a catalog containing a variety of premiums. In order to keep the interest of consumers who may not use large amounts of the brand, producers sometimes accept cash in lieu of the full number of coupons. *Trading stamps* used by retailers are similar to coupons and serve much the same purpose.

TRAFFIC BUILDERS Premiums used to promote store traffic were discussed earlier in the chapter, under the heading "Free offers."

COMBINATION OFFERS Just when a promotion ceases to be a premium and becomes a *combination offer* is rather arbitrarily decided.

Capture the great taste of Minute Maid®

And save a lot on a great little camera.
Here's an offer that'll have you taking beautiful pictures in a flash.

The makers of great tasting, 100% pure Minute Maid® frozen concentrated orange juice, now bring you a great camera. Kodak's new STYLELITE Pocket Camera. With f/8 lens and a built-in electronic flash.

But the best feature of this camera is its price, a comparable $37 retail value for only $19.95 and proofs of purchase. And for each camera ordered we'll contribute 50¢ to the 1980 U.S. Olympic Team.

Clip this coupon today. You'll enjoy the great taste of Minute Maid and picture perfect photographs every time.

Minute Maid.
Goodness you can taste.

Flash! Special Camera Offer

Please send me _____ of Kodak's STYLELITE Pocket Camera(s) with built in 1/1000 second stop action electronic flash (batteries included). For each camera ordered. I enclose $19.95 in check or money order (not cash) payable to "Camera Offer" PLUS either six (6) plastic opening strips from any 6 oz. can or three (3) strips from any 12 oz. or 16 oz. can of Minute Maid® Frozen Concentrated Orange Juice.

Name_____
Address_____
City_____State_____Zip_____

Mail to: Camera Offer
P.O. Box 9709
St. Paul, Minnesota 55197

Please allow six (6) weeks for delivery. Offer good in USA only. Void where taxed, prohibited or otherwise regulated. Mail strips per postal regulations. OFFER EXPIRES August 31, 1979. Offer fulfilled by Sports International, 1300 Hwy. 8, St. Paul, Minnesota 55112.

"Minute Maid" is a registered trademark of The Coca-Cola Company.

FIGURE 10-6

An advertisement publicizing a self-liquidating premium. (Original in color) *By permission: The Coca-Cola Company.*

Generally, combination offers differ from premium offers in that the items offered in combination may also be bought separately from the dealer. A combination offer combines two or more products in one selling unit at a price below that of the two items if purchased separately. Its main appeal to the consumer is savings. For the producer, it may be a way of introducing a new product by means of an established one, promoting a slow-moving product with a popular one, or introducing a new product with a sample of the same product. The products of a combination offer usually, but not necessarily, belong to one producer. When two different items are combined in an offer, it is important that there be a relationship between them. Otherwise, consumers may be unwilling to take advantage of the saving to obtain items for which they have no use.

SAMPLING   All the forcing techniques discussed above are in a sense forms of sampling, for they are all designed to induce consumers to try the product. The most obvious means of giving consumers a chance to try the product, however, is simply to give them a sample of

Sales Promotion
217

it. Of course, not all products can be sampled. For sampling to be successful, a product must be one that can be judged in small amounts and that normally is purchased at frequent intervals. Samples may be given free, or there may be a nominal charge. The argument for charging is that it will eliminate most of the uninterested consumers who just want something for nothing. A good sample should be of sufficient size to give the consumer an adequate opportunity to judge the product. Sometimes a *trial-size* package containing one serving or one use is sold for a nominal charge. This was used recently, for example, on a new dog food brand.

There are a variety of ways to distribute samples. Direct sampling places the sample in the hands of the consumer through house-to-house distribution, which is very costly, or through the mail. The Postal Service permits addressing mail to "occupant," making costly mailing lists unnecessary. Samples may be distributed to customers by dealers. It is difficult, however, to be certain that the retailer distributes the samples properly, if at all. Samples may also be offered through advertisements containing coupons or "hidden offers" that may be mailed to the producer for the product or redeemed at the retail store. These coupons may offer the product free or at a reduced price. Demonstrators in retail outlets may distribute samples and at the same time show the customer how to use the sample properly. Finally, sampling may be done through sample kits, generally sold, that contain a variety of samples. One manufacturer of pipe tobacco, for example, offered a package containing a number of different blends so that the consumer could choose the most appealing one.

CONSUMER PRICE INCENTIVES   In recent years, in the ever-growing competition to increase their share of the market, producers have engaged heavily in consumer price incentives. These include *cents-off* packages; *cents-off* coupons in advertisements or included in or on the package and usable for the next purchase of the product or as a price reduction for another of the manufacturer's products; multiple-unit price reductions of merchandise that is banded (for example, buy three at the regular price and get the fourth free); and send-in offers, where boxtops or labels are mailed to the manufacturer for cash refunds (rebates) or coupons good on the next purchase. When used with the package, these are known as *price packs*.

Price packs became so popular several years ago that virtually all packages carried special labels almost continuously. As a result, the FTC imposed certain controls on the frequency of such offers, the range of discount, and how the discount could be communicated to consumers. Although this action reduced the use of price packs, the slack was taken up by coupon cents-off incentives.

These consumer price incentives give producers control over price reduction instead of leaving it in the hands of retailers, who might not pass the price reductions on to consumers. Producers can also tie these promotions in with other promotional efforts for a well-coordinated program. They are strong inducements for consumers to try the product.

They also induce dealers to increase their stocks in anticipation of larger sales. Because they are a promotion, they often receive special retail display. Although they attract new customers, however, they do not necessarily keep them; many consumers show no interest in any brand loyalty, shopping price in terms of which brand is offering a price incentive that day. At the same time, those customers who are loyal to the brand are receiving a price advantage even though they would have bought the brand anyway. To compound this problem, such loyal customers frequently hoard during deals to take advantage of the savings. After a deal, the sales volume usually returns to normal. Nevertheless, it is an easy promotional technique to use and will generally be successful.

Some retailers have in recent years used producers' cents-off coupons to build store patronage by advertising "double coupon" deals in which they will double the amount of the coupon offers.

To ensure the maximum effectiveness of national advertising, the retailers handling the advertised brands must be cognizant of that advertising. Efforts to inform retailers about the advertising campaigns of the

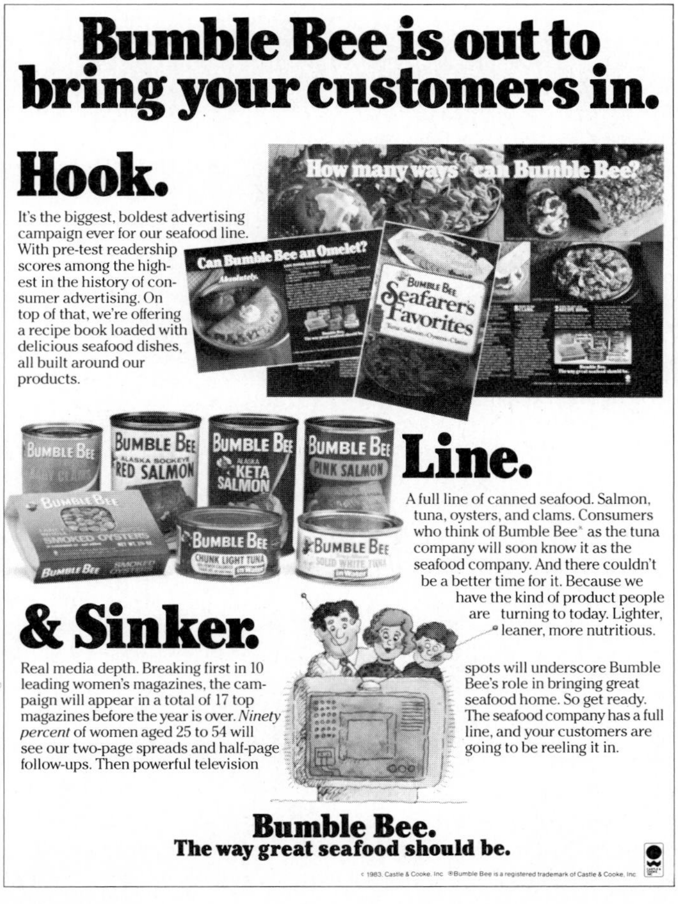

MERCHANDISING THE ADVERTISING

FIGURE 10-7

This advertisement in trade publications merchandises the consumer advertising for Bumble Bee to dealers. (Original in color) *By permission: Bumble Bee Seafoods.*

producer are known as *merchandising the advertising.* Through a sound program of merchandising the advertising, dealers can be made more enthusiastic about brands that are being aggressively promoted by their producers. Frequently, they can also be induced to tie in their own promotional efforts with those of the producer.

The responsibility for merchandising the advertising may rest with the advertising, sales, sales promotion, or product manager areas, or with all of them. The merchandising efforts may be through advertisements in the trade press and through brochures, preprints, portfolios, and the like mailed to dealers or presented to them by the producer's sales force. In some instances, the media carrying the advertising may do the merchandising for the producer.

TO SUM UP

Sales promotion involves all those special marketing activities between the producer and dealer to stimulate dealer sales, and between the producer and consumer to stimulate consumer demand.

Producers depend upon retailers for the sale of their products. Producers use advertising to consumers to *pull* products through their dealers, but they can also use sales promotion to *push* products through their dealers by making dealer selling efforts more effective.

Producers frequently offer dealers point-of-purchase display materials that afford the opportunity for one last promotional effort at the point of sale. They may also assist dealers with their own advertising by providing artwork and proofs of advertisements, and through dealer cooperative advertising, in which producers share the cost of retail advertisements. Finally, producers help stimulate store traffic through such devices as free offers, demonstrations, merchandise counseling, and special events.

Producers also use sales promotion to get *consumer* response. The techniques used are called *forcing methods* or *trial inducers* and are designed to get quick buying action from consumers. Techniques used vary with the nature of the product and the kind of action being sought. Among these are contests and sweepstakes, premiums, combination offers, sampling, and price incentives.

To get support at the dealer level to producers' national advertising to consumers, these advertising plans are promoted to dealers in trade publications and mailing pieces. This is known as merchandising the advertising.

QUESTIONS AND PROBLEMS

1. Of what importance is sales promotion activity to the advertiser?
2. What steps can the national advertiser take to ensure better use of point of purchase display by retailers?
3. What are the advantages and disadvantages of dealer cooperative advertising from the point of view of the national advertiser and of the retailer?
4. What are some of the techniques of sales promotion to stimulate store traffic?
5. Select an advertisement from a magazine for a food product, a clothing item, and an appliance. For each product, suggest the kinds of dealer sales promotion that might be used.
6. What are the various kinds of forcing methods or trial inducers that can be used in consumer promotion?
7. Choose a brand that to your knowledge is not using a contest or sweepstakes to promote it, and design either a contest or sweepstakes for it.

8. Choose a product and suggest five kinds of direct premium offers that could be used appropriately.

9. For each product chosen for question 5, suggest the kinds of consumer sales promotion that might be used.

10. What is meant by "merchandising the advertising"?

---

[1] *Journal of Marketing*, XIII, No. 2 (October 1948), 211.

[2] *Ibid.*, p. 214

[3] From brochures and correspondence from the Sales Promotion Executives Association International.

[4] "FTC Issues New Rules on Games of Chance." *Code News*, II (October 1969), 3–4.

The Advertising Expenditure

After completing this chapter, you should be able to:

1. Appreciate the difficulty in determining what advertising expenses are
2. Describe the procedure for advertising budget and cost control
3. Explain the budget buildup method of setting the advertising appropriation
4. Evaluate the various other methods of appropriating advertising dollars

How much should be spent for advertising? This is a familiar question to all who are engaged in the field. The answer is not a simple one, and there is no general agreement on how much should be spent or how one should arrive at the amount of the expenditure. There is as yet no absolute measure of the results that can be expected from a given advertising expenditure, and it is difficult to determine how much to spend to accomplish a particular objective. Recognizing the difficulties encountered in determining the appropriation is the purpose of this chapter. The importance of the subject can be appreciated when it is known that in some firms producing consumer goods, the advertising expenditure represents one of the largest budget items. In many more firms, it is the single largest marketing expenditure.

BUDGETING AND APPROPRIATION

The terms *advertising budget* and *advertising appropriation* are frequently used synonymously by advertising practitioners. Yet there is technically an important difference. An advertising appropriation is the *total* amount granted or earmarked by management for advertisng. Unfortunately, this sum is sometimes arrived at arbitrarily and, under these circumstances, may produce waste. An advertising budget, on the other hand, is divided into amounts set aside for specific activities. These separate figures make up the total appropriation. Budgeting suggests planning the size of the advertising appropriation on the basis of specific advertising objectives and the cost of accomplishing them. The practical difficulties of doing this should be recognized and are discussed below.

ADVERTISING EXPENSES

Which expenses are legitimately charged to advertising, and which are not? Before the advertising investment can be determined, some conclusions must be reached on the classification of advertising expenses. Unfortunately, there is no generally accepted practice regarding such classifications. What might constitute an advertising expense for one firm might be called a selling expense by another. One of the difficulties is that firms differ in their definitions of advertising. Where adver-

223

tising is defined broadly to include sales promotion, many expense items not directly related to advertising will be classified as advertising expenses.

The shortcomings of the practice of assigning nonadvertising expenses to the advertising budget are obvious, for the advertising investment is appraised in terms of an unfair burden. The advertising dollar, under such circumstances, buys less advertising and thus appears less productive.

The difficulty in classifying expenses lies in the gray area—the expenses that are neither clearly advertising nor clearly something else. The cost of television time is clearly an advertising expense; salespersons' expenses clearly are not. But where does the cost of sampling, or store signs, or sales exhibits belong? There are many items that must be arbitrarily assigned to an expense account or that may be charged to one account at one time and to another account at another time. For example, certain expenses may benefit the advertising effort and yet may be incurred by a department other than advertising. On the other hand, the advertising department may spend money preparing some work that benefits another department, either wholly or in part.

Take, for example, packaging. A package may be designed by production, although its use may be very important to advertising; or the package may be designed by the advertising department for use by production. Regardless of where the expenses are charged, both production and advertising will benefit. Obviously, every department wants to maximize the size of its budget and minimize expenses charged to it. The advertising department or product management is no exception, for the budget will be used as a measure of effectiveness. In fairness, then, one should take into account charges against the advertising account that are incurred for the benefit of others, transferring such expenses to the proper account when evaluating the advertising department, marketing services, or product managers.

Larger advertisers frequently establish an advertising chart of accounts to set forth what constitutes advertising expense and to provide a system of classification to aid in analysis and control. Such a chart of accounts will contain an assigned account number together with the name of the account (for example, "01 Network Television"), a description of what is meant by this account name and what is included in it (such as, "Program and facilities for all network television including activities designed specifically to attract attention to this programming"), charges included and excluded [Include: Cut-ins-Local or regional 'preemption' of network commercials (time and mechanics)"], and when expense is recorded (in the month commercials are aired). For firms using such a system, there is little likelihood of arbitrary or mistaken accounting of advertising expenses.

BUDGET AND COST CONTROL PROCEDURE

One of the more important functions of the advertising or product manager is the preparation of the budget. The physical preparation may be delegated to subordinates, and it is more than likely that the advertising agency will prepare media expenditure schedules and production cost estimates, but the overall responsibility belongs to the advertising or product manager. Although the amount spent on advertising continues to rise, media costs have tended to rise at a faster rate. This means that unless the manager can continually increase the efficiency of the advertising, ground will have been lost. Therefore, the manager must give careful attention to finding the right answers to the following questions:

Are advertising dollars buying the best values?
Are advertising dollars effectively budgeted and controlled?
Does performance compare favorably with plans?
Is there flexibility to meet the need for change?
What areas of expenditure can best be improved?

Requiring an advertising budget rather than an arbitrary appropriation forces planning, not only of the budget but also of the whole advertising strategy. A budget provides for order in purchasing, evaluation of goods and services received, and the necessary cash flow and reserves to pay for them. It also provides a valuable yardstick for measuring progress, detecting any deviations from the marketing plan, and making comparisons with past performance. The four main stages in the advertising budgetary process are preparation, presentation, execution, and control.

BUDGET PREPARATION   Preparation of the budget requires substantial time. To keep current, many companies have adopted a rolling budgeting system, whereby at the end of each quarter, projections are made for the next twelve months. In this manner, planning and budgeting can be kept current. To start with, one has to gather facts about the market, sales, distribution, and competition. Actually, a good marketing plan will contain this background information in its analysis and can be used advantageously for budget preparation. The next step is to build the budget by costing out the advertising segments of the marketing plan. These figures must be carefully evaluated to be certain that strategy objectives will be met with the smallest expenditure of funds. Consideration must be given to alternative courses of action and their costs. For example, can a media schedule at a lower cost achieve the same results as the suggested schedule at a higher cost? Also to be kept in mind is the relationship of the advertising budget to budgets for other marketing activities. As Chapter 7 makes clear, the marketing plan is an integrated effort, and top management will appraise the advertising budget in terms of the overall marketing expense and the contribution of advertising to achievement of marketing plan goals. It is well to remember that an advertising budget is a monetary statement of the advertising strategy of the marketing plan.

The final budget proposal must contain not only the cost of the advertising but also the costs of preparation of the advertisements, agency services not covered by commissions, related outside services such as research and rating services, and department administration. Recognition must be given to the dynamic nature of advertising; the budget

Bon Voyage. *In St. Peter, Minn., the weekly* Herald *ran a classified ad:* "WANTED: Man to handle dynamite. Must be prepared to travel unexpectedly."

TIME

FIGURE 11-1

Advertising Volume in the U.S. in 1981 and 1982

MEDIUM	1981 $ MILLIONS	PERCENT OF TOTAL	1982 $ MILLIONS	PERCENT OF TOTAL	PERCENT CHANGE
Newspapers					
Total	16,528	27.4	17,694	26.6	+ 7.1
National	2,259	3.8	2,452	3.7	+ 8.6
Local	14,269	23.6	15,242	22.9	+ 6.8
Magazines					
Total	3,533	5.8	3,710	5.6	+ 5.0
Weeklies	1,598	2.6	1,659	2.5	+ 3.8
Women's	853	1.4	904	1.4	+ 6.0
Monthlies	1,082	1.8	1,147	1.7	+ 6.0
Farm Publications	146	0.2	148	0.2	+ 1.5
Television					
Total	12,650	20.9	14,329	21.5	+ 13.3
Network	5,575	9.2	6,210	9.3	+ 11.4
Spot	3,730	6.2	4,360	6.6	+ 16.9
Local	3,345	5.5	3,759	5.6	+ 12.4
Radio					
Total	4,230	7.0	4,670	7.0	+ 10.4
Network	230	0.4	255	0.4	+ 11.0
Spot	879	1.4	923	1.4	+ 5.0
Local	3,121	5.2	3,492	5.2	+ 11.9
Direct Mail	8,944	14.8	10,319	15.5	+ 15.4
Business Papers	1,841	3.1	1,876	2.8	+ 1.9
Outdoor					
Total	650	1.1	721	1.1	+ 10.9
National	419	0.7	465	0.7	+ 10.9
Local	231	0.4	256	0.4	+ 10.9
Miscellaneous					
Total	11,908	19.7	13,133	19.7	+ 10.1
National	6,334	10.5	7,067	10.6	+ 11.6
Local	5,574	9.2	6,046	9.1	+ 8.5
Total					
National	33,890	56.1	37,785	56.8	+ 11.5
Local	26,540	43.9	28,795	43.2	+ 8.5
Grand Total	60,430	100.0	66,580	100.0	+ 10.2

Source: Prepared for Advertising Age by Robert J. Coen, McCann-Erickson, Inc. By permission: Advertising Age, 54, No. 23 (May 30, 1983), p. 42. Copyright 1983 by Crain Communications Inc.

should provide for the necessary flexibility to meet changing conditions. Because being caught short of funds to meet unforeseen developments can upset the whole budget and consequently the marketing plan, the budget should provide a contingency fund for unexpected expenses.

Obviously, in arriving at a total budget figure, the advertiser must know whether or not it is realistic. A budget so large that sufficient funds to cover it are not available is hardly likely to be approved. On the other hand, the budget for a year may be determined at a point when the amount allocated for advertising may exceed profits. This may be especially true for new products. Still, such a budget may be justified in terms of long-range objectives, assuming that sales stimulated by that budget will be sufficiently great in two or three years to justify the loss during the first year.

Ideally, in terms of profit maximization, the final advertising budget should be set so that the marginal revenue produced by that advertising will equal the marginal cost of that advertising. This ideal is virtually impossible to achieve because there are so many unknowns. Yet it is possible to set broader limits of minimum and maximum expenditures if these are not too rigid. Certainly it is possible to ascertain, at least in broad terms, the minimum funds necessary to elicit *any* response to the advertising. It is *not* true that for every advertising dollar spent, there will be a proportionate increase in the sales of the product. The necessary minimum will vary with the situation and depend upon such factors as the nature of the product, the amount of promotional effort by competition, and the complexity of the selling task. At the other extreme is a maximum expenditure beyond which there is a diminishing return. To say that the more money spent on advertising, the more profitable it will be is also untrue. Somewhere between these two points is the optimum. Through sound budget planning, it is possible to set the budget at some point between reasonable minimum and maximum expenditures.

BUDGET PRESENTATION When the budget is presented to management for approval, it should contain breakdowns by appropriate categories. These may include expenditures by product, by media, and by geographic areas such as sales territories. It should also show allocations by type of expenditure, such as commissionable media, production, noncommissionable advertising, advertising agency services, other outside services, and department administration. Finally, there should be data that compare present allocations with expenditures in previous years as well as with expenditures by the industry and by individual competitors.

It seems reasonable to expect management to challenge a budget request, not because of lack of faith in the advertising or product manager's ability but because management's function is, in part, to be certain that errors have not been made and considerations overlooked. The degree of formality of this process will vary from firm to firm, but in any case, the advertising or product manager must be ready and able to present an intelligent rationale for the budget.

BUDGET EXECUTION After the budget has been approved, responsibility for implementing the advertising aspects of the marketing plan and budget remains with the advertising or product manager. The manager should determine which incumbrances shall be made internally and which by the advertising agency. To ensure prudent spending, procedures must be established for placing orders and delegating authority to buy; for checking and approving invoices; for making payment. Failure to establish sound procedures for the execution of the budget can result in the loss of media quantity and cash discounts, uneconomical production costs, and the general dissipation of advertising funds.

BUDGET CONTROL Budget control involves knowing where you stand financially in relation to advertising plans and current conditions. Control can be divided into three phases: expenditure control, commitment control, and management control.

EXPENDITURE CONTROL This phase is concerned with the approval and payment of invoices for advertising materials and services. Of course, a sound plan of budget execution will simplify expenditure control. Because of the pressure of time and the complexities of media rates, there is a tendency to be less thorough, so that the advertising or product manager must inculcate in the staff a recognition that they should maximize the value received from advertising dollars expended. In larger organizations, a position of advertising controller may be established to oversee expenditure control.

COMMITMENT CONTROL In addition to money already spent, a good deal of money is usually committed several months before the receipt of invoices. These commitments arise chiefly from approved media schedules and the cost of preparing jobs in production or from preparation of estimates. In order for the advertising or product manager to know how the budget is being spent from day to day so as to plan intelligently, the manager must be aware not only of actual expenditures but also of committed funds. This is the task of commitment control.

MANAGEMENT CONTROL This control phase is, in essence, an occasional management review to determine the relation of the advertising effort to results. It provides management with information for making the decision to maintain or change the current rate of advertising expenditure.

There is no such thing, in my book, as an advertising appropriation. It is a sales appropriation. Every advertisement is supposed to sell. This is why advertising has been referred to as "Salesmanship in Print."

BERNARD C. DUFFY, Advertising Agent

READER'S DIGEST

METHODS OF SETTING THE APPROPRIATION

In actual practice, a number of methods are used in setting the advertising appropriation, probably as a result of the difficulty of setting the appropriation and of measuring the effectiveness of advertising. Each of the methods has its adherents, although each has definite limitations and none is completely accurate. Still, there is one method, at least, that seems sound from both an accounting and managerial point of view. This is the *budget buildup method.*

BUDGET BUILDUP METHOD   The budget buildup method of setting the advertising appropriation, also known as the *task method* and the *research-objective method,* is essentially the one described in the preceding section of this chapter. In recent years, it has gained considerable popularity and now appears to be the only logical method of appropriation determination. To reiterate, the object of this approach is to determine from the marketing plan the advertising task to be done and then to cost out that task in order to arrive at a budget estimate. Its lack of universal acceptance is undoubtedly due to the herculean job it presents in time and effort.

THE ARBITRARY APPROPRIATION METHOD   At the other extreme from the budget buildup method is the arbitrary appropriation. Like the others mentioned below, it is not truly a budgeting method, because instead of building up the appropriation from specific anticipated costs, it suggests that the advertising expenditure should be the result of sales and not the cause of sales. It is the weakest form of appropriation determination, because it is based upon the whim of the executive —the executive's intuitive judgment. (Even in the buildup method there is the need for intuitive judgment, but in that method, this judgment is based on facts.) Most frequently, the arbitrary method is employed by the smaller, inexperienced advertiser who has not learned the advantages of advertising and marketing planning.

One great factor in advertising as in all teaching is repetition. Repetition makes reputation.

ARTHUR BRISBANE (1864–1936), Editor

READER'S DIGEST

THE AFFORDABLE FUNDS METHOD   There are times when an advertiser's appropriation will be made up of all affordable funds. Usually this method is used by an advertiser of new products who has limited capital. This advertiser may actually have used the budget buildup method only to find that the budget request is greater than the funds available. Then all the funds that can be afforded will be used, even though these may be insufficient to meet the budget needs. Such a plan can prove satisfactory provided the available funds are sufficient to meet the requirements of a minimum advertising expenditure, as previously described. After the successful completion of a campaign, the advertiser may plow back the profits into the next budget in order to come closer to reaching the optimum advertising expenditure. This method is not used often, for eventually the affordable funds will be more than sufficient. At this point, the advertiser will have to select some other method—ideally, the budget buildup method.

Occasionally an advertiser will use the affordable funds method in a different manner. It might be believed that the more spent on advertising, the greater the profits, and the manager will therefore divert any funds that can be made available from other areas to advertising. Unfortunately, the advertising expenditure will eventually reach a point of diminishing returns. The strong advocates of this method are those who have never spent a sufficient sum to have reached the point of diminishing returns.

THE COMPETITIVE PARITY METHOD

"We've got to meet our competition. How much are they spending on advertising?" This is the competitive parity method of appropriation determination. It presumes that advertising should be used defensively to maintain the firm's position in the market. If competitive appropriations rise, so will this firm's. There are several hazards in this method. For one thing, what is an appropriate expenditure for a competitor may not be appropriate for this firm. That is, the competition may have different objectives, and its method of accomplishing its marketing plans may involve a different marketing mix; for example, it may use more personal selling and sales promotion and less advertising. Second, the competition may be looking to this firm while this firm is looking to it. Third, the competition's appropriation may not be on a sound basis, and to follow its lead would be to compound the error. Finally, there is no assurance and, indeed, little likelihood that following competition will help this firm accomplish its own objectives.

THE PERCENTAGE OF SALES METHOD

One of the most popular methods used to determine the advertising expenditure is the percentage of sales. Appropriations are based on a percentage of either past sales figures or anticipated sales estimates. The crucial factor here is arriving at the percentage, which is based sometimes on the industry average and sometimes on company experience of its past ratio of advertising to sales. In some few cases, it is just arrived at arbitrarily.

To base the percentage on industry averages assumes that all members of the industry have the same objectives and marketing mix. This is highly unlikely. Basing the percentage on company advertising history presumes a highly static market picture, which is also unlikely. To choose a figure arbitrarily is ridiculous. Still, some firms using the

FIGURE 11-2

Top 100 Advertised Brands for 1982

RANK	BRAND (CLASSIFICATION) CORPORATION	MAGAZINES	SUPPLEMENTS
1	SEARS (Retail) Sears, Roebuck and Co.	48,231	505
2	K MART (Retail) K mart Corp.	8,933	—
3	PENNEY'S (Retail) J. C. Penney Co.	11,285	—
4	FORD (Cars, Trucks) Ford Motor Co.	47,444	34
5	CHEVROLET (Cars, Trucks) General Motors Corp.	26,636	
6	WARDS (Retail) Mobil Corp.	105	—

percentage of sales method have been highly successful. This can be explained by the fact that some firms experience a rather smooth growth in a continually expanding market without overaggressive competition. If the long-range plans of the firm remain unchanged, there should be a roughly constant relationship between advertising dollars and sales. Thus, if the right percentage was picked in the first place, it should remain applicable as long as marketing plans remain unchanged. But the big question is how the percentage was picked in the first place. If the percentage was chosen originally by determining the advertising objectives and how to accomplish them, costing this out, and then relating it to sales, then the budget buildup method has been used. If periodic checks are made in the same manner to see that the ratio has not changed, there is nothing wrong with the method. But this is the budget buildup method and might as well be recognized as just that. On the other hand, if the percentage, once arrived at, is not checked regularly for its validity, then the method is weak and cannot be recommended.

THE FIXED SUM PER UNIT METHOD   Sometimes an advertising appropriation is set by putting aside a specified amount for each unit produced or for each anticipated unit to be produced. This method is really quite similar to the percentage of sales method, with much the same shortcoming. If it has any justification, it is in its use in assessing members of horizontal cooperative advertising programs by associations. Using this method, each member firm contributes equitably according to its production. However, the sum per unit should vary from year to year, depending upon the objectives to be accomplished and the cost of accomplishing them. Actually, the budget should be determined by the budget buildup method and then a fixed sum per unit should be allocated to the members to provide the necessary budget total.

NEWSPAPERS	NETWORK TV	SPOT TV	NETWORK RADIO	SPOT RADIO	OUTDOOR	TOTAL
(000 OMITTED FOR ALL MEDIA)						
394,000	87,540	12,631	11,072	2,084	5	556,068
270,000	32,470	7,447	761	5,638	23	325,302
237,000	23,788	13,522	2,203	738	27	288,563
31,593	98,437	34,208	3,907	35,572	2,538	253,733
30,022	76,035	33,268	327	13,958	4,924	185,170
157,000	—	9,310	—	1,345	18	167,878

(continued)

FIGURE 11-2 *(continued)*

RANK	BRAND (CLASSIFICATION) CORPORATION	MAGAZINES	SUPPLEMENTS
7	McDONALD'S (Restaurants) McDonald's Corp.	878	297
8	AT & T/BELL (Communications) American Telephone & Telegraph Co.	39,369	818
9	TOYOTA (Cars, Trucks) Toyota Motors	10,895	—
10	MILLER (Beer) Philip Morris	1,555	—
11	KRAFT (Cooking, Dairy, Prepared Foods) Dart & Kraft Inc.	17,711	379
12	BUDWEISER (Beer) Anheuser-Busch	2,560	—
13	CHRYSLER (Cars) Chrysler Corp.	8,849	—
14	KELLOGG'S (Cereals) Kellogg Co.	8,437	296
15	PURINA (Pet Foods) Ralston Purina Co.	7,855	1,246
16	WOOLWORTH (Retail) F. W. Woolworth	11	—
17	ATARI (Games) Warner Communications	8,559	21
18	DATSUN (Cars, Trucks) Nissan Motors	6,656	99
19	MATTEL (Toys) Mattel	8,188	317
20	HONDA (Cars, Cycles) Honda Motor Co.	15,446	343
21	MARLBORO (Cigarettes) Philip Morris	41,677	4,104
22	KOOL (Cigarettes) B.A.T. Industries	26,813	8,228
23	BENSON & HEDGES (Cigarettes) Philip Morris	29,261	5,076
24	MERIT (Cigarettes) Philip Morris	28,264	4,114
25	PEPSI-COLA (Soft Drinks) PepsiCo	271	—
26	BARCLAY (Cigarettes) B.A.T. Industries	29,025	8,600
27	VOLKSWAGEN (Cars, Trucks) Volkswagenwerk A.G.	13,993	—
28	DODGE (Cars, Trucks) Chrysler Corp.	10,078	731
29	BURGER KING (Restaurants) Pillsbury Co.	94	134
30	PIZZA HUT (Restaurants) PepsiCo	—	—
31	KODAK (Cameras, Film) Eastman Kodak	14,637	597

NEWSPAPERS	NETWORK TV	SPOT TV	NETWORK RADIO	SPOT RADIO	OUTDOOR	TOTAL
(000 OMITTED FOR ALL MEDIA)						
n.d.	59,876	94,156	1,718	2,138	4,143	163,206
6,248	94,971	11,668	7,319	1,076	287	161,756
15,610	21,244	63,890	250	3,623	2,524	118,036
490	74,651	19,868	—	16,051	661	113,276
3,955	37,074	46,020	470	1,395	47	107,051
1,929	50,479	21,905	4,572	20,261	3,191	104,897
16,789	34,471	12,185	813	28,293	583	101,983
2,044	57,413	27,292	—	794	254	96,530
2,163	71,570	11,440	—	221	110	94,605
87,720	—	3,564	—	2,222	—	93,517
8,520	50,838	13,415	1,178	1,894	19	86,338
9,711	14,458	42,313	—	11,383	920	85,540
4,805	55,533	16,052	—	155	14	85,064
6,792	29,887	14,556	1,239	11,866	3,043	83,172
13,207	—	—	—	—	16,877	75,865
19,138	—	—	—	—	19,340	73,519
24,219	—	—	—	—	8,260	66,816
23,681	—	—	—	—	9,978	66,037
1,786	13,319	40,784	—	8,825	999	65,984
13,851	—	—	—	—	14,501	65,977
11,657	22,355	14,653	—	1,867	74	64,599
12,406	24,063	11,304	2,107	4,387	300	65,376
87	35,400	28,759	—	—	691	65,165
n.d.	13,283	22,403	—	—	51	62,945
3,623	33,267	5,843	1,609	1,818	593	61,987

(continued)

FIGURE 11-2 *(continued)*

RANK	BRAND (CLASSIFICATION) CORPORATION	MAGAZINES	SUPPLEMENTS
32	SALEM (Cigarettes) R. J. Reynolds	17,275	2,764
33	GENERAL MOTORS (Corporate) General Motors	17,525	1,458
34	UNITED (Passenger Travel) United Air Lines	1,187	—
35	POST (Cereals) General Foods	3,558	182
36	OLDSMOBILE (Cars) General Motors	10,740	—
37	ANACIN (Medicines) American Home Products	1,376	215
38	COCA-COLA (Soft Drinks) Coca-Cola USA	276	—
39	AMERICAN EXPRESS (Financial, Travel) Shearson/American Express	11,978	495
40	PONTIAC (Cars) General Motors	10,240	—
41	MICHELOB (Beer) Anheuser-Busch	4,910	—
42	WINSTON (Cigarettes) R. J. Reynolds	19,141	2,839
43	MAZDA (Cars, Trucks) Toyo Kogyo	12,324	—
44	CLAIROL (Hair Products) Bristol-Myers	13,162	586
45	MAXWELL HOUSE (Coffee) General Foods	2,773	815
46	AMERICAN (Passenger Travel) American Airlines	891	376
47	EASTERN (Passenger Travel) Eastern Air Lines	4,263	55
48	WRIGLEY (Gum) Wm. Wrigley, Jr.	—	—
49	BUICK (Cars) (General Motors)	8,217	106
50	IBM (Office Machines) International Business Machines	12,530	740
51	DELTA (Passenger Travel) Delta Air Lines	798	—
52	KENTUCKY FRIED CHICKEN (Restaurants) Heublein	—	—
53	TYLENOL (Medicines) Johnson & Johnson	3,977	53
54	CANON (Cameras) Canon U.S.A.	11,683	—
55	VANTAGE (Cigarettes) R. J. Reynolds	20,591	714
56	XEROX (Office Machines) Xerox Corp.	16,928	19

NEWSPAPERS	NETWORK TV	SPOT TV	NETWORK RADIO	SPOT RADIO	OUTDOOR	TOTAL
(000 OMITTED FOR ALL MEDIA)						
30,652	—	—	—	—	10,887	61,551
16,769	17,777	3,646	1,186	3,098	6	61,465
6,077	13,793	25,747	—	13,603	48	60,455
443	42,906	11,535	—	11	—	58,635
10,427	9,632	20,470	—	3,999	514	55,782
223	50,051	3,192	612	—	—	55,669
2,535	17,197	26,878	—	6,123	2,602	55,611
8,658	17,639	13,745	—	1,829	18	54,362
5,292	20,450	16,770	—	809	97	53,658
727	34,691	6,156	1,727	5,230	156	53,597
19,571	—	—	—	—	11,617	53,168
512	26,710	12,958	—	46	133	52,683
1,282	31,534	3,348	1,251	442	65	51,670
1,188	31,953	8,087	4,470	2,292	—	51,578
18,634	12,289	10,759	—	8,429	186	51,564
21,218	5,203	7,758	—	10,238	2,499	51,234
—	37,642	10,868	—	37	—	48,547
7,242	13,763	15,100	2,893	249	933	48,503
7,228	17,633	3,861	1,590	2,774	68	46,424
24,276	—	6,979	—	11,746	1,854	45,653
n.d.	27,184	14,845	—	1,429	601	44,059
452	36,752	2,753	—	—	—	43,987
705	21,618	6,104	2,104	2	335	42,557
9,978	—	—	—	—	10,804	42,087
5,779	15,804	558	1,658	975	13	41,734

(continued)

FIGURE 11-2 *(continued)*

RANK	BRAND (CLASSIFICATION) CORPORATION	MAGAZINES	SUPPLEMENTS
57	PILLSBURY (Bakery, Cooking, Prepared Foods) Pillsbury Co.	2,893	72
58	VIRGINIA SLIMS (Cigarettes) Philip Morris	19,010	4,109
59	MORE (Cigarettes) R. J. Reynolds	13,131	5,510
60	GE (Appliances, Radio, TV) General Electric	8,592	400
61	TWA (Passenger Travel) Trans World Corp.	2,825	218
62	CREST (Dental Supplies) Procter & Gamble	2,773	26
63	MERCURY (Cars) Ford Motor Co.	4,658	—
64	POLAROID (Cameras, Office Machines) Polaroid Corp.	4,558	118
65	CAMEL (Cigarettes) R. J. Reynolds	10,518	—
66	CADILLAC (Cars) General Motors	5,150	46
67	SEAGRAM (Liquor) Seagram Distillers Co.	24,042	602
68	COLUMBIA (Movies) Coca-Cola	428	112
69	RENAULT (Cars) American Motors	9,394	—
70	20th CENTURY-FOX (Movies) 20th Century-Fox	431	319
71	CBS (Communications) CBS, Inc.	16,152	—
72	WENDY'S (Restaurants) Wendy's International	—	—
73	NABISCO (Bakery, Prepared Foods, Confectionery) Nabisco Brands	4,405	2,123
74	UNIVERSAL (Movies) MCA, Inc.	1,276	37
75	JELL-O (Desserts) General Foods	8,811	28
76	DU PONT (Paints, Fabrics, Fibers, Pest Control) E. I. duPont	20,270	3,848
77	CAMPBELL'S (Prepared Foods) Campbell's Soup Co.	5,094	770
78	RCA (Communications) RCA Corp.	4,735	520
79	SEVEN-UP (Soft Drinks) Philip Morris	1,073	7
80	COLGATE (Dental Supplies) Colgate-Palmolive	4,072	504
81	COVER GIRL (Cosmetics) Noxell Corp.	9,690	—

NEWSPAPERS	NETWORK TV	SPOT TV	NETWORK RADIO	SPOT RADIO	OUTDOOR	TOTAL
		(000 OMITTED FOR ALL MEDIA)				
267	31,364	6,954	—	—	—	41,550
9,312	—	—	—	—	8,924	41,355
12,800	—	—	—	—	9,381	40,822
4,544	24,583	1,897	177	399	83	40,675
19,774	—	10,086	185	6,205	34	39,327
47	32,351	4,073	—	—	—	39,270
3,958	19,208	9,281	1,285	597	128	39,115
1,388	31,037	753	—	—	—	37,854
11,290	—	—	—	—	16,026	37,834
16,752	6,992	5,792	—	690	669	36,091
3,418	—	—	—	—	6,217	34,279
156	25,638	5,923	28	1,608	148	34,041
3,075	12,763	8,650	—	—	144	34,026
621	22,771	8,821	78	765	182	33,988
15,577	—	851	485	393	50	33,488
n.d.	13,817	17,793	6	1,120	676	33,412
4,377	18,663	2,995	275	561	—	33,399
349	19,467	7,882	56	3,821	6	32,894
73	21,330	2,648	—	—	—	32,890
139	3,725	2,616	852	1,349	17	32,816
731	16,958	3,215	4,416	1,578	19	32,781
11,650	12,645	2,145	890	143	8	32,736
892	20,098	4,361	—	4,414	1,889	32,734
151	22,778	3,103	—	1,751	—	32,359
—	21,975	95	—	—	—	31,760

(continued)

FIGURE 11-2 *(continued)*

RANK	BRAND (CLASSIFICATION) CORPORATION	MAGAZINES	SUPPLEMENTS
82	NOW (Cigarettes) R. J. Reynolds	12,902	1,571
83	KENT (Cigarettes) Loews	13,033	583
84	REVLON (Cosmetics) Revlon	9,511	276
85	LIPTON (Prepared Foods, Beverages) Thomas J. Lipton, Inc.	6,400	407
86	JOHNSON'S (Hair Products, Lotions, First Aid) Johnson & Johnson	8,739	91
87	THE NATIONAL ENQUIRER (Newspapers) National Enquirer Inc.	—	—
88	SANKA (Coffee) General Foods	920	218
89	WARNER (Movies) Warner Communications	566	—
90	CLOROX (Laundry Preparations) Clorox	1,896	—
91	NESTLE'S (Confectionery, Beverages, Cooking) Nestle Enterprises	1,632	485
92	GOODYEAR (Tires) Goodyear Tire & Rubber	1,830	—
93	RED LOBSTER (Restaurants) General Mills	2	—
94	TRUE VALUE (Retail Hardware) Cotter & Co.	3,585	—
95	COLUMBIA (Records) CBS, Inc.	7,603	11,746
96	U. S. ARMY (U. S. Government) U. S. Army Recruiting Command	5,138	—
97	COORS (Beer) Adolph Coors Co.	56	—
98	MAYBELLINE (Cosmetics) Schering-Plough	9,892	—
99	FOLGER'S (Coffee) Procter & Gamble	—	—
100	OIL OF OLAY (Cosmetics) Richardson-Vicks	4,796	—

In addition to the media included here, many of these brands would also devote media dollars to business publications, direct mail, point-of-purchase, specialty advertising, and other media. Because so many large firms today are so diversified, these brand figures are more meaningful than would be total corporate advertising investments. Corporate names are given here in short form and brand classification is broad and general.

EXPERIMENTS IN BUDGET DETERMINATION

As was pointed out earlier, the most logical budgeting method is the *budget buildup* or *task* method. The fact that it is not used more universally is undoubtedly due to the difficulty of setting up a budget by this method. Ideally, of course, the budget should be set by determining the point at which the last dollar spent on advertising contributes that same amount in revenue for the firm. In economics, this is stated as equating

NEWSPAPERS	NETWORK TV	SPOT TV	NETWORK RADIO	SPOT RADIO	OUTDOOR	TOTAL
		(000 OMITTED FOR ALL MEDIA)				
17,206	—	—	—	—	16	31,635
9,770	—	—	—	—	7,752	31,141
471	14,957	5,352	368	13	—	30,948
1,133	15,543	7,399	—	—	65	30,947
127	19,456	1,214	369	455	—	30,451
—	27,515	2,171	—	69	—	29,755
655	21,414	4,492	1,880	142	—	29,721
598	19,394	7,989	—	816	28	29,391
—	25,183	1,933	—	—	—	29,012
489	14,340	9,435	2,225	146	—	28,752
21	15,291	10,267	609	402	210	28,630
n.d.	—	25,866	—	2,666	92	28,626
—	3,291	14,102	7,461	—	3	28,442
7,066	370	1,468	—	3	18	28,274
1,323	12,311	2	3,374	5,871	246	28,265
1,153	7,069	11,367	—	8,081	451	28,179
—	15,570	2,531	—	76	—	28,069
145	16,595	10,779	—	132	—	27,651
—	18,909	3,893	—	—	—	27,598

By permission: "The Top 200 Brands, 12th Annual Report," Marketing & Media Decisions, 18, No. 7 (July 1983), pp. 49-129.

marginal cost to marginal revenue. Thus, at least theoretically, marginal analysis would set the advertising budget at the optimal point. A number of researchers therefore have attempted to set up models for determining advertising budgets through marginal analysis.[1] But the models have their shortcomings, and they are still largely experimental. As one practitioner put it:

Many quantitatively oriented types are still looking for the magic formula which predicts the intersection of *marginal cost* and *marginal revenue,* the so-called optimum spending level. Personally I do not think anyone will find this answer for two reasons: (1) The marketing process is still a function of human frailty, and, (2) P & G [Procter and Gamble is the single largest and a highly sophisticated advertiser] has not done it yet. Furthermore, I consider it a naïve notion. Guys who trade dollars even up wind up in limbo.[2]

FIGURE 11-3

This advertisement explains how one advertising agency uses a model to determine how much to spend on advertising. *By permission: Ogilvy & Mather.*

In terms of practical reality, marginal analysis models have not as yet developed the "optimal" method. Still, the need is there, and as business develops greater knowledge, these models will perhaps reach a point where they can improve upon the budget buildup or task method of budget determination. Certainly, such research should be encouraged so that the marketing process is not always "a function of human frailty."

Traditionally, advertising has been thought of as a current expense. It is so treated by the accountant and so accepted by the Internal Revenue Service. But there can be an argument for treating advertising as a long-term capital investment. It is true that advertising costs are incurred to meet short-range objectives of immediate sales, but there is also long-range investment, for advertising has a cumulative effect. That is, in addition to stimulating immediate sales, each advertising dollar spent makes a contribution toward building a lasting consumer franchise and enhances the firm's goodwill—that is, the reputation and value of its name to the public. The immediate advertising expenditure may move a consumer to purchase a breakfast cereal initially, but it may also be responsible for the next purchase and the one after that. Furthermore, in addition to moving the consumer to the initial purchase of that particular breakfast cereal, it may also be responsible in full or in part for the same consumer's purchasing additional varieties of the same firm's breakfast cereals.

When advertising is looked upon as a current expense, management is bound to try to keep it to a minimum. When looked at as an investment, however, it might receive a better hearing. Because every advertising dollar is used for expense *and* investment, an exact accounting may be impractical. But it is vital that management be aware of the investment contribution of advertising dollars.

There is an important difference between "advertising budget" and "advertising appropriation." *Appropriation* refers to the total number of allocated advertising dollars, but *budget* suggests planning the size of the appropriation based on accomplishing specific advertising objectives.

There has always been some difficulty in determining which business expenses should be charged to advertising. Care is needed to avoid padding the advertising budget, because improper expenses make for an unfair burden in evaluating advertising efforts.

The advertising or product manager is under continual pressure to increase advertising efficiency, which suggests the need for careful budget and cost control. Such control suggests a budget buildup method of setting the advertising appropriation. But such a method is difficult, and many firms operate by choosing an arbitrary amount, using available affordable funds, meeting competition through competitive parity, taking a percentage of sales, or allocating a fixed sum per unit. These methods all leave something to be desired. The object is ideally to arrive at an appropriation in which marginal revenue equals marginal cost. Researchers continue to develop models to achieve this aim, but so far they have not achieved one.

ADVERTISING AS AN INVESTMENT

TO SUM UP

The Advertising Expenditure

QUESTIONS AND PROBLEMS

1. Explain the difference between an advertising budget and an advertising appropriation.
2. Which of the following items would be charged to the advertising budget? Why?
   (a) Package design
   (b) Design for a trade character
   (c) Preparation of a sales manual
   (d) Filming a television commercial
   (e) Preparing a management advertisement for a labor dispute
3. What is a "rolling" budgeting system, and what is its advantage?
4. How does budgeting for advertising relate to the marketing plan?
5. Explain the budget buildup method of setting the advertising appropriation. What problems are there in using this method?
6. What shortcomings are there in the percentage of sales method of setting the advertising appropriation?
7. Why should all advertising budgets contain contingency funds?
8. Why is it so difficult to determine how much to spend on advertising?
9. Why is it so difficult to develop a model of advertising budgeting in which marginal revenue and marginal cost are equated?
10. How might advertising be justified as an investment?

ENDNOTES

[1] For more information on these models, see the discussions in Philip Kotler, *Marketing Management*, 4th ed. (Englewood Cliffs, N.J.: Prentice-Hall, Inc., 1980), p. 500; and David A. Aaker and John G. Myers, *Advertising Management* (Englewood Cliffs, N.J.: Prentice-Hall, Inc., 1982), Chap. 3.

[2] Robert A Rechholtz, "Budgeting for Growth and Profit," speech presented at Association of National Advertisers Advertising Financial Management Workshop, April 1978.

12

Advertising and Consumer Behavior

After completing this chapter, you should be able to:

1. Understand how the study of consumer behavior helps to create better advertising
2. Show how organizations make use of consumer behavior in advertisements
3. Explain the stages of the hierarchy of effects model
4. Define cognitive dissonance

In order for advertising to be effective, it has been established that it must be part of a marketing plan in which the advertising strategy is designed to meet marketing objectives. It is necessary to decide what we want to say in our advertising and to whom. Thus, the first thing we must determine is the market or segment of the market we want to reach. Once we know whom we want to reach, we want to know something about how they think, their values, and their attitudes. We can then determine what to say in our advertisements so that we can persuade them. In short, we want to know why people behave as they do.

Advertising's interest in understanding consumers is not new. Advertising people like Walter Dill Scott were investigating consumer psychology shortly after the turn of the century. But most consumer behavior understandings until after World War II were intuitive, broad generalizations with little or no evidence to back them up. However, highly competitive business activity constantly seeks ways for improvement, and when the study of worker behavior began to suggest applying social science research techniques, it wasn't long before marketing and advertising people also turned to the social sciences like psychology, sociology, cultural anthropology, and social psychology for understandings of *consumer* behavior.

In just a few short decades, a whole new field of study—consumer behavior—has developed, with its substantial literature based on substantial research efforts. To be sure, the knowledge of consumer behavior is still highly limited, and there are new knowledge breakthroughs regularly. And although there is still much to learn compared to how little we really knew about why people buy, we have come a long way.

The purpose of this chapter is to very briefly review some of the literature of consumer behavior to provide you with a basic understanding of that behavior so that effective advertising can be produced.[1] Obviously, there is much more to learn than can be presented in a few pages.

Values that are shared by a particular group of people influence their behavior and thereby affect their response to appeals of advertising messages. These shared values are called *cultures*, and the groups that hold to them are called *societies*. Nations are usually individual societies and have different cultures. An advertisement in Japan showing a Japanese family bathing together in a public bath is reflective of that society's culture and could be a useful vehicle for selling soap. A similar advertisement in this country with an American family would be perceived as lewd and incestuous. In a society like ours, *enculturation,* or adapting to a culture, is primarily the result of the influence of the family, school, and church; the family inculcates each succeeding generation with its cultural values. But as needs change, so will cultural values, because culture is adaptive and will respond to pressures on the society. The continuing social upheaval since World War II combined with economic well-being has substantially altered cultural values in this country, as reflected in the increasing importance of leisure, an increasing proportion of emphasis on youthfulness, a decreasing interest in the established religions, and a changing set of values about sex. These changing cultural values are noted by advertisers and are reflected in the products and services they sell and the advertisements by which they sell them. The "Pepsi Generation" and "Coke adds life" are reflective of youthfulness and leisure time. Advertisements using Christmas themes have greater emphasis on Christmas as a holiday rather than a *holy* day. And a sensuous actress announcing on a television commercial, "All my men wear English Leather or they wear nothing at all," reflects a change in values regarding sex.

SUBCULTURES Within every society with its dominant culture, there are smaller groups that are at variance with the dominant culture. We call these *subcultures*. In a large and heterogeneous society like the United States, there are many subcultures of sufficient size with sufficient differences in values to make them attractive markets for special goods and services or for regular goods and services through special appeals. There are four kinds of subcultures: nationality, religious, geographic, and ethnic.

NATIONALITY SUBCULTURES Usually in metropolitan areas, there are pockets of first- and second-generation Americans who still cling to many of the cultural values of their national origins. Italian-Americans are a case in point, as are Mexican-Americans or Chicanos. These nationality groups tend to continue using their old language, eating "old country" foods, and observing many other aspects of the culture from which they or their forebears came. These subcultural groups are heavy users of many products as compared to their demand by the population as a whole; therefore, special advertising efforts may be directed toward them, sometimes even in their "old country" languages through special media.

"BACK TO SCHOOL"
Visa 60-Second
Television Commercial
1982-83

(Music under throughout)
Anncr. (VO): If you can
imagine it, you can achieve it.
If you can dream it,
you can become it.

Singers: You can open up your
world and make it shine.
You can do it.

You can squeeze that extra
something out of life.
Yes you can.

You can set a goal then do it,
add your own style to it.

It's your world. It's your life.
It's your time.

Every minute—you can do it.
Every day—yes you can.
You can grow in your own way.

You can do it,
and we'd like to help.

You can do it.

You can set a goal then do it,
turn your spirit to it.

It's your world. It's your life.
It's your time.

Every minute—you can do it.
Every day—yes you can.
You can grow in your own way.

You can do it,
and we'd like to help.
Anncr. (VO): Visa

FIGURE 12-1

A commercial recognizing a changing culture and the roles of women. *Reprinted courtesy of Visa U.S.A. Inc. All rights reserved.*

RELIGIOUS SUBCULTURES Jews in America represent an example of a religious subculture. Diamond Brand Walnuts found their buying power for walnuts to be sufficiently strong during Jewish holidays to warrant special advertisements to them. Moving from the subculture to the mass culture, manufacturers of the bagel have promoted a once-Jewish food item to a broader base and with less and less relation to its origins, so that ultimately the bagel may become as American as apple pie.

GEOGRAPHIC SUBCULTURES When you say, "California living" today, everybody knows what you mean. It suggests a regional or geo-

graphical way of life. Californians have their own style of dress, architecture, and entertainment, and all of it says "casual." Advertisers have appealed to this region with special advertising on local radio and television, in local newspapers, and in regional and local magazines such as *Sunset*. Since much of California living reflects the direction of contemporary American values as a whole, this subculture has been successfully sold to the rest of the country.

ETHNIC SUBCULTURES There are ethnic subcultures such as blacks and Orientals, and because of the large number of blacks in this country, this particular subculture is a very important one to advertisers. In many ways, blacks are as diverse as whites, but studies have shown that there are certain distinct black cultural values that are fairly uni-

BURRELL ADVERTISING INC.

As-filmed Photoboard:

CLIENT: McDonald's Corporation
TITLE: "Double Dutch"

COMMERCIAL NO.: MCBM1223
COMMERCIAL LENGTH: :30

(SFX: NATURAL SOUNDS)...

...

CHANT: Big Mac, Filet-O-Fish, Quarter Pounder, French Fries...

Icy Coke, Thick Shakes, Sundaes and Apple Pies.

Big Mac, Filet-O-Fish, Quarter Pounder, French Fries,

Icy Coke, Thick Shakes, Sundaes

and Apple Pies.

SINGERS: If you're hungry,

then for goodness sake

give yourself a

tasty break

with Big Mac, Filet-O-Fish,

Quarter Pounder, French Fries, Icy Coke, Thick Shakes,

Sundaes and Apple Pies.

At McDonald's.

FIGURE 12-2

This commercial shows a firm's awareness of subcultures in its advertising efforts. *By permission: McDonald's Corp.*

versal. For example, blacks respond more favorably to advertisements using all black models. They are also more responsive to advertisements in general than are whites.

Advertising nourishes the consumer power of men. It creates wants for a better standard of living. It sets up before a man the goal of a better home, better clothing, better food for himself and his family. It spurs individual exertion and greater production. It brings together in fertile union those things which otherwise would never have met.

WINSTON CHURCHILL (1874–1965), Statesman

READER'S DIGEST

SOCIAL CLASS

Within the society, we find that people may be classified into rather homogeneous groups that hold to common life-styles, values, interests, and behaviors. Individuals having the same amount of disposable income may not be interested in the same kinds of products, or if they are, their interests may reflect appeals to different values and life-styles. This is probably because these individuals are parts of different social classes.

WARNERIAN SOCIAL CLASSES Social class theory is adopted from sociology, and the standard classification is based on the work of W. Lloyd Warner, who divided American society into six classes. These may be described as follows:

1. The Upper-Upper or "Social Register" Class is composed of locally prominent families, usually with at least second or third generation wealth. Almost inevitably, this is the smallest of the six classes—with probably no more than one-half of 1 percent of the population able to claim membership in this class. The basic values of these people might be summarized in these phrases: living graciously, upholding the family reputation, reflecting the excellence of one's breeding, and displaying a sense of community responsibility.

2. The Lower-Upper or "Nouveau Riche" Class is made up of the more recently arrived and never-quite-accepted wealthy families. Included in this class are members of each city's "executive elite," as well as founders of large businesses and the newly well-to-do doctors and lawyers. At best, only $1\frac{1}{2}$ percent of Americans rank at this level—so that all told, no more than 2 percent of the population can be counted as belonging to one layer or the other of our Upper Class. The goals of people at this particular level are a blend of the Upper-Upper pursuit of gracious living and the Upper-Middle Class's drive for success.

3. In the Upper-Middle Class are moderately successful professional men and women, owners of medium-sized businesses, and "organization men" at the managerial level; also included are those younger people in their 20s or very early 30s who are expected to arrive at this occupational status level—and possibly higher—by their middle or late 30s (that is, they are today's "junior executives" and "apprentice professionals" who grew up in such families and/or went to the "better" colleges). Ten percent of Americans are part of this social class, and the great majority of them are college-educated.

Only one will bloom this year

Tulip Bowl, by Luciana G. Roselli, is copper wheel engraved in meticulous detail.
The first was made in 1981 and only one will be made each year until
the limited edition of five is complete. Diameter 12½". $27,500. Signed Steuben.

Steuben Glass, Fifth Avenue at 56th Street, New York, N.Y. 10022.
Major credit cards accepted. You may order by phone: 1-212-752-1441. Out of State:
1-800-223-1234. (For the Steuben Catalogue, send $5.00.)
Steuben is part of Corning Glass Works and has been since 1918.

STEUBEN GLASS

FIGURE 12-3

This advertisement by a distinguished producer of art glass recognizes that the product being advertised is not for everybody. *By permission: Steuben Glass.*

The motivating concerns of people in this class are success at career (which is the husband's contribution to the family's status) and tastefully reflecting this success in social participation and home decor (which is the wife's primary responsibility). Cultivating charm and polish, plus a broad range of interests—either civic or cultural, or both—are also goals of the people in this class, just as in the Lower-Upper. For most marketing and advertising purposes, this class and the two above it can be linked together into a single category of "upper status people." The major differences between them—particularly between the Upper-Middle and the Lower-Upper—are in degree of "success" and the extent to which this has been translated into gracious living.

4. At the top of the "Average Man World" is the Lower-Middle Class. Approximately 30 or 35 percent of our citizenry can be considered members of this social class. For the most part, they are drawn from the ranks of nonmanagerial office workers, small-business owners, and those highly-paid blue-collar families who are concerned with being accepted and respected in white-collar-dominated clubs, churches, and neighborhoods. The key word in understanding the motivations and goals of this class is Respectability, and a second important word is Striving. The men of this class are continually striving, within their limitations, to "do a good job" at their work, and both men and women are determined to be judged "respectable" in their personal behavior by their fellow citizens. Being "respectable" means that they live in well-maintained homes, neatly furnished, in neighborhoods which are more or less on the "right side of town." It also means that they will clothe themselves in coats, suits, and dresses from "nice stores" and save for a college education for their children.

5. At the lower half of the "Average Man World" is the Upper-Lower Class, sometimes referred to as "The Ordinary Working Class." Nearly 40 percent of all Americans are in this class, making it the biggest. The prototypical member of this class is a semiskilled worker on one of the nation's assembly lines. Many of these "Ordinary Working Class" people make very good money but do not bother with using it to become "respectable" in a middle-class way. Whether they just "get by" at work, or moonlight to make extra, Upper-Lowers are oriented more toward enjoying life and living well from day to day than saving for the future or caring what the middle-class world thinks of them. They try to "keep in step with the times" (indeed, one might say the "times" are more important than the "Joneses" to this class), because they want to be at least Modern, if not Middle Class. That is, they try to take advantage of progress to live more comfortably, and they work hard enough to keep themselves safely away from a slum level of existence.

6. The Lower-Lower Class of unskilled workers, unassimilated ethnics, and the sporadically employed comprises about 15 percent of the population, but this class has less than 7 or 8 percent of the purchasing power, and will not concern us further here. Apathy, fatalism, and a point of view which justifies "getting your kicks whenever you can" characterize the approach toward life, and toward spending money, found among the people of this class.[2]

Mass marketing and advertising concerns itself primarily with the lower-middle and upper-lower classes, which represent about 70 percent of the population. These groups are the major targets of television and radio advertising and advertising in most newspapers and magazines. But the approximately 10 percent in the upper-middle class and

On Second Thought. *In East Paterson N.J., the* Shopper *carried this ad:* *"For Rent—Widow would like to share apartment with another woman. Middle-aged. Or gentleman with references . . . ."*

TIME

the few percent that make up the upper classes can be appealed to through advertising media that have special appeal to these classes, such as the *New Yorker, House & Garden, Vanity Fair,* and *Gourmet.* Because the 15 percent that makes up the lower-lower class has such a small purchasing power, it is of marginal interest to most advertisers.

In order to classify people into the various groups, researchers developed certain "objective" measurements, which include occupation, income, education, size and type of dwelling, ownership of personal possessions, and organizational affiliations. Still, social stratification must be looked at as only approximations to give the advertising decision maker a feel for consumer behavior.

SOCIAL MOBILITY AND NONCONFORMITY IN SOCIAL CLASS   In American society, there is considerable opportunity for *social mobility.* That is, a person may advance from one social class to another by achievement, with education being the main criterion for social advancement. Still, some people are relatively immobile because of race, religion, family position, or simply because they prefer the status quo. Yet within any social class there are some who are nonconformists and who, because of their relative income, could consume at a higher level but do not choose to do so. They can be described as *overprivileged* consumers. There are other nonconformists who, because of their relative income, cannot maintain the consumption pattern of others within the class. They are described as *underprivileged* consumers.

Overprivileged consumers tend to buy the top of the line, whereas the underprivileged might buy lower-priced articles. Further, when these income differences become more profound, the overprivileged in one class may buy products very similar to those purchased by the underprivileged in the class immediately above theirs in the social class hierarchy. Social class rankings do not help us to identify meaningful market segments where such people are concerned.

REFERENCE GROUPS   Earlier it was mentioned that groups such as the family, church, and school affect a person's values, norms, and behavior patterns. They are also influenced by a number of other groups of which the person may be a part or that the person may reflect. Most of us are a part of several groups, but in some instances, the influence of the group in terms of our behavior may be negligible. If we actually aspire to be a part of the group, we are more likely to follow the group's values, norms, and behavior patterns. Such groups are called *reference groups*, and consumer consumption and use habits reflect those of such groups. For the individual, the reference group may be positive or negative, and it may be a membership group (one with which the person has contact or disclaims) or a nonmembership group (one to which the person would like to belong or to avoid).

Appeals may be made by advertisers to particular reference groups as a way to reach their markets. When Bruce Jenner talks about

FIGURE 12-4

This print advertisement, based on a television commercial campaign, makes excellent use of an appeal to a reference group. *By permission: Tropicana Products, Inc.*

Tropicana orange juice in a television commercial, many people will identify with him because he represents the epitome of what they would aspire to. In addition to celebrities, advertisers may also use "common" people in their advertisements, with these people being typical of the market. Consumers can then relate to the situation depicted because the spokesperson in the advertisement "is just like me."

INFORMATION PROCESSING

As consumers, we are exposed every day to a vast number of stimuli from a wide variety of sources, including advertising. As we receive these stimuli, our brain interprets them and gives them meaning. Information processing refers to the system of dealing with these stimuli by consumers until they are used to make decisions. The brain mechanism picks up the stimuli, but in the process, the brain filters out and discards a great many. Thus, studies have shown that although consumers are exposed to a large number of advertisements each day, they are conscious of only a very small portion of these and remember even fewer.

**EXPOSURE, ATTENTION, COMPREHENSION, AND RETEN-
TION**   There are four steps that consumers use in processing information. These steps are exposure, attention, comprehension, and retention.

Through the use of sound, color, action, subject matter, and other
devices, advertisers attempt to stimulate the various senses of sight and
hearing, and to some extent, smell, touch, and taste. But consumers expose themselves selectively to stimuli; that is, they "hear only what
they want to hear" and "see only what they want to see."

Some of the stimuli to which consumers are exposed are stored
momentarily while they go through another stage—attention. The first
part of this attention stage is known as preattentive processing and is
based on physical properties. Thus, a boldface headline in an advertisement or a musical fanfare in a commercial will trigger a response that
says look or listen. Further attention processing takes the form of determining the pertinence of the stimuli. This pertinence is related to the
need and values the consumers hold. For example, if you were thirsty
and beer was your kind of drink, you would find a beer commercial
stimulus pertinent, but if you were not thirsty and alcoholic beverage
consumption was against your moral values, you would undoubtedly reject the stimulus.

Being favorably processed at the attention stage does not assure
the success of the stimulus because it must still be comprehended, and
there are certain problems here in terms of misinterpretation of the
stimulus. Thus, for example, an advertisement by a firm for its brand
may be seen as one for a competitive brand by the consumer who subconsciously wants to reinforce a brand preference already held.

This information processing system will, of course, pick up many
stimuli and even store some of them for future reference. In the case of
advertising, however, retention of the stimuli tends to be low. This is
obvious when the importance of advertising stimuli versus others is
considered. This is one of the strong reasons for repetition in advertising: Repetition increases the likelihood of retention. For advertising, retention seems to be higher for brands that are already owned by the
consumer. Ask yourself how many advertisements you can remember
for your brand of car or stereo as against those for competitive brands.

PERSONALITY

Those psychological characteristics that determine how the consumer
will respond to stimuli in the information processing system are called
personality. There are a number of theories of personality. One is based
on *Freudian* psychoanalysis and suggests that consumers are motivated
unconsciously in terms of their behavior. By motivation is meant the
force that impels us to seek satisfaction of wants, needs, and desires.
Thus, to find out why consumers buy, it becomes necessary to discover
and categorize these motives. This is done primarily through projective
tests in which the consumers tell why others behave as they do in a
given situation, thereby revealing their own subconscious motivation.
(See Chapter 13.)

Social psychology suggests another clue to consumer personality, arguing that consumers are social (rather than biological, as Freudians contend) and that they are conscious of their needs and wants. Therefore, personality is based on the ways they go about satisfying them. This neo-Freudian approach, as in the Freudian approach, makes use of qualitative techniques like projection.

TRAIT THEORY A rather different approach to understanding personality is *trait theory*. Trait theory is based on the idea that people have inborn psychological traits and that the degree of these traits can be measured through questionnaires.

All these approaches to understanding consumer personality have contributed to the understandings of advertisers, yet none has provided the final answer. From an advertiser's point of view, understanding personality can provide direction toward advertising strategy, for if we know what motivates consumers, we can appeal to them in our advertising.

Communication is not just words, paint on canvas, math symbols or the equations and models of scientists; it is the interrelation of human beings trying to escape loneliness, trying to share experience, trying to implant ideas.

WILLIAM A. MARSTELLER, Advertising Agent

LEARNING THEORY

Advertisements are persuasive communication. Advertisers must therefore understand how people learn in order to "teach" them to respond to their advertising strategies. Learning takes place when the consumer alters a response or behavior as a result of some experience. Learning is made up of three components: motivation, experience, and repetition. Every time we see a commercial on television for a refreshing drink of iced tea, pop, beer, or powdered drink mix on a hot summer evening, there is a strong motivation to learn so that our thirst can be satisfied. It is also easier to have our message learned for hot chocolate when the weather turns cold. If the commercial presents the message so that it provides for a strongly perceived experience, learning is more likely to take place. Thus, when Nestea shows a hot and thirsty person drinking iced tea and then falling backward into cooling, refreshing water, the viewer can experience the brand benefit and is more likely to learn it. (This is referred to by behavioral scientists as *covert involvement*.) But even with good commercials, the experience can only be vicarious and is therefore weak in comparison to being able to have the announcer hand a glass of iced tea through the picture tube to the hot and thirsty viewer. Therefore, if advertisements are to be learned, there is a need for substantial repetition. It should be noted, however, that too much repetition can result in consumer fatigue as the message falls on "deaf ears." The advertiser can avoid this problem, however, by eventually changing the message.

Consumers learn to generalize from originally learned ideas. Therefore, advertisers will sometimes copy a highly successful campaign idea that has been well learned by consumers. The highly successful "Marlboro Country" advertising for cigarettes has led to "Ford Country" for automobile dealers and "Cadbury Country" for chocolate bars. Or the advertising that has successfully sold one product under a family brand may be used to sell additional products.

More frequently, advertisers want to use the knowledge of learning theory that shows that consumers can learn to discriminate between brands. Therefore, the promotional strategy may be based on positioning the brand (see Chapter 9) so that consumers will differentiate it from the competition.

In many instances, learning becomes so entrenched that a habit develops and the consumer buys the same brand without even being aware of the learning experience that originally led to the purchase. Under such circumstances, it is extremely difficult for advertising to get consumers to switch brands. To counter strongly entrenched buying habits, significant innovation and a heavy level of promotion are usually needed.

EVALUATIVE CRITERIA

What are the bases on which consumers make buying decisions? Advertisers must know these if they are to maximize the effectiveness of their advertisements. For example, in Chapter 9 we saw that Gillette discovered that consumers had developed negative attitudes about aerosol antiperspirants and had moved to a preference for roll-ons. But they disliked the "wetness" of roll-ons, and therein was the challenge and opportunity to develop Dry Idea. Even though some experimental products were more effective than the one finally marketed, they were rejected because the evaluative criterion of consumers was that if it went on *feeling* dry, it was more apt to keep you dry.

The study of consumer behavior quickly shows that not all people have the same evaluative criteria and that for any one segment of the market, these criteria may not be the same at all times and under all circumstances. Evaluative criteria are developed as a result of such things as personality, social factors, demographic factors, and market forces.

PERSONALITY FACTORS By the nature of the personality of some consumers, they are highly motivated to be the "first on the block" to try a new product. These innovators are frequently the market segment appealed to in advertising a new brand. As soon as everyone else is buying the brand, these consumers are looking for something new.

SOCIAL FACTORS Social factors also affect the evaluative criteria of consumers. These include the family, church, social class, and reference groups. For example, if at home you learned that the only good cake was one made from scratch, then given the opportunity to bake on your own, you will probably avoid cake mixes. On the other hand, you may be working and not have much time and therefore feel that you cannot bake. But your working friends all bake from mixes, justifying their behavior in terms of time. Therefore, you may accept a mix, especially when it is advertised as tasting just like one made from scratch.

DEMOGRAPHIC FACTORS   Probably the most frequently used basis for segmenting markets is to study the evaluative criteria of consumers as affected by demographic characteristics such as age, sex, education, religion, occupation, family size, and income. Since consumer evaluative criteria are often made as and for a family group, advertisers frequently look at the family as a dynamic entity, recognizing that the family changes over time. This has been referred to as the *family life cycle.* It can be divided into nine categories:

1. Bachelor State: young single people not living at home
2. Newly Married Couples: young with no children
3. Full Nest I: young married couples with youngest child under 6
4. Full Nest II: young married couples with youngest child 6 or older
5. Full Nest III: older married couples with dependent children
6. Empty Nest I: older married couples, no children living with them, household head in labor force
7. Empty Nest II: older married couples, no children living at home, household head retired
8. Solitary Survivor in labor force
9. Solitary Survivor, retired[3]

For products that are purchased for family consumption, such as food, drug sundries, and household equipment and supplies, it is therefore useful to measure demographic characteristics in terms of the family unit. In other situations, the evaluative criteria are for individual consumption, such as personal grooming, clothing, and hobbies. Here the demographic characteristics of the individual are important.

MARKET FORCES   Businesses and other organizations can also affect the evaluative criteria of consumers. Consumer advocates have made consumers conscious of safety factors in evaluating automobile brands. Environmentalists have affected consumer evaluative criteria for furs, automotive emission controls, and throw-away bottles. Through advertising efforts, businesses can influence consumer evaluative criteria by suggesting additional evaluative criteria for product categories. Thus, Minute Rice advertises that you get perfect rice every time because it eliminates conventional cooking.

To properly understand advertising or to learn even its rudiments one must start with the right conception. Advertising is salesmanship. Its principles are the principles of salesmanship. Successes and failures in both lines are due to like causes. Thus every advertising question should be answered by the salesman's standards.

CLAUDE HOPKINS, Advertising Agent

READER'S DIGEST

The consumer's evaluative criteria include an assessment of alternative means of satisfying consumption that is referred to as *attitude*. According to the classical model of attitude, attitude consists of three components: cognitive, affective, and conative. The cognitive component in consumer behavior refers to how information about the product (or service) is perceived by the consumer. That is, at this stage, attitudes are expressed as beliefs, opinions, or perceptions of the product—for example, "United Airlines is efficient and dependable," "Coke is too sweet," and "Miller Lite beer is less filling." The affective component refers to evaluations, feelings, and emotions. At this stage, consumers express their likes or dislikes. Examples are statements such as, "I love flying United," "I can't stand the taste of Coke," and "Miller Lite is my kind of beer," The affective component is closely related to the cognitive component. That is, feelings tend to be consistent with belief. Thus, if one believes Miller Lite beer is less filling, one is more likely to like this brand. The last component is conative or motivational. That is, it suggests the consumer's behavior, intention, or preference. Examples here would be, "I plan to take United to New York," "I always insist on Pepsi," and "I need some Miller Lite for the party tonight."

HIERARCHY OF EFFECTS   This classical model of attitudes led to an interesting and useful model of attitudes in advertising, referred to as the *hierarchy of effects theory*.[4] It was argued that although all product advertising is ultimately to produce sales in the long run, not all advertising can or does do this in the short run. This is true because consumers do not go from being unaware of the product to immediate purchase, for they must first hold certain beliefs, then have a liking, and finally a preference for the brand. This model depicts a hierarchy of six stages in the movement toward purchasing, and each two stages represent one of the three major advertising functions. (See Figure 12-5.) *Awareness* and *knowledge*, the first two stages, relate to the cognitive component of attitude. Here advertisements provide facts and information to establish consumer beliefs. Next, *liking* and *preference* relate to the affective component, with advertisements designed to positively affect attitudes and feelings. Finally, *conviction* and *purchase* relate to the conative component, and advertisements are designed to produce action through acquisition of the product. Through the use of this model, advertisers can set measurable goals for their advertising, such as increasing awareness of the brand (or a liking or a conviction) by a certain percentage. These goals can then be measured to determine the effectiveness of the advertising.

COGNITIVE DISSONANCE   Advertising may indeed be effective in moving consumers through the various stages of attitude until they purchase. But after purchasing, consumers sometimes question the wisdom of their choice. This is referred to as *cognitive dissonance*. There are postpurchase second thoughts that may be brought about by a number of factors, including competitive advertisements. In extreme cases, consumers may make returns or replace the purchase with a new

FIGURE 12-5

Advertising and Advertising Research Related to the Model

RELATED BEHAVIORAL DIMENSIONS	MOVEMENT TOWARD PURCHASE	EXAMPLES OF TYPES OF PROMOTION OR ADVERTISING RELEVANT TO VARIOUS STEPS	EXAMPLES OF RESEARCH APPROACHES RELATED TO STEPS OF GREATEST APPLICABILITY
CONATIVE—the realm of motives. Ads stimulate or direct desires	PURCHASE ↑ ↑ ↑ CONVICTION ↑ PREFERENCE	Point-of-purchase Retail store ads Deals "Last-chance" offers Price appeals Testimonials	Market or sales tests Split-run tests Intention to purchase Projective techniques
AFFECTIVE—the realm of emotions. Ads change attitudes and feelings.	↑ LIKING	Competitive ads Argumentative copy "Image" ads Status, glamour appeals	Rank order of preference for brands Rating scales Image measurements, including checklists and semantic differentials Projective techniques
COGNITIVE—the realm of thoughts. Ads provide information and facts.	KNOWLEDGE ↑ ↑ ↑ AWARENESS	Announcements Descriptive copy Classified ads Slogans Jingles Skywriting Teaser campaigns	Information questions Playback analyses Brand awareness surveys Aided recall

Model of the hierarchy of effects from Robert J. Lavidge and Gary A. Steiner, "A Model for Predictive Measurements of Advertising Effectiveness," Journal of Marketing, XXV, No. 6 (Oct. 1961), 61, published by the American Marketing Association.

brand. More often, consumers will attempt to rationalize their purchasing behavior by blocking out competitive advertisements and seeking out advertisements for the purchased brand so as to reinforce their behavior.

The study of consumer behavior provides advertisers with a greater understanding of the market and how people act in it. Consumer behavior can be a vital ingredient in developing sound advertising strategies to meet the objectives of marketing plans. Behavioral science, however, is not an exact science, and the fact that it can have holes poked in it by those who deal in more quantitative and statistically precise research methodologies should not diminish the importance of such research. *It simply means that it must be taken for what it is worth.* Insofar as it can provide advertisers with a series of broad generalizations that, when used prudently, can provide one more basis of effective advertising strategy, consumer behavior is a valuable and useful tool.

SOME CONCLUSIONS

TO SUM UP

For advertisers, it is important to know why people behave as they do. Research has provided some useful insights into consumer behavior.

Culture is a shared set of values of a society and will affect its response to advertising. Advertisers recognize that there are also *sub*cultures within the American society, which can be appealed to based on national origins, religion, geography, and ethnics.

People may be classified into groups having similar life-styles, values, interests, and behaviors and representing different social classes. Mass marketing and advertising is generally directed at the 70 percent of the population that is found in the lower-middle and upper-lower Warnerian social classes.

Individuals relate to a variety of different groups. These reference groups influence the person's consumption habits. Therefore, advertising may make appeals using particular reference groups in order to reach their markets.

Information processing refers to the way consumers deal with the stimuli to which they are exposed until the stimuli are used to make decisions. Personality research deals with consumer motivation and makes use of qualitative research methods. Learning theory involves the study of how consumers learn, so that they can be taught to respond to advertising and other promotional tools.

Attitude theory focuses on the process of how the consumer moves from brand unawareness to purchase. The best-known model of this process is the hierarchy of effects theory.

After purchase, some consumers have second thoughts, referred to as cognitive dissonance.

QUESTIONS AND PROBLEMS

1. Why is the study of consumer behavior important to advertisers?
2. How has the changing status of women in our society been reflected in today's advertisements?
3. How can a knowledge of subcultures be used in advertising?
4. Identify different magazine advertisements for different brands of the same generic product appealing to (1) the top three Warnerian social classes, and (2) the next two social classes.
5. In a current magazine, find several advertisements that appeal to reference groups through celebrities and through "common" people, and explain how they relate to the market.
6. Explain information processing and its relation to advertising.
7. Show how learning theory may be applied to advertising.
8. Explain how demographic factors affect evaluative criteria by consumers in making purchasing decisions.
9. Suppose you were going to advertise a new brand of ready-to-eat cereal. What approaches would you use at each stage to move consumers toward purchase? Follow the hierarchy of effects model.
10. What is meant by cognitive dissonance, and how can advertisements contribute to it?

ENDNOTES

[1] For more information on the consumer behavior topics discussed in this chapter, see Carl E. Block and Kenneth J. Roering, *Essentials of Consumer Behavior*, 2nd ed. (Hinsdale, Ill.: The Dryden Press, 1979); and Leon G. Schiffman and Leslie Lazar Kanuk, *Consumer Behavior* (Englewood Cliffs, N.J.: Prentice-Hall, Inc., 1978).

[2] Richard P. Coleman, "The Significance of Social Stratification in Selling," in Martin L. Bell, ed., *Marketing: A Maturing Discipline* (Chicago: American Marketing Association, 1961), pp. 173–75.

[3] Block and Roering, *Essentials of Consumer Behavior*, pp. 138–39.

[4] Robert J. Lavidge and Gary A. Steiner, "A Model for Predictive Measurements of Advertising Effectiveness," *Journal of Marketing*, XXV, No. 6 (October 1961), 59–62.

13

The Marketing Information System

After completing this chapter, you should be able to:

1. Define the marketing information system and its component parts
2. Differentiate between secondary and primary data
3. Outline the steps in a research study
4. Describe the three methods of marketing research

I n earlier chapters, we saw that advertisers and advertising agencies have a constant need to gather and interpret information in order to make intelligent decisions regarding their marketing and, more specifically, their advertising strategies. They want to know who their markets are and where they are located. They want to find out why and how consumers behave in the marketplace. They need information to prepare the marketing plan and the media plan and the copy for their advertisements, and to evaluate the effectiveness of their advertising efforts. This chapter deals with developing a system for gathering marketing and advertising information and using the tool of marketing research.

As business has become more and more complex and as computer technology has developed, information processing has become a vital factor in business success. This total processing system is called the *management information system* and pervades the entire organization. Our concern here, however, is with the problems related to marketing information in general, and advertising information in particular. As stated before, advertising is a part of marketing, and in most organizations today, advertising information processing is a part of the *marketing information system* (MIS).

There are four possible components in the MIS: internal data processing, marketing intelligence, marketing science, and marketing research. Not every organization having an MIS will have all these component parts.

From the internal accounting records of the firm there is a wealth of *internal data* on the advertiser's sales, costs, inventories, cash flows, and the like that can be processed through the MIS to provide valuable data for decision making.

Census data, trade-association data, and syndicated market data can provide a current picture of the marketing environment. Systematizing such data provides the firm with *marketing intelligence* inputs of great value. Other intelligence sources include observations reported by

MARKETING INFORMATION SYSTEMS

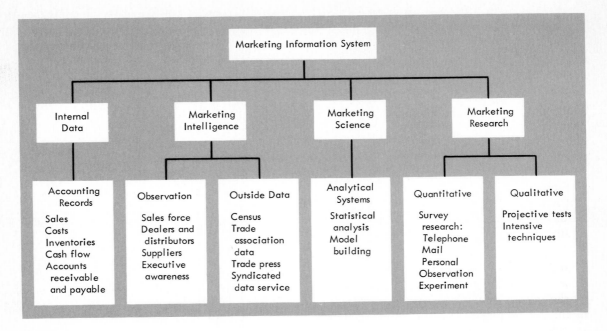

FIGURE 13-1

The marketing information system.

salespeople, dealers, and suppliers. Intelligence inputs, combined with internal data, provide an ongoing statement of what is happening.

Some larger advertisers have endeavored to develop a *marketing science* through mathematical models and sophisticated statistical analyses. These have been prepared to find answers to media planning, determination of advertising budgets, and appraisal of the success of new products on an ongoing basis.

When the advertiser wants to obtain information for a special marketing problem on a one-time basis, *marketing research* is needed. Such research can make heavy use of data collected internally, marketing intelligence, and marketing science models. The remainder of this chapter will cover marketing research activity.

THE MARKETING RESEARCH FUNCTION

Generally, the marketing research function is centralized in one location in the firm (sometimes as a part of the marketing services department) and one in the agency, to serve the needs of all the people in each organization. Although smaller advertisers and agencies may not have such departments, the larger ones almost always do. These marketing research departments seldom do all the research work themselves; they rely upon various types of outside organizations to supplement their own activities. How much of their own work they do varies considerably from firm to firm. In addition to the marketing research carried on by advertisers and their advertising agencies, a good deal of research work is also done by trade associations, advertising media, and government agencies.

Outside marketing research organizations are used for a number of reasons. For purposes of cost efficiency, it may be appropriate to have the research project done outside. (Of course, for smaller firms without any internal organization, this is a necessity.) Most advertisers and their agencies with research departments will farm out (also for cost efficiency) such work as field interviewing and tabulating to firms that specialize in handling these activities. Certain research firms conduct ongoing research of interest to a number of advertisers, agencies, and media. It is cheaper for a firm to buy syndicated research such as that of Simmons (discussed in a previous chapter) than to do the research itself and bear the whole cost burden alone. Finally, there may be certain kinds of research design requiring special skills or knowledge that is available only through external research sources.

There are two broad sources of marketing research data: secondary data and primary data. Not all marketing research requires original marketing information. There are vast amounts of information available to those who want it. Thus, in the gathering of data for marketing research, they are generally collected from secondary sources first and from primary sources second.

SECONDARY DATA   Primary data are those that are original and specifically gathered to get the information for the problem being considered. But before going to primary sources and undertaking costly marketing research, the firm should always turn first to secondary data —that is, information that has already been collected. There are two general sources of secondary data: internal and external. Within the firm there may be previously prepared research studies that can contribute to solving the present problem. The large volume of data from accounting and sales figures can frequently be of value. Sometimes these data are not in a useful form, but generally they can be reworked far more easily and less expensively than they could be gathered starting from scratch.

Externally, there is a considerable amount of secondary data available to the advertiser. Media studies, government studies (for example, census data), and association studies are generally available for the asking or for relatively small charges. Various previously described, specialized independent research organizations (such as syndicated services) carry on research that they will sell at a cost far lower than what advertisers would have to pay to get this information themselves.

Data collected from secondary sources may be sufficient to provide the answers needed by advertisers. For example, company sales records, *Survey of Buying Power* data, and information provided by Simmons may be sufficient to determine a target market for a new brand. In such situations, research needs have been satisfied, and it is unnecessary to go to the next step of gathering primary data.

SOURCES OF MARKETING RESEARCH DATA

ARIZONA

ARIZ. SRDS ESTIMATES	POPULATION—12/31/81								RETAIL SALES BY STORE GROUP 1981					
METRO AREA County City	Total Population (Thousands)	% Of U.S.	Median Age of Pop.	% of Population by Age Group				Households (Thousands)	Total Retail Sales ($000)	Food ($000)	Eating & Drinking Places ($000)	General Mdse. ($000)	Furniture/ Furnish./ Appliance ($000)	Automotive ($000)	Drug ($000)
				18-24 Years	25-34 Years	35-49 Years	50 & Over								
PHOENIX	1,618.2	.7005	30.5	13.4	17.2	16.6	25.7	598.3	7,204,212	1,728,413	624,994	863,648	522,579	1,479,298	237,962
Maricopa	1,618.2	.7005	30.5	13.4	17.2	16.6	25.7	598.3	7,204,212	1,728,413	624,994	863,648	522,579	1,479,298	237,962
Mesa	178.2	.0771	28.9	13.5	19.3	14.7	23.4	64.8	1,066,870	238,679	53,750	163,165	94,470	221,861	37,805
• Phoenix	822.1	.3559	29.7	13.4	18.5	17.2	23.0	303.8	3,395,677	753,501	382,231	426,575	247,711	695,424	121,131
Scottsdale	91.4	.0396	36.4	12.2	13.8	20.7	31.3	36.3	803,229	121,330	49,928	130,588	50,234	217,600	13,822
Tempe	115.5	.0500	25.9	24.3	20.1	16.7	15.0	41.3	672,426	201,790	80,453	53,930	53,786	150,810	10,154
SUBURBAN TOTAL	796.1	.3446	31.5	13.4	16.0	15.9	26.4	294.5	3,808,535	974,912	242,763	437,073	274,868	783,874	116,831
TUCSON	568.1	.2459	30.4	14.6	17.8	15.7	26.1	214.2	2,405,601	599,468	173,562	310,171	140,631	494,188	86,370
Pima	568.1	.2459	30.4	14.6	17.8	15.7	26.1	214.2	2,405,601	599,468	173,562	310,171	140,631	494,188	86,370
• Tucson	338.0	.1463	29.5	17.1	18.4	14.5	25.4	131.6	1,809,127	411,687	118,409	284,742	123,181	466,476	55,269
SUBURBAN TOTAL	230.1	.0996	31.9	10.9	16.6	17.6	27.2	82.6	596,474	187,781	55,153	25,429	17,450	27,712	31,101
OTHER COUNTIES															
Apache	55.8	.0242	21.6	12.7	14.8	14.5	14.5	13.8	71,564	12,819	4,209	23,296	331	3,255	2,169
Cochise	89.8	.0388	29.7	12.1	15.7	16.7	24.9	31.0	250,439	69,071	15,226	27,317	12,136	52,180	10,490
Coconino	79.8	.0346	24.0	20.8	18.6	14.4	14.1	24.0	339,643	80,449	39,451	45,599	13,428	33,138	5,334
Gila	38.5	.0166	31.8	9.7	14.1	15.9	29.6	13.6	121,699	41,505	10,730	7,084	2,830	23,186	3,076
Graham	24.1	.0105	26.9	12.4	15.0	15.2	22.6	7.0	65,697	18,668	3,487	6,021	2,463	16,258	1,817
Greenlee	11.6	.0050	26.5	10.7	16.6	15.8	20.0	3.8	30,001	14,722	936	2,231	1,852	2,070	1,398
Mohave	61.6	.0267	37.6	8.9	13.1	16.0	36.8	23.8	242,985	75,444	15,938	6,460	7,174	33,495	6,925
Navajo	71.6	.0310	23.3	11.8	15.1	15.3	17.0	19.9	231,129	68,790	14,671	23,986	6,423	22,902	2,505
Pinal	94.9	.0411	29.0	11.9	15.4	15.9	24.8	30.4	216,022	82,419	14,073	11,482	4,212	33,766	9,487
Santa Cruz	21.8	.0094	28.0	10.3	15.2	16.0	23.4	6.5	121,504	31,189	8,244	19,947	8,001	9,616	4,898
Yavapai	74.0	.0320	39.6	8.9	13.0	14.8	40.0	29.4	269,062	91,633	24,683	15,984	10,462	26,101	12,128
Yuma	95.2	.0412	28.8	13.6	15.1	15.5	25.1	32.0	360,797	86,607	29,433	50,112	13,541	67,986	9,823
TOTAL METRO COUNTIES	2,186.3	.9464	30.5	13.7	17.5	16.3	25.8	812.5	9,609,813	2,327,881	798,556	1,173,819	663,210	1,973,486	324,332
TOTAL STATE	2,905.0	1.2575	30.0	13.4	17.0	16.1	25.5	1,047.7	11,930,355	3,001,197	979,637	1,413,338	746,063	2,297,439	394,382

ARIZ. SRDS ESTIMATES	EFFECTIVE BUYING INCOME 1981							Buying Power Index
METRO AREA County City	Total EBI ($000)	Median Hsld EBI	% of Hslds. by EBI Group (A) $10,000–$14,999 (B) $15,000–$24,999 (C) $25,000–$49,999 (D) $50,000 & Over					
			A	B	C	D		
PHOENIX	13,757,446	20,225	13.3	28.2	31.7	5.1		.6865
Maricopa	13,757,446	20,225	13.3	28.2	31.7	5.1		.6865
Mesa	1,423,529	19,977	13.7	30.1	31.5	3.5		.0811
• Phoenix	6,883,741	20,115	13.0	28.8	31.2	4.8		.3387
Scottsdale	1,052,578	27,237	7.9	23.6	47.8	8.8		.0569

ARIZ. SRDS ESTIMATES	EFFECTIVE BUYING INCOME 1981							Buying Power Index
METRO AREA County City	Total EBI ($000)	Median Hsld EBI	% of Hslds. by EBI Group (A) $10,000–$14,999 (B) $15,000–$24,999 (C) $25,000–$49,999 (D) $50,000 & Over					
			A	B	C	D		
Tempe	1,103,822	24,174	11.2	26.1	41.8	6.0		.0565
SUBURBAN TOTAL	6,873,705	20,349	13.4	27.4	32.2	5.4		.3478
TUCSON	4,778,700	19,048	13.4	27.9	28.7	5.2		.2362
Pima	4,778,700	19,048	13.4	27.9	28.7	5.2		.2362
• Tucson	2,726,590	17,981	14.4	29.0	26.8	3.5		.1484
SUBURBAN TOTAL	2,052,110	20,960	11.9	26.2	31.8	7.8		.0878

FIGURE 13-2

There are numerous sources of secondary data available to advertisers. This is a sample page from *Sales & Marketing Management: Survey of Buying Power.* By permission: *Sales & Marketing Management.*

PRIMARY DATA Much original research to collect primary data would be almost impossible or terribly expensive if it were not undergirded with secondary data. For example, the data of the Bureau of the Census are indispensable to much primary research of advertisers and agencies, for they become the basis for sampling that is so essential to most marketing research.

If, after examining secondary data, the firm finds that it still needs additional marketing research, it must turn to means of obtaining primary data. The rest of this chapter is devoted to the ways and means of collecting primary data.

It is not the purpose of advertising to be remembered, admired, or liked. The purpose of advertising is to make the product remembered and liked and, therefore, purchased—even at the risk that the advertising will soon be forgotten.

ALFRED POLITZ,
Advertising Researcher

READER'S DIGEST

Although there may be some slight deviation in practice, there is a generally accepted procedure in any research operation. Essentially, it is the *scientific method*. The steps described below follow this method, but they are put in a frame of reference directly applicable to the needs of the advertising practitioner.

DEFINING THE PROBLEM   The first step in all marketing research, regardless of the method, is to formulate the hypothesis—a step referred to as *exploratory research*. It is an extremely important step in the research procedure, because an incorrect definition of a problem will produce useless findings. Marketing and advertising problems are usually rather complex, so after the problem is defined, it must be refined and subdivided to isolate the individual marketing research problems it presents.

INFORMAL INVESTIGATION   In order to isolate the individual research problems, an informal investigation is usually instituted. Its purpose is to help the researcher get the "feel" of the problem informally, through interviews with company executives, retailers, consumers, and the like. Additional information may be sought through readily accessible secondary data. On the basis of the informal investigation, the researcher will generally either decide to conduct further research or recommend that no additional research be undertaken.

DEVELOPING THE RESEARCH PLAN   Once the problem is defined and refined, the next step is to develop a research plan that will provide the necessary information for its solution. The first step is to determine the objectives of the research—that is, what is to be accomplished. The second step is to determine the specific information desired. Care in this task will prevent the problem of ending up with useless information. Step 3 is to determine the possible methods for obtaining the required information. (Some of the more widely used methods are discussed below.) Each method must be weighed in the light of such factors as cost, time, accuracy, dependability, and completeness. The fourth step is to write a formulation of the research plan in complete detail; the complexity of this written report depends upon the complexity of the planned research. This report becomes the working plan for the research. Frequently, it is submitted for approval before the research is undertaken.

SAMPLING   Sampling is one of the most valuable and essential tools for marketing research. As a result of the development of statistical techniques, sampling has become an extremely complex matter. To discuss it fully here would require more space than can be allotted in a basic advertising textbook. Nevertheless, anyone interested in advertising should have at least an understanding of its rudiments.

Stated simply, a statistical sample provides a means of drawing conclusions about the many (the universe) by sampling the few. The problem is to get a sample in which the few will be representative of the many. The technique of selection is *probability sampling*, by which each person in the universe has a known chance of being represented. Probability sampling depends upon "random" selection. Random selection is not to be confused with haphazard selection. Rather, it is a precise mathematical concept designed to ensure that every group, regardless of its characteristics, will be represented in a probability sample in about the same proportion as it exists in the universe.

In addition to this method, there are various other kinds of sampling techniques. The one to be chosen will depend upon the nature of the problem. In all sampling there is some degree of error. But the magnitude of error can be predetermined and controlled if care is exercised in the sampling procedure. Sampling error, however, is only a minor source of research inaccuracy when contrasted to other sources of error, such as improper definition of the problem or misinterpretation of findings.

TABULATION, ANALYSIS, AND INTERPRETATION   After the plan has been executed, a body of information has been gathered. This information must now be tabulated, analyzed, and interpreted. Tabulation involves the arrangement and presentation of quantitative data so that the reader can understand the finished report easily. Quantitative data are generally tabulated by machine, whereas data of a more qualitative nature require hand tabulation. There are six steps in the analysis and interpretation of the research data. These are:

1. Reviewing the statement of the problem and objectives of the research to be certain as to what is the purpose of the research
2. Separating relevant from irrelevant data and omitting those that have no bearing on the problem
3. Determining significant relationships in the data that bear on the research problem
4. Developing new combinations from the data whenever it is possible to do so and whenever such combinations are meaningful
5. Looking for unanticipated findings from the data that may contribute to the solution of the problem being researched or other problems faced by the firm
6. Organizing all relevant data in such form that it contributes to the solution of the problem being researched

PREPARATION OF THE REPORT   No research task is completed until a report is prepared and passed along to the appropriate people. A good research report communicates its findings in a manner that the recipients can understand, for frequently their knowledge of research techniques and statistical methods is limited. A good research report will contain a title page; introductory material (purpose, method, and scope of the research); a statement of the organization of the report; a table of contents; a summary of the research findings; the body of the research report; and appendices and supplementary material, if relevant. Illustrations in the form of charts or diagrams, for example, may prove helpful.

Three major types of marketing research are generally used to assist advertisers in answering questions and making decisions. These include survey, observation, and experiment. Each has its advantages and shortcomings. As mentioned above, factors such as cost, time, accuracy, dependability, and completeness must be considered in choosing the one to use. In some instances, sound research might recommend using more than one type.

THE SURVEY METHOD Probably the best-known marketing research technique is the survey method. Many people have conducted "surveys" among friends or classmates in order to get information. Usually these attempts leave something to be desired, for a survey is really a very complex and difficult technique if the results are to be reliable. This method is designed to secure information, usually by means of a questionnaire, from a sample of respondents representative of a larger group (although if the whole group is relatively small, a census may be used instead of a sample).

The survey method can be used to provide various types of information. One type of information is *facts,* like the number of households using liquid detergents, determined from a question like, "Do you use a liquid detergent?" Another is *quasi facts;* for example, the answer to a question that requires recall, as, "When did you last buy a liquid detergent?" (Because of the time lapse, the respondent may give misinformation. If questions involve personal situations or cause embarrassment, respondents may deliberately give misinformation.) Still another type of question tries to reveal *awareness,* or whether information has penetrated; for example, whether the consumer is aware of product features that have been advertised for a particular brand. Awareness can be determined by asking a question like, "Can you name a liquid detergent that contains [name of special ingredient]?" A survey may also be used to get *opinions,* through questions like, "Are liquid detergents better for clothes washing than powders?" Another use is for determining attitudes—for example, "In comparison with other brands of liquid detergents, would you say that [brand name] is better, about the same, or not as good?" The method may be used for discovering *future action plans:* "What brand, if any, of liquid detergent do you plan to buy next time?" Surveys may reveal *reasons* for choices, by posing a question like, "Why do you plan to buy that brand of liquid detergent?"

Surveys can be made from a sample on a one-time basis, or they can be made in a series with the same sample. In the latter case, the group surveyed is known as a *panel.* The major advantage of the panel is that it permits the surveyor to measure trends. Although a survey of two different samples at two different times may show an apparent change, the difference may indicate a genuine trend or simply a difference in the two samples. The panel, however, being the same sample, should indicate real trends.

The use of panels, although highly desirable, presents some problems. For one thing, a greater degree of cooperation is required of respondents when more than one interview takes place, and invariably some respondents will drop out of the panel. Another problem is the undesirable but unavoidable conditioning of panel respondents, who after a while no longer act as a representative sample but begin to concern themselves with the problem, which in turn affects their actions.

ATTITUDE SCALING   As mentioned above, surveys may be designed to collect data about attitudes. One way to determine consumer attitudes is by *scaling*. Attitude scaling in marketing research is borrowed from the behavioral sciences. There are a number of different scaling techniques, but basically they all involve respondents rating themselves on an attitudinal continuum. The basic scale is the *bipolar* scale, in which the respondent is asked to choose between two extremes, such as "good" or "bad," or "like" or "dislike." A variation of this technique is the *semantic differential,* in which the bipolar words are separated typically by seven positions, the middle one being neutral. Respondents are asked to mark the position that expresses their attitude toward the situation.

Another scaling test is the *Likert* scale, in which a group of statements is drawn up about the subject under study. The respondent is then provided with a scale of agreement-disagreement: (1) Strongly agree; (2) Agree; (3) No opinion; (4) Disagree; (5) Strongly disagree. The replies are then tallied by the number weight assigned to each. There are, of course, other techniques. The use of scaling devices is helpful in researching consumer behavior.

THE SURVEY QUESTIONNAIRE   Questionnaires can be used in three principal ways: by mail, by telephone, and by personal interview. Each way has its advantages and disadvantages. It is important that care be taken in planning questionnaires, because poor questions beget poor responses.

THE MAIL QUESTIONNAIRE In the mail survey, questionnaires are sent to a predetermined list of potential respondents. There is generally a covering letter explaining the questionnaire and soliciting the recipients' cooperation. Because some people choose to ignore questionnaires, a gift or premium is frequently offered as an inducement to cooperate. The major advantages of the mail questionnaire are many. It is generally economical. It provides an easy means of getting information from a widespread geographical area. It eliminates interviewer bias. It provides a greater possibility of reaching hard-to-interview respondents. It permits more time and more convenient circumstances for respondents to answer the questions. Through the anonymity of the mails, respondents may give information that they would not give in a personal interview.

On the other hand, there are some important disadvantages to using the mail questionnaire. There may be no suitable mailing list available to cover the universe the survey seeks to sample. Frequently, many of those on the list do not return the questionnaire and may thereby upset the accuracy of the sample. Complex or lengthy questionnaires are apt to discourage return. There is no opportunity for supplementing the questionnaire by observation as one can do in a personal interview. The opportunity for qualitative information is limited. Finally, misinterpretation of questions by respondents cannot be corrected.

THE TELEPHONE SURVEY The second type of questionnaire is given by telephone call to the proposed respondent, with the interviewer recording the answers. This survey is much like the personal interview except for the distance separating the two parties. The advantages of this technique are several. There is economy, because the interviewer saves the time and expense of travel. The interviewing can be closely supervised. A more complex questionnaire than the mail questionnaire can be used. It is possible to establish good rapport over the telephone. People who are difficult to reach personally can often be reached readily by telephone. Questions are asked and answered one at a time, permitting logical sequences not possible in mail questionnaires, in which all questions are seen at once.

But the telephone questionnaire has certain weaknesses, especially compared to the personal interview: It is almost never possible to get a truly representative sample, simply because not everyone has a telephone; telephone questionnaires must generally be kept short to keep the respondent from hanging up; and, as in mail questionnaires, there is no opportunity for observational information.

THE PERSONAL INTERVIEW A face-to-face interview is known as a personal interview. It includes the following advantages: The best opportunity is afforded for sound sampling design. Usually, more information can be secured during a single interview than through telephone or mail questionnaires. The interviewer can control the interview. Additional information can be sought and recorded. In addition to verbal questions, audiovisual devices of all kinds can be used to aid in questioning.

There are also shortcomings. For one thing, the personal interview is relatively costly because of the travel and hence additional time of the interviewer. There are a whole host of problems connected with the adequate selection and training of interviewers. Some respondents are difficult to reach personally. Interviewers are more apt to introduce biases into the respondents' replies, because they are generally required to interpret these replies in filling out the questionnaire.

PLANNING THE QUESTIONNAIRE The problems of wording questions and designing the questionnaire form are very complex, and only a few general points can be made here. Considerable skill and knowledge are necessary in planning the questionnaire if it is to provide information of value.

In framing questions, care should be taken to use simple and understandable words, remembering the characteristics of the sample. Conversational language should be used and ambiguous words should be avoided. Questions should be confined to kinds of information the respondent can supply. Questions should not contain more than one el-

Rosy Dawn. *In Jacksonville, the* Florida Times-Union *carried a personal announcement: "In Retraction to a statement made previously in this column, I wish to state that I am [again] privileged to be responsible for my lovely wife's debts. Robert A. Colson . . ."*

TIME

ement. They also should avoid eliciting generalizations from the respondent. Questions should be specific. Generally, leading and emotionally charged questions are to be avoided and provision should be made for conditional answers.

In designing the questionnaire form, the first question or two should be planned to establish rapport between interviewer and respondent. Early questions are best kept simple. Questioning should follow a logical order, but care should be taken that earlier questions do not bias answers to later questions.

As important as the form of the questionnaire and the nature of the questions is the preparation of adequate instructions for the interviewer, to eliminate bias. (In the case of the mail questionnaire, similar instructions must be provided the respondent.) Instructions should be written and designed to secure completely uniform questioning. In addition, checks should be made on field work to be sure that the interviews were correctly handled.

THE OBSERVATION METHOD This method of data collection involves either mechanical or human observation of the subject to find out what *is* happening rather than to explain what *has* happened. This method can be used alone or, as is more often the case, in combination with other methods.

Observation is used when no other method will provide the needed information—for example, in a traffic count for outdoor advertising. It is also used when there is a question about the accuracy of the information supplied by other methods. Thus, when a survey interviewer asks respondents to recall what magazines they read, the respondents may contribute to serious bias by not admitting that they read magazines considered socially inferior. With observation, however, respondents may be asked to show their copies of the magazines they read; this test reduces bias.

Finally, this method is very useful when a high degree of accuracy is desired and cost is not an important factor. The observation method has been popularly used for "pantry checks" (seeing what items are on the consumer's pantry shelf), "store audits" (physically checking movement of products through a retail store), and collecting data on television viewing habits by means of mechanical devices attached to sets in consumers' homes. (This mechanical "observation," however, indicates only what is on, not who, if anyone, is watching.)

Although observation is a valuable method, it has two shortcomings. It is expensive, because it requires being where the action is occurring; and, although observation can tell *what* is happening, it does not tell *why*. It does not explain attitudes and motives, although certain behavioral research techniques might be considered observational.

THE EXPERIMENTAL METHOD Experimental research involves experimentation under carefully controlled conditions to establish cause-and-effect relationships between variables or courses of action. The method is widely used in the various fields of science and is being used increasingly today in marketing research. Its chief value is that it provides a way to test the likelihood of success with small-scale risk before proceeding on a large scale.

Experiments may be conducted in the laboratory or in the field. The most widespread use of field experimental marketing research is in test marketing, in which a product is sold in a limited geographic area where national marketing conditions and activities are duplicated on a small scale. Not only the product but also all the marketing activities can be tested in this way. For example, three similar test markets might be chosen. In one area, television advertising might be used; in the second, print advertising might be used; in the third, perhaps no advertising would be used. If all other variables are held constant, the effectiveness of the different media can be judged. Or, using the same set of test markets, television advertising might be used in two markets, with each market using a different type of commercial or different selling proposition, and no advertising in the third market. For products already enjoying national distribution, it is still possible to test changes in marketing strategy experimentally. While a national advertising campaign is running, for example, new advertising approaches may be tested by substituting the experimental advertising for the national advertising in certain market areas and measuring its effectiveness. Laboratory experimental research is frequently used in copy testing. For example, television commercials may be pretested by showing them in a theater to a selected group of consumers to get their reactions. (See the next chapter.)

The major shortcomings of experimental research are its relatively high cost and the long time generally necessary to complete the experiment. Considering the value of this research, however, it may well be worth the cost and time in terms of long-run profitability.

The consumer is not a moron. She is your wife.

DAVID OGILVEY,
Advertising Agent

READER'S DIGEST

QUALITATIVE RESEARCH   Thus far, the discussion of research has centered on the *quantitative* techniques of measurement. That is, questions are asked whose answers can be quantified and tested for statistical probability. But there are some kinds of marketing information that the advertiser needs that cannot be quantified. That is, the advertiser wants to know how people think and feel. The advertiser is searching for subjective feelings and impressions instead of hard numbers. This is *qualitative* research, a relative newcomer to marketing research and a most helpful one. Peter Sampson says:

> Qualitative research is usually exploratory or diagnostic in nature. It involves small numbers of people who are not usually sampled on a probabilistic basis. . . . In qualitative research no attempt is made to draw hard and fast conclusions. It is impressionistic rather than definitive.[1]

Two kinds of qualitative research are used: projective and intensive.

PROJECTIVE TECHNIQUES   One group of methods used in qualitative research, projective techniques, is borrowed principally from psychiatry. The principle of projection is that even though people may be

FIGURE 13-3

Picture used in a Thematic Apperception Test. *By permission: The Chicago Tribune.*

Now I'd like you to tell a story about the picture, telling what's going on, who the people are, how it all came about and what will happen.

unwilling to admit their own feelings directly, they may do this indirectly in the way they describe other people, situations, or events. The techniques used to reveal these feeling are *indirect*; that is, the interviewer asks questions in such a manner that the interviewer's objectives are hidden from the respondent.

THEMATIC APPERCEPTION TEST One of the major projective techniques is the Thematic Apperception Test (TAT), developed by Henry A. Murray. It consists of a series of cards containing different photographs, paintings, and drawings. The respondent is shown a card and asked to make up a story around the picture; to explain the situation, the events leading up to it, and the outcome, and to describe the thoughts and feelings of the characters. The responses are then recorded and later analyzed. In adaptations for consumer behavior study, special illustrations are used that relate to the specific area of investigation. A respondent may be shown a drawing of a man grooming himself and asked to tell a story the picture suggests. A young man might describe a situation of somebody getting ready for a big date, but an older man might tell a story of somebody getting ready for work. The premise is that we express the behavior in the drawing in terms of projecting our own values and beliefs. Therefore, young people are more apt to think of personal grooming in terms of dating and older people in terms of career goals. More conventional approaches might not reveal the same information, because people are either unaware of their motivations or do not wish to admit to them.

OTHER PICTURE TECHNIQUES In addition to the Thematic Apperception Test, there are a number of other picture techniques, including the Paired Picture technique and the Rosenzweig Picture-Frustration Study (P-F). The Paired Picture technique is similar to the TAT, except that a pair of pictures is used—one, perhaps, showing a woman reaching for a

These women are talking about housecleaning. One of them just got married. She never helped at home and doesn't know about house-cleaning. What might the other woman be telling her about it?

FIGURE 13-4

Illustration used in a picture asso-ciation test. It is simpler in form than the Rosenzweig Picture-Frus-tration test. *By permission: The Chicago Tribune.*

package of butter from the grocer's dairy case and another showing the same woman reaching for a package of margarine. The respondent is asked to tell a story about each. Since the only variation in the pictures is the product, variations in response will reflect attitudes toward the product.

The Picture-Frustration Study involves a series of cartoons, each different, each containing two key figures with facial features and other individualizing characteristics omitted. The balloon above one figure says something that is potentially frustrating to the other figure, and the balloon of the second figure remains blank. Respondents are asked to fill in the blank, thus projecting their own biases into the situation. Ad-aptations of this technique for consumer research have proved very popular.

WORD ASSOCIATION TESTS One of the oldest projective techniques is the word association test. In the 1930s, such tests were already being applied to problems of consumer behavior.[2] Essentially, they consist of a crucial word or group of words, randomly placed in a list of neutral words. The respondent is asked to listen to each word and give another word as quickly as possible. The respondent's words are then analyzed for clues to attitudes and opinions. These tests have been used to study brand names and advertising themes and slogans as well as products.

SENTENCE COMPLETION TESTS Sentence completion tests are also widely used. Simply defined, these are partial sentences that the re-spondent is asked to complete. Consumer feelings, attitudes, and specif-ic reactions to people and things can be probed through such partial sentences as these:

The new model automobiles are _____
Television commercials are _____
A woman who uses lipstick is _____

INTENSIVE TECHNIQUES The intensive technique of depth interviewing is one developed by psychiatry using Freudian theory. It is the technique associated with the psychiatrist's couch, where the patient's unconscious mind is penetrated deeply through extended interviews over a period of months. The technique is nondirective, in that the interviewer remains neutral and does not guide the conversation any more than is necessary. Obviously, this technique requires much time and highly specialized skills. As depth interviewing is used in consumer behavior research, the interviewer minimizes specific questioning, although there are specific information goals in mind. The interviewee is encouraged to freely voice attitudes and beliefs, and the interviewer looks for important clues that may show up in remarks considered unimportant by the interviewee. In contrast to the typical quantitative research interview, these depth interviews usually last a long time. The application of this technique to consumer research falls short of its clinical use in that it is usually a one-session interview rather than a series of interviews extending over a period of months; the conversation must be "steered" to the subject of the research, whereas clinical patients steer their own paths; and the subject must be representative of some larger group of "normal" consumers if the interview results are to be meaningful, whereas the clinical patient's behavior is being probed to ascertain abnormalities. Still, it is used with some effectiveness in getting to the underlying motivations of consumers and probably goes beyond conventional fixed-answer questionnaires.

An interesting variation of depth interviewing, referred to as the *focused group interview*, works with groups and their interactions rather than with individuals. It is essentially a variation of group psychotherapy and takes a number of different forms.

PROBLEMS OF QUALITATIVE RESEARCH Some people are highly critical of qualitative research because *hard* generalizations are difficult when based on *soft* research that involves small samples and judgmental interpretation. Nevertheless, these research methods are helpful because they provide for a feel of the situation. Such research is often most helpful in an exploratory way for developing a basis for quantitative research. Because consumer behavior is so complex and deals to so great an extent with subconscious and unconscious levels of behavior, as was seen in the last chapter, these qualitative methods provide an opportunity to make advertising strategy decisions based on new understandings of the consumer, albeit with obvious limitations. The only thing that one can do wrong with using qualitative research findings is to assign them more value than they are due.

It should be noted that both observational and experimental research techniques and both qualitative and quantitative methods may be used. For purposes of understanding, the discussion of research techniques has had them separated and categorized, but in actual practice, they may well be used in combination, each helping to make the other more meaningful and relevant.

Whether you use secondary data, prepare original marketing research, or receive its findings, you should be concerned about the quality of the research, because bad research can lead to bad advertising decision making. The Advertising Research Foundation has set up a list of criteria for judging research results. Even if you are not a researcher yourself, the answers to these questions can help you substantially, for knowing how much weight you should place on the research will help you to make the correct advertising decisions.

1. Under what conditions was the study made?
   a. Full statement of the problems to be resolved by the study
   b. Who financed it
   c. Names of organizations participating in the study, together with their qualifications and extent of their interest, if any, in the findings
   d. Exact period of time covered in collection of data, with a statement as to the representativeness of the time period regarding subjects surveyed
   e. Date of publication of report
   f. Definition of terms used
   g. Copies of questionnaires and instructions to interviewers
   ḥ. Sources of collateral data
   i. Complete statement of methodology to be used concurrently with the findings
2. Has the questionnaire been well designed?
3. Has the interviewing been adequately and reliably done?
4. Has the best sampling been followed?
5. Has the sampling plan been fully executed?
6. Is the sample large enough?
7. Was there systematic control of editing, coding, and tabulating?
8. Is the interpretation forthright and logical?[3]

EVALUATING THE RESEARCH

The Advertising Research Foundation (ARF) is a nonprofit organization that is supported by advertisers, agencies, and media. It is organized to develop new research techniques and methods, analyze existing techniques and evaluate them, and set standards and criteria for advertising research. The ARF appraises published research and analyzes syndicated advertising research services. It also publishes the *Journal of Advertising Research*.

ADVERTISING RESEARCH FOUNDATION

This introduction to marketing information systems is meant to be just that—an introduction. For some it will have been elementary, serving only as a brief review. For others it will point to some basic consider-

SOME CONCLUSIONS

ations and developments in advertising and marketing research and perhaps will prompt them to look elsewhere for a more thorough grounding in this all-important facet of advertising. There are two vital points to remember: (1) Research is necessary to every step in the advertising process; (2) the techniques of marketing research are complex and require special skills. They are not for the amateur. To appreciate them is to recognize the need for highly competent and skilled personnel.

New techniques of marketing research are continuously being developed. They offer great promise of improving advertising. However, they are not the final answer to the problems of advertising. They are not a substitute for executive judgment; they merely help make those judgments better.

TO SUM UP

The need for information pervades the whole process of marketing and, hence, advertising. The total system by which a firm gathers marketing and advertising information is called the *marketing information system*. MIS has four components: *internal data processing* from accounting records; *marketing intelligence* from outside data sources and observation by salespeople, dealers, and suppliers; *marketing science*, through the development of models and statistical analyses; and *marketing research* of special marketing problems.

Marketing research is usually a function of the advertiser's marketing organization, but it is also found in most advertising agencies and can be obtained through independent research services companies, including some who syndicate their research.

There are two kinds of marketing research data: secondary data, which are data already collected in other forms, both inside and outside the organization; and primary data, which are collected from new research conducted by the research organization only after exhausting the search for secondary data.

There are a number of procedural steps in conducting a research study. It starts with the definition of the problem through exploratory research. This is followed by an informal investigation, which may suggest development of a research plan or abandonment. The plan spells out methods to be used to accomplish the research objectives. A sample of respondents representative of the universe is chosen. The results are then tabulated, analyzed, and interpreted. Finally, a report is prepared.

The *survey method* is the best known type of research. It may take the form of a mail questionnaire, a telephone survey, or a personal interview. The *observation method* uses mechanical or human observation of the subject to find out what is happening. The *experimental method* uses controlled conditions to establish cause-and-effect relationships between variables or courses of action, either in the laboratory or in the field.

The research methods above are all *quantitative* in nature. There is also *qualitative* research, usually exploratory or diagnostic, to provide the respondents' subjective feelings and impressions.

QUESTIONS AND PROBLEMS

1. What is meant by a marketing information system? Of what importance is it to advertising?
2. Why do firms with marketing research departments use the services of outside research organizations?

3. What are the differences between secondary and primary data? Suggest three sources of secondary data.

4. What are the steps in a research study?

5. Explain what is meant by the survey, observation, and experimental types of marketing research.

6. Differentiate qualitative research from quantitative research.

7. What is the basic principle behind projective techniques of qualitative research?

8. What is meant by intensive techniques of qualitative research?

9. What problems are there in using qualitative research?

10. Select an advertisement in a consumer magazine. What kinds of information might the advertiser have wanted in order to develop the advertisement? How might that information be obtained?

ENDNOTES

[1] Peter Sampson, "Qualitative Research and Motivational Research," in Robert M. Worcester, ed., *Consumer Market Research Handbook* [London: McGraw-Hill Book Company (UK) Ltd., 1972], p. 7.

[2] Dale Houghton, "Method of Advertising Evaluation," *Printers' Ink*, XXXII (June 1936), 18–20.

[3] *Criteria for Marketing and Advertising Research* (New York: Advertising Research Foundation, 1968).

Evaluating Advertising Effectiveness

After completing this chapter, you should be able to:

1. Appreciate the difficulty in measuring advertising effectiveness
2. Differentiate between measuring sales effects and communications effects
3. Explain the values of pretesting and posttesting advertisements
4. Summarize the various techniques of evaluation

Advertising is a most nebulous facet of business activity. Everyone knows it works, but it becomes rather difficult to spell out just how much and how well it works, although many researchers have tried to determine just that. The value of knowing the effectiveness of advertising should be evident at once. If we can measure the effectiveness of advertising, we can determine the optimum expenditure of advertising dollars necessary to achieve a particular sales goal. Thus, we want models and techniques that will permit *sales* evaluation of advertising effectiveness. But even though sales is the ultimate end for commercial advertising, individual advertisements and, indeed, whole campaigns may have shorter goals (as discussed in Chapter 12 in the hierarchy of effects theory), such as creating brand awareness, or brand preference, or the like. And here again, if we measure the effectiveness of advertising, we can determine the optimum creative strategy to achieve a particular communications goal. Thus, we also want techniques that will permit *communications* evaluation of advertising effectiveness. This chapter will take a look at evaluating advertising effectiveness in terms of *both* sales and communications.

Although many advertisers can and do conduct their own measurement of advertising effectiveness, a large part of it today is purchased from independent research firms that sell syndicated services. These firms are not mentioned here specifically, for new ones are constantly starting into business and old ones are constantly revising their techniques.

There has been a substantial debate over the relative merits of advertising *sales* measurement versus advertising *communications* measurement. Charles Ramond comments:

No controversy has wasted more marketing managers' time than that of whether advertising should be evaluated in terms of what it communicated or what it sold. The correct answer is *both*, for at least two reasons, one empirical and one rational.[1]

Ramond goes on to point out that studies have shown that advertisements have communicated without having sold, and vice versa. And rationally, although it is true that sales as a function of advertising cannot be isolated from other contributing factors such as price and personal selling, the same is true for communications, which are affected by word-of-mouth, brand familiarity, and the like, as well as advertising.[2]

The great art in writing advertisements is the finding out a proper method to catch the reader's eye; without which a good thing may pass over unobserved, or be lost among commissions of bankrupt.

JOSEPH ADDISON (1672-1719), Essayist

READER'S DIGEST

MEASURING THE SALES EFFECT OF ADVERTISING

Obviously, every advertiser would like to know to what extent advertising increases sales. To be sure, in a limited number of instances this is a relatively simple task. If you sell a product by direct marketing, for example, and the only knowledge customers have of your offer is through an advertisement, then the dollar volume of your sales would largely be a direct function of your advertising effort. Unfortunately, most marketing situations are not that simple, and there are many other variables that can also affect sales. This, then, has been the dilemma that some years ago led James Wallace to write, with tongue in cheek:

The demand for "proof of performance" of advertising has been fairly widespread and occasionally insistent. I sympathize with it.

Sometimes this demand asks for proof *quantified* in terms of sales or profit. Again, I sympathize—but that's about all anyone can really do, in a rigorous sense, at this time in history.

It seems odd to me that this widespread and frequently recurring demand for proof of performance is almost uniquely focused on advertising. I hear little of parallel demands for such measured proof with reference to other functions of business.

How do you answer the advertiser, when you know he cannot get as good an answer as he wants? How do you make him *understand* why he cannot have his measured proof?

It was against these uncomfortable questions that I came up with a "method" for defining precisely, either in sales or profit terms, the contribution made by advertising.

Step-by-step, here it is:

—First, make a list of all the working functions of the business (research and development, maintenance, accounting, sales, etc., etc.). *But do not include advertising.*
—To each one of the listed functions, allocate the exact amount of sales or profit which can properly be credited to that activity. —Add up the allocations.—Deduct the sum of these allocations from the known total of sales or profit for the business.
—What remains is the contribution of advertising.[3]

SALES-RESULTS MEASUREMENT TECHNIQUES Although direct marketing businesses minimize the number of variables that affect sales, advertising is not the only influence on sales of the firm. External factors such as competition, the generic product life cycle, technology, economic conditions, and societal factors can all have as much or more effect on sales than advertising. Additionally, for products sold through retailers, there are all the internal factors of the marketing mix for the manufacturer to consider. Still, for many such manufacturers, advertising represents so large a factor in sales that it is reasonable to assume that a cause-and-effect relation exists. A number of research efforts purport at least to show the effects of advertising on brand sales.

STUDYING CONSUMER PURCHASES One means of checking the sales effect of advertising is to check the purchases of consumers. A sample of consumers is taken, and the consumers are interviewed prior to the running of the advertisements to be tested. Data are collected on whether these consumers have purchased the generic product, what brand or brands have been purchased, how frequently the brand or brands have been purchased, and what inventory is on hand. After the advertisements have been run, these same consumers are interviewed again to determine the percentage of change in sales of the advertiser's brand. Not only does the information show the sales effects of the advertising, but this information can also be broken out by the demographics of the sample interviewed.

STORE INVENTORY Another technique is the store inventory check or store audit. Retailers' stocks are inventoried before and after the advertising effort, including not only the advertiser's brand but also the competition. Inventory checks are made every several weeks to check both the cumulative movement of merchandise and the trend of movement, which might be particularly revealing of the relative merits of each when a series of advertisements in a campaign is run. The inventories generally continue for some time after the advertising effort to test the longevity of the advertising pull as well as to isolate other factors that might have been responsible for the change in demand.

Retail store audits are syndicated by several firms. Field auditors check the sampled stores, say every two months, and take a physical inventory. To the opening inventory is added purchases (or warehouse withdrawals) less closing inventory. The difference represents sales for the period. The data may include sales by package size, inventories on hand, retail prices, and dealer promotional support and may be presented by geographic region, county size, and store type.

TEST MARKETS Test markets permit testing in the field where the respondents react under normal environmental conditions, frequently unaware of being tested. Even when they are aware of the test, the fact remains that they are still being tested under circumstances that approach normal conditions.

Test markets are generally used for new-product launches on a small scale before going national. In such tests, the advertisements and media strategies can both be tested. Not just single advertisements, but whole campaigns can be tested. The procedure involves making plans for the national campaign and then scaling them down for the test market so as to simulate the experience of the campaign on a national scale.

For brands for which there is no full-scale test marketing, *in-market testing* techniques can be used to pretest advertisements. For example, test advertisements can be substituted in certain editions of magazines, individual newspapers, and spot radio and television markets. A variety of different testing techniques may be used. One firm offers a system for measurement that utilizes a dual-cable CATV system and two balanced consumer purchase diary panels in three test market areas.

STRENGTHS AND WEAKNESSES. If advertising were the only variable, such techniques would provide a significant measure of advertising effectiveness. But because sales are also influenced by other factors, from competition to the weather, it is difficult to put too much faith in such data for measuring sales effects. On the other hand, once the limitations are recognized, such techniques can be a considerable help in planning marketing and advertising strategies for future campaigns. But if these techniques tell us anything about the sales effects of the advertising, they tell us nothing about the communications effects of the advertising.

EXPERIMENTAL DESIGNS FOR MEASURING SALES EFFECTS

Some major advertisers, dissatisfied with the available techniques for measuring sales effects of advertising and unwilling to settle for the James Wallace approach mentioned above, have resorted to experimental designs for measuring sales effects. A set of matched markets is chosen that would normally have the same level of advertising expenditure. For the experiment, however, the advertiser increases the advertising expenditure in some markets, decreases it in other markets, and continues the normal expenditure in still other markets in the set in order to provide for a control. At the close of the experiment, the advertiser measures the sales gains or losses relative to the changes in advertising expenditures. Two firms that have used experimental designs are du Pont and Anheuser-Busch.[4] These designs seem like the most promising approach to getting at the answer to the sales effect of advertising, but Ramond comments:

> By now it should be clear that there are few ways to evaluate the profitability of advertising or other marketing expenditures. The state of the art may be sound, but the art itself is costly and complex.
>
> Advertising experiments are expensive and tricky, yet they are often the only way to get unambiguous measures. They do not guarantee unambiguous results in those cases; they merely make them possible. For firms with large advertising budgets, their promise has outweighed their risks and costs. For these companies the ideological question of whether profit yardsticks are possible has given way to the practical question of the *condi-*

tions under which such yardsticks can be obtained and acted on to advantage.[5]

One of the problems of measuring the sales effect of advertising is that advertisements do not necessarily have sales as their immediate goal. By measuring the communications effect of advertisements, advertisers can determine the most effective means of advertising persuasion. This whole area of measuring the communications effect of advertisements is known as *copy testing* or *copy research*, although the concept is broader-based than the term. "Still anachronistically named after a variable which is but one aspect of advertising, copy research today investigates everything from the physical or mechanical characteristics of advertisements to the humor and sensuousness of TV commercials."[6] Thus, it should perhaps more correctly be called *stimuli testing*, but *copy testing* remains the term commonly used.

It is an amazing fact of advertising life that despite the high cost of advertising, a relatively small percent of advertising dollars is invested in researching the likelihood that the advertising message will be effective. In fact, advertising practitioners often argue that through years of experience, they have developed a sixth sense that tells them when an advertisement is a good one. Although there is undoubtedly some validity to intuitive judgment, it should not be trusted as the sole determinant of good advertisements, even with all the shortcomings of copy research. Therefore, it is foolish for creative personnel to disdain inputs from copy research when creating advertisements. Nor should research be a substitute for intuitive judgment. Instead, the two should work hand in hand. The various copy-testing techniques described in this chapter are indicators; they are not absolutes. The value of using them is in interpreting their meaning as an input into the decision-making process.

The safest conclusion is that copy research, like medicine, will remain an essentially clinical discipline, its best practitioners being those who have walked the wards long enough, mastered a few diagnostic principles, and perfected an effective bedside manner with their creative colleagues.[7]

PRETESTING AND POSTTESTING ADVERTISEMENTS The copywriter and art director think it is a good advertisement. The account group is enthusiastic. The client is in full agreement. But the advertisement fails in the one place it must succeed—in the marketplace.

MEASURING THE COMMUNICATIONS EFFECT OF ADVERTISING

Because it is not possible by judgment alone to tell if the advertisement will succeed, researchers have devised methods of pretesting advertisement effectiveness. Where should they start? There are some advertising practitioners who begin by researching the basic advertising concept before the advertisements are actually developed.

There are several different ways to evaluate advertisement concepts (not to be confused with *product* concepts). These techniques use qualitative measures such as those discussed in the last chapter, but they are not meant to provide hard-and-fast conclusions.

One technique is the *focused group interview*, in which alternative advertising concepts can be discussed to provide the moderator with a "feel" for the way to go. Another technique is to use *card sorting*, in which a series of respondents are asked to select from various possible product benefits (which could be used in advertising) written on a series of cards those benefits they believe are most important. After making their selections, respondents are asked to explain their choices. Although this technique might appear to be more quantitative, it should not be used that way. If anyone argues that such techniques are not valid, then the point of this research is misunderstood. The object of concept research is to *add* a consumer input to the creative practitioner's judgment, not to replace it.[8]

If pretesting of advertisements were an entirely accurate process, there would presumably be no need for testing advertisements after they are run. But pretesting usually does not provide conclusive answers. Sometimes it happens that an advertisement that has performed well in pretest research does poorly when it actually runs in the media. The reason for posttesting the communications effect of advertisements is to evaluate the advertisements under actual exposure conditions so that advertisers can ideally produce more effective advertisements in the future.

In both pretesting and posttesting advertisements, the effectiveness of the whole advertisement may be researched, or individual components such as headlines, body copy, illustrations, etc., or some combinations may be tested. The remainder of this chapter will consider the techniques of communications testing. Many of these techniques may be used for both pretesting and posttesting.

CHECKLISTS   Probably the oldest form of advertising evaluation, *checklists*, hardly falls into the category of scientific research. Checklists do have some value, however, if not to pick the winner, then to eliminate the loser. The technique is to make up a list of significant factors that should be contained in an advertisement. Responses can be of the "yes-no" variety, or they can be scaled. Checklists can be used by those responsible for creating the advertisement, or they can be given to a sample of consumers.

ADVERTISING RANKING   Two pretesting methods involve ranking of advertisements, either by comparing several different test advertisements or by evaluating one test advertisement with a number of others that have already been run. The two techniques that are used for print advertisements are *order of merit* and *paired comparison*. The object of the order-of-merit test is to have a group of consumers rank the advertisements from best to worst. The results are tabulated to show the combined ranking. The object of the paired-comparison test is to have consumers select the better of each of two advertisements. Each advertisement is paired with every other advertisement being tested. The result is an ultimate ranking of all the advertisements. A problem with both tests is that the panelist may be choosing an advertisement that is better than the rest but not really good.

THEATER TECHNIQUES   For pretesting broadcast advertisements —both radio and television commercials—the testing techniques discussed above would be cumbersome. The most popular procedure, therefore, is to obtain consumer reaction to the messages in a theater or studio. A number of research firms offer this service where test commercials can be evaluated.

Respondents representative of the proper universe are invited to a theater, where they are exposed to the commercial being tested in the course of viewing a television program.[9]   After the viewing, recall and playback measures are obtained through self-administered questionnaires containing attitude, persuasion, and diagnostic questions. The commercial is now replayed without the program context. Telephone recall several days afterwards is also sometimes used. The cost of such testing tends to be low to moderate. Although this technique covers a broad range of measurements in one test, it has not proved to be outstanding for any one of them. Respondents tend to be reluctant in providing sufficient information, because questionnaires are self-administered. They are also subject to the effects of theater-group interaction.

SHOPPING-CENTER TECHNIQUES   One of the shortcomings of theater-testing techniques is that what consumers say in the laboratory environment of the theater and what they do in the marketplace can be two different things. Therefore, another technique has been developed, called *shopping-center testing*, in which consumers' actual purchases are checked.

Respondents are recruited by interception at shopping malls.[10] There they are shown an advertisement (or commercial) in a program context or alone. Then they are questioned on what the main idea was, the credibility, the perceived effect on interest in the product, and what they liked and disliked. When the commercial is presented in the context of a program, an immediate recall score may be obtained.

PHYSIOLOGICAL TECHNIQUES   Physiological techniques of pretesting advertisements rely on what readers of an advertisement do rather than on what they say about the advertisement. The more commonly used methods of objective pretesting are the eye-movement camera, the psychogalvanometer, and Pupilometer.

Change of Address. *In Merrill, Wis., four independent truckers put an ad in the* Herald: *"Notice . . . . We are able to take care of our pulp hauling jobs even though we are now in the county jail . . . . Visitors welcome. Hours: 2 to 4 and 7 to 8:30 p.m. . . . ."*

TIME

Evaluating Advertising
Effectiveness
287

EYE-MOVEMENT CAMERA The eye-movement camera was invented by psychologists as a useful tool in remedial-reading projects. The first eye-movement camera was demonstrated in 1890, but it was nearly fifty years later that advertisers first thought to use it. Results of the first advertising testing with the eye-movement camera were reported in 1938. In these tests, a person sat before the camera and looked at an advertisement for fifteen seconds. The subject was not told how much time was to be allowed for looking at the advertisement. The camera photographed the subject's eye movement and recorded what spots were looked at and how long the subject looked at each spot.

Although the eye-movement camera is the only completely accurate means the advertiser has of discovering what people look at in an advertisement and how much they actually read, it does have certain drawbacks as a testing method. For one thing, the operational and time costs are high, and translation of data into understandable and practical language is sometimes difficult. Furthermore, the test does not indicate whether the impressions made by the advertisement or various elements in it are favorable or unfavorable. Still, the eye-movement camera is one of the few truly objective testing methods advertisers have at their disposal.

PSYCHOGALVANOMETER A psychogalvanometer is an instrument psychologists have used for many years to measure people's emotions and their reactions to various psychological stimuli. An adaptation of this device specifically designed for testing advertisements is the Electropsychograph, which is a supersensitive galvanometer. It is used to measure sweat-gland activity in the palm of the subject's hand. Electrodes are attached to the palm and to the forearm of the subject. A 25-milliampere current is passed through the subject, in at the palm and out at the elbow. When the person is "aroused," sweat-gland activity increases, electric resistance decreases, and the current passes through faster. Changes in the current rate are recorded on a graph. As the subject is exposed to various advertisements or various elements of advertisements, the subject's emotional activity is recorded objectively by the machine.

It takes a highly skilled expert to interpret the results of a psychogalvanometer test. After the test with the machine is completed, the tester interviews the subject and relates the answers to questions about the advertisements seen to the high and low points made on the graph by the machine. The graph accurately points up any discrepancy between these responses and the answers the subject may give in the subsequent interview.

The psychogalvanometer method is best used in testing advertisements for products about which people have strong emotional feelings, such as those that combat bad breath or body odor and those connected with such emotionally charged subjects as sex. Unfortunately, advertisements for food, staples, household cleaning supplies, and similar items have little emotional content for the majority of people, and the psychogalvanometer is of little use in testing them.

PUPILOMETER This method involves measuring dilation of the pupil of the eye by instrument. After the respondent's normal dilation is measured, the respondent is exposed to a series of test illustrations, and any deviations from normal dilation are recorded as each illustration is viewed. A major value in this technique is the ability to rule out bad artwork, which is too embarrassing to be talked about or about which people tend to speak in clichés.

None of these physiological techniques has won widespread acceptance among advertising researchers. Still other methods use brain waves, voice pitch, and heart rate.

INQUIRY TESTS Many advertisers measure the effectiveness of their advertisements by counting the number of inquiries each advertisement causes. These advertisements, of course, must contain some sort of offer to which the prospect can be expected to reply. In a print advertisement, such an offer may take the form of a coupon to be clipped and mailed or may be hidden in the body of the copy so that the reader must read the copy to find the offer. Broadcast advertisements also can be phrased to invite listener response. These advertisements should not be confused with mail-order advertisements; inquiries do not require the purchase of the product. Offers may include additional product information, sampling, or premiums.

As described, inquiry tests are a kind of posttest, but they can be used for pretesting advertisements when applied in a test market.

SPLIT-RUN TESTS. A variation of the inquiry test used for pretesting is the *split-run test.* It may be used for both print and broadcast media. Many newspapers, some magazines, and, through CATV, some television markets provide facilities for split-run testing. In a newspaper providing split-run facilities, for example, the advertiser can run different advertisements in alternating copies of the same issue of the paper. Thus, it is possible to compare two advertisements that have different approaches but make the same offer, each offer containing a key for identifying the advertisement to which the consumer is responding. Alternating copies of the newspaper are collated so that each of the advertisements will get equal distribution by neighborhoods and thus by income levels, education, occupation, and so forth. (This technique is frequently used for pretesting in one market; the better advertisement is then used nationally.) In the case of CATV, two panel groups of consumers with similar demographic characteristics in the same market are identified. Then, on the same programs, different commercials with keyed offers will be shown to each.

One shortcoming of inquiry tests is that they are applicable only to advertisements that can logically make use of an offer to arouse inquiries. Furthermore, the measure of the test is the number of inquiries received, a number that may not reflect the amount of interest generated by the advertisement in buying the product advertised. Thus, the offer may attract many readers because of its nature or value, but there may be little correlation between inquiries and readership or buying.

FIGURE 14-1

A sample advertisement from *Reader's Digest* showing Starch Advertisement Readership Ratings. (Original in color) *By permission: Oldsmobile Division of General Motors Corporation and Starch INRA Hooper, Inc.*

RECOGNITION OR READERSHIP TESTS   Readership tests are obtained by surveying representative cross-sections of people exposed to the advertisements. The interviewer approaches the interviewee with a copy of the periodical containing the advertisement to be tested. The interviewee is asked what magazines or newspapers have been read recently, and if the one to be tested is named, the interviewer brings it forth and asks the interviewee to thumb through it and point out the articles and advertisements that particularly attracted attention when it was read. Questions are so framed as to weed out false and inaccurate replies. Similar studies are made of consumers exposed to particular radio and television commercials.

Although these tests appear to be valid in testing readership when sound procedures are followed, there is no evidence to prove that any correlation exists between advertisement readership and purchase of the product. The advertiser can only hope that those people who remember the advertisement, as indicated by such a test, will remember to buy the advertiser's brand instead of a competing brand.

RECALL TESTS   Recall tests provide an opportunity of evaluating what a consumer remembers about an advertisement, after a time lapse of from 24 to 72 hours after exposure. The test can be administered in both *pure* and *aided recall* formats. In the case of pure recall, no assistance is given in identifying the advertisements; in aided recall, as the name suggests, assistance is offered, but not to the degree found in recognition tests.

Aided recall tests are helpful to the firm in determining how well its advertisements are pulling, compared with those of its competitors, and the extent to which ideas have been implanted in the respondents' minds. In readership tests, interviewees are shown advertisements and are asked if they remember them. In an aided recall test, however, the interviewee may be asked to identify an advertisement in which all brand identification has been masked. Another form of this test is to ask a series of questions, such as, "What brand of canned soup have you seen or heard advertised lately?" Caution must be taken, however, to be sure that the amount of help given does not exaggerate actual recall. These techniques also encourage guessing. Unfortunately, these tests do not indicate the influence of the advertisement on the consumer's decision to buy. Such tests also may be used for pretesting in test markets, mock magazines, and television commercial testing.

MOCK MAGAZINES AND PLACED-ISSUE TECHNIQUES A popular variation of the aided recall test for *pretesting* print advertisements is to include them in *mock magazines*. These magazines include the advertisements to be tested together with editorial matter and other advertisements. Copies of a mock magazine are distributed to a sample of consumers, who are asked to read the magazine. Subsequently, these readers are interviewed to find their reactions to the magazine. Questions are designed to lead from the readers' general impression of the whole magazine to their feelings about the specific advertisements being tested and which they recall.

Placed-issue testing involves tipping in copies of the advertisement to be tested into advance copies of a magazine. The magazines are then placed in homes of a sample under the guise of asking each participant to review the editorial material of the issue. The following day, the respondent is called in order to obtain information on how much of the test advertisement can be recalled and on how persuasive the test advertisement is.

TELEVISION Several research firms use telephone interview recall tests to evaluate television commercials the day after they are shown on television for both pre- and posttesting.

Advertisements are placed in regular television shows, preferably those with high ratings.[11] Telephone calls are made the next day to find program viewers and determine the percentage who recall seeing the commercial (total recall), can describe the commercial well enough to identify it as the test commercial (proved recall), and can describe the

BURKE INTRODUCES THE ULTIMATE CONCEPT IN TELEVISION COMMERCIAL TESTING... selector✓

For years, the Burke Day-After Recall technique has been recognized as the industry standard for evaluating television commercial effectiveness... for very good reasons. But we never stopped looking for ways to make television commercial testing better.

Now there's Burke SELECTOR.

At Burke, we have been measuring the recall effectiveness of television commercials for a long time, knowing full well that commercial recall is only part of the advertising effectiveness equation. While attention and memorability are very important first steps in successful communication, the bottom line of every commercial's success or failure is sales effectiveness. **Validly** measuring sales effectiveness, however, is no easy task. Other systems have tried to accomplish this, but have failed to provide the industry with **convincing** evidence that they are indeed measuring sales effect. At Burke, however, we have a unique opportunity. Adtel, another Burke company, provides us with a means for providing the kind of copy test validation the industry has been asking for. And we intend to do just that! That's why we developed SELECTOR.

Burke SELECTOR is a system that combines both a recall and persuasion measurement of a commercial's effectiveness with exposure taking place on-air and in the home.

The system utilizes a recruited audience for greater control, easier set-up, no cut-ins or cut-in

charges, and consistent samples that include working women. Best of all, the cost of a SELECTOR test is about half the total cost of a conventional on-air day-after recall test.

So make the move to SELECTOR. The **complete** copy testing system the industry has been waiting for.

Contact your Burke representative for more information about SELECTOR and our Adtel validation proposal.

Burke... **still** the first name in television commercial testing.

Burke Marketing Research

2600 Victory Parkway • Cincinnati, Ohio 45206

Offices in:
- Westport (203) 226-5400
- Philadelphia (609) 772-1394
- San Francisco (415) 937-0660
- Los Angeles (213) 393-0477
- Chicago (312) 693-0800
- Cincinnati (513) 961-8000
- Detroit (313) 559-8160
- Atlanta (404) 434-4100
- Dallas (214) 233-5755
- Louisville (502) 452-2472

Burke A Division of Burke Marketing Services, Inc.

FIGURE 14-2

A marketing research firm advertises a new television commercial testing method. *By permission: Burke Marketing Services, Inc.*

commercial but cannot specifically pinpoint the test commercial (related recall). Measures are made of recall, playback based on coding the respondent's descriptions of the commercial, and verbatim descriptions. When pretesting is desired rather than posttesting, the commercial is placed in spot markets by paying a cut-in charge, and the same methods are used.

SOME CONCLUSIONS

In judging the effectiveness of the marketing plan in achieving its marketing objectives, it is vital to know to what extent the advertising strategy has contributed to achieving those objectives. Although measuring the sales effectiveness of advertising may be difficult and imperfect, it *can* be done.

Not all advertisements are designed to achieve immediate sales results. In preparing those advertisements or future advertisements, it is important to know the communications effectiveness of such efforts.

Pretesting and posttesting advertisements can provide a measure of the communications effectiveness of advertisements.

The fact that testing techniques are not perfect should not prevent their being used, for they are meant to be not an absolute measure but rather an input into executive judgment in decision making.

Evaluating advertising effectiveness may be expensive and time-consuming. But the money and time are cheap enough when the greater likelihood of successful advertising as a result of this advertising research is considered. When the large investment in time and space costs for advertising is considered, the advertising research investment appears to be a small insurance premium to pay.

By now it is clear that advertising does not act alone. An advertising strategy that has been carefully tested must be combined with other ingredients in the marketing mix to achieve the goals of the marketing plan. Advertising is not an end in itself. It is a means to the end—achieving marketing objectives.

Although sales is the ultimate end for commercial advertising, individual advertisements may have shorter goals of communications. Thus, there is a need to evaluate both the sales and communications effects of advertising. Unfortunately, this is not easy to do because of the many variables affecting both sales and communications.

Pretesting of advertisements permits the advertiser to ascertain the likelihood of success of the advertisement. Posttesting helps in preparing future advertisements.

There are a variety of testing methods, from market tests of sales to advertisement ranking, theater testing, physiological measures, inquiry tests, readership tests, and recall tests.

Money spent on evaluating advertising is worthwhile despite the lack of perfection in testing techniques. They can provide one more judgment in decision making for advertising that is a much greater expense than the small investment in evaluation.

QUESTIONS AND PROBLEMS

1. Why is it important to evaluate the effectiveness of advertising?
2. Why is it usually so difficult to measure the sales effect of advertising?
3. Of what value are pretesting and posttesting of advertisements?
4. Describe the two methods of advertisement ranking.
5. How are commercials pretested through theater techniques?
6. What are the physiological techniques of copy testing, and how are they used?
7. What can the advertiser learn from recognition and recall tests?
8. How are mock magazines used to test the communications effect of advertising?
9. How can day-after recall tests of television commercials be used for pretesting them?
10. Select an advertisement from a current magazine and suggest the kinds of pretesting and posttesting that could be done for it.

ENDNOTES

[1] Charles Ramond, *Advertising Research: The State of the Art* (New York: Association of National Advertisers, Inc., 1976), p. 3.

[2] *Ibid.*, p. 4.

[3] James M. Wallace, "A Perfect Measurement of Advertising's Contribution to Marketing," *Journal of Marketing*, XXX, No. 3 (July 1966), 16.

[4] For details of these experiments, see Robert D. Buzzell, "E. I. du Pont de Nemours & Co.: Measurement of Effects of Advertising," in Robert D. Buzzell, ed., *Mathematical Models and Marketing Management* (Boston: Division of Research, Graduate School of Business Administration, Harvard University, 1964), pp. 157–79; and Russell L. Ackoff and James R. Emshoff, "Advertising Research at Anheuser-Busch, Inc. (1963–68)," *Sloane Management Review*, XVI, No. 2 (Winter 1975), 1–15.

[5] Ramond, *Advertising Research*, p. 106.

[6] *Ibid.*, p. 48.

[7] *Ibid.*, p. 52.

[8] See Mark Lovell and Jack Potter, *Assessing the Effectiveness of Advertising* (London: Business Books, 1975), Chap. 3.

[9] *Evaluative Pre-testing of Advertising* (New York: N.W. Ayer, n.d.) n.p.

[10] *Ibid.*

[11] *Evaluative Pre-testing.*

15

The Scoop Ice Cream Mix Marketing Plan

After completing this chapter, you should be able to:

1. Understand how a marketing plan is put together
2. See how the material included in Part II of the book is applied in the development of a marketing plan

I n the preceding chapters, we saw how advertising is tied to marketing and how it may be used as a tool to meet marketing objectives. It was pointed out that if commercial advertising is to be effective, there must be a plan—a marketing plan—that describes marketing objectives and strategies and the role advertising is to play.

This chapter presents an example of a marketing plan for a consumer product. The marketing plan for Scoop Ice Cream Mix is a hypothetical case that follows the design for a marketing plan presented in Chapter 7.[1] The advantage of using a hypothetical example here is that we can present *all* the pertinent data, much of which would be considered of a confidential nature by an actual firm.

It should be remembered that this example is only one illustration of the many ways firms may develop marketing plans. Each will vary depending upon its unique circumstances. Yet despite the variations in the format of marketing plans, certain basic planning must be included in all of them. These are presented in this example.

SCOOP ICE CREAM MIX: 1984 MARKETING PLAN

I. CURRENT YEAR'S PERFORMANCE

Scoop Ice Cream Mix is expected to achieve its target objectives this year of 2.7 million cases, representing $62.8 million in sales and $8.8 million in net profits. Shipments to date are 102 percent of sales goals.

It is of major significance that a competitive entry to Scoop, Admiral's "Confectionery Ice Cream Mix" has been successfully tested in the Kansas City area. The latest share for this brand is 2.9 percent, and trade sources indicate that it may be expanded nationally next spring. Scoop's marketing plan for next year assumes that this expansion will take place.

The 1984 objective of Scoop Ice Cream Mix is to obtain a 2.5 percent share of the retail ice cream market, representing shipments of 2.7 million cases and factory sales of $62.8 million. To achieve this objective, the brand will spend $10.7 million in advertising and $5.0 million in promotion.

	ACTUAL 1982	ESTIMATED 1983	PROPOSED 1984
Volume:			
Value	$49.7	$57.8	$62.8
Cases	2.2	2.5	2.7
Percent increase	+11%	+14%	+8%
Share	2.0%	2.3%	2.5%
Cost of goods	$24.9 (50%)	$28.9 (50%)	$30.8 (49%)
Advertising/sales promotion	$12.4 (25%)	$14.4 (25%)	$15.7 (25%)
Other costs	$5.5 (11%)	$7.0 (12%)	$7.5 (12%)
Pre-tax profits	$7.0 (14%)	$7.5 (13%)	$8.8 (14%)

1. THE MARKET

SIZE The total retail value of the ice cream market is approximately $2.2 billion, representing an estimated consumption rate this year of slightly over 1 billion gallons. No noticeable growth was observed this year over last year, although the market traditionally increases at an annual rate of about 1.5 percent. The static nature of this year's market is attributed to the cool summer experienced in most of the United States and to the increase in new types of desserts and frozen snack foods being offered to the public.

Competition consists of about 750 small regional companies, of which 15 account for about 65 percent of total ice cream production. None has a dominant position in the market nationally.

CONSUMER Although women between the ages of 25 and 54 having a household income of $15,000 plus with children under 18 years of age are the prime purchasers of ice cream, the prime consumers are the 7- to 12-year-olds (accounting for 50 percent of consumption) and the 13- to 18-year-olds (accounting for 30 percent of consumption). Consumption is universal among all socioeconomic groups, with consumption among large households being 50 percent greater than small households.

The appeal of this product category is strongest in the Northeast region of the United States and is weakest in the South:

	PERCENT POPULATION	USERS*		RELATIVE VOLUME†	
		%	INDEX	%	INDEX
Northeast	23.6%	25.5 %	108	29.7	126
Central	25.4	27.5	108	27.2	107
South	32.8	28.6	87	26.5	81
West	18.3	18.4	101	16.6	91

*Used ice cream in last month.
†Gross volume of distribution of ice cream tonnage.
Source: SMRB.

This consumption pattern is expected to be maintained next year.

PRICING The price for a gallon of ice cream can vary significantly, depending upon its quality. Average prices are as follows:

	1982 RETAIL PRICE/GALLON
Premium-price brands	$4.95
Medium-price brands	3.95
Low-price brands	1.85
Scoop	2.10

Source: Market research.

COMPETITIVE SPENDING Very little spending is done in this market except for short, periodic promotion and advertising campaigns in support of new flavor introductions. The annual advertising budget for the 10 largest producers ranges from $0.2 million to $3.1 million. Sales promotions on new flavors are typically 50 cents case allowances to the trade. Ice cream is essentially a commodity business, with sales favoring those firms offering the lowest price to the trade.

Projected on a national basis, Admiral's "Confectionery Ice Cream Mix" spending in its Kansas City test market is considerably higher than Scoop's. Introductory year one spending nationally by this competitor is estimated as follows:

	FIRST 6 MONTHS	SECOND 6 MONTHS	TOTAL
Media	$8.3	$5.5	$13.8
10¢ mailed coupon	2.2	—	2.2
Other promotions	2.0	1.5	3.5
Total	$12.5	$7.0	$19.5

Source: Agency.

FLAVOR VARIATIONS There is a slight movement away from the two basic flavors in favor of other varieties:

FLAVOR	1980 CONSUMPTION	1982 CONSUMPTION
Vanilla	50%	48%
Chocolate	20	17
Strawberry	7	8
Vanilla fudge	5	7
All other	18	20
Total	100%	100%

Source: Market research.

SEASONALITY Ice cream is consumed throughout the year, with the June–September period running somewhat higher than the rest of the year.

2. SCOOP ICE CREAM MIX

THE PRODUCT Scoop is a freeze-dried mix, made up in chocolate and vanilla flavors, which requires no refrigeration until it is prepared for serving.

Packets of the mix are sold in two container sizes:

SIZE	GROSS MARGIN
½ gallon, pack 24s	$13.00
1 gallon, pack 12s	$11.15

MANUFACTURING Production confirms that plant capacity is adequate to meet next year's sales objectives but that additional capacity will be required after that if the growth rate continues. Estimates are being prepared now on the cost and timing of acquiring this additional capacity.

PRODUCT RESEARCH Blind product tests conducted in May 1983 reveal that Scoop is preferred over all major competitive products:

PREFERENCE	TOTAL RESPONSE	REASONS FOR PREFERRING SCOOP	RESPONSE
Scoop	69%	Better flavor	61%
Regular brands	19	Better taste	76
No opinion	12	Doesn't crystallize	73
	—	Like overall quality	71
Total	100%		

Source: Market research.

MARKET RESEARCH Research conducted in March 1983 indicates that Scoop has a negative image in terms of the time and trouble it takes to prepare it for serving (58 percent of respondents) and that a significant portion of those housewives who have yet to try Scoop do not believe that it would taste better than regular ice cream (33 percent of respondents).

A special survey in the Kansas City area indicated that consumers preferred Scoop about equally to the Admiral product for the same reasons and to the same degree.

TRADE STUDY Scoop is preferred by all major trade accounts over regular ice cream because of its higher trade margins and because it doesn't need refrigerated space for stocking and display.

V. OPPORTUNITIES AND PROBLEMS

1. OPPORTUNITIES

Continued growth is anticipated for the following major reasons:

A three-year track record of sales increases in excess of 10 percent per year

A superior-tasting product

The brand's dominant advertising expenditures in the market, which exceed that of competition in any one area by at least 300 percent

Trade preference and higher trade margins which regular ice creams have difficulty meeting

Broader acceptance of the product by consumers, the March 1983 study reflecting a 12 percent increase in new users

2. PROBLEMS

Potential problems include:

The completion of test market activities on a similar product produced by Admiral and the anticipated national expansion of its product within the next four months

The marginal fall-off in repeat purchasers by older users, owing primarily to the time and trouble required to prepare Scoop

The continuing inability of technical research to develop viable new flavors other than vanilla and chocolate in the face of a consumer trend away from these basic flavors. Initial results of the latest new flavor tests appear promising, however, and progress is expected in this area before the end of the year

1. **MARKETING**   The objective of Scoop is to achieve a 2.5 percent share of the regular ice cream market, representing an increase of 8 percent over the current year in case shipments.

To achieve this objective, the brand's basic marketing strategy is to:

Position Scoop as a high-quality ice cream that children prefer but that costs less than regular ice cream

Continue spending in advertising and promotion at an A-to-S ratio of 25 percent to build distribution and trial and to preempt consumer awareness of the product category in terms of Scoop's superior quality

Spend more heavily during the warmer months of the year to capture new users during this period

Maintain a generally higher trade margin and lower retail price than competition in order to capitalize on Scoop's low-cost production process which refrigerated products cannot match without sacrificing quality

Invest more in consumer promotions during the summer to offset the anticipated expansion of Admiral's "Confectionery Ice Cream Mix"

2. **ADVERTISING**   The objective of Scoop's advertising is to convince mothers of children (ages 7 through 17) that their families will prefer the taste of Scoop over store-bought ice creams and that it costs less.

To achieve this, advertising will:

Continue to employ the proven success of the current theme, "Kids are crazy for Scoop"

Emphasize the superior, "home-made" taste of Scoop due to its exclusive freeze-drying process

Maintain the high recall demonstration of Scoop's lower retail price vs. store-bought ice cream

The brand's TV rotation policy will be to place 60 percent of its weight on the two new vanilla commercials and 40 percent weight on the two chocolate commercials. A new pool of commercials is being developed to replace the current pool immediately following the summer season.

3. **MEDIA**   Scoop's media are planned to reach the target audience of women between 25 and 54 having a household income of $15,000 plus with children under 18 years of age.

Television will continue to be the brand's major medium, as it:

Has the ability to build high levels of target reach within a relatively short period of time

Affords the opportunity of "targeting" against a specific population segment while delivering impressions against a secondary audience, children under 18

Has the ability to demonstrate, create appetite appeal, and show package to build brand identity

Is the primary medium of Scoop competitors. Offers a merchandisable commodity to use in presenting to the trade

Print is recommended to complement the television effort by:

Increasing reach against the light television viewer

Offering readers the opportunity of a lengthy, leisurely examination of the advertising copy

Providing a visual presentation of the product and especially product packaging to build brand awareness

Offering a vehicle for couponing to stimulate trial

Providing merchandisability to the trade

Next year's strategy is designed to meet the competition from Admiral in the Kansas City area by adding that market to the Group A markets for spot television and scheduling television to begin in February for network and Group A spot markets.

4. SALES PROMOTION Scoop's sales promotion objective is to develop a strong position in trade merchandising—i.e., in-store displays and advertising features, especially during the high-consumption season. To achieve this, the brand's strategy is to:

Maintain trade margins generally above that of regular ice cream brands by responding instantly with case allowances to match that of major new flavor introductions by competition

Offer two display allowances averaging $1.10 per case during the periods of May–June and July–August

Conduct two national consumer-oriented promotions, one in May–June and the other in July–August, involving premiums for children

Total planned sales promotion expenditures will be allocated by sales regions as follows:

	NORTH	SOUTH	CENTRAL	WEST
Dollars per case:				
Current year	$1.55	$2.25	$2.15	$1.60
Next year	1.30	2.15	2.05	1.65
Percent in trade deals:				
Current year	46%	60%	55%	51%
Next year	40	53	50	47

1. Blind product tests of three new flavors:	$150,000
2. Sales district test of a mailed sample:	$300,000
3. District test of free coupon packed in ½-gallon sizes and good on gallon sizes:	$60,000
4. Media-mix test	$85,000

EXHIBITS: 1984 MARKETING PLAN

Scoop Ice Cream Mix   Profit and Loss Statement   1984 Budget (in millions)

	PREVIOUS YEAR	(PERCENT SALES)	CURRENT YEAR	(PERCENT SALES)	NEW YEAR	(PERCENT SALES)
1. Total market:						
Value	$2,170.0		$2,170.0		$2,200.0	
Cases	—		—		—	
Percent increase/ decrease	1.3%		—		1.5%	
2. Brand share	2.0%		2.3%		2.5%	
3. Brand shipments:						
Value	$49.7	100%	$57.8	100%	$62.8	100%
Cases	2.2	—	2.5	—	2.7	—
Percent increase/cases	11%	—	14%	—	8 %	—
4. Cost of goods:						
Fixed cost	$21.4	43%	$21.9	38%	$23.3	37%
Variable costs	3.5	7%	7.0	12%	7.5	12%
Total costs	$24.9	50%	$28.9	50%	$30.8	49%
5. Gross margin:	$24.9	50%	$28.9	50%	$32.0	51%
6. Marketing expenses:						
Media/production	$6.9	14%	$8.5	15%	9.4	15%
Advertising reserve	0.5	1%	0.2	—	0.6	1%
Sampling/couponing	2.9	6%	2.3	4%	0.0	—
Trade allowance	1.5	3%	2.3	4%	1.9	3%
Other promotions	0.5	1%	1.1	2%	3.8	6%
Total marketing expenses	$12.4	25%	$14.4	25%	$15.7	25%
7. Other expenses:						
Market research	$0.2	—	$0.2	—	$0.6	1%
Sales force cost	2.4	5%	3.4	6%	3.1	5%
Distribution cost	2.0	4%	2.3	4%	2.5	4%
Administration	0.9	2%	1.1	2%	1.3	2%
Miscellaneous income and expense	—	—	—	—	—	—
Total other expenses	$5.5	11%	7.0	12%	7.5	12%
8. Profit contribution	$7.0	14%	$7.5	13%	$8.8	14%
Increase/decrease	5.5%		7.2%		17.4%	

Scoop Ice Cream Mix   Price and Profit Structure   1984 Budget

	MEDIUM	LARGE	AVERAGE PER STATISTICAL CASE
Packed	24 s	12 s	
Unit	½ gal.	gal.	
Unit retail price	$1.15	$2.10	$1,625
Retail price/case	$27.60	$25.20	$26.40
Manufacturer's price/case	24.00	21.15	23.26
Percent trade margin	15%	19.2%	13.6%

(*Continued on page 305*)

Scoop Ice Cream Mix   Sales Promotion Spread Sheet   1981 Budget

	JAN.	FEB.	MAR.	1ST QTR.	APRIL	MAY	JUNE
Region-Northeast							
Shipments	33	42	50	125	75	92	100
Type of promotion	—	—	—	—	—	$1.10 per case and premium	$1.10 per case and premium
Promotion cost	—	—	—	—	—	$350	$385
Region-South							
Shipments	18	21	25	62	38	46	50
Type of promotion	—	—	—	—	Free coupon test	$1.10 per case and premium	$1.10 per case and premium
Promotion cost	—	—	—	—	$100	$175	$190
Region-Central							
Shipments	21	28	33	82	51	61	66
Type of promotion	—	—	—	—	—	$1.10 per case and premium	$1.10 per case and premium
Promotion cost	—	—	—	—	—	$245	$270
Region-West							
Shipments	30	34	42	106	61	76	84
Type of promotion	—	—	—	—	Mail sample test	$1.10 per case and premium	$1.10 per case and premium
Promotion cost	—	—	—	—	$100	$230	$255
Total shipments	100	125	150	375	225	275	300
Percent of year	3.7%	4.6%	5.5%	13.8%	8.3%	10.2%	11.2%
Total cost	—	—	—	—	$200	$1,000	$1,100
Percent of year	—	—	—	—	4%	20%	22%
Cost per case	—	—	—	—	$.88	$3.64	$3.66

	MEDIUM	LARGE	AVERAGE PER STATISTICAL CASE
Cost per case	$11.00	$10.00	$11.40
Gross margin/case	13.00	11.15	11.86
Percent of mfr's. price/case	54.0%	52.7%	51.0%
Est. case shipments (000)	2,000.0	700.0	2,700.0
Total sales value	$48,000.0	$14,800.0	$62,800.0
Total profit margin	6,680.0	2,120.0	8,800.0
Percent of total sales value	13.9%	14.2%	14.0%

2ND QTR.	1ST HALF	JULY	AUG.	SEPT.	3RD QTR.	OCT.	NOV.	DEC.	4TH QTR.	TOTAL YEAR
267	392	116	125	100	341	83	50	34	167	900
—	—	$1.10 per case and premium	$1.10 per case and premium	—	—	—	—	—	—	—
$735	$735	$455	$490	—	$945	—	—	—	—	$1,680
134	196	58	62	50	170	42	25	17	84	450
—	—	$1.10 per case and premium	$1.10 per case and premium	—	—	—	—	—	—	—
$465	$465	$255	$24	$465	—	—	—	—	—	$930
178	260	77	83	67	227	56	33	24	113	600
—	—	$1.10 per case and premium	$1.10 per case and premium	—	—	—	—	—	—	—
$515	$515	$315	$340	$655	—	—	—	—	—	$1,170
221	327	99	105	83	287	69	42	25	136	750
—	—	$1.10 per case and premium	$1.10 per case and premium	—	—	—	—	—	—	—
$585	$585	$305	$330	$635	—	—	—	—	—	$1,220
800	1,175	350	375	300	1,025	250	150	100	500	2,700
29.7%	43.5%	13.0%	13.8%	11.2%	38.0%	9.3%	5.5%	3.7%	18.5%	100%
$2,300	$2,300	$1,300	$1,400	—	$2,700	—	—	—	—	$5,000
46%	46%	26%	28%	—	54%	—	—	—	—	100%
$2.87	$1.96	$3.71	$3.73	—	$2.63	—	—	—	—	$1.85

Scoop Ice Cream Mix
Marketing Plan

	1983 CURRENT YEAR		1984 NEW YEAR		DIFFERENCE ±000
	(000)	%	(000)	%	
I. NATIONAL EXPENDITURES					
Television:					
Network TV	$2,132	22%	$1,988	18%	$ −144
Spot TV	4,324	45	5,155	48	+831
Cable TV	—	—	270	3	+270
Production	300	3	164	2	−136
Total TV	$6,756	70%	$7,577	71%	$ +821
Print:					
Magazines	$1,268	13%	$1,178	11%	$ −90
Newspapers	888	9	1195	11	+307
Supplements	716	7	641	6	−75
Preparation	89	1	82	1	−7
Total print	$2,961	30%	$3,096	29%	$ +135
Other media	$ —	—%	$ —	—%	$ —
Total media expenditures	$9,702	100%	10,672	100%	$ +970

	1ST QTR.	2ND QTR.	3RD QTR.	4TH QTR.	TOTAL
II. QUARTERLY EXPENDITURES					
Television	$736	$2,574	$3,426	$677	$7,413
Print	163	993	1,475	382	3,013
Other	—	—	—	—	—
Total working media	$899	$3,567	$4,901	$1,059	$10,426
Percent of year	9%	34%	47%	10%	100%
Planned shipments (000)	375	800	1025	500	2,700
Percent of year	14%	30%	38%	18%	100%

QUESTIONS AND PROBLEMS

1. How would you evaluate the strategy suggested in the marketing plan?
2. What bearing do the profit and loss data have on the advertising strategy in the plan?
3. Can you suggest any marketing intelligence that was not included but that might have been useful?
4. What ingredients of the marketing mix have been included, and how are they interrelated?
5. If you were the chief executive officer of the firm, would you have accepted this plan?

ENDNOTE

[1] Adapted from E. Beaven Ennis *Effective Marketing Management* (New York: Association of National Advertisers, Inc., 1973), pp. 21–32. I am especially indebted to Herbert Ahlgren, vice-president of the Association of National Advertisers, for permission to adapt this material.

16

Advertising Media Planning

After completing this chapter, you should be able to:

1. Identify those who are involved in the planning and scheduling of media
2. Suggest sources of advertising media data
3. Summarize the factors in media decision making
4. Explain the various considerations involved in media scheduling

In order for the advertising message to reach the prospect, it needs some communications carrier. These carriers are called advertising *media* (or in the singular, *medium*). A particular advertising medium is also referred to as a *vehicle*. Advertisers can produce their own medium, such as direct advertising (broadsides, catalogs, and handbills, for example) or point-of-purchase advertising (for instance, signs, posters, or displays). Or advertisers can make use of the various commercial mass communications media, including newspapers, magazines (both consumer and business publications), television, radio, out-of-home media (outdoor and transit), directories, and films.

Some people may look upon media planning and selection as rather mechanical and matter of fact, but in fact, they can be as creative a part of advertising as copywriting and art. The success of any advertising effort depends as much upon the medium as the message. The mechanical part of the media function is likely to be as routine as any record-keeping or housekeeping operation. But the planning and selection of the right media to match the advertiser's marketing objectives as delineated in the marketing plan can be both an imaginative and a rewarding endeavor. It is also a vital one, because the greatest portion of all advertising dollars is spent on media.

Media are dynamic. Over the years, new advertising media have appeared—some successful, others not. Radio brought the voice of the advertiser into the American home and became the glamorous medium during the 1930s and 1940s. Then, after World War II, a new medium—television—took the limelight to revolutionize the American way of life in many ways and become a major advertising medium. But the older media have not remained static. Newspapers developed run-of-paper color for advertisers. Magazines, once thought to be strictly national media, developed regional editions. And every so often, someone comes up with a new advertising medium idea—from skywriting to Beetle Boards (advertising painted on the bodies of privately owned Volkswagen Beetles).

In the late 1890s, advertisers became possessed with a craze for presenting messages where the public would least expect to find them. Bald-headed men were seated in the front row of a theater, each with one letter of a famous trade name painted on his shining dome. Processions of costumed advertising characters paraded the avenues. Sign wagons, ringing bells and drawn by mules, dogs, or ostriches, toured the residential areas of a city. At the circus, space was sold on the side of elephants and camels. Clowns made vocal announcements. Men with carts on which phonographs were mounted played music and gave selling spiels. At night, slide projection apparatus was used to throw captions and pictures on the screen of low-hanging clouds. Surprised patrons of barbershops looked up from their semireclined chairs to find advertising messages on the barber-shop ceiling. Sailboats cruised back and forth in front of crowded bathing beaches with signs painted on their sails. Fans and canvas caps were distributed for advertising at parades and picnics. Free advertising postcards, some of them perfumed, were handed out to willing takers. The John H. Woodbury soap company started the "Facial Purity League," with buttons for all its members. Soon buttons became a nation-wide fad; decorated with all kinds of slang phrases and jokes, they blossomed out on the lapels of men, women, and children everywhere. Advertising rhymes and jingles earned equal popularity. Sheet music for advertising songs was distributed. Trading stamps were issued by department stores with each purchase and by saloons with each drink. They became so widely accepted that for a time they were practically legal tender. Counterfeiters even imitated them.[1]

Many of the novelty media come and go quickly, and even the more stable media are constantly undergoing change. At the same time, the product, competition, and market continue to change, so that each new advertising campaign requires a new look at media and the media plan.

The basic problem of media selection is choosing media that reach the markets or market segments the advertiser is trying to sell. Accomplishing this involves, broadly speaking, three steps or decisions. First, the general type or types of media must be decided upon. That is, should the advertiser use newspapers, magazines, television, and so forth, or a combination of these? Second, a decision must be made as to the class of media within a particular medium type. For example, if the advertiser decides upon magazines, should women's magazines or home magazines be used? If television is decided upon, should network or local spots be used? And should the commercial be placed in the format of news, drama, variety, or music? Third, the particular medium must be decided upon. In the case of women's magazines, should it be *McCall's,* or the *Ladies' Home Journal,* or *Good Housekeeping,* or some combination of these? For network television, should it be "As the World Turns," "Cheers," or "NFL Football"?

The number of possible choices and combinations makes this no simple task. But even more important is the complexity of the problem behind media selection—the marketing plan itself.

SELECTING ADVERTISING MEDIA

THE ORGANIZATIONS INVOLVED IN MEDIA PLANNING

Although the advertiser has an obvious stake in media plan and must ultimately approve, modify, or reject it, the bulk of media work is generally done by the advertising agency, media buying services, and the media. In the advertising agency, the media planning and buying function is delegated to the media department. In the media, the selling of space and time is delegated to the medium's advertising department and its sales force.

THE MEDIA DEPARTMENT In the smaller advertising agency, the media department functions primarily in the capacity of media buyer, with the account executive largely responsible for media planning. In the large agency, both planning and buying are the responsibility of the media department. Such a department is typically headed by a director of media, with a number of associate directors (or supervisors) and media buyers. The associate directors in a large agency are responsible for the media plan. Generally, each is assigned to one or more accounts; if

FIGURE 16-1

There is no end to the possibilities of media to reach specific markets, and they are not limited to the "major media." This advertisement in the business press suggests a unique medium to reach a highly selective and important market. *By permission: The Directory of Classes published by University Communications Inc.*

WHAT EVERY COLLEGE STUDENT NEEDS BESIDES MORE MONEY FROM HOME.

If you think college kids are lost now, imagine what it would be like without us.

The Directory of Classes. We're the official publication on over 65 campuses nationwide, serving over 1.7 million readers* three times a year.

We're must reading. Literally. Our book lists all the class schedules, registration information, times, dates, places. Without it, your typical European History major could very well end up spending his days knee deep in Feminist Literature.

You wouldn't want that. Neither would Toyota, Honda, Kawasaki, Pioneer, Hewlett Packard, Bose, the U.S. Navy, Teac, Suzuki, Kenwood and all the other big guys who advertise in the Directory regularly.

They tie in their national stuff with local dealer ads in our back-of-the-book Shopper's Guide. They read with great care our National Student Survey that questions 2000 respondents on product and buying attitudes annually.

Playboy's terrific. National Lampoon's a blast. But they're like textbooks. No college student has to even look at them.

They have to look at the Directory of Classes.

That's why, if you're buying the college market, so do you.

THE DIRECTORY OF CLASSES.

1.7 million college students. Guaranteed.

Publisher: Doug Bornstein, P.O. Box 1234, Rahway, N.J. 07065, (201) 382-6161 • In the EAST COAST contact Jeffrey Richard Associates, 310 East 44th, Suite 17108, N.Y., N.Y 10017, (212) 687-6036 • MIDWEST contact the Pattis Group, 4761 W Touhy Avenue, Lincolnwood, Illinois 60646, (312) 679-1100 WEST COAST contact Lowell Fox & Associates, 16200 Ventura Boulevard, Encino, California 91436, (213) 990-2950 *Publisher's statement.

ADVERTISING MEDIA
PLANNING AND
SELECTION

310

the agency uses the account group organization, the associate directors are the media department members of the account groups. In order to develop media plans adequately, they must be well versed not only in media but in marketing and the creative aspects of advertising as well.

Media buyers are specialists, their degree of specialization depending upon the size of the agency. There may be space buyers for newspapers and magazines and outdoor media and time buyers for radio and television. Each is responsible for being an expert in the media buyer's own media area. They interview media representatives, negotiate for space and time, and issue contracts on behalf of clients.

THE INDEPENDENT MEDIA BUYING SERVICE In recent years, a new kind of media organization—the independent media buying service—has assumed some degree of importance. There are essentially two varieties of the service. A few provide complete media planning and buying services, which are sometimes used by small advertising agencies that do not have adequate media departments of their own. Most, however, are hired to buy media that are in plans already developed. They deal primarily with broadcast media in which advertising rates are generally *negotiated*. Their usefulness, of course, lies primarily in their ability to negotiate more efficient buys. Usually they are compensated by getting a percentage of the difference between the dollars originally budgeted and the actual cost of the time they have purchased. Some advertisers test their agencies to see if they can come up with better buys than the buying services. Large agencies claim that they can match the buying services' performances.

MEDIA REPRESENTATIVES The media advertising departments are the sales departments for advertising space and time. They prepare sales presentations, conduct research projects on their audiences and effectiveness, and structure advertising rates. Their salespeople are known as media representatives. A medium may have its own salespeople or may use the services of agent sales representatives if they find it economically impractical to maintain their own representatives in various key cities where the majority of advertising agency business is located. These agents will represent a group of noncompetitive newspapers or television stations, for example. Not only do they offer a distinct service to the media, but together with the media's own sales force, they have much to offer to media buyers as well. A good portion of the media representative's time is spent making sales presentations. A good representative has a comprehensive knowledge of the market and the medium and can save the buyer's time by providing this information.

At the heart of media operations is the plan. In many smaller advertising agencies, as indicated above, media planning is handled by the account executive. But because this planning is a key factor in the overall advertising strategy and accounts for the major portion of advertising

THE MEDIA PLAN

Advertising Media
Planning

expenditures, it is strongly recommended that it be left to experts—the media director and associate directors.

Media planning is formalized in a written document called the *media plan.* It is based on objectives developed in the marketing plan. Different agencies will, of course, organize their media departments differently and use different techniques for constructing the media plan. Nevertheless, any soundly conceived technique of media planning should contain the same basic elements. First, and basic to all advertising activity, there is a recognition and understanding of the objectives of the marketing plan and the target market. Second, there is a consideration of the creative strategy. Obviously, creative strategy and media strategy must be compatible. For example, a creative strategy based on television demonstration will not work with a media plan that is centered on consumer magazines. Third, the media plan is developed into specific strategies that are consistent with the marketing objectives, target market, and creative strategy. Fourth, media selection translates the general strategies into specific media tactics. Thus, if the strategy suggests using women's magazines, this stage involves specific choices of *Ladies' Home Journal* or *McCall's* or *Good Housekeeping,* etc., or some combination of these. Fifth, there is a rationale for the media strategy and tactics. Putting all these elements together spells out a sound media plan.

The substance of a media plan is summarized in the marketing plan (as shown in Chapter 7), but although that is sufficient for the overall marketing plan, a more detailed media plan is needed to serve as a working document to guide and direct the media staff. A media plan might contain the following:

1. *Summary statement of marketing objectives.* Although the marketing objectives are stated in the *marketing* plan, they are summarized in the *media* plan to show that they were indeed recognized and provide the direction for media decisions.
2. *Summary statement of the creative strategy.* This is included to ensure that it is recognized in the media plan. It should be noted, however, that creative strategy and media strategy are interdependent, and although in some instances one may come before the other, more often they are developed jointly.
3. *Summary statement of market data.* These data should identify the target market and its demographic characteristics.
4. *Summary statement of competitive environment.* This should include competitive media strategies in terms of types used and expenditures.
5. *Statement of media objectives and strategy.* This should be based on and relate to the marketing objectives and creative strategy. It should explain what market the media to be used will reach, the timing strategy, and the relation to competitive efforts. Rationales for media choices should be given. Also, rationales for frequency and reach strategy and for special medium, geographic area, or market group emphasis should be stated.
6. *Statement of media selection and schedule.* This should spell out specific media to be used, when, what size or length advertisements, and how much they will cost.
7. *Appendices.* This should contain backup data that support the first six points but that would only clutter the main body of the media plan.

MEDIA
INFORMATION

Obviously, media planning requires a great deal of information. Information relative to the brand, the marketing problem, and creative strategy is obtained from other parts of the marketing plan. Information relative to media strategy and techniques must be obtained and assembled by the media department. The material that follows is a brief description of the kinds of information available. In the chapters that follow, many of these are discussed in more detail.

REPORTS BY MEDIA The various media are a source of considerable information. They provide rate cards, information on coverage, and studies concerning their markets. Even though such information is very valuable, caution must be exercised in evaluating its worth—not because such studies are dishonest, but because each medium presents the information that puts it in the most favorable light.

REPORTS BY MEDIA ASSOCIATIONS The various classes of media—newspapers, magazines, television, and so forth—have associations, such as the Newspaper Advertising Bureau, the Magazine Publishers Association, and the Television Bureau of Advertising. These groups, among their other activities, conduct research and prepare reports on the nature and merits of their own media.

STANDARD RATE & DATA SERVICE This firm publishes monthly catalogs of rates, circulation, mechanical requirements, issuance and closing dates, and other information for most major media types. It provides a quick source of basic information regarding media, but this must generally be supplemented with more detailed information from other sources.

AUDIT BUREAUS The Audit Bureau of Circulations, the Business Publications Audit of Circulation, and the Traffic Audit Bureau are three of the major auditing bureaus that measure, check, and verify the circulation of many newspapers, magazines, business publications, and outdoor advertising plants.

INDEPENDENT MEDIA INFORMATION SOURCES A large number of independent firms conduct media research and collect media data. Among these are such services as Simmons Market Research Bureau, which provides data on media audience demographics and product usage. Media Records supplies figures on the volume of advertising linage carried by newspapers and tabulated by product classification. It also provides data on business publication advertising. Leading National Advertisers (LNA) provides similar information for magazines, newspaper supplements, network television, spot television, network radio, and outdoor. Starch INRA Hooper provides advertising readership studies of a number of newspapers, magazines, and business papers. The Arbitron Ratings Company and A.C. Nielsen Company provide a variety of media research data for broadcast media. Broadcast Advertiser's Reports (BAR) covers network and spot television and network radio expenditures.

ADVERTISING AGENCY MEDIA RESEARCH In addition to using the information sources mentioned above, the advertising agency may conduct its own research through the research department or media research department if there is one.

MAKING MEDIA DECISIONS

Once organization, planning, and the gathering of information are complete, the problem of making media decisions can be undertaken. The problem becomes complex, because in general, the media plan involves a combination of media types—what is referred to as the *media mix.* Newspapers, magazines, television, and outdoor advertising are all media, but they are sufficiently different to make difficult any comparisons among them. Yet choice among them depends upon comparison.

A QUANTITATIVE APPROACH The possibilities of using computers for routine calculations in media planning and scheduling were immediately obvious to media departments, and computers were quickly utilized for many of the clerical bookkeeping-type functions. Additionally, with the increasing complexity of media and available media data, there has been a need for more sophisticated planning tools. Therefore, a number of mathematical models using computers for media planning have been developed by advertising agencies and commercial research companies. These have included linear programming, "high assay," and simulation models capable of providing quick analyses in areas where the calculations otherwise would be too slow and cumbersome to be feasible. The effectiveness of such computer-based models is, of course, largely dependent upon the quality of inputs and the assumptions that are made. The possibilities of computer use are still far from being maximized, and the future promises new breakthroughs. But computers should not be thought of as providing media plans. They are simply a quick and efficient means of obtaining information to which executive judgment must be applied in making final plans. As an editorial comment in *Advertising Age* so aptly put it:

> Money mechanics, gross audience totals, dollar comparisons and the hard CPM rankings produced by computer programs will always be an integral part of the media process, and they should be. But media efficiency calls

for seasoned judgments, analysis, common sense and painstaking study of alternatives which require experienced professionals both among buyers and sellers.[2]

FACTORS IN MEDIA DECISION MAKING   The starting point for making decisions should always be the basic marketing objectives. Beyond these, there are certain media factors to be considered, differing slightly according to individual circumstances but fundamentally similar. Let us now examine some of these considerations.

BUDGET The choice of media will depend to some extent upon the size of the advertising budget. Certain media types may be too expensive for the funds available. For example, the cost of network television is high, perhaps too high for a particular advertiser. Or an advertiser may use the complete budget on one medium and then not be able to include any other media in the mix. However, when the budget is determined in accordance with marketing objectives, as suggested in a previous chapter, it will take into account the cost of the media necessary to accomplish those objectives.

COMPETITIVE ACTIVITY The media department will either select media for the client that will cover essentially the same audience as that reached by the competition, or attempt to find a separate audience not being reached by the competition. Both these approaches require that one study the competitive media strategy. Of course, competitive media expenditures should not be the total basis for media decision making.

When competitors' advertising copy and intensity are similar, their choice of media will be the prime factor explaining their success or failure. By examining competitive media data, therefore, the advertiser can gain considerable insight into how to make media decisions. Information on competitive media expenditures is fairly easily obtainable from such sources as Media Records and Leading National Advertisers, mentioned above.

FREQUENCY VS. REACH Frequency refers to the number of times the advertiser reaches the same person; *reach* refers to the total number of people covered. The greater the frequency with which you reach the same person by virtue of the media selected, the smaller the reach will be, and vice versa. The decision rests upon the media strategy and marketing objectives. The problem is to determine the right combination of frequency and reach. Each situation will be different, but in general the ideal frequency will be the number of advertising messages it takes to move a prospective customer to action. What this number is and how to design the media plan to meet it can be determined only in a general way. Some prospects will require fewer messages than others, and some will see fewer messages than others. For products with wide general markets, reach is rather simply achieved, but it becomes more difficult to achieve as greater selectivity becomes necessary. Not all the people in the media markets may be prospects for the product brand. A

Piecework. *In Eagle Pass, Texas, the* News Guide *carried a classified ad* "*Wanted at once—Am desperate account of continued livestock thefts. Need watchman that can shoot. Will pay by hour or by head. C. S. Lee.*"

TIME

stantial amount of media audience information is available to help
ke more accurate frequency and reach decisions possible.

NTINUITY A decision must be made regarding the length of time a
paign should make use of one media type. There is a cumulative ef-
from *continuity*: A greater audience will be reached, in terms of
h frequency and coverage, by advertisements continually placed in
medium. That is, not only will a part of the audience see all the ad-
isements, but for each advertisement there will be some new audi-
e. For products with repeat sales, continuity in a medium is
cially important. On the other hand, when repeat sales are unlikely,
it may be desirable to change media so as to reach different audiences.

IMPACT ON DISTRIBUTION Although consumer media are chosen primarily to affect the consumer, the impact of media upon distribution
channels—that is, intermediaries—should not be overlooked. For one
thing, certain media carry considerable prestige for wholesalers and retailers, and thus they can impress these intermediaries as doing an effective local advertising job. Again, the use of certain media (for
example, newspapers) by the advertiser may induce retailers to run
their own tie-in advertising in the same media. Finally, the promotional
or merchandising support given by the medium can prove important in
maximizing the advertiser's overall promotional effort by eliciting greater cooperation from channel intermediaries.

FLEXIBILITY The ability of media to adapt to changing and special
needs of advertisers is known as *flexibility*; certain products require a
flexible medium. Certain media will allow for changes in the advertising
message, changes in the amount to be spent, and changes in geographical areas for the advertising, for example. The advertiser using flexible
media can make whatever changes are necessitated by competitive activity. Or the advertiser can adjust the schedule to special needs; for
example, an instant-cocoa manufacturer may have an arrangement for
spot television announcements to be aired when the temperature in a
given market drops below a certain point.

FRANCHISE POSITION Advertisers using a particular medium over a
period of time may enjoy special *franchise positions*. These can take
the form of special page positions in a magazine or an acknowledged
franchise to preferred position on television. In making media plans,
keep in mind the benefits of maintaining these franchise positions. They
can provide plus values in advertising effectiveness without any additional cost.

STANDARDS OF ACCEPTANCE Certain media must be ruled out of
consideration for some advertisers because they will not accept the advertiser's products. Liquor advertising, for example, is not accepted by
most broadcast media and by certain newspapers and magazines.

COST PER THOUSAND (CPM) A very important consideration in media decision making involves cost. Although cost is sometimes considered in terms of total expenditure, more often it is looked at in terms of the cost of reaching an individual prospect and expressed in terms of *cost per thousand* (not cost per person). The equation for computing cost per thousand is:

$$\text{Cost per thousand} = \frac{\text{Price of the medium to the advertiser}}{\text{Circulation or delivered audience (000 omitted)}}$$

Certain points should be noted in using this equation. Circulation represents the delivered number of copies of a publication or the equivalent number of households tuning into a radio or television station in the particular time period. It is on this basis that rates are determined, and they rise and fall with the rise and fall of circulation. However, more than one person may read a newspaper or magazine, and several members of a household may listen to a radio program or watch a television show. Thus, such information, when available, is more valuable in determining the cost of advertising in relation to the number reached. These figures are called *delivered audience* (or *readership,* in the case of publication advertising). Audience or readership figures are obtained on a sampling basis and have a greater degree of error than circulation, but they are more meaningful for media decision making. Therefore, the advertiser may want to use delivered audience instead of circulation as a denominator in the CPM equation. But the total audience delivered may include people who are not part of the target market. For example, a magazine might have a readership of a million, with only half that number being women. If the target market is women, then this figure might be used as the denominator in determining the CPM of *effective* delivered audience. Although a medium may look very inexpensive vis-à-vis several others on the basis of CPM of the *total* delivered audience, a comparison on the basis of *effective* delivered audience may point to very different conclusions.

Furthermore, there is no assurance that the circulation, delivered audience, or even effective delivered audience will see or hear the advertising message.

Another problem of the cost-per-thousand equation lies in the price of the medium to the advertiser. Negotiation of price, a very important factor for certain media types, can result in variations of actual cost, thus making it difficult to calculate accurate costs in advance. Discounts are another important factor. By taking advantage of discounts, the media buyer may be able to increase the audience at a lower cost per thousand. But again, these adjustments cannot always be made at the planning stage.

In the final analysis, cost-per-thousand computations must be tempered by judgment, because data are not available to make completely accurate computations.

EFFECTIVENESS OF SELLING MESSAGE The effectiveness of the selling message will be determined partly by the appropriateness of the medium. For example, a product requiring a lengthy message will be more effective in newspapers and magazines than in posters and car cards. Visual requirements such as color, motion, and ease of reproduction will all influence media choice. Sound (a jingle, for instance) precludes anything but broadcast media. Other factors are product image (the need for prestige or the news value), association with a specific personality or editorial material, and immediacy of action desired (reminder advertising or quick sale).

PROSPECTIVE CUSTOMERS Finally, media decisions must be made on the basis of who the prospective customers are. Among the many considerations in this area are the geographic concentration or spread of the customers, buying power or economic status, sex, specific age groups, and any other demographics that might be appropriate. One aspect of the marketing process has been described as the bringing together of products with known appeals and people with known characteristics. The catalyst in this process is the advertising medium. Each medium will vary somewhat in the characteristics of its audience, as will the characteristics of the product's customers. The key is to identify media that come as close as possible in their audience characteristics to those of the product's audience. Syndicated services like Simmons provide market and media data to facilitate matching media to markets.

> *The American standard of living is due in no small measure to the imaginative genius of advertising, which not only creates and sharpens demand, but also, by its impact upon the competitive process, stimulates the never ceasing quest of improvement in quality of the product.*
>
> *ADLAI E. STEVENSON (1900–1965), Statesman*
>
> READER'S DIGEST

MEDIA SCHEDULING AND RELATED MATTERS

Once the media plan has been approved and the media decided upon, the job of scheduling must be undertaken. The media department must determine the size of advertisements, their position in the media, and what mechanical possibilities to consider, such as color, bleed pages, inserts, or gatefolds. Then negotiation with media must be undertaken, space and time schedules prepared, contracts written, and finally, insertion orders issued.

SIZE, POSITION, AND MECHANICAL POSSIBILITIES   Size is a factor in print advertising just as length is in broadcast advertising. These are important considerations in media selection and scheduling because they will directly affect the advertising budget. But they are also a problem of creativity and marketing management. It is not possible to generalize about size, except to say that the advertisement should be as big as is necessary to accomplish the objectives of the advertising strategy. Creative factors influencing size include the length of copy, the nature of the illustration, and the visualization technique. Marketing management factors include the nature of the product, its competition, and the marketing objectives. Media considerations affecting size include not only the budget but also the effective audience potential of the medium, requirements of the media (some media specify minimum advertising space or time units), and readership habits of a print medium's audience (a hobby magazine may have extremely high readership, so that even the smallest advertisement will not be overlooked).

Proponents of large and small size are continually arguing the merits of their respective cases. In the final analysis, size must be related to cost: The size must be large enough and the cost must be low enough to produce the most sales at the least expense.

Qualifications. *In Portland, Ore., an* Oregonian *advertiser offered to rent a "newlyweds' dream house" to a couple with "no children under 12."*

TIME

POSITION The position of the advertisement or commercial plays an important role in determining its effectiveness. Advertising rates of media are generally based upon *run of paper* (r.o.p.)—that is, position to be determined by the medium. Certain positions, like the back cover of a magazine, are particularly desirable and command premium rates. In broadcast media, "position" is determined by time periods, with prime time periods (those commanding larger audiences) getting higher rates.

Although most advertisers place print advertising on an r.o.p. basis, some feel that preferred positions are worth the additional cost. Special position may be especially desirable because of the physical layout of the advertisement (e.g., one laid out for a right-hand page) or because it is appropriate for an advertisement to be close to specific editorial matter. For example, a food product advertisement may appear in the cooking section of a women's magazine. It is obvious that station-break spot announcements following television programs with extremely high ratings are much sought after. But although position is important, it is relative to the quality of the medium. Even using r.o.p., there is some opportunity for position choice, for the advertising agency will express preferences and will usually be accommodated by the medium as much as possible. Of course, long-term contracts help advertisers to earn franchise positions.

MECHANICAL OPPORTUNITIES Some media offer certain mechanical possibilities, at additional cost, to improve the effectiveness of advertisements. For instance, many publications offer color, which may be of value to the advertiser in securing greater attention or making the illustration more realistic, as in food advertising. Bleed pages, offered by certain media, permit the advertisement to run off the edges of the page, which may give it stronger impact than it would have on a normal page.

Certain media offer gatefolds for oversize advertisements, inserts permitting the use of special papers and printing processes, coupon inserts, consecutive numbering of coupons, and so forth. These, plus the reproduction limitations of the media, must be taken into account, usually by both media buyers and creative personnel, who also must take into account the relationship of additional cost to impact.

SPACE AND TIME BUYING   Media buyers still have the problem of actually purchasing space and time. To do so, they need a negotiating skill and a comprehensive knowledge of rate structures. Today, broadcast purchasing is almost totally based on negotiation, with rate cards serving as only a starting point in accomplishing a buy. Print purchasing, on the other hand, still is done mostly from rate cards, although print packages at negotiated prices are sometimes available. When negotiations are completed, contracts will be written by the media department on behalf of the client and the media. Finally, after the schedule has been decided upon, *insertion orders* will be written to designate the particular date, space, and position for each advertisement within the terms of the contract.

SCHEDULING   Before insertion orders can be issued, a schedule must be drawn up stating when the advertisements are to appear. This schedule is not determined haphazardly but is designed to ensure that advertisements are timed for maximum effectiveness.

There are several patterns of scheduling generally in use. One might be described as the *regular* or *even* schedule. Uniform time and space are used at regular intervals—every day, every week, every month. In contrast, advertisers are today increasingly making use of *flights* or *waves* of advertising. In flighting, the schedule is concentrated in short periods broken by periods without advertising. This is especially valuable when the advertiser has a limited budget and would lose much of the impact of the advertising if it were spread evenly over time. Thus, the advertising is bunched in high concentration *flights* to ensure impact. A variation of this pattern is *pulsing,* in which advertising is scheduled continually, but at high levels followed by low levels, and then repeated.

Another pattern is the *skip schedule,* in which advertisements are scheduled every other day, week, or month. In some instances, the advertiser may alternate media—for example, *McCall's* one month, the *Ladies' Home Journal* the next, then back to *McCall's*—so that the overall effect is similar to the regular schedule. The *seasonal schedule* emphasizes seasonal sales opportunities by running irregular schedules that peak the advertising during the seasonal periods. The *buildup* or *step-up* schedule starts out with small advertisements and eventually builds up to an all-out campaign of considerable intensity. The *blitz* or *step-down* schedule simply reverses the previous procedure. Both of the last two schedule patterns are used to introduce new products or established products to new markets. The choice is a matter of strategy preference.

Media must be chosen to reach the markets the advertiser wants to sell. At the heart of media operations is the media plan. There are many sources of media and market information available to media planners.

Beyond marketing objectives, the media planner needs to consider such factors as the budget, competitive activity, frequency and reach, continuity, impact on distribution, flexibility, franchise position, standards of acceptance, cost per thousand, effectiveness of the selling message, and prospective customers.

Matters to be considered in media scheduling include size, position, and mechanical requirements. Scheduling is keyed to media plan objectives and can vary from an even schedule with such techniques as flighting, pulsing, skip schedule, buildup, and blitz.

1. Why is media planning so important to the success of advertising?
2. What purpose does the media buying service serve? Who can use it, and how can it be used?
3. What elements should be included in a media plan?
4. Choose a consumer product you would like to advertise and suggest the kinds of data you would need to construct a media plan for it.
5. Name three sources of media information and explain the information they provide.
6. What is the media mix?
7. How can information about competitive media activity help in planning a media strategy for the advertiser?
8. What is meant by "frequency" and "reach"? What is their significance in media planning?
9. What is the equation for determining "cost per thousand"? For what is it used?
10. How do size and position affect media scheduling?

QUESTIONS AND PROBLEMS

[1] Ed Brennen, *Advertising Media* (New York: McGraw-Hill Book Company, 1951), pp. 210–11.
[2] "The Human Element in Media Planning." *Advertising Age*, XXXIX, No. 39 (September 25, 1978), 14. Copyright 1978 by Crain Communications, Inc.

ENDNOTES

Newspapers

After completing this chapter, you should be able to:
1. Define the characteristics of newspapers
2. Understand the advertising rate structure for newspapers
3. Explain newspaper circulation structure
4. Evaluate newspapers as an advertising medium

Newspapers, magazines, television, radio, out-of-home, and other media deserve consideration in separate chapters. They differ in nature and in advertising purpose, and therefore, each has a unique place in the firm's advertising strategy.

The critics of advertising seem to devote little attention to newspapers, and the advertising industry appears to take them for granted. Yet in terms of dollars expended, newspapers have consistently been the leading advertising mass medium. This fact is undoubtedly accounted for by the heavy volume of retail advertising carried by newspapers, for they are by far the leading retail advertising medium. They are also a key advertising medium for manufacturers. In 1981, it is estimated that $17.446 billion was spent by advertisers in U.S. newspapers, of which $9.631 billion was for retail advertising, $5.062 billion was for classified advertising, and $2.753 billion was for national advertising.[1]

Although people tend to think that one newspaper is much the same as another, a number of characteristics distinguish them from each other.

CHARACTER OF NEWSPAPERS

TYPES OF NEWSPAPERS   Most important as an advertising medium in terms of advertising dollars spent are the daily and Sunday newspapers. According to *Editor & Publisher*, there are 1,730 daily newspapers in this country with a combined circulation of 61,430,745. Of this number, 408 are morning newspapers, 1,352 are evening newspapers, and 30 are "all day" newspapers. There are 755 Sunday editions of daily newspapers, which have a circulation of 55,180,004.[2] These daily and Sunday newspapers are big business.

Although the daily and Sunday newspapers represent the most important advertising medium among newspapers, there are also 8,201 triweekly, semiweekly, weekly, biweekly, semimonthly, monthly, and bimonthly newspapers in the United States.[3] Most of these are small-town and rural papers and are sometimes referred to as *country* newspapers.

The vast majority of United States newspapers are of the general editorial type and in English, but there are special presses that may be of importance to the advertiser. For example, there are several hundred foreign-language newspapers.

There are also the religious press, the labor press, the college and high school press, the black press, the financial and commercial press, and shopping newspapers.[4] Each of these can give the advertiser an opportunity to select special audiences.

Many Sunday editions of newspapers have magazine supplements and color comic sections. Advertising space here is sometimes sold on an individual basis and sometimes on a group basis—that is, the advertiser can buy space in individual supplements or in a group of supplements. Sunday newspaper magazine supplements are in many ways similar to consumer magazines, and much of what is said regarding consumer magazines in the next chapter is applicable to them.

NEWSPAPER MECHANICAL REQUIREMENTS Newspapers come in standard and tabloid sizes. For many years, newspapers were fairly standardized at eight columns wide by 22 inches deep, but today, because of technological developments in printing and other factors, the trend is toward six and nine columns, with variations on the length of somewhat more or less than 22 inches. The tabloids (there were fewer than fifty of these) generally have five columns and are fourteen inches deep.

Newspaper space is generally measured in *agate lines*. The agate line is one-fourteenth of a *column inch* deep, so that in one column inch (one inch deep by the width of the column, which will vary with each newspaper), there are fourteen agate lines. A standard newspaper page, therefore, will contain approximately 1,800 to 2,700 agate lines, depending upon the number of columns and the length of page, and a tabloid page will contain approximately 1,000 agate lines. Advertising space in newspapers is generally sold by the agate line and is referred to as *linage*. Some of the smaller-circulation newspapers, however, sell space by column inches.

To overcome some of the problems of the variety of page formats, a distinct disadvantage in placing national schedules, the industry has developed the Standard Advertising Unit (SAU) system of 25 individual advertising sizes that can be accepted by all broadsheet newspapers regardless of their format or page size.

Because newspapers are for the most part printed on newsprint (a coarse paper stock) by high-speed presses, there are difinite limitations on the kinds of illustrative material that can be effectively reproduced. Many newspapers today offer run-of-paper options for black and white and for one, two, or three colors. To get better color reproduction, however, many newspapers will accept roll-fed preprints (also referred to as Hi-Fi). These are color advertisements preprinted by the advertiser on better-quality paper. Preprints are shipped to the newspaper in continuous form rolls, permitting the newspaper to back up the sheet with its own news and advertising and then collate it with the rest of the newspaper without losing the effectiveness of the color advertisement. Another color printing technique is known as Spectacolor. It is similar to roll-fed preprints, except that it makes possible the collation of the page in the whole newspaper and the registration of color work so that each copy of the advertisement is properly positioned when the newspaper prints on the other side. Many newspapers also will accept multipage preprinted inserts from advertisers, thus giving the advertiser a choice of printing processes. In r.o.p. color advertisements, it is possible to obtain improved color reproduction on fractional pages as well as full pages by using AdPro Inks. This system requires only three colors instead of the conventional four for full-color reproduction.

In addition to innovative color techniques, newspapers are adding other opportunities for advertisers. Flexform advertising offers the advertiser the opportunity to design an advertisement in any conceivable shape. Those parts of the newspaper page not containing the advertisement are filled with editorial matter. Such unconventional layouts, surrounded by editorial matter, are hard for the reader to ignore. Free-standing stuffers, also known as Flag-wavers, Ansecards, and Ad-A-Card, are basically advertising inserts with the advertisements printed on different-size cards that are attached to the advertisement by a special printing-press attachment. The reader pulls off the self-addressed card and mails it in for an order or inquiry.

Newspaper national advertising rates are generally quoted in terms of agate lines. There are, however, different rates for different types of advertising. First, rates differ for retail or local and for general or national advertising. The retail rate is lower than the general rate, but it is not commissionable. There are different rates for classified advertising (the "want ads") and display advertising. Classified advertising rates are usually based on cost per word or on the type line rather than on the agate line. There are some special rates for inserts, preprints, and comic-page advertising, special-position charges, and the like. In many newspapers, different classifications of advertising are charged different rates: one for amusements, another for real estate, a third for political advertising, and so on. Color rates, of course, are higher than black-and-white rates.

Retail advertising rates are substantially less than general advertising rates. As a result, many national advertisers have not been using newspapers to the degree they might otherwise.

Some newspapers offer special forced and optional combination rates. Forced combinations require an advertiser to buy space in more than one newspaper (usually a morning and an evening paper). Optional combinations give the advertiser the opportunity to buy space in more than one newspaper at a reduced line rate. Of course, daily newspapers with Sunday editions have different daily and Sunday rates all along the line. Newspaper rates are published on rate cards—one for retail rates and another for general rates. General rates and other data are also available in *Standard Rate & Data Service.*

St. Petersburg Times and Evening Independent
Advertising Rates
490 First Avenue South
St. Petersburg, Florida 33701
Phone 813-893-8249

Member of
Audit Bureau of Circulations (ABC)
Sunday Mag/Net
Magazine and Color Comics Group (Metro)
Newspaper Coop Network (NCN)
Newspaper Advertising Cooperative Network (NACON)
Newspaper Advertising Bureau, Inc. (NAB)

1. Personnel
President and Editor .... Eugene C. Patterson
Publisher .... John B. Lake
General Manager .... John O'Hearn
Advertising Director .... Leo L. Kubiet
General Advertising Manager .... Walter R. Stecher
National and State Advertising Sales Manager .... Michael H. Pearson
Retail Advertising Manager .... James E. Doughton
Classified Advertising Manager .... Richard E. Riggins
Cooperative Advertising Manager ... Gregory L. Huffman
Commercial Services/Job Printing Manager ... Vernon Firchow
Advertising, Marketing, Creative Manager ... Andrew Kahut
Research Manager .... Phillip J. Vernon

2. Representatives:
Story & Kelly-Smith, Inc. (See back page for addresses and phone numbers.)

3. Commission and Cash Discount
Terms net 15th of month following. 15% commission to recognized agencies. 2% cash discount applies when accounts are paid in full in accordance with the terms stated on advertising statements.

4. Rate Policy
Times Publishing Company guarantees that no advertiser enjoys any rate not covered by its rate cards.

a. General Rates
All advertising placed by a manufacturer, wholesaler, jobber or distributor for products or services sold generally through retail outlets or by mail or any other manner is classified as general advertising, except for Co-op (Cooperative) advertising where several options are available.
Veloxes or photoprints made for advertisers, when necessary, by the Times Publishing Co. or a commerical photoprinter will be charged to the advertiser.
Any tax levied against advertising will be added to the advertising space charges.

b. State Rates
15% discount on General rates available to distributors, wholesalers, manufacturers and brokers with homes or district offices located anywhere in the state of Florida but outside the 11-county Times/Independent Retail Area of Pinellas, Hillsborough, Pasco, Hernando, Citrus, Manatee, Sarasota, Charlotte, Lee, Marion and Collier Counties. Not commissionable to agencies at 15% discount from General rates, otherwise, usual 15% commission to agencies at General rates.

c. Retail Rates
Retail rates are applicable only to advertising placed by qualified retail outlets (selling direct to consumers) located within the 11-county Times/Independent Retail Trading Area.

d. C.A.P. Rates
Coop Action Plan advertising rates are available for product and service advertising that contains dealer listings. See C.A.P. rate card for details.

5. Black and White Rates (Run of Paper)

Full Run	Per Line
Morning and Evening*	$2.78
Morning	2.50
Evening	.48
Sunday	2.98
Sunday and Evening*	3.26

*See Combination Rates, page 3.

National Newspaper Sales Plan (NEWS PLAN)
Volume discounts for contracted number of pages or equivalent amount of space. Contracts to be effective for one year from date of first insertion.

6 pages	5% discount
13 pages	10% discount
26 pages	15% discount
52 pages	20% discount
65 pages	20.5% discount
78 pages	21% discount
91 pages	21.5% discount
104 pages	22% discount

These NEWSPLAN discounts apply to run of paper (R.O.P.), Spreel and regional edition advertising only and do not apply to color premiums, FLORIDIAN, Color Comics or TV Dial.

a. Standard Advertising Units (S.A.U.)

SAU Size	Morn.	M&E	Sun.	S&E	Eve.	CLE

(detailed rate figures by unit size)

b. Regional Area Editions

	Per Line Morning	Sunday
Clearwater Times	$.61	$.68
Largo-Seminole Times	.74	.83
Pasco Times	.52	.62
Hernando/Citrus Times	.72	.38
Clearwater and Largo-Seminole Times	1.17	1.31
Pasco/Hernando/Citrus Times	.70	.78
Clearwater/Pasco Times	.98	1.17
Clearwater/Pasco/Hernando/Citrus Times	1.37	1.39
Pasco/Clearwater/Largo-Seminole Times	1.39	1.57
Clearwater/Largo-Seminole/Pasco/Hernando/Citrus Times	1.57	1.74

c. Neighborhood Times (Monday or Thursday)

Part Run	Per Line
Northwest Zone	$.58
Northeast Zone	.71
South Zone	.45
NW and NE	1.26
NW and S	1.00
NE and S	1.13
All three zones	1.69

6. Combination Rates
a. All morning products may run in combination with the Evening Independent within 7 day period at 28 cents a line.
b. Spree edition may be purchased in combination with any Times or Independent edition with identical copy at the following rates per line:
SPREE I add 22 cents — SPREE I & II add 45 cents
SPREE II add 24 cents — SPREE I & III add 42 cents
SPREE III add 21 cents — SPREE II & III add 44 cents
SPREE I, II & III add 65 cents
Published on Wednesdays. May also be purchased separately from any Times or Independent edition at double the above rate.

7. Color Rates (Run of Paper)
Minimum size is 14 lines

	Applicable Color Unit Charges		
	Black & 1 Color	Black & 2 Colors	Black & 3 Colors
Morning & Evening	$487.00	$642.00	$798.00
Morning	418.00	544.00	671.00
Evening	198.00	282.00	367.00
Sunday	418.00	544.00	671.00
Sunday & Evening	487.00	642.00	798.00
Morning, Double Truck, Facing or Companion Pages	607.00	755.00	904.00
Evening, Double Truck, Facing or Companion Pages	240.00	367.00	494.00
Morning & Evening, Double Truck, Facing or Companion Pages	727.00	938.00	1,151.00
Sunday, Double Truck, Facing or Companion Pages	607.00	755.00	904.00
Sunday & Evening, Double Truck, Facing or Companion Pages	727.00	938.00	1,151.00
Clearwater Times	198.00	296.00	394.00
Double Trucks, Facing or Companion pages	240.00	367.00	494.00
Clearwater/Largo-Seminole Times	226.00	325.00	424.00
Double Trucks, Facing or Companion pages	282.00	424.00	562.00
Pasco Times	165.00	241.00	318.00
Double Trucks, Facing or Companion pages	200.00	294.00	400.00
Hernando/Citrus Times Combo	118.00	147.00	200.00
Double Trucks, Facing or Companion pages	147.00	224.00	306.00
Pasco/Hernando/Citrus Times	200.00	294.00	388.00
Double Trucks, Facing or Companion Times	235.00	365.00	494.00
Clearwater/Pasco Times	212.00	312.00	412.00
Double Trucks, Facing or Companion pages	247.00	365.00	494.00
Clearwater/Pasco/Hernando/Citrus Times	226.00	325.00	424.00
Double Trucks, Facing or Companion pages	282.00	424.00	565.00
Pasco/Hernando/Citrus Times	259.00	395.00	530.00
Double Trucks, Facing or Companion pages	360.00	560.00	770.00
Spree I	142.00	206.00	272.00
Double Trucks, Facing or Companion pages	174.00	259.00	353.00

Color Rates and Data (Continued)

Minimum Size is 14 lines	Black & 1 Color	Black & 2 Colors	Black & 3 Colors
	$142.00	$206.00	$272.00
Spree II			
Double Trucks, Facing or Companion pages	174.00	259.00	353.00
	142.00	206.00	272.00
Spree III			
Double Trucks, Facing or Companion pages	174.00	259.00	353.00
Any Spree edition in Combination with any other edition	71.00	97.00	127.00
Double Trucks, Facing or Companion pages	120.00	184.00	248.00

Color rates are doubled when all Spree editions are used.

	Black & 1 Color	Black & 2 Colors	Black & 3 Colors
Northwest Zone	175.00	265.00	340.00
Double Trucks, Facing or Companion pages	225.00	350.00	475.00
Northeast Zone	190.00	275.00	350.00
Double Trucks, Facing or Companion pages	240.00	365.00	490.00
South Zone	165.00	250.00	325.00
Double Trucks, Facing or Companion pages	215.00	340.00	465.00
NW and NE	250.00	375.00	500.00
Double Trucks, Facing or Companion pages	325.00	515.00	700.00
NW and S	225.00	350.00	475.00
Double Trucks, Facing or Companion pages	300.00	490.00	675.00
NE and S	240.00	365.00	490.00
Double Trucks, Facing or Companion pages	315.00	500.00	690.00
All three zones	282.00	424.00	565.00
Double Trucks, Facing or Companion pages	382.00	593.00	805.00

When run in combination with the Evening Independent add 28 cents a line space cost plus additional color charge.

Evening Independent color charge in combination with FLORIDIAN, Color Comics, TV Dial or any part run regional edition:

	Black & 1 color	Black & 2 colors	Black & 3 colors
Single Page Units	$71.00	$97.00	$127.00
Double Truck, Facing or Companion pages	120.00	184.00	248.00

10% discount if color used is same as and companion to that published in a news feature.

8a. Special Classification/Rates Inserts — Hi-Fi
(Note: Because of seasonal circulation/variance, paper requirement should be ascertained 60 days or more in advance of each insertion date.) Per M. Circulation of date carried:

Flat Rate	$16.00 PER M
Vertical Half Page Rate	8.00 PER M

Additional service fee $120.00 per unit

Availabilities: Times — Thursday and Sunday; other days occasionally by prior arrangement. Independent — Monday, Tuesday, Wednesday, Thursday, Friday and Saturday.

Closing dates for space reservations and cancellation: 10 days prior to publication date. Both papers are standard size, 55 inch web.

2   3

FIGURE 17-1

Sample pages from a general rate card for a newspaper, using the new standardized format. *By permission: St. Petersburg Times/Evening Independent.*

OPEN AND FLAT RATES General advertising line rates are *open* or *flat*. Open rates provide for rate discounts; flat rates are given if no discounts are offered. There are three types of newspaper advertising rate discounts. One discount is offered on the basis of agate lines purchased during a given time period (usually one year). This is known as a *bulk contract rate*, which has decreasing line rates on some predetermined scale, such as 1,000 lines, 2,500 lines, 5,000 lines, and 10,000 lines. Some 950 newspapers also offer national advertisers a continuity discount called *Newsplan*. Under this plan, discounts are offered if annual cumulative space equals 6, 13, 26, or 52 pages.

Another type of discount is offered by many newspapers on the basis of the number of full-page advertisements run during a given time period. This is known as the *frequency page contract rate* and may be structured, for example, on rates for full-page advertisements in multiples of ten. The *cash discount*, usually amounting to 2 percent, is offered by almost all newspapers whether they quote open or flat rates. Some newspapers offer *earned rates*, which means that the advertiser does not contract for any set frequency or quantity of advertising but receives the lowest rate after a certain time period according to the fre-

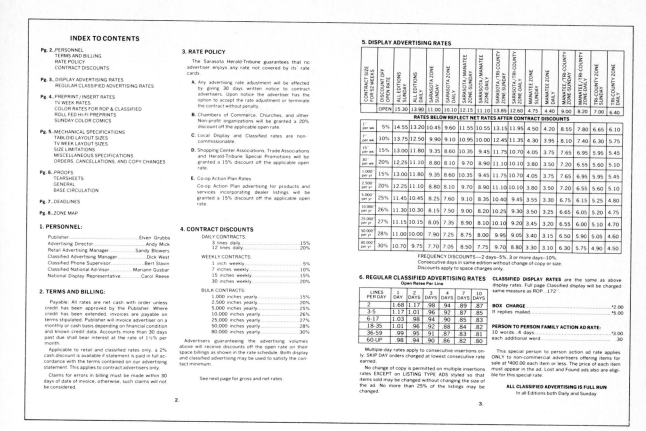

FIGURE 17-2

Part of a retail advertising rate card for a newspaper. *By permission: Sarasota Herald-Tribune.*

quency and quantity used. Finally, some newspapers offer *no-change rates* for advertisers who run the same advertisement without change over a period of time.

REBATES AND SHORT RATES Some newspapers require that advertisers pay the full agate line rate even though they have a contract for bulk or frequency rates. At the end of the contract period, they will adjust the rates and *rebate* the difference. On the other hand, some newspapers will charge the advertiser on the basis of the lowest contracted line rate from the outset. However, if the advertiser does not meet the terms of the contract at the end of the contract period, the advertiser must pay the difference between the contract rate and the rate earned. The difference is known as the *short rate*.

CIRCULATION

Newspapers are sold in three ways—by home delivery, on newsstands, and by mail subscription. The price charged for the first two delivery methods is usually the same, but mail subscriptions may be more or less expensive. In evaluating the circulation of a newspaper, several as-

FIGURE 17-3

A newspaper listing from *Standard Rate & Data Service*. By permission: *Standard Rate & Data Service, Inc.*

pects of circulation should be examined by the advertiser. First, circulation claims should be verified, for audience is what the advertiser is buying, and advertising rates are based on circulation. The Audit Bureau of Circulations was organized in 1914 to audit circulation claims and attest to their validity. ABC reports provide the following information:

Amount of net paid circulation

Circulation in city and retail trading zones

Net press runs by editions, time of issue, and where distributed

Number of copies sold in bulk

Amount of unpaid circulation

What territory is in city and retail trading zones

Prices paid for newspaper

Publisher's policy on returns and allowances

Inducements offered for subscriptions

Number of subscribers in arrears

Circulation of newspapers by counties and outside towns

Newspaper circulation has traditionally been divided into three geographical classifications: city zone, retail trading zone, and other. City zone circulation is that within the city limits; trading zone circulation is that outside the city limits but within the retail trading area of the city; and "other" circulation is that outside the city and trading zones. Such circulation breakdowns may be useful to retailers, but they leave much to be desired for national advertisers. Most national advertisers tend to define their markets in terms of metropolitan areas. Therefore, to make their medium more attractive to potential national advertisers, many newspapers today break out their circulation data by metropolitan areas, using Standard Metropolitan Statistical Areas (SMSA) as defined by the U.S. Office of Management and Budget. But even this analysis does not help those national advertisers who plan their advertising around television. There is a special geographical market designation for television, based on the area in which the station signal is received. These markets have been defined as Areas of Dominant Influence (ADI) and become the basis for media strategy for such advertisers. Therefore, some newspapers have also described their circulation by ADI market designation. Both SMSA and ADI circulation analyses are available to advertisers through a special volume of *Standard Rate & Data Service* and through other sources.

Many large newspapers sell advertising space for either all or only a part of their circulation, whereas some run special sections that are included only in those copies of the newspaper going to certain geographic areas. A number of the larger dailies have gone to zoned editions beyond the kinds mentioned above. The development of these additional zoned editions follows the population migration to suburbia, for many former city newspaper readers now live in the suburbs and want suburban news. These zoned editions provide this additional suburban news and at the same time provide the opportunity for suburban retailers to advertise in the newspaper without a large amount of waste circulation.

Because publishers are constantly trying to increase their circulation, it behooves advertisers to determine and evaluate how the circulation was obtained. If special inducements such as reduced rates or premium offers were used, the subscriber may have purchased the newspaper more for the bargain rate or premium than for the paper itself and may not read the newspaper as thoroughly and thus not see the advertisements.

The advertiser is also interested in the demographic characteristics of newspaper readers—age, sex, occupation, income, education, home and car ownership, buying habits, and the like. In single-newspaper cities, the newspaper readers are apt to be similar to the population as a whole. In multiple-newspaper cities, however, readers of each newspaper may differ substantially. Circulation represents copies sold, but generally more people read the newspaper than buy it. According to the Newspaper Advertising Bureau, 2.095 people read a single copy of a newspaper daily. Information on reader characteristics and brand preference is generally prepared by newspaper research and is available to advertisers. Such information may also be purchased from independent research firms.

Newspaper circulations and rates vary widely, and average figures are meaningless. If an advertiser were to run an advertisement in all the 1,730 daily newspapers listed in the 1982 *Editor & Publisher International Year Book,* the aggregate agate line cost based on minimum rates would be $968,723 for a combined circulation of 61,430,745. Assuming a full-page advertisement of 2,400 agate lines (without adjustment for tabloids), the cost of a full page in all dailies would be over $2 million.

The buying of newspaper advertising space will depend upon the media strategy and marketing objectives of the advertiser. When general newspaper coverage is desired, advertisers may buy the largest ten, twenty, or more markets. In other instances, they may want to reach markets of a certain size, such as cities with populations between 5,000 and 25,000. Or they may want to reach certain states or regions, or to relate their newspaper coverage to sales volume for their products. Finally, they may use newspapers to supplement other media they have chosen to get national coverage if they need additional market coverage, perhaps because of local or regional brand competition.

THE MILLINE RATE AND COST PER THOUSAND The traditional basis for newspaper rate comparison has been the *milline rate.* The equation for the milline rate is:

$$\text{Milline} = \frac{1,000,000}{\text{Circulation}} \times \text{Line rate}$$

The line rate for newspapers with open rates will vary according to the number of lines used. Therefore, the milline rate is frequently cal-

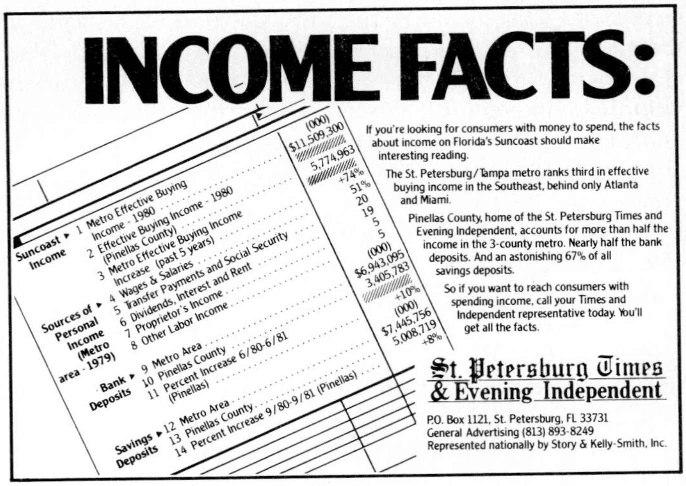

FIGURE 17-4

A newspaper advertises to business to attract advertisers. *By permission: St. Petersburg Times/Evening Independent.*

culated on the basis of the highest line rate—the *maximil*—and on the basis of the lowest line rate—the *minimil*. To make these computations meaningful, it may be necessary to adjust the circulation figure as well, for advertisers are interested only in effective circulation. They may therefore find it valuable to compute the milline using only city zone circulation, trading zone circulation, or SMSA or ADI circulation.

But milline rates are becoming less and less popular as a measure, primarily because they are not compatible with the measure used in other media—cost per thousand. For newspapers, cost per thousand is calculated on the basis of a 1,000-line black-and-white advertisement cost, which is equal to the milline rate.

$$\text{Cost per thousand} = \frac{\text{Agate line charge} \times 1,000}{\text{Circulation or delivered audience (000 omitted)}}$$

The advertiser, in calculating the CPM of newspapers, may use circulation as the denominator because this is frequently the only hard data available, especially with smaller newspapers; but a more effective calculation would use the delivered audience or readership. When there is some leeway in the degree of accuracy in the calculations and delivered audience data are not available, since it is known that the national average of newspaper readership is 2.095, this can be multiplied by the circulation to provide an estimated readership of the newspaper.

However, the milline rate and the cost per thousand are quantitative measures and must not be the only factors in selecting newspapers. A newspaper with a low milline rate or cost per thousand but with a poor audience from the advertiser's point of view does not represent a good buy. Therefore, qualitative as well as quantitative values must be considered.

Before buying newspaper space, advertisers should check both the market (by whatever market designation they use) and the newspaper. In examining the market, they should determine the market area, the size of the market (including population and households), economic factors such as consumer disposable income and retail sales, and any special market characteristics. Turning to the newspaper, they should examine circulation and how well it covers the market area; reader characteristics and reading and buying habits; editorial content, including philosophy and policy as well as physical makeup; advertiser acceptance in terms of linage by type of advertiser; and newspaper services available, such as mechanical facilities and merchandising aids. Only after having accumulated and analyzed this information can advertisers make an intelligent selection of individual newspapers for advertising.

We do not want to sail under false colors. The New York Times is not published solely for the purpose of attracting advertisers. We hope, however, to attract by the number and class of our readers. We are seeking to secure the goodwill and confidence of intelligent, discriminating newspaper readers. The advertiser is a secondary consideration . . . .

ADOLPH S. OCHS (1858–1935), Publisher

READER'S DIGEST

STRENGTHS AND WEAKNESSES OF THE MEDIUM

Before newspapers can be considered a part of one's media mix, some knowledge of the medium in general, and its strengths and weaknesses, is essential. Each medium, through its associations and individually, tries to present itself in the best light, but obviously not all media can be the best. On the other hand, each medium may be best in some particular situation.

The Newspaper Advertising Bureau promotes the use of newspaper advertising by disseminating research and market analyses to advertising agencies and advertisers. According to the Bureau, newspaper space should be used by advertisers for the following reasons: The newspaper's daily audience is actively seeking editorial and advertising information. It includes practically all the advertiser's customers, who become more interested in the advertising as they are ready to buy. Sixty-eight percent of adults (18 and older) read a newspaper on an average weekday. Newspapers reach an accumulated 89 percent of all adults (18 and older) over five weekdays. Eighty-six percent of all newspaper readers will turn to the page (excluding classified) carrying the advertiser's message.

The interest of readers in the advertisements is as high as for the editorial matter, primarily because so much retail advertising is carried. It is the second most popular part of the newspaper with women after the general news, and third only to general news and sports with men. In addition, the news value of newspapers adds an element of immediacy to the advertising. Newspaper reading habits are constant throughout the year.

Newspapers provide flexibility in a number of ways. You can run advertisements from one inch to multiple pages. Advertisements can be run on any schedule on any days or weeks. Closing dates are very late.

There is also flexibility in geographic selection of markets, allowing advertisers to correlate their newspaper advertisements with their market areas and strength.

Some additional comment seems appropriate. One of the major advantages of the newspaper as an advertising medium is also one of its greatest weaknesses. Nearly everyone reads a newspaper. Thus, although newspapers afford an opportunity for very intensive coverage, they generally lack selectivity of audience except geographically. Advertisers appealing to specific groups in the market—by sex or age or occupation, for example—will find that they must buy much waste readership.

Although all media offer merchandising services, newspapers are particularly effective in providing such services at the local retailer level. Retailers believe in newspapers and newspaper advertising. The newspaper's sales force may be used to supplement the advertiser's sales force in calling on dealers in connection with launching a campaign. Newspapers can generally provide valuable route lists to the advertiser's sales force. And they can be used to solicit retail tie-in

FIGURE 17-5

This advertisement to business suggests an important advantage of advertising in newspapers. The amount spent to buy newspapers continues to rise, and for 1982 it was over 6.5 billion dollars. *By permission: Newspaper Advertising Bureau, Inc.*

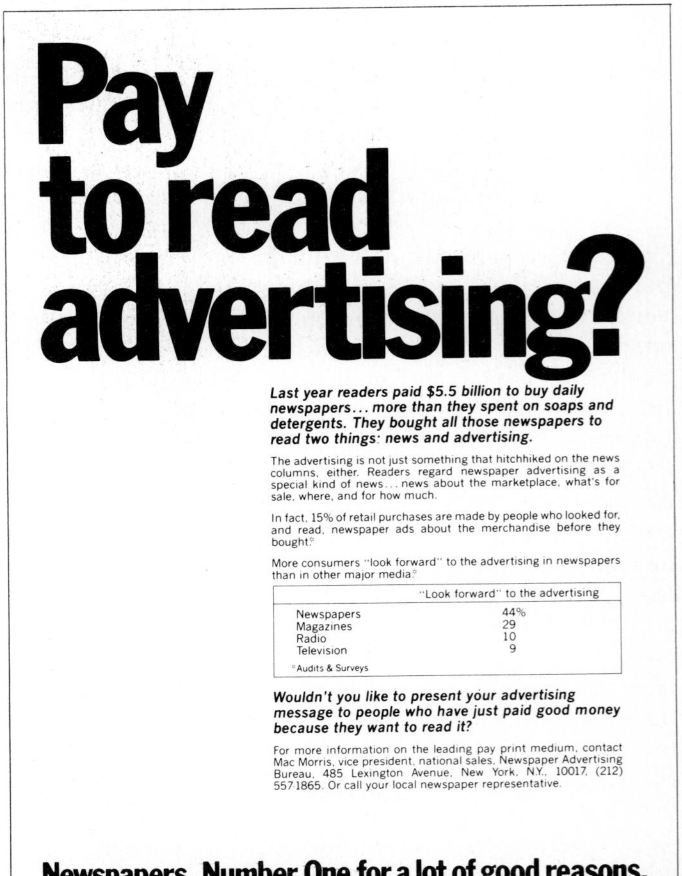

Pay to read advertising?

Last year readers paid $5.5 billion to buy daily newspapers... more than they spent on soaps and detergents. They bought all those newspapers to read two things: news and advertising.

The advertising is not just something that hitchhiked on the news columns, either. Readers regard newspaper advertising as a special kind of news... news about the marketplace, what's for sale, where, and for how much.

In fact, 15% of retail purchases are made by people who looked for, and read, newspaper ads about the merchandise before they bought.

More consumers "look forward" to the advertising in newspapers than in other major media.

	"Look forward" to the advertising
Newspapers	44%
Magazines	29
Radio	10
Television	9

*Audits & Surveys

Wouldn't you like to present your advertising message to people who have just paid good money because they want to read it?

For more information on the leading pay print medium, contact Mac Morris, vice president, national sales, Newspaper Advertising Bureau, 485 Lexington Avenue, New York, N.Y. 10017, (212) 557-1865. Or call your local newspaper representative.

Newspapers. Number One for a lot of good reasons.

advertising for the manufacturer's advertising. Newspapers also offer excellent opportunities for testing advertisements through split runs. Under such arrangements (available through many, though not all, newspapers), the advertiser can run two advertisements, alternating copy, in the same issue of the newspaper. By keying each advertisement and making an offer in each, the advertiser can see from the tabulated results which advertisement pulled best.

One of the greatest shortcomings of newspapers is their mechanical or production limitations. Many newspapers today accept color advertisements, but the quality of reproduction in either color or black and white frequently leaves something to be desired compared to reproduction quality of other print media. Finally, newspapers have a relatively short life. This means the time opportunity for observing an advertisement is limited, and more than one exposure of the same reader to an advertisement is unlikely.

An additional drawback stems from the fact that, whereas television provides visual, oral, and motion communication, and radio is oral, newspapers, like other print media, are only visual. Thus, they must depend upon sight communications, which some psychologists will argue are less penetrating than appeals to the ear.

Newspapers have consistently been the leading advertising mass medium. Daily and Sunday newspapers are the most important classifications for advertising. Space is generally sold by agate lines. There are considerable variations in page size and column widths, making national advertising campaign space buying awkward. Standard Advertising Units represent an industry attempt to standardize advertising space units among newspapers.

Advertising rates in newspapers differ between retail or local rates, which are lower and noncommissionable, and general or national rates, which are higher but commissionable to advertising agencies. Discounts include quantity, frequency, and cash bases.

Traditionally, newspaper circulation was divided by city zone, retail trading zone, and "other." Because national advertisers organize their media plans around Standard Metropolitan Statistical Areas or Areas of Dominant Influence (television market coverage areas), newspapers today also break out their circulation figures this way.

Comparisons of newspaper advertising rates are made on a *milline* basis, but because other media use cost-per-thousand comparisons, these are increasingly used also for newspapers.

TO SUM UP

---

1. Why are newspapers such an important advertising medium when measured by the amount of dollars spent on advertising?
2. What is the difference between national or general and retail or local advertising rates?
3. What is an agate line? How much would an advertisement cost that measures four columns wide and ten inches deep when the agate line rate is 85 cents per line?
4. What are combination rates?
5. What are rebates and short rates as used in newspaper advertising?

QUESTIONS AND PROBLEMS

6. What is the difference between the open rate and the flat rate?

7. Newspaper circulation data may be available to national advertisers on what bases?

8. What is milline rate? What is its major shortcoming?

9. What arguments could be advanced for using newspapers as an advertising medium?

10. What is the main reason for the popularity of retail newspaper advertising?

ENDNOTES

[1] Research Department, Newspaper Advertising Bureau, Inc.

[2] 1982 *Editor & Publisher International Year Book* (New York: The Editor & Publisher Co., Inc., 1982).

[3] *The IMS '83 Ayer Directory of Publications* (Ft. Washington, Penn.: IMS Press, 1983), p. viii.

[4] Shopping newspapers are generally made up exclusively of advertisements (mostly retail) and distributed free (mostly in metropolitan areas).

18

Consumer Magazines, Farm Publications, and Business Publications

After completing this chapter, you should be able to:

1. Discuss periodicals as advertising media
2. Describe how consumer magazines can be used by advertisers
3. Explain the unique position of farm publications
4. Evaluate the use of business publications by advertisers

Exactly what constitutes a magazine is somewhat difficult to describe. The lay public refers to consumer magazines, farm publications, and business publications all as magazines, but the publishing and advertising worlds make a distinction among these three groups. The term *magazines* appears to have been preempted by consumer magazine publishers. For purposes of simplicity and clarity, the term *periodicals* will be used here when referring to the three categories collectively. Some publications are difficult to classify, or even to distinguish from newspapers. Altogether, there are 10,873 periodicals published in the United States.

There are enough similarities among consumer magazines, farm publications, and business publications that certain aspects of their use as advertising media can be discussed at one time. In addition, each has certain unique features, and some attention must be paid to each individually.

PERIODICALS AS MEDIA

Periodicals vary considerably both in frequency of publication and in mechanics. There are dailies, weeklies, semimonthlies, biweeklies, monthlies, bimonthlies, seasonal periodicals, quarterlies, semiannuals, annuals, and publications issued at frequent intervals that do not fit any of the other patterns.

They vary in size and shape. But most are in a standard size like *Sports Illustrated* or *Mademoiselle,* or in pocket size like *TV Guide* or *Reader's Digest.* In addition, there are periodicals of various odd sizes.

Printing reproduction in periodicals is generally good, although quality varies widely and different printing methods are used. Most periodicals accept color advertising. Many offer bleed page opportunities. Many periodicals also offer various forms of physical flexibility, such as gatefolds, inserts of various kinds, special paper stocks, and consecutive numbering of coupons.

Periodical space is generally sold in units such as whole page, half page, and quarter page, and by the column, half column, quarter column, and so forth.

FIGURE 18-1

An advertisement in the business press, promoting magazines as an advertising medium. *By permission: Magazine Publishers Association.*

ADVERTISING RATES   Periodicals most generally quote advertising rates on the basis of the space units mentioned above, although they also quote rates by the agate line.

Many, although not all, periodicals give discounts. Discounts are of two principal types—*frequency* and *volume*. The more popular frequency discount is offered on the basis of the number of insertions, with different rates depending upon the number of insertions. Volume discounts are offered according to the total space used during a specified period, and, as in the case of newspapers, short rates and rebates are applicable. It should be noted, however, that many periodicals offer only flat rates. Almost all also offer cash discounts—usually 2 percent. Besides the rates for black-and-white advertisements, there are special additional charges for color, special position, and sometimes bleed. The most expensive special positions are the covers. Some periodicals also have classification rates for different types of advertisements, such as retail, restaurant, amusement, and book advertisements. About half of all magazines also have shopping advertising pages for retail and mail-order advertising, which have special rates.

GENERAL ADVERTISING-NATIONAL RATES

4-Color	1X	6X	12X	18X	24X	36X	48X	60X	72X	84X	96X	108X	120X
Full page	$53,925	$52,580	$49,995	$47,505	$46,060	$44,850	$44,190	$43,800	$43,335	$42,875	$42,165	$40,985	$40,280
2/3 page	39,365	38,080	36,345	34,370	33,860	33,495	33,230	31,980	31,650	31,305	30,870	30,005	29,490
1/2 page	31,575	30,720	29,490	27,815	27,345	27,005	26,865	26,190	25,600	25,340	24,980	24,280	23,870
1/3 page	21,770	20,685	20,000	19,160	18,810	18,615	18,375	17,680	17,505	17,305	17,070	16,590	16,310

2-Color	1X	6X	12X	18X	24X	36X	48X	60X	72X	84X	96X	108X	120X
Full page	$48,170	$47,120	$44,660	$42,490	$41,190	$40,205	$39,725	$39,270	$38,960	$38,555	$38,010	$36,945	$36,315
2/3 page	35,075	33,745	32,100	30,095	29,605	29,175	28,925	28,655	28,360	28,060	27,680	26,900	26,440
1/2 page	27,460	26,720	25,455	24,055	23,565	23,195	23,055	22,870	22,635	22,405	22,110	21,485	21,115
1/3 page	18,365	17,455	16,775	15,860	15,505	15,350	15,200	15,070	14,905	14,760	14,560	14,145	13,900
1/6 page	9,260	8,845	8,490	8,020	7,850	7,730	7,690	7,650	7,580	7,500	7,395	7,190	7,065

B&W	1X	6X	12X	18X	24X	36X	48X	60X	72X	84X	96X	108X	120X
Full page	$38,510	$37,670	$35,710	$33,970	$32,920	$32,145	$31,745	$31,475	$31,150	$30,825	$30,395	$29,535	$29,040
2/3 page	28,115	27,050	25,730	24,120	23,725	23,375	23,190	22,980	22,740	22,500	22,185	21,565	21,195
1/2 page	21,555	20,985	19,995	18,890	18,500	18,215	18,100	17,955	17,770	17,585	17,360	16,875	16,590
1/3 page	14,590	13,875	13,330	12,595	12,300	12,195	12,085	11,970	11,850	11,720	11,570	11,240	11,055
1/6 page	7,430	7,080	6,800	6,430	6,285	6,190	6,170	.6,145	6,075	6,015	5,920	5,760	5,665

REGIONAL PAGE RATES

		1X	6X	12X	18X	24X	36X	48X +
New England	4-Color	$ 4,455	$ 4,345	$ 4,260	$ 4,100	$ 4,035	$ 3,840	$ 3,640
Circulation—170,000	2-Color	3,665	3,585	3,505	3,380	3,325	3,165	3,005
National equivalent—.04 pp. B&W		2,995	2,940	2,875	2,770	2,720	2,590	2,455
Southwestern	4-Color	$14,335	$14,050	$13,760	$13,255	$13,045	$12,400	$11,755
Circulation—675,000	2-Color	12,005	11,770	11,525	11,105	10,925	10,390	9,845
National equivalent—.15 pp. B&W		9,520	9,335	9,135	8,810	8,665	8,235	7,810
Southeastern	4-Color	$12,060	$11,820	$11,580	$11,155	$10,975	$10,430	$ 9,885
Circulation—550,000	2-Color	10,100	9,895	9,695	9,340	9,195	8,750	8,280
National equivalent—.13 pp. B&W		8,010	7,855	7,685	7,415	7,290	6,935	6,565
North Central	4-Color	$18,325	$18,015	$17,645	$17,000	$16,720	$15,880	$15,050
Circulation—910,000	2-Color	15,285	15,035	14,720	14,175	13,950	13,245	11,950
National equivalent—.21 pp. B&W		12,085	11,835	11,595	11,165	10,985	10,420	9,870
Mid-Atlantic	4-Color	$15,950	$15,630	$15,315	$14,755	$14,515	$13,800	$13,085
Circulation—775,000	2-Color	13,330	13,060	12,795	12,330	12,130	11,530	10,930
National equivalent—.18 pp. B&W		10,575	10,360	10,150	9,785	9,620	9,145	8,670
Western	4-Color	$18,265	$17,900	$17,535	$16,900	$16,615	$15,805	$14,980
Circulation—905,000	2-Color	15,300	14,990	14,685	14,265	13,920	13,235	12,545
National equivalent—.21 pp. B&W		12,135	11,890	11,645	11,215	11,045	10,500	9,950

METRO PAGE RATES

		1X	6X	12X	18X	24X	36X	48X +
New York	4-Color	$ 6,565	$ 6,430	$ 6,240	$ 6,170	$ 6,035	$ 5,740	$ 5,415
Circulation—265,000	2-Color	5,480	5,370	5,205	5,145	5,040	4,795	4,530
National equivalent—.06 pp. B&W		4,345	4,260	4,125	4,090	4,000	3,800	3,590
Southern California	4-Color	$ 7,960	$ 7,800	$ 7,560	$ 7,480	$ 7,320	$ 6,970	$ 6,565
Circulation—325,000	2-Color	6,640	6,510	6,310	6,245	6,110	5,805	5,475
National equivalent—.07 pp. B&W		5,270	5,160	5,005	4,955	4,845	4,610	4,345
Northern California	4-Color	$ 5,380	$ 5,275	$ 5,110	$ 5,060	$ 4,945	$ 4,710	$ 4,435
Circulation—210,000	2-Color	4,490	4,400	4,270	4,220	4,130	3,935	3,705
National equivalent—.05 pp. B&W		3,555	3,490	3,380	3,345	3,275	3,115	2,935
Chicago	4-Color	$ 4,005	$ 3,925	$ 3,815	$ 3,765	$ 3,690	$ 3,505	$ 3,305
Circulation—145,000	2-Color	3,345	3,275	3,175	3,135	3,070	2,925	2,755
National equivalent—.03 pp. B&W		2,650	2,595	2,520	2,490	2,440	2,315	2,185

STATE PAGE RATES

		1X	6X	12X	18X	24X	36X	48X +
Texas	4-Color	$ 7,180	$ 7,040	$ 6,825	$ 6,745	$ 6,600	$ 6,280	$ 5,925
Circulation—285,000	2-Color	6,005	5,880	5,705	5,645	5,525	5,250	4,955
National equivalent—.06 pp. B&W		4,775	4,670	4,525	4,475	4,385	4,170	3,935
Florida	4-Color	$ 5,300	$ 5,195	$ 5,035	$ 4,985	$ 4,885	$ 4,640	$ 4,370
Circulation—195,000	2-Color	4,420	4,340	4,210	4,160	4,075	3,880	3,655
National equivalent—.04 pp. B&W		3,505	3,435	3,330	3,290	3,220	3,070	2,880

FIGURE 18-2

Part of a magazine rate card for *Playboy. By permission: Playboy Magazine.*

Like newspapers, periodicals may offer optional combination rates for two or, in many cases, more periodicals. This is especially true for consumer magazines, newspaper supplements, and farm publications. These combinations are referred to as *groups*. For example, the McFadden's Women's Group consists of *True Story, True Romance, True Experience, True Love, True Confessions, Modern Romances, Photoplay,* and *Secrets. True Confessions* and *Photoplay* can each be bought separately or advertising space can be bought for all eight publications collectively. There are over 60 magazine group buying opportunities.

COST PER THOUSAND   Periodical rate comparisons are made on the basis of *cost per thousand* for a full page in black and white. Advertisers, however, may want to make certain variations in computing cost per thousand. For example, they may want to adjust the cost per page to the actual cost in color or for a bleed. Instead of circulation, they may substitute audience or target audience (those readers who are prospective buyers of the product). There is a growing trend toward using demographic characteristics of the target market rather than circulation in these CPM (cost-per-thousand) calculations. Calculations based on households, heavy users, prime prospects, and the like are much more meaningful to the media planner. Cost-per-thousand figures in periodicals vary considerably because page sizes, editorial content, distribution methods, and the selective quality of circulations vary so much between one periodical and another. The result may be a considerably higher CPM for one periodical than another. It is important to remember that CPM alone is not the basis for choosing a periodical, and advertisers may well pick periodicals with a higher CPM if they will serve their media objectives more effectively.

CIRCULATION AND READERSHIP   Most periodicals have national circulations and readerships consisting of very general to highly specialized audiences. Circulation may be by mail subscription or retail store sales or a combination. It may be paid or, as is the case for many business periodicals, qualified (free), or a combination of the two.

VERIFICATION OF CIRCULATION Since circulation is the basis for advertising rates and one of the prime considerations in media selection, circulation figure credibility is of great importance. There are three circulation auditing groups. The Audit Bureau of Circulations, in addition to auditing newspaper circulation, audits periodicals with both paid and qualified circulation. There is also the Business Publications Audit of Circulation (BPA), which also covers both paid and qualified circulation. Both the ABC and BPA are nonprofit associations controlled by advertisers and advertising agencies. A third auditing organization for business publications, a privately operated venture for profit, is the Verified Audit Circulation Corporation (VAC), which will also audit both paid and qualified circulation.

Kit. *In Titusville, Pa., a for-sale ad in the* Herald *offered wool blankets, furniture, a shotgun, a wedding ring.*

TIME

GUARANTEED CIRCULATION AND THE CIRCULATION RATE BASE
Because the circulation for the particular issue of the periodical in which the advertiser's advertisement appears may fall below the previous circulation on which the advertising rates are based, some periodicals base their rates on *guaranteed circulation.* If circulation falls below the guarantee, the advertiser receives a rebate. In order to minimize the likelihood of rebating, however, periodicals generally set conservative guaranteed circulations, and the excess in actual circulation results in a bonus for the advertiser.

Today most of the large-circulation periodicals and many others have gone to a circulation rate base instead of the guaranteed circulation. In this system, the rates are based on a set average circulation figure, which is almost always below the actual circulation delivered in a given issue. Where the rate base is used, there is no guarantee of circulation. The guaranteed circulation tended to be unfair to publishers because they had to rebate the advertisers if their circulation fell off, but when they delivered circulation over the guarantee, the advertisers got the extra circulation without charge. Of course, with the rate base system, the advertisers take the risk that circulation will fall below it, but this is not a likely occurrence, since publishers would find it hard to attract advertisers if circulation regularly fell below the rate base. Also, for periodicals with most of their circulation by subscription, there is little likelihood of much circulation fluctuation.

QUALITATIVE CHARACTERISTICS When choosing periodicals, as when choosing newspapers, advertisers must weigh qualitative as well as quantitative factors. They should ascertain audience buying potential, including share of the total market, spendable income for the primary and secondary audience, and consumer expenditure patterns. They should also evaluate the degree of advertiser acceptance. Attention must also be paid to editorial matter. And advertisers will want to examine audience composition in terms of individuals and households. Finally, they should evaluate what services are available to advertisers.

Experience has taught me that, just as unmined gold is valueless, so are articles and manufactured goods hidden away in warehouses and factories useless until they are made known and made desirable by the art of advertising . . . it is uneconomic to build factories and buy machinery and raw materials unless adequate financial provision is also made to meet the cost of advertising the good produced.

DUKE OF WINDSOR

READER'S DIGEST

CONSUMER MAGAZINES

Over 1,200 consumer magazines are available to advertisers. They range in editorial content from *general editorial* to highly specialized classifications, from *airline inflight* to *youth. Standard Rate & Data Service* lists 67 classification groupings in all. This wide variety of specialized magazines permits the advertiser to reach both very general and highly selected audiences. About 48 percent of magazine pages contain advertisements. Forty percent of total magazine advertising revenue is for advertising smoking materials, automotive, alcoholic beverages, toiletries, and food.[1]

The Magazine Publishers Association (MPA) Marketing Division is the advertising promotional arm of the industry. In promoting the use of consumer magazines as an advertising medium, it suggests the following reasons why magazines sell:

1. *Authority.* Magazine authority dates back to man's very acceptance of the printed word as dependable . . . to his own signature which is accepted as a binding pledge.
2. *Color.* Magazine color spreads before the reader a spectrum of exciting visual pleasure. Color stimulates interest . . . creates desire . . . enhances image . . . identifies the package. Color sells.
3. *Believability.* Magazine believability builds reader confidence. Its influence affects ideas . . . opinions . . . desires. People believe what magazines have to say.
4. *Permanence.* Magazines last. People save them . . . set them aside for future reference . . . return to them again and again. The permanence of magazines gives your advertising the time it needs for careful consideration . . . the time that it deserves.
5. *Selectivity.* Magazine selectivity targets places and people. It reaches your best prospects . . . wherever they are . . . while they are most receptive to ideas and information.
6. *Flexibility.* Magazines offer a full range of prospects . . . with divergent interests . . . in one or all of the nation's key markets. The degree to which an advertisement stimulates . . . dramatizes . . . sells products is entirely at the discretion of the advertiser.
7. *Efficiency.* The ability of magazines to offer the widest range of incomparable values which can be translated into dollar sales makes magazines the choice of leading advertisers.[2]

The advertising man is liaison between the products of business and the mind of the nation. He must know both before he can serve either.

GLENN FRANK, Educator

READER'S DIGEST

In general, consumer magazines correlate well with population density and buying power for the whole country. For many advertisers, this provides a boon. However, not all advertisers are interested in this kind of coverage, for many times they wish to reach only certain geographic markets. To meet these needs there always have been some magazines of a regional nature and others that, because of their highly specialized editorial content, reach consumers with certain demographic characteristics. In the past, however, most magazines offered only national circulation, and those of a less specialized nature could deliver only a general audience. In recent years, however, there has been a growing trend among magazines to offer geographic and demographic editions to advertisers. *Better Homes and Gardens,* for example, offers 56 top markets (major metropolitan areas) and virtually any combination of regions and states. It also offers a demographic edition called Super Spot (high-income edition). Research has shown that the less-than-full-run advertising accounts for approximately 20 percent of total magazine advertising revenues. Thus, magazines have found a way of overcoming some of their market inflexibility.

Consumer Magazines, Farm Publications, and Business Publications

FIGURE 18-3

A consumer magazine listing from *Standard Rate & Data Service.* By permission: *Standard Rate & Data Service, Inc.*

Mademoiselle

A Conde Nast Publications Inc. Publication
(This is a paid duplicate of the listing under classification No. 50.)

Ⓐ ⒷⒸ   ⓂⓅⒶ

Media Code 8 728 0950 4.00   Mid 001298-000
Published monthly by The Conde Nast Publications, Inc., Conde Nast, 350 Madison Ave., New York, NY 10017. Phone 212-880-8800.
For shipping info., see Print Media Production Data.

PUBLISHER'S EDITORIAL PROFILE
MADEMOISELLE is edited for the woman 18-34, and addresses the needs of this fast-growing consumer segment with coverage of career topics, fashion, beauty, health, home decorating, travel, entertaining and the arts. Food, alcoholic beverages, automotive, personal finance, home sewing and crafts are treated in regularly scheduled columns. In addition, Mademoiselle publishes in-depth articles on subjects of current interest. Rec'd 2/25/82.

1. PERSONNEL
Publisher—Joseph L. Fuchs.
Advertising Director—Elliot Marion.
Mgr. Adv. Make-up—Agnes Kent.

2. REPRESENTATIVES and/or BRANCH OFFICES
Los Angeles 90010—Jerome S. Bronow, 3921 Wilshire Blvd. Phone 213-385-9141.
Boston 02116—Henry L. Shuster, Statler Bldg. Phone 617-426-6850.
Chicago 60611—Donald J. Henry, 875 N. Michigan Ave. Phone 312-943-2710.
Boca Raton, FL—Publishers' Representatives Of Florida, Inc.
Marietta, GA—Carbonara & Company.

3. COMMISSION AND CASH DISCOUNT
15% to recognized agencies. 2% cash discount 10 days; net 30.

4. GENERAL RATE POLICY
Announcement of any change in rate will be made at least 2 months in advance of black and white closing date for issue affected. Orders for issues thereafter at rates then prevailing.

ADVERTISING RATES
Rates effective February, 1983 issue. (Card No. 36.)
Rates received July 26, 1982.
Card received September 20, 1982.

5. BLACK/WHITE RATES

1 page	12,850.	1 column	4,340.
2 columns	8,680.	1/2 column	2,200.
1/2 page	7,890.		

5a. COMBINATION RATES
Also sold in combination—see listing for The Conde Nast Package Of Women in this Classification.

6. COLOR RATES

	b/1c	4 color
1 page	15,780.	18,720.
2 columns	11,700.	14,600.
1/2 page	10,890.	13,830.
1 column	7,650.	9,790.

7. COVERS
Non-cancellable.

2nd cover (4 color)	20,500.
3rd cover (4 color)	18,720.
4th cover (4 color)	21,710.

Options on cover positions must be exercised at least 30 days prior to four-color closing date. If order is not received by such date, cover option automatically lapses.

8. INSERTS
All special space units such as gatefolds, inserts requiring metallic inks, multiple page ads necessitating special positioning or other than normal printing treatment must be discussed in advance with publisher to establish feasibility and rates.

9. BLEED
Extra 15%

10. SPECIAL POSITION
Orders specifying positions other than those known as preferred not accepted. Orders specifying "right" or "left" accepted but cannot be guaranteed.
Card position reservations: Insertion order from agency concerned is required to guarantee a specific post card position. All orders calling for supplied inserts non-cancellable 60 days before closing date.

11. CLASSIFIED/MAIL ORDER
DISPLAY CLASSIFICATIONS:
MAIL ORDER
BLACK AND WHITE RATES:

	1 iss	3 iss	6 iss	12 iss
1 page	10,920.	10,374.	9,828.	9,282.
2 columns	7,280.	6,916.	6,552.	6,188.
1 column	3,640.	3,458.	3,276.	3,094.
3/4 column	2,720.	2,584.	2,448.	2,312.
1/2 column	1,830.	1,739.	1,647.	1,556.
1/4 column	920.	874.	828.	782.

COLOR RATES:
4 color:

	1 iss	3 iss	6 iss	12 iss
1 page	15,630.	14,849.	14,067.	13,286.
2 columns	12,000.	11,400.	10,800.	10,200.
1/2 page	11,240.	10,678.	10,116.	9,554.

COLLEGE AND SCHOOLS
BLACK AND WHITE RATES:

	1 iss	3 iss	6 iss	12 iss
1 page	9,000.	8,550.	8,100.	7,650.
2/3 page	6,000.	5,700.	5,400.	5,100.
1/2 page	4,500.	4,275.	4,050.	3,825.
1/3 page	3,000.	2,850.	2,700.	2,550.
84 lines	1,750.	1,663.	1,575.	1,488.
71 lines	1,500.	1,425.	1,350.	1,275.
56 lines	1,160.	1,102.	1,044.	986.
49 lines	1,025.	974.	923.	871.
42 lines	880.	836.	792.	748.
35 lines	745.	708.	671.	633.
28 lines	593.	563.	534.	504.
21 lines	445.	423.	401.	378.
14 lines	297.	282.	267.	252.
Line rate				21.25

FREQUENCY DISCOUNTS:
Discounts based on the use of 3, 6 or 12 separate issues within a 12 month period. Frequency refunds will be credited as earned during each advertiser's contract year.

MECH. REQUIREMENTS:

143 lines	2-1/4" x 10-3/16"
71 lines	2-1/4" x 5-1/16"
56 lines	2-1/4" x 4"
35 lines	2-1/4" x 2-1/2"
28 lines	2-1/4" x 2"
14 lines	2-1/4" x 1"

TRAVEL
BLACK AND WHITE RATES:

1 page	8,440.
2 columns	5,630.
1 column	2,815.
1/2 column	1,410.
35 lines	705.
28 lines	565.
21 lines	420.
14 lines	280.

COLOR RATES:
4 color:

1 page	13,160.
2 columns	10,340.
1/2 page	7,580.

FREQUENCY DISCOUNTS:
Frequency discounts are for total issues used within any 12-month period. Combinations of units in the one issue are considered as one insertion for rate purposes. Frequency refunds will be credited as earned during each advertiser's contract year. Schedules combining large and small space units are entitled to these discounts, except that any increase in total discount shall not exceed the net billing of the smallest unit.

RETAIL
BLACK AND WHITE RATES:

1 page	9,840.
2 columns	6,570.
1/2 page	5,760.
1 column	3,290.

COLOR RATES:
Black and 1 color:

1 page	12,120.
2 columns	8,840.
1/2 page	8,040.
1 column	5,530.

4 color:

1 page	14,040.
2 columns	11,010.
1/2 page	9,940.
1 column	7,460.

12. SPLIT-RUN
True A/B and "cluster" splits, regional inserts and off-set—available.

14. CONTRACT AND COPY REGULATIONS
See Contents page for location—items 1, 2, 3, 4, 7, 10, 18, 19, 24, 30, 35.

15. MECH. REQUIREMENTS
For complete, detailed production information, see SRDS Print Media Production Data.
Printing Process: Rotogravure, limited offset available.
Covers And Regionals Offset.
Trim size: 8-1/8 x 10-7/8; No./Cols. 3.
Binding method: Saddle-stitched.
Covers offset follow MPA standards.

DIMENSIONS-AD PAGE

1	7 x 10-3/16	1/2	3-1/2 x 10-3/16
2 col	4-5/8 x 10-3/16	1 col	2-1/4 x 10-3/16
1 col	4-5/8 x 5-1/16	1/2	2-1/4 x 5-1/6
1/2	7 x 5-1/16	1/2 col	4-5/8 x 2-1/2

16. ISSUE AND CLOSING DATES
Published monthly; on sale 15th of month preceding date of issue.
Cover closing 1st of 3rd month preceding date of issue.
Color and black and white closing 20th of 3rd month preceding date of issue.
Supplied inserts non-cancellable 60 days before closing date. Inside 4 color, 2 color and black and white order cancellation dates 10 days prior to closing date.

17. SPECIAL SERVICES
A.B.C. Supplemental Data Report released February 1982 issue.

18. CIRCULATION
Established 1935. Single copy 1.75; per year 12.00.
Summary data—for detail see Publisher's Statement.
A.B.C. 12-31-82 (6 mos. aver.—Magazine Form)

Tot. Pd.	(Subs.)	(Single)	(Assoc.)
1,283,510	405,205	878,305	

Average Total Non-Pd Distribution (not incl. above):
Total 24,127
TERRITORIAL DISTRIBUTION 9/82—1,420,625

N.Eng.	Mid.Atl.	E.N.Cen.	W.N.Cen.	S.Atl.
92,522	257,060	210,570	99,883	212,310
E.S.Cen.	W.S.Cen.	Mtn.St.	Pac.St.	Canada
65,649	125,766	63,141	187,445	85,057
Foreign	Other			
14,773	6,449			

Rate Card No. 36 effective February, 1983 issue states: "Rates based on a yearly average of 1,050,000."

(D-C, C-C2)

FIGURE 18-4

This advertisement explains how the use of MNI permits a local advertiser to advertise in national magazines without having to buy unwanted circulation. *By permission: Media Networks, Inc.*

From the advertiser's point of view, the problem of market inflexibility has also been solved to some extent through a service offered by Media Networks, Inc. This service permits an advertiser to use magazines in metropolitan areas that are too small for separate geographic editions. MNI will preprint the advertisements for local and national advertisers wishing to buy any of 125 specific metropolitan markets and will then arrange for a demographically compatible group of magazines to bind these into those subscriptions and selected single-copy sales going into that market. This service makes it economically feasible for the magazine and the advertiser, because the magazine does not have to prepare a special edition and the advertiser can effect economies of scale in preprinting the same advertisement for a number of different magazines.

Inflexibility has also resulted from the early closing dates (the dates on which an advertisement must be in the publisher's hand) of magazines, but recent innovations have moved closing dates up nearer to issue dates. Some magazines now offer, for a premium rate, *fast*

No hang-ups.

"Sorry, right number." That was the response Boston Traders—distributors of high-quality sportswear for men and women—got from their first-ever ad in PLAYBOY.

Boston Traders is a growing concern. Growing so rapidly, in fact, that they decided to expand from trade advertising to a consumer campaign. And to make that move in regional editions of PLAYBOY.

Crossed wires.

Boston Traders—and Maslow, Gold & Rothschild of Boston, their agency—decided to run the same ad in the April 1983 PLAYBOY that

had run in the trade publications. The only difference: For their PLAYBOY appearance, the telephone number and address of their New York showroom would be omitted.

But somewhere along the line a wire or two got crossed. The showroom information remained in the ad. PLAYBOY readers got ahold of it. And that was the end of any peace and quiet for Boston Traders.

Busy signals.

"As soon as that issue of PLAYBOY hit the stands," says Joe Lynch, executive vice-president of Boston Traders, "our phones started ringing off the hook." Joe adds, "Our showroom isn't all that easy to find. But PLAYBOY readers found us—by the hundreds. I guess they couldn't get through on the phone."

Will Boston Traders advertise in PLAYBOY again? "PLAYBOY has a phenomenal impact on the men's fashion field," says Lynch.

PLAYBOY means business.

"PLAYBOY will be at the top of our media list from now on." In fact, the company plans to go national beginning with the September issue.

If you'd like to find out how many calls your switchboard can handle, call on PLAYBOY—and the more than 13 million men who read it every month. We have no hang-up about giving you our phone number, either—212-688-3030 in New York; 312-751-8000 in Chicago; 213-934-6600 in Los Angeles.

FOR THE LATEST IN FINE IMPORTED SPORTSWEAR, CHECK THE LINES AT BOSTON TRADERS, 212-245-2919 OR 617-599-5345. OR WRITE FOR DETAILS TO BOSTON TRADERS, 15 WEST 55TH STREET, NEW YORK, N.Y. 10019.

Source: MRI, Spring 1983. © 1983 by Playboy.

FIGURE 18-5

A consumer magazine advertises to business to explain its advantages as an advertising medium. *By permission: Playboy Magazine.*

close availabilities, which bring the closing dates closer to publication dates. However, the relative infrequency of magazine issues, with many appearing only once a week and the largest number published monthly, remains a problem, because it means that the advertiser must have advertisements appear on the publisher's issuance date, which may not be most convenient for the timing of the overall sales effort. Advertisements must be prepared months in advance. Between the time an advertisement is started and the time it appears in the magazine, many factors can alter its effectiveness: Competitive conditions can change, consumer attitudes can change, and news events can become stale.

Although, on the basis of cost per thousand, magazines are not necessarily expensive, the total cost per page represents a substantial investment and may make it difficult for a small advertiser to use the medium and still have funds for other media or allow for spreading the advertising effort over a longer period of time. In addition to the space cost, the cost of production for magazine advertisements is relatively high. The rates charged by magazines are for the space only, and the advertiser also has all the costs involved in preparing the advertisement itself, including costs for artwork, typography, engravings, and so forth.

However, magazines offer the finest opportunity for excellent graphic reproduction. Food advertisements in color, for example, can look realistic and very appetizing. Magazines are prestige media and can enhance the reputation of the advertiser through association.

Although magazines cannot always reach special geographic markets, they are (with the exception of general editorial magazines) unexcelled in reaching audiences with special interests. The advertiser selling boating supplies can reach a market with almost no waste circulation by advertising in a publication like *Rudder* or *Boating*. The dress producer can use *Harper's Bazaar* or *Mademoiselle*, for example. In fact, in this last classification there are enough different magazines with

FIGURE 18-6

A farm publication listing from *Standard Rate & Data Service. By permission: Standard Rate & Data Service, Inc.*

Florida Cattleman and Livestock Journal, The

Official publication of:
Florida Cattlemen's Assn., Eastern Brahman Assn., Southeastern States Brangus Assn., Georgia-Florida Charolais Assn., Florida Hereford Assn., Inc., Florida Angus Assn., Florida Santa Gertrudis Assn., Florida Shorthorn Breeders' Assn., Florida Meat Packers Assn., Florida Beef Council, Florida Cutting Horse Assn., Florida Simmental Assn., Association of Florida Rodeos, Florida Polled Hereford Assn., Florida Limousin Assn., Florida Assoc. of Livestock Markets.

(ABC)   APA

Media Code 8 917 2100 3.00   Mid 001510-000
Published monthly by the Florida Cattlemen's Association at Cody Publications, Inc., P. O. Box 1403, 410 Verona St., Kissimmee, FL 32742. Phone 305-846-2800.
For shipping info., see Print Media Production Data.
PUBLISHER'S EDITORIAL PROFILE
FLORIDA CATTLEMAN AND LIVESTOCK JOURNAL, THE is written primarily for commercial cow and calf ranchers, pure bred cattle producers, dairy farmers and horsemen. Articles include current industry news; educational features on practical cattle operations; and from researchers—covering breeding, feeding, pasture management, parasite control, marketing, financing, and managing on large scale ranches.
1. PERSONNEL
Editor—James J. Flanagan.
Managing Editor—Donald E. Berry.
Advertising Coordinator—Lou Allen.
3. COMMISSION AND CASH DISCOUNT
15% to agencies; 2%—10 days after billing. Agency discount not allowed when ring services are required on breeder sale ads.
4. GENERAL RATE POLICY
Alcoholic beverages advertising not accepted.
ADVERTISING RATES
Rates effective December 1, 1982. (Card No. 41.)
Card received September 30, 1982.
5. BLACK/WHITE RATES

	1 ti	12 ti		1 ti	12 ti
1 page	450.	350.	1/6 page	86.	68.
2/3 page	318.	252.	1/12 page	44.	34.
1/2 page	242.	192.	1/24 page	22.	14.
1/3 page	166.	134.			

Dimensions different from those above charged at the 1" rate 18.00.
Subject to short rate for difference between rate earned and rate charged.
6. COLOR RATES
Standard AAAA color, per page, extra .... 80.
Matched special color, extra 125.00
Process color 250.00

7. COVERS
Available by contract.
8. INSERTS
Rates on preprinted inserts available.
9. BLEED
No charge.
10. SPECIAL POSITION
Advertisers specifying special positions will be accommodated where possible.
11. CLASSIFIED/MAIL ORDER
.35 per word, minimum charge 6.00 per issue.
Payable in advance.
DISPLAY CLASSIFICATIONS
Commercial advertisers must use minimum 1/12 page per month, 12 consecutive months in order to be eligible for 12 issue rate on all space or insert 12 full pages during a 12 month period. Livestock advertisers may hold 12-issue rate by using minimum "rate-maker" (approx. 17 agate lines) at cost of 14.00 per month. 12-issue rate is 20% off transient rate.
14. CONTRACT AND COPY REGULATIONS
See Contents page for location—items 1, 2, 8, 10, 11, 15, 24, 25, 27, 28, 34, 36, 39.
15. MECH. REQUIREMENTS
For complete, detailed production information, see SRDS Print Media Production Data.
Printing Process: Offset, sheet fed.
Trim size: 8-1/4 x 11; No./Cols. 3.
Colors available: Standard colors.

DIMENSIONS-AD PAGE

1	7 x		10	1/3	2-1/6 x		10
2/3	4-7/12 x		10	1/6	2-1/6 x		4-11/12
1/2	7 x		4-11/12	1/6	4-7/12 x		2-5/12
1/2	4-7/12 x		7-5/12	1/12	2-1/6 x		2-5/12
1/3	4-7/12 x		4-11/12	1/24	2-1/6 x		1-1/4

16. ISSUE AND CLOSING DATES
Published monthly. Issued 25th of preceding month.
Closing date for color and forms 5th of month preceding
Proofs close 1st of month preceding.
Contracts or insertions may be cancelled prior to closing date.
18. CIRCULATION
Established 1936. Single copy .35; per year 5.00.
Summary data—for detail see Publisher's Statement.
A.B.C. 12-31-82—(6 mos. aver.—Farm Form)

Tot. Pd.	(Subs.)	(Single)	(Assoc.)
6,533	6,516	17	5,036

Average bulk sales (not incl. above):
Total 788
TERRITORIAL DISTRIBUTION 12/82—6,630

N.Eng.	Mid.Atl.	E.N.Cen.	W.N.Cen.	S.Atl.	E.S.Cen.
4	20	27	16	6,388	62
W.S.Cen.	Mtn.St.	Pac.St.	Canada	Foreign	Other
41	13	14	2	26	17

enough differences in reader characteristics to allow the advertiser to reach the particular age and income groups desired. Because in so many consumer magazines the editorial content relates so closely to the advertising, many readers are very interested in the advertising.

FARM PUBLICATIONS

The nearly 250 farm publications listed in *Standard Rate & Data Service* are hard to classify. Inasmuch as farming is business, it might be argued that farm publications should be included with business publications. On the other hand, some farm publications appeal to all members of the farm family, and they could therefore be classified as consumer magazines, although there is a trend toward catering to farming as a business rather than a "way of life." At any rate, there is a definable market called the farm market, which can be, and in many marketing plans is, considered separately in discussing media.

Standard Rate & Data Service classifies farm publications by subject: dairy and dairy breeds; diversified farming and farm home; farm education and vocations; farm electrification, farm organizations and cooperatives; field crops and soil management; fruits, nuts, vegetables, and special products; land use, irrigation, and conservation; livestock and breed; newspaper distributed farm publications; and poultry. Farm publications are also classified by territorial groupings—national, sectional, and state. As with consumer magazines, advertisers can buy regional editions, split runs, color, bleed, inserts, and other special features in many farm publications. These publications have many of the same strengths and weaknesses of other periodicals, and the media buyer will make analyses for selection in much the same manner as for other periodicals.

The Agricultural Publishers Association (APA) is made up of a group of farm publications, all of which have their circulations audited by the Audit Bureau of Circulations. The main function of the organization is to promote increased advertising in farm publications.

There is nothing so absolutely unimportant as copy for copy's sake. Copy is only the telephone wire that carries the message: if only it carry the message clearly, swiftly, accurately, powerfully, the wire itself may be as rusty and bent as an old nail.

KENNETH M. GOODE, Advertising Writer

READER'S DIGEST

BUSINESS PUBLICATIONS

There are several thousand business publications, with a combined circulation of over 70 million. *Standard Rate & Data Service* lists 176 different classifications, which run the gamut from *advertising and marketing* to *woodworking*. Every conceivable kind of business and professional field appears to have one or more business papers. The names of just a few will indicate the high degree of specialization: *Aviation Week & Space Technology, Ohio Tavern News, Recycling Today,*

Constructor

Official publication of:
The Associated General Contractors of America, Inc.

▽BPA   𝖲𝖭𝖠𝖯

Media Code 7 245 2560 5.00   Mid 002998-000
Published monthly by AGC Information, Inc., a subsidiary of The Associated General Contractors of America, Inc., 1957 E. St., N. W., Washington, DC 20006. Phone 202-393-2040.
For shipping info., see Print Media Production Data.
PUBLISHER'S EDITORIAL PROFILE
CONSTRUCTOR is AGC's management magazine for the construction industry. Editorial emphasis is on new ideas for management as well as reviews of management trends in construction. Articles feature market data, economic analysis, interpretation of government controls and regulations, ideas on computers, bidding, public relations, purchasing, man-power and training, education, legal matters and taxation. Rec'd 9/27/79.

1. PERSONNEL
Publisher—Hubert Beatty.
Managing Editor—John Berard.
Marketing Manager—Becky Lower.
Editor—Diane Snow.

2. REPRESENTATIVES and/or BRANCH OFFICES
New York 10016—Glenn Spaeth, ParQuil Associates, Ltd., 210 E. 36th St. Phone 212-683-8600.
Chicago 60611—Fox and Associates, Inc., 200 E. Ontario St., 2nd Floor. Phone 312-649-1650.
Dallas 73238—Marc Bryant, Marketing Communications, Inc., P. O. Box 38212. Phone 214-349-2756.
Los Angeles 90036—Bruce Bigler, Zander & Bigler, 6030 Wilshire Blvd. Phone 213-938-0111.
Kansas City—Marc Bryant. Phone 816-842-8571.
Atlanta—Marc Bryant. Phone 404-524-1926.

3. COMMISSION AND CASH DISCOUNT
15% to agencies on space, color, bleed and position provided account is paid within 30 days; 2% if paid within 10 days. Bills rendered about 15th of publication month. Commission does not apply on mechanical charges such as back-up, photo conversion, special binding, insert printing.

4. GENERAL RATE POLICY
Rates subject to change upon notice. At time of change contracts already started will be completed at no penalty. When full schedule is not run, advertiser will be rebilled for space actually used.

ADVERTISING RATES
Effective June 1, 1982. (Card No. 31)
Card received May 13, 1982.

5. BLACK/WHITE RATES

	1 ti	3 ti	6 ti	12 ti	18 ti
1 page	1200	1125	1075	1035	1000
2/3 page	890	835	790	760	735
1/2 page	700	665	630	600	575
1/3 page	510	470	435	420	400
1/4 page	385	355	330	325	315
1/6 page	310	290	275	265	260

Multiple frequency rates based on number of issues used during a 12-month period (no bulking of space permitted.) Each page of a spread will be counted as 1 insertion toward warning frequency rate. 1/6 page rateholder.

6. COLOR RATES
Black and color available in all sizes, standard
AAAA colors: yellow, orange, red, blue, green, purple and brown, per color, extra .... 225.
Matched colors, per color, extra .... 325.

4-color process:

	1 ti	3 ti	6 ti	12 ti	18 ti
1 page	1900	1835	1770	1705	1640

Fractional ads at earned black/white rate plus .... 660.

7. COVERS
Non-cancellable.
2nd & 3rd covers:

	1 ti	3 ti	6 ti	12 ti
Black/white	1480	1410	1340	1270
2-colors	1650	1580	1510	1440
3-colors	1835	1765	1695	1625
4-colors	2015	1945	1875	1805
4th cover, 4-colors	2240	2170	2100	2030

8. INSERTS
Furnished complete, no back-up:
2-page inserts. earned black/white rate, plus folding and binding ROP .... 400.
4-page inserts. earned black/white rate, plus folding and binding ROP .... 635.
Postcard inserts with lip:
Ad dimension size rate for 2 sides, plus folding and binding ROP .... 400.
Back-up charge (non-commissionable).
Per page .... 240.

9. BLEED
Acceptable in spreads, full page and 2/3 page units. No charge for bleed.

10. SPECIAL POSITION
Non-cancellable, extra 15%

11. CLASSIFIED/MAIL ORDER
For complete data, refer to Business Publication Rates and Data - Classified.

13a. GEOGRAPHIC and/or DEMOGRAPHIC EDITIONS
Regional full page ads—available.

14. CONTRACT AND COPY REGULATIONS
See conditions page for location—items 1, 2, 3, 5, 6, 7, 8, 12, 13, 14, 15, 17, 18, 19, 21, 22, 25, 26, 27, 28, 30, 31, 32, 35.

15. MECH REQUIREMENTS
For complete, detailed production information, see SRDS Print Media Production Data.
Printing Process: Web Offset. Covers: Offset, sheetfed.
Trim size: 8-1/8 x 10-7/8; No./Cols. 3.
Binding method: Saddle-stitched.
Colors available: AAAA/ABP; Matched; 4-Color Process (AAAA/MPA).

METALLIC.

DIMENSIONS-AD PAGE

1	6-13/16 x 9-5/8	1/3	2-1/8 x 9-5/8
2/3	4-1/2 x 9-5/8	1/3	4-1/2 x 4-1/2
1/2	6-13/16 x 4-13/16	1/4	3-5/16 x 4-1/2
1/2	3-5/16 x 9-5/8	1/4	6-13/16 x 2-7/16
1/2	4-1/2 x 7-3/8	1/6	2-1/8 x 4-1/2

16. ISSUE AND CLOSING DATES
Published monthly, issued 10th of publication month. Copy and insertion orders due 1st of month preceding publication. Mechanicals, negatives or other printing materials due 10th of month preceding publication. Cancellations and changes due 1st of month preceding month of issue.

17. SPECIAL SERVICES
MCC Media Data Form registered 5/18/82
Reader service card. Reprints available.

18. CIRCULATION
Established 1919. Single copy 1.00; per year 10.00.
Summary data—for detail see Publisher's Statement.
B.P.A. 12-31-82 (6 mos. aver. qualified)

Total	Non-Pd	Paid
31,712	16,028	15,684

Average Non-Qualified (not included above):
Total 3,517
TERRITORIAL DISTRIBUTION 11/82—32,113

N.Eng.	Mid.Atl.	E.N.Cen.	W.N.Cen.	S.Atl	E.S.Cen.
1,036	1,879	3,792	3,880	5,985	2,163

W.S.Cen.	Mtn.St.	Pac.St.	Canada	Foreign	Other
6,142	2,758	4,184	24	65	205

BUSINESS ANALYSIS OF CIRCULATION
TL —Total.
1 —Gen. contractors.
2 —Other contractors or material producers.
3 —Industrial Companies, Utilities, Mining & Logging
4 —Government:
4-1 —Federal.
4-2 —State.
5 —Consulting engineers.
6 —Architects (industrial, commercial, institutional, public buildings, & tract development).
7 —Unions, engineering schools, libraries, trade associations.
8 —Insurance & financial services.
9 —Others related to the field.

TL	1	2	3	4-1	4-2	5	6	7	8
32113	11654	17840	233	...	890	54	153	193	589	135
9
372

FIGURE 18-7

A business publication listing from *Standard Rate & Data Service. By permission: Standard Rate & Data Service, Inc.*

Southern Funeral Director, Petfood Industry, Medical Economics, Pipeline, Intimate Fashion News, Seed World, and *Pit & Quarry.*

Business publications may be divided into three types—*industrial publications,* serving manufacturers and closely related businesses, such as construction as well as the transportation industry; *merchandising* or *trade publications,* serving retailers and other channel intermediaries; and *class* or *professional publications*, serving the professions and service fields. Business publications can also be divided into *vertical* and *horizontal* papers, depending upon the function they serve. Vertical business papers have an editorial content appealing to all the different levels within one industry. Thus, they may be read by everyone from the president down. Examples include *The Iron Age* in the metalworking industry and *Engineering & Mining Journal* in the mining industries. Horizontal business papers cut across industry lines at some functional level of business. Examples are *Advertising Age*, which reaches advertising practitioners in all kinds of businesses, and *Purchasing Magazine*, read by purchasing agents for many different industries.

Qualified or *controlled* free circulation, which is used to a limited extent in newspapers and magazines, is widely used in the business paper field. Instead of selling copies, some papers control their circulation by deciding upon who should receive the publication and sending copies only to them, at no charge. There is also a group of publications that has *both* paid and qualified circulation. Each group, of course, argues in favor of its own technique. Advocates of paid circulation say that people who buy subscriptions are more likely to read the publications than those who get free copies. On the other hand, the advocates of qualified circulation argue that such circulation is the only way to ensure coverage of the market and that it has no effect on readership. (It should be noted that paid circulation publications also "qualify" their circulation in a sense, by specifying that only persons fitting into the kind of circulation they want to build may subscribe.)

STRENGTHS AND WEAKNESSES OF BUSINESS PUBLICATIONS

Business paper publications are represented by their association, the American Business Press, Inc. (ABP). It devotes much of its time and effort to improving the quality of expertise of business publications and also helps promote more effective business paper advertising. The ABP requires that its member publications be audited by the ABC or BPA, that they adhere to the association's code of publishing practice, and that they be independently owned.

The arguments advanced for the use of business paper advertising are these: Business publications reach the business readers at work, where they are not distracted by social matters. They are devoted exclusively to business matters. They are looked to by business as an authoritative source of news and information about their industries. Business paper advertisements assist salespeople by setting the stage for their sales presentation in advance. The reputation of many business papers can add to the prestige of the advertiser. Most business people read the advertisements in business publications with as much interest as they read the editorial matter. The editorial content of business publications is a "continuing education" for businesspeople, because it keeps them abreast of new developments in their fields long after they have completed their formal education.

FIGURE 18-8

This classic advertisement to business presents some sound reasons for business publication advertising. *By permission: McGraw-Hill Publications Company.*

Business papers can be extremely selective. Cost per thousand figures vary widely according to the field covered. Where the cost per thousand is high, this can generally be attributed to small audiences and high production costs. But considering the small amount of waste circulation, even high costs per thousand may not be excessive. Then, too, the total dollar outlay for any particular business publication is still relatively small.

The main selling point of business papers is selectivity and quality of audience. Therefore, unlike other media, business publications are rather restrictive about who may obtain their publications. Both publications with qualified circulation and those with paid circulation demand that their subscribers meet certain standards. Many do not permit newsstand sales. Thus, business papers are in a position to report the exact makeup, in detail, of their circulations. They report circulation in terms of both territorial distribution and a business analysis of subscriptions.

Consumer Magazines, Farm Publications, and Business Publications

CUT YOUR AD BUDGET LATELY?

Honesty compels us to admit that you're not alone.

Whenever the cost/price squeeze gets really tough, it's a temptation to regard advertising as a cost...and to cut.

Not at every company, however.

In recent years, a significant change has taken place in the thinking of many management men about advertising budgets. No longer are appropriations cut automatically when the pressure is on.

Why?

For a number of reasons. Among them are:

1. *With the growth of the marketing concept*, advertising is no longer looked upon merely as an expense, but as an integral part of the company's marketing mix.

2. *Firms that maintain advertising during recession years do better in sales—and profits—in those and later years*. That was proved conclusively in studies of five separate recessions made by ABP and Meldrum and Fewsmith.

3. *The cost of a salesman's call today makes it imperative to make maximum use of advertising*. The average cost of an industrial sales call soared to a record $96.79 according to the latest report by McGraw-Hill's Research Laboratory of Advertising Performance. Yet studies show that a *completed* advertising sales call—that is, one ad read thoroughly by one buying influence—literally costs only pennies. Why deny yourself such efficiency?

4. *In some cases, there is no way to reach customers except by advertising*. The "Paper Mill Study" shows (1) the number of buying influences in the average plant is far greater than marketers are aware of, (2) the vast majority of these influences are unknown to salesmen, (3) no salesman has the time to contact all influences even if he knows them.

5. *Selling costs are lower in companies that assign advertising a larger role in marketing products*. So advertising is an investment in profit, just like a machine that cuts production costs.

6. *Memories are short*. There is an estimated 30% turnover every year among buyers. It isn't surprising, then, that lack of advertising contact can quickly result in loss of share of market.

7. *Most down periods turn out to be shorter than expected*. The history of every postwar recession is that it didn't last as long as predicted. Why gamble your market position for short-term gain?

8. *Consider lead time*. Very few products sold to business and industry are bought on impulse. The advertising you are doing—or missing—right now will have its effect years from now.

9. *Advertising works cumulatively*. It would be nice to think that every reader reads all of your ad. We know it doesn't work that way. To be most effective, advertising must have continuity.

10. *Did your competitor cancel his budget, too?* If not, you may be taking a big risk.

11. *Will you lose salesmen?* They know that their chance of getting an order is better if they are backed up by advertising. Can you be sure of keeping them when they learn that that support has gone?

12. *You know better*. Survey after survey of executives shows that they expect a *drop* in sales if advertising stops.

But there is need for efficiency...

whenever advertising budgets are being assembled—never more than in these inflationary times. Significantly, a recent survey shows that nearly 40% of the average budget for advertising to business and industry is invested in business publication space and preparation. That's *more than double* the next largest item.

Why? Because specialized business publications remain the most effective and efficient method of reaching target audiences in business, industry and the professions.

And we can prove it.

Write for your copy of "The ABP Library of Publishing, Advertising & Marketing" to American Business Press.

★ ABP

American Business Press, Inc.
205 East 42nd Street
New York, N.Y. 10017
212 661-6360

FIGURE 18-9

The ABP presents the case for continuing to advertise to business when business is poor. *By permission: American Business Press, Inc.*

Unlike other periodicals, business papers vary from the magazine format, running the gamut from newspaper style to "slick" magazine style. Most permit a great deal of flexibility in color, bleed, and especially inserts. Like other periodicals, they also offer geographic and demographic flexibility.

TO SUM UP

Periodicals can be divided among consumer magazines, farm publications, and business publications. Advertising space is usually sold in them on the basis of space units. Rates are generally discounted by frequency and volume, and cash discounts are also offered. Rate comparisons are made on a cost-per-thousand basis.

There are more than 1,200 consumer magazines. They range from rather general editorial appeal to highly selective appeals. Geographic and demographic editions of many magazines offer magazine advertisers greater flexibility in reaching specific markets.

Farm publications are highly specialized periodicals designed to reach the various segments of the agriculture business.

Business publications reach producers, retailers, and professions through industrial, trade, and professional publications respectively. They can also be divided between vertical papers, which are directed at all levels in a single industry, and horizontal papers, which are designed to cut across industries at a particular functional level. Whereas other periodicals must typically be purchased by readers, business publications are often distributed free to a selected audience, a practice referred to as qualified circulation.

1. Explain how frequency and volume discounts work for advertisers buying space in periodicals.
2. What is meant by *guaranteed circulation* and the *circulation rate base*?
3. What are the major strengths and weaknesses of consumer magazines as advertising media?
4. Suppose you had to make a decision for advertising your brand in one of several magazines in the same classification. What kinds of information would you want, and where would you get it?
5. What are geographic and demographic editions of consumer magazines? Of what value are they to the advertiser?
6. How is Media Networks, Inc., used in reaching selected markets through magazines?
7. Why might farm publications be logically included with business publications?
8. Explain the difference between *horizontal* and *vertical* business publications.
9. What are the claims made for *qualified* and *paid* circulation among business publications?
10. What are the arguments for using business publications?

ENDNOTES

[1] From promotional literature of the Magazine Publishers Association, Inc.
[2] *Ibid.*

Television
and Radio

After completing this chapter, you should be able to:
1. Explain the new technologies and how they affect television advertising
2. Describe the advantages in both network and spot advertising
3. Evaluate audience ratings services
4. Understand the nature of the radio medium

In the preceding two chapters, we looked at print media. Now we shall consider the broadcast media—television and radio. In some ways these broadcast media are very similar, but for the advertiser, they serve quite different media strategy purposes. Both have seen tremendous growth and change in recent years.

Flamboyant, lively, loud, talked about, the master showman—that's television. It has everything—sight, sound, movement, and color; the only thing lacking is smell—and some of its critics say it has that, too. Probably no other medium has ever had such an immediate impact on the American scene. In a few short years, it grew from a baby to a giant and has had a profound effect upon this country's whole way of life. It affected both radio and the movies, and it has rapidly gotten a firm hold on America's leisure habits and created new ones, such as eating TV dinners and watching the late show. It has profoundly affected media planning as well. In just a few decades, it has grown to be the second largest advertising medium in dollars expended.

Actually, television is not so new. In 1923, a picture was televised between New York and Philadelphia. By 1928, a regular television schedule was begun by WGY, Schenectady. In 1941, full commercial television was begun, but its growth was delayed by World War II.

Television as a communications medium and television advertising have come under heavy attack by critics—some of it well founded and some not. Television's rapid growth and popularity have made it the glamour area of advertising media, with the result that many people consider it almost synonymous with advertising.

Television operates on two sets of channels, the older "very high frequency" (VHF) and the more recent "ultrahigh frequency" (UHF). The video (picture) is transmitted by AM signal and the audio (sound) by FM signal. The structure of the industry is composed of networks and individual stations. In the United States, there are three commercial networks—American Broadcasting Company, Columbia Broadcasting Sys-

TELEVISION BROADCASTING

NATURE OF TELEVISION AS AN ADVERTISING MEDIUM

tem, and National Broadcasting Company. Networks figure prominently in television, and most of the prime television time is devoted to network programs. The networks own and operate only five stations each; the remainder are either affiliated with a network or completely independent.

In contrast to radio, which has already become a rather selective medium, television still remains a mass audience medium, extremely popular with all members of the family and with people in all walks of life. There were 81.5 million television households in the United States in 1982, which amounts to 98 percent of all households. Yet, with the increasing number of multiple-set television homes (43,280,000 in 1982, or 53 percent of television homes) and the potential of cable-originated advertising, there is a growing opportunity for demographic selectivity in the medium. There is, of course, some opportunity for selectivity now. Instead of buying network, an advertiser can buy individual or spot markets. Demographic analysis of television audiences by programs also provides an opportunity to place advertising that will be seen by target markets. The popularity of the medium can be attested to by the fact that 88 percent of all television households view television daily, spending an average of seven hours and 22 minutes of viewing.[1]

TECHNOLOGICAL DEVELOPMENTS IN TELEVISION Cable television, a system of picking up station signals by central receiving antenna or microwave radio relay and then delivering them by coaxial cable to subscriber homes, was originally designed to bring improved reception to homes in weak signal areas or where there was heavy interference. But this technology has opened a whole new concept in television viewing that promises substantial changes in buying television as an advertising medium. Today, there are about 5,000 cable systems in this country, with over 21 million subscribers. This represents approximately one quarter of all television households, and the number of cable households is growing rapidly.

Cable penetration has resulted in fragmentation of the television market, as viewers have more channel options. In addition to network and independent stations (over-the-air stations), there are also cable-originated stations bringing continuous specialized progamming such as news, music, sports, and other narrower-appeal programs to viewers, and carrying *commercial advertising messages*. This programming concept is called *narrowcasting,* as contrasted to the traditional *broadcasting* approach. Cable has also made possible the expansion of satellite transmission. For example, *superstations,* independent stations such as WTBS in Atlanta and WGN in Chicago, can now be seen by cable system subscribers all over the country just like the network stations.

All this programming is included in the basic cable charges. However, by paying an additional charge, cable viewers can pick up noncommercial *pay television* entertainment, such as Home Box Office (HBO) and Showtime. A less successful alternative to this is *subscription television,* which does not need cable but can be received at home by paying to have the transmission signal unscrambled in the subscriber's set. Both these services compete for audience shares without commercial advertising and therefore take away a part of the audience available for commercial-carrying stations. Public broadcasting also competes for audience without advertising, but its position has remained static. Many firms contribute to program sponsorship of public broadcasting as part of their corporate public relations efforts. There is some possibility that any or all of these services may in the future accept some amount of advertising. Home recorders of television (VTR) have become quite popular and permit owners to tape shows (with or without commercials) for future viewing and to play bought or rented entertainment tapes without commercials.

The role of television in information processing is in its infancy, but the potential is indeed great. The result of video games was to shut out programs in favor of using the television receiver screen for game playing. From this has evolved the home computer, using the television screen as a monitor. The potentials of all these new technological developments are hard to predict. Possibilities exist for the delivery of a wide range of information as part of this communications explosion. It may be possible through satellites, cable, and computers to provide total direct marketing operations—for example, with the consumer accessing the marketer's "catalog" via the home computer and two-way cable. The merchandise could be displayed on the television screen, purchase could then be made by proper computer input and paid for through electronic transfer of funds from the consumer's bank account.

Certainly the television medium is changing so fast that it is difficult to describe the state of the medium at any given time. This much can be said. Television audiences have been and will continue to be fragmented as cable grows and technology develops. Although at present the networks continue to dominate the market and deliver mass audiences, their position will be eroded over time, with a resulting segmentation of television audiences. This means that the cost per thousand for television audiences will increase as each channel (the number of channels is almost limitless) takes a share of audience. But the delivered audience will contain much less waste, so that the additional cost will be offset by more effective audiences.

NETWORK VS. SPOT ADVERTISING Most prime-time television programming—as well as some programming at other times—is done by the networks. Therefore, if national advertisers wish to reach their markets during these hours, the greatest availabilities are through participations on network programs.

In buying network time, the advertiser has close control over the commercial and the quality of its transmittal. There is more likelihood that the commercial will not be subject to following or being followed by a competitive commercial. The advertiser is also more apt to have simultaneous coverage in a time zone in the individual markets making

You can tell the ideals of a nation by its advertisements.

GEORGE NORMAN DOUGLAS (1868–1952),
Author

READER'S DIGEST

up the network lineup. Bookkeeping is substantially simplified, because the advertiser gets only one bill. Thus, if the advertiser is interested in national coverage, networks are a convenient and efficient means of achieving it.

On the other hand, networks present some problems to the advertiser. The network selected may not have the strongest affiliate in each market. Although it is possible to buy smaller numbers of stations than the full network lineup, the networks give preference to those advertisers buying the largest lineup. Thus, the advertiser whose market is smaller than or does not coincide with the lineup of the network may have difficulty in obtaining the network participations wanted or in reaching the market desired.

Before we proceed further, some definition of terms is in order. There is a difference between spot advertising and the frequently used term *spot announcements*. Spot advertising refers to buying time on a station-by-station or market-by-market basis instead of buying time by network. Spot announcements are individual commercial messages presented between programs or as participations during programs.

Spot advertising offers greater flexibility for the national advertiser, because it permits the advertiser to choose the time and place. Unfortunately, spot advertising availabilities during network programming are limited to station breaks (called adjacencies), some specific nonsponsored shows and movies, and occasions when network advertisers buy less than the full lineup, in which case the network allows the local station to sell on a spot basis time that was not bought, cutting into the program with the locally originated commercial. But there are other programs, especially during the nonprime-time dayparts, that are local and that the advertiser can buy on a participating basis in the same manner as a network program. Of course, buying spots is much more complex than buying on a network basis in terms of the multiplicity of buys and the complexity of bookkeeping. Station representatives play an important role here, letting media buyers know about availabilities and helping local stations determine realistic rates.

Although spot television probably originated as a means of permitting regional advertisers to use television, today it is also used by national advertisers who may not want extra advertising weight in certain markets. Spot television can cover the nation as evenly as network television, but more often it is used to cover markets unevenly, as dictated by marketing strategies and needs. Advertisers with limited budgets and those with limited distribution generally find it more efficient to use spot television, which provides much more flexibility. Even for the national advertiser who wants to cover the whole country, spot television provides an opportunity to more effectively choose the amount of weight to be assigned to each market on the basis of market potential.

For 1982, it was estimated that national advertisers spent $5.575 billion on network television and $3.730 billion on spot television. In addition, $3.345 billion was spent on television by local advertisers.[2]

PARTICIPATIONS, SPOT ANNOUNCEMENTS, AND PROGRAMS

As television quickly developed as an important advertising medium, it followed the format of radio in its own heyday. Advertisers sponsored programs in prime time, and the shows were identified by the name of the sponsor—the *Texaco Star Theater*, the *Firestone Hour*, the *Bell Telephone Hour*, the *United States Steel Hour*, and the *Armstrong Circle Theater*. Undoubtedly, there was a considerable advantage to be gained from consumer identification of the program with the sponsor. But there were shortcomings, too. As television costs mounted, the advertiser had to commit a considerable amount of the advertising budget to such programs at the cost of greater flexibility and greater reach and frequency.

Many of these programs were the properties of the advertisers, but the networks saw an advantage in ownership of such programs, and soon most of them were either produced by the networks themselves or bought by the networks from *package houses* (independent producers who develop and produce shows for sale as a package). With fewer opportunities to own a show and because of high costs with the resultant problems mentioned above, advertisers began to participate in co-sponsorship of programs, either by dividing a show into segments or by sponsoring it on an alternate-week basis.

With the problems of high costs continuing unabated, advertisers sought new ways to gain flexibility for their dollars. This has led to the practice in which virtually all television program buys are *participations*. Here, a number of advertisers each buy perhaps 30 seconds of a program. This practice provides the advertiser with an opportunity to spread television budget dollars over a much greater number of shows at different times and with appeals to different market segments. It also makes it easier to get in and out of a program without any long-term commitments, so that the advertiser who is operating on a flighting schedule can buy heavily for a short time and then pull out until the next scheduled flight. The use of participations permits the advertiser with limited dollars to buy announcements in a program format without the high total investment necessary for program sponsorship. This practice is known as the *magazine approach*, because it affords the advertiser the same flexibility in scheduling to be found in magazines.

Today, program sponsorship is largely limited to specials. These one-time or few-time programs are usually tied to seasonal promotion peaks by the advertiser. With networks producing more specials and mini-series in attempts to enlarge their audience shares, however, even specials are being sold increasingly as participations.

It is possible, as indicated earlier, to buy a participating 30 seconds on programs initiated by individual stations in the same way as on network-initiated programs. In spot television, however, the advertiser also has the option to buy spot announcements, which are purchased at times between programs, usually as 30-second announcements. In contrast to program participations, which are fixed as to day and time,

> *Too many ads in trying not to go over the reader's head end up beneath his notice.*
>
> LEO BURNETT,
> *Advertising Agent*
>
> READER'S DIGEST

such station-break spot announcements may be bought on a nonpreemptible basis or as preemptible spots that can be bumped by the station if it has oversold the time or if another advertiser is willing to purchase the spot at the higher fixed rate. Buying preemptions offers the advantage of lower rates. These spot announcements may also be purchased on a fixed position basis (preemptible or not) or on a run-of-station basis where they are placed in available slots at the station's option. Of course, run-of-station buys are again less expensive.

Independent stations must face the problem of having to originate all their own programs, whereas affiliates face this problem only for those times when network shows are not available. Because of the very high cost of producing programs, these stations generally produce few programs of their own, except for local news and sports. Instead, they depend upon syndicated programs, which may be obtained from firms specializing in the production and sale of such programs. Sources of syndicated programs include networks selling old network shows as re-runs and, more recently, advertisers who provide shows on a barter basis, with the station receiving the program without charge in return for running a fixed amount of commercial minutes of the advertiser providing the show. The stations sell participations on these shows to national and local advertisers. In the case of the advertiser-originated syndication, the excess minutes may be sold to other advertisers by the local station.

TELEVISION COVERAGE AND CIRCULATION

When you buy advertising space in print media, you also buy circulation—you are assured that a known number of copies of the publications will be placed in the hands of a known number of people. You still do not know if they will look at your advertisement, and you do not know with absolute certainty how large the total audience will be. But at least you are getting space in a minimum *known* number of copies of the publication that will be sold or given to a *known* number of subscribers and single-copy buyers. Not so, however, in the broadcast media. To be sure, potential audiences can reasonably be expected, but they are not guaranteed. They may tune to another station for any number of reasons, and if they do, they will never hear the program or commercial. Thus, it is the responsibility of the stations to build the audience for the advertiser's commercial.

The two main terms used to describe the quantity of a television or radio market are *coverage* and *audience.* Frequently used synonymously, the terms nevertheless have distinct meanings. *Coverage* refers to the geographic area where the station's signal can be heard by people who *want* to listen; *audience* refers to the number of people who *do* listen, or the *reach.* Television audiences have been measured in grade A and grade B coverage, representing, respectively, good reception all the time and good reception most of the time. However, because the signal patterns of stations in one market overlap those stations in other markets, firms measuring audiences use maps that provide a more precise definition of television markets instead of the traditional maps that give the usual market definitions. The Arbitron Ratings Company introduced the concept of the Area of Dominant Influence (ADI). This is a geographic market design that defines each market exclusive of another based on measurable viewing patterns. It consists of all counties in which the home-market stations receive a preponderance of viewing. The Arbitron Ratings Company uses a series of maps to outline each of its markets in terms of the metropolitan area (generally corresponding to Standard Metropolitan Statistical Areas as defined by the U.S. Office of Management and Budget), the Area of Dominant Influence, and the total survey area (a geographic area comprising those counties in which The Arbitron Ratings Company estimates approximately 98 percent of the net weekly circulation of commercial home-market stations covered). (The same is true for radio, and maps of a similar sort are used by The Arbitron Ratings Company in its radio audience studies.) A.C. Nielsen Company, using a similar technique, refers to ADI as the Designated Marketing Area (DMA). Although measurement of circulation for stations is more complex than for the print media, it is possible to measure program audiences through the syndicated audience measurement services.

AUDIENCE MEASUREMENT SERVICES   Perhaps no single aspect of advertising activity had stimulated greater controversy in the past than audience ratings. The various rating services made claims and counterclaims, much to the dismay of advertisers. This confusion and controversy has largely been eliminated through a greater understanding of the theory of marketing research. The audience measurement services and the broadcast industry today support the Electronic Media Rating Council, which monitors the procedures and performance of accredited-rating services. Although audience measurement has its limitations, it can be a valuable tool in the media selection process if used correctly. Audience measurement is the most valuable measure of television "circulation and readership" and is therefore vital to media buying.

DEFINITION OF AUDIENCE MEASUREMENT TERMS   Simply stated, audience ratings are the percentage of all television households or persons tuned to a specific station. Essentially, there are three major terms used in audience ratings. Each of these is defined in exact terms by each of the rating services; they are here described in general terms. The terms are *households using television, rating,* and *share of audience.*

HOUSEHOLDS USING TELEVISION The percentage of homes with the television set turned on gives us the *households using television* (HUT) index. In a sample of 1,000 homes with television, if 400 of these sets are turned on, the HUT would be 40 percent.

RATING The rating may be defined as the percentage of homes in a sample tuned to a specific station at a specific time period. If, in the sample mentioned above, 200 homes out of the 1,000 have reported tuning to a specific station at a specific time period, the station would have for that time segment a rating of 20 percent, or, as it is usually expressed, 20.0 rating points. When the sample is representative, which is not always the case, it is said to be *projectable* and may be used to indicate the total number of homes tuned to the station for the time segment. When it is desirable to project the rating in terms of the number of individual viewers, the number of viewing homes must be multiplied by the number of viewers per set.

Audience estimates are based on a projection of the unduplicated audience having viewed a station for a minimum of five minutes within a specific quarter hour. These quarter-hour total audiences, when combined in time, become *average* quarter-hour audiences.

SHARE OF AUDIENCE The percentage of HUT reached by a station during a specific time period is known as the *share of audience* (share). The share is the percentage of viewing households estimated to have been acquired by each reported station during a reported time period. The computation is made by dividing individual station ratings by the HUT. Using the examples above, if a rating of 20.0 is divided by the HUT figure of 40.0, the share is 50 percent. Thus, during the reported time period, 50 percent of all sets were tuned to this particular station. Because of multiple-television-receiver homes, share can exceed 100 percent because of two or more sets tuned to different channels simultaneously.

FIRMS PROVIDING AUDIENCE RATINGS Several firms offer audience measurement services to broadcasters and advertisers. Each has its own methods and techniques, and each furnishes somewhat different data. The fact that there are differences in the data of the various services does not diminish their value. It merely indicates different assumptions, sampling techniques, and computing methods. In short, it shows again that advertising is not an exact science. The major research methods used include diaries, electronic devices, personal interviews, and telephone surveys. The Arbitron Ratings Company and the A.C. Nielsen Company provide local audience measurements. Nielsen also provides national measurements. Trendex supplies special national and local reports. Home Testing Institute TvQ gauges viewer enthusiasm toward network and syndicated programs.

THE ARBITRON RATINGS COMPANY This firm collects information on local television audiences by means of diaries in which families record television viewing habits for each television set in the home. Arrangements with randomly selected homes are made by experienced telephone interviewers. In addition to television viewing information, the diaries record a number of demographic characteristics of the household. These local market reports are prepared from three to seven times

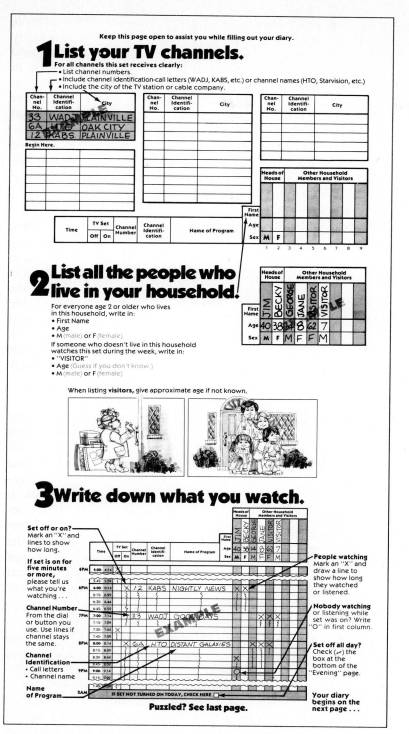

FIGURE 19-1

Instruction page from the Arbitron television diary. *By permission:* © *The Arbitron Ratings Company.*

a year for more than 200 Arbitron-defined ADI markets. They cover the diary-reported viewing over a period of four weeks.

In the New York, Chicago, San Francisco, and Los Angeles markets, because of the demand for fast and frequent television measurement, The Arbitron Ratings Company makes use of an electronic measuring device that is attached to each television set in the sample households. The device sends information on viewing by wire to computers in a central station, so that instantaneous information is available. The meter reports are similar in format to the diary reports, although different information is included and reports are issued daily.

A.C. NIELSEN COMPANY For local television, the Nielsen Station Index (NSI) uses diaries to sample the viewing habits of some 100,000 households in over 200 markets four times a year. The procedure and reports are similar to those of The Arbitron Ratings Company. Overnight television ratings based on meter measurements are available for New York, Los Angeles, Chicago, Boston, Detroit, Philadelphia, and San Francisco.

Nielsen also prepares national estimates of network television audiences, called the Nielsen Television Index (NTI). For these surveys, Nielsen uses the Audimeter, a complex electronic instrument attached to receivers in a national sample of 1,700 households. Tuning of all television receivers in these sample homes is automatically recorded every 30 seconds in the Audimeter's electronic memory system, and these data are retrieved daily by telephone line to a central office computer. Results are available daily and weekly, two days after collection. Every two weeks, the NTI report, popularly called the "pocket piece," is is-

FIGURE 19-2

A fieldperson installing an instantaneous Audimeter ® in a Nielsen household. *By permission: A. C. Nielsen Company.*

PROGRAM AUDIENCE ESTIMATES (Alphabetic)

1ST FEB. 1983 REPORT

AUDIENCE COMPOSITION

VIEWERS PER 1000 VIEWING HOUSEHOLDS BY SPECIFIED CATEGORIES

PROGRAM NAME / WK # DAY / START TIME / DUR NET PROG TYPE	1/C THIS SEASON	STA WK 1	STA WK 2	KEY	AVG AUD %	SHARE %	AVG AUD (0,000)	TOTAL PERSONS (2+)	LADY OF HOUSE	WORK-ING WOM.	W TOTAL	W 18-34	W 18-49	W 25-54	W 35-64	W 55+	M TOTAL	M 18-34	M 18-49	M 25-54	M 35-64	M 55+	TEENS TOTAL	TEENS FÉM.	CHILD TOTAL	CHILD 6-11
EVENING CONT'D																										
KNOTS LANDING	15	193	191																							
THU. 10.00P 60 CBS GD		99	99	A	18.8	29	1566	1440	769	257	868	315	512	461	411	279	428	166	269	226	194	134	90	41^	54^	28^
				B	17.7	29	1474	1435	786	271	861	279	477	446	417	308	426	139	245	227	209	149	94	46	54	34
10.00 - 10.30				A	18.6	28	1549	1453	770	258	868	315	516	458	412	278	433	166	271	233	198	136	94	41^	58^	26^
10.30 - 11.00				A	19.0	30	1583	1422	766	256	867	316	510	464	409	278	424	165	268	221	191	132	83	39^	48^	28^
LAVERNE & SHIRLEY	16	195	203																							
TUE. 8.30P 30 ABC CS		97	99	A	15.9	23	1324	1703	619	254	700	296	448	381	274	215	452	203	307	262	186	108	293	132	258	183
				B	18.5	27	1541	1901	675	291	749	348	531	424	299	175	479	230	350	293	198	97	318	179	355	241
LITTLE HOUSE NW BEGINNING	16	201																								
1 MON. 8.00P 60 NBC GD		97		A	17.1	24	1424	1734	767	299	821	208	352	328	340	408	451	177	231	179	129^197		190	99^	272	182
				B	17.8	26	1483	1789	808	268	880	242	419	388	386	408	495	148	254	238	218	211	153	97	261	169
8.00 - 8.30				A	16.6	24	1383	1717	778	301	824	199	343	326	341	423	450	166^	216	169^	127^207		195	92^	248	169^
8.30 - 9.00				A	17.6	25	1466	1737	754	292	813	215	358	328	337	393	449	185	241	182	129^191		185	105^	290	191
LOVE BOAT	16	199	203																							
1 SAT. 9.00P 60 ABC CS		98	99	A	23.6	37	1966	1765	801	298	865	256	429	422	401	367	531	187	303	268	231	203	186	83	183	127
2 SAT. 9.00P 120				B	20.6	34	1716	1795	789	307	865	278	478	429	401	330	555	196	323	302	247	194	17J	90	202	148
9.00 - 9.30				A	20.7	32	1724	1824	790	281	859	264	425	410	385	369	507	179	286	261	217	197	205	94	253	178
9.30 - 10.00				A	25.4	40	2116	1791	797	287	867	254	430	423	398	367	521	186	297	260	224	199	194	83	209	150
10.00 - 10.30				A	24.7	40	2058	1699	787	299	844	239	406	413	401	370	586	221	349	292	247	217	162	79^	107^	69^
10.30 - 11.00				A	25.1	42	2091	1659	821	345	876	262	451	440	420	360	539	173	305	269	255	207	158	75^	86^	53^
MAGNUM, P.I.	16	196	198																							
THU. 8.00P 60 CBS PD		99	99	A	25.0	36	2083	1797	727	303	814	251	449	426	412	300	622	205	374	343	307	205	200	114	161	102
				B	22.7	35	1891	1746	724	270	782	220	410	402	398	307	630	204	362	334	311	230	163	55	171	113
8.00 - 8.30				A	23.9	35	1991	1802	729	303	815	256	447	421	406	305	618	202	371	344	304	204	200	110	169	108

FIGURE 19-3

A page from the Nielsen Television Index Pocket Piece showing some program audience estimates and audience composition. (The key symbol A is to identify the current report and B is to identify the seasonal average to date.) *By permission: A. C. Nielsen Company.*

sued. In addition, Nielsen also produces related audience composition data based on a national sample of 3,200 diary-keeping households. Perhaps the most used report is the monthly National Audience Demographics report, with some 550 pages of detailed audience research in two volumes.

PROBLEMS AND USE OF AUDIENCE RATINGS

As previously indicated, audience ratings have been a source of considerable controversy in the advertising industry. Critics of advertising contend that they encourage programming on television designed to produce the largest possible audience, regardless of the entertainment value or social worth of such programs. This criticism misses the point to some extent, because ratings were never intended to measure the worth of programs in terms of performance. Rather, they are audience measurements. An audience rating will be affected not only by the nature of the program, but also by its time slot, competition, and preceding and following programs, as well as weather and season.

Even from the advertiser's point of view, the size of the audience must be evaluated carefully, for like circulation figures for print media, cost per thousand is not as significant as cost per *effective* thousand. A time period with a lower audience rating may be superior to a higher one for an advertiser if the demographics of the lower audience ratings better match the target market audience of the advertiser. Ratings should not be used as the only criterion in buying television time. There are qualitative measures in buying time as well as quantitative measures. Misuse of audience data is dangerous. Local data cannot be used to compute national estimates, and national data will not provide insights into the worth of specific local markets. Finally, it should be noted that *ratings are not absolute figures; they are only estimates.*

TELEVISION ADVERTISING RATES

Networks loom large in the media plans of many national advertisers who include television in their media mix. Network rates are the sum of the time charges for each station in the lineup. Each station is usually paid a percentage of its time charge for network participation. A certain minimum number of stations must be bought for network advertising, but the advertiser need not buy all available stations.

Time charges vary with the daypart, and for television the prime time is during evening hours (7:30 P.M. to 11 P.M. on the East and West coasts and 6:30 P.M. to 10 P.M. in the Midwest). Prime time is obviously the most expensive. The next most expensive time is *fringe time,* the hours immediately preceding and following prime time and sometimes designated as early and late fringe. Then there is the loosely defined time known as *daytime,* from sign-on to early fringe time. Finally, there is *late night time,* which follows the late fringe (after the late news) until sign-off, or for all night stations until daytime.

Network rates are based on prime-time hourly charges. These rates vary according to calendar time periods, with the lowest rates during the summer months, when audience viewing drops off sharply. Less than full-hour time rates are figured at a proportionately higher percentage of hourly rates. Rates also vary *within* dayparts by half-hour intervals.

Aside from time charges, the once-popular but now rare television network program sponsor bears the cost of the program itself. In general, talent and production costs run slightly less than the amount of time charges, although they can run considerably higher. When a sponsor buys a "package" show (a program owned by the network), payment is a single price for time and talent. Such package prices are likely to vary between 150 percent and 250 percent of time charges. *These figures for program time and talent or show costs are merely base information for negotiation of price, for in reality the price is subject to supply and demand.* The network is committed to running programs. If there are sufficient takers to use up its available commercial time at the published rates, it has the options of running public service or promotional announcements, or making the selling price more attractive to potential advertisers. Those advertisers who wish to assure a franchise position will buy prior to the season at a premium rate; others will negotiate later on, when rates depend upon whether it is a buyer's or seller's market. Of course, program rates and buying are of little importance today, when most of the activity on networks involves the negotiation of prices for participating 30-second commercials. With the greater flexibility of participants for short-time buys, demand may vary considerably from one time to another, thus creating a good deal of flexibility in price.

In spot television, the rates also vary by daypart, with costs and discounts varying, in addition, by markets and stations, usually on the basis of market size and audience shares. Naturally, in a market where demand for commercial time is high, this will reflect itself in higher rates. Here, too, rates are set by daypart, although the daypart definition will change from station to station. These dayparts are usually classified by an alphabetical system, generally from a high prime-time "A" to a low, after 1 A.M., "D." Larger stations attracting larger advertising revenues will have finer definitions of dayparts, with prime time divided, perhaps, into "AAA," "AA," and "A," and running to "E" at the lowest end of the rate scale. There are rates for spot announcements, participations, and program time. Frequently there also are package plans affording savings to advertisers buying a special assortment of announcements. Participants will command a premium rate because they involve program costs as well as time. Although program time is available, there is seldom any demand for it in spot television. As in the case of network rates, despite rate card prices, there is considerable opportunity for negotiation on price.[3]

In buying television time, advertisers are endeavoring to reach markets. Where the market is geographically broad, the network may provide the answer in getting the kind of coverage they are looking for. Where they have specific geographic areas they want to reach, spot television will probably be their choice. Or they may use both, with network buys providing the broad reach while spot buys supplement this with more intensive coverage of prime markets. Spot buys may also be used to equalize variations in network buys caused by the fact that ratings may dip below the network average in some markets.

The advertiser is concerned with getting the most for the dollars invested in television advertising. How many people are exposed to the commercials (reach), and how often are they exposed (frequency)? The reach or unduplicated audience in television is called the *cumulative audience,* or *cume.* This can be calculated by determining the audience in a particular time period. If the advertiser buys an announcement in that time period each day for five days and a person sees the program each of the five days, that person will be counted only once in that time period's cume. However, the frequency will be five. Frequency is generally determined for a four-week time period and is most often expressed as the *average* frequency for a large number of individuals or households. The cume multiplied by the frequency will give the total number of times a commercial is viewed, or *gross impressions.* If an advertiser runs a commercial *across the board* (Monday through Friday at the same time) and the cume is 100,000 with an average frequency of three, then the gross impressions delivered will be 300,000. If the advertiser's media objectives are to get as many different people as possible to see the announcement, then the advertiser will be interested in maximizing the cume and minimizing the frequency. An across-the-board buy would not be wise strategy here. If the advertiser wants to expose the same people to this message many times, then frequency is the objective and buying across the board is a step in the right direction.

A term frequently referred to in television is *gross rating points* (GRPs). It is based on the total number of rating points for a selected group of time periods. Rating points, as discussed earlier in this chapter, are the percentage of homes in a sample tuned to a specific station at a

---

KOTV
(Airdate November 30, 1949)
TULSA

Corinthian
Television Sales

CBS Television Network

ncb   TvB

A Corinthian Station
Media Code 6 237 0412 9.00   Mid 007703-000
KOTV, Inc.
302 S. Frankfort, Tulsa, OK 74120. Phone 918-582-6666,
TWX, 910-845-2256.
Mailing Address: Box 6, Tulsa, OK 74101.
1. PERSONNEL
Vice-Pres. & Gen'l Mgr.—John Irvin.
General Sales Manager—Joseph R. Matthews.
National Sales Manager—Jim Bisagni.
Program Manager—Bob Allen.
2. REPRESENTATIVES
Corinthian Television Sales, Inc.
3. FACILITIES
Video 100,000 w., audio 20,000 w.; ch 6.
Antenna ht.: 1,330 ft. above average terrain.
Operating schedule: 155 hours per week. CST.
4. AGENCY COMMISSION
15% to recognized agencies applicable to time charges
only; no cash discount.
5. GENERAL ADVERTISING See coded regulations
General: 1b, 2a, 3a, 3d, 4a, 5, 8.
Rate Protection: 10f, 14c.
Contracts: 22a, 25, 26, 32, 32c, 33, 34e.
Basic Rates: 40b, 41a, 41c, 43a, 47b, 51e, 52.
Comb.; Cont. Discounts: 52a.
Cancellation: 70b, 70n, 71, 72.
Prod. Services: 85, 86, 87c.
Affiliated with CBS Television Network.
6. TIME RATES
No. 982-1 Eff 9/13/82—Rec'd 8/5/82.
Rev. Rec'd 1/6/83.
7. SPOT ANNOUNCEMENTS
30 SECONDS

	— Section —		
	I	II	III
MON THRU FRI:			
1-5 am, CBS Nightwatch	20	15	10
5-5:30 am, CBS Morning News	20	15	10
5:30-6 am, Morning Stretch	20	15	10
6:30-7 am, Tulsa Morning	20	15	10
7-9 am, CBS Morning News	40	30	20
9 am-12:30 pm, CBS AM Rotation	120	80	50
PM:			
Noon-12:30, Eyewitness News at Noon	140	110	80
12:30-3, CBS PM Rotation	160	140	100
3-4, Bonanza	120	90	60
4-5, Tulsa Afternoon	150	110	80
6:30-7, Entertainment Tonight	450	350	250
5-6, Eyewitness News	225	175	125
5-5:30 Sat & Sun, Eyewitness News	175	150	100
10-10:30 Mon thru Sun, Eyewitness News	425	375	325
10:30 pm-1 am Fri & Sat, Late Movie	90	70	40
1-2 am Sat, Entertainment This Week	30	20	10
10:30-midnight Sun thru Thurs, CBS Late Movie I	110	90	70
Midnight-1 am Sun thru Thurs, CBS Late Movie II	40	30	20
WEEKEND			
SAT:			
7 am-concl, Kids Rotation	120	100	80
PM:			
5-5:30, Thirty Minutes	70	55	40
1-2 am, Entertainment This Week	30	20	10
SUN:			
6:30-10 am, Religious/Various	70	50	30
10-11:30 am, CBS Sunday Morning	70	50	30
PM:			
5:30-6, Wild Kingdom	250	200	150
PRIME TIME			
MON:			
7-8, Archie Bunker/Foot In The Door	600	500	400
8-9, MASH/Newhart	1200	1000	800
9-10, Cagney & Lacey	900	700	600
TUES:			
7-8, Ace Crawford/Gun Shy	650	550	400
8-10, CBS Movie	700	600	500
WED:			
7-8, Zorro & Son/Square Pegs	600	500	400
8-10, CBS Movie	700	600	500
THURS:			
7-8, Magnum, P.I.	1200	900	700
8-10, Simon & Simon/Tucker's Witch	800	650	500
FRI:			
7-8, Dukes of Hazzard	1200	1000	900
8-10, Dallas/Mississippi	1200	1000	900
SAT:			
6-7, Hee Haw	400	350	300
7-8, Wizards & Warriors	650	500	400
8-10, CBS Movie	600	500	400
SUN:			
6-7, Sixty Minutes	1300	1100	900
7-9, Archie Bunker's Place/Gloria/One Day/Jeffersons	800	700	600
9-10, Trapper John, MD	1200	850	700
60 sec: double the 30 sec.			
10 sec: 1/2 the 30 sec.			

10. PROGRAM TIME RATES
Class A—6-10 pm.
Class B—All other times.

	A	B		A	B
1 hr	4900	2900	1/2 hr	3300	1900

15% discount on 52 week buy.
11. SPECIAL FEATURES
COLOR
Schedules network color, film, slides, tape and live.
Equipped with high band VTR.
13. CLOSING TIME
72 hours prior advertising copy, film, slides and artwork; 1
week program copy and material.

FIGURE 19-4

A television station listing from *Standard Rate & Data Service. By permission: Standard Rate & Data Service, Inc.*

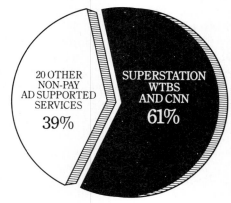

Cable buying made simple.

SuperStationWTBS and CNN dominate viewing to ad supported services.

If you're an advertiser who's been waiting for cable services to "shake out" to a dominant few, we have good news for you.

Most of the "shaking out" is over.

Of the more than 20 non-pay, advertiser-supported cable services available, two are attracting the lion's share of viewers—SuperStationWTBS and Cable News Network. Together they account for a staggering 61% share of this category.

20 OTHER NON-PAY AD SUPPORTED SERVICES 39%

SUPERSTATION WTBS AND CNN 61%

Cable's most dynamic duo.

SuperStationWTBS now reaches over 22 million homes nationally, with a 47% share of the non-pay ad supported cable audience. CNN reaches more than 14 million homes with a 14% share in the same category.

That's why it's now just as simple to make a national cable buy as it is to make a national broadcast network buy.

And, you can use the two dominant services, SuperStationWTBS and Cable News Network, to target special interest segments. Or you can use them to reach a broad upscale audience.

The unstoppable trend.

Based on February-May NTI Reports, network prime time ratings in cable homes were 10% below the average U.S. rating.[1]

Where have all these households gone? To cable alternatives, and the ratings leaders of advertiser-supported cable—SuperStationWTBS and CNN, the number one and two non-pay cable services. And, the first services measured by Nielsen meter.

With the drop-off in traditional network viewing, cable has become a necessary buy. Now it's a simple one too.

For more information, contact Gerry Hogan at (404) 892-1717.

#3 in a series. In coming weeks, Turner Broadcasting will examine other aspects of the Unstoppable Trend—the move of viewers and advertisers from broadcast networks to cable.

1. NTI NAD Reports, February-May '82, 7-11 PM all programs.

SuperStationWTBS/CNN

TURNER BROADCASTING SYSTEM
The leader in telecommunications.

Turner Broadcasting System, 1050 Techwood Drive, NW, Atlanta, Georgia 30318

FIGURE 19-5

This advertisement to business suggests why advertisers should use this cable alternative to the broadcast networks. *By permission: Turner Broadcasting System.*

specific time period. For each particular time period, there is a rating (expressed as rating points) that indicates the number of households tuned to a particular station as a percentage of the total households in the market. For advertising in a number of these time periods, the sum of the rating points for each is the GRP. A television buyer is often given the objective of achieving a specific weekly GRP level for the dollar investment.

Today's television advertiser is generally not as interested in the *total* audience delivered as in the *effective* audience. That is, the advertiser has determined the demographic characteristics of the market and wants to reach these people with commercials. Even though the total number of viewers in an audience may be the same for several different programs, the demographic composition may be significantly different. Suppose, for example, the advertiser wants to reach men between the ages of 18 and 34. Chances are the advertiser can reach more of them with less waste audience through sports programs and late night shows. Since the audience rating services break down audiences by demographic factors, this information can be included in the planning. Of course, this is not as simple as just examining Nielsen or Arbitron reports, inasmuch as the demographic breakdowns they provide are limited and may not provide the specific analytical information needed.

Network buys are more directly with the network concerned. Spot buys, however, are more often made through station representatives, mentioned earlier, located in the major cities, rather than directly with the individual stations. In either case, the advertiser must determine the availabilities, for certain times may have been sold already. The advertiser can buy commercials varying in duration from 60 to ten seconds. The most popular time period today is the 30-second commercial, which research has shown has a recall value approximately two-thirds of that of a one-minute commercial. The length of commercials has decreased, but the number of individual messages in a given time frame has increased, with the psychological effect on consumers that the channels are cluttered with commercials. Certainly, three 20-second commercials back to back appear to take a lot more time than one 60-second commercial.

The promotional arm of the industry, the Television Bureau of Advertising (TvB), suggests that television as an advertising medium has a number of strengths. Television combines all the elements of the best personal salesmanship—sight, sound, motion, and demonstration—and it does this in color. Television advertising arouses interest in the product and informs the potential consumers by involving them emotionally and by demonstrating the specific value of the product. In an average day, television reaches 88 percent of all television households; and within television homes, 73 percent of all men, 78 percent of all women, 68 percent of all teenagers, and 83 percent of all children are reached. In static media, the reader must act to receive the advertiser's message, but in a dynamic medium like television, the viewer must act to avoid

TELEVISION STRENGTHS AND WEAKNESSES

the message. Television knows no audience ceilings set by product interest levels or by page size. Every television message is equally full-screen, center stage. Of the total daily time spent with media by adults, 52 percent is with television, 33 percent with radio, 9 percent with newspapers, and 6 percent with magazines.[4]

Television is today's glamour medium. It combines sight, sound, color, and motion. It is extremely flexible. Advertisers can cover the whole country (network) or individual markets (spot) any day of the week and nearly any hour of the day. In most instances, new copy may be submitted as late as two days before broadcast. Nearly everyone watches television, so it is possible to reach nearly everyone. On a cost-per-thousand basis, television is inexpensive.

However, television can be an expensive medium for the advertiser in terms of total dollars expended, especially for the national network advertiser. Although there is a large audience potential, the size of the audience rests to a large degree with the station's programming as well as the programming of competitive stations. The nature of television does not make it a highly selective medium, although there is some opportunity to identify demographic market segments. The advertiser who uses television to reach only certain segments of the population frequently pays for a good deal of waste coverage. As in the case of radio, the television viewer, like the radio listener, has only one fleeting chance to see and hear the message, for there is no turning back. Perhaps, however, the greatest drawback to television advertising is the increasing tendency of viewers to block out many commercials mentally. Because of this tendency, advertisers must work hard to develop attention-getting and -holding commercials.

RADIO BROADCASTING

The growth of television after World War II had a profound effect on radio; the result was that whereas television has become the major *mass* market electronic advertising medium, radio has become the major *selective* market electronic advertising medium. Because television has occupied the limelight with big-show entertainment, there might be a tendency to think of radio taking a back seat to television. But radio is a dynamic medium in its own right, serving its unique functions in the media plans of advertisers. Today, radio is a more important advertising medium than ever before, and it is growing more rapidly than the rest of advertising. In a single decade, 1,324 new stations have come on the air.

Radio stations have program formats designed to deliver selective markets. There are classical music stations, contemporary music stations (with variations of rock and roll, pop, and "top 40"), country and western music stations, and "middle of the road" or standard music stations (many stations fall into this category, varying their musical offerings with news, interviews, sports, and special events). There are ethnic stations directed toward blacks or various foreign-language-speaking groups, all-news stations, and talk or conversation stations with interviews at the station or by telephone with listeners. Today's radio stations direct their programs to specific market segments. The nature of the programming selects the audience, with the result that rather specific demographic markets can be identified for specific stations. Market segmentation is the principle of radio station programming, providing a highly selective medium for the advertiser.

Modern radio has changed as an advertising medium from what it was before television and has grown tremendously. Today there are more than 4,600 commercial AM radio stations, compared to fewer than 1,000 in 1945. In addition, there are some 3,300 commercial FM stations and some 1,100 noncommercial (public) FM stations. There are also four wired national radio networks—the American Broadcasting Companies (which are segmented into several networks, each appealing to specific programming formats of its various affiliated stations), Columbia Broadcasting System, Mutual Broadcasting System, and National Broadcasting Company. In addition, through satellites, a considerable number of nonwired networks have been established, some being little more than advertising sales packages permitting buys on several stations through one purchase.

Radio networks account for only a small portion of advertising dollar volume, but they have been growing in importance in recent years. Whereas there is usually only one newspaper in a market (except for the larger metropolitan areas where there are several), there are many more radio stations in a market. With this growth in their number, radio stations have catered increasingly to specialized audiences through specialized program formats, as mentioned above. Thus, stations can deliver specific demographic segments such as teenagers, housewives, older adults, blacks, farmers, and ethnic groups speaking foreign languages. In this last category, there are stations broadcasting all or part of their programs in Spanish, German, Italian, Portuguese, Greek, Hungarian, Japanese, Persian, Sioux, Tagalog, Swahili, Lithuanian, Armenian, Croatian, French, Slovenian, Polish, Finnish, Pennsylvania Dutch, Basque, Serbian, Ukrainian, Latvian, Arabic, Swedish, Pueblo, Yiddish, Korean, Vietnamese, Zuni, Hindi, Romanian, Syrian, Maltese, Navaho, Cajun, and Russian, among others!

For the radio station to be an effective advertising medium, there must be many radio receivers. Estimates are that there are 425 million sets in use. This figure includes 115 million car radios.

Of course, audience size is also important. Radio audiences mount up to over 80 percent of the over-18 population in a single day and to over 95 percent in a week. Radio listening patterns generally seem to be the reverse of television viewing patterns: When television viewing is at its peak, radio listening is at its low ebb, and vice versa. In the summer months, when television viewing falls off, radio listening picks up. Television has replaced radio in the family living room, but the radio has not disappeared—it has only moved. About 71 percent of bedrooms are equipped with radios, as are 56 percent of kitchens. Total household coverage of radio sets is 99 percent. People also listen in their cars, 95 percent of which have radios.[5] And portability permits radio to go anywhere—even with joggers.

As in any other medium, in addition to the cost for time or space, there are production costs for the advertisements. Unlike costs in other media, the production costs for radio commercials are quite low.

NETWORK VS. SPOT ADVERTISING

Before television, radio was dominated by the networks. Today, aside from network news shows and a few other news or sports features, most radio programming is local. Therefore, most national advertisers buy *spot* (individual station) advertising, which this chapter will emphasize.

Spot advertising has a number of advantages. For one thing, it provides for individual market selection, so that the advertiser can have custom-made market coverage. By the selection of individual stations, the one most appropriate to the advertiser's needs and the best one in each market can be chosen, irrespective of network affiliation. There is also a timing advantage: Spot commercials permit the advertiser to present the message at the most favorable times in the individual market.

Commercials can be tailored to each market, which is an especially important consideration when there are different consumer characteristics and buying habits in different markets. Advertisers can frequently make use of local personalities by buying participations on shows in which the personalities help build local acceptance of their products. By buying spot advertising, they can get valuable merchandising support in local markets. Spot advertising means flexibility—flexibility in markets, stations, time, and copy.

To be sure, spot advertising presents problems. Buying spot advertising is complex, and so is its administration. Still, in the final analysis, cost and effort are secondary to advertising effectiveness and profits. If spot advertising on radio is profitable, then it is eminently worthwhile.

RADIO COVERAGE AND AUDIENCE

As with television, radio "circulation" is of great importance to the advertiser. This is measured in terms of *coverage* and *audience*. Coverage refers to the geographic area that receives the station's signal. Audience refers to the reach of the station; that is, the number of listeners to the station's programs.

COVERAGE Coverage varies from station to station for several reasons. Stations operate on different frequencies and have different power outputs or wattage. A *clear-channel* AM station of 50,000 watts will have the greatest coverage. *Regional* stations operate on not more than 5,000 watts and usually cover an area about the size of an average state. *Local* stations operate on 1,000 watts or less and will usually not carry for more than 25 miles. In addition to power and frequency, coverage is affected by the antenna system, soil conductivity, and the Heaviside layer, an atmospheric condition that bounces AM radio waves back to earth at night. As a result of the Heaviside layer, night

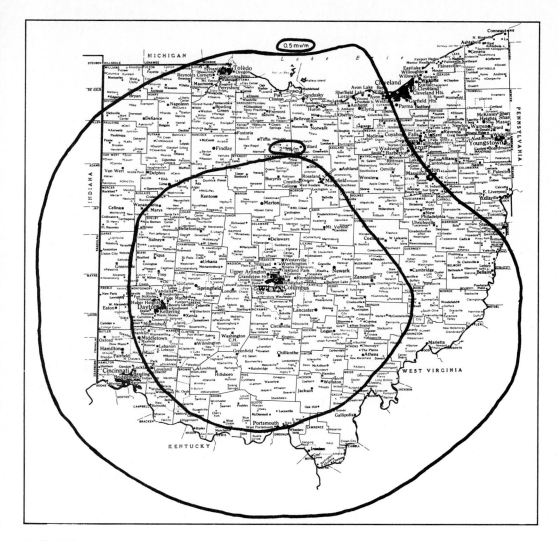

FIGURE 19-6

This map shows the primary and secondary coverage areas of radio station WTVN, Columbus, Ohio. *By permission: Taft Broadcasting Company.*

coverage for a station is generally greater than day coverage. In order to prevent interference of one station with another, the Federal Communications Commission may require a station to operate at a lower wattage at night.

Coverage is measured by *field intensity*, using portable measuring equipment sent in a field car to record station signal strength at various distances and in different directions. On the basis of the measurements, coverage maps are drawn, showing primary coverage (areas where reception is good virtually all the time) and secondary coverage (areas where reception is good most of the time).

Television and Radio

AUDIENCE A station with a very large coverage may have a relatively small audience. Determining the size of the audience (reach) is difficult, but the industry has developed several techniques to measure radio listening in and out of homes. The major firms that conduct local radio station audience studies are The Arbitron Ratings Company and Birch. They issue reports that include estimates of station audiences by age and sex on an average quarter-hour basis for dayparts and on a station cumulative basis for dayparts and the total week. Additionally, they provide other demographic breakdowns of audiences. These data are collected by diary for The Arbitron Ratings Company and by telephone for Birch.

Because radio listening is fairly stable—in contrast to television viewers, who change stations on a program-to-program basis, radio listeners tend to be far more loyal to a favorite station—it is possible to project current audience measurement information ahead, even taking into consideration seasonal fluctuations.

RADIO ADVERTISING RATES

Radio time is sold today primarily on the basis of station-break spot announcements and participations. Such rates are generally quoted for one-minute, 30-second, and ten-second announcements. Usually there are also package plan rates, which attract business by selling substantial quantities of time for commercials at greatly reduced rates. Different stations have different package plans. Finally, there is still some opportunity to buy program time; at one time, most radio time was sold on this basis, but it is now pretty much limited to what is referred to as "special features"—mostly news and sports. In a few instances, other program time is available, and when this is purchased, the advertiser has the additional costs of the program itself. Despite published rate structures, buying radio commercial time today is largely negotiated, depending upon the skills of agency time buyers and independent time buyers.

Rates vary according to the time of the day. Time periods are divided into classes, differing somewhat from station to station. An example would be: Class AA, 6:00 A.M. to 10:00 A.M., Monday through Friday; Class A, 4:00 P.M. to 7:00 P.M. and 11:00 P.M. to 11:15 P.M., Monday through Friday; Class B, 10:00 A.M. to 4:00 P.M., Monday through Friday, and 6:00 A.M. to 7:00 P.M., Saturday and Sunday; Class C, 7:00 P.M. to midnight daily. Some stations identify these time periods as *drive time, daytime and weekend, evening*, and *overnight*.

Discounts are generally available. *Frequency discounts* are based on the number of programs or spot announcements, and *dollar-volume discounts* are based on total dollars expended. Generally, radio stations do *not* offer cash discounts. Discount policies vary widely from station to station. Today, however, the most popular discount is the weekly package plan, also referred to as the total audience plan. In such plans, stations offer a specific number of commercials distributed over various time segments.

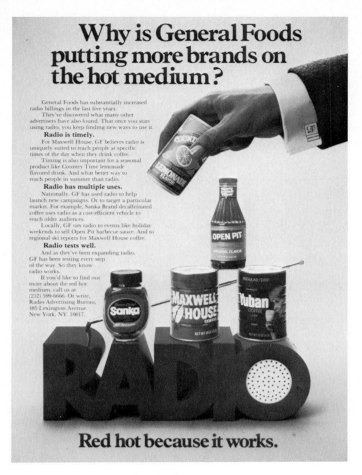

FIGURE 19-7

An advertisement to business that presents the case for radio as an advertising medium. *By permission: Radio Advertising Bureau, Inc.*

Stations also may have two sets of rates—national advertisers and another, lower one for local (retail) advertisers, although many stations have only one rate. Sometimes rates are offered in combination with other stations, or for a combination of AM and FM broadcasting.

Much of the rate structure described here for individual radio stations is equally applicable for networks. However, most of radio advertising sales are for spot advertising, and networks carry only a small volume of advertising.

BUYING RADIO TIME

Before buying advertising time on radio, advertisers should examine the station's audience and the station itself. They should ascertain the coverage of the station in terms of their own needs. Advertisers should study the demographics the station delivers to see how well they fit the market segments they are trying to reach. They should also consider program format and ratings in the same light. Because there are so very many stations, advertisers should know something about the station's management, reputation, and policies. Of course, they must consider

If you think rock radio is kid stuff, think again.

We're affiliated with The Source, America's #1 young adult network. The Source reaches more 18-34 year olds than any other radio network. And has more 18-34 year old listeners with household incomes of $25,000 plus.*

These listeners have spending power and they use it.**

The Source, compared to any other radio network, reaches more young adults who own compact cars and motorcycles. More consumers of domestic, imported, light and draft beers as well as those who drink canned colas.

A larger percentage of The Source's audience attends movies and concerts. And buys records, tapes, head phones, stereo speakers, turntables and AM/FM cassette radios.

They are also buying and taking care of homes. Acquiring mortgages. Investing in Keogh plans. And buying dishwashers, calculators, coffee makers, electric mixers, diamond rings, and disposable diapers.

So, if you thought rock radio was kid stuff, think again. Want more information? Give us a call.

* RADAR® 25, Vol. 2, M-S, 6A-12M, Average Audience
** SMRB®, 1981 Study of Media and Markets, 18-34

THE SOURCE

NBC Radio's Young Adult Network

FIGURE 19-8

This advertisement to business by a radio network attempts to position a rock'n'roll network as having upscale listeners. *By permission: NBC Radio.*

time costs, and because time charge policies and the possibility of package deals vary so much, they must negotiate carefully. It is always helpful to look to the experiences of others; therefore, the degree of advertisers acceptance is a valuable guide. Finally, station services and facilities should be examined. What merchandising aids does the station offer? What market and audience studies has the station prepared?

STRENGTHS AND WEAKNESSES OF RADIO AS A MEDIUM

The Radio Advertising Bureau (RAB), the sales development arm of the radio medium, suggests the use of radio as an advertising medium for the following reasons:

1. Women listen to radio an average of three hours and 21 minutes daily. Men average three hours and 24 minutes daily.
2. Radio reaches more adults than television during the summer, when many business sales peak.
3. Auto radio listeners, 95 percent of car radio owners, average 42 minutes of listening daily.

FIGURE 19-9

An advertisement that explains how one radio broadcaster provides selectivity by offering six network alternatives to target the advertiser's market. *By permission: ABC Radio Networks.*

4. More than 100 million radios were sold in the last two years.
5. Radio's selling personality has such qualities as sincerity, warm personal appeal, and friendliness.
6. Radio offers room-to-room coverage in homes.
7. Radio is preferred when fast-breaking news events occur.
8. There are 465 million working-order radio sets in the United States, about $5\frac{1}{2}$ for every household.

FIGURE 19-10

A radio station listing from *Standard Rate & Data Service.* By permission: *Standard Rate & Data Service, Inc.*

Radio is a medium that affords the opportunity to match the advertiser's demographics to those of the station, because stations position themselves to attract specific market segments. There are those who say that radio is no longer a primary advertising medium. To be sure, it is used today by many advertisers as a supplement to other media, but it can be and is used by other advertisers as an effective primary medium. No generalization about its relative importance can fairly be made. Like any other medium, its use depends upon the media plan objectives and strategy.

Spot advertising on radio provides for considerable flexibility. Markets can be picked individually. Timing of commercials can be pinpointed. Specialized audiences can be reached through station programming appeals. On a cost-per-thousand basis (the measure used in radio as in the other media), radio is inexpensive, as it is also in terms of total dollars per commercial bought. Thus, the size of the appropriation needed for an advertiser to enter radio advertising is relatively low, making the medium available to small as well as large advertisers. An advertiser can use the medium nationally (through networks, if desired, or through spot), regionally (through regional networks or spot), or locally.

On the other hand, radio has its limitations. Radio is an aural medium—communication to the ear. Aural communications may have certain advantages over the printed word, but often it is important that a product or advertising idea be visualized pictorially. However, evidence has shown that retailers, long used to "visual merchandising" in newspaper advertisements, have successfully used radio for their merchandise.

Another problem of broadcast media is that once the advertising message is presented, there is no turning back to it. An audience may not pay attention, and a radio is easily turned off. One can listen to only one station at a time, missing other stations' commercials. Because radio is often used as a background while someone is reading, or working, or driving, or doing some chore around the house, the radio commercial must fight these distractions to be heard. But because radio is inexpensive, frequency in presentation can overcome these problems.

TO SUM UP

Television, the second largest advertising medium in dollars expended, is certainly the most talked about of the media.

Cable televison has had a major effect on changing television and will have a greater effect in the future. It has challenged continuation of network dominance. By making possible many more station options, it has fragmented the market. The result has been higher cost per thousand, but greater segmentation. And technology in communications has revealed only the tip of an iceberg and the new dimensions of the medium in the future.

Network television programming dominates prime time, and many large advertisers find buying network time advantageous. But spot advertising also has a great appeal for national advertisers because of greater flexibility in matching stations to its markets.

Most advertisers today buy *participations* on television. Program sponsorship is usually limited to specials. Local station programming, aside from news and sports, tends to be mostly syndicated shows.

Because there are no hard circulation numbers for television as compared to print media, audiences are measured by rating service estimates. Television commercial rates are based on the ratings and dayparts. The most popular commercial time unit is 30 seconds. Dollar allocations for the medium are frequently based on achieving a particular level of gross rating points.

Radio stations deliver selective markets. Most radio is bought as spot advertising, but networks put together via satellite are growing in importance. A good part of radio listening takes place while driving—and portability has even brought radio to joggers.

---

1. What are some of the possibilities of cable for television advertisers?
2. Explain the advantages and disadvantages of buying spot and network advertising for radio and television.
3. Why has most television advertising moved to participations? What are the advantages of buying participation?
4. What is the "magazine approach" to buying time?
5. How do measurement services measure audiences?
6. What are gross rating points? How do advertisers use them in buying television time?
7. What are the strengths and weaknesses of television and radio as advertising media?
8. How and why is radio so effective in reaching selective markets?
9. How do radio listening patterns differ from television viewing?
10. For each of the following products, evaluate the probable effectiveness of television and radio as media for a national advertiser:
    (a) Livingroom furniture
    (b) Toothpaste
    (c) News magazine
    (d) Automobiles
    (e) Women's sportswear

ENDNOTES

[1] From the Television Bureau of Advertising, Inc.
[2] Figures from the Television Bureau of Advertising, Inc.
[3] For a more detailed examination of television advertising rates, see Warren A. French and J. Timothy McBrayer, "Managing Television Commercial Time," *Journal of Advertising*, VII No. 4 (Fall 1978), 17; and "Arriving at Television Advertising Rates," *Journal of Advertising,* VIII, No. 1 (Winter 1979), 15.
[4] From the Television Bureau of Advertising, Inc.
[5] Data from various documents of Radio Advertising Bureau, Inc.

Out-of-Home Media

After completing this chapter, you should be able to:

1. Describe the different kinds of outdoor posters available for advertising
2. Explain how outdoor is bought
3. Differentiate between using interior and exterior transit advertising
4. Tell how transit advertising is sold

Among the oldest forms of advertising is the outdoor sign. From the hieroglyphics cut in the *stellae*, or tablets, of ancient Egypt to today's standardized posters, bulletins, spectaculars, and car cards, signs have persisted as an advertising medium. Other varieties of signs continue to be seen all about us—on stores and other business establishments, on the sides of barns, on the highways and byways of America. Some are elaborate and artistic; others are crude and ugly and an eyesore on the American scene. This chapter will be devoted primarily to a consideration of the two main organized out-of-home media—standardized outdoor advertising and transit advertising—for it is in these forms that outdoor signs are most significant as an advertising medium. This does not mean that other forms of outdoor signs have no advertising value. Certainly the merit of store signs and many other nonstandardized signs should be evident.

Over the years, outdoor sign advertising has come under considerable criticism. There has been not only public pressure but also legislative action to restrict and prohibit such advertising. It would be unfair to say that the criticism has no foundation. Yet it seems equally unfair to condemn all outdoor sign advertising. Most of the criticism has been provoked by certain nonstandardized or on-premises signs. Although many such signs are in good taste, well executed, and thoughtfully placed, many others are amateurish, in poor taste, and a blot on the landscape. Unfortunately, all outdoor sign advertising comes under attack along with the obvious eyesores. The contention that outdoor signs on highways present a traffic safety hazard appears to be arguable, for there is considerable evidence that such signs prevent boredom and highway hypnotism, thus keeping the driver alert and safe.

Outdoor and transit advertising are unique as advertising media. Unlike most other mass communications media, these media serve no other purpose than carrying advertising. Another feature of these media is that the advertising message is not *delivered* to the audience, as are newspapers, magazines, radio, and television, which enter the home or office. Rather, the advertising messages are placed in strategic nonhome locations where they are exposed to audiences on the move. Thus, they are referred to as *out-of-home* media.

Although standardized outdoor advertising and transit advertising both include forms of outdoor signs, they are organized separately in the advertising industry. For this reason, they will be considered separately here. Within the industry, standardized outdoor signs are generally referred to simply as outdoor advertising, and the same term will be used here. Transit advertising will be so designated, and other forms of outdoor signs will be referred to as nonstandardized signs.

The trade of advertising is now so near to perfection, that it is not easy to propose any improvement. But as every art ought to be exercised in due subordination to the public good, I cannot but propose it as a moral question to these masters of the public ear, whether they do not sometimes play too wantonly with our passions? . . .

DR. SAMUEL JOHNSON (1709–84), Lexicographer

READER'S DIGEST

TYPES OF OUTDOOR ADVERTISING

A number of different types of outdoor advertising signs have been standardized and together represent the major portion of the outdoor sign industry. These include posters, painted bulletins, and spectaculars and are considered in detail below.

POSTERS Of the several forms of posters, the 30-sheet poster is most widely used. In lay language, these posters are generally referred to as billboards, the name deriving from the old practice of posting paper playbills for theatrical performances. The 30-sheet poster is 25 percent larger than the 24-sheet poster, which for many years was the standard size but which has lost in popularity to the larger version. The names 24-sheet and 30-sheet are somewhat misleading. Originally, because of the limitations of lithographic printing presses, it took 24 sheets measuring 24 inches high and 41 inches long to cover a poster panel. Today, through technological advancement, a panel can be covered with as few as ten sheets (or fourteen, in the case of 30-sheet posters). The copy area for a 24-sheet poster is 104 inches high and 234 inches long. For the 30-sheet poster, the copy area measures 115 inches high and 259 inches long. The basic poster panel in use today is the Loewy panel, which is a gray or white frame supported by one or more uprights. The single-pole units in both posters and bulletins have become very popular and account for most new and replacement construction. The area between the poster and the frame (which measures 12 by 25 feet) is known as the "blanking area" and is covered with plain white paper acting as a mat for the poster. A very popular poster is the *bleed* poster, which extends the artwork to the edge of the panel frame by printing on the blanking paper. All three poster sizes fit the same single-size panel, with only the blanking area changing. Most posters are reproduced by lithography, although for small runs, the silk-screen process is often used. These posters account for approximately 60 percent of sales volume for national outdoor advertising.

Much less widely used, but increasing in popularity, are the smaller eight-sheet or *junior panels*, which are about one-quarter the size of 30-sheet posters. These are generally found in suburban shopping areas and on neighborhood store walls. There are also three-sheet posters, which measure 8 feet 7 inches high and 4 feet 10 inches wide. They are generally placed on walls of retail stores. Some three-sheet panels appear in train stations and are then considered a part of transit advertising.

BULLETINS The second major type of outdoor advertising is the bulletin. Bulletins may be painted at the location (permanent bulletins) or, in the case of bulletins containing removable sections, at a paint shop (rotary bulletins). When the design is painted in sections, it may be rotated from one location to another on a scheduled plan to obtain maximum exposure. Today, some bulletins are *posted* rather than painted, in order to get uniformity around the country.

Bulletins differ somewhat in size, but they are most commonly 14 feet by 48 feet. Most bulletins today are in bleed form without frame.

Still another form of display is known as the *embellished bulletin*. This variation of the bulletin, becoming increasingly popular, adds to the bulletin such embellishments as cut-outs, special illumination, and animation and may extend beyond the physical limits of the bulletin frame.

SPECTACULARS Spectaculars are not standardized in size or shape. They are large permanent signs making use of elaborate lighting and action effects. Because of their relatively high cost, they are generally confined to the highest traffic areas in metropolitan centers. The most famous location of spectaculars is the Times Square area of New York City.

Outdoor poster panels and bulletins are owned not by one firm nationally but by regional and local firms. These organizations are known as *outdoor advertising plants* (the term here has nothing to do with factories). The plant is made up of a group of poster panel properties, bulletin properties, or both in a particular area and is headed by a plant operator. Several plants may be owned by one outdoor advertising company. There are over 500 plant operators providing service in over 8,000 markets.

The plant operator arranges to lease or buy property for the erection of panels and bulletins, erects such panels and bulletins, posts the panels and paints bulletins, and maintains the areas surrounding the structures so that they are clean and attractive.

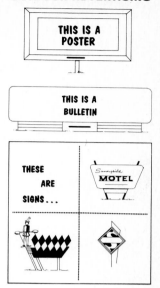

OUTDOOR ADVERTISING

THIS IS A POSTER

THIS IS A BULLETIN

THESE ARE SIGNS...

MOTEL

FIGURE 20-1

The two illustrations at the top are of standardized outdoor advertising. The four signs below are nonstandardized. *By permission: Outdoor Advertising Association of America, Inc.*

THE OUTDOOR ADVERTISING PLANT

Out-of-Home Media

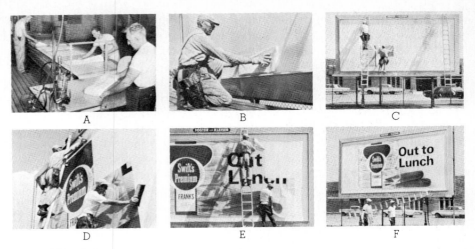

FIGURE 20-2

A. Printed poster sheets are collated, prepasted, and vacuum sealed in plastic bags. The glued sheets will remain moist for weeks. Each bag is identified and scheduled for posting routes. B. Now, "blanking paper" is pasted down to form a border. Then, beginning from the bottom, the bill poster takes the prepasted sheets and applies the first section to the panel. C. Next, starting at the bottom and working upward each sheet overlaps the previous section. This forms a "rain-lap" and helps prevent flagging or tearing of the outdoor poster copy. D. Then, because the sheets have been prepasted, the bill poster is able to use a dry brush to adhere the paper to the panel. Prepasting techniques eliminate glue streaks from dark backgrounds. E. Since a poster is a series of sheets, a flexibility of sheet arrangement is possible. The advertiser can localize a campaign to an area, include a dealer's name, or change a package. F. Finally, sheet by sheet, the giant paper mosaic is assembled to build the advertiser's message into a clean, colorful 25' × 12' display. This poster will be exposed to the mass public for 30 days. *By permission: Foster and Kleiser, a Metromedia Company.*

OUTDOOR ADVERTISING ORGANIZATION

Because the outdoor advertising business is essentially local, organization is needed to make it a feasible national medium. The organization of the outdoor advertising industry is the Outdoor Advertising Association of America, Inc.

OUTDOOR ADVERTISING ASSOCIATION OF AMERICA The Outdoor Advertising Association of America, Inc. (OAAA), has a membership of more than 90 percent of the plant operators in the country. The Association recommends standards for structures to ensure uniformity of size; it is the representative of the industry in legislative activity.

The Institute of Outdoor Advertising (IOA) is the marketing arm of OAAA. It compiles expenditure, rate, and market data; and it develops research on the audience and advertiser use of the medium. Some of the other responsibilities of the IOA include selling the concept of the use of outdoor advertising, promoting the use of the medium through its own advertising, developing case histories, making presentations, and providing creative assistance to users of the medium.

REGIONAL SALES GROUPS Individual plant operators lease panel and bulletin space to local advertisers. A few of the large plants maintain representatives in key cities to sell the medium to national ad-

FIGURE 20-3

A three-sheet billboard. *By permission: Criterion Advertising Company.*

vertisers. For most plant operators, maintaining a national sales force would be difficult and expensive. Therefore, they are faced with the same problem of national sales as are newspapers and local radio and television stations. For this reason, several regional market groups have evolved to handle sales on a regional or multiple-market basis.

Outdoor advertising audiences are exposed to the medium in the course of traveling from place to place. Unlike other media, it calls for no conscious effort to read, view, or listen and thereby note the advertising message. Circulation cannot be measured in terms of subscribers or sets tuned in. Outdoor advertising circulation is measured instead by reporting the number of cars that pass outdoor posters or bulletins. These figures are converted to potential viewers by multiplying automobiles by an "automobile load factor,"—that is, the average number of people in a car.

OUTDOOR ADVERTISING TRAFFIC

FIGURE 20-4

A spectacular for Pepsi-Cola in a high traffic count area facing the East River and the East Side Drive in Manhattan. The sign assumes more dramatic proportions at night when it is illuminated but is shown here by day so that the detail and size of the structure may be seen. *By permission: Pepsi-Cola Company.*

TRAFFIC AUDIT BUREAU, INC. In order to provide uniform, impartial data on outdoor advertising circulation, the Traffic Audit Bureau, Inc. (TAB), was organized by the Association of National Advertisers, The American Association of Advertising Agencies, and the Outdoor Advertising Association of America. TAB activity is twofold. First, it audits circulation for posters and bulletins by markets. Second, it publishes these data for use by the advertisers and/or their agencies. The TAB circulation audit is comparable to the Audit Bureau of Circulations audit for newspapers and magazines.

The Audited Circulation Values of Outdoor Advertising, prepared by TAB for advertisers and agencies, is an audit of circulation and space position value for individual panels and bulletins. Samples of the circulation and panels in each market are made to authenticate that the records of the plant are valid and reflect averages as published by the TAB.

Effective traffic circulation figures are obtained by either the use of official traffic counts or manual counts (hand sample counts). These traffic counts are converted into potential viewers by use of multiplying factors which convert cars into persons for 18 or 12 hour exposures [for illuminated and non-illuminated posters respectively]. The hours of exposure are 6 A.M. to midnight and 6 A.M. to 6 P.M., respectively. These figures represent potential viewers as the circulation reflects the number of people approaching a poster or bulletin.[1]

OUTDOOR ADVERTISING GRPs AND SHOWINGS

Plant operators set up poster panels in individual markets in high-traffic areas. An advertiser buys groups of these poster panel locations in order to get a certain amount of exposure to the population in the market. These units of sale are known as *gross rating points* (and are rather similar to the GRPs used in television). One hundred gross rating points does not refer to the number of panels bought; it indicates the number of panels (from as few as one in a small community to as many as several hundred in a large metropolitan area) necessary to give the advertising message a daily exposure equal to the total population of the market. Thus, 100 GRPs equals 100 percent of the market population. The TAB measurement of traffic for each panel provides the basis for determining the number of panels in a given number of GRPs. Traffic for these panels will vary according to location and whether they are illuminated or not.

The concept of gross rating points in outdoor advertising is relatively new and may be used to replace an older term, *showings*, which is still used by many plants either in place of GRPs or together with GRPs. The terms are interchangeable, and a #100 showing is equal to 100 gross rating points. The most popular designations are the #25 showing, the #50 showing, and the #100 showing.

Panel selection may be specialized or tailored to the advertiser's needs. Panels may be designated to reach specific parts of a market or types of outlets. They may be ethnic, sectional, highway, high-density, keyed to supermarkets, and so forth. Therefore, an airline might tailor its selection of sites to the highway leading to the airport, where its message is exposed to the most likely prospects.

OUTDOOR ADVERTISING RATES

Rates for outdoor advertising poster panels are based on the number of GRPs or showings bought for 30-day periods, but they will differ from plant to plant. Differences in rates are influenced by rentals for property on which structures are erected, wage scales for bill posters, and the size of the market, with larger markets commanding higher rates. Cost per thousand is the measure used here, as in other media. On this basis, outdoor advertising is very inexpensive. There is a wide spread in cost per thousand, however, from market to market. In large metropolitan markets, where there is heavy traffic, cost per thousand is apt to be lowest. In smaller markets, where the traffic volume is less, the cost per thousand is higher. In the case of bulletins and spectaculars, there are

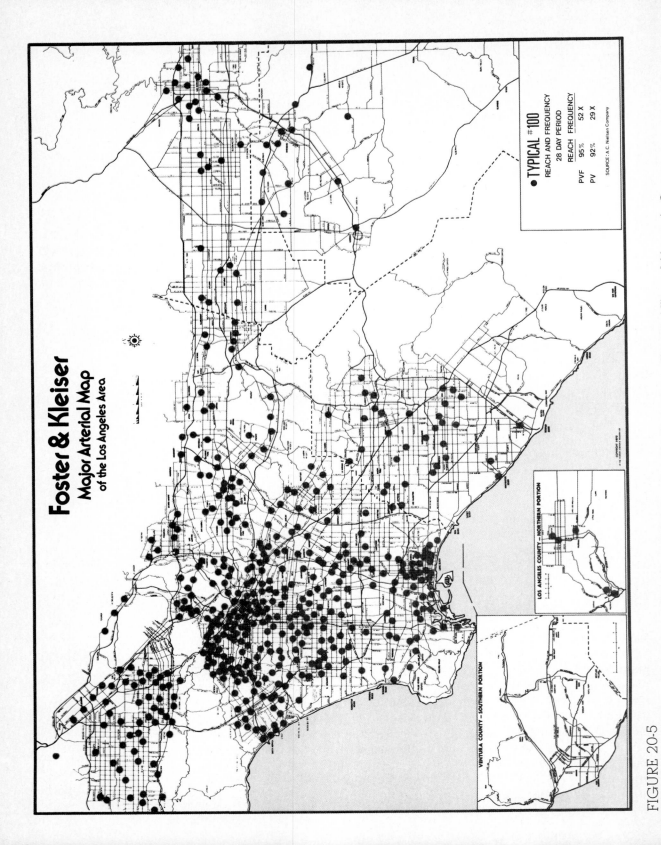

FIGURE 20-5

A typical poster map for a #100 showing. Each dot represents a panel location. *By permission: Foster and Kleiser. A Metromedia Company.*

Within the image:

Foster & Kleiser
Major Arterial Map
of the Los Angeles Area

TYPICAL #100
REACH AND FREQUENCY
28 DAY PERIOD

	REACH	FREQUENCY
PVF	95%	52 X
PV	92%	29 X

SOURCE: A.C. Nielsen Company

LOS ANGELES COUNTY — NORTHERN PORTION

VENTURA COUNTY — SOUTHERN PORTION

LOS ANGELES METRO MARKET				

Los Angeles-Long Beach; Anaheim-Santa Ana-Garden Grove;
Riverside-Ontario-San Bernardino; SMSA's.

SIZE	UNILL. PANELS	ILLUM. PANELS	TOTAL PANELS	COST PER MONTH
100	60	440	500	$177,840
50	30	220	250	88,920
25	15	110	125	44,460
10	6	44	50	17,784

When applicable a 10% continuity discount will be allowed.
Rotating/Permanent Bulletin Service Available.

Rates and Allotments quoted above are for general showings only. Coverages other than general in composition are available on an individual quotation basis.

FIGURE 20-6

Outdoor poster panel rates for various showing sizes in the Los Angeles market. *By permission: Foster and Kleiser. A Metromedia Company.*

so many variables that advertising rates will run quite a gamut. Spectaculars may cost as much as $10,000 per month. Contracts for bulletins and spectaculars generally run for a year or more.

There is no difference in rates for local and national advertisers as there is in many other media. Also, unlike other media, many outdoor plants grant advertising agencies a $16\frac{2}{3}$ percent commission. Discounts are given by some plants for continuity and for frequency.

All outdoor advertising rates, allotments, discounts, circulation, and market data are available in the *Buyers Guide to Outdoor Advertising,* published by the IOA.

In addition to the cost to the advertiser of poster panel and bulletin leases, there are the costs of production and printing of the poster panels and the painting and embellishment of bulletins. These are relatively high in relation to the medium cost.

Most cities have only one outdoor advertising plant, but some, especially in the larger markets, do have competition. In buying outdoor advertising, the advertiser should consider distribution and coverage of the outdoor plant, including acceptability of locations, distribution of locations in a specific GRP buy or showing as they apply to the advertiser's product, and details on the number of illuminated panels and their locations. The visibility of the specific GRP buy or showing should be considered, and the traffic, in terms of effective circulation, should be examined. A check should be made on the plant's quality of posting and standards of maintenance. Copy restrictions by the plant or by law should be checked. An analysis of rates and costs between competitive plants and competitive media should be made. Advertisers should ascertain what services, such as merchandising aids and market data studies, are available. They also should consider the market in terms of its size: market area, population, and households. Finally, they should

BUYING OUTDOOR ADVERTISING

Out-of-Home Media

examine such economic factors of the market as consumer spendable income and retail sales.

Because of the large number of availabilities, it is not practical for a national advertiser to buy a 100 GRPs or a #100 showing on a complete national basis. For this reason, advertisers frequently purchase the medium on a selective basis, buying the top 100 markets or those markets where their sales are highest.

In many instances, outdoor advertising is bought cooperatively by the manufacturer and retailer, with the name of the retailer included in the poster so as to identify the local retail outlet. Retailers, of course, also initiate outdoor buys.

OUTDOOR ADVERTISING STRENGTHS AND WEAKNESSES

Outdoor advertising offers many advantages to the advertiser. It can deliver a message nationally or on a market-by-market basis. In the latter case, it can be tailored to reach specific kinds of markets and to obtain specific frequencies and coverages. A really mass medium, it is

FIGURE 20-7
An advertisement to business explaining the advantages of outdoor as a supplement to television. *By permission: Institute of Outdoor Advertising.*

exposed to all economic and social groups, delivering messages to people on their way to work, to play, and to shop. As an out-of-home medium, outdoor is unique as compared to other media, which deliver messages primarily during a period of indoor activity. Outdoor speaks quickly and repeatedly. Its low cost enables it to be used as an impulse trigger, because it delivers at a time the prospect is apt to recognize the need for the product.

Outdoor advertising offers a great deal of flexibility for the advertiser. It can be used as a primary medium or as a secondary medium. It can be used nationally or pinpointed to key market areas. Its mass audience is a drawback as well as an asset, for the medium cannot be very selective and may be wasteful for some advertisers. On the other hand, its low cost makes it available to advertisers with limited budgets. The fact that its audience views the message on the move limits the copy to a short, quick message. Long reason-why copy cannot be used. Still, the poster's very size gains attention. It is likely to be seen many times and is valuable for its repetition. No effort on the part of the audience is required to buy the medium or tune it in.

A man who makes a specific claim is either telling the truth or a lie. People do not expect an advertiser to lie. They know that he can't lie in the best mediums. The growing respect for advertising has largely come through a growing regard for the truth.

CLAUDE C. HOPKINS, Advertising Agent

READER'S DIGEST

NON-STANDARDIZED SIGNS

One valuable kind of nonstandardized sign is the store or on-premise sign. Some national advertisers, recognizing this value, make available to retailers store signs with the retailer's name that include the brand name, slogan, or trademark of the national advertiser as well.

No discussion of sign advertising would be complete without mention of the private efforts of the advertisers with their own nonstandardized signs. Perhaps the most famous of these were the humorous Burma Shave jingles that dotted the countryside. A number of firms offer special sign advertising facilities to advertisers. One example is sign facilities in shopping center parking lots.

TRANSIT ADVERTISING

Another form of out-of-home advertising is transit or transportation advertising. This type of advertising is considered a medium in its own right and consists primarily of interior displays, exterior displays, station and terminal posters, and station and terminal clocks.

INTERIOR DISPLAYS Car cards are used in interior displays appearing in subway trains, buses, rapid transit systems, and commuter trains. Most of them appear in wall racks above the seats, but some are placed in other locations. The standard sizes of car cards are all 11

FIGURE 20-8

A bus car card. *By permission: The Transit Advertising Association, Inc.*

inches high, with widths of 28 inches, 42 inches, and 56 inches. The 11-by-28-inch size is the most popular. (Measurements for transit advertising specify height first and width second.) Advertisers can change their copy every month, but usually do so only every two months.

Other interior displays may also be available. On rail transit vehicles, including commuter trains and some buses, for example, there may be space for *square-end* displays (22 inches by 21 inches) located near doors, and *top-end* or *over-door* displays (16 inches by 39 or 44 inches).

Take-ones are brochures or coupons attached to interior transit advertisements. After reading the message, the passenger may take one of the brochures or coupons to request more information or receive some benefit in connection with the advertised product.

EXTERIOR DISPLAYS Exterior displays are advertising units appearing on the outsides of buses. They are placed on the sides, front, and rear of vehicles. There are a number of standardized varieties and sizes. King-size displays (30 inches by 144 inches) appear on the sides of buses. In some markets, there are also queen-size posters (30 inches by 88 inches). Traveling displays (21 inches by 44 inches) vary as to position by market. Taillight spectaculars (21 inches by 72 inches) appear, as the name suggests, on the backs of buses and modern trolleys. Bus-O-Rama (21⅞ inches by 144¾ inches) is a roof-top illuminated transit advertising panel backlighted by means of fluorescent tubes. There are two Bus-O-Rama positions on each side of the bus, which can be bought combined as a single advertising unit. In recent years, in some major markets, paper posters inside frames have been replaced by vinyl

FIGURE 20-9

Bus carrying exterior displays, including Bus-O-Rama at top. *By permission: The Transit Advertising Association, Inc.*

displays directly applied to the bus exterior and requiring no frame. This allows for sizes up to 30 inches by 240 inches.

STATION POSTERS   Station posters are in reality a variety of poster panel not unlike the 30-sheet poster. Because they are displayed in and on stations of subways, rapid transit systems, and suburban railroads, they are sold by the the same firms selling car cards and exterior transit diplays and therefore are considered a part of transit advertising. They are available in one-sheet size, with the inside dimensions of the panel measuring 46 inches high by 30 inches; two-sheet size, with inside dimensions of 46 inches high by 60 inches; and three-sheet size, with inside dimensions of 84 inches high by 42 inches. There is also a six-sheet size, the dimensions of which vary slighly by market area.

OTHER FORMS OF TRANSIT ADVERTISING   In addition to these major types of transit advertising, there are also floor exhibits, diorama displays, and clock spectaculars at train and airline terminals and some subway systems. These are generally custom-designed for advertisers and can be likened to outdoor advertising spectaculars. Clock spectaculars consist of a large clock set in a backlighted display that also may incorporate a moving message.

Out-of-Home Media

391

FIGURE 20-10

A two-sheet station poster in a New York subway station. *By permission: The Transit Advertising Association, Inc.*

Another form of transit advertising is the merchandising bus. These buses may be chartered by advertisers, usually in connection with a major promotional effort. A regular bus is converted into a mobile showcase and taken to the offices of retailers or wholesalers, or, in the case of consumers, to a shopping center. The interior and exterior advertising display space of the bus is completely utilized by the advertiser's messages, and merchandise and exhibits are placed in the bus on "stages" over the seats. The buses may be used effectively to sell merchandise to specific audiences by actually taking orders or by providing information.

TRANSIT ADVERTISING ASSOCIATION

There are about 50 transit advertising companies in the United States and Canada. They are known as *operators,* and their activity is similar to that of outdoor advertising plants. The national trade organization of transit advertising operators is the Transit Advertising Association (TAA). Its functions are the establishment of standards and promotion of the medium, conducting research and publishing a rate directory. Members of the TAA represent approximately 90 percent of the transit advertising volume in the United States and Canada.

TRANSIT ADVERTISING SHOWINGS

Car cards are sold primarily on the basis of *runs.* A *full run* is, in most instances, a card in each vehicle in the fleet. There are also one-half and one-quarter runs with cards placed in half or one-quarter of the vehicles respectively.

Outside displays are sold on a showing basis. Because market characteristics vary, transit advertising companies provide a range of alternatives for exterior showings in the market.

Mutual Transit Sales, a subsidiary of one of the major transit advertising companies, represents many of the transit advertising companies in selling national campaigns for several hundred markets.

An attempt has been made to measure audiences for exterior displays by employing an electronically controlled camera to count the eyes exposed to posters on a moving bus. Another technique has been to have randomly selected adults record in a diary the exterior displays they have seen in the course of a day and a week. These findings are then projected for reach, frequency, and gross rating points for the market on the basis of a month. By contrast, traffic for car cards is rather easy to measure by counting the fares in the fare box. Transit advertising companies provide sworn statements every year reporting the average monthly number of riders carried in transit company vehicles. The re-

```
                                          LOUISIANA        PAGE 73
                                          SHREVEPORT

OPERATOR:  TRANSPORTATION ADVERTISERS, INC.
NATIONAL SALES MANAGER:  GEORGE W. PRECHTER JR.
NATIONAL SALES OFFICE:  7915 MAPLE ST., NEW ORLEANS, LA. 70118
LOCAL MANAGER: JAMES N. RONCO  (504) 897-3333
LOCAL OFFICE:  7915 MAPLE ST., NEW ORLEANS, LA. 70118
SHIPPING ADDRESS:  LOUISIANA TRANSIT MANAGEMENT INC., 1115 JACK WELLS BLVD.,
                   SHREVEPORT, LA. 71107
```

EXTERIOR RATES

	Size Showing/# Units		1 Mo.	3 Mos.	6 Mos.	12 Mos.
30 x 144	#100	24	1,800	1,710	1,620	1,440
King Size	# 50	12	900	855	810	720
Street Side	# 25	6	450	428	405	360
	Unit	1	75.00	71.25	67.50	60.00
30 x 108	#100	24	1,500	1,425	1,350	1,200
Curb Side	# 50	12	750	713	675	600
	# 25	6	375	356	338	300
	Unit	1	62.50	59.35	56.25	50.00
21 x 40	#100	24	900	855	810	720
Headlight	# 50	12	450	428	405	360
	# 25	6	225	214	203	180
	Unit	1	37.50	35.65	33.75	30.00
21 x 72	#100	24	1,200	1,140	1,080	960
Rear Space	# 50	12	600	570	540	480
	# 25	6	300	285	270	240
	Unit	1	50.00	47.50	45.00	40.00
21 x 44	#100	24	600	570	540	480
Traveling	# 50	12	300	285	270	240
Displays	# 25	6	150	143	135	120
	Unit	1	25.00	23.75	22.50	20.00

INTERIOR RATES

			1 Mo.	3 Mos.	6 Mos.	12 Mos.
11 x 28	Full	60	325	309	293	260
2 cards	Half	30	188	178	169	150
22 x 21	Full	60	525	499	473	420
Bulkhead	Half	30	300	285	270	240
22 x 21	Full	60	394	374	354	315
Hi-Lite	Half	30	225	214	203	180

```
No. Vehicles Operating:  60
Transit System:  SporTran
Area Served:  Metropolitan Shreveport including Barksdale Air Force Base, Bossier City
Avg. Monthly Rides:  404,263  (Source:  Transit System)
SMSA Population:
```

FIGURE 20-11

A page from the *TAA Rate Directory of Transit Advertising. By permission: The Transit Advertising Association, Inc.*

ported audience is based on one person riding a display-carrying vehicle for one trip. The count includes paying passengers, paid and nonpaid transfers, free passengers, schoolticketers, etc. It allows only a single count for a zone rider who passes through more than one zone.

The rate structure for transit advertising is similar to that for outdoor advertising. It also enjoys a low cost-per-thousand rate. Like the other major media, it pays a 15 percent commission to advertising agencies. As in outdoor advertising, there is the additional cost of production and printing of cards and posters.

Advertisers can buy transit advertising on an individual market basis or in any combination of 380 major markets available in the United States. Although most advertisers buy on a selective market basis, some buy groups of top markets. In larger markets, it is possible to buy runs for individual sectors, affording greater selectivity for the advertiser.

STRENGTHS AND WEAKNESSES OF TRANSIT ADVERTISING

Transit advertising is, in a way, two media. Inside displays can use detailed copy because of the time spent by passengers in transit and their close proximity to the message. In this sense, they are not unlike magazine advertisements. Exterior displays are brief and, because of size, dramatic; in many ways, they are similar to outdoor advertising. Transit advertising is carried by over 70,000 vehicles throughout the urban United States and Canada.

Research shows that transit advertising costs average 30 cents per thousand average on a national basis. A transit rider averages 24 rides per month, 61 minutes a day.[2]

For the advertiser desiring high frequency, the medium is excellent, because riders for the most part repeat their trips frequently. Because of the close proximity to the point of purchase provided by the vehicles, there is the opportunity to expose the consumer to the advertising message just before buying takes place.

Although public transportation has faced some difficult years, a new interest appears to be developing in rapid transit systems that would provide new strength to the transit medium. A big problem in the use of car cards has been their high production cost relative to their low advertising rates. This has been overcome to some extent by the fact that advertisers increasingly have gone to adapting newspaper and magazine layouts and art to transit advertising campaigns.

OTHER OUT-OF-HOME MEDIA

There are, of course, other out-of-home media. Taxicabs frequently have exterior and interior advertising space for sale. Various truck fleets have used exterior space for advertising. Even U.S. postal trucks have carried advertising about the Postal Service on their sides.

Other out-of-home media of a different nature from outdoor and transit advertising include point-of-purchase advertising and exhibits. These are discussed in the next chapter.

394

Outdoor signs are one of the oldest forms of advertising. The medium has come under substantial social criticism, but this is directed primarily toward nonstandardized and on-premises signs. Unlike the media we have considered previously, out-of-home media serve no other purpose than to carry advertising.

Standardized outdoor advertising is made up of posters, bulletins, and spectaculars. Poster panels and bulletins are owned by regional or local firms called plants. Plant operators frequently own plants in a number of different markets. These operators usually sell directly to local advertisers, but national advertisers more often buy from regional market groups representing a large number of plants.

Outdoor "circulation" is called traffic and is a measure of the number of cars passing posters and bulletins. The medium is sold in gross rating points or showings. A 100 GRP or *showing* indicates the number of panels necessary for an exposure equal to the total population of the market.

Transit advertising includes car cards in the interior of public transportation and displays on the exterior. Station posters are also considered part of the medium. Interior transit advertising is sold in *runs*. A full run includes a card in every vehicle in the fleet. Exterior displays are sold as *showings*.

1. Some people advocate banning outdoor signs, or else placing severe restrictions on their use. Why do you agree or disagree?
2. Name and briefly describe the three types of standardized outdoor advertising signs.
3. What is an outdoor advertising plant?
4. Each of the following organizations plays a role in out-of-home media. Describe the role of each.
   (a) TAB
   (b) TAA
   (c) OAAA
   (d) IOA
5. Explain what is meant by buying 100 gross rating points in outdoor poster panels.
6. What is outdoor circulation called? How is it measured?
7. What are the strengths and weaknesses of outdoor advertising?
8. What are the major types of transit advertising?
9. What is a transit advertising run?
10. What are the strengths and weaknesses of transit advertising?

[1] Traffic Audit Bureau, Inc.
[2] *TAA Rate Directory of Transit Advertising,* October 1981, p. 2.

Other Media

After completing this chapter, you should be able to:

1. Understand the place of direct mail advertising in media planning
2. Appreciate how point-of-purchase display can be an effective part of advertising
3. Explain the uses of specialty advertising
4. Show how directories can be used as an advertising medium

So far, consideration has been given to the major commercial mass communications media that advertisers can "buy" to carry their messages, but there are other important media. Advertisers can buy some; others they must produce themselves.

By one measure—the amount of money spent—some of these media would be considered rather insignificant, although for others the expenditures are quite large. The real measure of the importance of any medium, however, must be its effectiveness in achieving the goals of the firm's advertising plan. Some advertisers rely on these media quite heavily; others use them as supplements to the media discussed in the previous chapters. This discussion of media is meant to be introductory rather than exhaustive. The media introduced here include direct mail, point-of-purchase, exhibits, films, specialty advertising, and directories.

DIRECT MAIL ADVERTISING

It is somewhat difficult to measure the dollar volume of direct mail advertising, but the Direct Mail/Marketing Association, using an equation it has devised, estimates the annual volume to be in excess of $10 billion. The volume of direct mail advertising in terms of mailing pieces is staggering. It is estimated that 95 percent of all third-class mail is direct mail advertising, and that more than 30 billion pieces of third-class mail are posted annually in this country. In addition, direct mail advertising is a significant part of other classes of mail, so that the number of pieces attributable to direct mail exceeds 34 billion.[1] And, of course, there are many other pieces of direct mail advertising used in countries all over the world.

A distinction must be made between *direct mail* and *direct marketing*. *Direct mail* refers to a vehicle for advertising where the advertising message is delivered through the Postal Service or similar delivery system. *Direct marketing,* also known as *direct response marketing,* is a system of marketing in which goods are transferred without the use of retail store or industrial supply house physical facilities. It is a redefinition of "mail-order" selling, in which the seller makes use of various advertising media (including direct mail) to elicit a direct response to purchase the offer. Direct marketers are major users of direct mail advertising, but they also make use of every other type of advertising that can also be used to elicit a direct response. Direct mail advertising is also used by virtually every kind of advertiser—both national and retail—as part of the media mix and is directed to consumers and other businesses.

NATURE OF THE MEDIUM The broad scope of advertisers using direct mail is evident by the fact that some 350,000 separate businesses hold third-class mailing permits from the Postal Service. Direct mail advertising ranges from used-car-dealer postal card announcements to the Sears, Roebuck catalog.

In the media previously discussed, national advertisers almost always make use of advertising agencies to prepare the advertisements for the media. For direct mail, however, until recently, the more general procedure was for advertisers to do it themselves. The major reason was that direct mail advertising is not commissionable, so that the agency must charge for those services that are paid for out of commissions when other media are used. But this picture is changing. More and more major agencies are setting up departments to create direct mail advertisements, and in some instances, full-fledged divisions have been created by major agencies for this function. So the old criticism that direct mail lacks the professional creative imagination an agency can provide is not valid today. There are also direct mail specialists who will provide clients with creative counseling as well as production services.

FIGURE 21-1

Various pieces from a direct mail campaign to physicians. Each mailing featured a color print of a different Continental soldier which could be detached and framed for decorating the physician's office. In addition, each contained a sample of a button from the uniform depicted, and a set of these buttons, suitable for a blazer, could be obtained as a self-liquidating premium offer. *By permission.*

For most media, the form the advertisements take is fairly well dictated by the mechanical specifications of the medium. Media will provide for some latitude in size (but these are usually fixed units), the use of color, or the option of bleed pages in magazines, for example. Direct mail imposes almost no limits short of cost, other than the technological limitations of the graphic arts and postal regulations regarding minimum and maximum size and legal limitations of copy. Therefore, the preparation of direct mail involves decisions on size, shape, enclosures, printing processes, and so forth, as well as copy and layout.

CIRCULATION Unlike advertisers using most other major media, advertisers using direct mail can have complete control over who and how many will receive their messages by choosing the specific list of people who are to receive the advertisements. Although they have rather tight control over who will receive their messages, obviously there is no assurance that all or even very many of these people will read it. Because many high-income and/or multi-interest people receive a disproportionate share of the direct mail sent, it is falsely believed that most people receive many pieces of direct mail. Actually, the average household in the U.S. receives no more than one piece of direct mail per day. As with any other advertising medium, people will read or pay attention only to those appeals that interest them. Unfortunately, direct mail advertising is frequently referred to as "junk" mail by the public. Still, studies of consumer attitudes toward direct mail show that most was opened and read, and the reception was largely that the direct mail was either useful information or, if not, was still interesting or enjoyable.[2]

Advertisers have several sources for mailing lists. One of these is their own resources. They may have lists of present or past customers, called *house lists,* or they may prepare lists from such sources as birth or marriage announcements in the newspapers, telephone or city directories, and salespeople's reports. If they do not wish to prepare their own lists, they can turn to list compilers. These firms specialize in preparing mailing lists, which may be highly specialized by such classifications as occupation, hobby, income, geographic location, ownership (of homes, brands of automobiles, and so forth), age, or family size. Many firms that have built their own lists, such as magazine publishers, rent these lists to interested direct mail advertisers. Such lists are segmented by geographic, demographic, and/or psychographic factors and can thus be highly correlated with the advertiser's prospects—for example, a photographic equipment manufacturer who uses the subscription list of a photography magazine. Finally, there are mailing-list brokers. Although they themselves do not own any lists, they act as agents in obtaining for advertisers the use of others' lists. For the advertiser, the broker's major value is his or her knowledge of what lists are available; for the list owner, the broker provides a source of business. Standard Rate & Data Service publishes semiannually a catalog called *Direct Mail List Rates and Data.* This catalog lists some 21,000 direct mail lists available and includes sources, cost per thousand, and other specifications.

Sound Investment. *In Long Beach, Calif., Mrs. Agnes Roche, 39, divorcee with eight children, was swamped with answers to her newspaper ad offering to marry "a nice man who wants a lot of income-tax exemptions."*

TIME

COLLEGE FACULTY AT HOME ADDRESS

Media Code 3 091 2767 8.00 **Mid 025955-005**

Member: D.M.M.A.

Market Compilation & Research Bureau, Inc.

11633 Victory Blvd., North Hollywood, CA 91609. Phone 213-877-5384, QWIP, 213-980-6453.

NOTE: For basic information on the following numbered listing segments 1, 5, 6, 7, 8, 10, 11, see Market Compilation & Research Bureau, Inc. listing under classification No. 45.

2. DESCRIPTION

College faculty at home address. Recompiled annually at start of each school year with computer selection by state, zip, sex, subject taught and faculty rank.

List is computerized.

ZIP Coded in numerical sequence 100%.

3. LIST SOURCE

College directories. Derived 100% through roster.

4. QUANTITY AND RENTAL RATES

Rec'd May, 1982.

	Total Number	Price per/M
Total list (No. 39T)	200,000	35.00
Selections by academic rank surcharges:		
College administrators	16,000	4.50
Professors & assoc. professors	90,000	1.50
Assistant professors	4,000	8.00
Instructors & assistants	24,000	3.50
Mixed college faculty	90,400	1.50
Selections by subject specialty charges:		
Agricultural sciences	1,000	8.00
Business data processing	13,000	4.50
Education	7,000	6.00
Engineering	8,000	•
English	9,000	•
Foreign language	4,000	8.00
Home economics	1,000	•
Vocational education	1,000	6.00
Librarians	3,000	•
Mathematics	5,000	6.00
Medical, includes medicine, dentistry, nursing, pharmacy veterinary	13,000	4.50
Music, includes music, band choir	4,000	8.00
Physical & biological sciences	27,000	3.50
Physical education	1,000	8.00
College administrators	3,000	8.00
Social sciences, law, religion & humanities	17,000	4.50
Mixed college faculty	103,400	N/C
Selection surcharges:		
Over 350,000 names	...	N/C
175,000 to 350,000 names	...	1.50
50,000 to 175,000 names	...	3.50
Under 50,000 names	...	4.00
Geographic	...	5.00
ZIP Code	...	5.00
All college faculty	...	N/C
Male only	...	1.00
Female only	...	2.00
Complete state counts by selection factors (automatically produced & billed unless otherwise requested)	...	1.25
Counts for analysis of results:		
Test surcharges:		
Random selection of names from area selected	...	3.00

Analysis of results including reinput of responses and computerized counting & reporting (request price).

Minimum order 400.00.

FIGURE 21-2

A listing for a direct mail list from *Standard Rate & Data Service. By permission: Standard Rate & Data Service, Inc.*

In most instances, advertisers rent lists instead of using their own. The list owners run labels or addresses directly onto envelopes. The labels or envelopes are sent to the advertisers' in-house mailing operations or mailing houses where labels are affixed to mailing pieces or envelopes are stuffed.

COST OF DIRECT MAIL Unlike the previously discussed media, direct mail involves no cost for time or space; instead, it pays the cost of postage. Otherwise, direct mail's biggest cost factors are creative (copy and layout), production, lists, and mailing. Production costs range from inexpensive mimeograph and multilith to high-priced letterpress jobs in full color with special die-cutting, or tip-ons. List prices differ according to the quality of the list. An average list today rents for about $50 per thousand names. Mailing costs will vary with postal rates for first- and third-class mail and the weight of the mailing pieces. In recent years, there have been considerable increases in postal rates.

Figured by cost per thousand, direct mail is undoubtedly an expensive medium. However, when costs are examined in terms of effectiveness, it seems much less expensive, because waste circulation is considerably lower than in other media. Advertisers can select their lists to include a high percentage of prospects. On the other hand, there is no assurance that every mailing list will be a good prospect list or that the message of the mailing pieces will be effective.

STRENGTHS AND WEAKNESSES OF DIRECT MAIL The major organization concerned with direct mail is the Direct Mail/Marketing Association (DMMA). Its membership is composed of users, producers, creators, and suppliers of direct mail advertising. The main purpose of the DMMA is to promote the effectiveness of the medium. It advances the following advantages of direct mail advertising:

1. It can be directed to specific individuals or markets with greater control than any other medium.
2. It can be made personal to the point of being absolutely confidential.
3. It is a single advertiser's individual message and is not in competition with other advertising and/or editorial.
4. It does not have the limitations on space and format as do other mediums of advertising.
5. It permits greater flexibility in materials and processes of production than any other medium of advertising.
6. It provides a means for introducing novelty and realism into the interpretation of the advertiser's story.
7. It can be produced according to the needs of the advertiser's own immediate schedule.
8. It can be controlled for specific jobs of research, reaching small groups, testing ideas, appeals, reactions.
9. It can be dispatched for accurate and in some cases exact timing, both as to departure of the pieces as well as to their receipt.
10. It provides more thorough means for the reader to get or buy through action devices not possible of employment by other media.[3]

Although the cost per thousand may be high for direct mail advertising, the total cost of a direct mail advertising campaign can be small enough to be within the means of even the smallest firm. The flexibility of the medium offers an opportunity for reaching the specific prospects of the advertiser, with little or no waste circulation. It also has flexibility in geographical coverage, in the format of the mailing piece, and in the timing of the mailing. Perhaps its greatest disadvantage is that it is solely an advertising message carrier, without entertainment value. Therefore, getting the reader's attention may be a problem.

American advertising has learned to tell the truth attractively about American products. When the product is good, and the truth is told, we have the appealing combination that secures sales and keeps the wheels of industry turning.

NORMAN V. PEALE, Clergyman

READER'S DIGEST

POINT-OF-PURCHASE ADVERTISING

The last opportunity for the advertiser to promote a sale is at the point of purchase, which, for consumer goods, is most often the retail store. Some promotional persuasion may be made by retail salespersons, and some by store displays. Good retailers are generally quite cognizant of the importance of promotional effort at the point of purchase, and they provide displays and train sales personnel to maximize the selling effort. However, national advertisers still have some problems. First of all, they recognize that not all retailers will maximize the selling effort. Second, even when retailers promote the sale of goods effectively at the point of purchase, they may be promoting their own private brands or competitive brands at the expense of the national advertiser. Third, to an increasing extent, retailers have resorted to self-service operations with little or no personal selling. National advertisers recognize that although national advertising in other media may presell consumers, they may change their minds at the point of purchase; they may switch brands, or they may be persuaded to make unpremeditated purchases on the basis of impulse. Most national consumer-goods advertisers, therefore, devote a portion of the advertising effort to point-of-purchase (P-O-P) advertising, making this one more out-of-home medium.

Point-of-purchase advertising makes use of an almost infinite variety of formats. The on-premise store sign, mentioned in the preceding chapter, is properly considered P-O-P advertising. It can be window displays and banners, counter displays, interior or exterior wall signs, merchandise racks for counters and aisles, or shelf edgers or can toppers. In fact, the variety is endless. All signs, displays, devices, and structures used as sales aids in a retail store are point-of-purchase advertising. It may be as simple as a printed card or as elaborate as illuminated, animated, talking displays, with corresponding costs from pennies to hundreds of dollars.

The trade association for P-O-P is the Point-of-Purchase Advertis-

Other Media

ing Institute (POPAI), which estimates that advertisers are spending $5.5 billion annually on point-of-purchase advertising. There are 26 different major types of P-O-P units, ranging from pole toppers to clocks to various forms of signs. These major types of P-O-P units break down into three major categories. The first category includes short-term signs and displays that are designed to last only a few weeks. Signs, banners, and cardboard or corrugated dump bins are examples of these. The second major category includes long-term displays, which have a life of at least three months but may be constructed to last for many years. These units are made of wood, wire, metal, or plastic. The third category is long-term signs that are maintained in service for many years. For some advertisers, investment in these outdoor signs is substantial, and the signs are a major vehicle for establishing company image. As it is a noncommissionable medium, less than 5 percent of P-O-P is handled through advertising agencies; and although some advertisers create their own P-O-P advertising, it is usually prepared by P-O-P houses. About 60 percent of these houses have their own production facilities. They will design, engineer, and produce anything from a unit to an entire promotion. Many of the larger houses have national coverage involving plants, their own sales force, and sales representatives.

It is difficult to measure cost per thousand for P-O-P with any high degree of accuracy, but it is reasonable to say that it is low compared to other media. An outside retail store sign that might represent a substantial investment could still be in use a dozen years after it was installed, thus bringing the cost per thousand down to less than a penny.

FIGURE 21-3

Two of the almost limitless varieties of point-of-purchase advertising materials. To the left is a permanent display. To the right is a temporary display. *By permission: Point-of-Purchase Advertising Institute, Inc.*

The POPAI says that temporary corrugated counter cards, having a two-week life expectancy, average less than 12 cents per thousand exposures. The more expensive the display, the longer it lasts. Therefore, the cost per thousand remains low for expensive as well as for inexpensive displays.

Point-of-purchase advertising by manufacturers is referred to as a kind of dealer help or dealer aid. (This was discussed in Chapter 10.) It might be expected that dealers would welcome all the aid they could get, but although most do, this is not always the case. Some advertisers find it difficult to get P-O-P accepted by some of the retailers because the retailers prefer to use their own display materials or because the retailers are simply poor businesspeople. In some cases, advertisers find it difficult to have P-O-P used correctly and effectively. Dump bins filled with a competitive brand and display clocks in the retailer's family room do not help its effectiveness. Because of the great quantity of P-O-P, there is much competition for the limited amount of retail display space. National advertisers generally use their sales force (or the wholesaler's sales force) for the distribution of P-O-P, or include it in the shipping carton with the merchandise. But some retailers cannot be bothered to install the display, and when the display is installed by the salesperson, the next salesperson from the next firm replaces the display with another display.

In most instances, P-O-P advertising is provided free to retailers. In some cases, however, the retailer pays a part or all of the cost for the item. The reason for such charges may be that the manufacturer believes that the retailer will use the item more effectively if the retailer has a financial investment in it. On the other hand, some P-O-P materials, such as store signs and display racks, may be quite costly but may be a real convenience for the retailer as well as an advertising aid. For example, a retailer may need an ice cream freezer display case. The manufacturer may be willing to supply one with brand advertising at a cost lower than a retailer would pay for one without advertising. In some cases, the only way the manufacturer can get advertising at the point of purchase is to pay the retailer for the privilege of using the display space. This, in reality, becomes a form of advertising allowance, and care must be exercised to see that there is no violation of the Robinson-Patman Act, which prohibits discrimination in advertising allowances.

In summary, it can be said that the greatest advantage of P-O-P is that it is the "last word" before the purchase. It is closer than any other medium to the point where the sale takes place. At this point, it provides information, identification, and merchandising for the national advertiser. Point-of-purchase advertising can create the excitement of change for special events. It can provide a means of holding special promotions without disturbing the retailer's shelf arrangements. It can stimulate impulse purchases. Coordinated with national advertising in other media, P-O-P recapitulates the whole promotional effort at the most vital time in the consumer decision-making process—just before buying.

Between the Lines. *In Oakland, in its classified advertising columns, the* Tribune *offered: "Hollywood bed frame, mattress, springs; wedding veil, reasonable. LO 9-2365."*

TIME

Progressive retailers recognize the value of P-O-P, but their space is limited, and they demand that such advertising materials be good. The national advertiser thus must "sell" quality P-O-P to the retailer.

> *Advertising is an invaluable and indispensable part of modern business and modern life. . . . Advertising is the cheapest and most efficient method of announcing new products . . . helps to reduce seasonal variations in sales and so tends to stabilize employment. By speeding up turnover, advertising makes distribution more efficient and makes capital go farther.*
>
> *HARRY A. BULLIS, Manufacturer*
>
> READER'S DIGEST

INDUSTRIAL AND CONSUMER EXHIBITS

In contrast to point-of-purchase advertising, which is primarily a consumer medium, another form of display—the exhibit—is primarily an industrial medium. Point-of-purchase is also used occasionally in industrial sales, especially for those items that are sold through industrial distributors, such as mill supply houses that maintain showrooms, as in the case of the building trades. The major use of exhibits is at trade shows, and thousands of these are held each year, usually in connection with association conventions. Exhibits provide the exhibitor with an opportunity to demonstrate the product, which is especially important for bulky equipment that cannot be carried by a salesperson when making a call. Exhibits are also frequently used for institutional advertising.

There are four major cost factors in exhibit advertising. The first of these is space rental. The cost of booths at shows will vary greatly. The second is exhibit design and construction. This activity usually is handled by specialists, many of whom are members of the Exhibit Producers & Designers Association. Fixed fees are generally charged, depending upon the complexity and elaborateness of the exhibit. Third, there are miscellaneous expenses, including transportation, installation, and furniture rental. The fourth cost involves staffing the booth. Since it is usually staffed by salespeople, this cost is usually charged to personal selling. Because the cost of design and construction is frequently high, many exhibits are moved from show to show.

Circulation for exhibits is readily measured, because those manning the booths can keep a traffic count. However, it is difficult to use this information to predict circulation for future shows.

In addition to industrial exhibits, there are certain consumer-goods manufacturers who participate actively in county and state fairs and home, sport, and garden shows. Some major manufacturers also maintain exhibits at world's fairs and the Disney EPCOT Center, with huge investments not only in the exhibits themselves but also in the buildings to house them. In recent years, a number of firms have set up traveling exhibits in trailers. These move from shopping center to shopping center and offer demonstrations or more diversified samples of the line than those usually carried by the retailers.

American business has used motion picture film in a number of important ways. Nontheatrical films, for showings typically to schools and club groups, serve as an advertising and public relations medium. Business films are used by salespeople as a selling aid. Finally, theater screen commercials, shown in motion picture theaters between features, are not unlike spot announcements on television.

There is no yardstick for measuring whether nontheatrical films should be classified as advertising or public relations, and the firm would have to assign the costs for such films to the appropriate accounts arbitrarily. The cost of such films will obviously depend upon their production complexities and their length.

Whereas the advertising department may prepare films to be used by the sales force as sales aids, the cost of these films is considered a selling expense and therefore will not be discussed here.

In other parts of the world, especially where television has not developed as a strong medium or is noncommercial, theater screen advertising is an important advertising medium. Although it is not as strong a medium in this country, the majority of movie theaters accept theater screen advertising. Rates for theater screen advertising are based on weekly showing. Rate books give average weekly attendance figures for each theater, together with national and local rates. The cost per thousand figure for this medium is higher than for most, but it is argued that audience viewers are actual viewers rather than estimated circulation.

It is estimated that over $3.5 billion is spent annually by American business firms for specialty advertising. A specialty is a useful item usually imprinted with the name of the advertiser and sometimes other copy and given free to prospects and customers with no obligation. There are three classes of specialty advertising. One is imprinted advertising specialties, generally inexpensive items such as pens, pencils, balloons, ice scrapers, key chains, and the like. The second is calendars, the most popular item of all specialty advertising. The third is executive gifts. These are distinguished from other specialties mainly by higher prices and are distributed primarily to business executives. They are further distinguished by the general absence or concealment of an advertising imprint.

The possibilities for using specialty advertising are myriad, but it is most ideally suited to promoting branch openings by retailers, introducing new products, opening new accounts for service businesses, developing trade show exhibit traffic, changing names and products, motivating consumers through premiums, creating excitement at the point-of-purchase, building an image, and providing a constant brand or retailer reminder.

The cost of advertising specialties will depend upon the item used and the quantity purchased. There are some 15,000 to 20,000 articles of merchandise used by specialty advertisers, assuring the advertiser of a suitable item that will fit the budget. Their distribution can be tightly controlled to ensure a minimum waste. A research study indicates that

FIGURE 21-4

Two assortments of advertising specialties. Above: To commemorate the anniversary of a college bar and to increase patronage, the bar employed a promotion that spoofed the penchant of college preppies for designer labels. The Green Dolphin bar distributed dolphin appliqués that could be attached to clothing and bumper strips reading "Drink the Dolphin." The theme was supported with flyers and newspaper advertisements. Below: To increase space sales to advertisers, the publisher of an industrial business paper used specialty advertising to carry its message to 500 advertising and marketing executives. Mailed or personally delivered by space salespeople over a six-month period were tennis balls, executive basketball games, stadium cushions, sports duffle bags, and towels. These were all tied in with the theme "Hard to reach," explaining how *Chemical and Engineering News* reaches chemical buyers and specifiers. *By permission: Specialty Advertising Association International.*

70 percent of recipients of advertising specialties remember the advertiser's name.

There are three types of organizations within the industry. A *supplier* either manufactures, imports, or otherwise converts items for sale through distributors. A *distributor* or *counselor* develops ideas on how specialty advertising items can be used, buys them from suppliers, and sells them to advertisers. A *direct selling house* combines the functions of supplier and distributor in the one organization. The trade association for this industry is the Specialty Advertising Association International (SAAI).

Specialty advertising has many advantages. First, specialties are useful items and are sought after, or at least appreciatively accepted. Because they generally have a long life, their advertising messages are repeated over and over again. Considering their repetitiveness, they are inexpensive. Because of their material value, their advertising message is more readily accepted.

We regard our advertising program as an essential to the growth of this business and our advertising appropriation as a business investment which should be the last to be curtailed and among the first to be expanded.

A.P. SHANKLIN, *Manufacturer*

READER'S DIGEST

Directories are a form of periodical sufficiently different from other periodicals to merit some special consideration. Directories may be defined as listings of people, professions, institutions, or the like. Generally, they are published infrequently and may be sold or distributed free. They may be published by firms specializing in this kind of publication, such as Standard Rate & Data Service, Inc., which publishes catalogs of major media accepting advertising. They may be published as an adjunct to other periodicals; the *Directory of NECA Members and Electrical Materials,* for example, is published annually as an extra issue of the *Qualified Contractor.* They may also be published as a service by a business; the telephone directory is an example. Most important directories that accept advertising are listed in the *Business Publications* and *Consumer Magazines* volumes of *Standard Rate & Data Service,* and the problems of using them are similar to those of using other periodicals. Classified advertising in telephone directories, however, is somewhat different and will be considered further here.

YELLOW PAGES ADVERTISING   Telephone directory advertising is available in the Yellow Pages, which are to be found either appended to the regular directory or, in the larger cities, as a separate volume. Many retailers have found this classified advertising indispensable. For national advertisers, the Yellow Pages have found a place in their media mixes by providing sophisticated demographic data for target mar-

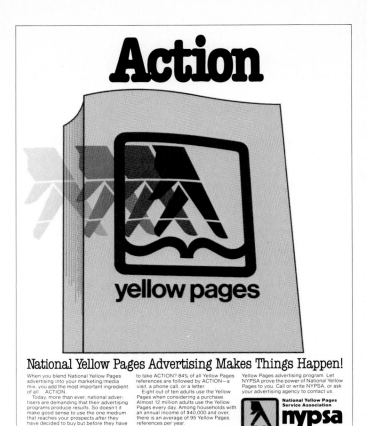

Action

yellow pages

National Yellow Pages Advertising Makes Things Happen!

When you blend National Yellow Pages advertising into your marketing/media mix, you add the most important ingredient of all...ACTION.

Today, more than ever, national advertisers are demanding that their advertising programs produce *results*. So doesn't it make good sense to use the one medium that reaches your prospects *after* they have decided to buy but *before* they have decided which brand to buy or where to buy?

And doesn't it make even more sense to use the medium that gets your prospect

to take ACTION? 84% of all Yellow Pages references are followed by ACTION—a visit, a phone call, or a letter.

Eight out of ten adults use the Yellow Pages when considering a purchase. Almost 12 million adults use the Yellow Pages every day. Among households with an annual income of $40,000 and over, there is an average of 95 Yellow Pages references per year.

The National Yellow Pages Service Association has all the research, the facts, and the tools you need to help you plan a more effective, cost-efficient National

Yellow Pages advertising program. Let NYPSA prove the power of National Yellow Pages to you. Call or write NYPSA, or ask your advertising agency to contact us.

National Yellow Pages Service Association

nypsa

888 W. Big Beaver Road
Troy, Michigan 48084
Telephone: (313) 362-3300

**the medium that puts the "closing touch"
on your marketing/media plans**

FIGURE 21-5

An advertisement by NYPSA explaining the advantages of Yellow Pages to national advertisers. *By permission: National Yellow Pages Service Association.*

kets. There is also information in the *NYPSA Rates & Data* publication, which covers more than 5,800 telephone directories in the United States.[4] Usually the Yellow Pages are used by a prospect after need is established and the prospect is ready to buy. Ultimate consumers and industrial users have long recognized the value of the Yellow Pages in finding names, addresses, telephone numbers, and additional information regarding sources of goods and services. Telephone directories, published each year, are received and retained by all homes and businesses having telephones. They are also available wherever there are public telephones. All businesses and services having telephones are listed in the Yellow Pages, but in addition, there is an opportunity to purchase advertising space. Advertising revenue for the Yellow Pages approximates $1.5 billion annually.

In addition to the regular listing that is free to all businesses having telephone service, a firm may buy the following: *bold listings* that are the same as the regular listings but set in boldface capital letters; *extra lines* of copy describing features of the business; *space listings* in single-column widths and sold in half-inch increments with permissible variations in type size, enclosed by a line border; and *trade names,* appearing in boldface type with dealer listing below. Other possibilities are *trademarks,* which include the brand name, trademark, several lines of copy, and the phrase, "Where to buy it," followed by dealer listing; and *display spaces,* permitting regular advertisements within ruled borders, which may include illustrations and special typography.

Yellow Pages advertising may be bought in individual directories, but the national advertiser planning to use many directories can place advertising nationally, regionally, or locally through National Yellow Pages Service in some 5,000 directories in the United States and Canada. This provides the advertiser with a single contract and a single bill. Such advertising is commissionable to advertising agencies. National advertisers using the medium may use the Yellow Pages emblem in their other advertising to advise consumers that dealers are listed in the Yellow Pages.

Probably the chief characteristic of Yellow Pages advertising is its directionality, appealing as it does to specific audiences. It generally reaches people *after* they have decided to buy but do not know where to buy. As a result of aggressive advertising of the medium to consumers and business, people have learned increasingly to use the Yellow Pages and let their "fingers do the walking."

A Yellow Pages study by Audits & Surveys, Inc. indicates that from a base of the entire adult population of the United States aged 20 or older, Yellow Pages reach 76.8 percent of the adult population with a frequency of 40.1 times per person in a year. There were 3.69 billion references to the Yellow Pages in a twelve-month period, with 89 percent of these followed by a telephone call, visit, or letter. Of these, 38 percent were for business use and 62 percent were for personal use. Fifty-one percent of these references were made without a name in mind.[5]

OTHER MEDIA

Many other, less-used media are available, and new ones are coming into being from time to time. Any medium, if it does the job for the advertiser, is important, at least to that advertiser. Some of these media are skywriting, supermarket shopping carts, textbook covers, time tables, theater ticket envelopes, postage meter indicia, and bus-stop benches, to mention but a few. (It has recently been proposed that the Postal Service sell advertising space on postage stamps!) Most such media do not have established advertising rates or certified circulation. Most are noncommissionable. But if they do the job and fit the media plan of the advertiser, they should be used.

TO SUM UP

The volume of direct mail advertising is staggering. Direct mail advertisers control who and how many will receive their messages, although they cannot be assured that the recipients will read them. Advertisers may have their own mailing lists or buy them. On a cost-per-thousand basis, direct mail may appear expensive. But there is little waste circulation, which really makes it economical.

Point-of-purchase displays provide a last opportunity to deliver a sales message where goods are bought. P-O-P makes use of a wide variety of formats. Displays may be permanent or temporary in nature. They are especially valuable in cases of self-service retailing. It is difficult to measure the cost per thousand for this medium, but its popularity with both national advertisers and retailers suggests its worth.

Exhibits are more often used as a business-to-business advertising medium, although world's fairs and the Disney EPCOT Center have proved the value of exhibits for consumers.

There are three classes of specialty advertising: imprinted advertising specialties such as key chains; calendars; and executive gifts. Because specialties have a long life, their advertising messages are repeated frequently.

There are a variety of directories that carry advertising, but the most important are the telephone directory Yellow Pages. Their main purpose is to inform consumers and businesses as to where goods and services can be obtained.

QUESTIONS AND PROBLEMS

1. Differentiate between direct mail and direct marketing.
2. What are the various ways an advertiser might obtain a mailing list for direct mail advertising?
3. What are the strengths and weaknesses of direct mail as an advertising medium?
4. Why is point-of-purchase advertising important to advertisers who manufacture consumer package goods?
5. Visit a supermarket and identify as many examples of point-of-purchase advertising as you can. For each, list the advertiser, the type of P-O-P advertisement, and its location.
6. What are some of the problems the P-O-P advertiser faces in using the medium?
7. Name and describe the three classes of specialty advertising.
8. Look around your living quarters, car, pockets, purse, and so on. Make a list of the specialty advertising items you find, indicating the advertiser and kind of specialty.
9. What are the four major cost factors in exhibit advertising?
10. Select a national advertiser of shopping goods and describe how the firm could effectively use the Yellow Pages.

ENDNOTES

[1] Direct Mail/Marketing Association.
[2] *Ibid.*
[3] "Advantages of Direct Advertising," *Direct Mail/Marketing Manual* (New York: Direct Mail/Marketing Association, Inc., n.d.), manual file: 1201.
[4] The National Yellow Pages Service Association (NYPSA) is an organization made up of publishers of Yellow Pages directories and authorized selling representatives.
[5] *Yellow Pages Usage: A New Study by Audits & Surveys, Inc.*, n.d.

22

The Scoop
Ice Cream Mix
Media Plan

After completing this chapter, you should be able to:

1. Understand how a media plan is put together
2. See how the material included in Part III of the book is applied in the development of a media plan

From the discussion in the foregoing chapters, it should be obvious that the development of an actual media plan is an imaginative and complex operation. Most advertising agencies prepare media plans for their clients in formalized, written documents. But there is much work to be done prior to writing the plan, and a good part of this, representing many hours of work, would not be included in the writing of the final plan. To present all the planning and figuring that go into the final product would require much more space than can be devoted to it here. Still, although the shortcomings of presenting only a part of the total input of media planning are recognized, the media plan for Scoop Ice Cream Mix is presented as an example.[1] The marketing plan in Chapter 15 would have been developed based on this document and other data. The section of that marketing plan that covers media is a summarization of this media plan. It might prove helpful to review the Scoop Ice Cream Mix marketing plan before reading this media plan.

Since this media plan is presented as an example, a word of caution is in order. This is a specific plan for a specific product for a specific year. It is not meant to be "typical," for it is doubtful that there are any typical plans. Each situation calls for its own plan. Each client and each advertising agency has its own media philosophy. Each plan must be approached by the agency media department personnel as a unique and challenging problem. For instance, it is reasonable to assume that an advertiser such as Scoop Ice Cream Mix would probe into the uses of cable television. As opposed to traditional broadcasting, cable television allows for targeting to a small but selective audience. "Narrowcasting," as the concept is referred to, is easily incorporated because of the thematic nature of several cable networks. In order for you to get a realistic look at a media plan, the jargon of the advertising business has been left intact here.

PRODUCT DESCRIPTION Scoop Ice Cream Mix is made up in chocolate and vanilla flavors and requires no refrigeration until it is prepared for serving.

I. BACKGROUND

Packets of the mix are sold in two container sizes:

SIZE	GROSS MARGIN
1/2 gallon, pack 24s	$13.00
1 gallon, pack 12s	$11.15

The additional ingredient needed to prepare the mix is either whole, low-fat, or skim milk. The mix and milk are blended in a rotary mixer and frozen in a home freezer or the freezer compartment of the refrigerator.

PRODUCT DISTRIBUTION AND ADVERTISING Because of special distribution problems that are inherent in the dairy industry, the majority of its distribution is restricted to small geographic areas. Of primary concern is the limited shelf life of most dairy products that does not permit warehousing but instead requires delivery of the products directly to the individual store units.

TARGET AUDIENCE Because Scoop's primary source of volume is expected to be the same as purchasers of regular ice cream, the target audiences are the same. That is:

PURCHASERS Women 25 to 54 having a household income of $15,000 plus with children under 18 years of age.

	ICE CREAM USERS					
	USED IN LAST MONTH			USED IN LAST MONTH 3 TO FEWER THAN 10 QUARTS		
	(000)	PERCENTAGE OF USERS	INDEX	(000)	PERCENTAGE OF USERS	INDEX
Women 25–54 years	36,855	54.8%	106	14,095	61.7%	119
Household income $15,000 +	40,618	60.4	106	15,153	66.3	116
Presence of children under 18 years	31,992	47.6	109	13,673	59.8	137
Combined	17,493	26.0	113	8,228	36.0	157

Source: SMRB.

413

REGIONALITY Ice cream consumption is strongest in the Northeast and Central regions of the United States and weakest in the South.

	% POPULATION	USERS*		RELATIVE VOLUME OF CONSUMPTION†	
		%	INDEX	%	INDEX
Northeast	22.0%	22.1%	100	23.2%	106
Central	25.8	27.1	105	28.4	110
South	33.5	32.4	97	30.8	92
West	18.7	18.4	98	17.6	94

*Used any ice cream in last month.
†Gross volume in quarts.

Source: SMRB.

SEASONALITY Ice cream is consumed throughout the year, with the March and June through September periods accounting for 46 percent of all consumption.

Larger-size units (gallons) are purchased during the summer months. It seems reasonable to assume that this seasonal consumption pattern has not changed significantly. (The following research is the latest available.)

	VOLUME*	PERCENTAGE	INDEX	PERCENT VOLUME BY MONTH	
				1/2 GALLON	GALLON
1973:					
January	70.9	7.7%	92	81.3%	11.0%
February	69.0	7.5	90	80.4	11.7
March	83.6	9.1	109	81.0	11.6
1972:					
April	69.5	7.6	91	80.8	12.6
May	71.5	7.8	94	83.1	10.7
June	85.2	9.3	112	81.4	11.6
July	83.9	9.1	109	80.5	12.5
August	86.1	9.4	113	80.9	12.0
September	83.4	9.1	109	80.6	12.6
October	72.4	7.9	94	82.2	10.9
November	71.1	7.7	92	81.8	11.1
December	71.8	7.8	94	82.2	11.7
	918.4	100.0%			

*Volume in millions of equivalent 1/2=gallon units.
Source: United Dairy Industry Association, "The Household Market for Ice Cream and Related Products," April 1972/March 1973.

Manufacturers of ice cream
Manufacturers of ice cream mixes

A. ICE CREAM MANUFACTURERS Ice cream manufacturers are considered to be our current competitors, consisting of approximately 750 small regional companies, of which 15 account for about 65% of the total ice cream production. However, owing to the dairy-to-store distribution pattern of the dairy business, no one brand has a dominant national position.

Ten companies accounted for $8,178,200, or 84% of advertising dollars.
Two companies accounted for $5,317,500, or 54% of advertising dollars.

Companies Accounting for the Top Advertisers

	1981 TRACEABLE MEDIA	
	TOTAL DOLLARS (000)	PERCENTAGE
Breyer's	$ 3,160.1	32.3
Sealtest Ice Cream	2,157.4	22.0
Klondike	573.5	5.9
Weight Watchers	556.1	5.7
Pet	462.4	4.7
Eskimo Pie	316.7	3.3
Hood	255.4	2.6
Häagen-Dazs	241.3	2.5
Kemps	228.0	2.3
Meadow Gold	227.3	2.3
Subtotal	$ 8,178.2	83.6%
All others	1,606.9	16.4
Total reported	$ 9,785.1	100.0%

Source: Leading National Advertisers Inc., and Media Records for January–December.

Although the majority of competitors are regional or local in nature because of their distribution situation, they cannot be overlooked as critical advertising forces. A smaller company, such as Abbott, which focuses all its advertising weight into the Philadelphia marketing area, has the potential of generating as much as 20 percent to 30 percent of the ice cream advertising "share of voice" in that one area (while accounting for less than 5% of national advertising dollars). If its media schedule were translated into national media (network television and national Sunday supplements), its national advertising budget could easily be 20 to 25 times its current size.

The following example from 1978 illustrates this relationship in terms of communication weights (reach and frequency) by a small company (Abbott) into Philadelphia and actually lesser weights going into Philadelphia (as well as other markets) by a large company (Breyer's). The big difference in budgets really relates more to the number of markets covered, not the "share of voice" in individual marketing areas.

Advertising Expenditures and Number of Markets, Abbott's and Breyer's

	SPOT TV	NEWSPAPER	TOTAL
Abbott's expenditures	$ 257,200	$ 35,200	$ 292,400
Abbott's number of markets	1	5	
Breyer's expenditures	$4,215,300	$ 111,300	$ 4,326,600
Breyer's number of markets	49	16	

Average Four-Week Market Reach and Frequency, Abbott's and Breyer's

	PERCENTAGE HOUSEHOLD REACH	AVERAGE FREQUENCY
Abbott's	89%	6.7
Breyer's	68%	4.9

Source: Leading National Advertisers, Inc., and Media Records, January–December.

B. ICE CREAM MIXES One product, Admiral's "Confectionery Ice Cream Mix," falls into this category. It has been successfully tested in the Kansas City area and is anticipated to be national by next spring. This is currently the only direct product competitor to Scoop. Projecting Admiral's Kansas City test market to national spending indicates a total of $15.0 million to be allocated to media. This is considerably higher than Scoop's spending. Introductory year-1 nationally projected expenditures would be:

	FIRST SIX MONTHS (MILLIONS)	SECOND SIX MONTHS (MILLIONS)	YEAR's TOTAL (MILLIONS)
Media	$ 9.3	$5.7	$15.0
Ten-cent mailed coupon	2.8	—	2.8
Other sales promotions	2.5	1.9	4.4
Total	$14.6	$7.6	$22.2

Source: Agency.

COMPETITIVE MEDIA VEHICLES The majority of media spending in the ice cream category is concentrated in spot television and newspapers. Inspection of competitive advertising indicates a large degree of couponing.

TOP TEN ICE CREAM ADVERTISERS, PERCENT SPENDING BY MEDIUM

Spot television	80.2%
Network television	0.1
Newspapers	9.8
Magazines	8.7
Outdoor	1.2
Total	100.0%

Source: Leading National Advertisers Inc., and Media Records for January–December.

MEDIA OBJECTIVES Scoop's media objectives in order of importance are:

1. Provide for selected market emphasis to combat competitive ice cream advertising as follows. Expenditure in key and secondary markets should exceed 67%.

MARKETS	PERCENTAGE UNITED STATES HOUSEHOLDS	PERCENTAGE FOOD SALES	PERCENTAGE OF BUDGET
Key markets	50.6%	51.4%	67%
Secondary markets	16.5	16.1	
Remaining United States	32.9	32.5	33%

2. Provide within the primary medium varying reach levels of the primary target audience (women 25 to 54 having a $15,000 plus household income with children under 18 years of age) as follows:

MARKETS	FEBRUARY TO APRIL	MAY TO SEPTEMBER	OCTOBER TO NOVEMBER
Key markets	60%	80%	60%
Secondary markets	60	80	60
Remaining United States	40	40	40

3. Provide for national support of the brand.
4. Provide for a continuous program covering as much of the year as possible.
   (a) Disproportionately allocate dollars to higher consumption months:

	BUDGET: WORKING MEDIA (000)	PERCENTAGE
1st Quarter	$ 899	9%
2nd Quarter	3,567	34
3rd Quarter	4,901	47
4th Quarter	1,059	10
	$10,426	100%

(b) Start as early as February to combat Admiral's national introduction, which is anticipated to be in the spring of 1984.

(c) Support two national consumer sales promotions consisting of premiums for children: May/June; July/August.

5. Select media vehicles and elements within these vehicles that will also provide reach against the secondary target audience of children under 18 years of age.

6. Select couponing vehicles to promote trial and to combat Admiral's introduction.

7. Select vehicles that may provide merchandising support to the trade and/or consumer.

8. Select vehicles that, in themselves, are merchandisable to the trade.

9. Select vehicles compatible with creative executions: television, magazines, Sunday supplements, newspapers.

MEDIA STRATEGIES

A. Television
1. Utilize television as the primary communication vehicle to reach both primary and secondary audiences.
2. Utilize television to provide for a visual usage of product as well as of product packaging.
3. Utilize network television to provide continual national support.
4. Utilize spot television to provide selected market support as well as seasonal support:
   (a) Group A markets: top 25 markets plus Kansas City.
   (b) Group B markets: 26 to 50 markets minus Kansas City.
   (c) October for one flight to provide year-end continuity.
5. Schedule television advertising in:
   (a) February to combat Admiral's introduction (network television plus Group A spot markets only).
   (b) June to provide seasonal emphasis, combat competitive advertising, and provide support of two consumer promotions (network television base plus Groups A and B spot markets).
   (c) October for one flight to provide year-end continuity.
6. Utilize the following daypart mix:
   (a) Daytime to reach the primary audience.
   (b) Early fringe and prime time to provide reach of the primary and secondary audiences and to provide visibility to the trade.
7. Utilize a pulsing strategy to provide coverage over more of the year while maintaining sufficient levels to combat competitive advertising.
8. Utilize television as a merchandisable commodity to the trade.

B. Cable
1. Utilize cable television to provide continual national support.

2. Schedule cable concurrent with network television.
3. Utilize the following cable vehicles:
   (a) "Daytime"—women's interest programming. Targeted to women 25–54.
   (b) Music Television—24-hour video music channel. Targeted to children 18 years and under.

C. Magazines
   1. Utilize magazines to provide national support.
   2. Utilize magazines to provide regional support.
   3. Utilize magazines to provide continuity by scheduling from March through October.
   4. Utilize magazines to provide for a coupon vehicle.
   5. Utilize magazines to provide support for the two national consumer sales promotions in May/June and July/August.
   6. Utilize magazines to provide merchandising to the trade.

D. Sunday supplements
   1. Utilize supplements to provide for selected market support.
   2. Utilize supplements to provide for seasonal support by scheduling May through September
   3. Utilize supplements to provide support for the two sales promotional events as well as preholiday support to Memorial Day, Fourth of July, Labor Day.
   4. Utilize supplements to provide for additional four-color advertising weight.

E. Newspapers
   1. Utilize newspapers to provide for selected market support.
   2. Utilize newspapers to provide for seasonal emphasis by scheduling June through September.
   3. Utilize newspapers to provide for preholiday promotions as with supplements.
   4. Utilize newspapers to provide for fast close ability to drop in a coupon to combat competition.
   5. Utilize newspapers to provide for couponing in support of the two consumer sales promotions.
   6. Utilize newspapers to provide merchandising to the trade and consumers.

MEDIA TACTICS Although the objectives, strategies, and media plan flow chart outline the direction needed to implement the media support activity, there are also a number of more subtle tactics that could be utilized to extend the value and impact of the program. These implementation tactics for Scoop are presented below.

TELEVISION

1. Schedule as much weight as possible on the three primary best food days (BFD), Tuesday, Wednesday, and Thursday, to provide an emphasis on the days when most food shopping is done and to create the image of a larger campaign to break through competitive advertising and other advertising clutter.
2. "Roadblock" commercials to achieve a higher reach potential. [Note: "Roadblocking" refers to buying television commercial time on all stations in a market at the same time so that a reach of 100 percent of all households tuned in can be obtained.]
3. Use a 30-second commercial.

DOLLAR EXPENDITURES (000)

	1ST QUARTER	2ND QUARTER	3RD QUARTER	4TH QUARTER	TOTAL	GRAND TOTAL
Network television (100% daytime) 38 target GRPs per week X 21 weeks, daytime	$405.2	$741.1	$564.8	$276.4	$1,987.5	
Spot television Group A (top 25 plus Kansas City) 27 target GRPs per week X 21 weeks, early fringe 48 target GRPs per week X 9 weeks, prime	330.8	1,371.4	2,069.4	252.6	4,024.2	
Group B (26–50 less Kansas City) 27 target GRPs per week X 12 weeks, early fringe 48 target GRPs per week X 9 weeks, prime	—	343.2	690.4	96.8	1,130.4	
Cable television Daytime 10 ROS per week	—	30.1	25.8	12.9	68.8	
Music Television 14 ROS per week	—	88.2	75.6	37.8	201.6	
Total television	$736.0	$2,574.0	$3,426.0	$676.5		$7,412.5
Magazines (digest size, four-color bleed)						
Better Homes and Gardens (4)						
Good Housekeeping (3)						
Family Circle (4)						
McCall's (4)						
Reader's Digest (2)						
Redbook (3)						
Woman's Day (4)						
Parents (4)						
Sunset (3)						
Essence (4)						
Forecast for Home Economics (4)						
Total magazines	$162.8	$498.0	$373.8	$143.1	$1,177.7	
Sunday supplements (digest size or two-fifths page, four-color) Sunday Metro 55 papers		$256.4	$384.6	—	$641.0	
Newspapers Group A (top 25 plus Kansas City) five 1000-line black-and-white						
Group B (26–50 less Kansas City) five 600-line black-and-white						
Total newspapers		$239.0	$717.0	$239.0	$1,195.0	
Total print	$162.8	$993.4	$1,475.4	$382.1		$3,013.7
Total working media	$898.8	$3,567.4	$4,901.4	$1,058.6		$10,426.2
Television production						$164.0
Print production						$82.0
Grand total						$10,672.2

MAGAZINES

1. Schedule a mass circulation publication to carry pop-up coupon cards in the spring.
2. Schedule a wall chart to run in *Forecast for Home Economics* to prompt usage in classroom.
3. Utilize a special section "Summer Table" of *Reader's Digest* to take advantage of their sales promotion support to the trade.
4. Investigate possible use of the *Good Housekeeping* seal.
5. Utilize trade leaflets published by *Better Homes and Gardens, Family Circle,* and *Sunset*.
6. Use digest-size four-color bleed to take advantage of production savings.

SUNDAY SUPPLEMENTS Use digest or two-fifths page, four-color bleed.

NEWSPAPERS

1. Utilize merchandising support such as newsletters to the trade.
2. Schedule on best food day.
3. Use two advertisement units: 1,000-line black-and-white (Group A—top 25 markets plus Kansas City) and 600-line black-and-white (Group B—26–50 less Kansas City).

MEDIA OVERVIEW

IV. RATIONALE

1. Television is recommended as the primary communication vehicle because:
   (a) Television has the ability to build high levels of target reach within a relatively short period of time. This will be important in view of the three-month hiatus from the previous year's plan and Admiral's introduction in the spring.
   (b) Television affords the opportunity of "targeting" against a specific population segment, while at the same time delivering impressions against secondary audiences—i.e., children under 18 years of age.
   (c) Television has the ability to actually demonstrate the product's usage, create appetite appeal, and visually show product package to help build brand identity.
   (d) Television is the primary medium of Scoop's competitors (both ice cream manufacturers and ice cream mixes).
   (e) Television offers a merchandisable commodity to use in presenting to the trade.
2. Print is recommended to complement the television effort by:
   (a) Increasing reach against the light television viewer.
   (b) Offering the readers the opportunity of a lengthy, leisurely examination of the advertising copy.
   (c) Providing a visual presentation of the product and especially product packaging to build brand awareness.
   (d) Offering a vehicle for couponing (price-off or mail-in form for sales promotions) to stimulate trial of the product.
   (e) Providing merchandisability to the trade and, in some instances, actual merchandising to the trade.

Scoop Ice Cream Mix
Media Plan

CAMPBELL-EWALD COMPANY — ADVERTISING — SCOOP ICE CREAM MIX

Numbers denote spots per week — not GRP's.

LEGEND: tgt = target; GRP's = gross rating points; KC = Kansas City; mkt = market; E.F. = early fringe; ROS = run-of-station

	JAN	FEB	MAR	APR	MAY	JUN	JUL	AUG	SEP	OCT	NOV	DEC	TOTAL DOLLARS
NETWORK TV (:30) Day 38 tgt (GRP's/wk) — 21 Weeks		38	38		38	38	38	38	38	38			$1,987.5
SPOT TV (:30) •Group A (top 25 plus KC mkt) E.F.: 21 wks @ 27 tgt GRP's/wk		27	27		27	27	27	27	27	27			$4,024.2
Prime: 9 wks @ 48 tgt GRP's/wk						48	48	48	48				
•Group B (26–50 less KC mkt) E.F. 12 wks @ 27 tgt GRP's/wk						27	27	27	27	27			$1,130.4
Prime: 9 wks @ 48 tgt GRP's/wk						48	48	48	48				
CABLE TELEVISION* Daytime — 10 ROS per week				10	10	10	10	10	10	10			
MUSIC TELEVISION 14 ROS per week				14	14	14	14	14	14	14			
QUARTERLY TV BUDGET:	$761.0			$2,559.0			$3,451.0			$701.5			$7,412.5 (TOTAL TV)
MAGAZINES Digest size, 4 color bleed — Better Homes & Gardens, Good Housekeeping, Family Circle, McCall's, Reader's Digest (A = P4C and pop-up coupon; B = P4C, special edition), Redbook, Woman's Day, Parents, Sunset, Essence, Forecast			A			B							$1,777.7 (TOTAL MAGAZINES)
SUNDAY SUPPLEMENTS Sunday Metro — 55 papers					X	X	X	X	X				$ 641.0
NEWSPAPERS •Group A (top 25 plus KC mkt)						X	X	X	X	X			$ 974.4
•Group B (26–50 less KC mkt)						X	X	X	X	X			$ 220.6
QUARTERLY PRINT BUDGET	$162.8			$993.4			$1,475.4			$382.1			$3,013.7
TV PRODUCTION													$ 164.0
PRINT PRODUCTION													$ 82.0
TOTAL													$10,672.2

TELEVISION DAYPART SELECTION The recommended daypart selection is as follows:

1. Daytime provides an efficient base of communication.
2. Early fringe and prime extends the reach in combination with daytime.
3. Both early fringe and prime (especially prime) have the ability to reach the secondary audience of children under 18 years of age.
4. All dayparts are merchandisable to the trade, but the trade has more opportunity to actually see the commercials during early fringe and prime.

The daypart mix for the three levels of advertising provides for potential reach and frequencies as shown:

	AVERAGE FOUR-WEEK PERCENT REACH	WOMEN 25 THROUGH 54 AVERAGE FREQUENCY
38 D, 27 EF, 48 P = 113 target GRPs per week (33% D, 25% EF, 42% P)	81.1	4.2
38D, 27 EF = 65 target GRPs per week (58% D, 42% EF)	62.3	3.1
38 D, = 38 target GRPs per week (100% D)	41.8	2.7

TELEVISION GROSS RATING POINT ALLOCATION Television weight is allocated according to three marketing groups:

1. Group A represents high category development markets that are the top 25 ADIs plus Kansas City. (Note: The two major advertisers, Breyer's and Sealtest, concentrate advertising in these markets as well as many regional and private label brands. Kansas City, though ranked as the 27th ADI, is included due to its usage as Admiral's test market for the past year.)
2. Group B represents moderate category development markets consisting of ADIs 25 to 50. (Note: These markets receive a moderate amount of competitive advertising within the television medium.)
3. Group C represents the remaining United States. (Note: These markets receive a low level of ice cream advertising.)

Network television is recommended to provide an efficient base of national advertising, with spot television providing the ability to adjust weight levels according to market development. All markets are to receive 21 weeks of television support in three-week flights. However, below is an outline of the varying weight levels by group.

The February-to-May activity provides a competitive stance in key markets to offset Admiral's introduction. The higher levels during June to September provide for seasonal support at increased levels to combat competitive advertising. The last flight in October to November provides for continuity to help carry over to the following year's advertising.

GROUP	(NUMBER OF 3-WEEK FLIGHTS)	TARGET GRPs PER WEEK		NETWORK (NTV) SPOT (STV)
A	(3) February—May to offset Admiral	38	daytime	NTV
		27	early fringe	STV
		65	per week	
	(3) July–September seasonal support	38	daytime	NTV
		27	early fringe	STV
		48	prime	STV
		113	per week	
	(1) October–November postseasonal support	38	daytime	NTV
		27	early fringe	STV
		65	per week	
B	(3) June–September seasonal support	38	daytime	NTV
		27	early fringe	STV
		48	prime	STV
		113	per week	
	(1) October–November postseasonal support	38	daytime	NTV
		27	early fringe	STV
		65	per week	
C	(7) February–November	38	daytime	NTV

MAGAZINE SELECTION The recommended magazines have been selected to provide:

1. Reach against the primary audience of women 25 to 54 with children under 18 years of age
2. Regional emphasis
3. Special merchandising opportunities
4. Special marketing opportunities
5. Merchandisability to the trade

The recommended list of magazines is:

Women's service publications: *Better Homes and Gardens, Good Housekeeping, Family Circle, McCall's, Redbook*, and *Woman's Day*
Mass audience: *Reader's Digest*
Regional: *Sunset*
Special marketing opportunities: *Parents, Essence*, and *Forecast for Home Economics*

All the selected publications provide reach of the target audience. Additional values are:

1. Food editorial environment: All women's service publications, *Parents, Sunset*, and within the special section of *Reader's Digest*.

2. Good reproduction quality: All.
3. Special merchandising opportunities:
    (a) *Reader's Digest* special issues include special merchandising to the trade.
    (b) *Family Circle, Better Homes and Gardens*, and *Sunset* prepare trade promotion leaflets for product releases.
4. Special marketing opportunities:
    (a) *Parents* has a concentrated audience of women with children.
    (b) *Essence* provides a vehicle to carry special copy within an environment that may lend credibility to the product message and identification within the black audience.
    (c) *Forecast for Home Economics*, the home-economics teacher's publication, may stimulate usage in the classroom as well as having children then making it at home to show their parents. A special pull-out insert (wall chart) will be used for one advertisement so that teachers may post it in the classroom.
5. All publications are known by the trade, thereby being merchandisable.

SUNDAY SUPPLEMENTS AND NEWSPAPERS These vehicles are recommended to provide timely heavy-up support for selected markets.

1. Sunday supplements provide this support in four-color, thus creating more appetite appeal. This complements the magazine schedule. *Sunday Metro* has been selected because its list most closely correlates to key ice cream markets.
2. Sunday supplements and newspapers will be scheduled prior to Memorial Day, Fourth of July, and Labor Day in order to give holiday support.
3. Newspapers will be scheduled in the two groups: Group A: Top 25 markets plus Kansas City are key ice cream markets. (Note: They are also higher population areas; therefore the newspapers are generally larger in size. To increase advertisement visibility, they will receive a 1,000-line advertisement.) Group B: Markets 26 through 50 less Kansas City are moderate ice cream markets. (Note: These newspapers generally have fewer pages and therefore can carry a smaller advertisment, providing cost efficiencies without loss of potential advertisement visibility.)

MEDIA NOT RECOMMENDED Radio has not been considered, primarily because it lacks the ability to visually show and/or demonstrate the product and product packaging. Because of this, it is difficult to create appetite appeal as well as recognition of the package.

Although outdoor could be used to provide local market support generating strong reach with a relatively high frequency of message exposure, spot television has been recommended because of its ability to actually demonstrate the product in use, which would subjectively create more appetite appeal.

Additionally, in order to include any other medium, it would be necessary to decrease one or all of the media in our currently recommended media mix, diluting their effectiveness within their specific audience as well as the combined audiences.

Scoop Ice Cream Mix
Media Plan

QUESTIONS AND PROBLEMS

1. How would you evaluate the strategy suggested in the media plan? What would you say are its strengths and weaknesses?
2. Evaluate the plan in terms of the suggested ingredients in a media plan as discussed in Chapter 16.
3. Would you include any other media classifications in the plan? Why, or why not?
4. What kinds of media information would be necessary in order to prepare this media plan?
5. If you were the client, would you have accepted this media plan?

ENDNOTE

[1] I am indebted to members of the media department of Campbell-Ewald (whose names appear in the Preface) for creating this hypothetical example.

23

Advertising and the Creative Process

After completing this chapter, you should be able to:
1. Define creativity and the creative personality
2. Describe the creative process
3. Summarize the process of persuasion
4. Explain the concept of the advertising campaign

When all is said and done, someone has to prepare the advertisements. Most of the other activities of the advertising process are means to the end of creating advertisements; and the final end of creating advertisements is the maximization of profits for the firm employing the advertising tool. In the next several chapters, therefore, consideration will be given to the work of copywriters, art directors, and print and broadcast producers. It is in order to enable them to produce better advertisements that advertising planning, research, media planning, and the like are in the main undertaken. In this day of management-oriented thinking, there are those who would argue that we frequently give too little recognition to the importance of the creative side of advertising, with the result that the management skills and technological know-how become somewhat meaningless in the face of ineffective advertisements.

A historical examination of the creative aspects of advertising would indicate that, like a pendulum, creativity swings back and forth. In the 1930s and the economic chaos that accompanied those years, business looked for a more scientific approach to advertising, and research became the buzz word—even taking precedence over creativity. The slide rule became more important than the typewriter and drawing board. But the economic boom of the post–World War II period saw a return to creativity above all else. New agencies were born that were labeled "creative houses," and the "creative boutique" sold creative talent alone. Many of the established advertising agencies that had developed solid reputations for their marketing orientation lost business in this race for creativity. As one copywriter described them, they were too "fat, slow, and dull." But, it seems almost inevitably, there came the recession of the 1970s, with tight money, diminished advertising budgets, and nervous clients. Again there was the need for stability, certainty, and "proven results." Again it was a time for the big, full-service agency complete with researchers, marketing strategists, media planners, and the like. But this does not have to be nor should it be at the expense of creativity. Creativity can and does flourish even within the ever more confining borders of legal, social, and economic constraints.

Thus, advertising today might be described as part of a solid marketing strategy within which there is a solid, *creative* campaign.

Advertising creativity is never an end in itself. It is not for art's sake. Instead, it must be a means to the marketing objectives and strategy of the advertiser. But such restraints should not inhibit advertising creativity. They are simply the challenge for the truly creative to exercise their creativity. Thus, instead of "it's them or us," creative personnel need to become more familiar with marketing planning, research, and media strategy and use the facets of the "advertising mix" to make creative advertisements that are also *effective*.

CREATIVITY DEFINED

To begin with, it is important to define *creativity*. The simplest explanation: "Creativity is defined as the ability to formulate new combinations from two or more concepts already in the mind."[1] Such a definition is applicable to all endeavors, including both the arts and the sciences. It is therefore also appropriate to the making of advertisements, with which we are primarily concerned here.

The definition is a simple one, but the act of creating is not so simple. For one thing, it does not just "happen." It requires hard work and a keen mind. Second, although all people are undoubtedly endowed with some degree of creative ability, some are superior in this respect.

ADVERTISING AND CREATIVITY

The work of copywriters, art directors, and print and broadcast producers is today generally referred to as the *creative* side of advertising. The terms *creative* and *creativity* have been much used and abused in recent years. In fact, some advertising practitioners have discontinued using them on the grounds that they have been overworked or ill used. Despite such objections, the terms persist, and even though some purists might take exception, they do provide a shorthand way of expressing an important concept in advertising.

By implication, the application of the term *creative* to copy, art, and production precludes all other aspects of advertising from being creative. To be sure, for advertising management, marketing research, media planning, and the like to be effective, they too must be creative. In fact, there is a need for greater creativity in all phases of American business. Still, creativity has taken on a special meaning in advertising and refers to the making of advertisements. The term will be used largely in that sense here.

THE CREATIVE PERSONALITY

What are the requisites of superior creative ability? There are those who will argue that there is no creative personality. Certainly the image of the creative person as an "oddball" is misleading. Creative people do not have a "creative look" that distinguishes them from others. Some advertising creative people want to *look* creative and there is no harm done, but wearing the "creative" costume, whatever that happens to be at the moment, does not make you creative. During the 1960s and early 1970s, many people tried to dress the part, with far-out clothes and hair,

Advertising and the Creative Process

429

Keep It Simple

Strike three.
Get your hand off my knee.
You're overdrawn.
Your horse won.
Yes.
No.
You have the account.
Walk.
Don't walk.
Mother's dead.
Basic events
require simple language.
Idiosyncratically euphuistic
eccentricities are the
promulgators of
triturable obfuscation.
What did you do last night?
Enter into a meaningful
romantic involvement
or
fall in love?
What did you have for
breakfast this morning?
The upper part of a hog's
hind leg with two oval
bodies encased in a shell
laid by a female bird
or
ham and eggs?
David Belasco, the great
American theatrical producer,
once said, "If you can't
write your idea on the
back of my calling
card,
you don't have a clear idea."

FIGURE 23-1

The principle of keeping language simple as presented in this advertisement is a sound principle for creative people to remember. *By permission: United Technologies Corporation.*

but there has never been any known relationship between a good advertisement and the creator's hair length and sandals and beads. In fact, during the heyday of creative dress, some of the most creative people were the most conservative dressers. And today, with the changing social codes, you cannot tell an account executive from a copywriter from a media representative.

Nevertheless, it is reasonable to assume that the drive to want to write or draw is reflected in a certain kind of personality. After making a study of a number of authors on this subject, James F. Lawrence came up with the following creative profile:

1. *In relations to others*:
   (a) Not a joiner
   (b) Few close friends
   (c) Independent
   (d) Dominant
   (e) Assertive, bold, courageous
   (f) Little interest in interpersonal relations
   (g) Independence from parents
   (h) Independence of judgment, especially under pressure
   (i) Conventional morality
2. *In job attitudes*:
   (a) Preference for things and ideas to people
   (b) High regard for intellectual interests
   (c) Less emphasis on and value in job security
   (d) Less enjoyment in and satisfaction from detail work and routine
   (e) High level of resourcefulness and adaptability
   (f) Skeptical

(g) Precise, critical
(h) Honesty, integrity
(i) Ability to toy with elements—capacity to be puzzled
(j) High tolerance for ambiguity
(k) Persistence
(l) Emphasis on theoretical values
3. *Attitudes toward self*:
   (a) Introspective, egocentric, internally preoccupied
   (b) Openness to new experiences
   (c) Less need to protect self
   (d) Great awareness of self
   (e) Inner maturity
   (f) Great ego strength, strength of character
   (g) Highly responsive emotionally
   (h) Less emotionally stable
   (i) Less self-acceptance
4. *Other characteristics*:
   (a) Spontaneity, enthusiasm
   (b) Stubbornness
   (c) Originality
   (d) Adventurousness
   (e) High excitability and irritability
   (f) Compulsivity
   (g) Impulsivity
   (h) Complexity as a person
   (i) Anxiety[2]

But Edward Buxton says:

. . . Creative people as individuals defy classification. As they see themselves, no two are alike. And if they were, each would be the last to admit it. The usual myths and shibboleths about creative people fall apart upon the first cursory view of creative people at work in groups. This is especially so in the world of commerce and business. To be sure, even in groups, some are unique—and others make a concerted effort to appear unique. Observable credentials and occupational badges are inordinately important to many creative people—which leads to the one generalization we will make.

Creative people are vain. According to psychologists and other people who have studied them, the general view is that creative people have a stronger, more pronounced sense of self. Call it ego, pride of authorship, a larger-than-normal need for praise and approval. In any case, successful creative people do indeed seem to have a need—often bordering on a compulsion—to "express themselves"—and to the largest and most appreciative audience possible. So be it—it is an integral part of their equipment. It can fuel a burning ambition—or cause untold misery. It usually does both.[3]

Everyone has some creative ability, although some undoubtedly have more than others. Perhaps of more significance, however, is the fact that people may not be aware of their creative ability—they may not have the need, or the environment, to develop it. In his preface to *Applied Imagination*, Alex Osborn, a well-known former advertising executive, said:

All human beings, to a greater or lesser degree, possess the imaginative faculty. Whether this talent can be enlarged by training is questionable. The point is that the student can be trained to use more productively the talent which he innately possesses. This training is subject to disciplines similar to those applicable to the mastery of any subject. . . .

One of [the blocks to creativity] is student unawareness of the fact that everyone is gifted with a creative potential. Other blocks include lack of understanding of how creativity works, and failure to realize that all of us can keep ourselves from becoming less creative, and can do much to make ourselves more creative.[4]

Advertising primarily is a business of words, of communication. It must convey ideas so clearly and provocatively that masses of people who vary widely in education will understand and act on them.

CHARLES L. WHITTIER, Advertising Agent

READER'S DIGEST

THE CREATIVE PROCESS

If a person's creativity can be developed through learning, there must be some method that can be learned for creating ideas. When creative people are asked to explain how they came upon an idea that resulted in some outstanding creative work, they are usually hard put to come up with an explanation. On the other hand, there have been some serious attempts to develop a formula for creativity. Still, different people will create in different ways. Osborn says:

There can be no set formula for the production of ideas. A research laboratory can apply to its problems a more or less formal program of procedure, but even that must be subject to frequent change. The usual personal or business problem calls mainly for continual concentration in which one step usually suggests another. And so it is that in almost every ideation process, the talent which plays the leading part is that which is known as *association of ideas.* . . .

Although physical facts are easier to unseal than psychic facts, nobody yet knows exactly how babies are born. No wonder, then, that we are still at sea as to exactly how ideas are born. Perhaps neither of these mystic processes will ever be fully comprehended. For this reason it is unlikely that creative procedure can ever be strictly formulated.[5]

On the other hand, James Webb Young, a famous former advertising agency executive and master copywriter, said that:

. . . the production of ideas is just as definite a process as the production of Fords; that the production of ideas, too, runs on an assembly line; that in this production the mind follows an *operative technique* which can be learned and controlled; and that its effective use is just as much a matter of *practice in the technique* as is the effective use of any tool.[6]

THEORIES OF THE CREATIVE PROCESS   One of the early writers to suggest a process of creativity was the English political scientist and sociologist, Graham Wallas, who formalized the thought of the German scientist, Hermann von Helmholtz. The latter suggested that creative thought developed in three stages: preparation, incubation, and illumination.[7] To this Wallas added an additional step, *verification*, which relates to the development or elaboration of ideas.

Working without reference to any existing theory, James Webb Young formulated *A Technique for Producing Ideas,* as follows:

> First, the gathering of raw materials—both the materials of your immediate problem and the materials which come from a constant enrichment of your store of general knowledge.
>
> Second, the working over of these materials in your mind.
>
> Third, the incubating stage, where you let something beside the conscious mind do the work of synthesis.
>
> Fourth, the actual birth of the Idea—the "Eureka! I have it!" stage.
>
> And fifth, the final shaping and development of the idea to practical usefulness.[8]

Alex Osborn developed a theory of the steps in the creative process:

> . . . those who have studied and practiced creativity realize that its process is necessarily a stop-and-go, catch-as-catch-can operation—one which can never be exact enough to rate as scientific. The most that can honestly be said is that it usually includes some or all of these phases:
>
> 1. *Orientation*: Pointing up the problem.
> 2. *Preparation*: Gathering pertinent data.
> 3. *Analysis*: Breaking down the relevant material.
> 4. *Hypothesis*: Piling up alternatives by way of ideas.
> 5. *Incubation*: Letting up, to invite illumination.
> 6. *Synthesis*: Putting the pieces together.
> 7. *Verification*: Judging the resultant ideas.
>
> In actual practice we can follow no such one-two-three sequence. We may start our guessing even while preparing. Our analyses may lead us straight to the solution. After incubation, we may again go digging for facts which, at the start, we did not know we needed. And, of course, we might bring verification to bear on our hypotheses, thus to cull our "wild stabs" and proceed with only the likeliest.[9]

THE "CREATIVE COMPUTER" No matter how they are expressed, the theories of the creative process have much in common. And any and all can be useful. They will not, of course, make the noncreative person creative, but they *will* help the person who has not yet developed creative skills come closer to achieving mastery of those skills through systematizing the process, for system is possible in every endeavor, even creating advertisements.

Today, the greatest tool for management systems is the computer. When we examine the way a computer works, we can see that there are great similarities between it and the advertising creative person's mind. After all, the computer is an extension of the human mind. And, as in the case of the computer, we feed information into the mind and it regurgitates the various inputs in a new arrangement that can be employed in this case in better advertising efforts. Thus, the creative advertising process that follows might be dubbed the "creative computer."

Dull people always write dull copy, but bright people write bright copy only when they work hard at it.

WILLIAM A. MARSTELLER, Advertising Agent

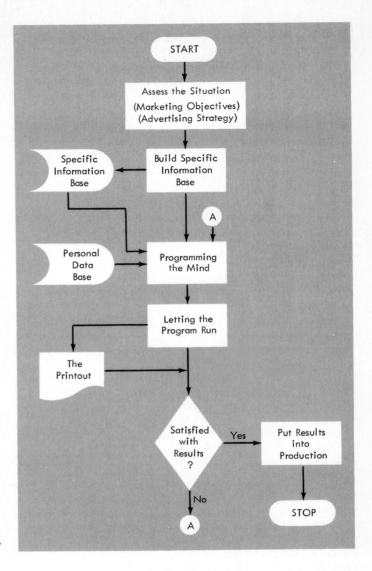

FIGURE 23-2

Flow chart for the "Creative Computer."

ASSESSING THE SITUATION When advertising creative personnel receive an assignment, their first question should be, What is the purpose of the advertisement? Therefore, before they can write one line of copy or draw one line of a layout, they must look over the situation to understand the environment for the advertisement. They must get answers to key questions such as the following: What are the marketing objectives? What is the advertising strategy?

BUILDING THE INFORMATION BASE Advertisements are not created in a vacuum. Closely related to a knowledge of marketing objectives and advertising strategy are such questions as, What marketing research data are available? Who are the consumers in the target market? How do they behave? What is known about the generic product (or service)? What is known about the advertiser's brand? competitive brands? (Whenever it is feasible, creative people should try the brand and the competition to discover the advantages and disadvantages of each and to have a hands-on experience with the product rather than a theoretical one.) What is the competitive advertising like? What are related products like, and how are they advertised? (For example, if you were going to advertise luncheon meats, it would be helpful to also know something about bread, sandwich spreads, relishes, cheeses, and the like.) What restrictions are given, such as media types, advertisement size or commercial length, color or black and white, legal restrictions, and advertisers do's and don'ts?

PROGRAMMING THE MIND Now that the creative people understand the purpose of the advertisement and have built a body of knowledge, they try putting various combinations together as possible directions for the advertisement they must prepare. This may be a series of rough drafts pounded out on a typewriter, then ripped from the machine, rolled up into little balls, and shot at the wastebasket for two points. Or it may be staring out the window as the ideas are explored mentally, or talking over a long lunch with a colleague where ideas are sounded out by bouncing them off the listener, or any other technique that works. Regardless of the method, at this stage, information and ideas are being stored in that human computer, the mind. Over a lifetime, people store lots of data of a general but valuable nature. They store many of the great creative ideas of others that they have experienced through literature, music, theater, and art. They also store all the experiences they have had with people, and places, and things . . . and advertisements—things they have long since forgotten but that are still there in the innermost parts of the mind. (Since all these inputs are so valuable to creative productivity, it is important that you broaden your experience bases and that you learn to go through life always observant of all you encounter.)

It is interesting to see where many of the professional advertising creative people turn for creative inputs. In a nationwide survey of advertising creative people on how they "feed" their creative resources, they rated the importance of a list of possibilities as follows:

Watching, studying TV	73%
Reading general magazines	72%
Reading daily newspapers	69%
Reading trade magazines	54%
Seeing good movies	48%
Travel, weekend trips	45%
Plays and concerts	34%
Special interests, hobbies	32%
Visiting museums	26%
Books on advertising	22%[10]

LETTING THE PROGRAM RUN There comes a time at which it is no longer productive to try for additional inputs. Creative people recognize this when they start repeating themselves or new thoughts are hard to come by. This is the time to let the computer process the inputs they have provided. They should turn to something else. Work on other tasks. Sleep on it. Take in a show. Watch some television. Read a book. But they should not think about the advertisement they are trying to prepare. The subconscious, however, is still working. The computer is sifting through all the inputs in terms of all the possible combinations. Now, whereas modern-day technology can achieve through electronic wizardry almost immediate turnaround time, the human mind is still somewhat slow. But given sufficient time, the creative mind will ultimately find it is ready to spill out an advertisement.

RUNNING THE PRINTOUT This is the day. Now is the hour. The copywriter sits at the typewriter letting the fingers type the message the brain is transmitting. The artist takes the drawing pencil or marker and sees what the mind draws as a layout or storyboard.

DEBUGGING THE PRINTOUT It is possible that it is all there—the "Eureka! I have it!" situation. But more probably, it is either scrap it and start all over again (at the very worst) or this is a start in the right direction requiring refinement after refinement until like a knife it is honed to the point of razor sharpness. In most cases, a germ of an idea is taken and built upon until what is necessary to do the job has been found.

PUTTING THE RESULTS INTO PRODUCTION But it does not end there. The advertisement is finished when it is produced and the engravings or negatives are sent to the publication, or the commercial is "in the can" ready to be shipped to the television station. The advertisement or the commercial is still being created all the way through production. And there is an opportunity for more fine honing by inputs from copywriters and art directors who can suggest how the photographer can best shoot the illustration, or what type face has the best feel for the mood of the copy, or how the actors can most effectively interpret the action suggested in the storyboard, or what intonation by the "voice-over" can best express the ideas in the script.

These steps in the creative process are generalizations, and they must be adapted to fit each individual personality. But certain points should be clear. There is a computer principle known as "GIGO." It means "garbage in, garbage out." That is, if the inputs are not meaningful and relevant, the results will not be meaningful and relevant. To be sure, creative talents who have a way with words or pictures may be able to come up with "clever" or "entertaining" commercials. The point is that being clever or entertaining is not enough, for as stated at the beginning of this chapter, advertisements are not ends in themselves. Therefore, a good creative person must have an interest in and understanding of the marketing environment if the advertisements created are going to be effective. In a survey of creative management people, when

Craftsmen. *In Greensboro, N.C., a laundry proudly posted a notice in its window: "We don't mangle your clothes with machinery—we do it carefully by hand."*

TIME

asked to rank some nine talents and skills that might be important in an advertising creative person, they overwhelmingly chose "a strong marketing sense" as the most important.[11]

MAKING IT HAPPEN If one follows the creative process as suggested above, after the period of incubation in which the program is run, the ideas should presumably come freely from the computer printer (the typewriter or the layout pad). But this is generally not the case. The step of giving birth to an idea is more often most agonizing. S.R. Bernstein, a longtime chronicler of the advertising scene, makes an astute observation about the act of copywriting that is equally applicable to advertising art:

> For most people writing is a lonely, frustrating and sometimes unhappy experience. The writer who actually enjoys the process of writing seems to be unusual; most writers enjoy *having written* but get no joy whatever from the actual task of moving a pencil across a sheet of paper or hitting one key after another on a typewriter.

> Buckling down to the task of writing is a sort of horror, to be put off until the last possible minute. An infinitely complicated and pointless ritual, much like the contortions a baseball pitcher frequently goes through before he finally cocks his arm and actually starts the pitching motion, is often involved. Paper must be stacked just so; the typewriter or the pencils must be fingered, caressed, carefully lined up. Coffee must be drunk, or not drunk. The window must be opened, closed or adjusted. The chair must be raised, lowered, moved in, moved out, or replaced. That new, funny looking spot on the neck must be carefully inspected in the bathroom mirror; or the girl whose profile shows in the window across the business canyon must be speculatively regarded. Time moves on, and so does the pointless ritual, until at last the moment can no longer be postponed. It is time to *start writing.*[12]

The titles *copywriter* and *art director* are somewhat misleading, or at least confining. To be sure, copywriters write copy, but in addition, copywriters are generally the creative heads of the particular account or accounts to which the copywriters are assigned. (In many advertising agencies, there are copy chiefs or supervisors who work with several copywriters and frequently assume this role of creative head for the particular accounts.) Perhaps the most important function of copywriters is developing ideas for advertisements. Traditionally, they have been the principal visualizers of advertisements. In addition to writing the headlines and body copy, they have generally been responsible for coming up with the ideas for the advertisements and envisioning the advertisements in their totality. But many times, art directors operate in the same way. They not only prepare the layouts but create the ideas for the advertisements as well, especially when the advertising is largely pictorial. More and more, however, an idea-creating partnership is developing between teams consisting of a copywriter and an art director working together in visualizing advertisements, and sometimes interchanging their roles. This team concept has seen increasing recog-

THE CREATIVE PEOPLE

nition as an essential factor in maximizing the creative effort. It affords for the team members an opportunity to draw ideas out of each other, to become sounding boards and "alter egos"—so important in nurturing creativity.

Of course, not all ideas for advertisements come from copywriters or art directors. When the agency operates under the account group system, anyone assigned to the account may have a good creative idea for an advertisement, but then copywriters and art directors may have some contributions to make to media planning, research, and the like. The fact remains that the job of creating advertisements falls largely to copywriters and art directors.

VISUALIZATION DEFINED

Even in advertising circles, the term *visualization* causes a great deal of confusion and misunderstanding. Sometimes a rough layout is called a "visual." The term is used here to refer to seeing in the mind's eye the form of the idea as it will appear in the advertisement. The copy has not been written, the layout has not been drawn, but the very rough form of the advertisement as suggested by the creative idea can be seen in the visualizer's mind. When the visualization is the work of the copywriter, it may take physical shape in the form of some rough notes suggesting a headline and a copy theme and a rough sketch suggesting the illustration. When the visualization is the product of the art director, it will probably take physical shape in the form of thumbnail sketches or a rough layout. Or it can remain in the mind of either visualizer until there is a chance to put it down on paper in more finished form.

REINS ON CREATIVITY

Talk to any copywriter or art director and chances are pretty good that you will talk to a frustrated person. The frustration lies in the inability to have free rein in creative matters. Every copywriter and art director has seen work altered or restricted from the start by account executives, clients, and researchers. At least in one sense, their frustration seems reasonable. They are employed as creative experts to produce advertisements that reflect their creative talents. And yet all the others consider themselves experts. The account executive suggests a change here because of the "knowledge" that the client will not approve it as is; the client suggests a change there because of the "knowledge" of the market. And the marketing researcher suggests changes everywhere because research "shows" the advertisement will not "pull."

No wonder there are frustrations. It is natural that creative people, the real experts, should object to having their efforts emasculated by the "blue pencil." Still, commercial advertisements are not an end in themselves; they are a means to the end of maximizing profits. Suggestions and guides of account executives, clients, and researchers can improve advertisements, but their suggestions should not be accepted automatically. The creative people should listen with open minds, and if the suggestions are valuable and will improve the advertisements, they should be incorporated. If, however, the creative people believe the sug-

How to write clearly

By Edward T. Thompson
Editor-in-Chief, Reader's Digest

International Paper asked Edward T. Thompson to share some of what he has learned in seventeen years with Reader's Digest, a magazine famous for making complicated subjects understandable to millions of readers.

If you are afraid to write, don't be.

If you think you've got to string together big fancy words and high-flying phrases, forget it.

To write well, unless you aspire to be a professional poet or novelist, you only need to get your ideas across simply and clearly.

It's not easy. But it is easier than you might imagine.

There are only three basic requirements:

First, you must *want* to write clearly. And I believe you really do, if you've stayed this far with me.

Second, you must be willing to *work hard*. Thinking means work—and that's what it takes to do anything well.

Third, you must know and follow some *basic guidelines*.

If, while you're writing for clarity, some lovely, dramatic or inspired phrases or sentences come to you, fine. Put them in.

But then with cold, objective eyes and mind ask yourself: "Do they detract from clarity?" If they do, grit your teeth and cut the frills.

Follow some basic guidelines

I can't give you a complete list of

"dos and don'ts" for every writing problem you'll ever face.

But I can give you some fundamental guidelines that cover the most common problems.

1. Outline what you want to say.

I know that sounds grade-schoolish. But you can't write clearly until, *before you start*, you know where you will stop.

Ironically, that's even a problem in writing an outline (i.e., knowing the ending before you begin).

So try this method:

• On 3" x 5" cards, write—one point to a card—all the points you need to make.

• Divide the cards into piles—one pile for each group of points *related closely* to each other. (If you were describing an automobile, you'd put all the points about mileage in one pile, all the points about safety in another, and so on.)

• Arrange your piles of points in a sequence. Which are most important and should be given first or saved for last? Which must you present before others in order to make the others understandable?

• Now, *within each pile*, do the same thing—arrange the *points* in logical, understandable order.

There you have your outline, needing only an introduction and conclusion.

This is a practical way to outline. It's also flexible. You can add, delete or change the location of points easily.

2. Start where your readers are.

How much do they know about the subject? Don't write to a level higher than your readers' knowledge of it.

CAUTION: Forget that old-and-wrong advice about writing to a 12-year-old mentality. That's insulting. But do

---

remember that your prime purpose is to *explain* something, not prove that you're smarter than your readers.

3. Avoid jargon.

Don't use words, expressions, phrases known only to people with specific knowledge or interests.

Example: A scientist, using scientific jargon, wrote, "The biota exhibited a one hundred percent mortality response." He could have written: "All the fish died."

4. Use familiar combinations of words.

A speech writer for President Franklin D. Roosevelt wrote, "We are endeavoring to construct a more inclusive society." F.D.R. changed it to, "We're going to make a country in which no one is left out."

CAUTION: By familiar combinations of words, I do not mean incorrect grammar. *That* can be unclear. Example: John's father says he can't go out Friday. (Who can't go out? John or his father?)

5. Use "first-degree" words.

These words immediately bring an image to your mind. Other words must be "translated"

"Outline for clarity. Write your points on 3" x 5" cards—one point to a card. Then you can easily add to, or change the order of points—even delete some."

through the first-degree word before you see

First-degree words	Second/third-degree words	
face	visage, countenance	
stay	abide, remain, reside	
book	volume, tome, publication	

First-degree words are usually the most precise words, too.

6. Stick to the point.

Your outline—which was more work in the beginning—now saves you work. Because now you can ask about any sentence you write: "Does it relate to a point in the outline? If it doesn't, should I add it to the outline? If not, I'm getting off the track." Then, full steam ahead—on the main line.

7. Be as brief as possible.

Whatever you write, shortening—*condensing*—almost always makes it tighter, straighter, easier to read and understand.

Condensing, as *Reader's Digest* does it, is in large part artistry. But it involves techniques that anyone can learn and use.

• *Present your points in logical ABC order:* Here again, your outline should save you work because, if you did it right, your points already stand in logical ABC order—A makes B understandable, B makes C understandable and so on. To write in a straight line is to say something clearly in the fewest possible words.

• *Don't waste words telling people what they already know:* Notice how we edited this: "Have you ever

---

wondered how banks rate you as a credit risk? ~~You know, of course, that it's some combination of facts about your income, your job. But actually, Many banks~~ have a scoring system...."

• *Cut out excess evidence and unnecessary anecdotes:* Usually one fact or example (at most, two) will support a point. More just belabor it. And while writing about some-

"Cut your teeth and cut the frills. That's one of the suggestions I offer here to help you write clearly. They cover the most common problems. And they're all easy to follow."

thing may remind you of a good story, ask yourself: "Does it really help to tell the story, or does it slow me down?"

(Many people think *Reader's Digest* articles are filled with anecdotes. Actually, we use them sparingly and usually for one of two reasons: either the subject is so dry it needs some "humanity" to give it life; or the subject is so hard to grasp, it needs anecdotes to help readers understand. If the subject is both lively and easy to grasp, we move right along.)

• *Look for the most common word wasters:* windy phrases.

Windy phrases	Cut to . . .
at the present time	now
in the event of	if
in the majority of instances	usually

• *Look for passive verbs you can make active:* Invariably, this produces a shorter sentence. "The cherry tree *was chopped down* by George Washington." (Passive verb and nine words.) "George Washington *chopped down* the cherry tree." (Active verb and seven words.)

• *Look for positive/negative sections from which you can cut the negative:* See how we did it here: "The answer ~~does not rest with carelessness or in-competence. It is largely in~~ having enough people to do the job."

• Finally, to write more clearly by saying it in fewer words: when you've finished, stop.

The biota exhibited a 100% mortality response

Writing clearly means avoiding jargon. Why didn't he just say, "All the fish died!"

Today, the printed word is more vital than ever. Now there is more need than ever for all of us to read better, write better, and communicate better.

International Paper offers this series in the hope that, even in a small way, we can help.

If you'd like to share this article with others—students, friends, employees, family—we'll gladly send you reprints. We've already sent out more than 6,000,000 at requests from people everywhere.

Please write: "Power of the Printed Word," International Paper Company, Dept. 4Z, P.O. Box 954, Madison Square Station, New York, NY 10010.

Edward T. Thompson

△ INTERNATIONAL PAPER COMPANY
We believe in the power of the printed word.

FIGURE 23-3

One of a series of advertisements to college students to improve their reading and writing skills. Although it is not specifically directed to writing advertisements, what is discussed in this advertisement is most applicable. *Reprinted by permission of International Paper Company.*

gestions will weaken the advertisements, they should fight for their beliefs.

But the best solution is to avoid, as much as possible, any criticism in the first place. The creative person who understands business and the marketing function should not lose sight of the need to create advertisements that "sell," which is what advertising is all about. Then there is less likelihood of any criticism.

IDEAS INTO ADVERTISEMENTS

If this chapter gives the impression that all a successful advertisement needs is a good creative idea, that impression should be corrected. Creative ideas are vitally important, but they are only the start. The idea must be translated into words and pictures and sounds—the *right* words and pictures and sounds. Only then is the creative idea of any value to the advertiser. John Pullen aptly explained the importance of these when he said:

> . . . The idea is only the beginning. A good idea can be obscured by a beautiful smoke screen of ungoverned "creativity." It can be dropped before it has had time to penetrate. Or it can be expressed so poorly that the value of the idea is lost.
>
> The selling idea is the framework. But words give it flesh and blood, make it live and breathe in direct proportion to the vitality of a quality that seems to be inherent in words themselves.
>
> As proof of this, you can start with a selling idea and assign it to six writers. One will produce a great campaign, while the score for the others will be perhaps four good and one average. The idea is the same, but there are astonishing differences in the way it springs to life.
>
> Or take the idea, "a pretty woman," and give it to six artists. One paints the Mona Lisa, the others just pretty women.
>
> Or say the idea is to "dedicate a cemetery." Abraham Lincoln delivers the Gettysburg Address. Edward Everett speaks for two hours and his words vanish into oblivion.
>
> The English language is a mighty and melodious instrument, capable of almost infinite effects upon us. . . .
>
> It is fascinating to consider the differences words can make. "Cease motion, observe carefully and note sound of approaching train" can't compare with "Stop, look and listen!"
>
> "We won't let them get by" is a pale substitute for "They shall not pass!"
>
> "A diamond will last forever" would not last long in comparison with "A diamond is forever. . . ."
>
> The Bible says that a word fitly spoken is like apples of gold in pictures of silver. It is also like gold in the pocket of an advertiser.[13]

Leo Burnett was paying appropriate tribute to the importance of the writer when he said:

> After all the meetings are over, the phones have stopped ringing and the vocalizing has died down, somebody has to get out an ad, often after

hours. Somebody has to stare at a blank piece of paper. Probably nothing was ever more bleak. This is probably the very height of lonesomeness. He is one person and he is alone—all by himself—alone. Out of the recesses of his mind must come words which interest, words which persuade, words which inspire, words which sell. Magic words. I regard him as the man of the hour in our business today.[14]

It is far easier to write ten passably effective sonnets, good enough to take in the not too inquiring critic, than one effective advertisement that will take in a few thousand of the uncritical buying public.

ALDOUS L. HUXLEY (1894-1963), Novelist

READER'S DIGEST

THE PERSUASION PROCESS

Other kinds of writing and art may have a variety of purposes, but advertising copywriting and art have one main purpose—*persuasion.* When we considered the hierarchy of effects model in Chapter 12, we pointed out that advertisements are not all geared to directly producing sales. Advertising, indeed, may be used in several different stages of persuasion: learning (cognitive), feeling (affective), and acting (conative). Thus, in the Lavidge and Steiner model, a firm may first attempt through advertisements to achieve brand awareness and knowledge; then in another effort, the firm may attempt to achieve brand liking and preference; and finally, advertisements may take on the task of achieving brand conviction and purchase. Charles Raymond points out that since the Lavidge and Steiner model in 1961, there have been no less than fourteen other models and a substantial degree of controversy that is still unresolved.[15] But this controversy is a preoccupation of researchers; practitioners take a much more pragmatic approach. From a practical point of view, advertising strategies most often have objectives like those suggested by the model, so that in practice, advertisers obviously recognize that indeed there is a hierarchy of effects in consumer behavior.

There is another kind of hierarchy of effects *within* each advertisement. In the discussion above, we were talking about the ways consumers behave toward an advertisement. There is another model we shall use here, so old that no one knows when it was first devised and who first devised it, but this much is known: It was first used by salespeople in developing a logical method of making a sales presentation. It is known as the AIDA principle, and the acronym stands for Attention (cognitive), Interest, Desire (affective), and Action (conative).[16] As applied to advertisements, it suggests that in order to persuade the consumer, an advertisement must first attract *attention,* then create *interest,* next stimulate *desire,* and finally get *action.* Surprisingly, some creative people argue that AIDA is too academic! It is said that many consumers do not behave in this manner. (Could it be that they have been talking to the theoreticians?) Undoubtedly, writing advertisements is not always so simple; still, the process is basic to understanding the *art* of persuasion. Only after mastering it can creative personnel go beyond it.

ATTENTION   To begin with, if we are going to persuade consumers to buy our product, we must attract their attention. The best of advertisements or commercials are useless if nobody sees them.

There are two general types of attention-getting devices. One includes external factors over which the creative team has little or no control; the other involves internal factors that are to a large degree directly under the creative team's control.

The external factors include such things as the medium in which the advertisements appear and the size and position of the advertisements. For example, readers of some magazines regard advertising almost as editorial matter. A *Mademoiselle* reader is apt to be as interested in the fashions featured in the advertisements in the magazine as in the fashions considered in the editorial matter. Thus, when advertisements are closely related to editorial content, considerable attention is likely to be paid to the advertisements. In most television advertising, however, there is little relation between the commercials and program content; therefore, commercials elicit little spontaneous interest from viewers, and thus there is a need for stronger attention-getting devices.

Size is another external factor that influences attention. Obviously, the larger the advertisement or the longer the commercial, the more likely the reader or viewer will be to notice it. Similarly, position affects attention. An advertisement appearing on the fourth (back) cover of a magazine or just prior to the conclusion of a dramatic television show will attract greater attention than that same advertisement appearing in an r.o.p. position in a magazine or during a station break on television.

The creative team has several internal attention-getting devices it can use. In print, these are the headline and the illustration. The effectiveness of either is to some degree dictated by the layout, which can emphasize either or both in order to gain maximum attention. In radio, these include sound effects, music, and the opening words. In television, they include sound effects, music, the opening words, and the establishing shot.

A word of caution is in order on using attention-getting devices. An attention-getting device is simply a means used to attract an audience to the rest of the message. Therefore, the device used should be related to the rest of the advertisement or commercial. The audience whose attention is attracted by a headline or musical theme and then finds that it has little or no relation to the rest of the advertisement is apt to be turned off. Using sex appeal for attention to sell pocket calculators will hardly result in an orderly transition to the next stage of persuasion.

Because few advertisements are read in their entirety and because few viewers or listeners keep up with the content of commercials as they continue, the attention-getting devices should try to include as many of the other AIDA factors as possible. If the headline, in addition to gaining attention, can also promise some benefit to the consumer and identify the advertiser, it is likely that more people seeing the advertisement will get the message. For example: "The Rose's Gimlet. Four parts vodka, one part elegance" (for Rose's Lime Juice), or "Pontiac Grand Prix. You'll Find Something New to Love Every Time You Drive It." In addition, the illustration can be used to call attention to the product and the package.

INTEREST   Ideally, the attention-getting device should lead the audience to the body of the message and hold its interest. There is no better way of creating interest than by appealing to the audience's self-interest. All too often, advertisements are created in terms of advertiser interests instead of consumer interests. The approach to use is what is referred to as the "you" attitude. Consumers are not interested in how wonderful the company is; they want to know what the product or service will do for *them*.

DESIRE   Each step in the persuasion process is important, but none is so important that it can stand alone. Having created interest, the creative team's next task is to stimulate the audience's desire for the product or service. The easiest way to stimulate desire is to show that the product or service will benefit consumers, show that they will not be as well off without it, and then prove it. Again, the emphasis should be on consumer self-interest. Since claims may be met with skepticism, it is necessary to convince the audience that the claims are valid. Not only should the claims be substantiated, they must also be believable.

ACTION   No advertisement is complete if it does not "ask for the order"—ask the consumer to take action. Action does not have to sell the product, for often the advertisement may only be aiming for cognition, such as an awareness of the generic product or the brand. The action called for here may be to remember a brand name. An example of an obvious action statement is, "If you don't know your Steinway dealer, Mr. John H. Steinway will arrange an introduction. Write him at Dept. 17, 109 West 57th Street, New York 10019" (Steinway Pianos). In some instances, the urge to action may be implied in the message without being explicitly stated.

Most advertisements and commercials are not individual entities; instead, they are a part of a series that make up an *advertising campaign*. Therefore, before the creative people can turn their attention to any single advertisement, they must consider the nature of the campaign.

A campaign can be made up of a series of advertisements and/or commercials that are variations on a single theme. In such cases, they are usually markedly similar in format, perhaps using the same or very similar headlines, a series of related illustrations, and the same or similar body copy (or their equivalents, in the case of commercials). A campaign may also be made up of a series of advertisements building toward a planned end in the manner of the hierarchy of effects. For ex-

THE ADVERTISING CAMPAIGN

Human beings come in all sizes, a variety of colors, in different ages, and with unique, complex and changing personalities.

So do words.

There are tall, skinny words and short, fat ones, and strong ones and weak ones, and boy words and girl words and so on.

For instance, title, lattice, latitude, lily, tattle, Illinois and intellect are all lean and lanky. While these words get their height partly out of "t's" and "l's" and "i's", other words are tall and skinny without a lot of ascenders and descenders. Take, for example, Abraham, peninsula and ellipsis, all tall.

Here are some nice short-fat words: hog, yogurt, bomb, pot, bonbon, acne, plump, sop and slobber.

Sometimes a word gets its size from what it means but sometimes it's just how the word sounds. Acne is a short-fat word even though pimple, with which it is associated, is a puny word.

Puny words are not the same as feminine words. Feminine words are such as tissue, slipper, cute, squeamish, peek, flutter, gauze and cumulus. Masculine words are like bourbon, rupture, oak, cartel, steak and socks. Words can mean the same thing and be of the opposite sex. Naked is masculine, but nude is feminine.

Sex isn't always a clear-cut, yes-or-no thing on upper Madison Avenue or Division Street, and there are words like that, too. On a fencing team, for instance, a man may compete with a sabre and that is definitely a masculine word. Because it is also a sword of sorts, an épée is also a boy word, but you know how it is with épées.

Just as feminine words are not necessarily puny words, masculine words are not necessarily muscular. Muscular words are thrust, earth, girder, ingot, cask, Leo, ale, bulldozer, sledge and thug. Fullback is very muscular; quarterback is masculine but not especially muscular.

Words have colors, too.

Red: fire, passion, explode, smash, murder, rape, lightning, attack.

Green: moss, brook, cool, comfort, meander, solitude, hammock.

Black: glower, agitate, funeral, dictator, anarchy, thunder, tomb, somber, cloak.

Beige: unctuous, abstruse, surrender, clerk, conform, observe, float.

San Francisco is a red city, Cleveland is beige, Asheville is green and Buffalo is black.

Shout is red, persuade is green, rave is black and listen is beige.

Oklahoma is brown, Florida is yellow, Virginia is light blue and Massachusetts is dark green, almost black. Although they were all Red, at one point Khrushchev was red-red, Castro orange, Mao Tse-tung gray and Kadar black as hate.

One of the more useful characteristics of words is their age.

There's youth in go, pancake, hamburger, bat, ball, frog, air, surprise, morning and tickle. Middle age brings abrupt, moderate, agree, shade, stroll and uncertain. Fragile, lavender, astringent, acerbic, fern, velvet, lace, worn and Packard are old. There never was a young Packard, not even the touring car.

Mostly, religion is old. Prayer, vespers, choir, Joshua, Judges, Ruth and cathedral are all old. Once, temple was older than cathedral and it still is in some parts of the world, but in the United States, temple is now fairly young. Rocker is younger than it used to be, too.

Saturday, the seventh day of the week, is young while Sunday, the first day of the week, is old. Night is old, and so, although more old people die in the hour of the morning just before the dawn, we call that part of the morning, incorrectly, night.

Some words are worried and some radiate disgusting self-confidence. Pill, ulcer, twitch, itch, stomach and peek are all worried words. Confident, smug words are like proud, lavish, major, divine, stare, dare, ignore, demand. Suburb used to be a smug word and still is in some parts of the country, but not so much around New York anymore. Brooklyn, by the way, is a confident word and everyone knows the Bronx is a worried word. Joe is confident; Horace is worried.

Now about shapes.

For round products, round companies or round ideas use dot, bob, melon, loquacious, hock, bubble and bald. Square words are, for instance, box, cramp, sunk, block and even ankle. Ohio is round but Iowa, a similar word, is square but not as square as Nebraska. Boston is, too—not as square as Nebraska, but about like Iowa. The roundest city is, of course, Oslo.

Some words are clearly oblong. Obscure is oblong (it is also beige) and so are platter and meditation (which is also middle-aged). Lavish, which as we saw is self-confident, is also oblong. The most oblong lake is Ontario, even more than Michigan, which is also surprisingly muscular for an oblong, though not nearly as strong as Huron, which is more stocky. Lake Pontchartrain is almost a straight line. Lake Como is round and very short and fat. Lake Erie is worried.

Some words are shaped like Rorschach ink blots. Like drool, plot, mediocre, involvement, liquid, amoeba and phlegm.

At first blush (which is young), fast words seem to come from a common stem (which is puny). For example, dash, flash, bash and brash are all fast words. However, ash, hash and gnash are all slow. Flush is changing. It used to be slow, somewhat like sluice, but it is getting faster. Both are wet words, as is Flushing, which is really quite dry compared to New Canaan, which sounds drier but is much wetter. Wilkinsburg, as you would expect, is dry, square, old and light gray. But back to motion.

Raid, rocket, piccolo, hound, bee and rob are fast words. Guard, drizzle, lard, cow, sloth, muck and damp are slow words. Fast words are often young and slow words old, but not always. Hamburger is young but slow, especially when uncooked. Astringent is old but fast. Black is old, and yellow—nearly opposite on the spectrum—is young, but orange and brown are nearly next to each other and orange is just as young as yellow while brown is only middle-aged. Further, purple, though darker than lavender, is not as old; however, it is much slower than violet, which is extremely fast.

Because it's darker, purple is often softer than lavender, even though it is younger. Lavender is actually a rather hard word. Not as hard as rock, edge, point, corner, jaw, trooper, frigid or trumpet, but hard nevertheless. Lamb, lip, thud, sofa, fuzz, stuff, froth and madam are soft. Although they are the same thing, timpani are harder than kettle drums, partly because drum is a soft word (it is also fat and slow) and as pots and pans go, kettle is one of the softer.

There is a point to all of this.

Ours is a business of imagination. We are employed to make corporations personable, to make useful products desirable, to clarify ideas, to create friendships in the mass for our employers.

We have great power to do these things. We have power through art and photography and graphics and typography and all the visual elements that are part of the finished advertisement or the published publicity release.

And these are great powers. Often it is true that one picture is worth ten thousand words. But not necessarily worth one word. The *right* word.

The Wonderful World of Words

FIGURE 23-4

The importance of words in copy is eloquently stated in this famous advertisement. *By permission: Marsteller Inc.*

ample, the first advertisements may announce a new brand, the second may talk of certain brand features, and the third may suggest strong reasons for buying the brand now. Finally, a campaign may consist of a series of advertisements that appear on the surface to have little in common with one another. Such advertisements may all be related to the same set of objectives, but the advertiser may believe that by using different advertisements, it is possible to appeal to different market segments.

Although advertisements in a campaign center around one theme, they may differ from medium to medium in order to take advantage of the unique characteristics of each medium's market. Thus, if the media plan for the campaign includes *Reader's Digest, Playboy*, and *Motor Trend*, three different advertisements, each matching the medium and its market, may be prepared even though the basic theme remains the same.

Perhaps the most crucial step in the creative process is developing the campaign theme or *idea*. It is the heart of all the advertisements in the campaign. A good creative idea gives direction for developing the individual advertisements in the series. Once the creative idea has been established, new advertisements in the campaign become variations on that theme and are generally relatively easy to develop.

In most instances, an important task of the creative team is to work with other agency personnel and the advertiser to establish the creative direction. The creative idea can be developed from the advertising strategy, and the copywriter and art director can turn their attention to the creation of individual advertisements.

Advertising creativity is not an end in itself. It must be a means to the marketing objectives and strategy of the advertiser. Creativity involves formulating new combinations from other concepts already in the mind. Everyone has creative ability, although not everyone is aware of it.

There are numerous theories of the creative process, and they have much in common. Essentially, advertising creative people start with an assessment of the situation, followed by the building of an information base. Now they try putting various combinations together, seeking an advertisement idea. After they "sleep on it" for a while, the creative idea will come forth. But this is typically in rough form and takes a good deal of refinement. This advertising creativity process is increased by a team effort.

The advertising message recognizes the persuasion process, which suggests that there is an order in persuasion that moves from attention to interest to desire to action. If you are going to persuade, you must first get your audience to listen. Then you need to move them to have some interest in what you are saying, and there is nothing more effective than their own self-interest. Now it is necessary to stimulate desire in terms of perceived benefits. But nothing happens if you do not also "ask for the order"—that is, every advertisement should move for some response.

Individual advertisements are usually part of a bigger campaign. The campaign has at its core an idea—a *selling* idea—that is the basis for the individual advertisements.

QUESTIONS AND PROBLEMS

1. Why is creativity so important to advertising?
2. Explain the relationship of advertising creativity to marketing objectives.
3. Describe the functioning of the "creative computer."
4. What is meant by visualization in advertising?
5. Why are the titles copywriter and art director somewhat misleading?
6. Describe the four steps in the persuasion process.
7. Select three advertisements and show how each step of the persuasion process has been incorporated in them.
8. Select three examples of magazine advertisements you consider highly creative and explain why you think they are so creative.
9. Select three examples of magazine advertisements you consider highly lacking in creativity and explain why you consider them so.
10. Select several different advertisements from the same campaign and explain how they are all part of the same campaign.

ENDNOTES

1 John W. Haefele, *Creativity and Innovation* (New York: Reinhold Publishing Corp., 1962), p. 5.
2 Haefele, *Creativity*, pp. 122–23.
3 Edward Buxton, *Creative People at Work* (New York: Executive Communications, Inc., 1975), pp. ix–x.
4 Alex F. Osborn, *Applied Imagination*, rev. ed. (New York: Charles Scribner's Sons, 1957), pp. vii–ix.
5 *Ibid.*, pp. 110–14.
6 James Webb Young, *A Technique for Producing Ideas*, 4th ed. (Chicago: Advertising Publications, Inc., 1960), p. 15.
7 Graham Wallas, *The Art of Thought* (New York: Harcourt, Brace and World, Inc., 1926), p. 80.
8 Young, *A Technique for Producing Ideas*, pp. 53–54.
9 Osborn, *Applied Imagination*, p. 115.
10 Buxton, *Creative People at Work*, p. 239.
11 *Ibid.*, p. 247.
12 S.R. Bernstein, "Introduction," in Denis Higgins, *The Art of Writing Advertising* (Chicago: Advertising Publications, Inc., 1965), p. 8.
13 "The Idea Is Only the Beginning." *Printer's Ink*, CCLXXIV, No. 9 (March 3, 1961), 47.
14 Leo Burnett, *Communications of an Advertising Man* (Chicago: Leo Burnett Company, Inc., 1961), p. 84.
15 Charles Raymond, *Advertising Research: The State of the Art* (New York: Association of National Advertisers, Inc., 1976), p. 15.
16 It is reasonable to assume that this model was not based on any theoretical understandings of consumer behavior. The particular choice of words form the acronym *AIDA*, which is also the name of a popular Italian grand opera by Giuseppe Verdi and was therefore considered easy to remember.

24

Advertising Copy

After completing this chapter, you should be able to:
1. Identify the elements of a print advertisement
2. Explain the kinds of print advertising copy
3. Describe the kinds of broadcast commercials
4. Discuss the problems of creating television commercials

In this and the next several chapters, we will discuss the theory and techniques of combining words and pictures and sounds to produce advertisements. This chapter's emphasis is on the copy inputs in print and broadcast advertisements.

Since copywriters and art directors work as teams today, it is a bit difficult to say who will do what. And print and broadcast advertisements are both prepared by these same teams. That is, a particular creative team may be executing a print advertisement one day and a television commercial the next. For clarity here, copy and art are separated between this chapter and the next, and print and broadcast are separated within the chapters, but it should be noted that who does what and when is not that clearly separated in the day-to-day operation of the business. Instead, it is a team effort in the true sense of the words, with everyone contributing all that each can to develop the very best advertisements.

ELEMENTS OF A PRINT ADVERTISEMENT

As we shall see, any print advertisement is made up of several elements. Most advertisements use all of them. They include the headline or display line; the illustration; the body copy or text; the theme line or slogan, trade character, seal, and other marks; and the logotype or signature. Each will be considered in some detail below.

HEADLINES The headline or display line appears in most advertisements for several reasons. Along with the illustration, it is an attention-getting device. It also selects an audience by appealing to a specific group, as this line does: "Arthritics, reduce painful inflammation *and* get stomach upset protection." Finally, it is the key factor in getting people to read the body copy. Unfortunately, only a small percentage of those who see most advertisements read them completely. Thus, the headline, because it is the part most likely to be read, is especially important, and every care must be taken to make sure that it does the job.

ILLUSTRATIONS In addition to headlines, most advertisements contain illustrations. The illustration, like the headline, attracts attention, selects the audience, and stimulates interest in body copy. What is more, the illustration can be invaluable in showing the product or product use and explaining graphically certain ideas or situations that are cumbersome to put into words. The old saying that one picture is worth a thousand words has much merit in it. Illustration will be considered in detail in the next chapter.

BODY COPY To begin with, some explanation of the word *copy* is necessary. Sometimes it is used to refer to all the reading matter in the advertisement, including headlines, subheads, captions, and text. At other times, it refers to the completed artwork for the plate maker. To know what is meant by *copy*, one must know the context in which the word is being used. Frequently, the terms *body copy* and *text* are used to refer only to the copy, usually set in small type, in the body of the advertisement—that portion of the advertisement excluding the headline, illustrations, and logotype. Some advertisements use no body copy, but most use some, with the amount differing considerably from advertisement to advertisement. The job of body copy is to stimulate interest in the product or service or idea being advertised, create desire for it, and urge action. This is a big task and calls for the right words. Although headlines and illustrations clear the way, it is body copy that must carry the burden of the selling job.

There are many practitioners who argue that nobody reads body copy, or that at least nobody reads *much* body copy, so that body copy ought to be short if there is any at all. But John O'Toole takes exception to this, as is noted in this excerpt from an office memo to agency personnel:

It is true that some products require little or no copy. There isn't much substantive information you could provide a prospect about Coca-Cola or Wrigley's Spearmint gum that they don't already have or that they could conceivably require. But, for most products, information is the key to the sale. And since print is the only medium that lets us present a virtually limitless amount of information to the interested prospect, it is folly not to provide as much copy as necessary.

But the prospect must be interested. That's the job of the headline and illustration: To deliver a momentarily attentive, willing and intrigued reader to the opening sentence of the text. It is the job of the copy to turn that interest into a decision by means of information presented dramatically, engagingly, and economically.

Copywriting—real copywriting—is difficult, and those who can do it well are rare. The dumb idea that copy is not important has probably been responsible for their increasing scarcity. This is a shame, since the dumbness of that idea is becoming apparent and, in the last few years, copy seems to be regaining the emphasis and space it deserves.

I hope that, in all of our offices, we will continue to find and encourage real copywriters. And that we'll remember that nobody reads copy—except interested prospects.[1]

FIGURE 24-1

With such a well-known product, there is little need for a whole lot in the advertisement. Notice that there is no headline, body copy, or logotype—only an illustration of the bottle. (Original in color) *By permission: Chanel, Inc.*

Advertising Copy

THEME LINES, TRADE CHARACTERS, SEALS, AND OTHER MARKS

A number of different marks and devices may appear in an advertisement, including theme lines, trade characters, and seals. Generally, when an advertiser uses any of these devices, they appear automatically in all the advertiser's advertisements. For example, the Rock of Gibraltar is always included in Prudential insurance advertisements. General Foods uses a corporate identity symbol in all its advertisements. The automatic use of these elements in the advertisement, however, does not diminish their importance.

THEME LINES The theme line or slogan has become an easy, shorthand way for the consumer to remember a brand and salient brand features. Most people have little difficulty identifying brands with theme lines. Today the theme line has become a "war cry." It is that phrase or those words that sum up the campaign, fight the competition, and *internally*, give the sales force and others something to live up to—for example, "Nothing else is a Volkswagen." The theme line is the memorable encapsulation of the campaign idea, and hence it is tremendously important to continuity. Theme lines become "logo" lines for print advertisements, "supers" for television commercials, and "tag lines" for radio. Theme lines may be purposely designed, but often they come out of successful headlines. The problems of writing theme lines are similar to those of writing headlines and will be discussed later in the chapter.

TRADE CHARACTERS A trade character may be described as a characterization developed from a human being, an animal, or an inanimate object made animate. Examples are Betty Crocker, the Jolly Green Giant, Morris the Cat, the Cricket lighter cricket, and the Pillsbury Dough Boy, to mention but a few. The idea behind the use of trade characters is to encourage greater identification and to provide a vehicle around which to build a promotional program. Morris has been used by 9-Lives as the central character in most of its advertising. The Pillsbury Dough Boy, on the other hand, has generally been used in a subordinate role. Even when an advertisement does not feature the trade character, the character is often included somewhere in the advertisement. In addition to being used for print advertisements, trade characters have been most effectively used in television, where they can deliver animated advertising messages. They also lend themselves to good use in other promotional efforts. For example, Ronald McDonald has been seen in parades and greeting children in the restaurants. Like a product itself, the trade character must frequently be updated. As people's attitudes and tastes change, so does Betty Crocker. Generally, trade characters like Ronald McDonald and "Charlie" the StarKist tuna reflect an image of humor and warmth. They may also be used to add credibility and authoritativeness, like Betty Crocker, who has been considered a serious adviser in home economics as well as an emotionally appealing character.

SEALS Seals are offered by some organizations to companies whose products meet the standards established by these organizations. They are valuable to the advertiser as an endorsement by a recognized authority and add prestige to the advertiser. A number of seals, including such popular ones as the Good Housekeeping Seal of Approval, the Parents' Institute Seal, and the seal of the Underwriters' Laboratories, are much coveted by many advertisers. When advertisers have obtained permission to use one or more of these, they generally include them in all their advertisements. Their value is obvious. They provide an independent endorsement of the product being advertised. Unfortunately, from time to time, seals and awards of questionable integrity have been featured in advertisements. These have weakened the value of those that are valid.

OTHER MARKS Trademarks, discussed in an earlier chapter, are automatically included in most advertisements. In addition, certain advertisers have other marks and devices that are put in all their advertisements, including notice of patents, copyrights, guarantees, and the like.

LOGOTYPES Logotypes (logos), or signature cuts, are special designs of the name of the advertiser or product that are used repeatedly in that product's advertising. Most advertisers have such designs, which are frequently the same as the trademarks on the products themselves. A well-designed logotype will give the product individuality and provide for quick identification at the point of purchase. As in the case of trade characters, logotypes are constantly in need of updating to keep the company image modern.

Truth is essential in advertising today. You're not going to make it without it. But, while telling the truth may make you feel virtuous, it isn't its own reward. As far as your advertising budget is concerned, the truth isn't the truth until people believe you. And they can't believe you if they don't know what you're saying. And they can't know what you're saying if they don't listen to you. And they won't listen to you if you're not interesting. And you won't be interesting unless you say things freshly, originally, imaginatively. . . .

WILLIAM BERNBACH (1911–1982), Advertising Agent

KINDS OF PRINT ADVERTISING COPY

Different advertisements are designed to meet different problems in reaching their ultimate objective of maximizing the profits of the firm. There are various kinds of copy to handle these problems. Philip Ward Burton describes them as:

1. *Straight-line copy*, in which the body text begins immediately to develop the headline and/or illustration idea in direct selling of the product, using its sales points in the order of their importance.
2. *Narrative copy*, the establishment of a story or specific situation that, by its nature, will logically lead into a discussion of a product's selling points.
3. *Corporate advertising*, in which the copy sells an idea, point of view, service, or company, instead of presenting the selling features.

FIGURE 24-2

A straight line advertisement. (Original in color) *By permission: Colgate-Palmolive Company.*

4. *Dialogue and monologue copy*, in which the characters illustrated in your advertisement do the selling in their own words (testimonials, pseudo-testimonials, comic strip, and continuity panel).

5. *Picture and caption copy*, in which your story is told by a series of illustrations and captions rather than by use of a copy block alone.

6. *Gimmick copy*, unclassified effects in which the selling power depends upon humor, poetry, foreign words, great exaggeration, gags, and other devices.[2]

The legend of The Pendleton Shirt.

It all began in the Pacific Northwest. At the turn of the century, a pioneer family began weaving blankets, robes and shawls of exceptional quality in Pendleton, Oregon. Many designs were inspired by the motifs of the nearby Nez Perce Indian Nation.

It was an ideal place for such a beginning. Rich grasslands nurtured bands of sheep that grew wool of the highest quality. Soft, pure water was abundant for scouring and dyeing. And the family brought to the task a heritage of weaving which began generations before in England.

Through the years, Pendleton blankets and robes came to be considered a standard of value among settlers and Indians throughout the West.

And so the legend of excellence began.

The family then applied its skills to the creation of 100% virgin wool clothing fabrics. Fine, beautiful fabrics which were then tailored into shirts that loggers, ranchers and sportsmen of the region could wear a lifetime.

Each shirt was "warranted to be a Pendleton," to assure the buyer that the company stood behind its products, in quality and workmanship.

And the legend grew.

Today, four generations later, the family is still making shirts warranted to be Pendletons, to the same standards our forefathers set those many years ago.

We continue to use only pure, virgin wools, selected and graded by hand each shearing season.

We design the patterns, dye the wool, spin the yarn, weave the fabrics.

And then, in over 60 careful steps, these pure virgin wool fabrics are cut and sewn into Pendleton Shirts.

It is this commitment to quality and value in 100% virgin wool, this attention to detail every step, every stitch of the way, that makes a Pendleton Shirt different from every shirt in the world.

It is the commitment we have always made to a Pendleton Shirt. And always will.

The legend deserves no less.

FIGURE 24-3

Narrative copy can be used to tell a story that involves the product or service. (Original in color) *By permission: Pendleton Woolen Mills.*

Rather than further elaborating on these techniques, an example of each is presented in Figures 24-2 through 24-7.

A single advertisement may contain more than one of these kinds of copy. An analysis of the advertising objectives will usually suggest which ones to use. As might be expected, straight-line copy is most often used, for it is applicable to most situations. Copywriters cannot afford to specialize in one type of copy, however, for they may be called upon to write any kind of copy and they should be prepared to do so.

COMPARATIVE ADVERTISING In recent years, advertisements that make direct reference to competition have become quite popular. (See Figure 24-8.) There are those who would argue that such comparisons, which name names, are unethical or immoral, and there are others who would contend that such comparative advertising should be increased because it better informs consumers. But such advertising is not

FIGURE 24-4

A corporate advertisement, one of a series on health care. The campaign also makes use of television commercials. *By permission: Pfizer Inc.*

THE PFIZER HEALTHCARE SERIES

5,000,000
have diabetes and don't know it...

You could be one

It's estimated that 5 million Americans have diabetes and don't know it. The early symptoms are vague and may seem minor. As a result, they are often ignored or not taken seriously enough. Yet, if undiagnosed, diabetes can lead to serious complications affecting various parts of the body, including eyes, heart, kidneys, brain or even life itself.

What are the symptoms of diabetes?
There may be none. Or there may be such simple things as an increase in skin infections or a slower healing of bruises and cuts. Also, be aware of excessive thirst or hunger, frequent need to urinate and extreme fatigue.

These symptoms do not necessarily occur all at once and they usually develop gradually. So it's easy to understand how they can be overlooked or considered part of the normal aging process.

It is important, therefore, to be alert to changes in your body and report them directly to your doctor. You have a greater chance of being diabetic if you are over 40, overweight or have a history of diabetes anywhere in the family.

What is diabetes?
Diabetes is a disorder in which the body cannot control the levels of sugar in the blood. Normally the hormone, insulin, regulates the blood sugar level. But if your body does not produce or effectively use its insulin, diabetes results.

Treatment of diabetes.
Diabetes usually can be successfully managed. Some diabetics need no more than weight reduction, the right foods and moderate exercise to bring blood sugar levels under control. And, if these changes are not enough, a simple oral medication is all that may be needed. Today, even those who need insulin can be better and more comfortably managed by their doctors than ever before.

The diagnosis is easy.
But only your doctor can make it. And remember, if you are over 40 and overweight, or have diabetes in your family, you should have regular blood and urine tests. Early diagnosis in adults can lead to better management and fewer problems later on.

Only your doctor can prescribe treatment.
Follow your doctor's advice about diet, exercise and medication. Also, be aware that you have a support system, which we call...

Partners in Healthcare:

You are the most important partner.
Only you can see your doctor for a proper medical checkup. And it's you who must decide to accept the guidance and counseling of your physician, nurse, nutritionist and pharmacist. When medications are prescribed, only you can take them as directed.

Your doctor orders your tests and makes the diagnosis.
Your physician will advise you on your weight, your diet and your exercise, and also decide if you require medication. He will help you monitor your progress.

All those who discover, develop and distribute medicines complete the partnership.
Pfizer's ongoing research brings you essential medicines for a wide range of diseases. Through our development of these medicines, we are fulfilling our responsibility as one of your partners in healthcare.

For additional information on diabetes, please contact your local American Diabetes Association affiliate.

For reprints of this Healthcare Series, please write: Pfizer Pharmaceuticals, Post Office Box 3852D, Grand Central Station, New York, NY 10163.

 **Pfizer** PHARMACEUTICALS • A PARTNER IN HEALTHCARE

FIGURE 24-5

This advertisement makes use of the monologue technique in its copy, using a testimonial from a satisfied user. *By permission: The Maytag Company.*

a social issue. It *is* legal, and many advertisers contend that it is very useful. To be sure, in the early days of its popularity, some advertisers went overboard and were sued by their competitors. However, any advertising is subject to suit on the basis of violating laws or the rights of others, and this advertising is no different.

Because so much controversy was stirred up, the American Association of Advertising Agencies adopted a policy statement and guidelines for comparative advertising. (See Figure 24-9.) Since there is so much interest in comparative advertising and since it is a useful tool, it is helpful to review these points when considering its use.

Many authorities have indicated that the headline is the single most important element of the advertisement. (Sometimes it is the "theme line," discussed earlier.) Certainly it is an essential element in getting attention. David Ogilvy, who feels quite strongly about the headline, comments:

WRITING THE HEADLINE

FIGURE 24-6

A picture and caption advertisement. (Original in color) *By permission: The Coleman Company, Inc.*

The headline is the most important element in most advertisements. It is the telegram which decides the reader whether to read the copy.

On the average, five times as many people read the headline as read the body copy. When you have written your headline, you have spent eighty cents out of your dollar.

If you haven't done some selling in your headline, you have wasted 80 percent of your client's money. The wickedest of all sins is to run an advertisement *without* a headline.[3]

Me-ów

meower

n.\: *deriv.* cat **1:** word commonly associated with Mix, *as in* Meow Mix." **1a:** the only cat food cats ask for by name (*e.g.,* meow, meow, meow). **2:** Nutritionally complete meal. **3:** Tuna, liver and chicken flavors. **4:** *syn.,* great tasting. *archaic,* cry of a cat. **5:** *usu. usage,* only Meow Mix" tastes so good cats ask for it by name."

FIGURE 24-7

An advertisement for a brand that from its start has made effective use of humor—one of the "gimmick" varieties of copy. *By permission: Ralston Purina Company.*

TYPES OF HEADLINES   Headlines may be categorized into five different types: news, benefit, curiosity, selective, and directive. Each of these is explained below. Of course, it should be kept in mind that a given headline may be a combination of several of these types.

THE NEWS HEADLINE A headline that tells readers something they want to know about the product is a news headline. Wanting to keep up with the latest developments in any field is a very common human trait. The news headline plays upon this desire by telling readers what is new with the product advertised. Such news should be pertinent to the product advertised and of real interest to the readers. In other words, it should show how the product will benefit the reader. Here are some examples of news headlines:

> Panasonic introduces a thinner Mr. Thin.
> These two Mercedes-Benz cars just rewrote Diesel history—by adding the word "performance."
> This is the only wristwatch ever to be certified a marine chronometer. (Omega)
> The first air freshener so effective it fights odors two ways. New Twice as Fresh.

FIGURE 24-8

An example of a comparative advertisement. *Reproduced by permission of the copyright owner* © *Bristol-Myers Co.*

THE BENEFIT HEADLINE Some headlines suggest the benefits that will accrue to the reader by buying or using the advertiser's product. Of course, the product must be capable of fulfilling the promised benefit. Examples of this type of headline include:

You'll find something new to love every time you drive it. (Pontiac Grand Prix)
So much squeezable softness, you want to hug it. (Charmin)
So moist, it almost belongs in a pudding dish. (Duncan Hines)
Washing makes it better, not smaller. (Cross Creek shirts)

THE CURIOSITY HEADLINE A headline that deliberately conceals what the advertisement is all about is called a curiosity headline. The object is to make the reader want to read on. However, if the reader is not challenged to read the copy, it is likely that the advertisement will be completely wasted, for the headline does no selling. Examples are:

POLICY STATEMENT AND
GUIDELINES FOR COMPARATIVE ADVERTISING

The Board of Directors of the American Association of Advertising Agencies recognizes that when used truthfully and fairly, comparative advertising provides the consumer with needed and useful information.

However, extreme caution should be exercised. The use of comparative advertising, by its very nature, can distort facts and, by implication, convey to the consumer information that misrepresents the truth.

Therefore, the Board believes that comparative advertising should follow certain guidelines:

1. The intent and connotation of the ad should be to inform and never to discredit or unfairly attack competitors, competing products or services.

2. When a competitive product is named, it should be one that exists in the marketplace as significant competition.

3. The competition should be fairly and properly identified but never in a manner or tone of voice that degrades the competitive product or service.

4. The advertising should compare related or similar properties or ingredients of the product, dimension to dimension, feature to feature.

5. The identification should be for honest comparison purposes and not simply to upgrade by association.

6. If a competitive test is conducted it should be done by an objective testing source, preferably an independent one, so that there will be no doubt as to the veracity of the test.

7. In all cases the test should be supportive of all claims made in the advertising that are based on the test.

8. The advertising should never use partial results or stress insignificant differences to cause the consumer to draw an improper conclusion.

9. The property being compared should be significant in terms of value or usefulness of the product to the consumer.

10. Comparatives delivered through the use of testimonials should not imply that the testimonial is more than one individual's thought unless that individual represents a sample of the majority viewpoint.

FIGURE 24-9

A positive position toward the effective use of comparative advertising. *By permission: American Association of Advertising Agencies.*

We've become a nation of skeptics.

An American can put up with just about anything short of being made to look a fool. Yet, there always seems to be someone out to do that very thing—politicians, biographers, repairmen, husbands, wives. And since we're obviously not a nation of fools, we've become a nation of skeptics. To keep from believing something false, we've decided not to believe much of anything at all.

It is fashionable to point to advertising as a major contributor to the national distrust. And perhaps it is accurate. But for us in the business, what caused the skepticism is not nearly so important as what the skepticism has caused: an unreceptive audience for almost everything we say. Once, maybe, it was possible to fool someone into buying. Now it's hard to talk anyone into listening. People start to read between the lines as soon as they start to read. And they have become very

proficient in the art of recognizing fast talk and hollow claims.

In order for us to do our job, we have to make believers out of the skeptics. And our only chance to do that is to create advertising that will stand up to their scrutiny—advertising that contains honest ideas worth talking about. Every product has at least one, but not every advertiser has the stamina to find it. Most times it's easier to wrap an empty thought in cleverness and call it creativity. But people aren't buying empty thoughts today, no matter how cleverly they are disguised. Today it stretches the limits of creativity to make an honest idea stand out as an honest idea. That we can do, however. We have the skill to make our words heard if we find the thoughts worth hearing. For although this is a nation of skeptics, the skeptics are fair. And if they have learned to spot a trick, we can help them learn again to recognize the truth.

The truth about Northlich, Stolley
We try to win over the skeptics with our advertising. But sometimes we lose.
We think a lot of our abilities as an agency. But we're not the right agency for a lot of companies.
If you would like to know more about us, write for our new booklet to Northlich, Stolley, Inc., 200 West Fourth Street, Cincinnati, Ohio 45202.

Northlich, Stolley, Inc.

FIGURE 24-10

An advertising agency speaks to the increasingly important factor of credibility in advertisements. *By permission: Northlich, Stolley, Inc.*

In the summer of 426 A.D., Vili Vikkela, the Finn, took his girl sight-seeing, promising to bring her home before sunset. Three months later her parents grew quite concerned. (Finnair) [In case you are curious, the advertisement goes on to say the sun never really sets in Finland during the summer!]

"We'll have to allow for a little adjustment in the year 2100," he said. (Audemarks Piguet watches)

THE SELECTIVE HEADLINE If the objective is to single out a particular audience for the advertiser, the copywriter may use a selective headline. Such headlines may select the audience through the nature of the subject discussed or by addressing the particular audience. Examples of those headlines selecting an audience because of the nature of the subject include:

Feet hurt, burn? (Dr. Scholl's Foot Balm)
Relieve varicose vein problems. (Bauer & Black)

Examples of those headlines that select an audience by addressing them are:

Employers: (Phoenix of Hartford Insurance)
Tall and Big men: (The King-Size Co.)

THE DIRECTIVE HEADLINE Some headlines direct the reader to try or buy the product. The most effective use of such headlines is usually when a directive is combined with one of the other types of headlines. Examples are:

Open the indoor season with Lysol spray.
Bring yourself back to life. (Coast)

It should be noted that some advertisements have no headline at all. In some cases, such strategy can be very effective, because it forces readers to "headline" the advertisement themselves with appeals that are directly related to them.

HINTS ON HEADLINE WRITING It is rare for copywriters to come up with the final headline on the first try. A good technique is to put all ideas down on paper. Then you can rework, combine, and refine until you have it. David Ogilvy says he never writes fewer than sixteen headlines for a single advertisement.[4] In some instances, one headline will serve as a theme line for a number of advertisements in a campaign with little or no change.

Copywriters disagree on how long the ideal headline should be. To be sure, a short headline can be grasped more quickly as a person turns the pages of a magazine or newspaper. However, brevity can sacrifice effective statement of an idea. Ogilvy argues that a good headline should include the selling promise. This practice makes long headlines. Ogilvy feels that the best headline he ever wrote contained eighteen words: "At Sixty Miles an Hour the Loudest Noise in the New Rolls-Royce Comes From the Electric Clock."[5]

Subheads are additional display lines that provide the transition between the headline and the body copy. They usually amplify the main headline, and because they are generally set in smaller type, they may be considerably longer. The same kind of care must be taken in writing subheads as in writing the major headline. Frequently, readers will not go beyond the subhead, so it should carry as much of the sales story as possible.

The importance of the headline cannot be overstated. If the headline does not do the job it should, nothing will happen, for readers rarely overlook a headline and go into the body copy. Victor Schwab said:

Remember when writing your headline: You are really calling out a phrase or a sentence that will "flag" people—and will make as many of them as possible say, "I want that," or at least, "What *is* that? Tell me more."[6]

WRITING THE COPY

In most cases, the headline is written first; then the copywriter turns to the body copy. Although many critics of advertising will claim that copy is dashed off on a typewriter by the copywriter with machinelike ease, this is hardly the case. Good copy requires careful and painstaking thought and knowledge. Only when these factors have been brought to bear does the sheer ability to write come into play.

Back in 1925, J. George Frederick wrote the following remarks about copy, which have stood the test of time well:

> *Copy* is the soul of advertising. Picture and type may appeal to instincts, to the senses, but copy has no other entry-way into the reader except through his or her intelligence. And yet copy is more potent perhaps than type or picture to reach, if desired, either instincts or senses, for language has power to create an infinitely greater variety of images, symbols and associations than any other medium of communication. *Copy* is, therefore, a supreme consideration.[7]

GETTING THE FACTS   Although it has been stated earlier in the book, this deserves repetition and amplification here, because the point is so vital to the success of the advertising: Good copy is not written in a vacuum, but only after the creative people have thoroughly digested all the facts about the product, the marketing objectives, and the nature of the consumers in the target market. Copywriters must become as familiar as possible with the generic product and the advertiser's brand. Whenever possible, they should use the product themselves. They should make comparisons with competitive products, determine the brand's main benefits, and *believe* in the brand. It is terribly difficult to convince others to use something you yourself would not use.

Copywriters must also learn all they can about the consumers to whom they are talking. If they have a knowledge of the product and the consumer and an understanding of the marketing objectives, copywriters can begin to identify what appeals they can use most effectively to persuade consumers to buy. It is during this stage of getting the facts that they can make use of marketing research to find some of the needed answers. Even with all the facts at their command, however, creative people are in danger of failing to communicate properly because they have a tendency to lose perspective as they become more expert. Copywriters are usually not "typical" consumers, for by the very nature of their professional roles, they develop a distorted point of view. Seeking understanding of the consumer can help bring these practitioners back to reality.

THE CONSUMER VIEWPOINT   A well-written advertisement should seem to the reader to have been written for that reader alone. This effect depends upon what is referred to as the "you" attitude. Copywriters should avoid saying "they" when referring to the audience and "I" or "we" when referring to the advertiser. Copy should be *you, you, you!* Consumers, like the rest of us, are essentially self-centered, inasmuch as they are most concerned with their own problems and with those of the people close to them.

Copywriters communicate best when they write in the language of the readers, because that is how readers communicate, and the audience can appreciate best those situations and circumstances that are similar to their own, because that is how they think. Some copy critics say that you cannot write to Main Street from Madison Avenue. This is true only if the copywriters assume that the world *lives* on Madison Avenue. But if they recognize that different market segments of consumers have their own languages and their own life-styles and reflect these in their copy, they can write from the steel and glass towers of Madison Avenue and hit home on Main Street or the Sunset Strip or Peachtree Street or anyplace else. Being in tune with the audience is a vital link for good copy.

There are lots of young people who would have no trouble in communicating with target audiences for stereo components, records, soft drinks, shampoos, and jeans, because they would be talking to their peers. But could they talk to the audiences for washers and dryers, office forms, wrinkle creams, bran cereals, industrial equipment, and rose fertilizers? And what do they do when they are ten years older? The answer is that if you are going to write advertising copy, you have to be tuned in to the life-styles of your audience. That is no easy task, but getting out of your narrow routine and experience and seeing how the "other half" lives and trying it yourself will help a lot. The creative person who talks only to other creative people is going to lose touch with the market unless the copy assignment is to reach advertising creative people.

WRITING STYLE   Perhaps no phase of copywriting is as subject to differences of opinion as writing style. Some advertising experts warn copywriters to avoid clichés and corn—but there are some great advertisements that are filled with such. Some experts insist that writing style should be simple and to the point—but there are examples of great advertisements that are highly literate and verbose. Critics of advertising, however, attack all advertising as being generally illiterate. They point to grammatical murder, as in "*scratch* has met its match"; or coined words, such as "flavor-ific" chewing gum, "flavor buds" for instant coffee, and "secure-ance" for insurance; or the dropping of adverbs, as in "Fly Direct to Europe." They are shocked at what has been described as the "floating" comparative—faster, deeper, better, longer, with no mention of what the product is faster, deeper, better, or longer *than*. They question the use and abuse and tremendous frequency of words like "finest," "world's best," and "America's only."

If we agree with those who contend that people do not *read* advertisements, then none of this makes any difference. But people *do* read things that interest them—and good advertisements can create interest and will be read! The test of good copy is communication and persuasion. It is concerned with attention, interest, desire, and action—not formal, grammatical English usage. This is not to suggest that anything goes. Rather, the language that will be best comprehended by the audience is the language to use. When advertising a new English grammar text to profs like in that discipline, be sure youse pick the right form what to say it with!

Still, there are some general rules that should be kept in mind. The copywriter should write to the readers, not to the client. Copy should be factual, not vague. The more information provided in the copy, the more likely it is that a sale will be made. The message should be comprehensible to the readers, for they will not take the time to study copy that is not immediately clear. Finally, copy is not meant to be literature; it is designed to persuade the reader to buy.

CREDIBILITY   Perhaps the greatest problem facing advertising as an effective tool of business today is advertising's credibility. Society has become terribly cynical, and not without cause. The Gulf of Tonkin incident of the Vietnam war, the Watergate scandal, and the whole communications explosion have resulted in shaking people's beliefs in everything. It is no wonder that with all these experiences and the consumerism movement of the last decades, the public is highly suspicious of advertising credibility. To be sure, most advertising is truthful, but this does not ensure that the public will believe it. Copy must be believable, not just true; for truth that is beyond the realm of believability will result in disbelief. Advertising that concedes that audiences do not believe in it and argues that it is an exception, or advertising that builds its case on the lack of truthfulness in the competition, is not the answer, for it only increases the consumer's suspicious attitude toward advertising. After the copywriter has finished writing the copy, it should be put to the test (aside from the tests of the legal department). The copywriter should ask, If I were the consumer, would *I* believe it?

LENGTH OF COPY   How much should copywriters write? There is little question that they have to capture and hold their audiences; and the longer they have to hold them, the more likely they are to lose them. Yet the rule, "the shorter the copy the better," is not necessarily sound. There are advertisements that contain very lengthy copy and still get high readership. Perhaps a sounder rule is that copy should be as long as is necessary to tell the story, but without unnecessary verbiage.

The best advertising is fairly simple and proceeds step by step from an interesting start to a logical conclusion. Sometimes it is a long walk and sometimes a short walk, but with good advertising the direction, the pace and the purpose are easy to trace.

WILLIAM A. MARSTELLER, Advertising Agent

RADIO COMMERCIALS   Much of what has been said about copy for print advertisements is obviously applicable to broadcast commercials as well, but there are also differences. Print advertising must appeal to the eyes, but radio must appeal to the ears, and television must appeal to both eyes and ears. As a result, radio and television have certain differences in both format and copy approach. These differences will be discussed below.

FIGURE 24-11

One in a series of advertisements making extensive use of body copy. In the proper situation, long copy may be used effectively. *By permission: General Motors Corporation.*

TYPES OF RADIO COMMERCIALS Radio commercials may be classified by the kind of copy approach used. The *straight commercial,* as the name suggests, is simply an announcement about the merits of the product delivered by an announcer without the aid of any special effects or music. Because it is a problem to get attention with only a limited time for presenting a message, there are many who argue that this technique leaves something to be desired. Nevertheless, it is frequently used and is probably the simplest to write. In print, copywriters need to concern themselves only with choosing the right words to express their ideas, but in radio, copywriters must also be concerned with who is going to deliver the message. It is a well-known fact that the announcer makes all the difference in how the copywriters' words are delivered. As an illustration affects the words in a print advertisement, so the announcer affects the words in the radio commercial. Each announcer is different and brings a different feel to the commercial—from young and hip, to sincere and warm, to authoritative and newsy, to strident, to comical. Therefore, when copywriters write commercials of this sort, they should have a specific type of announcer in mind, and they should be involved in auditioning to select the right announcer.

Another variety is the *dialogue commercial,* a conversation about the product by two or more persons, one of whom is usually the announcer. These may be real people or imaginary characters. The conversation is usually an endorsement of the product in testimonial form. Although this technique can be used effectively, it presents a problem in creating believability and not sounding like a well-rehearsed play.

Still another approach to radio commercials is the *dramatic commercial.* This is a form of playlet with a brief story plot, generally employing professional actors. Usually it is followed by an announcer giving a straight commercial finish. Its main virtues are its strong attention-getting value and its ability to create interest. In both dialogue and dramatic commercials, there is a choice of playing it straight or using humor.

Finally, there is the *singing commercial.* This technique has been much criticized by listeners, probably because some very poor commercials have been made using this technique. Some of the better singing commercials have been very popular. The Boston Pops Orchestra has even made symphonic arrangements of them that never fail to bring a huge favorable response from the audience. One variation of the singing commercial that has been rather successful in recent years has been the musical theme that uses no lyrics but is accompanied by a straight announcement. Because the theme is repeated in a number of commercials, it becomes identified with a particular product. In most situations, music with or without lyrics becomes a part of a commercial using one of the other forms mentioned above. A good singing commercial or "jingle" will do more than just entertain; it will sing out the brand benefit, and because of its memorability, it will be sung by consumers after the radio is turned off. Commercial music is an important part of both radio and television advertising today and is a substantial business on its own. There are many musicians who work full or part time in this business and who work with copywriters to create music for advertising.

WRITING RADIO COMMERCIALS A number of considerations unique to the broadcast media must be borne in mind in writing radio commercials. Perhaps the most unique quality of broadcast is that once the commercial is given, it is gone. There is no turning back, although, of course, a given advertisement may be run more than once. There is no second chance. Therefore, it is essential to get the audience's attention at the very outset and to create sufficient interest so that the audience will stay with the commercial until it is completed.

The special challenge of radio is that because it appeals only to the ear, it must depend upon words and music and sound effects to "paint" pictures in the mind. The high quality of the great dramatic shows of an earlier day of radio attests that this can be done effectively.

Getting the all-important attention for radio commercials requires considerable ingenuity. Unlike audiences for other media, including television, radio listeners are generally preoccupied with other activities

LEO BURNETT U.S.A.
A DIVISION OF LEO BURNETT COMPANY, INC.
ADVERTISING

PRUDENTIAL PLAZA · CHICAGO, ILLINOIS 60601
312-565-5959

UNITED AIRLINES
50/10 Second Recorded Radio Announcement
"MUSIC" (FANTASTIC FABULOUS FLYING FARES) REV.
FARE ANNOUNCEMENT

02721-PASS-50/10

1	MSR:	"MUSIC" TRACK
2	ANNCR:	If you thought last summer's airfares were good, United's got some new ones
3		that are fantastic ... fabulous ... there's never been such flying fares as --
4	SINGERS:	UNITED'S FANTASTIC FABULOUS FLYING FARES
5		LOTS MORE WAYS TO SAVE, WE'LL FLY YOU ALMOST ANYWHERE.
6	ANNCR:	This summer, kids seventeen and under with an adult can fly for
7		half fare with --
8	SINGERS:	UNITED'S FANTASTIC FABULOUS FLYING FARES
9		LOTS MORE WAYS TO SAVE, WE'LL FLY YOU ALMOST ANYWHERE.
10	ANNCR:	Adults can save up to forty percent. Fifty percent on Night Coach.
11		So call your travel agent. Then get in on the summer savings.
12		They're better than ever with --
13	SINGERS:	UNITED'S FANTASTIC FABULOUS FLYING FARES
14		LOTS MORE WAYS TO SAVE WE'LL FLY YOU ALMOST ANYWHERE
15		WORKING TOGETHER
16		COME FLY THE FRIENDLY SKIES.
17	MUSIC:	(:10 LOCAL TAG)

FORM 8-44 R-73

FIGURE 24-12

A radio commercial script. *By permission: United Airlines Inc.*

while listening to the radio. If careful planning of the script is overlooked, the commercial may come and go without the listeners being cognizant of it.

One solution is to make use of unusual techniques to flag the listeners so that they will pay attention to the message. Poorly done, such techniques are resented, but they need not be poorly done. A technique for getting and holding attention that has become increasingly popular on radio is the humorous commercial, frequently in the form of situation comedy. Humor is one of the most difficult means of expression, and there is nothing worse than attempted humor that is not funny. Some copywriters, often freelancers, specialize in this kind of copy, and their proven talents are worth securing. Aside from humor, any device that will offer the listener a degree of entertainment is valuable.

When writing a radio commercial, one should remember that the words on the typewritten page will be spoken. It is a good idea to read the copy aloud constantly to judge it as it is written. To the greatest extent possible, copy should be conversational in tone. However, caution is necessary here, because some words and phrases that are acceptable in everyday conversation may cause resentment in some quarters when they come through the loudspeaker of the radio.

Complex ideas, words, and sentence structure should be avoided in any copy, but it is perhaps especially important to keep copy simple in radio commercials. The listener must be able to grasp every idea and word with a minimum of effort. Some words are poor to use orally because they tend to be indistinct, confused with similar words, not readily defined, or harsh on the ear.

As indicated in an earlier chapter, commercials are bought in time units. It is essential that the script fit the available time. In live commercials, the station may indicate a maximum number of words it will permit in a commercial for a given length of time. But beyond that, and more important for every commercial, there should be sufficient time to have the commercial presented at a pace commensurate with the mood desired.

Music and sound effects can be important aids to good radio commercials, and it is important that the copywriter appreciate these devices. This does not mean that a copywriter must be able to compose music. Rather, the copywriter should understand enough about music to know how and when it can be used effectively in a commercial.

Although the form for preparing radio scripts will vary somewhat among advertising agencies, these general observations can be made. First, it is essential that detailed instructions be included with the commercial. Words are frequently subject to varying interpretations that may or may not be consistent with the objectives of the copywriter. Second, care must be taken in the typing of the script to avoid putting stumbling blocks in the way of the announcer or actors. Hyphenated words should be avoided. Punctuation should make the meaning of each phrase clear. Difficult-to-pronounce words and names, when they must be used, should be accompanied by phonetic spelling to avoid mispronunciation. Best of all, the copywriter should participate personally in the production of the commercial.

Of course, all the marketing inputs and creative techniques that are applicable to print should be kept in mind in writing radio commercials. Radio audiences are highly segmented, and the copywriter must understand the life-style of the audience. An "all-rock" station is obviously for younger people, and radio commercials written to be placed here might have a young voice, a contemporary musical score, somewhat "hip" language, etc. A more conventional jingle for a "familiar music" station might be reworked in a rock version for the "all-rock" station.

THE FACT SHEET   It is sometimes considered desirable for the "personality" of a radio show, such as a disc jockey or a master of ceremonies, to give the commercial live. Although this is rare for national advertisers, it is popular among retailers. Some advertisers believe it is even more desirable to have these personalities deliver the messages in their own words, extemporaneously, to give it the flavor of their own personalities. In such cases the advertiser supplies the personality with a radio *fact sheet.* The fact sheet contains the major points in the copy platform. It may indicate certain points to be stressed and certain phrases to be used, but the rest is left to the discretion of the personality. Unfortunately, the advertiser surrenders any control of the commercial under such circumstances, and the results are sometimes disastrous. On occasion, the personality has used this opportunity to knock the product! When such a commercial is done well, however, it is usually better than anything the advertiser can prepare. This technique has also been used to a lesser extent in television.

The relative merit of television as an advertising medium may be arguable, but few would question that it is the most complex medium for which to prepare commercials. Television involves not only copy and art but also casting, set design, producing, directing, sound, and filming or taping. As mentioned in Chapter 19, the television advertiser may advertise by means of spot announcements placed between shows or by participations during programs.

TYPES OF TELEVISION COMMERCIALS   Television commercials may be classified by the type of copy approach. One kind, as in radio, is the straight or "stand-up" commercial. Here the burden of the commercial presentation rests with announcers who stand (or sit) in front of the camera and make their "pitch." They will probably use some selling aids, such as charts, a sample of the product, and other props. They may use a "hard sell" or a "soft sell." Variations of this approach include the use of "star" salespersons and announcers with reputations from stage, screen, or television and, usually, long association with the product. Joe DiMaggio, for example, has announced Mr. Coffee commercials. In a limited sense, these "stars" resemble trade characters. Another variation is the "personality" announcer, the star of a show, who will deliver the message. Ed McMahon is such a personality. These people frequently will not work from scripts prepared by the advertising agency, but work instead from fact sheets so that they may keep their own styles and personalities.

Dramatization is another approach to commercial presentation. Dramatized commercials are frequently referred to as *slice of life* commercials, for the dramatic plot of the script generally involves an episode designed to simulate real-life experiences. Their format may be

Client:	Orkin
Campaign:	Pest
Product:	
Title:	"Clean"
Media:	TV
Length:	:30
Comments:	As Produced Revision #3

CREATIVE DEPARTMENT
J. Walter Thompson Company
Atlanta

January 31, 1983

VIDEO	AUDIO
OPEN ON CLOSEUP OF MOPPING FLOOR.	VO: You can scrub every floor
CUT TO CLOSEUP OF SCRUBBING COUNTER.	every counter
CUT TO CLOSEUP OF CLEANING CUPBOARD.	every cupboard
CUT TO BUG SCURRYING ACROSS DISHES.	and still have bugs.
CUT TO TRUCK PULLING UP HEAD ON.	You need America's Number One choice in pest control.
CUT TO EXTREME CLOSE UP OF DOOR OPENING TO REVEAL LOGO ON DOOR.	The Orkin Army. We'll clean out your bugs with
CUT TO TREATMENT SHOTS WITH RD98 CHEMICAL. BY ELECTRICAL OUTLET, WHERE PIPE GOES INTO WALL, BY REFRIGERATOR.	proven chemicals like our famous RD98. So effective we give you a pest control guarantee.
CUT TO CLOSEUP SHOT OF GUARANTEE IN RAISED LETTERS, SUPER: LIMITED GUARANTEE PROVIDES FOR FREE RETREATMENT IF PESTS RETURN DURING CONTRACT PERIOD.	
CUT TO MEDIUM LONG SHOT OF ORKIN TRUCKS DRIVING BUY. CONTINUE SUPER UNDERNEATH.	It's another reason people choose one company far more than any other.
CUT TO 3 QUICK SHOTS OF REAL ORKIN CUSTOMERS FROM ATLANTA, GA. MIAMI, FL; AND DENVER, CO.	CUSTOMER #1: Orkin! CUSTOMER #2: Orkin! CUSTOMER #3: Orkin!
CUT TO ZOOM ON FLAG.	
SUPER: NUMBER ONE AGAINST PESTS.	SING: Call the Orkin Army. Number one against pests.

FIGURE 24-13

A television commercial script. *By permission: Orkin Exterminating Company, Inc.*

complex, compared to the format of the straight commercial. A series of commercials may have a related theme, sometimes using a "family" in a series of episodes and sometimes using different "families" in the same episode. Another variation of dramatization is the *testimonial,* which employs name personalities or ordinary users of the product. (In some instances, pseudo-testimonials are used, with actors assuming the roles of consumers.) The athletes who have presented messages about razor blades are almost too numerous to count. In fact, the use of "stars" in dramatic presentations or as star salespeople has become increasingly popular as the compensation has become very lucrative. Bill Cosby, Candice Bergen, Mariette Hartley, Orson Welles, and many other celebrities are now selling goods and services on television.

Demonstrations are another popular kind of commercial. Probably no other medium can provide so effective a vehicle to demonstrate the merits of the product as can television, where you can *show* how the product delivers the benefits.

Production commercials are the television counterpart of radio's singing commercials. They involve not only music and lyrics but usually dancing as well. They entertain while selling, and they can be very elaborate and expensive to produce.

KENYON & ECKHARDT INC. 200 PARK AVE..NEW YORK 17, N. Y.

CLIENT ___CHRYSLER/CORPORATION___   JOB NO. ___CRCK 3603___   TIME ___60 SECONDS___

PRODUCT ___CORPORATE___   TITLE ___"AMERICAN INDUSTRY REV. 3"___   DATE ___6/2/82___

1. LEE A. IACOCCA: There was a time when "Made in America" meant something.

2. It meant you made the best.

3. Unfortunately, a lot of Americans don't believe that anymore, and maybe with good reason.

4. But the time has come to restore the confidence of the American car buyer

5. in American technology, American workers and American cars.

6. It's time we in the auto industry convinced you that you can make a long term investment

7. in the quality of a new American car and not have to worry about it.

8. So Chrysler will protect every new American built Dodge, Chrysler and Plymouth passenger car three ways.

9. One, 5 years or 50,000 miles on engine and power train.

10. Two, 5 years or 50,000 miles rust-through protection on the outside of the car.

11. Three, 5 years or 50,000 miles free scheduled maintenance.

12. We in the car industry must make "Made in America" mean something again. We owe it to you.

13. So we invite GM and Ford to follow Chrysler. But until they do,

14. if you can find better protection, take it. If you can find a better car, buy it.

15. (SILENT)

FIGURE 24-14

This commercial makes use of the firm's well-known chief executive officer as a star salesperson to sell the product. *By permission: Chrysler Corporation.*

CREATING TELEVISION COMMERCIALS The task of creating television commercials is a complex one, for the creative personnel must think beyond words and pictures. The task might be likened to that of a playwright, but unlike a drama, which may be the product of a

Advertising Copy

471

1. (SFX: WAVES LAPPING) MUSIC: PIANO THEME.

2. (SFX: THUD) HE: Ow. . .

3. we need a taller cabin!

4. SHE: Maybe I need a shorter husband. HE: (VO) Oh yeah! (LAUGHTER)

5. SHE: Coffee, sailor?

6. HE: Good morning.

7. SONG: TIMES LIKE THESE. . .

8. ARE MADE FOR TASTER'S CHOICE. (Anncr VO): Taster's Choice.

9. A premium blend. . .

10. of some of the world's best coffee beans. . .

11. freeze-dried to keep its fresh-brewed flavor. . .

12. for your best coffee times.

FIGURE 24-15

From a series of television commercials that tell a story—the dramatization technique. *By permission: The Nestle Company, Inc. Copyright 1982.*

sole writer, the television commercial will more likely involve, in addition to words and action, music and lyrics and maybe dancing. Thus, whereas in the early days of television commercials, a copywriter wrote the words and an art director provided the visual element, today a commercial is so complex that there are few people who have sufficient talent to handle all facets of television commercial creation. For this reason, a commercial is more apt to be a group effort of a team, consisting of a copywriter, an art director, and a television producer. In some instances, a musical composer and a choreographer may be included.

The television creative team usually starts with a *script,* on typed sheets of 8½ -by-11 inch paper divided in half, with the *audio* (words,

FIGURE 24-16

An effective use of a testimonial in a television commercial. *By permission: Bic Corp.*

BIC SHAVER

CLIENT: BIC PEN CORP.

TITLE: "McENROE CLOSE SHAVE"

CODE NO.: WBBR2395

LENGTH: :30

UMPIRE: Mr. McEnroe, that's a very close shave.

McENROE: You must be joking. That ball was in!

UMPIRE: No, Mr. McEnroe, your shave. It's very close.
McENROE: Of course. I shave with Bic.

UMPIRE: You earn millions and shave with a 20 cent Bic.

McENROE: Look, why pay more for fancy handles and tricky tops when I get lots of close shaves with Bic.

UMPIRE: Advantage, McEnroe.
McENROE: He's right, I don't have to shave with a 20 cent Bic. . .but I do.

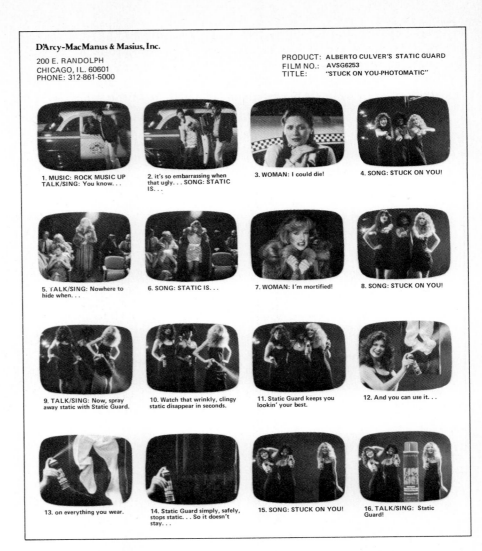

D'Arcy-MacManus & Masius, Inc.

200 E. RANDOLPH
CHICAGO, IL. 60601
PHONE: 312-861-5000

PRODUCT: ALBERTO CULVER'S STATIC GUARD
FILM NO.: AVSG6253
TITLE: "STUCK ON YOU-PHOTOMATIC"

1. MUSIC: ROCK MUSIC UP
TALK/SING: You know. . .

2. it's so embarrassing when that ugly. . . SONG: STATIC IS. . .

3. WOMAN: I could die!

4. SONG: STUCK ON YOU!

5. TALK/SING: Nowhere to hide when. . .

6. SONG: STATIC IS. . .

7. WOMAN: I'm mortified!

8. SONG: STUCK ON YOU!

9. TALK/SING: Now, spray away static with Static Guard.

10. Watch that wrinkly, clingy static disappear in seconds.

11. Static Guard keeps you lookin' your best.

12. And you can use it. . .

13. on everything you wear.

14. Static Guard simply, safely, stops static. . . So it doesn't stay. . .

15. SONG: STUCK ON YOU!

16. TALK/SING: Static Guard!

FIGURE 24-17

Television commercials provide an excellent opportunity for demonstrating the product as shown here. *By permission: Alberto-Culver Company.*

music, and sound effects) on the right-hand side and the *video* (instructions for settings and action) on the left-hand side. In order to coordinate the audio and video, the team must visualize the whole commercial before writing. But first there has to be the *idea* (like the headline before the body copy in the print advertisement). And the idea becomes the basis for the type of commercial. The creative team must consider the brand and the marketing strategy, because these will suggest the type of commercial.

The individual commercial may be a combination of several of the types described above. In addition, the creative team has several forms

YOUNG & RUBICAM INTERNATIONAL, INC.

CLIENT: DR PEPPER CO.
PRODUCT: DR PEPPER
TITLE: "GUS"

LENGTH: 30 SECONDS
COMM. NO. DPYT 9033
DATE: 12/7/78

1. (MUSIC UNDER)
MAN 1: Hey Gus, you special enough to skate with us?

2. MAN 2: I'm an all star skater.

3. There's nobody greater.

4. I score every game,

5. but being a Pepper's my fame.

6. PEOPLE: All right. We're Peppers too.

7. MAN 2 SINGS: I'm a Pepper, he's a Pepper...
CHORUS: We're a Pepper,

8. she's a Pepper, wouldn't you like to be a Pepper too. We're a Pepper,

9. he's a Pepper...FRED FLINTSTONE: Yabba dabba dew. I'm a Pepper too.

10. CHORUS: If you drink Dr Pepper,

11. you're a Pepper too.

12. Be a Pepper, drink Dr Pepper. Be a Pepper.

FIGURE 24-18

One of a series of production commercials in which there is singing and dancing. *By permission: Dr Pepper Company.*

at its disposal. One is *live* action, using real people and animals. It has the greatest realism, but because the vast majority of commercials use live action, it is not as distinctive as other forms. Another form, more interesting by contrast to live commercials and programs, is *animation.* This cartoon form may use drawings done by animated cartoon artists, or it may use puppets or dolls in place of drawings. Frequently the animated commercial suggests whimsy, but it is not limited to a humorous approach. Animation may be used effectively to portray certain action that does not lend itself to being represented live—for example, an illustration of the working of a drug as it passes through the body. *Stop motion,* a third form, can bring life to inanimate objects, such as the product or the package. It provides an excellent means of focusing attention on products as they dance or march across the screen.

The key, however, as to which type and form of commercial to use is to strive for originality and excellence. So often some type or form of

Advertising Copy

RIGHT GUARD

"Lime Twist Dance"

SONG: COME ON BABY

TRY THE RIGHT GUARD
LIME TWIST

COME ON BABY

TRY THE RIGHT GUARD
LIME TWIST

BRAND NEW RIGHT GUARD
LIME DEODORANT STICK

ANNCR: New Right Guard
Lime

The same all day protection
as regular Right Guard Stick
with a fresh lime twist.

SONG: TWIST IT AROUND

AND UP AND DOWN IT GOES

FOR ALL DAY PROTECTION

RIGHT GUARD KNOWS

IT'S THE RIGHT GUARD
LIME TWIST

ANNCR: New from Right
Guard

SONG: LIME DEODORANT
STICK

FIGURE 24-19

An example of a stop motion television commercial. Through this technique, inanimate objects appear to
have come to life. *Reprinted with the permission of The Gillette Company.*

commercial falls out of favor in the business until some creative team comes up with an idea that is so freshly original and so excellently executed that this type or form of commercial is "in" again, as it is imitated and run into the ground by others.

In general, the number of scenes in a commercial should be limited to avoid confusion, although some commercials deliberately go to quick cuts of many related scenes to achieve special effects. Audio and video should be coordinated so that one does not distract from the other. Key selling points and the brand name should be repeated frequently, because the audience cannot look back or "tear out" the advertisement but must commit major points to memory. Finally, the television copywriter should keep production cost in mind when writing the script, because making television commercials can be very expensive.

Print advertisements may include any or all of the following elements: headline, illustration, body copy, theme line, trade character, seal, and logotype.

There are a variety of kinds of advertising copy, which may be categorized as straight-line copy, narrative copy, corporate advertising, dialogue and monologue copy, picture and caption copy, and gimmick copy. Which is most appropriate should be determined by the objectives of the advertising. Using comparative advertisements in any of these cases may be a desirable technique.

Many people believe that the headline is the most important element in the advertisement. There is little agreement, however, as to the ideal length of a headline. Usually, headlines are written before body copy. Good copy should appear to have been written for each reader alone. To be effective, the writer must be tuned in to the life-style of the audience, and the copy must be believable.

In writing copy for radio, one must remember that the audience cannot turn back. Also, radio appeals only to the ear, and any illustrations are in the consumer's mind. Because radio is so often a background to other activities, getting attention is of considerable importance.

Creating a television commercial is not unlike writing a play. Because it involves putting together so many diverse elements, it is more apt to be a team effort. There are various types of commercials, which can be produced in a variety of forms. The keys are excellence and originality, whatever the type and form.

1. What are the elements of a print advertisement?
2. Select examples of current magazine advertisements for each kind of print copy.
3. Find several examples of comparative advertising and explain why you think they are either unethical or immoral or why you think they are good because they inform consumers better.
4. Illustrate the five types of headlines with examples taken from current advertisements.
5. What is the ideal length of a headline?
6. What is the ideal length of body copy?
7. Why is credibility so important in advertisements?

QUESTIONS AND PROBLEMS

8. Describe each of three types of radio commercials.

9. Describe each of three types of television commercials.

10. Explain what is meant by the following techniques for creating television commercials:
    (a) Live action
    (b) Animation
    (c) Stop motion

ENDNOTES

[1] *Advertising Age,* XLIX, No. 40 (October 2, 1978), p. 56. Copyright 1978 by Crain Communications, Inc.

[2] Philip Ward Burton, *Advertising Copywriting,* 5th ed. (Columbus, O.: Grid Publishing Inc., 1983), pp. 76–78.

[3] David Ogilvy, *Confessions of an Advertising Man* (New York: Atheneum, 1963), p. 104.

[4] *Ibid.,* p. 105.

[5] *Ibid.,* pp. 106–7.

[6] Victor O. Schwab, *How to Write a Good Advertisement* (New York: Harper & Row, Publishers, 1962), p. 41.

[7] J. George Frederick, *Masters of Advertising Copy* (New York: Frank-Maurice, Inc., 1925), pp. 29–30.

25

Layouts,
Storyboards,
and Art

After completing this chapter, you should be able to:
1. Describe the various kinds of layouts
2. Explain the principles of good layout
3. Discuss the use of storyboards and animatics
4. Identify the different kinds of advertising artwork

dvertisements are a combination of copy and art inputs. Just as the copywriter generally has a greater stake in the words, the art director generally has a greater stake in the illustrations and layouts. As indicated earlier, however, increasingly their efforts are those of a partnership that blends the talents of both to create effective finished advertisements.

Art directors contribute to the whole creative effort, but they are, of course, more concerned with some areas than with others. Because they have certain art skills, they will undoubtedly be the ones who physically prepare the layouts for the advertisements. Art directors, however, seldom *produce* art, at least in finished form. Rather, they are responsible for directing others—artists generally outside the advertising agency organization—in the preparation of finished artwork. They do this by determining the nature and composition of all the elements in the advertisements. This chapter will concern itself with these aspects of advertising—layouts and art for print advertisements, and storyboards for television commercials.

PRINT ADVERTISEMENT LAYOUTS

A major job of the art director is executing the layout of the advertisement. A layout may be defined as the format in which the various elements of the advertisement are combined. It is the physical visualization of the creative idea that was in the mind of the art director or the creative team.

KINDS OF LAYOUTS The several different forms of layout each serve a particular purpose; any one advertisement may use all of them or only some of them. They are thumbnail sketches, rough layouts, finished layouts, comprehensive layouts, and working layouts. They may be executed in several ways but are most frequently done with drawing pencils or felt-tip pens. They are generally drawn either on tracing paper or on bond paper. These layouts are used as guides in the various stages of advertisement development by those working on the advertisements and by those who must approve them. They are not only use-

480

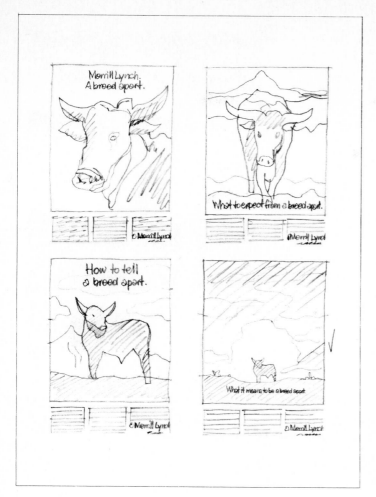

FIGURE 25-1
The start of advertising layout. These four thumbnail sketches suggest four different visual approaches to the advertisement. *By permission: Merrill Lynch and Young & Rubicam, Inc.*

ful to the art director and for presentation to the client. They also help the writer to see the words of the copy and headline in the "full dress" of the layout. Does the headline grab at you, or just lie there? Does it excite, stimulate, motivate? Layouts provide an opportunity for seeing the advertisement in its totality. Copy, headline, and illustration take on new meanings when they are combined. This, of course, is another reason for suggesting creativity as a team effort.

THUMBNAIL SKETCHES Thumbnail sketches are miniature sketches that are used by some art directors to convey the basic layout style and treatment without spelling out small details. They offer a quick and convenient method for putting alternative layout ideas on paper. They are drawn in proportion to the actual space, but much smaller—usually only a few inches high. Art directors may draw only a few or a great many, until they find one or more that seems worthy of being worked up more completely.

Layouts, Storyboards, and Art
481

FIGURE 25-2

Rough layout developed from one of the thumbnail sketches. *By permission: Merrill Lynch* and *Young & Rubicam, Inc.*

ROUGH LAYOUTS Rough layouts, or *visuals,* are prepared for almost all advertisements. They are the same size as the finished advertisement except for outdoor posters, when they are smaller but drawn to scale. Some layout artists prefer to start with rough layouts *instead* of thumbnail sketches, whereas others develop rough layouts *from* thumbnail sketches.

FINISHED LAYOUTS The next stage is the preparation of the finished layout, which is worked more carefully than the rough layout. Finished layouts suggest in considerable detail the style of the illustration and the headlines and therefore serve as a guide to artist and typographer. Generally, finished layouts are the ones submitted to clients for approval.

COMPREHENSIVE LAYOUTS Occasionally a client is unable to judge the effect of the finished advertisement by looking at a finished layout. In such circumstances, a comprehensive layout is prepared for the client. These layouts very closely resemble the finished advertisement. The illustrations are carefully drawn, or, when a photograph is used, a rough proof of the photograph may be pasted into position. Headlines are carefully hand-lettered to resemble the actual type face. And the body copy is sometimes actually set into type and a proof pasted into position. Comprehensive layouts are obviously very expensive. Frequently, they are prepared for the agency by a freelance artist or an art studio. Whereas advertising agencies generally absorb the cost of fin-

FIGURE 25-3

Finished layout for the same advertisement. *By permission: Merrill Lynch* and *Young & Rubicam, Inc.*

FIGURE 25-4

The finished advertisement as it ran in the *New York Times. By permission: Merrill Lynch and Young & Rubicam, Inc.*

ished layouts in the commission they receive from media, the client is generally billed for the additional expense of comprehensive layouts.

WORKING LAYOUTS A working layout is not really a layout but rather a sort of "blueprint" for production, indicating the exact position of the various elements and appropriate instructions for the typographer and plate maker. Working layouts are also known as *mechanicals;* in work prepared for offset lithography, they are called *keylines* or *pasteups.*

PRINCIPLES OF GOOD LAYOUT An infinite number of arrangements is possible for the elements of an advertisement. However, regardless of the arrangement of the elements, certain sound principles should be followed in a good layout. These include balance, movement, unity, clarity, simplicity, and emphasis.

BALANCE Balance, of considerable importance in a layout, involves artistically combining the various sizes and shapes that make up an ad-

FIGURE 25-5

An advertisement with formal balance. *By permission: Soloflex.*

We have been fascinated from the very beginning. By its beauty. The sheer simplicity of line. As a machine, the human body remains the supreme invention. While able to perform the most intricate, the most subtle of movements, it is, at the same time, capable of astonishing feats of strength. Strangely enough, the more that we demand of this machine, the more powerful, the more graceful it becomes.

To unlock your body's potential, we proudly offer Soloflex. Twenty-four traditional iron pumping exercises, each correct in form and balance. All on a simple machine that fits in a corner of your home. For a free Soloflex brochure, call anytime 1-800-453-9000.

BODY BY SOLOFLEX

CALL OUR 24 HR. TOLL-FREE NUMBER

Soloflex, Hillsboro, Oregon 97123.

Layouts, Storyboards, and Art

485

FIGURE 25-6

An advertisement with informal balance. (Original in color) *By permission: Baccarat, Inc.* and *Berger, Stone & Partners, Inc., Advertising.*

vertisement. Essentially, there are two forms of balance—*formal,* or symmetrical, and *informal,* or asymmetrical. Both are good, if well executed. However, informal balance is probably more frequently used in advertising because it creates more interest and excitement.

The artist achieves balance in a layout by so combining the elements that they are in scale in terms of size and weight. ("Weight," in layout, refers to the lightness or darkness of an element.) The concept of balance can be visualized by drawing an analogy to a seesaw. In formal balance, equal weight must be placed on both sides of the center in the same positions. In informal balance, different weights may be used, but they must be so positioned as to keep the seesaw level. Whereas the seesaw principle provides balance between right and left, *optical center* is the key to balance between top and bottom of an advertisement. The optical center of an advertisement is a point halfway between the right and left of the advertisement, approximately three-fifths of the way up from the bottom—the point to which the eye is naturally attracted. Formal or informal balance is achieved by the way the elements are positioned above and below this point in much the same manner as described for balance between right and left.

MOVEMENT If a print advertisement is to get the reader's eye to "move" through it, the layout should provide for *gaze motion,* or *structural motion.* Gaze motion involves placing the persons or animals in the illustration so that they are looking toward the next important element—such as the headline or body copy. The tendency is for the reader to follow the gaze in the illustration. Structural motion is designed to achieve the same results, but more subtly. Here, the reader's eyes are carried from place to place in the advertisement in a manner desired by the advertiser by the structure of the layout itself. Shapes, arrangement of elements, lines, and so forth are all designed to "move" the reader through the advertisement.

UNITY Unity in layout refers to keeping the elements of the advertisement together so that the advertisement does not "fall apart." The injudicious use of white space between elements of the advertisement, for example, can result in the advertisement's appearing to be several separate ones.

CLARITY AND SIMPLICITY Although it is important to make a layout interesting, care must be taken to see that it remains simple enough so as not to lose its clarity. The more elements added to an advertisement, or the more unconventional the arrangement of the elements, the more confusing it becomes. The result is lack of emphasis on the more important elements, lack of interest, and general confusion, which result in the reader's losing interest and abandoning the advertisement and its message. There is a noticeable exception to this rule, however. Certain advertisements announcing bargains may appear unclear and complex, with a crowded layout that looks as if it was just thrown together. These layouts are referred to as "borax" advertisements. Frequently, considerably more care is involved in making them than the reader would suppose.

EMPHASIS A good layout should make the advertisement as a whole prominent and also emphasize certain more important elements. One of the techniques for creating emphasis is *repetition*. A headline, an illustration, or a trademark, for example, may gain added emphasis if repeated several times. Another technique is *contrast* of size, color, or style. A small boy at the end of a row of six men, all six feet tall, will attract attention to himself. If you color just one element in a black-and-white advertisement, that element will be emphasized. In an illustration of a group of live models, include one mannequin and it will receive the emphasis. A third technique for achieving emphasis involves the use of white space. It must be used carefully if unity is to be achieved, but it can be used effectively for emphasis. Place a small pill in the optical center of an advertisement and surround it by lots of white space. It is as if a spotlight were on it!

CONTINUITY An advertisement is more often than not a part of a campaign. As such, it is helpful to establish a continuity in the layout design in order to achieve a cumulative effect. This helps to create an identity for the advertiser and provides for quick identification of the product and advertiser. This principle is useful in broadcast commercials as well.

MECHANICS OF LAYOUT Layout artists follow certain general rules in the mechanics of their production to achieve as nearly as possible the effect of the finished advertisement. One of these rules involves measuring out the space for the advertisement. If the space for an advertisement in a magazine measures seven inches by ten inches, the layout can use all the space contained within these dimensions. The margin of white space around the advertisement that appears in the actual publication is added to this size by the publisher. No rule should be drawn around the layout space unless it is purposely desired as a border. The proper technique is to define the outer limits of the space by drawing light, small guidelines away from the four corners.

By paying a premium charge, the advertiser may use the white margin around the advertising space. A page with no margin is called a *bleed* page, because the ink "bleeds" off the edges of the paper into the trim space of the page—that is, the part of the paper that is trimmed off in the binding process. The technique of handling guidelines mentioned above is applicable here.

In illustrations that are to have tonal values, such as photographs and wash drawings, the tonal values should be indicated by shading the drawing on the layout. Merely outlining the objects in the illustration fails to show the proper weight.

Headlines, subheads, and logotypes are lettered in on the layout to indicate the general type classification to be used and the weight of the type, which must be in keeping with the mood of the layout. Light

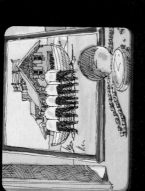

VIDEO: FADE IN: SNORKEL CAMERA EFFECT. SLOWLY WE ARE MOVING THROUGH OLD COAST GUARD ARTIFACTS CIRCA. 1800's. TELESCOPE, CAP, SEXTANT, OLD SHIP'S LOGS.

AUDIO:

ANNOUNCER(VO): Off the outer banks of North Carolina, where the seas are among the most treacherous in the world, there is a family known for saving lives.

VIDEO: TINTYPE OF GROUP OF COAST GUARD MEN STANDING BY THEIR LIFEBOAT.

AUDIO:

Their name is Midgett and they've been a Coast Guard family since the 1790's.

VIDEO: GROUP OF OLD MEDALS WITH RIBBONS. WE HESITATE ON ONE, BEGIN TO MOVE INTO IT.

AUDIO:

Over ten members of this remarkable family have received the Lifesaving Medal ...for their valor and courage.

VIDEO: CUT TO: E/C/U FLASHING RED LIGHT.

AUDIO:

SFX: OVEREMPHASIZE NATURAL SOUNDS, SIREN, ENGINE, ETC.

VIDEO: CUT TO: E/C/U HAND TURNS KEY.

AUDIO:

The Midgett family still serves in the Coast Guard. 32 strong. It's a tradition, helping others.

VIDEO: CUT TO: E/C/U WATER LEVEL EXHAUST PIPE BILLOWS SMOKE & WATER.

AUDIO:

You can start your own tradition in the Coast Guard...helping to protect our environment...

VIDEO: CUT TO: E/C/U PROFILE OF COAST GUARDSMAN FACE.

AUDIO:

saving lives...helping yourself to a fine, rewarding career.

VIDEO: CUT TO: CU: 44-FOOTER HEAD ON. BOW LIFTS. BOAT EXECUTES HARD PORT TURN AND HEADS AWAY FROM CAM. SUPER: HELP OTHERS/ HELP YOURSELF. 800-424-8883.

AUDIO:

The Coast Guard...America's foremost maritime law enforcement agency since 1790. See your Coast Guard recruiter. Or call us. Toll free.

Help others, help yourself.
800-424-8883

FIGURE 25-7

A television storyboard. (Original in color) By permission: U.S. Coast Guard.

guidelines should be used to keep lines straight. Hairline outlines of letters will not do, as they do not suggest the proper weight or the necessary amount of space for the type. The lettering should be careful enough to suggest the general type style that will be used.

Body copy, unless it is very large, is not lettered on the layout. Instead, it is indicated by drawing a series of parallel lines of appropriate thickness and darkness to indicate the weight of the type.

A finished layout to be submitted to a client for approval should contain no extraneous marks, such as mechanical instructions for typography and plate making, for these tend to distract from the appearance of the layout.

Advertising is a necessary lubricant for civilian economy. It keeps business flowing, prevents stagnation, introduces new products, develops new patents, promotes new business ideas. Taxing advertising would tend to reduce it; reduction of advertising would constrict business; constriction of business would result in fewer tax dollars: Therefore taxation on advertising would actually in the long run produce less revenue for the government.

CHARLES E. WILSON (1890–1972), Industrialist

READER'S DIGEST

SMALL-SPACE LAYOUTS

It is undoubtedly easier to prepare an attractive and effective layout for a full-page advertisement than for a smaller advertisement. Getting all the principles of good layout into a small space offers a real challenge to a layout artist. Such advertisements have a hard time competing for attention with larger advertisements and others the same size. The principles mentioned in this chapter are generally applicable to small advertisements, but small size requires greater ingenuity and creativeness on the part of the artist.

TELEVISION STORYBOARDS

After the television commercial script described in the last chapter has been agreed upon by those working on the account, the next step is usually the preparation of a *storyboard*. It should be noted, however, that there is nothing sacred about the sequence in developing the commercial. The script may not be written first. A creative team may, in fact, work backward, with an art director roughing out a storyboard before a word of copy is written.

The storyboard may be likened to the layout of a print advertisement. It will contain, in miniature size, sketches of the various scenes with instruction for video and the wording of the audio. It is used to get approval from the client for the commercial and as the basis for the production of the commercial.

Because the storyboard illustrations are stills, it is necessary to provide detailed instructions on the actions and camera techniques called for. This information is contained in the video instructions below each illustration. (These instructions are also used in scripts.) Since space is limited, abbreviations are commonly used. Some of the more frequently used instructions include:

CU	Close-up. This is a very close camera shot showing a single object or a single feature of that object in a scene.
ECU	Extreme close-up. This is simply a more extreme version of the instruction above. It is sometimes designated as BCU (big close-up) or TCU (tight close-up).
MCU	Medium close-up. It emphasizes the object but will include some other objects that are peripheral to it.
MS	Medium shot. This is a wide-angle shot of a number of objects, but not the whole set.
FS	Full shot. This is a shot of the entire set or object.
LS	Long shot. A full view of the object or set shot smaller than frame size to give the effect of distance.
Dolly	This refers to physically moving the camera toward or away from the subject. You can dolly in (DI) and dolly out (DO) or dolly back (DB).
Pan	This involves swinging the camera from one side of the set to the other to provide a panoramic view.
Zoom	Moving in or out from the object without blurring the image.
Super	To superimpose one image on another. This is frequently done to show the brand name over the scene being shot.
Diss	Dissolve (also DSS). Fading out one scene while at the same time fading in another.
Cut	Quick changing of one picture to another.
Wipe	An effect of erasing the picture from the screen.

In addition to carrying the spoken word, the audio will contain instructions on how these are to be delivered and instructions on music and sound effects. Two of the more frequently used instructions are voice-over (VO), an offstage voice (usually an announcer); and down-and-under, fading of music or sound effects so that voice can be heard over it. (The opposite effect is up-and-over.)

Unfortunately, even the best storyboards leave something to be desired, for the finished effect of the commercial will involve action, which the storyboard can only suggest. One technique for getting around this problem is referred to as *animatics*. There are several ways to produce animatics, but essentially it involves putting the storyboard frames on videotape and synchronizing this with the audio, which can be produced in rough form. It is possible to increase the amount of "action" in the video portion by adding more frames. In as little as a few hours, a commercial can be put together that can be heard as well as seen and that adds a sense of action even though stills are being used.

These animatics, which are relatively inexpensive to produce for commercials that will incur high time charges, are quite useful to research the effectiveness of alternative creative executions. They can be played to focus groups for quick pretesting to help determine impact and the communications effect of the commercial.

Layouts, Storyboards, and Art

ADVERTISING ART

Illustrations in advertising (including photography) are usually referred to as *art*. Most, although not all, print advertisements contain artwork, for art serves many important purposes. The decision to use artwork in an advertisement will depend on whether art will serve any of a number of purposes, such as to attract attention to the advertisement; to demonstrate the product or its effect; to emphasize certain features of the product; to clarify or illustrate headline and copy ideas; to transmit a visual image of the product or package or brand name to the mind of the consumer; to arouse interest in the advertising message or the product being featured; and to stimulate desire for the product.

Perhaps the first purpose of the major illustration in an advertisement is gaining attention. Beyond that, however, it should help to create interest—in the product advertised and in the advertisement. Thus, the artwork must be appropriate to the sales objective of the advertisement, and not an end in itself. Art can create interest in many ways. One is through depicting *action*. Because so much of our daily lives consists of action and observing action, we are very much aware of action, including that in the illustration of an advertisement. Another way art can be used to develop interest is through a *story* or *plot* illustration, which invites the reader to find out more. Art can use *realism* for interest; we tend to respond more easily to what we recognize. A wonderfully human quality possessed by everyone in some degree is *sentiment*. Who can turn the pages of a magazine without stopping to look at an advertisement showing a baby or a kitten? Despite critical condemnation, *sex* remains a much-used art technique for appealing to consumer interest. Provided that it is appropriately related to the selling situation, it is a powerful tool. *Adventure* also provides a useful theme for illustration. Its interest lies in escape and excitement, and it can take many forms, from pictures of far-off places to sports shots. Another form of illustration used to create interest is the *unusual*, which excites our curiosity, such as an illustration of how we may be living a hundred years from now. And, of course, there is *humor*. Everyone enjoys an amusing situation and a good laugh. These appeals to interest through art are not mutually exclusive, and any advertisement may combine several of them.

KINDS OF ARTWORK Once the art director and copywriter have determined the nature of the art, the next step is to determine the art medium. A host of art media are available for producing the illustration, and each has its own peculiar qualities that make it desirable, depending upon what is to be illustrated. The choice will be tempered somewhat, however, by production (technical) limitations, cost, and the time factor. Individual advertisements may use a number of illustrations involving several different art media. Furthermore, individual illustrations may combine several of these techniques; for example, a combination wash and line drawing, or a photograph with a line drawing superimposed. Among the more frequently used art forms are photography; wash drawings; line drawings; scratchboard; and pencil, crayon, and charcoal.

PHOTOGRAPHY As used in advertising, photography is generally considered a kind of artwork. Over the years, it has grown in popularity as an art form in advertising. Why use photography instead of some type of drawing? Because photography sees things in much the same way the eye sees them and has as its greatest attribute *realism*. Photography can show the pores in skin, the grain in wood, or the texture in cloth in a way few drawings can. It can bring an illustration to life. Furthermore, it tends to make the subject more believable. Photography can create a feeling of immediacy, giving the receiver a sense of being there. It can also stimulate emotional involvement, because people in a photograph are real. Commercial photography is by no means inexpensive, but in many cases, it can be more economical than drawings. Photography is not all "practical"; it can, indeed, be of such great beauty that it rivals other art forms.

Commercial photography has become quite sophisticated and increasingly flexible, so that many special effects are now possible. Probably most photographs have some imperfections or the need for corrections. Corrections are handled in part by the photographer in developing negatives and making prints and in part by retouchers, who work with air brush, dyes, and bleaches to improve the photograph. Whereas drawings sometimes require models and props, photographs always do. That is, there must be something physical to photograph. Sometimes photographers work "on location" to use natural settings, but more often they work in studios.

The art director must decide whether to use photography or drawings, depending upon the nature of the illustration. Suppose the task is to illustrate a cake. Obviously, no drawing can capture its texture and composition as well as a photograph. Here, a good photograph (especially in color) can make a picture so realistic that it activates the salivary glands. If a cake is to be photographed, one has to be baked, and baked just right, for the viewer is more critical viewing a two-dimensional picture than viewing the real thing. Then, of course, there must be just the right props—an appropriate cake plate, cake knife, and other accessories. If it is necessary to depict a small boy devouring a piece of that cake, a model must be hired. There are agencies for such purposes, but occasionally the art director or photographer will look for nonprofessional models if greater realism is wanted. Perhaps in this case, a red-haired, freckle-faced boy with a missing front tooth is called for. A

Dream House. *In Halifax, N.S., a pair of newlyweds advertised in the* Mail Star: *"Want modest home large enough to keep the bride from going home to her mother and small enough to keep the mother from coming to visit."*

TIME

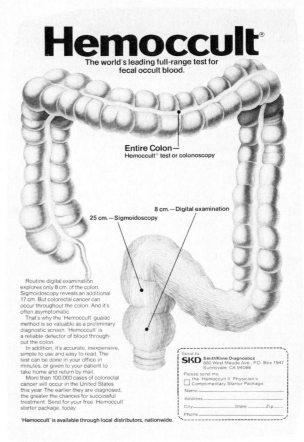

FIGURE 25-8

Tight wash drawings are frequently used in medical illustrations because although realism is desirable, photography would not be practical. (Original in color) *By permission: SmithKline Corporation.*

model agency may be unable to come up with such a model, and the "kid down the street" might do just fine.

WASH DRAWINGS Not all subjects to be illustrated can be photographed. Try photographing a person with eight arms! Or see if you can take a suitable picture of the inside of the stomach. When realism of the type that a photograph ordinarily captures is not possible photographically, a wash drawing comes close to it and overcomes the limitations of the camera, for drawing permits interpretation as photography does not.

Wash drawings are made with brush and India ink or lamp black diluted with varying amounts of water to give the desired tonal effect. There are two general types of treatment of wash drawings—*tight* and *loose*. A tight drawing is one that is detailed and tends more toward realism. People cannot always distinguish a tight wash drawing from a photograph in an advertisement. A loose wash drawing tends to be more impressionistic. This technique is used most frequently for fashion illustration, in which a sense of the fashion is desired rather than a realistic rendering of a specific item. Loose wash drawing omits much of the detail and may exaggerate; for example, the fashion figure tends to be quite elongated.

LINE DRAWINGS Line drawings are sometimes referred to as pen-and-ink drawings. They do not contain tonal values. An exception is the use of Benday; this is a photoengraving process in which continual tonal values are added to specific areas of line drawings to give body to the art. (This technique is also accomplished today through screen tint film, which can be applied directly onto the mechanical by an artist.) Except in these cases, however, line drawings tend to be simple and leave much to the imagination. Line drawings are typically less expensive than wash drawings or photographs and ideally suited to situations in which production limitations preclude good reproduction of tone and detail. Line drawings are probably most often used for small supplemental illustrations. Cartoons are generally drawn in this manner.

SCRATCHBOARD Scratchboard drawings are made by using a stylus to scratch through a surface of black on a white piece of drawing board. The result is a series of white lines on a black background (not to be confused with a reverse plate). This artwork has a special quality that gives an impression of fine workmanship, somewhat similar to the quality of an old woodcut.

PENCIL, CRAYON, AND CHARCOAL Pencil, crayon, and charcoal are used in advertising art less frequently than wash or line drawings. Therefore, they offer the advantage of novelty. These drawings tend to be informal and are therefore usually rendered in the form of a sketch.

OTHER ART MEDIA There is no limit to the media that can be used in advertising art. Any device capable of producing an illustration can be used, and occasionally an advertisement will even feature finger painting or collages. However, the techniques mentioned above account for most advertising art.

FIGURE 25-9

Three popular art techniques used in black-and-white advertisements. *Richard M. Schlemmer,* Handbook of Advertising Art Production, 2nd ed., *Englewood Cliffs, N.J.: Prentice-Hall, Inc., 1976. Printed by permission.*

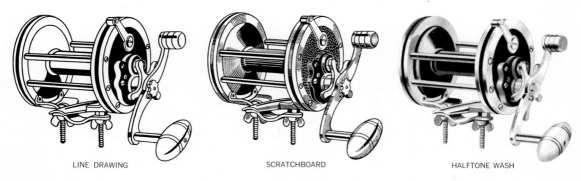

LINE DRAWING   SCRATCHBOARD   HALFTONE WASH

COLOR IN ADVERTISING ART   Over the years, the amount of color in print advertising has increased substantially, largely because of improved technology that has resulted in better color and lower cost. Because color advertisements cost more than black-and-white advertisements, they must offer some benefit to warrant the additional expense. Other things being equal, color offers the advantages of attracting attention; depicting subject matter more realistically; emphasizing a particular element; psychological stimulation or pleasure; and providing accurate representation of the product and package for easy recognition in self-selection at the point of purchase.

Whether color can achieve these ends better than black-and-white depends upon the nature of the product, the visualization, and the advertising objective. Illustrations of food, for example, do particularly well in color because color adds realism and appetite appeal and attracts greater attention. On the other hand, an advertisement for a different situation might do as well in black-and-white. In some cases, in fact, black-and-white is used because of its contrast in a book of mostly color advertisements.

The advertiser using color has two general choices. One is to use black and one additional color (sometimes, black and two colors, or two colors and no black). Color used in this manner serves primarily as an attention-getting device or to emphasize some particular element of the advertisement. The other option is to use the four-color process, which reproduces the full range of colors. When full color is used, color not only serves the purposes just mentioned but also creates great realism.

Almost all the art techniques mentioned earlier can be used with color. Color photography has advanced in technique to a considerable degree since photographers began working with color transparencies. The color counterpart of the wash drawing is the watercolor painting. In addition, oil painting is sometimes used for illustration art. Line drawings, pencil, and crayon can be worked in color. It should be noted that line illustration art or the other techniques drawn in black can be printed in color.

BUYING FINISHED ART   Because advertising agencies seldom have the art staff to do finished art, it must be bought from outside sources. There is a good reason for not maintaining a staff of artists to do finished art in an advertising agency. Different art techniques call for different talents, and one artist seldom excels in all the art media. Even a large advertising agency would probably not have enough art requiring any one technique to warrant the full-time services of an artist who excels in that technique. Moreover, different artists tend to specialize in different subject matter, such as fashion figures, action scenes, or lifelike furniture and appliances. Finally, different artists have different styles.

One job of the art director is to find the proper talent, negotiate with the artists or photographers, and guide them in producing the finished product. In addition to art directors, many large agencies employ art buyers, who, working with the art directors, specialize in this task alone. This is hardly surprising when one considers there are thousands of commercial artists in this country, not including photographers.

Artists generally work either freelance (frequently using a representative who also handles the business end) or through an art studio, which is a firm offering a variety of art talents. The art buyers and art directors keep extensive files on artists, including proofs or tear sheets of advertisements featuring their work. In addition, they continually interview artists and examine their portfolios. The cost of artwork will vary widely, depending on such factors as the reputation of the artist (some artists are so well known that their distinctive style and signature enhance the whole advertisement), the degree of difficulty, and the size of the artwork. The most important variable in the cost of art, however, is the medium in which it is to be used. Thus, national media will demand higher art prices than local media, and consumer more than trade.

Artwork is generally prepared larger than it is to appear in the finished advertisement (except in color photography, which uses transparencies, and art prepared for outdoor posters). The purpose of making artwork larger is to facilitate retouching and, through reduction, to make slight imperfections in the finished art less noticeable. In executing the finished art, constant attention must be given to the mechanical requirements of producing the advertisement, such as the paper stock, the printing process, and the type of press.

A major job of the art director is to prepare layouts for advertisements. There are a variety of layout forms, including thumbnail sketches and rough layouts used in the process of arriving at the finished layout, which is prepared for client approval. The comprehensive layout is a tighter version of the finished layout, prepared when the client is unable to adequately judge the advertisement in a rougher form. Working layouts are used as "blueprints" in the production of advertisements. Good layouts must consider factors such as balance, movement, unity, clarity and simplicity, emphasis, and continuity.

The counterpart of print layout in television is the storyboard. These still frame layouts of commercials are sometimes given movement through a technique called animatics, where the frames are put on videotape and a sound track synchronized to provide a dimension of movement.

Finished art for advertisements, in the form of drawings or photographs, is usually obtained by the art director or art buyer from freelance artists or studios. This provides greater flexibility in getting the most appropriate execution of the visual elements in the advertisement.

---

1. What is a comprehensive layout, and what is its purpose?
2. For what purposes are working layouts prepared?
3. Explain the principles of good layout and illustrate with examples of current advertisements.

4. What are animatics, and how are they used?
5. Where and how does an agency obtain finished art?
6. What purposes does art serve in an advertisement?
7. Why are photographs so frequently used in advertisements rather than drawings?
8. What is the difference between a wash drawing and a line drawing?
9. Why use color in advertisements?
10. Select current magazine advertisements to show five different kinds of artwork.

26

Print and Broadcast Production

After completing this chapter, you should be able to:
1. Understand the principles of good typography
2. Describe the various printing processes
3. Explain how radio commercials are produced
4. Outline the production of a television commercial

Although production details for print advertisements and broadcast commercials are handled by specialists within an advertising agency and advertising department and by suppliers on the outside, it is essential that people in all phases of advertising have some knowledge of these production operations. Production potentials and limitations in both print and broadcast will affect the whole advertising planning process and are especially important for copywriters and art directors in planning their basic approaches. They should also be directly involved in the production process to ensure that the finished advertisements are faithful to their creative conceptions.

PRINT PRODUCTION

Print production is a part of the graphic arts. Indeed, print production is itself a genuine art requiring great skill. With the great technological progress in the graphic arts, and especially the development of electronics, the problems of producing an advertisement have become very complex. There are many ways of handling almost every phase of production.

The job of the print production department in an advertising agency is to work with the creative departments in the preparation of reproducible artwork, to select the suppliers to do the various jobs (such as typography and photoplatemaking), to instruct them, and to check on the result to see that it meets the agency's standards. Type specifications may be handled by the production department, working with the art director, or they may be handled by a type director who is attached to the art department.

TYPOGRAPHY AND TYPESETTING

Typography is both art (design) and technology. It is that part of the graphic arts dealing with the selection and arrangement of type. Letters are composed photographically or by cathode-ray tube or laser output on photosensitive paper or film. Preparation of virtually all advertisements must include typographic considerations because of headlines and body copy. In some instances, because a special effect is desired that is unattainable through phototypography, the art director will have the headline hand-lettered. But even hand-lettering usually follows the principles applicable to good typography.

To most people, type is type. They do not generally take conscious notice of the fact that there are a great many kinds of letter styles. This is as it should be, because good typography does not draw attention to the type itself. But even though it is not consciously noticed, type is one more means of making an advertisement as effective as possible. Deciding which typeface is right for a particular advertisement is a complex task. Beyond the selection of the typeface, the designer faces the problem of using type correctly; for there are many factors to consider in getting the type to work for you.

LEGIBILITY Perhaps the single most important principle of typography is that type should be *legible*. Certain typefaces tend to be more legible than others, and type groups with which people are most familiar are generally most legible to them. Legibility, or, in a wider sense, readability, is also achieved through care in using the type. Generally *lowercase type* (small letters) is easier to read than *uppercase* type (capital letters). Proper spacing between words and letters increases not only the aesthetic qualities of type but also its readability. Likewise, spacing between lines of type (called *leading*, to rhyme with *heading*) can increase the legibility of the copy. The size of type also will affect legibility for obvious reasons.

Legibility also depends upon the length of the type line and where the line is broken. The eye is capable of spanning a certain number of words on the printed page at one time. If the line of type is too long, quick scanning of the line becomes more difficult. The reader is slowed down, the reader's place may be lost, and, most important, the reader may not get the message or may give up trying to read the advertisement. The correct line length will be determined, in part, by the type size. In body copy, it is not usually possible to complete a sentence in one line, so it is necessary to break the sentence and paragraph into a number of lines. Sometimes it will be necessary to split a word at the end of a line, but hyphenation should be kept to a minimum for highest legibility. Obviously, one would never want to hyphenate a brand name in the copy. Sometimes it may be necessary to break the line in a headline, but because the length of headlines can be varied, it should never be necessary to break a word. When a headline is broken into more than one line, the primary consideration is to break for meaning.

AESTHETICS OF TYPE Aside from enhancing legibility, good use of type will improve the "looks" of an advertisement, making it more effective. Type should be harmonious with the product advertised, the spirit of the advertisement, and the illustration. Different type faces suggest different feelings and moods. Some types suggest masculinity, others femininity. Some suggest the old, some the new. Some suggest delicacy, others strength. Some suggest formality, some informality.

TAgerta TAgerta TAgerta TAgerta TAgerta TAgerta TAgerta TAgerta TAgerta TAgerta TAgerta TAgerta TAge *6 Point*

TAgerta TAgerta TAgerta TAgerta TAgerta TAgerta TAgerta TAgerta TAgerta TAgerta TA *8 Point*

TAgerta TAgerta TAgerta TAgerta TAgerta TAgerta TAgerta TAgerta TAgerta *10 Point*

TAgerta TAgerta TAgerta TAgerta TAgerta TAgerta TAgerta *12 Point*

TAgerta TAgerta TAgerta TAgerta TAgerta TAgerta *14 Point*

TAgerta TAgerta TAgerta TAgerta TAgert *18 Point*

TAgerta TAgerta TAgerta T *24 Point*

TAgerta TAgerta TA *30 Point*

TAgerta TAgert *36 Point*

TAgerta T *48 Point*

TAgert *60 Point*

FIGURE 26-1
A type face in a variety of point sizes.

Contrasting type can be used for emphasis. One method is to use more than one type style, but caution should be taken so that contrast is not achieved by mixing too many different type faces, the result of which is a lack of unity. More subtly, contrast can be achieved by using variations on a single type family. (See Figure 26-2.)

TYPE GROUPS Some typefaces are similar enough in design to be regarded as a group. Authorities differ as to how many groups there are, but many agree on the following classifications: roman, sans serif, square serif, script and cursive, blackletter, and miscellaneous.

BODONI BOOK

ABCDEFGHIJKLMNOPQRSTUVWXYZ

abcdefghijklmnopqrstuvwxyz

1234567890

BODONI REGULAR

ABCDEFGHIJKLMNOPQRSTUVWXYZ

abcdefghijklmnopqrstuvwxyz

1234567890

BODONI BOLD

ABCDEFGHIJKLMNOPQRSTUVWXYZ

abcdefghijklmnopqrstuvwxyz

1234567890

ULTRA BODONI

ABCDEFGHIJKLMNOPQRSTUVWXYZ

abcdefghijklmnopqrstuvwxyz

1234567890

ULTRA BODONI ITALIC

ABCDEFGHIJKLMNOPQRSTUVWXYZ

abcdefghijklmnopqrstuvwxyz

1234567890

Ultra Bodoni Condensed

ABCDEFGHIJKLMNOPQRSTUVWXYZ

abcdefghijklmnopqrstuvwxyz

1234567890

FIGURE 26-2
Variations of a particular typeface.

ROMAN The most popular type group is *roman*. This group may be distinguished by the common characteristics of a combination of thick and thin strokes finished by *serifs*, short crosslines at the ends of unconnected strokes. Roman faces may be subdivided into two broad classifications: *old style* and *modern*, with a *transitional* group between these two. The old-style roman faces tend to be less severe and less formal than the modern faces. The modern roman faces have greater

Print and Broadcast
Production

formality and cleanness of line, reflected primarily in the serifs, which tend to be straight and thin.

SANS SERIF Sans serif types are the second most popularly used group of faces. They are also known as *block* (a term mainly used in Great Britain) or *Gothic*, but this latter term suggests Gothic architecture, the design of which is the very antithesis of block design. The sans serif group is characterized for the most part by its lack of serifs and the uniform (or relatively uniform) thickness of its strokes. Although the sans serif group is used for both display lines and body copy, it appears more frequently in the display lines, with roman for the body copy.

SQUARE SERIF Square serif letters usually have the same uniform (or nearly uniform) stroke thickness as sans serif styles. However, they are designed with rather pronounced square or slab serifs.

SCRIPT AND CURSIVE The *script* and *cursive* group is characterized by its similarity to handwriting. Script letters appear to be connected; cursives stand as individual letters. Because they are not very legible when set in quantity and in small sizes, these faces are used almost completely in headlines.

BLACKLETTER Blackletter or *text* is the oldest of all typefaces, having been used by Gutenberg, the inventor of metal typecasting. Its design, with heavy angular strokes and great ornamentation, makes it so illegible that its use in advertising is limited to brief special effects when a suggestion of great antiquity is desired.

MISCELLANEOUS A sizable number of ornamental typefaces do not fit into any of the other categories. Their designs differ considerably. They provide for novelty, and because of the special effects they can achieve in advertisements, they are frequently used for headlines.

TYPE FAMILIES Within the broad type groups, there are design families of related faces identified by names such as Caslon, Bodoni, and Futura. The design remains the same within a family, but there are variations in the weight, width, and angle of the characters. This provides contrast and emphasis without changing typefaces.

The most common variations within a type family are bold, extra bold, condensed, extended, and italic type. Not every family will contain all the possible variations. *Italics* were at one time a separate type group, but today they are designed as a slant version of other faces and therefore become a part of those families. In some sans-serif faces, italic is called *oblique*. There are also some other variations in type families, which usually have a novelty appeal. Letters may be *open* (tooled) or *shaded*, for example.

TYPE MEASUREMENT The graphic arts have their own system of measurement, which is generally used in advertising in place of the usual American system of measurement. Type size (height) is measured in

BODONI BOOK

ABCDEFGHIJKLMNOPQRSTUVWXYZ
abcdefghijklmnopqrstuvwxyz $1234567890

TIMES NEW ROMAN

ABCDEFGHIJKLMNOPQRSTUVWXYZ
abcdefghijklmnopqrstuvwxyz $1234567890

FUTURA MEDIUM

ABCDEFGHIJKLMNOPQRSTUVWXYZ
abcdefghijklmnopqrstuvwxyz $1234567890

NEWS GOTHIC

ABCDEFGHIJKLMNOPQRSTUVWXYZ
abcdefghijklmnopqrstuvwxyz $1234567890

STYMIE MEDIUM

ABCDEFGHIJKLMNOPQRSTUVWXYZ
abcdefghijklmnopqrstuvwxyz $1234567890

COMMERCIAL SCRIPT

ABCDEFGHIJKLMNOPQRSTUVWXYZ
abcdefghijklmnopqrstuvwxyz $1234567890

BERNHARD TANGO

ABCDEFGHIJKLMNOPQRSTUVWXY
abcdefghijklmnopqrstuvwxyz $1234567890

CLOISTER BLACK

ABCDEFGHIJKLMNOPQRSTUVWXYZ
abcdefghijklmnopqrstuvwxyz $1234567890

BROADWAY ENGRAVED

ABCDEFGHIJKLMNOPQRS
TUVWXYZ $1234567890

GALLIA

ABCDEFGHIJKLMNOPQRSTUVW
XYZ   1234567890

FIGURE 26-3

Examples of various type styles.

points. (There are 72 points to the inch.) The most common point sizes of type are 6, 7, 8, 9, 10, 12, 14, 18, 24, 30, 36, 42, 48, 60, 72, 84, 96, and 120 points. A unit of twelve points is known as a *pica*. (Thus, six picas equal one inch.) The pica measure is the most frequently used for measuring width in typography.

Another printer's measure is the *em*. The em measures in two directions at one time—height and width. Thus, it is a square measure. The size of an em depends upon the point size of the type. An 8-point em is 8 points high and 8 points wide; a 12-point em is 12 points high and 12 points wide and is generally referred to as a *pica em*. Half an em in width is known as an *en*.

The *agate line* is used as a measure in newspaper advertising. There are fourteen agate lines to the column inch. (Because the width of a column varies from one newspaper to another, an agate line measures 1/14 of an inch deep by the width of the particular newspaper column.)

PHOTOTYPOGRAPHY: DISPLAY COMPOSITION *Phototypography* encompasses the process of exposing letters of the alphabet (display or text) onto film or photosensitive paper, and the arrangement and makeup or stripping of such material. Photographic composition has become the major method of advertising typography, because of its economies, its sharpness, its aesthetic advantages (especially with regard to interletter and word spacing), its compatibility with the photoplatemaking processes, and its wide selection of available letter styles.

Photodisplay is the manual or semiautomatic composition and assembly of headlines and other display words. *Manual photodisplay* is usually called *process lettering* or *photolettering*. Photo images of individual letters (on film or paper) are assembled by hand into pleasing arrangements. This assembly is photographed to layout size. Alphabets are generally based on the work of lettering artists and calligraphers and are normally produced in a plethora of weights and widths. *Semiautomatic photodisplay* is produced photomechanically, one letter at a time, on photodisplay equipment like Photo Typositer or Staromat. Most of these machines permit the operator to see each letter image before exposing. This operator can determine the spacing between letter combinations, change the size of each letter, and modify letter proportions through built-in modification lenses. Photodisplay can also be produced on most automatic phototext equipment.

PHOTOTYPOGRAPHY: TEXT COMPOSITION Text composition is produced on a great variety of highly sophisticated computerized equipment. On one type of machine, text is composed photomechanically; on other equipment, it is generated on cathode-ray tubes or by laser beams. The photomechanical typesetter makes use of a light beam, which is flashed through negative letters on a disk, grid, or other master. The beam travels through a system of lenses and prisms and exposes film or photographic paper.

Many of these machines consist of two separate units, with computer memory included in both units: a front-end or input system, with a keyboard, etc.; and a photograph or printout output device. The front-end system normally performs all width calculations and the hyphenation and justification of the text. The data are stored on paper or magnetic tapes, which, in turn, activate the photographic output unit.

In the front-end systems, keyboards usually have a computer memory and a video display screen that allows the operator to read, edit, and frequently to position and make up the text input. Interfaces permit input from word-processing or from optical character-recognition equipment to be used directly for phototypesetting.

A more advanced equipment group, also highly computerized, does not use negative alphabet masters, but stores the letterforms as digital (binary) information in its computer memory. Characters are generated on a cathode-ray tube from which they are relayed through a lens system to film, photographic paper, or directly to lithographic printing plates. The characters can also be "written" with a laser beam. Digital typesetters work at ultrafast speeds of up to 10,000 characters per second. The front-end systems for digital typesetters are similar to those in the photomechanical equipment group.

Proofs made of photographically composed type fall into two categories: (1) submission or checking photographic proofs, usually made on diazo copying equipment; and (2) photographic reproduction proofs (repros), produced either by the diazo method or in a darkroom on photographic paper. Photographic repros can be pasted up by advertising agency art departments or studios into mechanicals (keylines) to be used by photoplatemakers as camera-ready copy. A more direct method is to have the typographer strip up all type film elements in exact position and size in the photomechanical. Contact films (either positive or negative) of the photomechanical are then sent to the photoplatemaker or printer to be combined with pictorial elements (halftones) for the production of printing plates or cylinders.

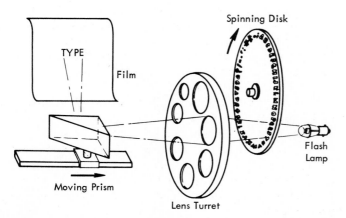

FIGURE 26-4

A schematic of the photocomposition method of setting type.

COLD-TYPE COMPOSITION Cold composition and *cold type* are misleading terms to describe phototypography, although they have been used in a wider sense to describe copy composed by means other than the use of outmoded metal type. A more specific name for cold type is *strike-on* or *direct-impression composition*, which is accomplished either on a standard typewriter, a Varityper, an IBM Selectric Composer, or any of the automatic justifying typewriter systems.

PRINTING PROCESSES

A number of methods of printing are available to advertisers. For magazine and newspaper advertisements, the printing method is dictated by the medium. In other advertising, the printing method is determined by such factors as production problems that may be encountered, quality desired, and costs. The three major printing processes are offset lithography, gravure, and letterpress. In addition, the screen printing process assumes some importance in poster advertising. The several other printing processes are not of sufficient importance to advertising production to be considered here.

OFFSET LITHOGRAPHY   The type of printing that has become the most widely used commercial printing method in recent years, used for most magazines and newspapers, is *lithography*. It is printing from a plane or flat surface. Therefore, it is sometimes called a *planographic* printing process. Its most important form for advertisers is called *photo-offset lithography*. Offset presses require the use of photographically prepared, flexible printing plates made of aluminum, zinc, or other lightweight image carriers. They are produced in much the same manner as photographic prints on paper. The plate is then bent over a cylinder of the press, and a roller applies water containing an additive. Because of the chemical properties of the plate, the water will adhere only to those parts of the plate that do not contain any printing images. The plate then comes in contact with the ink roller containing a greasy ink. Because grease and water will not mix, the ink adheres only to those portions of the plate that contain printing images and is rejected by the

FIGURE 26-5

The offset lithographic press. *From Richard M. Schlemmer,* Handbook of Advertising Art Production, 2nd ed., *Englewood Cliffs, N.J.: Prentice-Hall, Inc., 1976. Printed by permission.*

THE OFFSET LITHOGRAPHIC PRESS

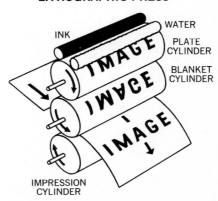

water. Now the inked plate comes in contact with another cylinder, called a *blanket*, and the ink is offset onto this rubber blanket, which in turn offsets it onto the paper.

Because the process is photographic, it is possible to work directly from phototypographic films or pasteups of reproduction proofs. As it requires little *make-ready* time and makes use of less expensive plates than most other printing methods, offset lithography is generally very economical. It is used extensively for direct mail advertising, posters, point-of-purchase advertising, catalogs, booklets, and book printing, in addition to newspapers and magazines.

GRAVURE   *Gravure* or *intaglio* printing is printing from a depressed surface and is usually done as *rotogravure* printing from cylinders on rotary presses. The ink is deposited by a roller in tiny cells on the cylinder. Because the roller also leaves ink deposited on the surface of the plate, it is followed by a knife, called a *doctor blade*, that removes the ink from the surface, leaving only the ink that is deposited in the cells. The paper, as it comes in contact with the plate, causes a suction that lifts the ink from it. Rotogravure can print only from copper cylinders, which are made directly from photographic positive films. These cylinders are chemically etched or electromechanically engraved to provide the cells, which differ in size and depth. The method is particularly well adapted to large-quantity printing and is generally used to print Sunday supplements to newspapers, large catalogs, folders, and packages. It is also used by many magazines.

LETTERPRESS   *Letterpress* or *relief* printing is the oldest printing process. Most newspapers and magazines used this method at one time, but in recent years, it has seen a very rapid decline. Essentially, it is

FIGURE 26-6

The gravure press. *From Richard M. Schlemmer,* Handbook of Advertising Art Production, *2nd ed.,* Englewood Cliffs, N.J.: Prentice-Hall, Inc., 1976. Printed by permission.

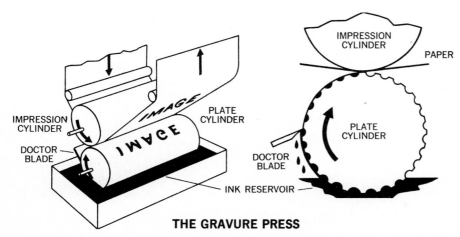

THE GRAVURE PRESS

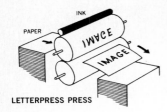

printing from a raised surface. Ink is applied by rollers across the raised surface. Then the paper is pressed against it and the image is transferred to the paper.

SCREEN PRINTING   *Screen Printing* or *silk screen* is a relatively simple printing process completely unrelated to the three mentioned above. Its use in advertising is primarily for limited production of posters and point-of-purchase display material. In its most basic form, screen cloth is fastened taut to a wooden frame. The design is then drawn on a lacquer film and the areas to print are cut away. The remaining film is bonded to the screen. Ink is then squeegeed through the screen onto the printing surface; the lacquer holds back the ink in the nonprinting areas. There are automatic and semiautomatic screen printing machines available, and synthetic materials are now generally used in place of silk.

COLOR PRINTING   All the printing processes discussed earlier in this chapter can perform in color. However, it should be noted that a press unit can print only one color at a time. Thus, if a job is to be printed in four colors, the paper must receive four impressions, one for

FIGURE 26-8

Silk screen printing. *From Richard M. Schlemmer,* Handbook of Advertising Art Production, 2nd ed., *Englewood Cliffs, N.J.: Prentice-Hall, Inc., 1976. Printed by permission.*

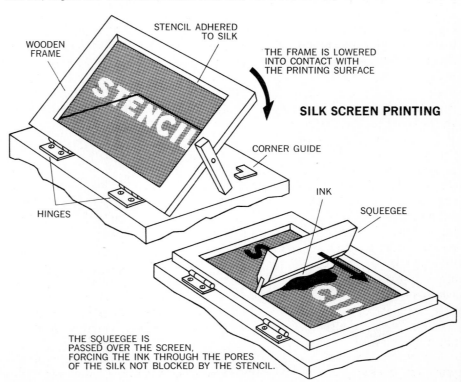

each color. Although there are presses that will print four colors (or more) with only one feeding of the paper, these presses are really a combination of several separate printing units, one for each color, and the paper, either in sheet or web form, is carried through the press from one cylinder to the next.

PHOTOPLATEMAKING In order to print by offset, rotogravure, or letterpress today, it is necessary to have an image carrier (plates or cylinders), and these are prepared by various photomechanical methods using negative or positive films of type and art (mechanical paste-ups) to prepare the printing surfaces. Lasers have also been used to scan mechanicals and transfer the image to photosensitive plates, but they have not figured importantly in advertising thus far.

There are two kinds of images, *line* and *halftone*. Line images consist of solid tones and white space. Most types make line images, as do pen-and-ink drawings. Halftones consist of continuous tonal values from light to dark, such as those found in photographs and wash drawings. When copy containing tonal values is reproduced, it appears to the eye that there are various shades. In black-and-white printing, these appear as shades of gray. But of course, black ink can print *only black*. The eye simply tends to blend black and white to create an illusion of gray. The more white in relation to black, the lighter the gray tones; the more black in relation to white, the darker the gray tones. Stated simply, halftone printing makes use of a screening process between the camera copy and the photographic film to break down the grays into a series of black dots (the printing ink) on a white background (the printing paper), in the proportion and size necessary to achieve the proper illusion. In the screening process, the *number* of dots per inch is determined by the screen size (usually between 65 and 150 lines to the inch), and the *size* of the dots will vary depending upon the intensity of the light reflection passing through the screen. If a halftone reproduction is enlarged through magnification, we see only solid black dots and white spaces. (See Figure 26-9.)

Films are thus made of the halftone art through screens and of line art without screening. In the case of an advertisement containing both halftone and line material, the films can be stripped and combined. The filmmaker will then use the film either to make an off-press proof with photosensitive materials, or to make a printing plate for press proofs. When the proof is approved, copies of the film and proof are sent on to the printer (for advertising, this is usually a newspaper or magazine), where printing plates are made.

For gravure printing, film supplied by the advertiser (in which line material as well as halftone material is screened) is placed over photosensitive cylinders, which are then exposed and developed. The cells that must receive the printing ink are then created through an etching process that cuts into those portions of the metal not protected by photographic emulsion.

Since there are still newspapers and magazines using letterpress printing, photoengravings must be made from the films of the mechani-

The most important job of an advertisement is to center all the attention on the merchandise and none on the technique of presenting it.

ROY DURSTINE,
Advertising Agent

READER'S DIGEST

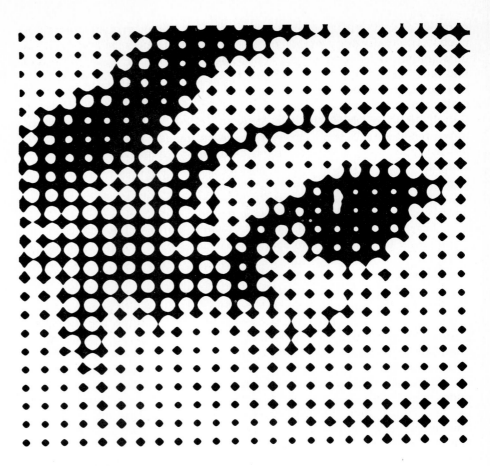

FIGURE 26-9

A greatly enlarged halftone showing the effect of screening. By propping up the book and moving away from it sufficiently, you should discover part of a photograph.

cal paste-up. As in the case of gravure, an etching process is used in this instance to eat away metal surrounding the raised printing surface.

COLOR REPRODUCTION   For the reproduction of full-color illustrations containing tonal values, it is necessary to separate the various colors so that a separate plate may be made for each. The most commonly used technique is the *four-color process*.

All colors can be reduced to the primary printing colors of magenta ("process red"), yellow, and cyan ("process blue"). That is, these primary colors, when combined, will produce all the colors of the spectrum. In addition to the primary colors, black will provide detail strength and neutral shades of gray. By photographing the color copy through filters of green for the magenta, violet for the yellow, orange for the cyan, and a special filter for the black, the colors can be separated from the original. After the separated colors are corrected (that is, improved for color accuracy by masking), the separations are photographed again, this time through a screen, to make halftone films. For each color, the screen is turned to a different angle so that the resultant dots, when they are combined on the press, will not completely overlap and will therefore reproduce an accurate rendition of the original color. In printing from four-color process plates the printing sequence is normally yellow, red, blue, and black. (See Figure 28-10).

Instead of separating the colors on camera, many engravers are now employing electronic color separation equipment called *scanners*. In electronic page make up systems, these scanners can automate the complete process from color separation to retouching to combining images in final page form, producing the final films or image carriers.

BROADCAST PRODUCTION

Although the same copywriters and art directors create both print advertisements and broadcast commercials, because of the technology involved with each, production for print and broadcast are two entirely different departments with different personnel. Broadcast production is in turn divided between radio and television, and each of these is considered below.

PRODUCING RADIO COMMERCIALS

Radio commercials may be *live* or *recorded*. Live commercials are infrequently used today by national advertisers, but retailers still use them to some extent, having them delivered by local station personalities. The perceived advantage is that these personalities may add a kind of endorsement value merely by presenting the advertiser's message, and by their very nature, they add a sense of immediacy. But despite the opportunity for last-minute copy correction, critics of live presentation argue that such live commercials sound like amorphous disc-jockey patter mixed in with the time, traffic conditions, weather, and other pat radio pap, and, of course, they run the risk of error.

Transcribed commercials offer the advertiser complete control over advertising, short of an equipment failure. They permit more complex scripts, calling for musical accompaniment, sound effects, and a number of voices. However, because they are usually more complex and involve the additional steps of recording, they are obviously more expensive than live commercials.

RECORDING RADIO COMMERCIALS The production problems a radio commercial presents will depend upon the complexity of the commercial. The format of live commercials is generally simple, requiring only a carefully typed script with adequate instructions.

Because recorded commercials are usually more complex, they involve more production problems. The advertising agency may have a radio commercial producer on its staff, or it may employ the services of a freelance producer. In either circumstance, the actual production of the commercial is generally done at a recording studio where the proper facilities and equipment are available.

The first problem is to cast the commercial. This may involve finding the right announcer with the right voice for a particular commercial, or it may involve casting professional actors. If music is used, the producer must decide whether to use music already recorded or hire a composer (or an arranger, if there is already a musical theme) and the necessary musicians. Sometimes it is possible to secure the services of name instrumental and vocal talent for such purposes, although the cost of name talent is high. Sound effects may be available from recorded sources, or they may be tailor-made for the occasion, depending on the demands of the commercial.

After all the talent components are gathered, a director will supervise rehearsals until the performers are ready to record. As a general rule, several takes will be made of the commercial and the best one selected. The recording is then put on the requisite number of tapes and supplied to the stations.

Radio commercials are often produced by a series of separately developed component steps that are ultimately combined in the finished product. A typical production schedule might involve having music tracks "laid down" in the morning and the announcer recorded in another session in the afternoon. All the elements on the various tape tracks are then put together in an editorial session called the *mix*. Here, music levels are adjusted, the announcer "laid on top" of the music, and then sound effects added to the tape where needed.

When advertisers wish to tie in with local distributors of products, the advertisers provide for *tagging* the commercials with the names and addresses of the local retailers, to be added by the local announcer at the end of the recording.

PRODUCING TELEVISION COMMERCIALS

Advertising agencies with large television commercial expenditures maintain television production departments. The agency television producer is responsible for the administrative end of producing the commercial after script and storyboard have been approved by the client. The job of the producer will vary somewhat depending upon whether the commercial is to be live, taped, or filmed. Live commercials are produced in the television studio. Taped and filmed commercials are made either on location or in production studios.

The agency producer acts as a liaison, conveying to the production company and the director for the commercial the intentions and requirements of the agency with regard to the commercial. The producer's responsibility is to see that the production company produces, at the very least, the storyboard that the agency "sold" to the client. The producer must also keep costs under control (within budget), since shooting a commercial tends to be a very expensive business.

Ideally, the copywriter and art director responsible for developing the commercial will stay involved, working with the producer, through all phases of the commercial's production. This is important to the integrity and interpretation of the original creative idea and it ensures that the finished product will reflect that idea. It also provides an opportunity to embellish the concept in actual production. No matter how much thought goes into the storyboard, when there are sets, people, sound effects, and action, there are bound to be changes and improvements, and the creative team can be very helpful in this process.

LIVE, TAPED, AND FILMED COMMERCIALS   The live television commercial, even more so than live programming, is almost a thing of the past. This is certainly true for most national advertising and for even a very large part of local television commercials with the growth and development of videotape. To be sure, live commercials are inexpensive when compared to film and tape, but they are so terribly limited in what can be done live—no set changes, no time lapses, no location shots, and most important, no opportunity to correct errors. When an occasional commercial is done live, it is usually done by a local station personality or a national star salesperson. Even in these cases, however, what appears to be live may have been taped some period before air time to permit editing and correcting errors.

Tape, or more correctly, *videotape,* and film offer considerably more flexibility than live production in terms of effects that can be achieved. These include stop motion (a means of providing "life" for inanimate objects), animation (a cartoon technique), freeze frame (an effect of stopping and holding the action), location shooting, time-lapse effects, and numerous optical effects. They also offer control to the advertiser, who can be assured of the commercial production before it appears on television. Initially, the sort of flexibility we have been talking about was available only on film, but as tape has advanced technologically, it has become possible to achieve all the same effects as film. What is more, tape has an additional advantage over film in that it provides for immediate playback, so that you can see what you have without having to wait for film developing. But film is still extensively used, because tape cannot equal the quality, subtlety, richness, mood, and versatility of film. Only if tape can catch up with film in aesthetic values will it overtake film in use. Still, tape has its place—for example, when shooting in a studio with an on-camera announcer. Here, tape can provide a visual quality of immediacy—the same effect as that of the news programs. Perhaps the decision on whether to use film or tape should be determined in terms of the particular creative idea and how it can best be presented. In practice today, the vast majority of national-advertiser commercials are done on film, although they are then in most cases distributed to stations on tape.

SHOOTING THE COMMERCIAL   After the commercial idea has been developed into a script and storyboard and is approved by the client, the television commercial has to be produced. In almost all cases, production takes place outside the advertising agency, by either a production company or a television station studio. Deciding where to have the commercial produced will depend, first of all, on the amount that can be spent. Of course, the very nature of the commercial (size of cast, complexity of the story, etc.) will affect the cost. But beyond that, there is a wide variation in cost, depending where the work is done. A television station studio videotape might be done for as little as a few hun-

Commandment 8-a. *In Levittown, Pa., thefts of top soil from the grounds of the Hope Lutheran Church stopped after the Rev. Charles L. Ertman posted a sign reading: "Thou shalt not steal church top soil."*

TIME

dred dollars, whereas a production company film can run as high as several hundred thousand dollars.

Starting with a budget figure in mind, a production company must be chosen from approximately 1,000 such firms. Different production companies charge different rates, depending upon their expertise, the production talent they employ, and the facilities at their disposal. Furthermore, different companies have different talents. And they may further be divided between animation and live action. Agencies usually have or can obtain sample reels of commercials these production companies have done for others. Having narrowed down the choices, say, to three companies, the agency television producer should then get bids based on scripts, storyboards, and other pertinent information submitted. Care should be exercised to be sure that it is known who pays for what, and the final selection should consider price, but only in terms of the quality of production anticipated. Bids may be made on a fixed or cost-plus basis.

After a contract has been issued to the production company, the casting director—from the agency, production company, or freelance—needs to start casting the commercial. Naturally, it is important to choose a cast carefully so as to avoid ruining a good, expensive commercial through poor performance. Commercials may use professional actors, including star personalities, or "real people" (amateurs chosen because their lack of acting skills can enhance credibility). These performers should be interviewed in tryouts, and it is helpful to view them on a television monitor to get a feel of how they will appear on the screen. Putting them on videotape affords an opportunity to compare different talent trying for the same role. Since the talent must be paid not only for making the commercial but also in residual payments each time the commercial is aired, the total cost for the cast can be quite substantial. Therefore, it is a good idea to minimize the number of performers needed, and to weigh the additional cost of star personalities against the benefits perceived.

Prior to the actual day of production, a meeting is held by the agency producer and creative team, the production company director, and such other people as the casting director, set designer, and, depending upon the nature of the commercial, perhaps a home economist and a fashion coordinator. At this meeting, all the details of the shooting should be reviewed. The cast should be definitely set; set designs and/or props should be decided; and any special considerations should be noted.

The day of the shooting is now at hand—either on a sound stage or on location. Besides all the previously mentioned personnel, there will be a film crew, including camera people, a script clerk, sound people, electricians ("gaffers"), grips, and, according to the nature of the production, numerous others. Cameras are ready to roll. Scenes will be shot out of sequence, with the most difficult ones first. Generally, several *takes* are made for each scene so that the best can be selected.

A 30-second television commercial will end up as 45 feet of 35-millimeter film (or 18 feet of 16-millimeter film); but chances are it will take a whole day of shooting and use from 4,000 to 15,000 feet of film! Bad takes will be discarded, but all the promising ones will be developed and the *dailies* (or *rushes*) will be viewed, usually the next day. Ideally, there will be enough good takes so that they can be edited without any further shooting.

Editing is done by the production company or by independent editing houses. The editor examines the dailies to select footage for a *rough cut,* with the remaining film (*outtakes*) being set aside. Editing is crucial to the whole production process if the very best frames from all the film that was shot are to appear in the finished commercial rather than on the "cutting-room floor."

This *rough cut* film and the sound track are now viewed in combination, through what is called an *interlock.* (Voice-over and other special sound and music effects are recorded separately.) After corrections are made, the film and sound are combined on a single film, and opticals (special effects, such as wiping and dissolving) and titles are added. The resulting print, known as an *answer print,* is viewed for adjustment of light balance in the various scenes. After these final corrections and client approval, the necessary number of *release prints* are prepared and sent to the networks and stations for their use.

When animated or stop-motion commercials are to be filmed, there are obvious changes from the procedure described above. In animated commercials, instead of a cast and props, drawings must be prepared and then photographed. Stop motion may involve the use of talent and props, but filming takes the form of a number of still shots with movement of talent or props taking place between shots.

Technology in the field of television commercial production moves so quickly that it is difficult to stay with the latest developments. Developments in electronics such as computer-generated graphics offer new opportunities for animation for everything from the product to the logotype. Every time you see a new technique in a movie or on a television show, chances are that it can be incorporated into a television commercial to more effectively attract and hold the audience in order to deliver the message and make the sale.

CREATING A TELEVISION COMMERCIAL: LITE BEER FROM MILLER

This is the story of the creation of a television commercial for Lite beer from Miller.[1] The individual creative effort behind the particular commercial is part of a bigger creative strategy that led to this now-famous campaign. And this, in turn, is part of the brand's overall marketing objectives and strategy. This campaign has won at least one award every year since the brand went national and shows no signs of weakening.

BACKGROUND　The first low-calorie beer was introduced in New York in 1964 but was abandoned after only six weeks. Three years later, two other breweries tried again, this time with some moderate success, but still with a problem—poor flavor. One of these was Meister Brau's Lite beer, targeted to dieting women. However, the amount of beer consumption by women had always been low, and although initial trial for the brand was good, repeat purchase was not.

In general, the brewing industry looked at low-calorie beer as a novelty for at best a marginal part of the market, and believed that it would therefore have no appeal to heavy beer drinkers.

In 1970, Philip Morris Incorporated acquired the Miller Brewing Company and sent in a new management team recruited from its tobacco operations. At that time, Miller was eighth in the industry, but the new management was intent on improving its position. Miller's principal brand, High Life, was repositioned, with a change in the advertising theme line from "The champagne of bottle beers" to "Miller time." And management looked for additional opportunities to increase its market share. Thus, in 1972, Miller bought a number of brands from the ailing Meister Brau brewery in Chicago, including Meister Brau Lite. Five years after its introduction, this low-calorie brand was still managing to hold onto some distribution in several midwestern states. Unlike most of the industry, Miller management believed that there was still a potentially good marketing opportunity for a low-calorie, low-carbohydrate beer, and that with better marketing strategies, packaging, and advertising, greater success could be achieved.

A study of sales data for Meister Brau Lite showed that it was doing quite well in Anderson, Indiana, a blue-collar steel town. So the Miller people set out to find out why. Research had shown that negative consumer attitudes toward low-calorie beers resulted from their poor *taste* and from an appeal to *diet* drinkers rather than heavy beer drinkers. But the real market for beer was among "heavy" drinkers (eight or more 12-ounce cans a week), because demographics for heavy beer drinkers showed that this 30 percent of the market consumed 80 percent of the volume. It was made up largely of men, aged 18 through 49, skewed lightly toward blue-collar workers.

Interviews with *heavy drinkers* in Anderson indicated that they drank Lite because *it did not fill them up as much as regular beers*, thus permitting them to drink more. Further research in other markets substantiated this contention—provided that such a beer would compare favorably in taste to regular beers. Universally among heavy drinkers, it was agreed that low-calorie beer was definitely feminine, and therefore it was reacted to negatively.

MARKETING OBJECTIVES The marketing objective was now clear: to position Lite beer as a beer that was less filling, thereby permitting greater consumption by heavy drinkers. It was essential to avoid a low-calorie or feminine beer image. And taste had to be there.

Miller's Master Brewing Department was assigned the task of developing a less-filling (low-calorie and low-carbohydrate) beer with all the taste of a regular beer. In a little over a year, they came up with just such a brew, and it was branded Lite (the registered trademark now owned by Miller), but without the Meister Brau name. Because it

FIGURE 26-10

A Lite advertisement showing the package designs.
By permission: Miller Brewing Company.

was felt that calling it *Miller's Lite* would result in cannibalization of the Miller name without any increase in total Miller volume, it was decided early on to refer to the brand as "Lite Beer from Miller." Although flavor was believed to be the key factor in the anticipated success of this new product, and the brand name *Lite* was an important shorthand way of summing up product attributes, packaging was also deemed to be a very important element—especially since consumers frequently held it in their hands for long periods of time.

The communications objectives for Lite appeared obvious. First, it would be necessary to overcome any negative perceptions that might arise when "low-calorie" was mentioned. Second, it was essential to masculinize the product. Finally, it was necessary to reassure heavy drinkers that the product was a legitimate, real beer—with an added benefit.

To accomplish these objectives, three promotional concepts were developed. These were (1) a less-filling concept, "Lite leaves room for

FIGURE 26-11

A newspaper advertisement for Lite. *By permission: Miller Brewing Company.*

more"; (2) a low-calorie concept, "I'm man enough to admit I was wrong about a low-calorie beer"; and (3) a taste concept, "The beer for bigger thirsts." Each of these was then tested with a concept/use predictive model. From these tests Miller hoped to get not only data on the new Lite trial and repeat sales but, more important, the kind of volume repeaters would continue to give to the brand—a vital factor in this heavy-user market.

Results of the tests showed a high interest in trying the brand. Repeat purchase was also extremely high. (In fact, the taste of the new Lite was so good that, where it was used as a "control" product, masquerading as a regular, popular, full-caloried brand, it was also very successful.) The key factor, however, was what happened to volume as a result of exposure to the "less-filling" concept. Heavy drinkers interpreted that concept as management had hoped—as their being able to drink more. One-third fewer calories was looked at not as a female-oriented diet appeal, but as the fact that heavy drinkers could drink

BANK SHOTS, TRICK SHOTS AND OTHER TABLE MANNERS.

by Steve Mizerak

I'm gonna teach you a coupla things that'll 1) impress your friends, and 2) maybe lose some friends.

All you need is good eyesight, a little dexterity, and three essentials: a pool table, pool cue, and some Lite Beer from Miller.

CHEAP SHOTS

Here's a goodie. I call it the "Cheap Shot." Place a ball on the edge of the corner pocket. Then, take a half-dollar and lean it against the side rail at the other end of the table. (If you don't have a half-dollar, you can always write home to your parents: they'd love to hear from you.)

Tell your friends you're gonna sink the ball in the corner, using the half-dollar as a cue ball. It's not hard. Hit the coin solidly on the edge, just above the center, and it will roll along the rail knocking the ball in the pocket. But don't forget to scoff up the half-dollar. Because you're not supposed to lose money doing trick shots—just win Lite Beers.

THE COIN TRICK

This one drives people nuts. Place a ball on the head spot. With the chalk, make a circle around it, approximately 8" in diameter. Then put a quarter or half-dollar on top of the ball. (Yes, you can use the same one from before, or you can write home to your parents again.) Place the cue ball behind the foot line and have your friends

LITE BEER FROM MILLER. EVERYTHING YOU ALWAYS WANTED IN A BEER. AND LESS.

try to knock the coin out of the circle. Chances are, they won't be able to (this is a good time to work on your Lite Beer and act smug).

When you shoot, do one of two things: hit the object ball head-on with follow-through so the cue ball knocks the coin out, or hit the cue ball very, very slowly so the coin rolls off the object ball.

TABLE MANNERS

Now for simple table etiquette. After you've "hustled" your friends, you gotta keep 'em. So do what I call "Clearing the Table." Simply offer to buy the next round of Lite Beer. They'll all clear the table fast and head for the bar (or to your room or apartment). Then, once they all have Lite (just one apiece—you're not too rich, remember), tell them with Lite in hand and a smirk on your face that your shots were no big deal—you were just showin' off.

FIGURE 26-12

A print advertisement for Lite. *By permission: Miller Brewing Company.*

three beers with the feeling of having consumed only two-thirds that amount.

THE CREATIVE STRATEGY   The heavy beer drinker was now clearly targeted as the Lite market. The objective of Lite advertising was thus to convince heavy drinkers that Lite was a regular beer, but better than regular beer *because it was less filling*. Therefore, the primary product attribute was that it was "less filling," with "one-third fewer calories" as the reason-why support. Lite was now competing directly with all other beers for a share of the heavy-drinker market. The theme would be, "Everything you always wanted in a beer. And less." This fun, play-on-words slogan was to provide direction for the whole advertising campaign.

The primary medium for the promotion of Lite would be television, so the creative strategy was to evolve around television commercials, and it went through a number of stages before it took its final format. It was generally felt that masculinity had to be the most important element, because it would make both the product and the selling proposition acceptable. It was also decided to use a spokesperson format—and to use well-known personalities whose very physical appearance, demeanor, and fame would be compatible with a regular beer.

The advantages provided by the personalities were perceived as providing endorsement value and masculinity that would be unquestioned. Because of the enjoyment and fun aspects of beer drinking, care was taken not to appear too serious. Brand management and agency personnel agreed that the spokesperson should not present a hard-selling pitch. What they wanted to achieve was an image that would suggest to a viewer that this was the kind of personality with whom you could sit down and have a beer. Its purpose was to provide some warmth and permit the consumer to empathize with the personality.

To reinforce the regular-beer positioning to Lite and to provide an appropriate forum for the personalities, the commercials would be filmed on location in unquestionably beer-drinking environments.

The first commercials featured mystery writer Mickey Spillane and former running back for the New York Jets football team, Matt Snell.

The brand was put into test market in July 1973 and was rolled out nationally by 1975. Initial sales were so much greater than anticipated that the roll-out was temporarily halted while production caught up with demand. Trial was good. Repeat sales were good. And those heavy drinkers to whom the campaign was targeted became heavy drinkers of Lite.

Additional commercials were executed. Appropriate nonathletes, people who were well known and would be perceived as regular, masculine beer drinkers, were hard to find. So former athletes were used primarily. They worked very well, presenting a great combination of "beeriness" and masculinity. Although humor was interjected into the commercials indirectly, it was decided to give it more emphasis. The personalities' poking fun at themselves served to humanize them in a

TWO OF THE NICEST, SWEETEST GUYS EVER TO PLAY FOOTBALL ON DRINKIN' DOWN BEER AND EATIN' UP QUARTERBACKS

by Bubba Smith and Dick Butkus

BUBBA: Now that we're not playin' football anymore, we spend more time poppin' tops off cans of Lite Beer from Miller than poppin' quarterbacks.

DICK: But our favorite topic of conversation over a couple of Lite Beers is still the art of playin' defense.

BUBBA: Yeah. The bigger we were, the harder they fell.

DICK: Very true. Being big helps give you presence. What I call *winning through intimidation.*

BUBBA: But you also have to play smart. Like watching the guy in front of you for a tip. Sometimes the position of a guard's feet'll tell you where he's gonna go once the ball is hiked. Feet can tell you a lot. I guess that's why shoes have tongues.

DICK: But smart guys remember they're on a team. Work with a partner. Try to draw players, so maybe *he* can get through. This technique also works well when you want to get a Lite Beer

in a crowded bar.

BUBBA: And drinkin' Lite Beer is one of the *smartest* things you can do. Because Lite's less fillin', so it won't slow you down.

DICK: Sure. And even though we're not playin' anymore, after years of eatin' up quarterbacks, it's nice to relax with the great taste of Lite Beer.

BUBBA: You might say we've gone from being heavy hitters to Lite drinkers. Right, Mr. Butkus?

DICK: Right, Mr. Smith.

EVERYTHING YOU ALWAYS WANTED IN A BEER. AND LESS.

© 1982 Miller Brewing Co., Milwaukee, Wis.

FIGURE 26-13

Another print advertisement for Lite. *By permission: Miller Brewing Company.*

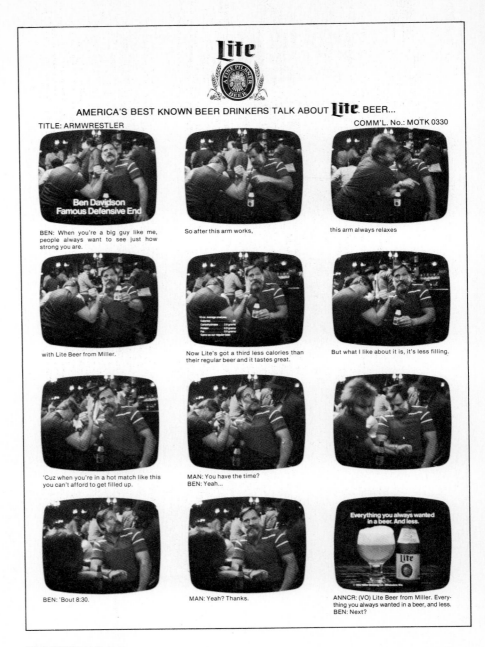

FIGURE 26-14

One of the Lite commercials. *By permission: Miller Brewing Company.*

way that cut the usual distance between viewers and spokespersons—particularly famous ones. The humor also served to make the whole proposition more credible.

As a final development in the executions, it was decided to reinforce the concept of good product taste with an argument format. Thus,

FIGURE 26-15

Another of the Lite commercials. *By permission: Miller Brewing Company.*

"Tastes good" was countered with "Less filling," and both points were reinforced.

Each year, in addition to the individual personality commercials, there was a Lite All-Star reunion commercial featuring the earlier personalities.

Print and Broadcast
Production

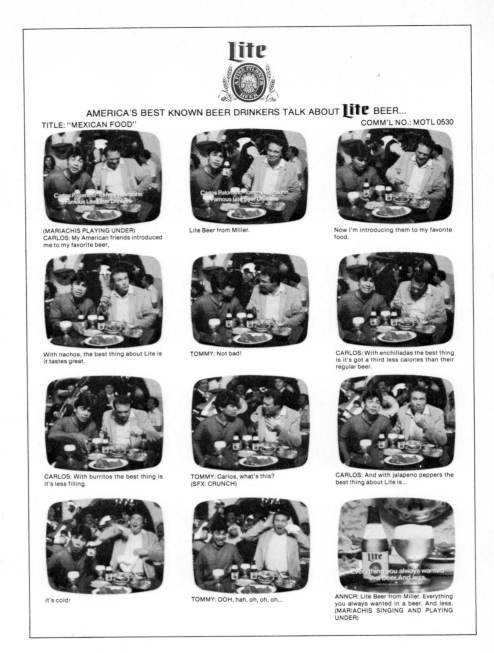

FIGURE 26-16

Still another of the Lite commercials. *By permission: Miller Brewing Company.*

While television was and continues to be the major medium, print has also been used. For the most part, the print advertisements represent "translations" for the television commercials, using the same television personalities.

AMERICA'S BEST KNOWN BEER DRINKERS TALK ABOUT Lite BEER...

COMM'L NO.: MOTK 0930   TITLE: "ALUMNI BOWLING"

JONES: Deacon's my name, and bowling's my game.

MADDEN: Gutter Ball! Gutter Ball!

BUTKUS: (VO) How you going to score that? MARTIN: Come on, three strikes and you're out.

HEINSOHN: We just won another round of Lite Beer from Miller.

RED AUERBACH: Well, Lite sure tastes great!

CROWD: LESS FILLING!!! TASTES GREAT!!!

POWELL: Hold it! Hold, it, Jim.

You're going the wrong way. There it is down there.

MIZERAK: Eight ball in the pocket.

BUTKUS: Hey Bubba, this ball doesn't have any holes in it.

SMITH: Now it does.

MEREDITH: The score is all even.
NITSCHKE: Last frame. Who's up?

CARTER: Rodney...

CROWD: RODNEY???
BUTKUS: Got to be a mistake.

DANGERFIELD: Hey you kidding. It's a piece of cake.

DAVIDSON: All we need is one pin Rodney.

ANNCR: (VO) Lite Beer from Miller. Everything you always wanted in a beer. And less.

MADDEN: I didn't get my turn yet. I'm gonna break this tie.

FIGURE 26-17

The previous year's alumni commercial for Lite. *By permission: Miller Brewing Company.*

AMERICA'S BEST KNOWN BEER DRINKERS TALK ABOUT Lite BEER...

TITLE: "ALUMNI SOFTBALL"

(SFX: CROWD CHEERING THROUGHOUT)
BILLY MARTIN: We're up 15.

We got this game won.
DICK WILLIAMS: Yeah! You get to buy the Lite Beer from Miller.

RED: Yeah, Lite's less fillin'.

TASTES GREAT TEAM: Tastes great!

LESS FILLING TEAM: Less filling!
TASTES GREAT TEAM: Tastes Great!

BILLY MARTIN: One out to go.
DICK WILLIAMS: Yeah, what can they do to us now?

(SFX: HORN BLOWS)
RODNEY: Here you are, keep the change.

DICK BUTKUS: Hey look, there's Rodney!
(TASTES GREAT TEAM ALL LAUGH)

LEE: (GIGGLING) My turn.
FRANK ROBINSON: Any pinch hitters left.

BOB UECKER: Here I am.

TASTES GREAT TEAM: Come on Lee! Come on Lee!
(LEE HITS HOME RUN & SCREAMS)

MICKEY SPILLANE: All right, Doll!

ANNCR: (VO) Lite Beer from Miller. Everything you always wanted in a beer. And less.

JOHN MADDEN: Wait a minute, this game isn't over yet. I caught that ball . . .

FIGURE 26-18

The current alumni commercial for Lite. *By permission: Miller Brewing Company.*

Since the acquisition of Miller by Philip Morris Incorporated, the brewery moved its industry position from eighth to second place with its brands: Miller High Life, Lite, Lowenbrau, and Magnum.

CREATING THE COMMERCIAL With 77 commercials completed, the advertising agency got under way with plans for the newest Lite All-Star reunion commercial. The marketing objectives and overall creative strategy remained unchanged, with the creative team looking for a fresh idea for the now standardized format.

It was decided to build this All-Star Reunion commercial around a softball game, because it would provide a change of pace from prior indoor commercials, offer the opportunity for a large number of cameo appearances, and make it possible to feature some All-Stars not extensively used before.

A script was prepared with Rodney Dangerfield as the key figure and including a number of comic miniplays with the various former athletes who appeared in earlier commercials. Because of the obvious time constraints (60 seconds), the script had to be cut until a tight, finished script was ready to be produced. A storyboard was also prepared to assist in the shooting.

Because the commercial was being shot out of doors in the winter, a mild climate was needed. Also, these All-Star Reunion commercial shootings had developed into an opportunity for major media events producing valuable publicity, and for these reasons it was decided to shoot in Los Angeles, which was a good location on both counts. As in the past, a big banquet for the cast and press preceded the shooting. The location was a little league ball park in the suburbs. Los Angeles was experiencing extremely heavy rains, but fortunately there were three good days—enough time to complete the shooting.

The commercial was shot on film rather than tape, as all Lite commercials are, because it was believed this medium provided a degree of warmth unattainable on tape. As was the usual practice, substantial extra footage was shot to assure the best editing and a tight finished product. Typically an establishing shot would be used, but it was decided to eliminate this shot and go right into the action so that the number of cameos could be maximized.

With the production mechanics completed, release prints on tape were prepared and distributed according to the media schedule. It was now time to start on the next set of commercials.

Print production is a true art form. The selection and arrangement of type is important to the success of the print advertisement. The most important consideration is legibility. Beyond that, good type makes the advertisement look better. Type can be classified into roman, sans serif, square serif, script and cursive, blackletter, and miscellaneous groups. Type is composed today by photographic and electronic means.

TO SUM UP

527

The most important printing process is now offset lithography, which involves printing from a plane surface. Next is rotogravure, a process of printing from a depressed surface. Finally, there is letterpress printing from a raised surface, but this technique is fast disappearing.

All printing processes require image carriers. These are made through photographic techniques that require advertisers to supply printers with films of the mechanicals of the advertisements.

Radio commercials are mostly recorded. This is done at recording studios, where the talent puts the message and sound effects and music on tapes. This may be done all at once or as separate components that are later combined in a *mix*.

Advertising agency television producers supervise the making of commercials. These may be live but are more apt to be filmed or videotaped. They may be live action or animation. Producers engage production companies to shoot commercials. Casts are chosen, sets built or locations selected, and a director from the production company directs the shooting of the spot. Many *takes* are made, and, in the case of film, *dailies* are viewed the next day; from these, an editor makes a *rough cut*. The film and soundtrack are then *interlocked*. Opticals are added and an *answer print* is made. After client approval, *release prints*, usually on tape, are sent to the stations.

QUESTIONS AND PROBLEMS

1. Explain the principles and importance of good typography.
2. Look through current advertisements and find examples of display type to illustrate each of the different groups.
3. Define the following printing terms:
   (a) Points
   (b) Pica
   (c) Em
   (d) Justified line
   (e) Pi
4. Explain the basic differences between lithography, gravure, and letterpress.
5. What are the basic differences between halftone and line photoplates?
6. What are the colors in the four-color process of printing? Why do they reproduce all colors?
7. Describe the typical production schedule for a radio commercial.
8. Discuss the pros and cons of live, taped, and filmed television commercials.
9. Describe the steps in producing a television commercial.
10. Of what value is a knowledge of print and broadcast production for advertising people in other ends of the business?

ENDNOTE

[1] I am indebted to the Miller Brewing Company and its advertising agency, Backer & Spielvogel, for providing the information for this example.

27

Retail Advertising

After completing this chapter, you should be able to:

1. Define the different types of retail advertising
2. Describe a retail advertising plan
3. Evaluate the various media for retail advertisers
4. Explain how a retail advertisement is prepared

Much of what has been said for national advertising applies to retail advertising, but there are also certain differences. (Retail advertising organization was discussed in Chapter 6.) Some new retail institutions, such as fast-food franchise retailers, have split advertising activities, with national advertising handled by the central office and advertising agencies in a similar manner to advertising by producers, and local advertising handled by the franchise owner, also often using an advertising agency. Direct marketers are also less similar to other retailers in both their media mixes and organizational structures. Thus, the discussion here is primarily related to advertising by department stores, departmentalized specialty stores, and larger specialty stores.

For retailers, advertising has become a very important part of their operation. Indeed, retail advertising, by any measure, is an important part of all advertising. Retailers are in the business of buying for resale. Their success depends in large part on buying merchandise that the customer wants and selling it at the right prices, at the right time, and in the right place. Locating in the right place is important in attracting customers to buy the merchandise, but location is not enough. Retailers must utilize well-planned advertising to inform prospective customers—both passersby and nonpassersby—about the availability and the desirability of the merchandise and the services they offer. Most retailers are now so acutely aware of this fact that they need to be told little about *why* they must advertise. They are keenly interested, however, in knowing *how* they should advertise.

TYPES OF RETAIL ADVERTISING

Retail advertising can be divided into two broad types: *product* and *patronage*. Product advertising is designed to sell specific merchandise and get immediate response. Patronage advertising, on the other hand, is designed to sell the store. Its effects are generally felt in the long run. Of course, product advertising may also generate store patronage, and patronage advertising may directly influence immediate purchase of specific goods.

PRODUCT ADVERTISING For the vast majority of retailers, product advertising represents the greatest part of the advertising effort. Product advertising can be further subdivided into *regular price-line* advertising, *sale* advertising, and *clearance* advertising. Advertisements are generally devoted to only one variety of the subdivisions, but it is possible to combine elements of more than one subdivision in a single "omnibus" advertisement.

REGULAR PRICE-LINE ADVERTISING A newspaper reader probably sees regular price-line advertising most frequently, especially when the economy is booming. Its purpose is to inform readers of the wide selection of merchandise at regular prices that the store has available, generally when this merchandise is timely. It is hoped that the consumer wanting the generic products will visit the store to purchase the particular advertised varieties. Thus, such an advertisement may feature children's wear for back-to-school, dresses and hats for spring, or swimsuits and sports clothes for summer. The emphasis may be on fashion, or variety, or exclusiveness, for example. This advertising is designed to ensure regular business and build store traffic.

SALE ADVERTISING Unfortunately, a steady diet of regular price-line advertising may result in the customer's putting off purchases. Also, it does not stimulate heavy store traffic during periods when retail sales are generally slow. Therefore, many retailers supplement their regular price-line advertising with *sale* or *price* advertising, which emphasizes special reduced prices. Some stores that are highly promotional use price advertising almost exclusively and appeal to the bargain hunter. Price advertising is frequently used to spread out a selling season by offering merchandise at reduced prices before or after the normal selling season. For example, there may be an August fur sale. When volume in a certain department is lagging, the retailer may run sale advertising. Whereas such advertising produces immediate mass response, those attracted are frequently bargain hunters who do not maintain any store loyalty. On the other hand, when customers shop for sale merchandise, they frequently buy other merchandise and thus increase the overall sales volume of the store.

CLEARANCE ADVERTISING Periodically, retailers want to move merchandise to make room for new assortments or models. There may be slow-moving lines, items that are no longer seasonal and that are undesirable to hold over to the next season, broken sizes and assortments, odds and ends, and shopworn merchandise, such as floor samples. In such cases, the retailer will resort to clearance advertising. Some stores run clearance advertising sporadically, whereas others run such advertising annually, semiannually, or monthly. Obviously, such advertising has its drawbacks. Clearance advertising is difficult, because the items offered are naturally those that others did not want. Still, it has an appeal to certain customers who are looking for very low-priced merchandise, and the merchandise must be sold.

Try Our Pick-Me-Up. In London, the New Statesman and Nation, *in its entertainment column, carried a notice by the Unity Theater: "Burlesque—The Loudest Show in Town. Nightly police raids."*

TIME

FIGURE 27-1

A regular price line advertisement by a furniture store. Compare the style of this advertisement with Figures 27-2, 27-3, and 27-4. *By permission: Kanes.*

FIGURE 27-2

A sale advertisement. *By permission: Kanes.*

FIGURE 27-3

A clearance advertisement. *By permission: Kanes.*

Bedroom & Dining room

LEWITTES - lattice back dining side chair, leather wrapped rattan
in a fruitwood finish, Reg. $239.00 . . . . **Sale $179**

THOMASVILLE - oriental style serving cabinet on casters, dark
fruitwood finish with black serving surface, Reg. $500.00 . . . . **Sale $298**

BARRY WOODARD - 6 piece contemporary bedroom, chocolate
high pressure laminate with tinted mirror fronts, includes:
3 drawer/2 door 72" dresser, with brass framed vertical mirror,
queen size panel headboard with frame, (2) night stands, and a
large armoire chest, Reg. $3800.00 . . . . **Sale $2795**

DESIGN SYSTEMS - rectangular dining table, split rattan laminated
base with 40x70x½" glass top, Reg. $495.00 . . . . **Sale $298**

KINDLE - 34" bamboo style extension table finished in distressed
bisque with two self storing 13" leaves, opens to 60",
Reg. $795.00 . . . . **Sale $488**

AMERICAN OF MARTINSVILLE - large man's chest with 6 drawers
and 4 doors, dark "mosaic" fruitwood finish with brass hardware,
Reg. $1180.00 . . . . **Sale $899**

DAVIS CABINET - 5 piece party set, from the "Rouen II" collection,
Louis XV style, in a rich bisque finish, 42" round table with one 18"
leaf and 4 arm chairs on casters, Reg. $2975.00 . . . . **Sale $1975**

DESIGN INSTITUTE AMERICA - 38" square antiqued brass dining
table with glass top, extends to 58" with one 20" leaf,
Reg. $800.00 . . . . **Sale $398**

THOMASVILLE - Louis XV "Camille Collections" antique white with
gold and celadon trim.

Bedroom - 5 pc. suite: 68" 9 drawer dresser, vertical mirror,
queen size cane headboard with frame and two drawer commodes,
Reg. $2515.00 . . . . **Sale $1995**
7 drawer semanier chest, Reg. $780.00 . . . . **Sale $599**
Large 6 drawer chest on chest, Reg. $1090.00 . . . . **Sale $859**
Dining room - 5 piece set includes 29x54 oval table with two 20" leaves,
fruitwood top and four side chairs, Reg. $2150.00 . . . . **Sale $1695**
53" china cabinet with lighted interior, Reg. $2070.00 . . . . . . **Sale $1699**
Mobile server - flip top design on hidden casters,
Reg. $1000.00 . . . . **Sale $799**

TABLEWORKS - custom beveled all mirrored dining table, on cube
base. 70"x40", Reg. $1150.00 . . . . **Sale $488**

BERNHARDT - 60" two piece breakfront, burl finish with antique
brass trim and glass doors with interior lighting,
Reg. $900.00 . . . . **Sale $578**

BARRY WOODARD - custom bedroom suite, 4 piece bed unit
includes queen size platform bed, extended queen size headboard
with attached nite stands, Reg. $1340.00 . . . . **Sale $995**
4 piece vanity wall unit includes (2) 32" 3 drawer chests with a 36"
glass shelve between and a full length arched mirror,
Reg. $1875.00 . . . . **Sale $1395**
All finished in a parchment high pressure laminate with brushed
brass trim.

7 piece dining room set, 58" oval dining table with one 16" leaf by
THOMASVILLE with 6 **AMERICAN OF MARTINSVILLE** cane back
side chairs, antique white with yellow trim, Reg. $1150.00 . . . . **Sale $688**

THAYER COGGIN - modular bedroom collection, dark mink finish
with brass accents, 32" 2 door cabinet, Reg. $495.00 . . . . **Sale $359**
32" 3 drawer chest, Reg. $515.00 . . . . **Sale $359**
32" lighted open bookcase, Reg. $425.00 . . . . **Sale $279**
18" radius end cabinet, Reg. $535.00 . . . . **Sale $359**
Queen size low profile headboard with frame, Reg. $385.00 . . **Sale $259**

CHAIRCRAFT - 42" buffet/serving cabinet, traditional style in
antique white with bright yellow trim, Reg. $550.00 . . . . **Sale $288**

THOMASVILLE - 5 piece oriental bedroom, mottled garnet red
finish, suite includes 60" dresser base with vertical mirror, queen size
panel headboard with two drawer commodes,
Reg. $1215.00 . . . . **Sale $658**

DAVIS CABINET - buffet cabinet from "Ro en II" collection,
Louis XV, in a rich bisque finish with hand carved doors,
Reg. $2475.00 . . . . **Sale $1895**

CENTURY - 60" contemporary rectangular dining table, rich burl
finish with beveled smoke glass top, with one 18" leaf,
Reg. $1195.00 . . . . **Sale $698**

DIXIE - 3 piece bedroom group includes lingerie chest, twin size
poster bed and one nite stand, in an antique white with yellow
trim and floral decoration, Reg. $750.00 . . . . **Sale $498**

PATRONAGE ADVERTISING   Relatively few stores put strong emphasis on patronage advertising, a kind of institutional advertising, but almost all major retail advertisers use some degree of it to supplement their product advertising. Such advertisements may be separate or part of product advertisements. Their appeal may be storewide or for a single department. The object of retail patronage advertising is to build store traffic and goodwill for the retailer.

Several approaches may be used in retail patronage advertising. It may be used to build prestige for the store or a department by talking about the high fashion or extensive assortment of the merchandise. It may stress the services the store offers, such as charge accounts, personal shoppers, or special hours. Finally, such advertising may be used to improve public relations—for example, by showing the store's support of civic enterprises. This last activity is similar to public relations corporate advertising.

Thus, retailers have used patronage advertising to announce that they have a couturier or designer shop in women's dresses; have a bridal shop with a consultant; are open evenings before Christmas; or as public relations advertising to urge you to support the United Way. Unfortunately, it is difficult to measure the effectiveness of patronage or public relations advertising. Furthermore, its results are generally not immediate, but long range. Because it does not offer specific merchandise information, it is not likely to have as high readership as product advertising. Still, if it is well done, it will be read, and it can help immeasurably to build the store image and attract regular customers.

Retailers may plan advertisements in a series over a period of time as a campaign, or they may run advertisements independent of any series. In practice, the store will probably run both varieties of advertising, having certain longer-range planned advertising objectives as well as advertising opportunities that present themselves at specific times.

Advertisements in campaigns are related through such devices as similarity in layout, illustration technique, copy style, logotype, and slogans. Through repetition, these devices help build store reputation. They permit the consumer to recognize advertisements easily. Campaigns provide for planned promotion, which can have a greater cumulative effect than independently run advertisements.

ADVERTISING CAMPAIGNS

If there is one enterprise on earth that a "quitter" should leave severely alone it is advertising. To make a success of advertising, one must be prepared to stick like a barnacle on a boat's bottom. He should know before he begins it that he must spend money—lots of it. Somebody must tell him that he cannot hope to reap results commensurate with his expenditure early in the game.

JOHN WANAMAKER (1838–1922), Merchant

READER'S DIGEST

FIGURE 27-4

A patronage advertisement designed to build store traffic. *By permission: Kanes.*

Planning is as essential to the success of the retailer as it is to the producer. For this reason, the retailer plans ahead for the store's operation, mainly by means of the merchandising plan. The function of advertising is to promote the sale of the store's merchandise; it follows that there should be an advertising strategy that is coordinated with the merchandising plan. Such a strategy or retail advertising plan, as it is called, will make the funds devoted to advertising more effective by helping to determine when and how often to advertise, what should be advertised, and how to advertise.

There are different types of advertising plans, but they all aim at the same objectives and have certain characteristics in common. They necessitate drawing on past experience, minimizing guesswork, and engaging in advance planning. They coordinate all phases of the advertising program. Taking into account current trends and developments, they coordinate advertising expenditures with sales potentials and provide for adequate consideration of all merchandise lines and the seasonal variations of some of them. They help in obtaining the lowest advertising media rates, manufacturers' cooperative advertising allowances, and better buying positions for the buyers.

Although the responsibility for the advertising plan for a department store rests primarily with the advertising manager or the sales promotion director or both, the plan must be developed in close cooperation with the merchandise manager, controller, and buyers. The advertising plan is as much needed by the small retailer as it is by the large department store, and the requirements set forth here can be readily adapted to the needs of the small retail store.

TYPES OF PLANS Depending upon the type of store and current business conditions, advertising plans may be developed on a seasonal (six months), quarterly, monthly, or weekly basis. Of these, the monthly plan is most popular among department stores. However, even when the monthly plan is used, it may be preceded by seasonal or quarterly plans. These longer-range plans might be used to establish whole-store objectives, whereas the monthly plan would deal with departmental objectives.

Because the monthly plan is the most popular, the steps in its formulation are discussed here. These steps are applicable, when adjusted, to the other plans as well. Formulation of the plan may start two months to one week before the month in question, but generally it starts about a month in advance.

STEPS IN THE FORMULATION OF A MONTHLY PLAN The first step is to review the planning data for the month for the whole store. These include such facts as current business conditions and their possible effects on sales for the period; sales figures for the same month last year and projections of sales figures for the month in question; past and planned advertising expenditures; past and planned selling events of the store, with an evaluation of the success of past events; past and anticipated selling events of competitors, with a consideration of how

1. (ANNOUNCER V.O.:) You work hard for your food dollars.

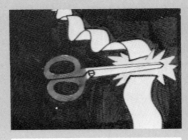

2. And nobody works harder to save them (SFX: SNIP) than Kroger...

3. with Cost Cutter prices!

4. (WOMAN #1 O.C.:) To me Krogering means you can save money and you get good stuff.

5. (WOMAN #2 O.C.:) I can find most of the things I want here cheaper.

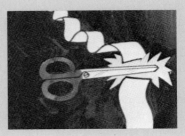

6. (ANNOUNCER V.O.:) (SFX: SNIP) Cut your costs everyday with Cost.

7. Cutter prices. Only when you

8. go Krogering.

9. Cut your costs up to 80 cents, now $1.18.

10. Cut your costs up to 50 cents. Now 99 cents.

FIGURE 27-5

A chain of food stores makes use of television commercials, as illustrated in this storyboard, to promote its services and goods. *By permission: Kroger Food Stores.*

these events might affect the advertising plan for the store; special dates and occasions; and current and anticipated fashion trends.

Next, sales quotas, advertising budgets, and major selling events for the month must be established. These are worked out for the whole store, for each merchandise division, and for each department.

Then, departmental planning data are distributed to the appropriate divisional merchandise managers and buyers. These plans follow the same basic procedure as those for the whole store, except that they are on a departmental basis.

After receiving the planning data, the buyer or department manager formulates plans for the department. Generally, a work sheet will be used, containing such pertinent data as previous years' sales records and the amount spent on advertising. The buyer will indicate what advertising is wanted on what days and in what media and will request such supports as displays or signs.

From these work sheets, the advertising manager prepares a preliminary master plan in which adjustments are made for a balanced advertising program for the month.

A meeting is then held with divisional merchandise managers and their buyers. At these meetings, departmental sales quotas and advertising budgets are confirmed and selling events for the month are agreed upon.

The sales promotion director, advertising manager, and merchandise manager now compile the final advertising plan for the month. The completed plan is then distributed to top executives; divisional and departmental plans are sent to divisional managers and buyers or department managers respectively.

THE RETAIL ADVERTISING BUDGET

Before a retail advertising plan can be conceived and put into operation, the retail advertising budget must be established. The difference between how much the retailer would *like* to spend on advertising and how much the retailer *can* spend must be reconciled, and the problem of how much *should* be spent on advertising must be resolved. Unfortunately, too many retailers allot a "magic" percentage of sales, frequently taken from average figures for the industry. The shortcomings of such a method should be obvious. An intelligent advertising budget should be based upon the particular needs of a particular store. Such factors as the size of the store, its location, the nature and amount of competition, business conditions, the availability and costs of advertising media, and the nature of consumers to whom the store is catering must be considered in arriving at how much to spend on advertising.

Ideally, the method of setting the retail advertising budget is the same as that suggested for producers—the *budget buildup method*. This involves an examination of sales projections for the whole store and the amount of advertising (together with other promotional techniques) necessary to meet established sales goals. This examination is difficult to make and requires considerable executive judgment, but it will probably come closest to maximizing the effectiveness of the advertising investment.

After the advertising budget for the whole store has been established, there remains the task of distributing the budget by time periods and by divisions and departments. Such breakdowns will go hand in hand with the advertising plan, with seasonal, quarterly, monthly, and weekly allocations. Next, the portion to be used for institutional advertising will be set aside. The remainder will then be distributed to divisions and departments.

The first step here is to distribute the remainder of the budget, less an amount set aside for contingencies, to the divisions and departments on the basis of projected sales for each. This, however, is an oversimplification. Adjustments, based on a number of important factors, must be made. The sales potential of a department must be examined in the light of the profit potential, because some departments are more profitable than others. The ability of a department's advertising to stimulate storewide traffic must be considered. The nature of the goods in a department and the likelihood of getting a buying response as a result of advertising may suggest more or fewer advertising dollars. Finally, the amount of advertising funds that will be supplied by other resources (such as cooperative advertising) must be taken into account.

Assuming that a monthly advertising plan is used, a department's budgeting procedure would be that described above for the monthly advertising plan. Some control is needed to ascertain the amount of funds used and the amount available for the remainder of the month, to be certain that the budget is not overspent and that funds do not remain unencumbered.

RETAIL ADVERTISING MEDIA

Retailers make use of virtually all the media producers use. However, some media that are very important to the producer are less important to the retailer, and vice versa. Which media to use will depend upon the store type, the kind of customers the store is trying to reach, location, trading area, competition, media costs, advertising budgets, and the kind of message to be delivered.

Most media have two sets of advertising rates—one for general or national advertising and another for retail or local advertising. The retail rate is lower, but it is not commissionable. Because the bulk of retail advertising is placed directly by the retailer rather than through an advertising agency, the advantage is a lower cost to the retailer for advertising media. In addition, media generally offer quantity and frequency advertising discounts that afford additional savings to the retail advertiser making extensive use of a particular medium.

NEWSPAPERS Newspapers remain the number 1 retail advertising medium. In fact, retail advertising constitutes the largest percentage of newspaper advertising linage. Nevertheless, the newspaper is not the answer for all retail advertisers. Many smaller retailers, especially those located in secondary shopping areas, find the newspaper impractical for their purposes.

The decision of which newspaper to use is becoming increasingly simplified as the number of multiple-newspaper cities becomes smaller. When a choice has to be made, it is determined by the nature of the market the newspaper reaches and the cost of reaching it. Having selected a newspaper, the advertiser must decide whether to run r.o.p. position or special position. For the most part, retailers are satisfied with r.o.p. at regular rates. Occasionally, however, they will pay the premium rate for a special position in order to increase readership, attract a special segment of the market, or gain prestige. Although most newspapers are now equipped with facilities for color printing, press limitations have in the past restricted the use of color in retail advertising primarily to attention getting. Improvements today, however, provide much more effective use of color. The finest opportunity for retail color advertising is in the Sunday magazine supplements printed by rotogravure, in which very good quality four-color process reproduction can be achieved.

Perhaps the main reason for the popularity of retail newspaper advertising is that consumers accept it. In fact, they seek it. Consumers have come to look at newspapers as a sort of retail buying guide. For large, centrally located retailers and those with a number of branch stores, newspapers are a relatively inexpensive means of reaching their markets. They are flexible because they are so frequently issued. They also permit illustration of goods for sale, which is of considerable importance for many products, especially fashion items.

However, newspapers have their limitations. They are not very selective in the markets they reach, which may mean sizable waste circulation. They carry considerable amounts of competitive retail advertising, which may diminish the impact of the retailers' advertising. Finally, use of illustrations is hampered by poor reproduction.

DIRECT ADVERTISING Even though it is difficult to get an accurate measure of how much retailers spend for direct advertising, its importance as a retail advertising medium is obvious. The largest single item of direct advertising is *direct mail* advertising, from envelope stuffers sent out to charge customers with their monthly bills to large catalogs offering merchandise for sale. Other direct advertising may consist of advertisements inserted in packages or handbills, broadsides, and circulars delivered to the consumer's doorstep.

Direct advertising can reach specific market segments, although it may also be used to reach the mass market. Direct advertising can be personalized, so that the recipient feels a greater willingness to read the message. It has little direct competition from other retail advertisers at the same time, and so is more likely to get the reader's undivided attention. It can fit the advertising budget, as it may be very inexpensive or very expensive. Finally, there is no limit to the graphic possibilities that can be used to meet the demands for any product.

There are few drawbacks to direct advertising. Generally, such advertising is slower in producing sales results than some of the other me-

Genuinely good advertising must give in wording something that will be read about the goods that are wanted and that will clearly state exactly what the goods are.

JOHN WANAMAKER (1838–1922), Merchant

READER'S DIGEST

Why we call ourselves Lands' End, Direct Merchants.

These days, on top of everything else, you don't need the added frustrations you often face when you go shopping.

Threading your way through traffic into parking lots, in distant suburbs. Shouldering your way through crowded malls into stores well-stocked with goods, but staffed too sparingly to serve you well.

Lacking clerks who know the stock, you paw over counters, and shuttle hangers back and forth on racks.

Finally, when you've found what you want, there's that added wait while a cashier communes with her computer, recording everything about the item sold except that you've been standing in line waiting to pay for it.

There has to be a better way. And there is.

Shop with Lands' End, Direct Merchants.

We call ourselves direct merchants because we provide a straight line service, from us to you, with *no middle men* (or *middle-persons*, if you prefer.) Our way lets you shop at leisure in your home. From a colorful catalog. 24 hours a day, 365 days a year. By mail if you like. But, better still, by phone.

You pay no toll. No parking fees. You burn no gas. You lose no patience. And you have direct access to an astonishing array of quality products, about which we give you no-nonsense information, and which we offer at no-nonsense prices.

We didn't originate this method of shopping. But not a day goes by but what we at Lands' End ponder ways to re-invent the system, simplify it, refine it, or add to it when appropriate.

We roam the world in your behalf.

The search for quality is endless at Lands' End. And we go to the four corners of the earth in quest of it. In so doing, we practice a tough philosophy. Simply stated, it goes like this:

First, *quality.* Then, *price.* And always, always *service.*

Once an item seems right for our customers, as direct merchants

we seek out the prime quality source; the one not only best suited to manufacture it, but the one that can make it most efficiently as well.

When we're sure we can offer you Lands' End quality at a Lands' End price, we pass the word on to you promptly in our catalogs. If we can't price a quality item so it's to your advantage to buy it from us, we don't offer it. But we continue to search for a new prime source of that item. And occasionally—as with our soft luggage lines—we undertake to make the items ourselves.

Millions use us. Millions more could.

We have served and satisfied millions of customers, but there remain millions more of you who have never experienced our direct service.

If you're among the latter group, why not try us now? Let us prove to you that you can trust us, too.

Ask us to send you a catalog by return mail. Better still, call us right now on our toll-free number (800-356-4444). We have over 100 friendly, well-informed operators waiting to answer your call personally, 24 hours a day. They're trained to serve you,

and serve you they do. With answers to questions on sizes, styles, shipments and prices. On colors, on

care, on delivery. Should an item be temporarily out of stock, they'll tell you and suggest an alternative. (Including, if need be, referring you to a respected competitor.)

What can you lose?

Understand, we're not all things to all shoppers. We don't initiate or pursue fads. We don't start or ride trends. We deal in clothing and accessories that know no time or season.

And we guarantee every item, in these unconditional terms: "*If you are not completely satisfied with any item you buy from us, at any time during your use of it, return it and we will refund your full purchase price.*"

Call us right now, and let us begin to serve you. From our brand-new Catalog, featuring pages of solid values, we can ship to you within 24 hours, or we'll know the reason why, and so will you.

Lands' End, Direct Merchants. The exciting new way to shop in today's world.

LANDS' END
DIRECT MERCHANTS

of fine wool and cotton sweaters, Oxford button-down shirts, traditional dress clothing, snow wear, deck wear, original Lands' End soft luggage and a multitude of other quality goods from around the world.

☐ **Please send free catalog.**
Lands' End Dept. J-09
Dodgeville, WI 53533

Name _____
Address _____
City _____
State _____ Zip _____

Or call Toll-free:
800-356-4444
(Except Alaska and Hawaii call 608-935-2788)

FIGURE 27-6

Direct marketing has become the fastest growing kind of retailing. This advertisement, appearing in consumer magazines, attempts to find new customers who will be added to the firm's mailing list to receive its catalog. *By permission: Lands' End Corporation.*

dia. Poor mailing lists for direct mail can result in considerable waste. Finally direct advertising has nothing to commend it to the reader but the advertising itself. Therefore, poorly thought out, poorly executed direct advertising is likely to be tossed in the wastebasket without being read.

BROADCAST For many years, radio and television were considered by most retailers as national advertising media, but the picture has changed considerably in recent years. Even so, these media have been used primarily as a supplement to other media, although more retailers are using broadcast as a primary medium today.

Both radio and television reach large segments of the mass market. They allow advertising to tie in with topical programs such as fashion and home economist shows. They are extremely flexible, so retailers can reach their market not only on any day of the week but also at any time of day. Production costs, especially for radio, can be very low. Finally, they provide an appeal to the ear through the spoken word and sound effects. Television can also provide sight and color.

With all these assets for the broadcast media, one would think that retailers would use them more. But broadcast has some severe limitations. For one thing, broadcast advertising requires brevity. Although retail advertising copy for any one item is generally quite short, there usually are many items to advertise. Another problem is the short life of a broadcast commercial, giving the consumer no opportunity to refer back or to make comparisons with competitive stores. Radio, in addition, cannot picture the merchandise. Television, which has been dominated by national advertisers, has made it hard for the retailer to obtain choice times, but the situation is changing, and the volume of spot television buying by retailers has grown tremendously in recent years.

SIGNS Signs used by retailers may be divided into three broad categories: store signs, outdoor advertising, and transit advertising. These are generally considered supplementary media. Although signs offer mass exposure, low cost per viewer, color, and size, they have some major shortcomings for retailers. First, they are changed infrequently, which limits their use for most merchandise promotion. Second, their message must generally be brief because they are read hurriedly. Third, they are not selective in the audience they reach. Signs are used primarily for institutional advertising to build store patronage and goodwill. When they are used for specific merchandise, it is usually for items that have continuous appeal, such as brand-name lines.

OTHER MEDIA All the other advertising media can be and have been used by retailers. Magazines, for example, have been used successfully by chains and large individual retailers. They can carry merchandise advertisements for store purchase or mail-order purchase. Frequently, they are used to help build store prestige, even though there may be considerable waste circulation; regional editions have cut down this waste substantially, so that it is no longer the drawback it once was. For example, a number of retailers use the advertisements in fashion magazines as a basis for local promotions.

On the other hand, some media used by retailers, such as souvenir programs, school yearbooks, and the like, may or may not be regarded as bona fide advertising media. The motive for such "advertising" is frequently public relations, and as public relations, this advertising should not be charged to the advertising budget, which is generally strained to begin with.

The technique of preparing retail advertisements will vary somewhat depending upon the advertising medium being used. The discussion here will be focused upon the preparation of newspaper advertisements —the most important type of retail advertising. The variations for other media should be apparent. Much of the technical detail resembles the technicalities of print production for national advertisers.

PREPARING THE RETAIL ADVERTISEMENT

543

The first unique feature of a retail advertisement is the time allotted for its creation. Whereas national advertisements may take six months from the time they are requested until the time they appear in the media, retail advertisements are more likely to take two weeks. Competitive conditions and closeness to the market do not permit long-range planning except in very general terms. Specific advertisements must generally be prepared in a very limited time.

Another point is that retail advertising is prepared, for the most part, by the advertising department of the retailer rather than by an advertising agency. In many ways, the relationship of the retail advertising department to the divisional merchandise managers and buyers is similar to the relationship of the advertising agency to the national advertiser.

As indicated earlier in the chapter, the preparation of a retail advertisement starts with the advertising plan. About two weeks before the publication date (the exact amount of time prior to publication that the advertisement is started will differ from retailer to retailer), the buyers or department managers are asked to submit certain information on *copy fact forms*. The forms will indicate the item to be advertised, the date of the advertisement, the newspaper, and the space. The buyers or department managers fill in important copy facts about the merchandise, including colors, sizes and prices. They also indicate any special requirements, such as the use of a producer's logotype, the use of a brand name in the headline or copy, or inclusion of mail-order information. The forms also contain due dates for the forms to be returned to the advertising department.

When the copy fact forms are returned to the advertising department, together with samples of the merchandise to be advertised, the advertising manager makes a last review of the advertising plans to be sure that the right merchandise is being promoted. Then instructions are issued to the staff for the execution of the advertisements. At this point, the advertising manager may rough out a layout and then turn the assignment over to a copy supervisor or copywriter; or may turn the advertisement responsibility over to the copy supervisor or copywriter without preparing the rough layout; or may have the art director or a layout artist prepare a rough layout and turn the copywriting task over to the copy supervisor or copywriter. Finally, the advertising manager may call for a coordinated effort, assigning the advertisement to the layout artist and copywriter simultaneously, expecting them to work together on copy and layout.

After the layout is prepared, the copywriter, working with the buyer or department manager, goes over the copy fact form for any additional information and to ascertain the best approach to advertising the merchandise. The copywriter also may turn to other sources, such as the manufacturer and reference books, for additional information. When the copy and layout have been prepared, they are sent to the advertising manager for approval. Frequently, they are checked by the buyer or department manager as well.

The advertisement is now ready for production. Artwork will be assigned either to staff artists and photographers or to freelancers. Copy and layout will be marked up to specify type. This may then be sent to the newspaper for composition, although this is increasingly done in-house. A mechanical layout (or keyline) is then prepared, from which *veloxes* (glossy photographic copies suitable for making printing plates) are made to be sent, together with release orders, to the newspapers being used.

The task is by no means completed at this point. The advertising department now sends proofs or photocopies of the advertisements to the buyers or department managers to remind them to have the merchandise available for sale and also to inform the salespeople in the department about the advertisements.

After the advertisements have been published, the advertising department will prepare complete records of the occasion. Copies of the advertisements and competitive advertisements are filed. Data on sales resulting from the advertisements are also gathered and filed. Finally, records are made of costs so that the appropriate departments can be charged, and bills are prepared for resources when cooperative advertising is used.

RETAIL COPY AND ART

The principles of copy and art for retail and national advertising are quite similar, but some differences should be noted. Most retail advertising is direct-action advertising, designed to bring an immediate response in sales. Therefore, copywriters have to do more than *announce;* they have to *sell.* Copywriters for national accounts may write on several different products, but the number is relatively small, and they can become experts on them. They will stay with them, preparing a good many advertisements for them over a period of time. Retail advertising copywriters, on the other hand, may have to write about several hundred different items. Frequently, they will write copy for a specific brand only once. Therefore, they do not have the opportunity to be as knowledgeable about the products as the national copywriters are.

Because the amount of space a retailer will assign to any specific merchandise is generally limited, so is the amount of copy. The copywriter must, therefore, make every word count to sell the goods. There is little room for frills. Retail copy must usually be specific if it is to induce consumers to act. Retail copy will generally include detailed information regarding models, sizes, colors, prices, and the like.

National advertising copywriters sell specific brands. There may be competition from similar products, but the brand is unique. However, the same brand may be sold in a number of stores in the same community. Retail copywriters must, therefore, build into their copy not only reasons for buying the product, but reasons for buying it from their stores rather than from competitors'.

In most national advertisements, only one item, or a group of related items, is featured. The retail advertisement more frequently features different items in one *omnibus* advertisement. The omnibus advertisement presents some real challenges to the layout artists, requiring them to design a cohesive layout while keeping the spirit of the omnibus advertisement, which is essentially several advertisements in one.

Because retailers want to develop their own readily identifiable images in their advertising, stores usually endeavor to establish layout styles that customers will recognize immediately and associate with the stores.

As pointed out earlier, most retail advertising appears in newspapers. Because newspapers have severe production limitations, retail advertising art for this medium must adapt to the restrictions. An illustration in a national advertisement generally refers to a specific item of merchandise. For retail advertising, however, the illustration may have to suggest a wide assortment of merchandise. Thus, while a furniture manufacturer may feature a detailed illustration of a specific sofa in an advertisement, the retail advertisement is more apt to suggest loosely a style of sofa to represent the wide assortment of different brands carried by the retailer.

CREATING A RETAIL ADVERTISEMENT: JACOBSON'S

Jacobson Stores Inc. operates a group of 16 stores in Michigan, Ohio, and Florida and specializes in fashion apparel and accessories for the entire family and furnishings for the home. The stores cater to customers with higher-than-average incomes and preferences for quality merchandise. Corporate offices and the merchandise distribution center for the northern stores are located in a facility in Jackson, Michigan.[1]

BACKGROUND The Jackson offices include centralized merchandising and sales promotion operations, but the individual stores are not branches of any main or "flagship" store, and each is organized to meet the special needs of the customers in its market. In the central offices are the buyers who report to merchandise managers and the general merchandise manager. Each store has department managers who report to supervisors and a store manager.

ADVERTISING AND SALES PROMOTION The advertising and sales promotion activities are centralized in Jackson under the supervision of the director of advertising and sales promotion. A business manager is responsible for media contracts, cooperative advertising agreements with resources, and buying outside printing for catalogs, statement enclosures, etc. There are also several art directors who supervise the creative aspects of the advertisements, including finished art and layouts. A copy chief is then responsible for getting copy written for the layouts. The production manager has responsibilities for type setting, preparation of keylines (mechanical paste-ups of the elements of the advertisements as they are to appear in finished form), and veloxes (photographic prints of the keylines, which are suitable for reproduction for plate making).

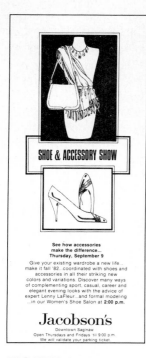

FIGURE 27-7

A special promotion for an individual store, showing a newspaper advertisement and invitations to be addressed by salespersons and mailed to their customers. *By permission: Jacobson Stores Inc.*

All newspaper advertisements, catalogs (with a few exceptions) and other direct mail pieces, and radio commercials are prepared in-house in Jackson. Advertising agencies are used to buy radio (and occasionally television) time and for photography for some national magazine advertisements, but JSI (Jacobson Stores Inc.), an in-house agency, places national advertisements directly.

ADVERTISING PLANS AND PROCEDURES Jacobson's uses a six-month advertising plan, which in turn is broken down to monthly advertising calendars. Management determines the overall dollar budget, and this is divided among the various stores. The initial planning for an individual advertisement takes place when buyers are in the market buying merchandise. These requests are submitted to the merchandise managers, who, together with the general merchandise manager and the director of advertising and sales promotion, meet to determine advertising strategies and coordination and to set up the monthly advertising calendar.

When the buyer wants a specific advertisement, an advertising request form is completed. This request is tabulated with others for the same period and is checked for cooperative advertising claims. A copy of the request form comes into the advertising and sales promotion department, usually together with a sample of the merchandise. The request is placed on the appropriate month's calendar and then goes to an

Retail Advertising

art director, who selects an artist (most of whom are freelancers) and sends instructions and the merchandise sample for a rendering. When the finished art is received, it is sent to the camera room, where a "stat" (photostatic copy) is made for ease of handling without wear and tear on the artwork. The art director reviews it and gives directions to the layout artist, who executes a layout. The layout is then sent to a copywriter, who writes the copy based on the information provided by the buyer on the advertising request form. The layout and copy then go to the buyer for approval, and next they go to the merchandise manager and general merchandise manager for their approval. The advertisement is then reviewed by the director of advertising and sales promotion.

After the layout and copy have been approved, they are sent to production. Type is set in-house by photocomposition, and a keyline layout is prepared. The advertisement is then checked by the production manager, copy chief, and art director; and the advertising and sales promotion director reviews it with the chairman of the board (to whom the director reports) or the general merchandise manager as a kind of "fail-safe."

The keyline is now returned to the camera room, where veloxes are made of it for each store. At the same time, three photocopies of the advertisement are also made for each store, to be supplied to the sales

FIGURE 27-8
The center-spread from a back-to-school catalog. *By permission: Jacobson Stores Inc.*

```
JACOBSON'S - Kalamazoo
30 sec. Sales & Clearances
Broadcast Dates:  Jan. 2 thru 26th



        It's always pleasant to shop at Jacobson's...and
        right now it's particularly appealing.  The holiday
        crowds have gone and the shopper who comes in from
        the cold finds a warm and welcoming oasis...soft
        lights and friendly sales people.  And in every
        department, Jacobson's has special values and
        clearances to make room for the new Spring merchandise.
        In the store-for-the-home the white sale's in progress.
        Jacobson's in January...a nice place to be.  And
        remember we'll validate your parking ticket from any
        city lot.
```

FIGURE 27-9

A radio commercial for one of the stores. *By permission: Jacobson Stores Inc.*

promotion manager, department manager, and store manager. When the store department manager notifies the sales promotion manager that the merchandise has been received, the sales promotion manager releases the advertisement to the local newspaper, notifies the department manager, and, when the advertisement runs, posts a tear sheet or a proof copy of the advertisement in the department. Either after closing time the night before or before opening time on the day on which the advertisement is to appear, an announcement is made over the store's public address system to all employees so that they are made aware of what is being featured in the advertisements for that day.

MEDIA Most of Jacobson's advertising is in print, with newspapers as the main medium. Newspaper advertising is placed on an r.o.p. basis in black-and-white. In most instances, the advertisements are for individual items rather than omnibus advertisements. From time to time a special promotion in color is run in the Sunday supplement of the newspaper. Catalogs are used extensively for seasonal promotions, such as Christmas, spring and summer fashions, and back-to-school. These catalogs are mailed to charge customers. (See Figure 27-8.) Advertising materials are also always included with monthly statements. And on the local store level, there are numerous printed invitations sent out to selected groups of customers for special events.

Jacobson's also makes use of radio advertising on a limited basis. Primarily, this advertising is directed to the junior market, which does not read the newspaper extensively but which is a major radio audience. (See Figure 27-9.) The commercials are written and produced by the advertising and sales promotion department. For special promotions, television has been used on occasion.

Although the company's markets are limited to Michigan, Northwest Ohio, and parts of Florida, Jacobson's periodically runs advertisements in national fashion magazines. (See Figure 27-10.)

ADVERTISING PHILOSOPHY Jacobson's endeavors to have each individual store stand for a center of high-quality fashion for the market area it serves. Each store also tries to provide a very high level of customer service. A feeling for personal service by salespersons is instilled in employees. They are also urged to develop "PTs" (personal trade

FIGURE 27-10
A Jacobson's magazine advertisement from Vogue.
By permission: Jacobson Stores Inc.

lists) and to contact those customers by telephone or mail when there is specific merchandise they believe the customer will like. Although the buying function and top management are centralized, each store enjoys a substantial degree of autonomy to serve the needs of the specific market it serves. Thus, each store is encouraged to develop events to tie in with the market.

In its advertising, Jacobson's tries to achieve a feeling representative of the atmosphere of the stores—high fashion, quality, and service. This is achieved through a variety of means, such as an airy, uncluttered look and single-item advertisements. Generally, the artwork

FIGURE 27-11

The advertising request. *By permission: Jacobson Stores Inc.*

consists of wash drawings instead of photographs because wash drawings create a higher fashion image, and great care is taken to secure the services of artists who can produce illustrations having a high-fashion flair. Photographs are used, however, for complex subjects such as electronic equipment, where wash drawings would not do them justice. Although price is included in most advertisements, it is not emphasized. In the case of sale advertisements, the sale price is never compared to the regular price. In some instances, price is omitted altogether, as in the case of high-fashion merchandise, where price is believed to be inappropriate.

CREATING A NEWSPAPER ADVERTISEMENT   On July 29, the buyer for designer suits and coats, having been to the market and bought thirty-four pieces from the Yves Saint Laurent Rive Gauche collection, completed an advertising request form (see Figure 27-11), scheduling an advertisement for the fourth week of September. When the request reached the advertising and sales promotion department, it was included on the calendar for the appropriate time and turned over to the art director.

FIGURE 27-12

The finished art for the Yves Saint Laurent Rive Gauche outfit. *By permission: Jacobson Stores Inc.*

FIGURE 27-13

The layout for the advertisement. *By permission: Jacobson Stores Inc.*

The art director indicated an appropriate shoe style to be used with the outfit and arranged for a freelance artist in New York City to do the drawing. A sample of the outfit was delivered to the artist in mid-August and the finished artwork was received by the central office on August 29 (see Figure 27-12). Over the next several days, a layout was prepared (see Figure 27-13), and then copy was written (see Figure 27-14). The advertisement was then sent around for approval, where some corrections were made in the copy.

Next, the advertisement was turned over to production, type was set, and the keyline was prepared. After the advertisement was finally

FIGURE 27-14

The corrected copy. *By permission: Jacobson Stores Inc.*

YSL RIVE GAUCHE

**FROM OUR INTERNATIONAL
DESIGNER COLLECTIONS...**

The independent spirit, incomparable
style and distinctive design concept
of Yves Saint Laurent remain constant
in his Rive Gauche Collection for fall
and winter. Classic examples: pure wool
olive or black poncho cape coat, prune
shorter spencer jacket, marine midcalf
dirndl skirt; soft blue satin charmeuse
stock-tie blouse. Sizes 4 to 12. We invite
you to see his collection at Jacobson's.

Jacobson's

Open Thursdays and Fridays until 9:00 p.m.   We will validate your parking ticket.

FIGURE 27-15

The finished advertisement. *By permission: Jacobson Stores Inc.*

approved, veloxes and three sets of photocopies were made for each store that was scheduled to run the advertisement. This material was then shipped to each store's sales promotion manager. After notification that the merchandise was in stock, the advertisement was released to the newspaper (see Figure 27-15), and salespeople were informed that the advertisement was running.

TO SUM UP

Retailers recognize the importance of advertising to their success. Retail advertising can be divided into two broad types: product and patronage. Product advertising features specific merchandise and may be regular price-line, sale, or clearance advertising. Patronage advertising is primarily aimed at building store patronage.

Good retail advertising makes use of plans. The most popular is the monthly plan. Planning data are reviewed for the whole store, then broken down for individual departments. Buyers or department managers then formulate plans for each department. These are then coordinated for the whole store, and a final plan is prepared and distributed to the department level.

The ideal way of setting a retail budget should be the same as for national advertisers—the budget buildup method. Retailers make use of all media, but newspapers are still the most important medium.

Retail advertisements are generally prepared in a rather short time, usually by the retail advertising department rather than an advertising agency. Buyers or department managers initiate a request for advertising by providing necessary data on a copy fact form.

Retail copy is generally written to get direct action. Thus, the copy *sells*. Copy tends to be limited in space, so every word must count.

QUESTIONS AND PROBLEMS

1. What is the difference between product and patronage advertising by retailers?
2. Name and describe the three kinds of product advertising by retailers. Find an example of each in a newspaper.
3. What is the purpose and nature of the retail advertising plan?
4. Indicate the steps in the formulation of the monthly retail advertising plan.
5. How is the retail advertising budget determined?
6. Why are newspapers such an important advertising medium for retailers?
7. Describe the steps in the preparation of the retail advertisement.
8. Select an item to be advertised by a men's clothing store in a college newspaper. Assuming that the advertisement is 560 agate lines, write the copy and prepare a rough layout.
9. Choose an advertisement by a department store. Visit the store and observe the kind of display support the merchandise receives. Shop the merchandise and find out how much knowledge the salesperson has of the advertised merchandise.
10. Find a national advertisement and a retail advertisement for the same brand. Compare the differences in the approaches and objectives of the manufacturer and the retailer.

ENDNOTE

[1] I am indebted to Jacobson Stores Inc. for providing the information for this example.

Advertising to Business

After completing this chapter, you should be able to:
1. State the purposes of advertising to industry
2. Give the reasons for advertising to the trade
3. Explain the value of advertising to professionals
4. Evaluate media and creativity in advertising to business

Business-to-business advertising involves three broad market groups: industry, the trade, and the professions. Each represents an important market to some firm that wants to sell its goods or services. Although personal selling is the most important selling technique for each market, advertising can and most frequently does play a role in the promotional mix.

INDUSTRIAL ADVERTISING

Industrial advertising is advertising of goods and services to be purchased by those who would use them in the production of other goods and services. Unlike the consumer, industrial users purchase products or services to be used directly or indirectly to facilitate their own production, which in turn must be sold to other industrial users or consumers through direct sale or intermediaries.

Whereas consumer goods are classified according to the way they are bought (as convenience goods, shopping goods, or specialty goods), industrial goods are classified according to the way they are used, as raw materials, semifabricated materials and parts, major installations and machinery, equipment, and operating supplies. These classifications include items from giant turbines to typewriter ribbons, requiring a wide variety of selling techniques.

NATURE OF THE INDUSTRIAL USER Industrial advertising deals with a market that is different in many ways from the consumer market. Not all industrial markets are the same, but all have some special characterisitics that should be noted.

The industrial market has a derived demand. It has fewer buyers than consumer markets have. The market is much more concentrated, it is more vulnerable to fluctuating demand, and it has a greater cash flow than the consumer market. Industrial buying is a rational process. It is done in large quantities. Purchasing criteria are specifically defined, and buyers and sellers must maintain extensive contact.[1]

THE PLACE OF ADVERTISING FOR THE INDUSTRIAL USER

As indicated above, the demand for industrial goods is a derived demand, based upon the demand of ultimate consumers for consumer goods. Therefore, the marketability of industrial goods depends upon the needs and desires of consumers. For the most part, then, industrial advertisers must use their advertising efforts where a demand exists for the generic product.

Because industrial sales are complex, with a relatively small number of prospects and large dollar transactions, personal selling is generally much more important to industry than advertising. For the most part, industrial sales are made through the personal sales force of the producer, the producer's agent, the industrial jobber, and the like. The role of advertising is largely supplementary. Industrial advertising is used primarily for purposes such as helping to open the door for the salesman by bringing the company name before prospects. It also acts as a reminder to industrial buyers between calls by salespeople. Such advertising can be used to gain new prospects for salespeople if the number of potential prospects is large and not clearly defined, or to broaden the existing market. It may also substitute for personal selling when peripheral prospects cannot be reached economically by the sales force. Finally, it is a means of helping to build a favorable image for the advertiser.

Not all industrial sellers use or should use advertising. Whether it should be used and the extent to which it should be used must be determined after deciding upon the overall marketing plan for the firm. Too often, the smaller industrial advertiser (and most industrial advertisers are relatively small advertisers when compared with consumer-goods advertisers) enters into advertising without adequate consideration of the importance and value of such advertising in the firm's overall marketing objectives.

In many instances, the industrial user is separated from the producer by *distributors*. These intermediaries have to be sold in the same manner as intermediaries in the consumer market. Advertising is used here by producers in much the same way as trade advertising (see below). Distributors also use advertising to reach their customers—the industrial users.

The Other Power. *In St. Louis, the Atlas Manpower Co. advertised in its window: "Women Wanted."*

TIME

ORGANIZATION OF INDUSTRIAL ADVERTISING

The advertising organization for industrial advertising is not unlike the organization of consumer-goods advertising, but there are some differences.

THE ADVERTISING FUNCTION The organization of the advertising function of the industrial advertiser is quite similar to that of the producer of consumer goods, with, perhaps, two exceptions. For one thing, in most instances the position of the advertising organization within the firm tends to be lower than it is in the consumer-goods advertiser's firm, especially for packaged goods. This is readily understandable, be-

What <u>can't</u> a Cat Wheel Loader do?

All these attachments make it a tough question.
If you think wheel loaders need buckets to be productive, think again. Because these Cat Wheel Loaders use buckets only part time — just when the job calls for it.

The rest of the time, you'll find them equipped with special tools for special jobs. Any number of tools . . . from booms, forks, and blades . . . to brooms, snow plows, and — yes — various buckets. For any number of jobs.

The quick coupler makes it easier.
Because it converts your Cat Wheel Loader from one special machine into many different specialized machines. All it takes is minutes and your operator can make the change without leaving his seat.

Here's how versatility works.
- A railroad service company uses a Cat 910 and 930 Wheel Loader with quick couplers to haul ties and rails with forks, then switching over to buckets for backfilling or to booms for lifting rail sections. Three-job versatility keeps costs down.
- A millyard uses a Cat 930 equipped with a quick coupler to unload trucks and feed the debarker. On top of this it will change from forks to bucket 4 to 6 times a day to load bark and sawdust on trucks. Two jobs, one machine — that's versatility saving money.
- In the oil fields, a drill rig contractor moves pipe casing with his Cat 966D, then couples on a bucket for clean up. Not only has he cut equipment costs, but he's even picked up new business because of the "extra" service he provides.
- A scrap metal company handles more than 400 scrap cars per day with a Cat 930 equipped with forks. For cleaning up the yard, they switch to a broom. Changing from forks to bucket to broom takes only minutes. Versatility — a way to stay competitive.

And here's how versatility pays.
Cat Wheel Loaders + the quick coupler + all these special tools make any material handling operation just that much more economical. Because about all a Cat Wheel Loader **can't** do is increase your material handling costs.

If you want to know more about Cat Wheel Loaders or the Quick Coupler, ask your local Cat Dealer for brochure AEDH8014. He's your single source . . . for material handling machines.

◨ CATERPILLAR

FIGURE 28-1

An example of an advertisement appearing in an industrial publication. (Original in color) *By permission: Caterpillar Tractor Co.*

cause for the industrial advertiser the position of advertising relative to personal selling is generally lower. Another difference is that the industrial advertising department tends to be more involved in the physical creation of advertising, because there is a greater amount of noncommissionable advertising, which is more likely to be prepared by the firm than by an agency. Also, the fact that industrial advertising tends to be more technical results in greater participation by company advertising personnel in the creation of copy and art.

Because a considerable amount of industrial advertising is noncommissionable (catalogs, direct mail, and exhibits, for example), and because many industrial advertisers spend very small sums on advertising, there are a number of services available to industrial advertisers in addition to those offered by advertising agencies. In fact, for the reasons mentioned above, a sizable number of industrial advertisers do not use advertising agencies at all, although the percentage is decreasing. Such industrial advertisers may themselves assume the functions normally handled by an advertising agency, or they may rely upon the advertising service departments of business publications to provide them with the needed assistance. Many commercial printers also maintain special service departments to help advertisers in the preparation of mailing pieces and catalogs. There are also direct mail specialists who offer counsel and prepare direct mail advertising. At one time, most advertising agencies had only limited experience in this noncommissionable form of advertising, so these firms offered valuable assistance and were used as a supplement to the advertising agency. Today, however, many agencies offer such services themselves.

The major shortcoming to these outside service companies is that they tend to promote their own specializations. Unless the producer's advertising personnel is of a caliber to coordinate and integrate the whole advertising effort, a lopsided advertising program may develop. An advertising agency can provide balance, although in fairness it must be pointed out that agencies, too, may display a bias toward commissionable media. Many industrial advertisers do not use an advertising agency for reasons of economy. Because space costs in business publications—the most important of the commissionable industrial advertising media—are relatively low, commissions do not supply a sufficient gross margin for advertising agencies that handle accounts using these media to provide the agencies with an adequate net profit. Therefore, the agencies must bill the clients for additional gross margin, and clients may end up spending 25 percent or more of their advertising budgets for agencies' services. On the surface this appears wasteful, but often industrial advertisers who think they are effecting real economies by not using agencies will find that they have paid dearly through less effective or ineffective advertising efforts.

THE ADVERTISING AGENCY Industrial advertisers may find that the technical nature of the advertising and their minimal use of commissionable advertising media limit their use of advertising agen-

Getaway. *In Hamilton, New Zealand, the Waikato* Times *ran an ad: "Engagement ring, 2-stone, diamond and platinum, value £50, swap for good 2-stroke motorcycle. . . . "*

TIME

cies' services. Yet agencies may provide considerable assistance to the advertiser, not only in preparing commissionable media advertising but also in preparing all advertising, doing advertising research, creating a sound advertising plan, carrying out sales promotion and public relations assistance, and coordinating advertising with the other marketing efforts necessary to maximize profits. Therefore, increasingly, industrial advertisers are using advertising agencies.

Two types of advertising agency are available to the industrial advertiser: the general advertising agency and the industrial advertising agency. Carefully chosen, each can afford the advertiser expert counsel. The criteria for making a choice of agencies are the same as the criteria for choosing an agency for consumer-goods advertising, discussed in Chapter 6. Many general advertising agencies maintain staff personnel to render service specifically to industrial advertisers, whereas the smaller number of industrial advertising agencies deal with industrial accounts almost exclusively. However, because general agencies are geared to consumer-goods accounts, with large portions of their budgets specified for commissionable media, they are generally not attuned to any but large industrial accounts that may also have considerable commissionable media schedules. The industrial agencies, on the other hand, are geared to the needs of the industrial advertiser and therefore find it possible to operate profitably for the agency and effectively for the client.

Whereas general agencies typically operate on a commission compensation plan, industrial agencies more frequently do not. The reasons have already been mentioned—the relatively small amount of commissionable media advertising used, and the low cost per page for business publication advertising. Almost the same expense is incurred in the preparation of an advertisement to appear in a business publication with a $1,000 per-page rate as in the preparation of one for a general editorial magazine costing $25,000 per page. Research is necessary, media plans must be made, copy needs to be written, artwork must be purchased, type has to be set, engravings must be made, and so forth. The result is that a 15 percent commission on a $1,000 advertisement ($150) is just not sufficient gross margin to cover agency expenses and give the agency a profit. Furthermore, the out-of-pocket expenses incurred in the production of the advertisement may approximate or even surpass the space costs. For this reason, the industrial agency will generally charge the client on a fee basis (frequently crediting commissions against the fee) or on a percentage-of-billing basis. The problem of high production costs has little solution, except to economize to the greatest extent possible without sacrificing quality.

In an effort to reduce the relatively high production costs, studies have been run on the effectiveness of repeating advertisements. By running the same advertisement several times, it is possible to reduce the cost of production as a percentage of media costs. Economizing on production costs is an area that calls for years of experience and a hard-nosed look at every invoice.

Trade advertising means the advertising of goods and services to intermediaries who buy these goods and services for resale. Intermediaries may be wholesalers or retailers, but most trade advertising is directed toward retailers. In fact, many wholesalers themselves engage in trade advertising to retailers. Although most trade advertising is designed to sell goods for resale, such advertising also promotes items such as display fixtures and equipment that retailers use in their businesses.

The retailer buys the same products as the ultimate consumer, but with a major difference in motive. The ultimate consumer buys goods for the satisfactions they will afford; the retailer buys goods expecting to sell them at a profit.

OBJECTIVES OF TRADE ADVERTISING Recognizing the profit motive of retailers, producers in their trade advertising take an approach different from their approach to consumer advertising. Satisfaction to be derived from the products they sell becomes secondary to the appeal to the motive of profits. They may use trade advertising to inform retailers of the existence and availability of their merchandise, but they will stress its desirability in terms of the profit that the retailer who handles these goods will make. They may also use advertisements to the trade to back up their sales promotional activity, described in Chapter 10. Thus, their advertisements to the trade may announce available dealer aids, such as point-of-purchase displays and dealer cooperative advertising programs. Such advertising may also be used to merchandise the producer's consumer advertising program.

Like industrial advertising, trade advertising is usually a supplement to personal selling. It helps open the door for the sales force and acts as a reminder between sales calls. However, in selling to retailers, the channels of distribution quite frequently involve wholesalers. Because producers cannot be certain that the wholesalers' sales force will do the job they desire, and because wholesalers may carry a great many products, which prevents their salespeople from devoting much time to any one product, producers may depend upon advertising to the trade as their major means of selling their brand features.

ADVERTISING ORGANIZATION FOR THE TRADE ADVERTISER Unlike the typical industrial advertiser, the trade advertiser is primarily an advertiser, frequently of packaged goods, to consumers. Therefore, producer advertising organizations are structured as de-

TRADE ADVERTISING

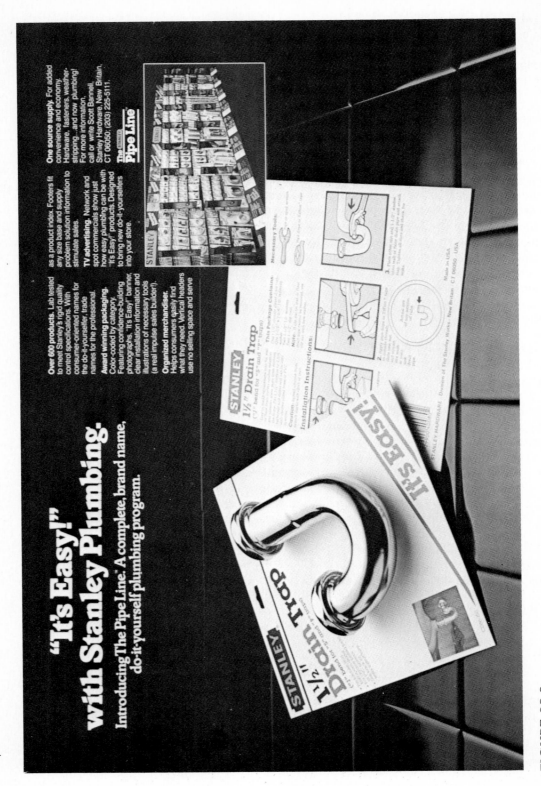

FIGURE 28-2

An example of an advertisement appearing in a trade paper. Notice that it emphasizes merchandising aids. (Original in color) *By permission: The Stanley Works.*

scribed in Chapter 6. The advertising agency usually handles the producer's trade advertising in commissionable media in the same manner as for the producer's consumer advertising. Collateral advertising may be prepared by the agency on a fee or cost-plus basis, or it may be prepared by the advertising department of the producer.

Professional advertising is the advertising of goods and services to professional people, such as doctors, dentists, lawyers, and the clergy. Probably its greatest use, however, is in advertising to doctors and dentists. These advertisers generally use personal selling as their major selling tool. Their salespeople are involved in a kind of missionary selling and are known as *detail persons* in this field. The personal selling and advertising efforts are designed for two major purposes. One is to sell things to doctors and dentists for their own use, such as equipment and supplies. The other is to convince them of the merits of the producer's products so that they will recommend the products to patients or write prescriptions calling for them. The advertising also helps to open the door for salespeople. Most professional advertising employs two media, professional publications and direct advertising.

Because professional advertising frequently involves highly technical copy, it is often prepared by someone with technical skills relating to the product rather than technical skills in advertising. Therefore, the producer rather than an advertising agency often handles the advertising, or at least the copy.

In most countries it costs less to catch a fish or to grow a lettuce than to carry it hundreds of miles, pass it on to the right retailer and have it available for the consumer, fresh, nearby and at the right time of the day.

SIR GEOFFREY HEYWORTH, Manufacturer

READER'S DIGEST

All kinds of advertising media can be and have been used in advertising to business, but business publications, direct mail advertising, catalogs, and exhibits are most often used. These media have been discussed earlier in the chapters on advertising media, but they will be considered further here in terms of the special problems of advertising to business.

BUSINESS PUBLICATIONS Business publications afford an excellent opportunity for business-to-business advertisers to reach a selected market with minimal waste circulation. Using vertical or horizontal publications, the advertiser can reach all levels of management within a particular industry or trade, or a particular level of management cutting across industries.

When more than one publication reaches a particular market, the problem for advertisers is to determine which business publication or

FIGURE 28-3

An example of an advertisement appearing in a professional journal. (Original in color) *By permission: Roerig, a division of Pfizer Pharmaceuticals.*

publications are the most valuable. First of all, they want the publication that will reach the people who are potential customers for their products. This may include not only those who actually do the purchasing but also those who influence buying decisions. Second, they must consider the editorial content of the publications, since there is a high correlation between editorial content and readership. Another factor to consider is the amount of merchandising service offered by the publication. Many business publications will provide advertisers with valuable market data and information regarding product use. Consideration must also be given to advertising objectives: Some advertisers are interested in securing inquiries and will seek publications with good inquiry-pulling records; others may be interested in disseminating information, building reputations, or establishing long-range preference for their products.

Some advertisers to business may find that because of their limited and readily identifiable markets, they can reach their markets economically and effectively through direct mail advertising. However, there is an important reason for including business publications in their media plans. These publications are the official and unofficial publications of the various industries. As such, they are respected by their readers and looked to as a source of information about the industry. The advertiser whose advertisements appear in these publications gains some of the prestige the publications enjoy. Even more important, perhaps, is the fact that they provide an excellent source of publicity for the advertiser.

DIRECT MAIL ADVERTISING Because advertisers to business usually know their market and the people in it, and because its size is small relative to the usual consumer-goods markets, direct mail advertising offers excellent advertising possibilities. Advertisers can reach the people they want when they want to reach them, with minimal waste circulation. Their messages are frequently technical and long, and direct advertising helps them avoid the limitations of the business publication's printed page size as well as the prohibitive cost of running multiple pages. Nor are size, shape, fold, color, paper, and the like restricted. Should they want to show X-ray views of their machines, they can use printed cellulose overlays. If they desire to include a sample of their lubricating oil, they need only find the right container. In short, the flexibility of direct mail advertising is almost limitless.

In addition to direct mail advertising, however, other forms of direct advertising can be delivered by messenger or salespeople or distributed at trade shows and exhibits.

One interesting form of direct mail advertising is the external house organ. Such publications, mailed regularly by the advertiser, usually contain articles of general interest to prospects as well as advertisements for the advertiser's products.

Because direct mail advertising contains information that is valuable to business prospects, it usually gets rather good readership. However, the volume of direct mail advertising is so large that the competition for attention is severe. If mailing lists are inaccurate or the advertisements unappealing, there can be considerable waste. Whereas direct mail advertising to ultimate consumers reaches them at home and must be discarded by them personally, direct mail advertising to business may be intercepted by an "efficient" secretary who wants to save the boss's time.

First Things First. *In San Diego, the* Evening Tribune *ran an advertisement in its Situations Wanted column:* "Woman, 35, general housework, loves children, live in. Husband welcome. TV not absolutely essential."

TIME

Advertising to Business

CATALOGS Catalogs really represent a form of direct mail advertising, but because of their unusual importance in advertising to business, they are considered separately here. Catalogs contain enough information on products offered for sale by the advertiser for the prospect to make a purchase. They are an important adjunct to other advertising efforts and personal selling. Because a well-prepared catalog is placed on file by the prospect, it provides a valuable source of information to the prospect between calls by salespeople. In peripheral market areas, it may serve as a substitute for the salesperson.

If a catalog is to be effective, it must be painstakingly prepared. Catalogs may have many costly illustrations and be quite extensive, sometimes as much as a hundred pages or more. As a result, they can be very expensive to produce. In an effort to keep unnecessary costs to a minimum, catalogs may be prepared with separate price lists that can be replaced as necessary without outmoding the catalog. If frequent changes in products occur, catalogs may be bound loose-leaf so that individual pages may be replaced. In addition to the more expensive *general* catalogs, firms frequently prepare smaller *special* catalogs for certain lines or classes of prospects.

Most catalogs are prepared and distributed directly by the advertiser by mail, messenger, or sales force. Another valuable means of catalog distribution, however, is the *prefiled* catalog or catalog file. Distributing companies like Sweet's collect catalogs of a number of firms, bind them together, and distribute them to a selected group of industrial users. Because of the convenience to the user in having all catalog material together, advertisers are assured greater life and greater use of their selections of the catalog file.

EXHIBITS Whether exhibits are advertising or sales promotion is beside the point. They are an important part of the promotional efforts in advertising to business and are generally the responsibility of the advertising personnel. Exhibits may be used at trade shows or at the advertiser's own shows. In either instance, they coordinate advertising through the distribution of direct advertising materials, demonstration, and personal selling by salespeople handling the exhibits.

OTHER MEDIA Some of the media thought to be ultimate consumer media, such as consumer magazines, newspapers, television and radio, can play and have played an important part in the media plans of many advertisers to business. Although these media provide much waste circulation, they may be valuable to the large advertiser with a budget that can afford them.

BROAD COVERAGE In an effort to reach everyone who may exert an influence on buying decisions, especially for industrial products with multiple markets, it well may be more economical to use consumer media rather than the more traditional business media. It is almost impossible to devise mailing lists or find combinations of business publications that can get this kind of coverage as effectively as

Advertising expenditures sustain the necessary demand to bring about savings in production costs which although they cannot be exactly calculated, are probably greater in amount.

SIR GEOFFREY
HEYWORTH,
Manufacturer

READER'S DIGEST

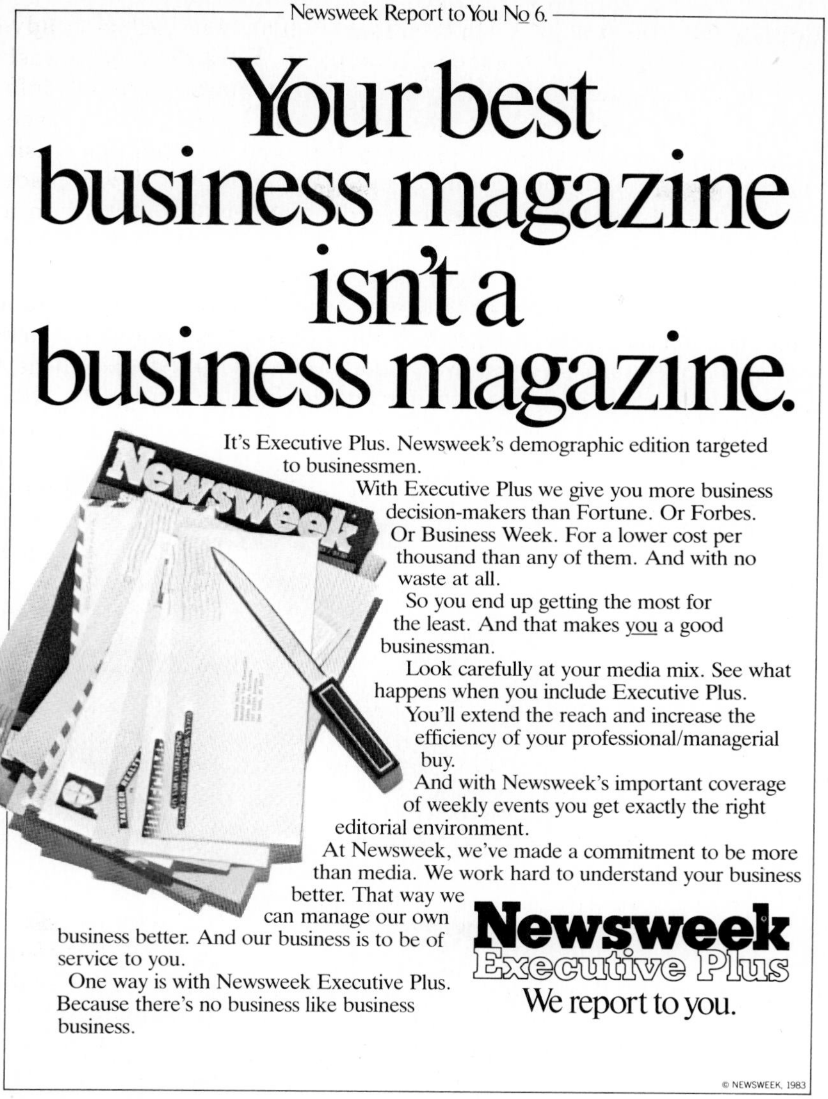
Newsweek Report to You No 6.
Your best business magazine isn't a business magazine.
It's Executive Plus. Newsweek's demographic edition targeted to businessmen.
With Executive Plus we give you more business decision-makers than Fortune. Or Forbes. Or Business Week. For a lower cost per thousand than any of them. And with no waste at all.
So you end up getting the most for the least. And that makes you a good businessman.
Look carefully at your media mix. See what happens when you include Executive Plus.
You'll extend the reach and increase the efficiency of your professional/managerial buy.
And with Newsweek's important coverage of weekly events you get exactly the right editorial environment.
At Newsweek, we've made a commitment to be more than media. We work hard to understand your business better. That way we can manage our own business better. And our business is to be of service to you.
One way is with Newsweek Executive Plus. Because there's no business like business business.
Newsweek
Executive Plus
We report to you.
© NEWSWEEK, 1983

FIGURE 28-4

A consumer magazine advertises to business to suggest its publication as an effective means of reaching business executives. *By permission: Newsweek Magazine.*

consumer media can. With some care in the selection of consumer media, such as *Newsweek* magazine with its special demographic editions, or the *New York Times*, which has high readership among businesspeople, it is possible to get broad coverage at relatively low cost per thousand effective circulation.

MINIMIZING BUSINESS COMPETITION Because such media are read away from the office, the business advertiser can reach prospects when they are not preoccupied with business problems and when there is less competition from other business advertisers. Executives are always interested in their businesses and can be appealed to even after hours.

PRESTIGE Some business advertisers use consumer media to increase their prestige among prospects. Such advertising also may help the financial position of the advertiser by attracting stockholders.

DERIVED DEMAND Increasingly, producers of fabricated parts used in consumer goods are advertising to ultimate consumers through consumer media. Names such as Talon, Ethyl, S.K.F., and Botany have become household words with considerable prestige among consumers, who may look for these parts in finished products they buy.

FIGURE 28-5

A firm selling to business reaches its market by selectively buying participations on television. *By permission: Burroughs Corporation.*

Burroughs
"Janzen"

COMM'L NO.: YB2C 8301   LENGTH: 30 SECONDS

CARL JANZEN: People usually think of IBM before Burroughs. After all, they are bigger.

I was with IBM for 14 years and bigger doesn't necessarily mean better.

Take small business computers. The Burroughs B20 has more memory, power, and growth potential than IBM's Datamaster.

And our hotlines will also answer your questions instantly. So, when it comes to IBM and Burroughs, believe me

the question isn't who's bigger. It's who's better.

PENCHINA, SELKOWITZ INC.

The result is a strong pressure on the producers of finished consumer goods to make use of these fabricated parts in manufacture.

The principles of good copy and art are universal in all advertising and so are applicable to business advertising. Nevertheless, some problems peculiar to business advertising creativity should be considered.

The point was made at the beginning of this chapter that whereas consumer advertising appeals to the emotions, business advertising appeals to reason. Because the business purchaser is buying to meet specific needs of the firm, buying behavior is apt to be strongly rational. Even so, the place of emotional appeal should not be underrated. After all, as a human being, the business buyer can also be moved by appeals to emotions.

Business advertisements have a great deal of competition. Business publications usually contain a large volume of advertising linage, and the advertiser must effectively gain attention if the advertisement is to be read. Unfortunately, all too often, amateurish attempts are made to secure attention as an end in itself. These devices may get attention, but they generally fail to bring the reader to read the advertisement and take action.

Business advertising should be interesting, but it should get to the point quickly. Extraneous copy and illustrations take readers' time and discourage them. They know why the advertisement is there and are more interested in reading it if they can expect some immediate reward for their efforts. Business copy need not be dull, yet it should not be frivolous. It should be specific, and it should tell the whole story.

Advertisements showing the product in use and promising benefits to the reader will gain favorable attention and interest as well. Readers respond well to advertisements telling of others' experiences in the form of testimonials or case histories, because businesspeople know and respect their colleagues. All the theoretical pleadings of a producer as to the potential worth of the goods are not nearly as effective and convincing as the successful experience of a user.

Another effective technique for gaining attention and interest in business advertisements is to use an editorial format. This "no-nonsense" approach appeals to the businessperson's seriousness of purpose and is also consistent with the editorial content of the publication in which the advertisement appears.

Business advertising tends to require a high degree of technical knowledge. Although the copywriter should therefore have technical competence, language should be kept as simple as possible without sacrificing technical accuracy. Copy should not be written "over the reader's head" or "written down."

As a final word of caution, business advertisers should avoid boasting in their advertisements. They are appealing to businesspeople who are serious-minded and knowledgeable. The advertising story should be told truthfully, directly, and specifically. In the final analysis, the reader will be convinced on the merits of the product, not the skill of the advertising copywriter.

Signode Corporation is the leading manufacturer and distributor of strapping systems in the free world. These systems are used in packaging and materials handling by a broad range of industries. They consist of steel or plastic strappings, together with seals and special machines and tools with which to apply them.[2]

BACKGROUND   Because of its long history of producing good products and of being an engineering innovator, Signode has become the dominant supplier in most industries using strapping. The extra services offered by Signode in package design and guidance in designing better-handling systems have played a major role in its success. As part of its marketing strategy, Signode emphasizes the sale of its application machines and tools to customers in order to establish a continuing demand for its strapping materials.

The corporation looks for future growth through new applications of its materials in new markets. Those industries not currently using strapping offer the greatest sales opportunity. The extra services offered by Signode are an extremely important factor for the firm in opening new markets. Experience has shown that the major buying influences for its products are top management, middle operating management, plant engineers, and purchasing agents.

COMPETITION The greatest threat to sales to large national account customers is from cut-price strapping suppliers. Signode believes that it can meet this threat by showing customers that it offers the lowest *total* price. In newer markets where Signode does not enjoy the top position, there is some competitive threat from a manufacturer's newly developed binder.

EARLY ADVERTISING EFFORTS Marsteller, Inc., through its Chicago office, took on the Signode account several years ago. Among the early advertising efforts was a series of case-history advertisements showing how Signode solved a variety of customer problems. (See Figures 28-6 and 28-7.) Initially, customer endorsements (that is, case histories) were difficult to obtain and, in some cases, therefore, the topics became more and more watered down.

Starch scores and other readership studies showed that the advertisements were moderately well read. As the campaign developed, however, readership fell. Follow-up creative research indicated that the subject matter in each advertisement was too narrow and thus excluded broad segments of the audience of *Business Week*, which carried the advertisements.

CURRENT PROMOTIONAL EFFORT   The marketing objectives behind the current promotional effort were to develop new markets for plastic strapping through the sale of equipment; to protect the existing

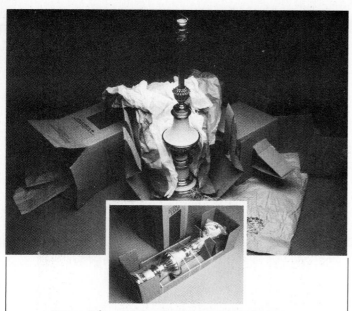

How 2¢ worth of Signode® strapping turned into a $45,000 savings.

Stiffel Company is known for its high-quality lamps. And to protect that reputation their products must be carefully packed.

Slow stuffing.

Until recently, their packing procedures required six people and tons of stuffing to be sure their lamps would not be damaged in transit. A costly and time-consuming method.

Safe in a cradle.

Stiffel, their container supplier, and Signode developed a new way to pamper the lamps. They're now carried in corrugated "cradle" trays. And held in position by Signode Contrax® strapping. This compact unit is then shipped in a corrugated sleeve.

Strapping is faster.

Now, one strapping machine and one operator make sure each lamp is safe and secure. Copolymer Contrax strapping holds the lamps but will not scratch or damage them. And it can easily be cut with scissors at its destination.

Ten feet of Contrax per package costs Stiffel less than 2¢. The labor savings alone is $45,000 a year.

Lamps, or you name it. We can help.

Improvement of packaging, unitizing and shipping methods are some of the ways we've helped industries save.

Modern strapping equipment and methods help you package your product better and faster.

Take a look at your packing lines. Think how a few cents worth of strapping could speed up your operation. Then call your local Signode representative. He's listed in the Yellow Pages, under Strapping.

▶◀ SIGNODE®

Signode Corporation, 2618 N. Western Avenue, Chicago, IL 60647

FIGURE 28-6

One of the early advertising efforts. (Original in color) *By permission: Signode Corporation.*

market share for steel strapping; and to begin to sell new plastic products in new markets before competition takes a leadership position. The specific objectives for the advertising in relation to the marketing objectives were to increase awareness of Signode capabilites in solving packaging, handling, and shipping problems; to convince those who influence buying decisions that Signode offers the lowest total cost; and to introduce new plastic products in appropriate markets.

TARGET AUDIENCE It was recognized that the advertising effort should be directed toward all those who influence purchase decisions. These could be divided into three target groups, and each would have the advertising effort tailored to it.

First, there was management, including presidents and financial officers, as well as vice-presidents of production, marketing, and purchasing. These people were seldom reached in any personal selling ef-

FIGURE 28-7

Another of the early advertisements. (Original in color) *By permission: Signode Corporation.*

fort, yet they exert considerable influence over purchase decisions. It was believed that they would be interested in the broad problems that Signode products could solve and how they could contribute to overall profitability.

Second, there was a functional audience of middle managers responsible for materials handling, packaging, physical distribution, and purchasing. This was the group called on by the Signode sales force. They would be interested in what Signode could do to solve their specific problems. Their concerns would be with the specific capabilities of Signode equipment and supplies. It would be important that they consult with Signode salespeople when they had a specific problem and when they were ready to buy.

Third, there were vertical industry audiences composed of all levels (top management and middle management) in individual vertical markets where Signode had something very special to say. Some of these were growth industries, and others were quite mature. The objective here would be to reach all levels in these specific industries to show how Signode could solve the problems peculiar to these industries.

MEDIA　For the management target market, demographics could be effectively matched through the demographic edition of the business publication *Business Week* known as "Business Week/Industrial." In addition, another business publication, *Industry Week,* was to be used. For the functional market target, a group of horizontal business publications was selected, and for the special vertical markets, the appropriate vertical publications were chosen.

CREATIVE STRATEGY　This creative strategy is for the top-management target market. The same advertisements were also used in those media chosen to reach the functional market target. For specific vertical markets, the same creative strategy was employed, except that the examples used were directly related to problems of particular industries. These advertisements were prepared in black-and-white for placement in the selected vertical media.

It was recognized by the agency account group that there was nothing glamorous about strapping. It was visually unappealing. There was nothing to significantly differentiate Signode's products from the competition's products. Strapping was looked upon as an expense by the people who bought it and it had to be on the bottom of the list of top-management concerns.

But despite all this, the account group recognized that what the product does and how it is used can be most interesting. It solves materials handling problems and it saves money. And saving money—especially large sums—the account group reasoned, had to be on top management's list of priorities. Thus, the strategy became clear. The account group needed to make top management aware of what Signode does with strapping that helps companies save money.

After a few sessions, the agency account group came up with a list of ways in which Signode helps reduce costs through problem solving:

1. By reducing in-transit damage
2. By reducing excess handling through product unitization
3. By making better use of warehouse space
4. By replacing more expensive methods of packaging
5. By reducing overpackaging
6. By improving plant efficiencies
7. By reducing load sizes through compression

The task of the advertising was now clear, but the account group still had to find the best way to communicate in advertisements how Signode solves problems. As indicated earlier, case histories had been used but were found wanting for the diversified kind of audience they would be reaching. It was strongly believed that if the advertisements

Advertising to Business

were to be effective, they would have to dominate the competition—not only other packaging supply advertisements but also advertisements for automobiles, liquor, and other products with more inherent interest than strapping that appeared in the particular media that would be used.

COPY RESEARCH Five different campaign creative approaches were developed. These emphases could be briefly described as technology, special market segments, damage and pilferage, cost control, and problem and solution. Their executions ran the gamut from cartoon illustration to serious advertisements showing how two cents worth of strapping material could save thousands of dollars. These were then tested by an independent research firm, using a sample of higher-management *Business Week* readers primarily from firms that were heavy users of strapping materials.

The advertisements to be tested were complete except for the copy. (See Figures 28-8 and 28-9.) The major research objective was to explore the main thrusts delivered by the illustrations, headlines, and

FIGURE 28-8

One of the test advertisements. Note the dummied body copy. (Original in color) *By permission: Signode Corporation.*

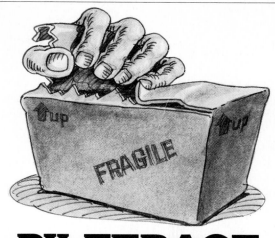

PILFERAGE.

How 2¢ worth of Signode strapping can save your product.

Nunquam ilisa custodibus horrebis ontrunum furem que stabulis insursus huproma ant impacatos ibers a tergo.

Saepe etiam agitabis timidos anagros cursu et leporuem canibus venabere damas et canibus. Saepe trubagis latra apros pulsos silverstribus que agens per altos montes preme ingentem crevum ad.

Quod mulsere die surgente horis diurnis premunt nocte quid jam tenebris et sole adit apros pulsos silverstribus que

Calathis sub lucem adit oppa aut contingunt parco sale que. Reponunt hiemi ncea cura canum fueit postrema tibi sed una pasce veloces catulos spartae wue acrem molossum.

Nunquam ilisa custodibus horrebis ontrunum furem que stabulis insursus huproma ant impacatos ibers a tergo.

Saepe etiam agitabis timidos anagros cursu et leporuem canibus venabere damas et canibus. Saepe trubagis latra apros pulsos silverstribus que

spartae wue acrem molossum.

Nunquam ilisa custodibus horrebis ontrunum furem que stabulis insursus huproma ant impacatos ibers a tergo.

Saepe etiam agitabis timidos anagros cursu et leporuem canibus venabere damas et canibus. Saepe trubagis latra apros pulsos silverstribus que agens per altos montes preme ingentem crevum ad.

Quod mulsere die surgente horis diurnis premunt nocte quid jam tenebris et sole adit

 **SIGNODE**®

Signode Corporation, 2699 N. Western Avenue, Chicago, IL 60647

FIGURE 28-9

Another of the test advertisements. (Original in color) *By permission: Signode Corporation.*

company identification and to evaluate their potential for gaining the attention of readers to the intended media, as well as inducing these readers to pursue the body copy when it was provided.

None of the approaches proved to be particularly outstanding. The one that tested best showed Signode solutions to common handling and shipping problems. The problem for these advertisements was that they were not communicating very quickly or effectively.

CREATING THE ADVERTISEMENTS The shortcomings of the problem-and-solution approach now became clear to the agency group creative members. They not only had to talk about various materials-handling problems in the body copy; they had to visualize them as well. Modification of the campaign idea came quickly after that. There were a number of ways they could visualize problems and solutions. They could, for example, show loading docks with loads arriving in bad and good condition—the latter with the help of Signode strapping systems. Or they could depict a warehouse using expensive hand labor and one using money-saving automation and Signode systems.

Advertising to Business

FIGURE 28-10

One of the early advertisements from the new campaign. (Original in color) *By permission: Signode Corporation.*

FIGURE 28-11

Another of the early advertisements from the new campaign. (Original in color) *By permission: Signode Corporation.*

Headlines were to be deliberately short so that they would communicate quickly. Body copy was also to be cut to a minimum because of the visual clarity of the approach. The account group believed that if the headline and illustration communicated well, and if prospects learned that Signode was in the business of helping to solve problems, then they had accomplished their objectives. Double-page spreads in full color and bleed would provide the kind of domination in the media that was deemed necessary, although in some instances, single-page, full-color bleed advertisements were to be used when the problem and solution could effectively be illustrated in a single page. Two of the early advertisements in the campaign are shown in Figures 28-10 and 28-11.

The creative team was now assigned the task of creating the next advertisement for the campaign. A member of the account group described the creative approach as follows:

> Because many industries ship goods by rail, as well as by truck, it was decided we should use the problem/solution technique for rail shipments. The agency discussed the problem with the client industry specialist for rail bracing and shipping methods. It was determined that many companies still ship loose containers that are not unitized or braced for rail shipment. The simple solution for these packages that get "all shook up" in transit is unitizing the containers and filling the dead space with "air bags." The latter are inflated to allow the load to move as desired by the

FIGURE 28-12

The rough layout for the "All shook up" advertisement. (Original in color) *By permission: Signode Corporation.*

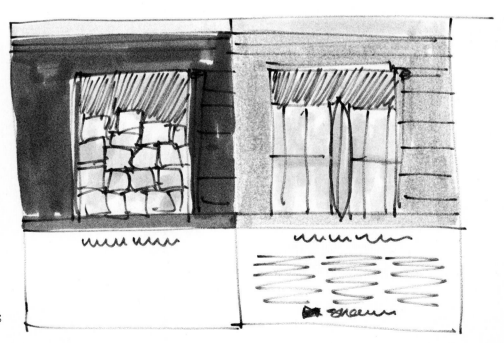

FIGURE 28-16

The combination of the yellow, red, blue, and black plates produces the finished advertisement shown here greatly reduced from the original size. *By permission: Signode Corporation.*

FIGURE 28-17

An enlargement of a portion of the four-color halftone screen showing the dot formation and how the colors are created by optical illusion. *By permission: Signode Corporation.*

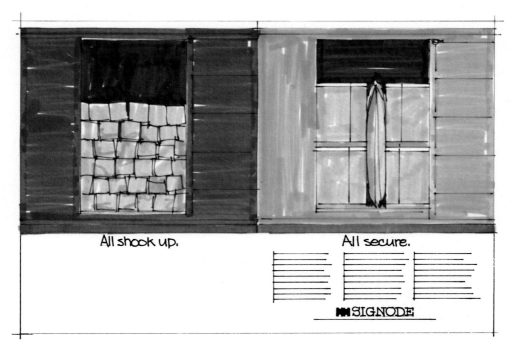

All shook up.

All secure.

◗◗SIGNODE

FIGURE 28-14

The finished layout. *By permission: Signode Corporation.*

FIGURE 28-15

See overleaf. The four-color process showing reproductions of progressive proofs. First is the yellow plate. Second is the red plate. Third is a combination of the yellow and red plates. Fourth is the blue plate. Fifth is a combination of the yellow, red, and blue plates. Sixth is the black plate, which also picks up the body copy. *By permission: Signode Corporation.*

All shook up.

All secure.

shipper. The creative approach is needed to follow the problem/solution format. Cartons that are shipped loose in rail cars get banged around or "all shook up." Cartons that are unitized (strapped) are easier to load and unload and they remain secure and in place with the simple addition of air bags.

The story was easy to tell: "all shook up . . . all secure," using the before/after photos.

FIGURE 28-13

The copy for the new advertisement. *By permission: Signode Corporation.*

NORTH AMERICA: CHICAGO · LOS ANGELES · NEW YORK · PITTSBURGH · WASHINGTON · TORONTO **SOUTH AMERICA:** SAO PAULO
EUROPE: BRUSSELS · FRANKFURT · GENEVA · LONDON · PARIS · STOCKHOLM · STUTTGART **ASIA:** HONG KONG · SINGAPORE · TOKYO · KUALA LUMPUR

Marsteller Inc.
CHICAGO

ADVERTISING COPY

Date March 9, 1978   Revision number:
Client SIGNODE   Ad number:
P.O. 15628   Ad subject/title: Shook Up

HEADLINE: All shook up.

            All secure.

COPY: Shipping damage wastes millions of dollars every year. Yet,

            most damage can be easily avoided. For just a few dollars

            per load, some simple bracing techniques developed by Signode

            can save thousands in the long run.

SUBHEAD: Get product and profit security.

COPY: No matter what or how you ship, there's a Signode Bracing

            System for all kinds of products and shipping carriers. For

            instance, for heavy loads shipped by rail or truck, Free

            Floating Load Control is an inexpensive way to prevent damage.

            This system allows the whole load to move slightly to

            gradually absorb the impact of sudden shocks.

            Or for light or compressible products, Wall Anchoring Systems

            holds loads firmly in place. Strapping is "anchored" to

            carrier tensioned walls around the entire load to act as a

            bulkhead.

SUBHEAD: More ways to cushion the blows.

(Continued)

Advertising to Business

```
COPY:      Signode Air Bags are placed between unit loads and inflated
           for cross car bracing.  They actually push loads against car
           sides to hold them firmly in place.

           There are even systems designed to protect your customers.
           Universal Retaining Strips are simple ways to keep products
           from falling into doorways or out of carriers when your
           product arrives and doors are opened.

SUBHEAD:   Let us help hold down costs.

COPY:      Signode Bracing Systems are just part of what we do.

           We're the world's leading supplier of all types of plastic,
           steel strapping and strapping equipment.

           Take a look at your loading dock.  If you think your load
           bracing methods are shakey, let's talk.  We're in the
           Yellow Pages under Strapping.

LOGO:      Signode Corporation
           2699,2675,2618,2626,2624,2690,2676,2678 N. Western Avenue
           Chicago, IL 60647
```

FIGURE 28-13 *(Continued)*

Copy was written and a rough layout was prepared (see Figure 28-12). After some small amount of revision in the copy (see Figure 28-13) and the preparation of a finished layout (see Figure 28-14), the advertisement was approved by the client and was ready for production. The first step was for the art director to arrange to have photographic color transparencies made for the illustrations of the boxcars. The photographs were shot at a train yard, where two boxcars were set up, one with unitized containers and air bags and the other with loose containers. In the meantime, the marked-up copy was sent to a typographer to be set.

Because the advertisement was to be printed by offset lithography, a keyline was made with photostats of the art and reproduction proofs of the typography pasted in place. This was sent, together with the transparency of the art, to a photoplate maker for positive separation films and proofing plates for progressive proofs. The films and "progs" were returned to the agency production department for color correction. After the necessary corrections and approval by the client, a set of the films and "progs" was sent to the publisher. (See Figures 28-15 and 28-16.)

Business-to-business advertising is to industry, trade, and professionals. The industrial market is divided according to the way industrial products are used. Personal selling is much more important in industrial sales than is advertising. Industrial advertising includes many noncommissionable media. Advertisers may use general or industrial advertising agencies.

Trade advertising is primarily directed toward retailers. Because it is designed to get retailers to stock and push the product, it emphasizes profitability rather than product benefits. Because most trade advertising is by producers of consumer goods, they usually make use of the general advertising agencies handling their consumer advertising.

Professional advertising is designed to reach professional people such as doctors and dentists. Because such advertising is often highly technical, there is a need to find people who can write about the product, rather than people with highly creative advertising skills.

All kinds of media can be used in advertising to business, but the major ones are business publications, direct mail advertising, and exhibits. Other media, however, can be used effectively to reach prospects out of their busy business environment. Through careful selection, business advertisers may make use of newspapers, consumer magazines, radio, and television.

QUESTIONS AND PROBLEMS

1. How do industrial markets differ from consumer markets?
2. How does the role of industrial-goods advertising differ from that of consumer-goods advertising?
3. What are the two main differences between the advertising organization for the industrial advertiser and for the consumer advertiser?
4. Why does the advertising agency generally charge the industrial advertiser on a fee or percentage-of-billing basis?
5. What is meant by trade advertising, and what are its objectives?
6. What is professional advertising?
7. What special media problems are encountered in advertising to business?
8. How can an advertiser to business justify using such media as consumer magazines, newspapers, and radio?
9. What special creative problems should be considered in advertising to business?
10. Find three examples of advertising to business in consumer magazines or general newspapers. In your opinion, what were the objectives of each advertisement?

ENDNOTES

[1] Maurice I. Mandell and Larry J. Rosenberg, *Marketing*, 2nd ed. (Englewood Cliffs, N.J.: Prentice-Hall, Inc., 1981), pp. 220–24.
[2] I am indebted to Signode Corporation and its advertising agency, Marsteller Inc., Chicago, for providing the information for this example.

International Advertising

After completing this chapter, you should be able to:
1. Explain the organization for international advertising
2. Describe advertising media in different countries
3. Explain the problems of creativity in advertising abroad

Although many firms have for many years been engaged in marketing their goods and services internationally, international business and international advertising have truly come into their own only since World War II. Not only has American advertising abroad increased tremendously in recent years, but domestic advertising in foreign countries has become increasingly important. What is more, foreign advertisers and advertising agencies are increasing their investments in this country.

International advertising has an interesting side effect. Although it would be difficult to find any exact measure of effectiveness, undoubtedly this activity has had some influence in "shrinking" the world and creating better understanding among nations. There is every reason to expect that the public relations aspect of international advertising by the private sectors of national economies helps to create an understanding between people in a way that government propaganda never can.

It is difficult to get an accurate estimate of the size of the advertising investment worldwide. Probably advertising volume in the rest of the world combined is about equal to that of the United States alone. Many principles of advertising in this country are equally applicable to advertising in other countries. Still, there are certain unique factors present in each country that justify separate consideration of international advertising by U.S. and foreign firms advertising abroad. Generalizations regarding international advertising are difficult, because the situation varies from country to country. This discussion will of necessity be sketchy, inasmuch as only very broad generalizations are possible.

The organization of the advertising function for the American firm engaged in international marketing is the same as that for domestic operations, described in Chapter 6. A question arises as to whether the advertiser should centralize or decentralize its foreign advertising organization. The degree of decentralization will usually be related to the nature of the product and the markets. For products that are rather standardized in use regardless of the country, there is greater central-

ADVERTISING ORGANIZATION

Ever get the feeling no one understands you?

Introducing Alliance… a dynamic, new way to make sure your international advertising message is crystal clear.

Alliance is a consortium of independent advertising agencies operating in six countries. Each agency is owner-operated, entrepreneurial in nature and expert at clearly communicating your message in the local language. Because, the fact is, your message may be getting lost in the translation. And that could translate to a loss of sales.

Each Alliance agency is headed and staffed by nationals. People who know and understand the local scene. So we will not only translate your message in "people talk," but will also tailor your message to fit the needs of the local market.

Alliance members have well-earned reputations for strong creative based on sound marketing strategies and planning. We believe in providing international advertisers with the very best native talent to create the most meaningful advertising.

And in providing the intimacy of a one-on-one relationship indigenous to a local agency.

Combined Alliance billings are almost $300,000,000. Our blue chip clients range from promising young enterprises to Fortune "500" companies.

The member agencies of Alliance are Arks in Dublin, C.F.R.P. in Paris, L.V.H. in Brussels, Prad in Amsterdam, The Kirkwood Company in London and Warwick Advertising in New York and San Diego. Further partners are being sought in Germany, Italy and Spain.

To find out more about how Alliance speaks their language, contact Tom O'Leary in Brussels (Alliance Coordination Office) at 02-242-0400. Or John Warwick in New York at 212-751-4700.

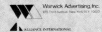
Warwick Advertising, Inc.
675 Third Avenue, New York, N.Y. 10022
ALLIANCE INTERNATIONAL

FIGURE 29-1

An advertisement that suggests a way to reach foreign markets by using a consortium of independent advertising agencies operating in six countries, thus assuring clear communication of advertising messages in the local language. *By permission: Warwick Advertising, Inc.*, and *Alliance International.*

ization of advertising; where the product is perceived and used differently in different countries, decentralization is more likely to be the case. In actual practice, the answer to whether to centralize or decentralize the advertising function will most likely be related to the firm's organization for international marketing in general, and may be centralized for some countries in which it markets, while being decentralized in others.

Most international advertisers will call on advertising agencies to assist them abroad. Today, most of the large U.S.-headquartered advertising agencies are *international agencies,* maintaining branches in those countries in which their clients advertise. They use mainly local personnel in those branches, and they solicit local business as clients in addition to handling the foreign advertising for their U.S. clients. In addition to, or in place of, wholly owned branches, these agencies sometimes operate joint ventures with local agencies in foreign countries. Of course, there are agencies headquartered in other countries that today have branches in the United States.

Where advertisers use American agencies without foreign branches, they can usually arrange to have international agencies handle only

FIGURE 29-2

Advertisers can use the *Reader's Digest* not only to reach the U. S. market but through its many foreign editions they can reach markets in many parts of the world. (Original in color) © *1983 The Reader's Digest Association, Inc. Used by permission of The Reader's Digest Association, Inc.*

their foreign advertising. Some medium agencies without foreign branches participate in international agency networks with similar agencies in different foreign countries.

Advertisers with decentralization of the advertising function may also "decentralize" their agency relations by choosing different foreign agencies in different countries. This, of course, suggests that there will be a considerable difference in their advertising from one country to another, but that is probably consistent with their decentralization.

INTERNATIONAL ADVERTISING ASSOCIATION

As there is for most other advertising activities, there is an association for international advertisers, called the International Advertising Association (IAA). The Association was organized in 1938 to advance the marketing and advertising of goods and services throughout the world. Among its many activities is the publication of *The International Advertiser* and its World Congresses, regional conferences, and the local meetings of its chapters in many countries. The IAA has also established a code of international advertising standards and practices for advertisers, agencies, and media.

There is no such thing, in my book, as an advertising appropriation. It is a sales appropriation. Every advertisement is supposed to sell. This is why advertising has been referred to as "Salesmanship in Print."

BERNARD C. DUFFY, Advertising Agent

READER'S DIGEST

MEDIA

Essentially the same media used for advertising in the United States are used elsewhere. However, there is generally a significant difference in how and to what extent they are used. To consider international advertising media collectively presents certain difficulties, for in each country, the problems involving media are different, if not unique. The important thing to remember is that the same media may differ in how they function from one country to another.

Unfortunately, although a good deal of reliable media data is available in the United States, such data are often sketchy or unavailable in other countries. Some information on foreign media is available from secondary sources. Great Britain publishes *British Rate & Data*. There are also *Tarif Media* for France, *Media Daten* for West Germany, and *Medios Publicitarios Mexicanos* for Mexico and Central America, for example. In the United States, there are two international media directories: *Business Media Guide International* and *Newspaper International*. Both give rates in U.S. dollars. If reliable secondary data are not available—and this is all too frequently the case—it is essential to collect primary data before making media plans. What was passing for a radio station in the interior of one country turned out on investigation to be a series of loudspeakers hung up along the street.

MEDIA SELECTION FOR DIFFERENT COUNTRIES Although there are certain universal principles of media selection that can be applied to international as well as domestic media, choice of foreign media will also depend upon special conditions in each country: the degree of literacy of the population, the relative cost of different media, the disposable income of the population, and coverage.[1]

LITERACY Media planning will vary from country to country, depending upon the degree of literacy of its people. In a country with a low literacy rate, print media are ineffective, but broadcast media can do the job. A low literacy rate generally reflects a low level of economic development—and, ironically, radio and television receivers are among the most expensive media for the consumer to buy.

RELATIVE COSTS OF DIFFERENT MEDIA Although it might be supposed that the relative costs of different media would be the same from one country to another, this is far from the case. Conditions peculiar to each country will affect media cost. These include restrictions imposed by government, media monopolies, and opportunity for circulation of the medium relative to the size of the country, among others.

Regardless of a medium's production cost, the price it charges an advertiser may vary from country to country because of its degree of popularity. It is difficult for advertisers to assess the relative value of media in foreign countries. They may select media they consider most suitable and pay the asking price. This may be satisfactory in countries where media rates are standardized. In other countries, media may take advantage of the foreign advertiser by charging exorbitant rates. As an alternative, some advertisers will pay less attention to the suitability of the media and choose those whose rates compare favorably with the rates of their counterpart in the home country.

DISPOSAL INCOME The distribution of income differs from country to country, and so, therefore, does the social structure. In some countries, there is a large middle class, whereas in others, there may be only the very poor and the very rich. Such income distribution patterns affect media planning, because the selection of media has to be adjusted to the habits and levels of discretionary spending of the different social classes.

These patterns of income distribution and the degree of discretionary spending are constantly changing as nations reach new levels of economic development. Therefore, markets must be analyzed continually as their size and patterns change as a result of overall economic change.

COVERAGE In this country, with its highly developed society, it is possible to reach just about any market segment. This is not always true in other countries, because of levels of literacy or income. Seldom, however, does an advertiser want total coverage in a foreign country, because

FIGURE 29-3

A magazine listing from the French media directory, *Tarif Media*. By permission: *Tarif Media, S.A.*

International Advertising

Why wait for Christmas?

12 YEARS OLD WORLDWIDE · BLENDED SCOTCH WHISKY · 86 PROOF · GENERAL WINE & SPIRITS CO., NEW YORK, N.Y.

FIGURE 29-4
Some consumer products, because of their nature and the universality of markets, can make use of the same advertisement simply by translating the copy into the appropriate language. Here is an advertisement for the U. S. market. Figure 29-5 is the same advertisement in Spanish for the Latin American market. Still, in other parts of the world, because the client uses local advertising agencies, the advertisements are different. (Original in color) *By permission: General Wine & Spirits Co.*

sales potential is usually limited to a minority of the population, the mass market being served by domestic producers.

PUBLICATION ADVERTISING   Publication advertising can be divided into two broad categories: international publications and national publications. Each can be useful in media strategies.

INTERNATIONAL PUBLICATIONS A number of publications, primarily but not exclusively published in the United States, are designed for distribution in foreign countries as well as domestically. These publications may be published in the native language of the country of publication, or they may be multilingual, using the languages of the countries in which they are distributed. They include newspapers, consumer magazines, and business publications.

The *International Herald-Tribune* is an example of an international newspaper. It is published in English and has circulation all over Europe. Its appeal is to a relatively small segment of highly educated and generally high-income Europeans and to Americans living or traveling abroad. It contains not only American advertising but also advertising of European firms.

¿Por qué esperar hasta Navidad?

Añejado por 12 años, mundialmente. Whisky Escocés Blended. 86 grados prueba. General Wine & Spirits Co., N.Y.

FIGURE 29-5

The Spanish language version of the advertisement in Figure 29-4 for the Latin American market. (Original in color) *By permission: General Wine & Spirits Co.*

Among American international magazines are *Time* and *Newsweek*, published in English in special foreign editions. These are similar in appeal to the newspaper mentioned above. On the other hand, there is *Reader's Digest*, with 38 foreign editions published in many different languages. The circulation of these editions is almost completely among citizens of the country in which the edition is published, and they contain advertisements by both American and foreign advertisers. Another type of publication is published in the United States but distributed *only* abroad. An example is *Vision*, a news magazine in the Spanish language published in New York and distributed in Latin America.

Advertisers wishing to reach businesspeople abroad use international consumer magazines because their highly select audiences generally include a considerable number of businesspeople. A group of international business publications is also available for this purpose. They can be categorized by language and circulation like the consumer magazines mentioned above and also can be divided into general and specialized publications. *American Exporter* is an example of a general business publication, whereas *El Farmaceutico* is designed to reach a special market.

These publications provide many services for advertisers, including foreign market data, translation, credit reports, and the like. They have the advantage of having dependable, honest rates and audited circulation. When an advertiser wants to get limited coverage of a number of foreign markets, they may prove to be quite valuable. On the other hand, they do not as a rule cover a single foreign country or cover a country in depth. Therefore, for advertisers who have limited their international business to a few countries or one, or for advertisers who want to reach the mass market, they are of somewhat limited value.

NATIONAL PUBLICATIONS Newspapers are found in all countries and are a popular advertising medium. However, they frequently differ in several respects from American newspapers. In many foreign countries, there are two varieties of newspapers: national and local. The national newspapers, such as Helsinki's *Helsingin Sanomat* and *Uusi Suomi,* are generally published in the capital but have heavy circulation all over the country, much like American national magazines. In addition, there are local papers with circulation confined primarily to the city's trading zone. A number of countries are bilingual, like Finland and Belgium, or multilingual, like India. In such countries, there are separate newspapers appealing to the different language groups. Then, too, the newspapers in many foreign countries tend to appeal strongly to select groups, for various reasons. For instance, there are strong political newspapers and strong religious newspapers that divide circulation according to readers' political leanings or religious affiliations. Thus, an advertiser may have to use several newspapers to cover the market.

Foreign magazines are quite similar to American magazines, although their quality of production is sometimes poor by comparison. In many countries with many poor people, their circulation is quite limited because of their high cost. However, because they are expensive, their readership per copy may be very large.

Foreign publications in some countries present many problems for international advertisers. For one, their rates are frequently unreliable and are quoted on the basis of what the publisher thinks the traffic will bear. Therefore, it is frequently necessary to haggle over prices, and advertisers can never be quite sure that they have obtained the most favorable rate. Then, too, circulation data are frequently unreliable. There are seldom any audits of circulation. Likewise, there is a dearth of data on readership with regard to such information as sex, education, and income. For the advertiser using publications in several different countries, language and custom differences may present problems.

BROADCAST ADVERTISING Broadcast is a most valuable advertising medium, but broadcast advertising is still unavailable in some countries, including some that are highly developed economically. Government prohibition of commercial broadcasting has been the reason. However, the development of television is breaking down these restrictions, because the cost of television is so high that advertising revenue is virtually an economic necessity.

FIGURE 29-6

This advertiser follows a policy of using the same advertisements in all countries. At the top is the U. S. version; next is the Spanish language translation; at the bottom is the Arabic translation. Because the language reads from right to left, the layout has been reversed. (Originals in color) *By permission: Eastman Kodak Company.*

RADIO In those countries where commercial radio is permitted, it is an important advertising medium, frequently more important than television. Even where few people own radio receivers, consumers have access to the broadcasts through public radio receivers in public squares, stores, and restaurants. The medium is particularly valuable because in many countries the literacy rate is low, even though many people have the money to buy the advertised goods.

TELEVISION In recent years, the number of both television transmitters and receivers sold outside the United States has grown tremendously. Still, the high cost of receivers has kept the number down except in Western Europe and Japan.

Three methods are used in the various countries to control television and therefore, indirectly, the possibility for commercials. The system of multiple enterprises permits a number of stations to be operated privately for commercial purposes. Under state monopoly, the govern-

FIGURE 29-7

This English-language version of an advertisement to business appeared in Australia, while the same advertisement appeared in other languages in other markets. *By permission: Burroughs Corporation.*

THE BURROUGHS B20. THE BUSINESS MICRO WITH THE BRAINS OF A MAINFRAME.

The more brains you have in business, the farther you'll go.

So it's no wonder the Burroughs B20 is doing so well.

With its powerful 16-bit processor and up to 640K bytes of RAM in each workstation, the Burroughs B20 gives each user his own computer, but with the power, data base and storage that were once associated only with mainframes.

Brains, however, are just part of the beauty of the B20.

Fact is, the Burroughs B20 is one of the most versatile, easy-to-use, expandable, stand-alone computers in the industry. The B20 can also be networked with other B20's so everyone is always working with the latest, up-to-date information. And because the B20 can have multiple workstations, it grows as your business grows. To operate, all you do is open the carton, plug it in,* choose one of our application software programs, tilt the screen to your desired height, and you're off. (Our step-by-step training manuals are so easy to use, you can be doing sales projections in a matter of hours.)

If you need any help, just call the Burroughs Resource Control Centre. Trained Burroughs computer specialists will help you with any problem—whether it's our hardware, software, or operating systems. (Being in the office equipment business internationally for 87 years has taught us a little something about service and support.)

You see, at Burroughs, we believe it's more important to be better than bigger.

So, if you're in the market for a business micro, consider the Burroughs B20. The one with the brains.

*B22 mass storage unit requires installation by a qualified Burroughs service representative.

I'm interested in the Burroughs B20 business micro. Please send me more information.

Name_____
Title_____
Company_____
Address_____
Telephone_____

Send to: Burroughs Limited
30 Alfred Street, Milson's Point
2061 N.S.W.

Burroughs

THE QUESTION ISN'T WHO'S BIGGER.
IT'S WHO'S BETTER.

**PRESENTAMOS
EL BURROUGHS B20,
EL MICROCOMPUTADOR COMERCIAL
CON LA INTELIGENCIA
DE UN GRAN COMPUTADOR CENTRAL**

Cuanto mayor sea su inteligencia para los negocios, más lejos llegará. Por eso estamos seguros de que el Burroughs B20 será un éxito.

Con su poderoso procesador de 16 bit y hasta 640 KB de memoria RAM en cada estación, el Burroughs B20 da a cada usuario su propio computador, pero con el poder, la base de datos y la capacidad de archivo que hasta hace poco sólo existían en los grandes computadores centrales.

Sin embargo, la inteligencia no es más que una parte del atractivo del B20. El Burroughs B20 es uno de los computadores independientes más versátiles, ampliables y fáciles de usar del ramo.

Los B20 pueden conectarse entre sí en una red, de manera que todos los usuarios tengan siempre a su disposición la información más reciente y actualizada. Y al poder utilizar varias estaciones de trabajo, el sistema puede crecer junto con su negocio.

Para operarlo, simplemente sáquelo de su caja, enchúfelo,* elija uno de los múltiples programas de aplicación disponibles, incline la pantalla al ángulo que más le acomode y… ¡listo! Nuestros manuales, donde se dan las instrucciones paso a paso, son tan fáciles de usar que en cuestión de horas estará usted haciendo proyecciones de ventas.

Si necesita ayuda, le bastará con llamar a Burroughs. Especialistas entrenados le podrán solucionar cualquier problema, ya sea de hardware, software o sistemas operativos. (87 años en el negocio de equipamiento de oficinas a nivel internacional nos han enseñado algo sobre el servicio y apoyo al cliente.)

En Burroughs creemos que, más importante que ser el más grande, es ser el mejor.

Si usted está pensando en adquirir un microcomputador comercial, piense en Burroughs B20, el inteligente.

Burroughs

LA CUESTION NO ES SABER CUAL ES EL MAS GRANDE, SINO CUAL ES EL MEJOR.

*Las unidades de almacenamiento masivo del modelo B22 tienen que ser instaladas por un representante calificado del servicio técnico de Burroughs.

Estoy interesado en el microcomputador comercial Burroughs B20. Sírvase enviarme más información.

Nombre_____
Cargo_____
Compañía_____
Dirección_____
Teléfono_____

Remitir a:
Burroughs de Chile S.A.,
Casilla de Correo 14285
Santiago

FIGURE 29-8

This advertisement, identical in format and copy to the advertisement in Figure 29-7, appeared in the Spanish language in Chile. *By permission: Burroughs Corporation.*

ment owns all television and no advertising is permitted. Finally, some countries have combination setups, with only some stations carrying commercials. Even where advertising is permitted, however, there are generally restrictions, and sometimes they are severe. In some instances, commercials are permitted only between programs. Sometimes they must be on film or tape. In some places, the filmed or taped commercial must be made in the country where it is to be broadcast.

Broadcast media in many countries do not provide reliable data on coverage, and their rates are frequently negotiated. The production costs of filming television commercials add to total expenses, especially because customs and language may differ sufficiently from one country to another to require separate films. Dubbing the audio, however, can solve the language problem.

FIGURE 29-9

With changes to fit foreign cultures the highly successful American "Mean Joe Green" commercial was effectively adapted to foreign markets by changing the football setting to soccer with "Mean Joe" Maradona in Argentina, "Mean Joe" Zico in Brazil, and "Mean Joe" Newat in Thailand. In Germany, on the other hand, where American-style football is growing in popularity, the concept worked without change. *By permission: CocaCola.*

MOTION PICTURE ADVERTISING Motion pictures have not been a major advertising medium in the United States, but in many other countries they play an important role, for several reasons. In countries where broadcast advertising is not permitted, the effect of television commercials can be attained to a considerable degree in movie houses. Motion pictures can also be a means of reaching an illiterate audience. They are an extremely popular form of entertainment in many countries, far more popular than in the United States, and therefore provide a mass audience for commercials.

The commercials are generally of the spot announcement variety, but sometimes they are long enough to be classified as "short subjects." Because the audience is in a sense a "captive" one, its size is easily measured, and reasonably accurate audience figures are generally available.

An interesting and valuable adjunct to motion picture advertising is the availability in many countries of sales promotion services. In addition to showing the film commercial, the theaters can distribute to the audience samples of products, coupons, and direct advertising pieces. They may also feature displays in their lobbies.

OUTDOOR ADVERTISING The use of outdoor advertising is very extensive throughout the world. In most countries, however, *non*-standardized outdoor advertising is much more important than it is in the United States. Red Coca-Cola signs can be found almost everywhere and in almost every language. It is not unusual to see this "sign of civilization" even in remote hut villages. Because economic conditions and the literacy rate in some countries keep the circulation of other media relatively small, outdoor advertising can be particularly effective. It costs the consumer nothing, and careful use of symbols and

FIGURE 29-10

The use of advertising in the People's Republic of China is increasing. In this photo from Beijing, the poster on the left advertises Japanese electronics while the one on the right advertises Chinese clocks. *By permission: Ruth Miller.*

illustrations can make comprehension possible even for those who cannot read.

Poster design, especially in European countries, is a highly developed art form and generally more readily accepted there than the more blatantly commercial design of American posters is accepted here. Outdoor poster boards are frequently placed along highways in virtually continuous succession extending for miles. An advertiser may buy a string of a dozen or more boards in a row, each containing the same poster.

OTHER ADVERTISING MEDIA   There are, of course, many other advertising media in various countries. Among these, probably the most important are fairs and exhibits and direct advertising.

FAIRS AND EXHIBITS Outside the United States, fairs and exhibits are considerably more popular than they are here and draw large audiences. There are both consumer and industrial fairs, which may show exhibits of many countries or of only one country. For example, Germany has held industrial fairs in a number of other European countries. Fairs offer an opportunity to display and demonstrate merchandise and distribute literature. Of course, they are also used to sell merchandise directly.

International Advertising

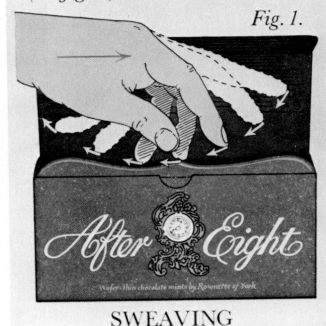

sweave_(sweev)_ vb. To finger through a box of After Eight mints at some speed in order to locate the last full envelope without drawing undue attention to oneself. _(See fig. 1.)_

Fig. 1.

SWEAVING

FIGURE 29-11

A British advertiser directs a promotion to the domestic market, using an English subsidiary of a U. S. based advertising agency. (Original in color) _By permission: Rowntree Mackintosh P.L.C._

DIRECT ADVERTISING The use of direct advertising abroad gives the advertiser a considerable amount of control over the advertising and the audience to whom it is directed. In addition to distribution of direct advertising material through theaters, stores, and fairs, direct mail may be used effectively and economically, because mailing lists can generally be obtained readily, and postage is usually low. Many organizations that want to stimulate trade will provide accurate mailing lists for prospective dealers and distributors.

CREATIVITY

There is considerable controversy regarding the creative aspects of international advertising. One school of thought is that people in all markets are alike in basic motives and can therefore be appealed to through essentially similar advertisements. Another school argues that local customs, habits, and the like dictate different creative strategies in

PEACHES AND CREAM.

FIGURE 29-12

A British advertisement by a British advertising agency with a play on words. (Original in color) *By permission: Saatchi &
Saatchi Garland-Compton Ltd.*

each country. After conducting research on the effectiveness of
standardized global advertising, the researchers concluded:

> . . . the results of the study appear to contradict the idea that international
> advertising should be standardized due to either the similarities among
> worldwide consumers or on the assumption that several products fulfill
> universal needs. Even though the basic product may serve essentially the
> same need in each country, the findings suggest that several cultural and
> environmental factors will influence the characteristics of the product that
> people emphasize in its purchase. A strong family orientation in the cul-
> ture may necessitate the use of family appeals. A relatively low level of
> income could dictate the emphasis of the functional qualities of the prod-
> uct, while a high level of income, which implies that all basic needs are
> being satisfied, may require an emphasis upon the more esoteric aspects
> of the product. In countries where the level of sanitation comes into ques-
> tion, advertising may have to mention the "purity" of the product.[2]

Undoubtedly, the time will come when we have one world, and
one advertising message will suffice for all people everywhere. Mean-

International Advertising

Vision

Open on a street at night and a man walking his dog.

Cut to Air Traffic Control Tower where we see controllers at work.

Cut back to man walking his dog in street, the dog pauses pulling on lead and begins to bark alarmingly at something in the sky. Man stops and looks up and is surprised at what he sees.

Cut back to Air Traffic Controllers in tower.

Cut back to Air Traffic Control Tower.

Cut to couple kissing on doorstep. Girl notices something strange in sky and nudges her boyfriend who also looks up and they both stand open-mouthed.

Cut to long shot of street and we see a spaceship type object travelling across the sky.

Cut to Air Traffic Controller close up.

Cut to two bikers sitting outside a fish shop. We then cut to a close-up of one of the bikers who is looking down and sees a reflection of the object in the sky and then looks up amazed.

Cut to housewife putting milk bottles out on doorstep, she pauses and looks up and is surprised by what she sees.

Cut to wide shot of street and a lot of awe-struck people standing in the road and on the pavement, all looking up at the sky. Manhattan now looms over the roof tops all very brightly lit. We cut to various people standing in awe and covering their eyes from the intense light.

Cut to reflection of Air Traffic Controller in Radar screen.

We cut back to see Manhattan landing on a runway until it totally fills screen.

Cut to logo device.

Sound

SFX: AIR TRAFFIC CONTROLLER TOWER

MUSIC: BEGINS

LONDON AIR TRAFFIC CONTROLLER:
Roger, Manhattan, continue descent to F.L. Eight Zero...

SFX: EERIE MUSIC CONTINUES

CO-PILOT:
Roger Heathrow, descending to Flight, Eight Zero...
SFX: MUSIC

LONDON AIR TRAFFIC CONTROLLER:
Manhattan, that's correct, contact Radar Director on One..Two..Zero.. Point..Four.

SFX: EERIE MUSIC CONTINUES

LONDON AIR TRAFFIC CONTROLLER:
Roger, Manhattan, continue to 2,000 feet, reduce speed to One Seven Zero Knots...

SFX: EERIE MUSIC CONTINUES

VOICEOVER:
Every year, British Airways fly more people to more countries than any other airline.

CO-PILOT:
Manhattan is established. Leaving 2000 feet on the glide path...

VOICEOVER:
In fact, every year we bring more people across the Atlantic than the entire population of Manhattan.

LONDON AIR TRAFFIC CONTROLLER:
Manhattan, you are clear to land, Two..Eight..Right...

SFX: MUSIC CLIMAXES INTO A LOUD CRESCENDO

VOICEOVER:
British Airways, the world's favourite airline.

SFX: AIRCRAFT

FIGURE 29-13

A television post-production script for the home market by a British agency. Note the differences in language, spelling, and concepts as compared to American English. *By permission: Saatchi & Saatchi Garland-Compton Ltd.*

while, there are some very real differences between foreign markets that must be recognized by the international advertiser.

One of these differences is language. Literal translations are not enough. To be effective, translations must capture the idiomatic differences in language. For example:

General Motors made an embarrassing mistake when, in Flemish, "Body by Fisher" translated as "Corpse by Fisher." In a similar case, Schweppes Tonic Water was rapidly dehydrated to "Schweppes Tonica" in Italy, where "il water" is the idiomatic expression for a bathroom. An American airline operating in Brazil proudly advertised plush "rendezvous lounges" on its jets, only belatedly discovering that "rendezvous" in Portuguese meant a room hired for lovemaking. Pepsi's familiar ad, "Come Alive with Pepsi," had problems in Germany because the translation of "come alive" meant "come out of the grave." Obviously, the ad had to be reworded.[3]

There are also differences between cultures. French is spoken in France and Vietnam and Quebec, but customs, tastes, and attitudes of the people are different in each market. Habits of dress, eating, and living are different in many ways. As R.R. Walker illustrates:

A Maidenform bra would not be appreciated by certain tribeswomen in Africa, since they refuse to wear any clothes at all. . . . For religious rea-

FIGURE 29-14

This brochure from Yugoslavia merchandises the advertising for Pepsi Cola. *PepsiCo, Inc. Reprinted by permission.*

Moi mes pulls, j'aime les porter à même la peau et leur douceur je ne la confie qu'à Woolite,

et à moi !

En machine ou à la main, Woolite lave la laine et tout ce qui est délicat

en douceur et en beauté.

Faites comme moi,

et comme moi, utilisez Woolite.

Je n'ai plus rien à dire !...

FIGURE 29-15

A television commercial for the French market prepared by a French agency for an American client. *By permission.*

Figure content (advertisement):

This is Sierra.
The changing shape of Ford.

Sierra breaks new ground. Perhaps, even a few traditions.

It's a car that, we believe, meets motoring needs through the eighties.

An unconventionally good-looking car. For all the right reasons.

A car that embodies the best available technology.

Above all a car that strives to bring man and machine into close harmony.

The shape of purpose. Parts the air with ease. Aerodynamically efficient. Gives more speed for less engine effort and fuel. And quietness. Especially at high speeds.

The shape of high technology. Windows flush-bonded to body for better aerodynamics, better seal. Integral, impact resistant bumpers. Hydraulic engine mounts for less vibration. Electronic safety display.

Optimum ride/handling balance. Sophisticated, fully independent suspension. Comfortable ride on all surfaces. Precise steering. Exceptional stability even on fierce corners.

Driver responsive instrumentation. Wrap-round, driver biased facia. Controls and instruments positioned for maximum command,

minimum fatigue. Overall interior well equipped, comfortable, luxurious. Space for 5.

The balance of power. 60 to 114 PS. Petrol or diesel. Instant power smoothly transmitted via 4 or 5 speed manual or automatic transmission, all computer matched to engine. For instance, 105 PS 5-speed manual capable of 0–100 km/h in 10.4 seconds and a top speed of 185 km/h.

Fifth door convenience. Assisted lift rear hatch. Fold down rear seat backs (60/40 split) for flexible, generous load/passenger space. Also available as a 5-door wagon.

The shape of economy. Up to 5.1 litres per 100 kms fuel economy (5-speed 2.3 diesel at constant 90 km/h). Low operational and service costs. 20,000 km major service intervals. 6 year anti-rust warranty.

The Sierra range from Ford. For availability, local specifications and price details, contact your nearest Ford Dealer.

SIERRA *Ford*
The shape of total driving pleasure.

Facia illustrated is from Sierra Ghia.

FIGURE 29-16
This advertisement, for a car made in Europe by a subsidiary of an American firm, was prepared by an agency abroad for a U. S. magazine and the U. S. market. (Original in color) *By permission: Ford of Europe.*

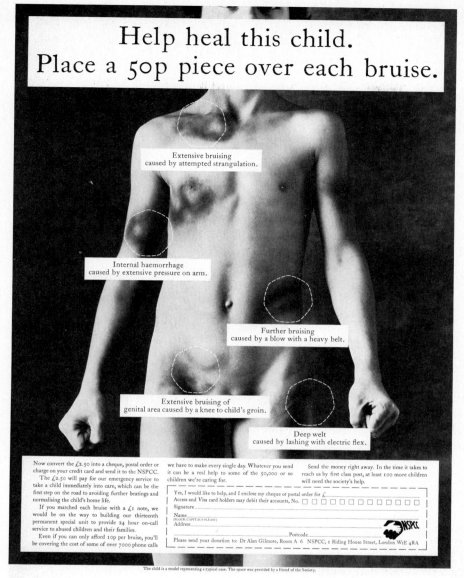

Help heal this child.
Place a 50p piece over each bruise.

Extensive bruising
caused by attempted strangulation.

Internal haemorrhage
caused by extensive pressure on arm.

Further bruising
caused by a blow with a heavy belt.

Extensive bruising of
genital area caused by a knee to child's groin.

Deep welt
caused by lashing with electric flex.

Now convert the £2.50 into a cheque, postal order or charge on your credit card and send it to the NSPCC.

The £2.50 will pay for our emergency service to take a child immediately into care, which can be the first step on the road to avoiding further beatings and normalising the child's home life.

If you matched each bruise with a £1 note, we would be on the way to building our thirteenth permanent special unit to provide 24 hour on-call service to abused children and their families.

Even if you can only afford 10p per bruise, you'll be covering the cost of some of over 7000 phone calls

we have to make every single day. Whatever you send it can be a real help to some of the 50,000 or so children we're caring for.

Send the money right away. In the time it takes to reach us by first class post, at least 100 more children will need the society's help.

Yes, I would like to help, and I enclose my cheque or postal order for £_____
Access and Visa card holders may debit their accounts, No. ☐☐☐☐☐☐☐☐☐☐☐☐☐☐
Signature _____
Name _____
(BLOCK CAPITALS PLEASE)
Address _____
_____ Postcode _____
Please send your donation to: Dr Alan Gilmore, Room A 6 NSPCC, 1 Riding House Street, London W1E 4RA

The child is a model representing a typical case. The space was provided by a friend of the Society.

FIGURE 29-17

This British public service advertisement uses strong shock appeal to make a point. Compare this with the American advertisement on the same topic in Figure 30-6. *By permission: Saatchi & Saatchi Garland-Compton Ltd.*

sons, a Sikh sees no value in a razorblade. A Hindu, however, prizes soap highly and considers that the European who takes a bath only once a day is a very dirty fellow indeed. African women want straight hair. The Japanese would like theirs wavy. In China red is lucky, white is for mourning. In many other territories, white signifies purity.[4]

For this reason, it is not enough to have a skilled translator. Only local creative talent can appreciate the peculiarities of local cultures.

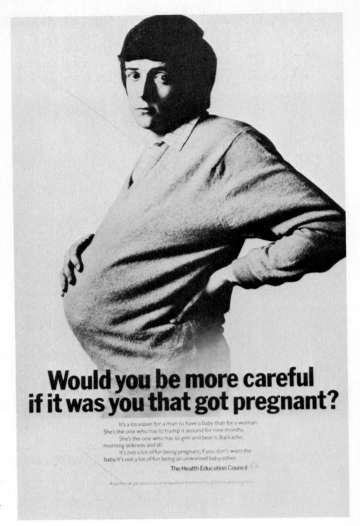

FIGURE 29-18

Another British public service advertisement which makes an important point by using excellent English humor. *By permission: Saatchi & Saatchi Garland-Compton Ltd.*

Therefore, when possible, it is probably wise to use advertising agencies in the local country. When an international advertising agency has branches in the various countries, these branches should employ local creative talent. Almost all countries also have legal restrictions on what can be advertised and what advertisements can say, and they are in a constant state of change. Thus, care must be taken not to violate local regulations.

Finally, there are the differences in economic development among countries. Thus, the creative approach will be affected by media development. As discussed earlier in this chapter, there are differences in the availability, effectiveness, and coverage of media from one country to another. This means that creative approaches must be tempered by media strengths and weaknesses in various countries. Likewise, the overall development of the economy will affect creative strategy. In one country, a product may have a mass market appeal, whereas in another, because discretionary income is limited, the same product may be sold effectively only to a small upper-class group.

On the other hand, some differences are perhaps largely imaginary, and advertising techniques that have proved successful in one country should generally prove successful in all countries, because if they are sound in principle, they should be universal.

International advertising will continue to grow in importance as the world shrinks and foreign markets become more accessible. We may one day achieve one world where all people react the same way to the advertising stimulus; but such a world is not here now. All women may be sisters under the skin, but consciously and even subconsciously, they react to the mores of their own cultures, and the advertiser must adapt the advertising to the differences of these different markets. Of course, there are exceptions to this, primarily among a small, elitist group of people in every country who are truly international in their customs and habits.

Total advertising in all other countries has grown rapidly and now is about equal to that of the United States. Firms engaged in international advertising need to develop an organization for the advertising function. This may be centralized or decentralized, depending upon the international marketing organization structure. International advertising agencies have branches in countries in which their clients have foreign marketing. Sometimes these branches are joint ventures with agencies in the foreign country. Other domestic agencies belong to networks of foreign agencies. Finally, there are local foreign agencies that can be used by the advertiser.

In considering media strategy for a foreign country, the advertiser must consider literacy, relative costs, income, and coverage. Foreign media vary considerably from country to country in terms of quality, rates, and audiences reached. In most other countries, both national and local newspapers are available. Some American magazines have foreign editions. National magazines vary substantially in quality from country to country. In some countries, broadcast media do not permit advertising or put considerable restrictions on it. Outdoor advertising is very popular in most parts of the world.

At issue in international advertising creativity is whether advertisements should be similar or different in each country. Care must be exercised in translations, legal regulations must be taken into account, and economic development levels must be recognized.

1. How does the volume of advertising in the rest of the world compare with that of the United States?
2. What kinds of advertising agencies does the international advertiser have available?
3. Compare centralized control and decentralized control of international advertising.
4. What are some of the media problems in international advertising?

5. What kinds of publications are available to the international advertiser?

6. How do broadcast media abroad compare to those in this country?

7. Why is motion picture advertising more important in many countries than it is in the United States?

8. What are some of the differences that must be considered in creating international advertisements?

9. Select three consumer-product advertisements from a domestic magazine. Would these advertisements need to be rewritten (aside from translation) to be used abroad, and if so, how?

10. International advertising has had some influence in "shrinking" the world and creating better understanding between nations. Do you agree or disagree? Support your stand.

ENDNOTES

1 Colin McIver, "Formulating Media Strategy for Foreign Markets," in S. Waston Dunn, ed., *International Handbook of Advertising* (New York: McGraw-Hill Book Company, 1964), pp. 135–39.

2 Robert T. Green, William H. Cunningham, and Isabella C.M. Cunningham, "The Effectiveness of Standardized Global Advertising," *Journal of Advertising*, 4:3 (Summer 1975), p. 30.

3 David A. Ricks, Jeffrey S. Arpan, and Marilyn Y. Fu, "Pitfalls in Advertising Overseas," *Journal of Advertising Research*, 14:6 (December 1974), p. 48.

4 R.R. Walker, "Marketing Opportunities in the Developing Countries of Africa and Asia," in Dunn, *International Handbook of Advertising*, p. 563.

Noncommercial Advertising

After completing this chapter, you should be able to:
1. Explain the concept of public service advertising
2. Describe the procedures of The Advertising Council
3. Understand the purpose of advocacy advertising
4. Evaluate the use of advertising in politics

$\mathbb{I}$f advertising has proved to be an effective tool for business, then could not this same tool be used effectively for noncommercial purposes? Who it was that first thought of using advertising for noncommercial purposes will probably never be known. Certainly, as will be shown later in this chapter, it is not a new idea. Yet in recent years, this use has grown tremendously.

PUBLIC SERVICE ADVERTISING

In Chapter 1, we discussed the use of advertising to sell ideas, which is known as corporate or institutional advertising. One such kind of advertising is *public service advertising*. In a broad sense, of course, all advertising conforming to ethical standards is *public service* advertising, if one accepts the tenet that the capitalistic system has resulted in the betterment of our society. Certainly this system has made effective use of the advertising tool and has contributed to our high standard of living. But public service advertising is used here in a narrower sense, to designate something distinct from what is termed commercial advertising. Its main purpose is the dissemination of information on a public problem and in the public interest. Advertisements to prevent forest fires, encourage driving safety, support higher education, and urge the public to register and vote are examples of public service advertising.

Most public service advertising in the U.S. is underwritten by business. It may result in building goodwill for the sponsor, but whether or not it is motivated by altruism, public service is its immediate end. Such advertisements may or may not have a relation to the sponsor's products. It would be unreasonable and unrealistic to ask that advertisements have no connection with the sponsor's business interests in order to be considered in the public interest. An advertisement is a public service advertisement if the message is designed to give unbiased information on some public problem and is in the public interest.

Use of public service advertising is not solely an activity supported by business. Various eleemosynary institutions have used this type of advertising effectively. Governments have also used it to good advantage. But business, through The Advertising Council, has developed public service advertising to its present importance and usefulness.

Thus, public service advertising has today become an important device for the transmission of information and ideas, a device to help a democracy maintain a well-informed citizenry. In addition to representing a significant development in the area of mass communication, this advertising has been significant in yet another way. Public service advertising represents a manifestation of the new philosophy of business —business with a social conscience.

EARLY PUBLIC SERVICE ADVERTISING   It is difficult, if not impossible, to know just when the first public service advertisement appeared. By the time of the Napoleonic Wars, however, there was a sizable amount of such advertising. An English recruiting poster for the Light Dragoons—which might today be considered exaggerated and in poor taste—read in part:

> You will be mounted on the finest horses in the world, with superb clothing and the richest accoutrements; your pay and privileges are equal to two guineas a week; your society is courted; you are admired by the fair, which, together with a chance of getting swished to a buxom widow, or brushing with a rich heiress, renders the situation truly desirable. There is a tide in the affairs of men, which taken at the flood, leads on to fortune. Nick it, and instantly apply.

Wars apparently brought forth considerable amounts of public service advertising. In World War I, both England and the United States used advertising extensively to help the war effort. In 1918, Woodrow Wilson issued an executive order creating a Division of Advertising to handle advertising for the Liberty Loan, Food Administration, Council of National Defense, and other bodies. The advertising was actually donated by business and was estimated at $5 million, a sizable sum for that day.

Wars were not the only time that public service advertising was used. In 1912 in several southern cities, civic-minded groups were using advertising to combat vice and corruption. In 1922, the Metropolitan Life Insurance Company launched a campaign for better health. Charles Frederick Higham wrote in 1918 and 1920 of the potential of advertising for public service. He advocated that governments (state, local, or national) use their own funds for such purposes.[1]

It was not until World War II, however, that public service advertising truly came into its own. Within days after the United States's entry into the war, the advertising industry had placed its services and resources at the disposal of the government to help win the war. From this effort was born the War Advertising Council. This organization worked closely with the government on numerous advertising campaigns for such things as war bonds; forest fire prevention; recruiting; prevention of inflation, espionage, and sabotage; victory gardens; and many others. All told, American business contributed an estimated $350

FIGURE 30-1

An early English public service advertisement. It was published in 1805 and sponsored by a private citizen.

million worth of advertising space and time in war-bond promotion alone.

THE ADVERTISING COUNCIL   With the war over, the advertising industry saw that the effort used for public service in war could also be used in peace. The board of directors stated that the Council's peace-time purpose would be:

> . . . to utilize some of the power of advertising in the interest of all the people; to give by its use an example of advertising as a social force in a nation at peace; to give a continuing demonstration of the willingness of business to cooperate with national leaders and leaders of government; and, by these means, to conduct on the highest plane the finest type of public relations possible for advertising and business.[2]

Thus, the organization was continued and its name changed to The Advertising Council, Inc. The Council receives its support from business, the various associations in the advertising industry, and individual advertisers, advertising agencies, and advertising media.

Before the Council will undertake a campaign, it screens requests made by government, private organizations, or individuals. They must be noncommercial, politically nonpartisan, and not aimed at influencing legislation. Further, they must be of national significance. The Public Policy Committee, composed of leading citizens from all walks of life, reviews all campaign requests from private sources and makes its recommendations to the Board, which is the final authority for action.

When a campaign is accepted by the Council, the American Association of Advertising Agencies recommends a volunteer agency to create the advertising, and the Association of National Advertisers recommends a volunteer campaign coordinator to guide the campaign. Customarily, the campaign coordinator is the advertising or marketing executive of a national corporation.

The task force and the coordinator meet with the client to determine the objectives of the campaign, necessary research, timing, financing of out-of-pocket expenses for the campaign, budget, and Council facilities and media to be used. A detailed report is then drawn up for approval. Since the formation of the Council, media have contributed approximately $8 billion of time and space, with recent media contributions running to almost $600 million annually.

Some recent campaigns have included aid to higher education: child-abuse prevention; high blood pressure education; forest fire prevention; rehabilitation of the handicapped; technical education; U.S. Savings Bonds; energy conservation; fighting pollution; crime prevention; alcoholism; and opportunities for minorities.

CONSIDERATIONS IN UNDERTAKING PUBLIC SERVICE ADVERTISING   When a firm contemplates undertaking public service advertising, it must consider several factors. The increasing awareness of the social responsibility of business can certainly justify such participation. Still, businesses are established to make profits for their stock-

As a profession advertising is young; as a force it is as old as the world. The first four words uttered, "Let there be light," constitute its character. All nature is vibrant with its impulse.

BRUCE BARTON,

READER'S DIGEST

The Great Imitator

HIDING behind a mask, man's most dangerous enemy strikes in the dark, and adds two out of every thirteen deaths to his score.

Just so long as men and women, and boys and girls approaching maturity, are not taught to recognize the cruelest of all foes to health and happiness—just so long will many lives be utterly wrecked, lives which could have been saved or made decently livable.

Strange as it may seem, tens of thousands of victims of this insidious disease (syphilis) are utterly unaware of the fact that they have it and that its malignant poison is steadily and surely robbing them of health and strength.

No other disease takes so many forms. As it progresses, it may mask as rheumatism, arthritis, physical exhaustion and nervous breakdown. It may appear to be a form of eye, heart, lung, throat or kidney trouble. There is practically no organic disease the symptoms of which it does not simulate. No wonder it is called "The Great Imitator".

It is the imperative duty of each man desirous of protecting his own health—and more especially the duty of every parent anxious to safeguard children—to know its direct and indirect results.

Syphilis is responsible for more misery of body and mind than any other disease. It destroys flesh and bone. Its ulcers leave terrible scars. It attacks heart, blood vessels, abdominal organs—and most tragic of all are its attacks upon brain and spinal cord, the great nerve centers, resulting commonly in blindness, deafness, locomotor ataxia, paralysis, paresis and insanity—a life-long tragedy.

Because of fear and ignorance, countless millions of victims have been wickedly imposed upon and hoodwinked by quacks, charlatans and worse—insidious black-mailers pretending to practice medicine.

The United States Government took a brave step forward during the Great War and told our soldiers and sailors the truth about this dread disease and what it would do if unchecked or improperly treated.

It can be cured by competent physicians if detected in time and if the patient faithfully follows the scientific treatment prescribed by his doctor. After the disease has been allowed to progress beyond the first stages, cures are less certain, but a great deal can often be done to help chronic sufferers.

Men and women should learn the truth and tell it in plain language to those dependent upon them for education and guidance. It is a helpful sign that the best educators deplore the old habit of secrecy and urge widespread knowledge and frank instruction.

It is estimated that more than 12,000,000 persons in the United States have or at some time have had syphilis.

From 5% to 40% of all the cases in the general hospitals of this country are found to be suffering — directly or indirectly — from this disease. The variance in the figures depends upon the character and location of the hospital.

According to Government statistics, the deaths of 200,000 Americans, each year, are directly caused by syphilis and associated diseases. But thousands of deaths charged to other causes are actually due to this disease.

Hospital and clinic records show that early infant mortality can be reduced one-half by pre-natal treatment of syphilitic infection.

The Metropolitan Life Insurance Company will gladly mail, free of charge, its booklet, "The Great Imitator." You are urged to send for it.

HALEY FISKE, President.

Published by
METROPOLITAN LIFE INSURANCE COMPANY ∼ NEW YORK
Biggest in the World, More Assets, More Policyholders, More Insurance in force, More new Insurance each year

FIGURE 30-2

This pioneer in American public service advertising published this controversial advertisement in 1927.

holders. To suggest using corporate funds for purely altruistic purposes might meet with some resistance from stockholders. If, however, it can be shown that public service advertising is good public relations, then perhaps this problem is solved. Certainly, considerable public relations value can accrue to such advertising. It is important to note, however,

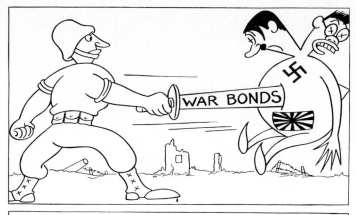

FIGURE 30-3

During World War II, many advertisers and publishers sponsored advertising to support the war effort. *By permission: The Advertising Council Inc.*

that public service advertising for public relations purposes is not commercial advertising, and expenditures should not be charged against the regular advertising budget.

It is not surprising that many firms supporting public service advertising choose themes that relate to their own businesses. For example, lumber companies might well be interested in and support forest fire prevention; the automotive industry might likewise support traffic safety. Although these firms may receive special benefits from such advertising, the benefits certainly do not diminish the social value of such advertising.

Many times, public service advertisements are devoted completely to the public service theme and carry only the name of the sponsor; other advertisements are regular product-reputation advertisements, into which a box or a slogan or a similar ingredient has been added as a public service message. In addition to the public service advertisements sponsored by advertisers, many are donated by media.

Although public service advertising tends to be noncontroversial in nature (there is probably no issue on which there is not *some* disagreement), not all noncommercial advertising falls into such a category.

ADVOCACY ADVERTISING

FIGURE 30-4

A World War II advertisement to combat inflation, prepared by the War Advertising Council. *By permission: The Advertising Council Inc.*

Both business and nonbusiness organizations have increasingly been using advertising to advocate some position on a controversial issue. Thus, *advocacy advertising* has been presented by individual corporations and by trade associations, and consumer advocate groups have also turned to advertising—sometimes to counter the positions of those corporate advertisements. Even among nonprofit organizations, there have been advocacies by one group and counters by another, as in the case of Handgun Control, Inc., and the National Rifle Association.

There are some who would argue that because of their immense financial power, corporations present an unfair balance on image/issue advertising. Ralph Nader argues that the public should have greater opportunity for response.[3]

ADVERTISING BY ELEEMOSYNARY INSTITUTIONS

Nonbusiness institutions have long recognized the value of advertising as a communications tool. Today many charities, churches, schools, museums, and other eleemosynary institutions engage in advertising. To be sure, their messages are sometimes underwritten by business, but often

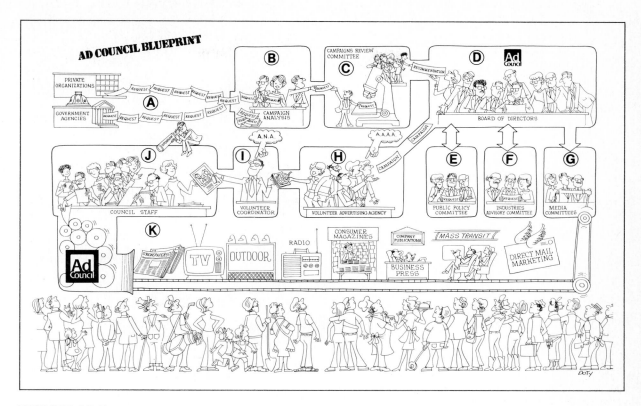

FIGURE 30-5

A flow chart for The Advertising Council.   A. Approximately 400 requests from private organizations and government agencies are received annually by the Advertising Council requesting campaign support.   B. These requests are analyzed and reviewed by the Council's Director of Campaigns Analysis and other staff executives. The Director gets any needed clarifications from the requesting organizations and forwards the information to the—   C. Campaigns Review Committee—a committee of the Advertising Council Board of Directors which considers the requests in detail and makes recommendations to—   D. The Board of Directors of the Advertising Council which, after discussing and acting on the committee's recommendations, votes on whether to accept the proposal as a major campaign or not.   E. The Public Policy Committee, an independent committee comprising leaders from many walks of life, recommends areas of concern and advises the Board of Directors about their importance to the public, acting as the Council's conscience, and reviewing ongoing campaigns and new proposals.   F. The Industries Advisory Committee, composed of leading business executives, assists the Ad Council and the board in financial development and other supportive areas.   G. Through the Media Committees of the Board and outside consultants the Council maintains liaison with all the media to help insure maximum usage of the Ad Council's public service advertising campaigns.   H. When a campaign is accepted, a Volunteer Advertising Agency is appointed by the American Association of Advertising Agencies to carry out the creative effort of all media, gratis, charging only for out-of-pocket costs. I. Too, a Volunteer Coordinator—usually an advertising or marketing executive from a major advertiser is appointed by the Association of National Advertisers, to coordinate all aspects of the approved campaign.   J. The Ad Council appoints a campaign manager from its staff to facilitate the progress of the campaign and maintain liaison with client, agency and coordinator. Staff media managers prepare the public service advertisements for mass duplication and distribution to—   K. All major media who each year contribute available time and space worth over a half billion dollars. *By permission: The Advertising Council Inc.*

The abused child will grow up someday.
Maybe.

Each year, over one million American children suffer from child abuse. Over 2,000 children die from it.

But what about those who survive?

Statistics show that an abused childhood can affect a person's entire life.

Many teenage drug addicts and teenage prostitutes report being abused children.

So do juvenile delinquents and adult criminals.

The fact is, a large percentage of many American social problems stem directly from child abuse.

Yet child abuse *can* be prevented.

The National Committee for Prevention of Child Abuse is a private, charitable organization that knows how to prevent child abuse.

But we need your help to do it. We need your money. We need more volunteers.

Send us your check today, or write for our booklet.

Because if we don't all start somewhere, we won't get anywhere.

National Committee for Prevention of Child Abuse

Help us get to the heart of the problem.
Write: Prevent Child Abuse, Box 2866, Chicago, Illinois 60690

Ad Council A Public Service of This Magazine & The Advertising Council.

Everybody deserves a chance to make it on their own.   Everybody.

The National Urban League is dedicated to achieving equal opportunity for all.
And there are things you can do to help. Contact your local Urban League or write:

National Urban League
500 East 62nd Street
New York, N.Y. 10021

Ad A Public Service of Trusted Advertising & The Advertising Council

FIGURE 30-7

Another campaign of the Advertising Council. *By permission: The Advertising Council Inc.*

they spend their own funds. Such advertising may or may not be of a public service nature.

Most universities, for example, engage in advertising. Their efforts may include direct mail advertisements, such as recruitment booklets about the facilities and programs at the university, posters announcing scholarships and fellowships, newspaper advertisements describing adult education programs, and entire advertising campaigns to raise money.

FIGURE 30-8

An outdoor poster from a campaign of The Advertising Council. *By permission: The Advertising Council Inc.*

All of us who professionally use the mass media are the shapers of society. We can vulgarize that society. We can brutalize it. Or we can help lift it onto a higher level. We must resolve to do all we can to use the skills we have worked so hard to develop in behalf of good causes, causes in desperate need of being talked about in clear, believable, penetrating and persuasive words.

WILLIAM BERNBACH (1911-1982), Advertising Agent

ADVERTISING BY GOVERNMENT

Governments have used advertising for many years. Many routine matters have always had to be brought to the attention of the public by means of advertisements, including the disposal of government property, contracts, court decisions, tax defaulters, and so forth. The *Congressional Directory* for 1901 showed that the contract division of the Post Office Department prepared advertisements, and War Department and Army advertising was the responsibilty of the chief clerk of the War Department. After World War II, the War Assets Administration spent $16 million on advertising to dispose of surpluses. Today, advertising by the armed forces is so huge that it makes the United States government a major advertiser. Recruitment advertising, and advertising by Amtrak and the U.S. Postal Service pay commercial rates for media and so such advertising is similar to the commercial advertising of business. It is a part of running the business of government. The U.S. government, however, has done little in the way of public relations advertising. Congress has been loath to appropriate funds for the same advertising tool that in the hands of business has often been criticized as manipulating human emotions and being ethically questionable. On the other hand, the government has readily accepted the public service advertising help of business through The Advertising Council.

ALCOHOLISM: A TREATABLE DISEASE

"JASON ROBARDS"	**CNAL-3130**	**30 SECONDS**

ANNOUNCEMENT (VO): Jason Robards!

JASON ROBARDS (VO): I am Jason Robards and I'm alcoholic.

I thought only losers became alcoholics.

Then I learned it's a disease that could have killed me.

I don't drink anymore. And now I really know what success is all about.

Not just with my career. . .but with my wife, my children, and my life.

I'm living proof you don't have to die for a drink.

ANNCR. (VO): Get help like Jason Robards got.

Call the National Council on Alcoholism in your area.

Get Help Like Jason Robards Got.
Call The National Council on
Alcoholism In Your Area.
Or write NCA, 733 Third Avenue,
N.Y., N.Y. 10017

A Public Service Campaign of the Advertising Council

Volunteer Agency: N.W. Ayer. Volunteer Coordinator: Edward M. Block, American Telephone & Telegraph Co. . **183**

FIGURE 30-9

A television commercial from a public service campaign. *By permission: The Advertising Council Inc.*

Undoubtedly, the use of the advertising tool by government could be an effective means of public relations. Perhaps, however, it would also be a danger. Such advertising, used to promote the public good in nonpartisan issues, could be an effective tool for the dissemination of information. But would it end there? Is it possible that such a tool as advertising, used improperly by government, could be a propaganda de-

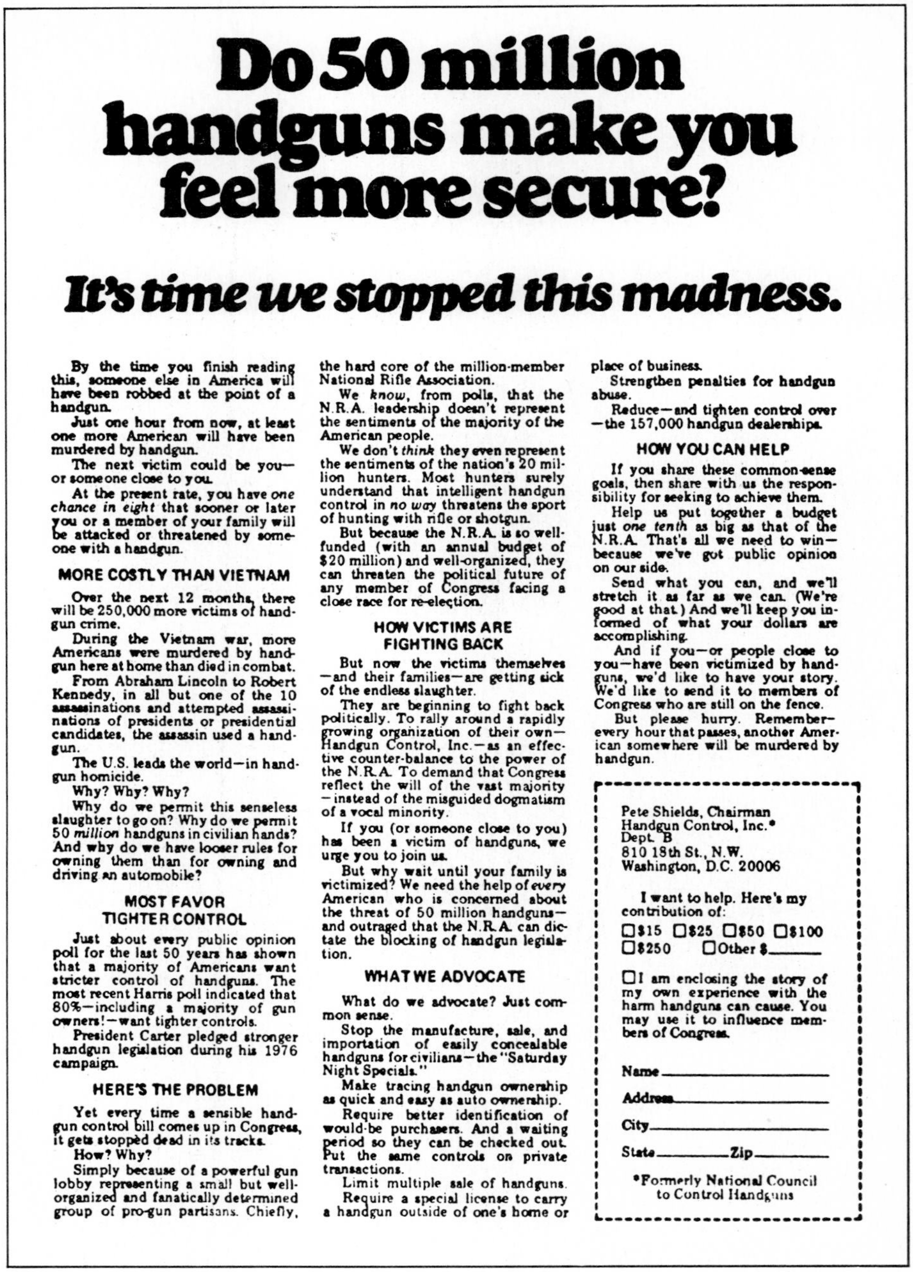

Do 50 million handguns make you feel more secure?

It's time we stopped this madness.

By the time you finish reading this, someone else in America will have been robbed at the point of a handgun.

Just one hour from now, at least one more American will have been murdered by handgun.

The next victim could be you—or someone close to you.

At the present rate, you have *one chance in eight* that sooner or later you or a member of your family will be attacked or threatened by someone with a handgun.

MORE COSTLY THAN VIETNAM

Over the next 12 months, there will be 250,000 more victims of handgun crime.

During the Vietnam war, more Americans were murdered by handgun here at home than died in combat.

From Abraham Lincoln to Robert Kennedy, in all but one of the 10 assassinations and attempted assassinations of presidents or presidential candidates, the assassin used a handgun.

The U.S. leads the world—in handgun homicide.

Why? Why? Why?

Why do we permit this senseless slaughter to go on? Why do we permit 50 *million* handguns in civilian hands? And why do we have looser rules for owning them than for owning and driving an automobile?

MOST FAVOR TIGHTER CONTROL

Just about every public opinion poll for the last 50 years has shown that a majority of Americans want stricter control of handguns. The most recent Harris poll indicated that 80%—including a majority of gun owners!—want tighter controls.

President Carter pledged stronger handgun legislation during his 1976 campaign.

HERE'S THE PROBLEM

Yet every time a sensible handgun control bill comes up in Congress, it gets stopped dead in its tracks.

How? Why?

Simply because of a powerful gun lobby representing a small but well-organized and fanatically determined group of pro-gun partisans. Chiefly, the hard core of the million-member National Rifle Association.

We *know*, from polls, that the N.R.A. leadership doesn't represent the sentiments of the majority of the American people.

We don't *think* they even represent the sentiments of the nation's 20 million hunters. Most hunters surely understand that intelligent handgun control in *no way* threatens the sport of hunting with rifle or shotgun.

But because the N.R.A. is so well-funded (with an annual budget of $20 million) and well-organized, they can threaten the political future of any member of Congress facing a close race for re-election.

HOW VICTIMS ARE FIGHTING BACK

But now the victims themselves—and their families—are getting sick of the endless slaughter.

They are beginning to fight back politically. To rally around a rapidly growing organization of their own—Handgun Control, Inc.—as an effective counter-balance to the power of the N.R.A. To demand that Congress reflect the will of the vast majority—instead of the misguided dogmatism of a vocal minority.

If you (or someone close to you) has been a victim of handguns, we urge you to join us.

But why wait until your family is victimized? We need the help of *every* American who is concerned about the threat of 50 million handguns—and outraged that the N.R.A. can dictate the blocking of handgun legislation.

WHAT WE ADVOCATE

What do we advocate? Just common sense.

Stop the manufacture, sale, and importation of easily concealable handguns for civilians—the "Saturday Night Specials."

Make tracing handgun ownership as quick and easy as auto ownership.

Require better identification of would-be purchasers. And a waiting period so they can be checked out. Put the same controls on private transactions.

Limit multiple sale of handguns.

Require a special license to carry a handgun outside of one's home or place of business.

Strengthen penalties for handgun abuse.

Reduce—and tighten control over—the 157,000 handgun dealerships.

HOW YOU CAN HELP

If you share these common-sense goals, then share with us the responsibility for seeking to achieve them.

Help us put together a budget just *one tenth* as big as that of the N.R.A. That's all we need to win—because we've got public opinion on our side.

Send what you can, and we'll stretch it as far as we can. (We're good at that.) And we'll keep you informed of what your dollars are accomplishing.

And if you—or people close to you—have been victimized by handguns, we'd like to have your story. We'd like to send it to members of Congress who are still on the fence.

But please hurry. Remember—every hour that passes, another American somewhere will be murdered by handgun.

Pete Shields, Chairman
Handgun Control, Inc.*
Dept. B
810 18th St., N.W.
Washington, D.C. 20006

I want to help. Here's my contribution of:

☐$15 ☐$25 ☐$50 ☐$100 ☐$250 ☐Other $______

☐I am enclosing the story of my own experience with the harm handguns can cause. You may use it to influence members of Congress.

Name ______________

Address ______________

City ______________

State ________ Zip ________

*Formerly National Council to Control Handguns

FIGURE 30-10

A nonprofit organization makes use of advertising in the *New York Times* to appeal for support on a controversial issue. *By permission: Handgun Control, Inc.*

GOV. VICTOR ATIYEH: Governor of Oregon; Former Businessman,
State Legislator and Senator;
Grandfather and Life Member of the National Rifle Association.

"You have to be somewhat of a romantic to be a gun collector.
I look at the eighty guns in my collection and wonder 'Who owned them?',
'Who shot them?'. They kind of hook me up with history
and make the days of George Washington, Lincoln and the pioneers much
more real than the pages of a history book ever could.

"I started gun collecting in college and it's become a lifetime hobby.
In 1946, I joined the NRA as a Life Member and 25 years ago I helped start the
Oregon Arms Collectors which is an NRA affiliated club.

"As a Governor, I'm concerned with crime protection and Oregon's penal system.
And like other NRA members, I want guns to be used safely and legally.
We believe strict punishment is
the best solution to crime with a gun." **I'm the NRA.**

Each year gun collector clubs and associations affiliated with the NRA
donate hundreds of thousands of dollars in firearms and contributions to museums, libraries and
education and training programs for the shooting sports. If you would like
to join the NRA and want more information about our programs and benefits, write Harlon Carter,
Executive Vice President, P.O. Box 37484, Dept. VA-20, Washington, D.C. 20013
Paid for by the members of the National Rifle Association of America.

FIGURE 30-11

Another view of the controversial issue discussed in Figure 30-10 is presented in this advertisement, which is one of a series. (Original in color) *By permission: National Rifle Association of America.*

vice to perpetuate the party in power and lessen freedom and democracy? The British advertising practitioner F.P. Bishop writes:

> The critics of modern commercial advertising often allege . . . that it prepared the way for totalitarian propaganda, and developed the technique which the dictators took over with such disastrous effect. Dr. Goebbels is

GUESS WHO HIRED MORE PEOPLE RIGHT OUT OF COLLEGE LAST YEAR THAN ANYONE ELSE.

Hiring college grads is something the Army has always done. And lately, we've been doing a lot more of it.

In fact, last year alone nearly 7,000 college grads chose to begin their future as Army officers.

Why? Some wanted the opportunity to develop valuable leadership and management skills early in their career.

Others were impressed with the amount of responsibility we give our officers starting out. And still more liked the idea of serving their country around the world.

Interested? Then you can start preparing for the job right now, with Army ROTC.

ROTC is a college program that trains you to become an Army officer. By helping you develop your leadership and management ability.

Enrolling can benefit your immediate future, too. Through scholarships and other financial aid.

So the next time you're thinking about job possibilities, think about the one more recent college graduates chose last year than any other.

For more information, contact the Army ROTC Professor of Military Science on your campus. Or write: Army ROTC, Dept. GE, P.O. Box 9000, Clifton, N.J. 07015.

ARMY ROTC. BE ALL YOU CAN BE.

FIGURE 30-12

The U. S. government is a major advertiser through such campaigns as military recruitment as illustrated in this Army ROTC advertisement. *By permission: United States Army ROTC.*

said to have declared in 1932, when the Nazis came into power, that he was going to use American methods on an American scale. Hitler himself in *Mein Kampf* pointed his arguments about propaganda with references to the methods and experience of commercial advertising. The similarities are indeed obvious, and the drawing of parallels . . . is hardly needed to reveal the fact that the methods of both rest upon the same basic principles. . . . Both are seen to be derived from the same teachings of the modern science of psychology, and from the same practical experience in the task of influencing the mass mind.[4]

The fact that the advertising tool can be used for evil purposes does not, however, diminish its value for good, as has been shown in the efforts of The Advertising Council. For government to use advertising effectively for propaganda purposes, it is necessary for government to have control of the mass communications media. In the free-enterprise system in the United States, however, the media are assured their freedom from political domination because business provides commercial advertising revenue. Certainly, within the structure of American democracy, there should be little fear of government advertising's being used as propaganda. Yet when a system of government becomes as complex as ours, there is always the potential threat of propaganda efforts going undetected or unchecked until it is too late. There are some people who believe, for example, that the extensive advertising and

KEEP THIS OFFER ALIVE.

This is your chance to help someone who really needs you.

It's an opportunity for you to take a child who is hungry and lonely and help give him the basic needs of life. Regular meals, warm clothing, even medical help.

It's also an opportunity to show that you care. By sponsoring a child through the Christian Children's Fund.

You needn't send any money right away. Just send the coupon. We'll send you a child's picture and background information. We'll tell you his age, how he lives, what he wears, and how your 50¢ a day—your $15 a month —can help make a world of difference in this poor child's life. We'll also tell you about the project where the child will be helped, and explain how you can write to him and receive his very special letters in return.

After you find out about the child and the Christian Children's Fund, then you can decide if you want to become a sponsor. Simply send in your first monthly check or money order for $15 within 10 days. Or return the photo and

other materials so we can ask someone else to help.

Since 1938 the Christian Children's Fund has helped hundreds of thousands of children. But so many more still need your help. Please send in the coupon today. It could be the chance of a lifetime.

For the love of a hungry child.

NNWK36

Dr. Verent J. Mills
CHRISTIAN CHILDREN'S FUND, Inc.
Box 26511, Richmond, Va. 23261

I wish to sponsor a ☐ boy ☐ girl.
☐ Choose any child who needs help.

Please send my information package today.
☐ I want to learn more about the child assigned to me. If I accept the child, I'll send my first sponsorship payment of $15 within 10 days. Or I'll return the photograph and other material so you can ask someone else to help.
☐ I prefer to send my first payment now, and I enclose my first monthly payment of $15.
☐ I cannot sponsor a child now but would like to contribute $

Name
Address
City
State   Zip

Member of American Council of Voluntary Agencies for Foreign Service, Inc.
Gifts are tax deductible. Canadians: Write 1407 Yonge St., Toronto, Ontario M4T 1Y8.
Statement of income and expenses available on request.

Christian Children's Fund, Inc.

FIGURE 30-13

A noncommercial advertisement sponsored by a charitable organization. *By permission: Christian Children's Fund, Inc.*

public relations programs of some branches of the government go beyond the legitimate needs of these branches and are designed to enlist public sentiment for the support of higher appropriations and political aims. Without debating the pros and cons of the charges of the critics, certainly there is a potential danger that, even if the charges are not founded, such advertising activities, left unchallenged, could possibly go beyond the bounds of legitimacy. Still, there is a wonderful opportunity for government to use the advertising tool to inform the public about the noncontroversial aspects of the problems of poverty, crime, intolerance, and the like. There is a need for an informed citizenry, and advertising is a potent tool for mass communication.

Promotional techniques have long been used by political candidates. There have been campaign buttons, slogans, songs, and posters. In recent years, however, many political candidates have turned to advertising on a big scale. Advertising agencies are retained to develop and execute complete marketing plans for candidates.

ADVERTISING AND POLITICS

623

If you drink too much there's one part that every beer can reach.

Your health isn't the only thing which suffers if you over-drink. A night of heavy drinking can make it impossible for you to make love.

And even if you think your drinking isn't affecting you, have you ever wondered how it might be affecting your partner?

Put it this way. How would you like to be made love to by a drunk?

The Health Education Council. **Everybody likes a drink. Nobody likes a drunk.**

FIGURE 30-14

In many other countries, public service advertising is also used. This advertisement appeared in England. *By permission: Health Education Council.*

But there are some who seriously question the use of advertising by political candidates. Martin Mayer states:

> The most common objection to the use of advertising to magnify political issues is that advertising oversimplifies. A good part of the techniques of advertising has the single purpose of simplification, of finding from the welter of causes which make people buy a product the one or two or three which can be refined down to "reason" and then blown up to a slogan. Applied to branded products, the technique at its worst can do little harm to society as a whole, because product purchases are trivial matters and because people do not buy even the most heavily advertised product a second time unless it has given satisfaction. Applied to political issues, however, the technique must partially misinform, create undesirable emotions, and destroy the realities, which, in theory, underlie the decision of the electorate.[5]

Regardless of its social worth, political advertising is a fact of life. In recent presidential campaigns, many millions of dollars have been spent at the national level, mostly in television—all in about twelve weeks of campaign time! Increasingly, politicians recognize the role that advertising can play. Lest one become alarmed at the thought of government's being the result of the creative capabilities of advertising agency executives, however, it must be remembered that, as in the case of commercial advertising, it is only one of many ingredients in the marketing mix.

Nevertheless, with each new election, there are more critics raising voices of protest against selling political candidates like breakfast

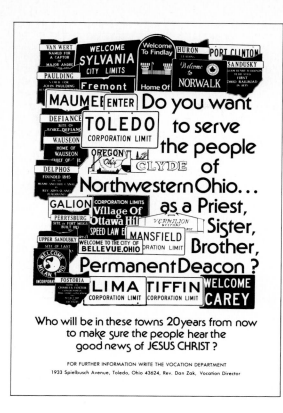

cereals. There have been attempts to curb political advertising by limiting the amount that can be spent. Even the advertising community is split on the issue of political advertising. But what are the alternatives? With all the technological advances in communications, they have not caught up to the growth and complexity of the population. Denying advertising privileges to political candidates still exposes the electorate to the influence of the powerful few who control the mass communications media, the political nuances of news analysts, the editorials of the press, the political machines, the ward healers, and the like. Should not candidates have the opportunity to present their positions when and where they choose? If some political advertising has been unethical or in bad taste, this only indicates that it must be kept in line. But there is little justification on these grounds for eliminating *all* political advertising.

It has been suggested that the broadcast media can better inform the electorate by having public service political programs of sufficient length to permit candidates to express their views and engage in orderly debate. A check of the program ratings for such programs indicates, though, that there are many people who do not listen. Yet these same people vote. They have been conditioned by the mass communications media and advertising to brevity in messages. Political advertising at least provides them with *some* information, granted that it may be woefully inadequate in terms of what is desirable.

Noncommercial
Advertising

TO SUM UP

Public service advertising is used to disseminate information on a public problem in the public interest. Most public service advertising is donated by business. Some public service advertising can be traced back to the Napoleonic Wars. It was not until World War II, however, that it truly came into its own. The War Advertising Council was set up by business, and after the war it continued, under the name of The Advertising Council. In addition, many businesses undertake public service advertising on their own—frequently related to their business and its problems.

Other businesses and nonbusiness organizations also engage in advocacy advertising—taking a position on a *controversial* issue. Many charitable and other nonprofit organizations also use advertising—sometimes in a similar manner to business advertising, and other times for noncommercial purposes. Even the government advertises. Recruitment advertising by the armed forces, however, is more akin to commercial advertising by business.

Political advertising has grown in importance as a major form of advertising. Some people, however, are highly critical of it, arguing that it does not really inform the electorate.

QUESTIONS AND PROBLEMS

1. Why can advertising be used effectively for noncommercial purposes?
2. How is public service advertising distinguished from other advertising?
3. Why should business firms sponsor public service advertising?
4. What is The Advertising Council? How does it operate?
5. Can advertising by antiestablishment groups be justified? Why, or why not?
6. Explain your position on whether or not government agencies should engage in advertising.
7. Are there any potential dangers in using advertising in political campaigns?
8. Assume that you are a candidate for the U.S. Senate from your state, and prepare an outline of a "marketing plan" for your campaign.
9. Select and evaluate three examples of current noncommercial advertisements.
10. What kind of future do you predict for noncommercial advertising? Why?

ENDNOTES

[1] Charles Frederick Higham, *Scientific Distribution* (New York: Alfred A. Knopf, Inc., 1918), pp. 138–39. Charles Frederick Higham, *Looking Forward* (New York: Alfred A. Knopf Inc., 1920), pp. 198–200.

[2] War Advertising Council, *The Council Looks Ahead* (New York: War Advertising Council, 1944).

[3] Ralph Nader, "Commentary Corner," *Advertising Age*, 54:4 (January 24, 1983), pp. M-12–M-14.

[4] F.P. Bishop, *The Ethics of Advertising* (London: Robert Hale Limited, 1949), p. 69. See also Robert Brandon, *The Truth about Advertising* (London: Chapman & Hall, Ltd., 1949), pp. 44–58.

[5] Martin Mayer, *Madison Avenue, U.S.A.* (New York: Harper & Row, Publishers, Inc., 1958), pp. 300–1.

A

Careers in Advertising

It seems appropriate in this introductory text to briefly consider career opportunities in advertising and how to get that first advertising job. From the text, it should be apparent that there are many different kinds of advertising jobs with a variety of different types of firms. Most advertising operations are relatively small in terms of the number of employees when compared to sales, production, and finance. As a result, there are few firms that recruit for advertising personnel through campus placement offices. This does not mean that the jobs are not there. It simply means that you must take the initiative to seek out firms that have advertising position openings.

KINDS OF ADVERTISING JOBS

In addition to positions with advertising agencies, there are job opportunities in advertising in the advertising departments of producers, service companies, and retailers; advertising media; art and photography studios; and other advertising suppliers, such as printers, typographers, television and radio commercial production houses, and the like. Finally, there is a growing demand for advertising and promotion people by nonprofit organizations such as museums, charities, health services, and schools and colleges.

All these organizations employ two kinds of personnel: those with advertising skills and those with other skills, such as secretarial, accounting, information systems, graphic arts, photographic, cinematographic, and others. Although these other skills may sometimes provide an entree to advertising positions, this discussion will be limited to those positions involving direct advertising skills, which were described in more detail in various parts of the text.

ADVERTISING AGENCY JOBS Advertising positions in the advertising agency may be divided into account management, media, research, and creative. To be proficient in any of these requires at least some understanding of the others, although these others may not be the strong points for a particular individual. Thus, a person employed in account management should have some understanding of media, research, and creative, although this person's main strengths will lie in marketing and advertising management.

ADVERTISING DEPARTMENT JOBS Advertising departments will differ in responsibilities from firm to firm, especially the manufacturer's advertising department and the retail advertising department. In most cases, the main job is managerial, but advertising departments may also employ media, research, and creative people. This is particularly true in retailer advertising departments. Additionally, firms that are organized on a product or brand management basis need managers whose major activity is apt to center around advertising.

ADVERTISING MEDIA JOBS For advertising media to exist, they need to sell advertising space or time. Even though these are sales jobs, they are *advertising* sales jobs, and such salespeople need a knowledge and understanding of advertising to be successful. Additionally, the media have advertising departments like other businesses, because they use advertising to sell advertisers on the merits of their medium and subscribers and viewers or listeners on the desirability of their medium.

ADVERTISING SERVICE COMPANY JOBS Frequently overlooked are the many job opportunities in the firms that supply the advertising agencies and advertisers. Art and photography studios need sales representatives who know the advertising business to sell their services to advertisers and agencies. The same is true in the graphic arts businesses and in the broadcast commercial production houses.

It should be noted that if you aspire to a position in an advertising agency or advertising department but cannot land one right away, one way of getting there is indirectly through jobs with suppliers or media. There are also many people who have moved from positions in advertising departments to advertising agencies and vice versa.

There is no one universally agreed-upon best way to prepare for an advertising career. Different practitioners offer different philosophies—frequently based upon their own experiences. Even college professors who teach advertising disagree on the best preparation for an advertising career. Still, there are certain generalizations that might be helpful.

PREPARATION FOR AN ADVERTISING CAREER

EDUCATIONAL PREPARATION There is fairly universal agreement today that for success in an advertising career, a college degree is essential. When it comes to deciding upon the course of study, however, there is widespread disagreement. While some still hold that a broad-based humanities or liberal arts degree is the best preparation for an advertising career (with no need to study advertising and related subjects), this philosophy is not borne out by the course of study of younger people employed in advertising today. And personnel managers in the business certainly suggest that they are more interested in students who have taken at least a part of their college work in advertising and marketing and related areas.

The college courses and program emphasis should undoubtedly be related to the major interest of the student. Through a combination of major and minor (or sequence, or area of specialization, as the terminology is variously expressed) and the judicious use of elective credits, a student should get an exposure to the following subjects: advertising, including its management and creativity; writing, through journalism or English courses; marketing, including management and research; visual and aural communications, through courses in interpersonal communications, broadcasting, graphics, and art design; and related activity areas, through such courses as public relations, personal selling, sales promotion, photography, cinematography, and business (especially basic accounting, electronic data processing, statistics, management, and finance). Of course, regardless of the program being followed, students must usually complete courses in general education. To the extent that it is possible to choose here, courses in psychology, sociology, social psychology, English literature, public speaking, art appreciation, theater appreciation, music appreciation, ethics, and logic are probably most valuable. A quick calculation might suggest that it will take eight years to complete all those courses! The idea is to pick and choose carefully in order to have a balanced program that will provide at least a basic understanding of the management, media, research, and creative functions of advertising.

OTHER PREPARATION To be sure, advertising education is not limited to formal course work in school. Extracurricular activity opportunities relating to advertising abound at most schools. There are advertising and marketing clubs. There are school newspapers and other publications and, perhaps, radio and television stations. Students can work in the editorial or business end, where practice in writing, art and photography, and advertising sales can be experienced. Serving as publicity or promotion officer for any club can afford an opportunity to practice advertising or advertising-related activities.

Many students work part-time while attending school and during summers. When feasible, jobs in sales (including retail stores) and in media are valuable and might be well worth any sacrifice in the rate of pay because of the experience gained.

A great deal can be learned by reading some of the nontexts written about advertising, which can be entertaining as well as informative. (See Appendix D.) Regular reading of one or more advertising business papers is also valuable. Finally, there is much to be learned by viewing, hearing, and reading advertisements and analyzing them as a practitioner rather than only as a consumer, now that you have completed an introductory course in advertising.

APPLYING FOR ADVERTISING JOBS

After having prepared for a career in advertising through a college program of study and extracurricular activities, and having had some work experience, you come to the time when you must seek a job. As pointed out, relatively few such jobs are filled by interviewing through college placement offices. In most cases, you must take the initiative to call on potential employers.

RÉSUMÉS AND PORTFOLIOS   Whether interviewing on or off campus, you should prepare a résumé. There are many books and some college courses that discuss how to prepare a good résumé. However, especially for those seeking advertising jobs, a résumé provides an opportunity to demonstrate creative ability. The real challenge is to be creative and still remain within the bounds of brevity, clarity, and completeness that a good résumé demands.

If you are seeking a job in copywriting or art direction, it is also vital to prepare a portfolio of samples of your creative work. This may include articles that appeared in school newspapers and literary magazines, and even unpublished works. In the case of art directors, the portfolio may include any art prepared for courses or included in shows. In addition, for both cases, any advertisements that might have been prepared for the school paper should be presented, as well as some copy and layouts that might have been part of course requirements or a series of hypothetical assignments. These might include advertisements for new-product ideas, improvements on existing poor advertisements, and additional advertisements for a successful campaign.

TAKING THE INITIATIVE   When the right kind of job interview is not available on campus, you must take the initiative. First, the type of job and firm desired must be identified. Then the geographic location must be decided upon. Although there is advertising activity and, hence, jobs in all the larger cities and many smaller ones, there are major concentrations in certain big cities, primarily New York, Chicago, Los Angeles, San Francisco, and Atlanta. You can use the geographic listings in the *Standard Directory of Advertising Agencies* to determine what agencies serve what accounts and where. Other directories, including the Yellow Pages, can help you to locate national advertisers, retailers, media, and suppliers. By reading the advertising journals, you can learn which agencies have landed new accounts and may need additional personnel to serve them.

Once you have decided upon whom you would like to interview, there are a number of ways to make contact. You may write a letter to the firm and enclose a copy of your résumé. The letter should be short and specific, but at the same time it should be creative if you want a favorable response. It should always be sent to a specific person by name —for example, the advertising manager, the media director, etc. When unsure of which person to write to, choose the one you would like to work for.

You may also make cold calls on companies, but you must be prepared to fill in application blanks and to leave your résumé. As a rule, it is less desirable to try to see people Monday mornings and Friday afternoons; and you should avoid arriving just as the firm opens or shortly before it closes. Be prepared to have to come back again at a more convenient time for the interviewer. If you are seeking a creative job, be sure to carry your portfolio.

There are, of course, other means of job hunting. You may check the help-wanted advertisements in the newspapers and the professional publications. You might also consider running your own situation-wanted advertisement. Another source of jobs is through employment agencies, which are sometimes paid by employers and sometimes by those seeking jobs. In the heavy advertising areas, there are employment agencies that specialize in advertising personnel.

One further source of job leads should not be overlooked—personal contacts. If you or a member of your family or a friend knows somebody in the business, ask for a referral. Frequently, a quick telephone call can set up an interview when nothing else will. This is not to suggest undue influence or pressure, for *you* will still have to perform well to get the job.

SOME ADDITIONAL THOUGHTS

People trying to break into advertising are frequently frustrated by being told that the employers are looking for people who have experience. Do not be dismayed. You may have more experience than you thought. Part-time jobs in selling, working for the school paper or radio station, entries in national student advertising competitions, some short stories you have written—all these are experience; and if you present any of these with imagination, you might well overcome this objection.

Never go into a company for an interview without finding out as much as you can about the company beforehand. You will perform better, and the interviewer will be impressed and flattered by your knowledge.

Do not try to be a "jack of all trades." Some people are so anxious to land a job that when they are asked what they want to do, they say, "Anything." But employers want writers for copywriting and managers for account management. Therefore, be specific—even though as your career progresses, you may change your direction.

Do some self-analysis. Determine your strengths and be prepared to "sell" them in the same manner that an advertisement sells the features of the product.

Get some interviewing experience. It is generally a disaster to make your first interview the one with the firm for which you most want to work. Develop your poise and interview technique through role playing with a tape recorder or a videotape machine first.

There is a temptation to "put on an act" during an interview. It does not usually work. It is far better to be yourself. This is not to suggest that you sit there like a bump on a log. As stated several times, advertising is a creative field, and you should be creative in your résumé, portfolio, letter writing—and in the interview itself. Be prepared to take the initiative in conversation (without being overwhelming), and by all means be enthusiastic!

Whenever you have had the good fortune to get an interview, be sure to follow it up immediately with a letter of enthusiastic appreciation.

When you try for your first advertising job and things do not go the way you had hoped, do not become discouraged. Just keep at it. I never knew a qualified student of advertising who *really* wanted a job in advertising who did not get one ultimately. If it is what you truly want to do, nothing else will give you more real pleasure and satisfaction—and the ends are well worth the efforts.

Good luck, and good advertising!

B

Media Data

T he media data that follow provide a quick and accessible source of information for advertising media planning and buying.[1] Such data are compiled by several large advertising agencies for use by their management personnel. The media data presented here are from *Media Modules* of Grey Advertising Inc.

Although these guides can serve as convenient references for media costs and audience data, they do have their limits. They can be useful as a source for roughing out the dimensions of a media plan but are not meant to be a substitute for the careful kind of information provided by professional media planners, who have substantially more media information available to them.

Because the business of advertising media is so volatile and rapidly moving, much of the data, especially cost information, can change rapidly. Therefore, it is suggested that the information's use be limited to making only approximations of media plan costs.

DEMOGRAPHICS OF THE U.S. POPULATION
POPULATION BY AGE AND SEX

Age Group	Total (MM)	%	%18+	Men (MM)	%	%18+	Women (MM)	%	%18+
Under 2	7.6	3	-	3.9	3	-	3.7	3	-
2-5	13.9	6	-	7.1	6	-	6.8	6	-
6-11	19.4	9	-	9.9	9	-	9.5	8	-
12-17	22.1	9	-	11.3	10	-	10.8	9	-
18-24	30.0	13	18	15.2	13	18	14.8	12	17
25-34	40.1	17	23	20.0	18	24	20.1	17	23
35-44	29.3	12	17	14.4	13	18	14.9	12	17
45-49	11.2	5	7	5.5	5	7	5.7	5	6
50-54	11.2	5	7	5.4	5	7	5.8	5	6
55-64	22.3	10	13	10.5	9	13	11.8	10	13
65+	27.1	11	15	10.8	9	13	16.3	13	18
Total	234.2	100	100	114.0	100	100	120.2	100	100
Under 18	63.0	27	-	32.2	28	-	30.8	26	-
2-11	33.3	14	-	17.0	15	-	16.3	14	-
18-34	70.1	30	41	35.2	31	43	34.9	29	39
18-49	110.6	47	65	55.1	48	67	55.5	46	62
25-54	91.8	39	54	45.3	40	55	46.5	39	52
25-64	114.1	49	67	55.8	49	68	58.3	49	65
35+	101.1	43	59	46.6	41	57	54.5	45	61
50+	60.6	26	35	26.7	23	33	33.9	28	38
55+	49.4	21	28	21.3	19	26	28.1	23	31
18+	171.2	73	100	81.8	72	100	89.4	74	100

Source: Bureau of Census, Series P-25, No. 917 (Series II) for 1981 Population Estimates. Percent Growth from 1981-1983 estimates based on increases shown in Series P-25, No. 704 (Series II)

Represents July 1, 1983, Population Bases

DEMOGRAPHICS OF THE U.S. POPULATION

ADULTS BY HOUSEHOLD INCOME

Income Group	Total (M)	%	Men (M)	%	Women (M)	%
Under $5.000	12.792	7.5	3.763	4.6	9.029	10.1
$5.000-$9.999	16.587	9.7	6.217	7.6	10.370	11.6
$10.000-$14.999	19.049	11.1	8.589	10.5	10.460	11.7
$15.000-$19.999	22.077	12.9	10.634	13.0	11.443	12.8
$20.000-$24.999	23.274	13.6	12.188	14.9	11.086	12.4
$25.000-$34.999	38.059	22.2	19.550	23.9	18.509	20.7
$35.000+	39.368	23.0	20.859	25.5	18.509	20.7
Total	171.206	100.0	81.800	100.0	89.406	100.0

ADULTS BY EDUCATION

Education Group	Total (M)	%	Men (M)	%	Women (M)	%
Graduated College	25.2b1	14.7	14.642	17.9	10.639	11.9
Attended College	28.858	16.9	14.642	17.9	14.216	15.9
Graduated High School	65.659	38.4	28.466	34.8	37.193	41.6
Did Not Graduate High School	51.408	30.0	24.050	29.4	27.358	30.6
Total	171.206	100.0	81.800	100.0	89.406	100.0

ADULTS BY HOUSEHOLD SIZE

	Total Adults (M)	%	Men (M)	%	Women (M)	%
1-2	74.029	43.2	34.601	42.3	39.428	44.1
3-4	67.029	39.2	32.965	40.3	34.064	38.1
5+	30.148	17.6	14.234	17.4	15.914	17.8
Total	171.206	100.0	81.800	100.0	89.406	100.0

ADULTS BY MARITAL STATUS

	Total Adults (M)	%	Men (M)	%	Women (M)	%
Single	33.663	19.6	18.732	22.9	14.931	16.7
Married	110.928	64.8	56.033	68.5	54.895	61.4
Divorced/Widowed/Separated	26.615	15.6	7.035	8.6	19.580	21.9
Total	171.206	100.0	81.800	100.0	89.406	100.0

Source: Bureau of Census. Series P-25. No. 917 (Series II) for 1981 Population Estimates. Percent Growth from 1981-1983 estimates based on increases shown in Series P-25, No. 704 (Series II)

Represents July 1, 1983. Population Bases

DEMOGRAPHIC CHARACTERISTICS OF MEDIA EXPOSURE GROUPS

Demographics	Total Adults	% Pop	Radio Heaviest 20%	Radio Lightest 20%	Magazines Heaviest 20%	Magazines Lightest 20%	Newspapers Heaviest 20%	Newspapers Lightest 20%	TV (Total) Heaviest 20%	TV (Total) Lightest 20%
Age	18-24	17.7	164	44	148	68	67	142	93	117
	25-34	22.4	112	71	129	64	83	115	87	113
	35-54	30.9	89	101	93	90	118	78	84	107
	55+	29.0	63	154	56	159	113	86	131	72
Education	Att./Grad. Col.	31.8	99	83	145	42	138	68	59	130
	HS Graduates	38.4	109	85	95	86	97	93	103	87
	Less	29.8	89	138	59	180	63	143	140	85
HH Income	$35M+	19.1	91	86	149	42	160	52	55	126
	$25M+	38.9	100	79	131	55	133	64	68	112
	$15M+	66.6	101	87	115	71	118	80	80	103
	$10-$15M	12.9	98	118	75	124	81	116	123	98
	Under $10M	20.5	98	132	64	180	54	77	150	91
HH Size	1-2	44.4	92	114	84	120	97	101	107	95
	3-4	38.8	103	91	113	83	100	99	98	102
	5+	16.8	114	82	110	87	108	101	85	108

To be read: An index of 164 in a demographic cell which accounts for 17.7% of the population indicates that 29.0% (17.7 x 1.64) of the quintile group are in that demographic cell.

Source: MRI, Spring 1982

CROSSTABS OF MEDIA EXPOSURE GROUPS

MEDIA EXPOSURE—ADULTS

		TV (Total) Heaviest 20%	TV (Total) Lightest 20%	Newspapers Heaviest 20%	Newspapers Lightest 20%	Magazines Heaviest 20%	Magazines Lightest 20%	Radio Heaviest 20%	Radio Lightest 20%
TV (Total)	Heaviest 20%	-	-	88	106	105	100	100	116
	Middle 20%	-	-	106	87	98	101	89	93
	Lightest 20%	-	-	96	125	106	112	117	100
Newspapers	Heaviest 20%	88	96	-	-	154	50	104	85
	Middle 20%	112	87	-	-	78	102	87	109
	Lightest 20%	106	125	-	-	56	192	104	125
Magazines	Heaviest 20%	105	106	154	56	-	-	143	60
	Middle 20%	96	91	99	79	-	-	101	96
	Lightest 20%	100	112	50	192	-	-	65	159
Radio	Heaviest 20%	100	117	104	104	143	65	-	-
	Middle 20%	92	87	99	95	95	94	-	-
	Lightest 20%	116	100	85	125	60	159	-	-

To be read: An index of 154 (see heaviest quintiles for newspapers and magazines) in a cell which accounts for 20% of the population indicates that 31% (20 x 1.54) of the quintile group are in that demographic cell.

Source: MRI, Spring 1982

MATHEMATICAL FORMULAS USED IN MEDIA

Ratings
1. Rating = Share x HUT
2. Share = Rating ÷ HUT
3. HUT = Rating ÷ Share
4. (a) Target Rating = (TVHH Rating x TVHH Base x VPVH) ÷ Total Target Base
4. (b) Target Rating = TVHH Rating x $\frac{\text{Program VPVH}}{\text{People per 100 TV·HH}}$

Audience
1. Print Audience = Circulation x RPC
2. TV Audience = TV Homes Delivered x Target VPVH
3. Audience = Population x Rating
4. Messages = Cost ÷ CPM
5. Turnover = 4 Week Reach ÷ 1 Week Rating

Reach
1. Reach = GRP ÷ Average Frequency
2. GRP = Reach x Average Frequency
3. Average Frequency = GRP ÷ Reach
4. Average Frequency = Gross Impressions ÷ Reach (000)
5. Gross Impressions = Average Audience x Number of Announcements

Cost
1. CPM = Cost ÷ Messages
2. Messages = Cost ÷ CPM
3. Cost = Messages x CPM
4. Cost per Rating Point = Cost ÷ GRP
5. Target CPM = TVHH CPM ÷ Target VPVH
6. $\frac{\text{Household Cost per Rating Point}}{\text{Demo Conversion Factor}}$ = Demo Cost per Rating Point
7. Demo Cost per Rating Point x Demo Conversion Factor = Household Cost per Rating Point

DISTRIBUTION OF ADVERTISING VOLUME BY MEDIA

Medium	1981 ($MMM)	% Total	% National	1982 Est. ($MMM)	% Total	% National
Television	12.7	21	-	14.5	21	-
Network	5.6	9	17	6.4	9	17
Spot	3.7	6	11	4.3	6	11
Local	3.4	6	-	3.8	6	-
Radio	4.2	7	-	4.6	7	-
Network	0.2	*	*	0.3	*	*
Spot	0.9	2	3	1.0	2	3
Local	3.1	5	-	3.3	5	-
Magazines	3.5	6	10	3.8	6	10
Newspapers	17.4	28	-	19.2	28	-
National	2.7	4	8	3.0	4	8
Local	14.7	24	-	16.2	24	-
Business Publications	1.8	3	5	2.0	3	5
Farm Publications	0.1	*	*	0.2	*	*
Direct Mail	8.8	14	26	9.6	14	26
Outdoor	0.7	1	-	0.8	1	-
National	0.4	1	1	0.5	1	1
Local	0.3	*	-	0.3	*	-
Miscellaneous	12.1	20	-	13.5	20	-
National	6.4	11	19	7.2	11	19
Local	5.7	9	-	6.3	9	-
Total	61.3	100	-	68.2	100	-
National	34.1	56	100	38.3	56	100
Local	27.2	44	-	29.9	44	-
U.S. Grand Total	61.3	100	56	68.2	100	56

*Less than one percent
Source: Advertising Age. Grey Estimates

	Total HH (000)	TV HH Penetr %	Total TV HH (000)	%	Color TV HH (000)	%	Multiset TV HH (000)	%
Jan. 1, 1982	83.120	98	81,500	100	71,390	88	43.280	53
Jan. 1, 1983	84.940	98	83,300	100	73,890	89	45.400	55
Jan. 1, 1984 Est.	86.840	98	85,100	100	76,600	90	48.500	57

HOUSEHOLD CHARACTERISTICS
TV HOUSEHOLDS

Household Income	(000)	%	County Size	(000)	%	Household Size	(000)	%	Presence of Children	(000)	%
Under $10.000	18.920	23	A	34.450	41	1	18.750	22	Any Under 18	32.610	39
$10,000-$14,999	11.550	14	B	24.960	30	2	26.560	32	Any Under 12	24.260	29
$15,000-$19.999	9.580	11	C&D	23.890	29	3	14.730	18	Any Under 6	15.088	18
$20,000-$29.999	17.840	21				4+	23.260	28	Any Under 3	9.210	11
$30,000+	25.410	31							Any 6-11	14.980	18
									Any 12-17	15.410	18

PERSONS IN TV HOMES

	Total People (000)	People 100 TV HH		Total People (000)	People 100 TV HH		Total People (000)	People 100 TV HH
2+	218.130	262						
Adults 18+	164.120	197						
Men 18+	77.770	93	Women 18+	86.350	104	Teens	21.680	26
18-34	33.030	40	18-34	33.910	41	Girls	10.640	13
18-49	52.240	63	18-49	54.140	65	Boys	11.040	13
25-54	43.470	52	25-54	45.470	55			
35-64	34.570	42	35-64	37.470	45	Children	32.330	39
55+	20.270	24	55+	26.510	32	2-5	13.210	16
						6-11	19.120	23

Source: A.C. Nielsen, Grey Estimates

TV DEMOGRAPHIC RATING CONVERSION FACTORS BY DAYPART

	Av. TV HH Rtg. %	Men 18+	18-34	18-49	25-54	55+	Women 18+	18-34	18-49	25-54	55+	Teens 12-17	Children 2-11
Fall/Winter													
Day Network	6.3	28	22	21	19	52	85	80	76	73	108	30	26
Prime Network-Regular	17.8	68	59	61	68	83	77	67	72	77	86	52	55
Network News	13.6	68	38	44	54	123	73	39	47	57	124	24	26
Late Night Network	5.3	58	57	59	61	56	63	59	63	65	63	24	5
Day Spot	4.8	30	23	21	19	54	81	77	72	70	101	28	32
Prime Spot	12.0	68	61	64	68	81	78	74	75	78	85	66	54
Early Fringe Spot	6.6	45	38	36	35	70	63	54	54	53	82	77	86
Late Fringe Spot	3.6	63	63	60	63	70	70	66	66	69	76	27	9
Fringe Spot	5.1	54	51	48	49	70	67	60	60	61	79	52	48
Summer													
Day Network	6.3	26	23	22	19	38	74	71	68	67	88	89	65
Prime Network-Regular	12.0	62	58	59	60	75	76	71	71	74	88	63	58
Network News	10.0	63	45	48	54	104	74	46	51	59	119	26	25
Late Night Network	4.9	55	58	56	54	54	59	59	62	63	59	48	13
Day Spot	4.7	26	21	19	17	44	75	72	68	64	90	79	55
Prime Spot	8.6	65	58	59	59	86	77	71	71	73	88	65	54
Early Fringe Spot	5.3	43	40	38	34	61	64	59	57	53	79	77	77
Late Fringe Spot	3.6	61	61	61	61	61	69	67	67	69	75	56	17
Fringe Spot	4.5	52	51	50	48	61	67	63	62	61	77	67	47

To be read: A 6.3 rated Day Network program will generate a 4.8 rating against Women 18-49 in Fall/Winter (6.3 x 76). For Spot, 100 rating points in Early Fringe will generate 40 rating points against Men 18-34 in Summer.

Source: Nielsen NAD Nov. '81. Feb.. July '82: DMA Planner's Guide Nov. '81. Feb.. July '82

TV HOMES—USAGE BY MONTH

		Year Avg.	Sept.	Oct.	Nov.	Dec.	Jan.	Feb.	Mar.	Apr.	May	June	July	Aug.
Daytime														
Mon.-Fri. 10:00am-4:30pm	%	27	25	26	26	27	32	29	27	27	23	23	27	28
	Index	100	93	96	96	100	118	107	100	100	85	85	100	104
Sat. 8:00am-1:00pm	%	23	22	23	24	25	26	25	25	25	21	21	19	19
	Index	100	96	100	104	109	113	109	109	109	91	91	83	83
Sat. 1:00pm-4:30pm	%	32	29	33	35	36	40	35	33	32	27	28	25	27
	Index	100	91	103	109	112	125	109	103	100	84	88	78	84
Sun. 9:00am-1:00pm	%	24	22	25	26	27	30	26	26	24	22	21	19	20
	Index	100	92	104	108	113	125	108	108	100	92	87	79	83
Sun. 1:00pm-4:30pm	%	37	37	42	42	45	52	38	37	33	30	30	28	30
	Index	100	100	114	114	122	141	103	100	89	81	81	76	81
Prime Time														
Mon.-Sun. 8:00pm-11:00pm	%	61	61	65	64	65	66	65	64	63	57	53	50	55
	Index	100	100	107	105	107	108	107	105	103	93	87	82	90
Mon.-Sun. 8:00pm-9:00pm	%	59	57	63	65	64	68	66	64	62	54	51	47	50
	Index	100	97	107	110	109	115	112	109	105	92	86	80	85
Mon.-Sun. 9:00pm-11:00pm	%	60	58	62	62	62	64	63	62	60	59	55	52	55
	Index	100	97	103	103	103	107	105	103	100	98	92	86	92
Mon.-Sun. 7:30pm-8:00pm	%	56	52	58	62	62	65	63	61	59	50	47	44	46
	Index	100	93	104	111	111	116	113	109	105	89	84	78	82
Early Fringe														
Mon.-Fri. 4:30pm-7:30pm	%	46	42	46	50	50	53	52	49	47	41	40	39	41
	Index	100	91	100	109	109	115	113	107	102	89	87	85	89
Mon.-Fri. 4:30pm-6:00pm	%	39	36	39	41	42	46	44	41	39	35	34	34	35
	Index	100	92	100	105	108	118	113	105	100	90	87	87	90
Mon.-Fri. 6:00pm-7:30pm	%	53	48	53	58	57	61	60	57	54	47	46	43	46
	Index	100	91	100	109	108	115	113	108	102	89	87	81	87
Late Fringe														
Mon.-Sun. 11:00pm-11:30pm	%	47	45	48	46	49	51	49	48	46	46	46	45	45
	Index	100	96	102	98	104	109	104	102	98	98	98	96	96
Mon.-Fri. 11:30pm-1:00am	%	28	26	27	27	29	31	28	28	27	28	28	28	28
	Index	100	93	96	96	104	111	100	100	96	100	100	100	100
Sat. 11:30pm-1:00am	%	32	32	32	31	35	36	34	33	32	32	31	29	31
	Index	100	100	100	97	109	113	106	103	100	100	97	91	97
Sun. 11:30pm-1:00am	%	26	25	25	25	28	29	28	25	25	25	27	27	27
	Index	100	96	96	96	108	112	108	96	96	96	104	104	104

Source: A.C. Nielsen, HUT Summary Reports, July-Dec. 1981; Jan-June 1982.

SOME USEFUL TOOLS

	4th Quarter		1st Quarter		2nd Quarter		3rd Quarter		Yearly Average	
	%	Index	%	Index	%	Index	%	Index	%	Index
Homes										
Daytime	26	96	29	107	25	93	27	100	27	100
Early Fringe	47	104	52	116	42	93	39	87	45	100
Prime Access	60	109	63	115	52	95	45	82	55	100
Early Prime 8-9pm	63	109	66	114	56	97	47	81	58	100
Late Prime 9-11pm	62	105	63	107	58	98	52	88	59	100
Prime	62	107	64	110	57	98	50	86	58	100
Late Fringe 11-11:30pm	47	100	49	104	46	98	45	96	47	100
Late Fringe 11:30pm-1am	28	97	29	100	28	97	29	100	29	100
Women 25-54										
Daytime	17	100	20	118	15	88	17	100	17	100
Early Fringe	29	107	32	119	23	85	23	85	27	100
Prime Access	42	114	45	121	32	86	29	78	37	100
Early Prime 8-9pm	49	117	50	119	37	88	32	76	42	100
Late Prime 9-11pm	49	107	51	111	45	98	40	87	46	100
Prime	49	107	51	111	42	91	38	83	45	100
Late Fringe 11-11:30pm	33	73	37	82	35	78	33	73	35	100
Late Fringe 11:30pm-1am	18	95	19	100	19	100	19	100	19	100
Men 25-54										
Daytime	6	100	7	117	5	83	6	100	6	100
Early Fringe	24	114	25	119	18	86	18	86	21	100
Prime Access	38	112	40	118	29	85	28	82	34	100
Early Prime 8-9pm	45	115	46	118	36	92	30	77	39	100
Late Prime 9-11pm	46	107	46	107	43	100	37	86	43	100
Prime	46	110	46	110	41	98	34	81	42	100
Late Fringe 11-11:30pm	34	100	34	100	34	100	33	97	34	100
Late Fringe 11:30pm-1am	19	96	20	100	20	100	20	100	20	100
Adults 55+										
Daytime	19	100	22	116	17	89	16	84	19	100
Early Fringe	43	110	45	115	35	90	31	79	39	100
Prime Access	60	115	61	117	48	92	40	77	52	100
Early Prime 8-9pm	59	116	60	118	48	94	38	75	51	100
Late Prime 9-11pm	52	100	53	102	49	94	52	100	52	100
Prime	54	108	55	110	48	96	42	84	50	100
Late Fringe 11-11:30pm	36	97	38	103	36	97	36	97	37	100
Late Fringe 11:30pm-1am	16	94	17	100	17	100	17	100	17	100
Teens 12-17										
Daytime	7	64	9	82	6	55	22	200	11	100
Early Fringe	23	100	27	117	20	87	23	100	23	100
Prime Access	28	104	32	119	23	85	23	85	27	100
Early Prime 8-9pm	36	109	39	118	30	91	28	85	33	100
Late Prime 9-11pm	30	100	32	107	29	97	30	100	30	100
Prime	32	103	34	110	29	94	29	94	31	100
Late Fringe 11-11:30pm	13	81	14	88	14	88	21	131	16	100
Late Fringe 11:30pm-1am	8	80	9	90	8	80	16	160	10	100
Kids 6-11										
Daytime	8	73	9	82	5	45	23	209	11	100
Early Fringe	34	106	40	125	26	81	28	88	32	100
Prime Access	44	119	48	130	26	70	28	76	37	100
Early Prime 8-9pm	50	111	55	122	39	87	35	78	45	100
Late Prime 9-11pm	24	92	28	108	21	81	31	119	26	100
Prime	33	100	37	112	29	88	32	97	33	100
Late Fringe 11-11:30pm	6	75	5	62	5	62	16	200	8	100
Late Fringe 11:30pm-1am	2	50	2	50	2	50	9	225	4	100

Source: A.C. Nielsen, HUT Summary Report; Demographics NAD Report; Nov., 1981. Feb., May. July 1982

TREND OF VIEWING IN TV HOMES
SHARE OF VIEWING

Total Week	Total	Affiliated Stations	Other Stations	Pay Cable	Cable Origination
1980/81					
4th Qtr. 1980	103	78	21	2	2
1st Qtr. 1981	102	77	22	2	1
2nd Qtr. 1981	103	74	24	3	2
3rd Qtr. 1981	103	73	24	4	2
Yearly Avg.	103	76	23	3	2
1981/82					
4th Qtr. 1981	102	74	23	3	2
1st Qtr. 1982	102	73	23	4	2
2nd Qtr. 1982	102	70	23	6	3
3rd Qtr. 1982	103	69	25	6	3
Yearly Avg.	102	72	24	5	3
Prime Time					
1980/81					
4th Qtr. 1980	102	84	15	2	1
1st Qtr. 1981	103	84	15	3	1
2nd Qtr. 1981	102	80	18	3	1
3rd Qtr. 1981	102	76	19	5	2
Yearly Avg.	102	81	17	3	1
1981/82					
4th Qtr. 1981	103	80	16	4	2
1st Qtr. 1982	103	80	16	4	3
2nd Qtr. 1982	103	76	18	6	3
3rd Qtr. 1982	103	72	22	6	3
Yearly Avg.	103	77	18	5	3

Source: Cable TV: A Status Report (Nov '80. Feb. Mar. July '81); Monthly Cable TV Status Report (Jan-Dec '82) A.C. Nielsen Company

NETWORK TV HOUSEHOLD EFFICIENCIES
DAYPART

	Jan-Mar '83			Apr-June '83			July-Aug '83			Sept-Dec '83			Year Average		
	Cost/30	HH Rtg.	HH CPM	Cost/30	HH Rtg.	HH CPM	Cost/30	HH Rtg.	HH CPM	Cost/30	HH Rtg.	HH CPM	Cost/30	HH Rtg.	HH CPM
	$ (M)	%	$	$ (M)	%	$	$ (M)	%	$	$ (M)	%	$	$ (M)	%	$
I. **Daytime** (Mon.-Fri.)	12.6	6.6	2.30	14.0	5.7	2.95	12.1	6.2	2.35	15.5	6.0	3.10	13.6	6.1	2.68
II. **Prime Time** (Sun.-Sat.)	85.8	17.6	5.85	93.6	14.5	7.75	66.1	12.2	6.50	102.7	17.0	7.25	87.0	15.3	6.83
III. **Fringe Time**															
Early Morning	6.9	4.5	1.85	9.1	4.1	2.65	6.6	3.7	2.15	9.1	4.1	2.65	8.0	4.1	2.33
News	45.1	13.7	3.95	51.3	11.2	5.50	34.5	10.1	4.10	56.1	12.7	5.30	46.7	11.9	4.71
Late Night	14.4	5.4	3.20	21.0	5.2	4.85	15.2	5.0	3.65	22.7	5.3	5.15	18.2	5.2	4.21
IV. **Weekend Children's Programs**	12.6	5.6	2.70	15.7	4.4	4.27	13.9	4.3	3.89	22.1	5.3	5.00	16.21	4.9	3.97

Note: These are broad estimates; actual costs subject to specific buys, etc. For special costs and ratings, consult media personnel.
Source: A.C. Nielsen. Grey Estimates.

NETWORK TV DEMOGRAPHIC EFFICIENCIES
DAYPART

Women Efficiencies By Quarter

	Jan-Mar '83			Apr-June '83			July-Aug '83			Sept-Dec '83			Year Average		
	18+ $	18-49 $	25-54 $	18+ $	18-49 $	25-54 $	18+ $	18-49 $	25-54 $	18+ $	18-49 $	25-54 $	18+ $	18-49 $	25-54 $
I. Daytime (Mon-Fri)	2.64	4.89	5.90	3.39	6.41	7.56	3.05	5.34	6.53	3.56	6.46	7.95	3.16	5.78	6.99
II. Prime Time (Sun-Sat)	7.22	12.45	13.93	9.81	17.22	19.38	8.23	14.13	16.67	9.18	15.76	17.68	8.61	14.89	16.92
III. Fringe Time															
Early Morning	2.47	6.38	6.17	3.44	8.28	8.28	3.03	7.41	7.41	3.58	8.55	8.55	3.13	7.66	7.60
News	5.13	12.74	12.34	7.24	17.74	18.33	5.32	12.42	12.81	7.07	18.28	18.28	6.19	15.30	15.44
Late Night	4.92	7.80	9.14	7.58	12.44	14.26	5.70	9.13	10.74	7.58	11.90	14.29	6.45	10.32	12.11

Men Efficiencies By Quarter

	Jan-Mar '83			Apr-June '83			July-Aug '83			Sept-Dec '83			Year Average		
	18+ $	18-49 $	25-54 $	18+ $	18-49 $	25-54 $	18+ $	18-49 $	25-54 $	18+ $	18-49 $	25-54 $	18+ $	18-49 $	25-54 $
I. Prime Time (Sun-Sat)	9.59	15.39	17.21	13.14	21.53	23.48	11.02	17.11	20.31	11.51	19.08	20.71	11.32	18.28	20.43
II. Fringe Time															
Early Morning	4.30	11.56	11.56	6.63	17.67	16.56	5.38	14.33	12.65	6.46	16.56	16.56	5.69	15.03	14.33
News	6.37	13.62	13.62	9.02	19.64	19.64	6.95	13.67	14.64	8.41	18.93	18.93	7.69	16.47	16.71
Late Night	5.82	8.42	9.70	9.15	13.47	15.65	7.16	10.43	13.04	9.09	13.16	15.63	7.81	11.37	13.51

Non-Adult Efficiencies By Quarter

	Jan-Mar '83			Apr-June '83			July-Aug '83			Sept-Dec '83			Year Average		
	Children 2-11 $	6-11 $	Teens 12-17 $	Children 2-11 $	6-11 $	Teens 12-17 $	Children 2-11 $	6-11 $	Teens 12-17 $	Children 2-11 $	6-11 $	Teens 12-17 $	Children 2-11 $	6-11 $	Teens 12-17 $
I. Weekend Children's Programs	3.10	5.63	14.21	4.80	8.90	21.35	4.32	7.34	18.52	5.88	10.20	26.32	4.53	8.02	20.10

Source: A.C. Nielsen, Grey Estimates

NETWORK AUDIENCE COMPOSITION BY DAYPART— VIEWERS PER 100 VIEWING HOMES

	Men					Women					Teens	Children*			Total
	18+	18-34	18-49	25-54	55+	18+	18-34	18-49	25-54	55+	12-17	2-5	6-11	2-11	2+
Daytime (M-F 10:00 AM-4:30 PM)															
Fall	25	9	13	9	11	88	34	50	41	33	7	5	3	8	128
Winter	27	9	13	10	13	88	31	48	41	35	8	6	5	11	134
Spring	24	8	12	9	11	87	30	48	40	34	9	4	5	9	129
Summer	24	9	14	10	9	77	29	44	36	28	24	8	18	26	151
Average	25	9	13	10	11	85	31	48	40	33	12	6	8	14	136
Prime Time (M-S 8:00 PM-11:00 PM)															
Fall	64	24	40	36	21	77	27	45	40	27	14	6	14	20	175
Winter	62	23	38	35	19	81	28	47	42	28	15	7	15	22	180
Spring	60	22	37	34	19	79	27	45	41	28	15	8	14	22	176
Summer	59	23	38	32	18	79	29	46	39	28	17	6	16	22	177
Average	61	23	38	34	19	79	28	46	41	28	15	7	15	22	177
Prime Time (M-S 8:00 PM-9:00 PM)															
Fall	63	22	37	34	22	78	26	43	39	30	15	11	19	30	186
Winter	62	21	36	33	22	79	26	43	40	31	16	12	21	33	190
Spring	60	21	35	31	21	77	25	41	37	31	16	11	21	32	185
Summer	58	23	35	29	20	77	27	42	35	30	18	10	19	29	182
Average	61	22	36	32	21	78	26	42	38	31	16	11	20	31	186
Prime (M-S 9:00 PM-11:00 PM)															
Fall	64	25	41	37	19	78	28	47	41	25	13	4	11	15	170
Winter	62	24	39	36	18	81	29	49	43	27	14	5	12	17	174
Spring	60	23	38	35	18	80	29	47	42	27	15	5	12	17	172
Summer	59	23	38	32	18	81	30	48	42	27	17	5	15	20	177
Average	61	24	39	35	18	80	29	48	42	27	15	5	13	17	173
Early Evening News															
Fall	62	15	28	28	29	75	15	29	30	40	6	4	5	9	152
Winter	62	15	28	28	29	77	16	31	31	40	7	4	6	10	156
Spring	61	16	28	29	28	76	16	31	31	40	7	4	5	9	153
Summer	59	18	30	28	25	77	19	33	32	38	7	4	6	10	153
Average	61	16	29	28	28	76	17	31	31	40	7	4	6	10	154
Late Night															
Fall	54	24	38	31	13	66	26	42	35	20	7	1	1	2	129
Winter	55	22	38	33	14	64	23	41	35	20	7	0	2	2	128
Spring	54	21	36	31	14	64	23	40	34	19	6	1	0	1	125
Summer	51	23	35	28	13	64	24	40	34	19	13	1	4	5	133
Average	54	23	37	31	14	65	24	41	35	20	8	1	2	3	130

*Boys and Girls are estimated to split about 50/50.

Source: A.C. Nielsen NAD Reports: Oct., Nov., Dec., 1981; Feb., Mar., Apr., May, July 1982.

NETWORK AUDIENCE COMPOSITION BY PROGRAM TYPE— VIEWERS PER 100 VIEWING HOMES

	Men					Women					Teens	Children*			Total
	18+	18-34	18-49	25-54	55+	18+	18-34	18-49	25-54	55+	12-17	2-5	6-11	2-11	2+
Weekend Daytime Children's (6:00am-6:00pm)															
Fall	24	15	19	13	5	30	16	22	14	7	19	36	49	85	158
Winter	26	14	19	15	5	32	16	23	15	8	19	39	49	88	165
Spring	23	13	17	13	5	27	15	20	13	7	20	41	48	89	159
Summer	23	14	18	12	4	30	17	23	14	6	21	37	53	90	164
Average	24	14	18	13	5	30	16	22	14	7	20	38	50	88	162
Daytime Drama															
Fall	24	8	12	9	10	90	35	52	42	33	7	4	3	7	128
Winter	24	8	12	9	11	92	33	52	42	35	8	4	4	8	132
Spring	22	7	11	8	11	92	32	51	42	36	9	4	3	7	130
Summer	23	8	13	9	9	86	33	51	41	30	19	5	13	18	146
Average	23	8	12	9	10	90	33	52	42	34	11	4	6	10	134
Daytime Quiz/Aud. Participation															
Fall	33	8	14	12	17	82	25	37	31	39	4	7	3	10	128
Winter	34	8	14	11	19	86	21	37	36	42	5	7	4	11	136
Spring	29	8	12	10	16	81	22	36	34	38	6	7	5	12	128
Summer	27	9	14	10	13	69	20	32	30	32	25	9	23	32	153
Average	31	8	14	11	16	80	22	36	33	38	10	8	9	17	138
Prime General Drama															
Fall	54	19	31	28	19	88	30	48	43	33	11	5	11	16	169
Winter	54	19	29	27	20	89	29	47	42	35	12	7	13	20	175
Spring	56	20	32	29	20	87	30	47	41	33	13	5	12	17	173
Summer	53	21	32	25	18	82	30	46	38	31	15	6	15	21	171
Average	54	20	31	27	19	87	30	47	41	33	13	6	13	19	172
Prime Suspense Mystery															
Fall	65	24	41	38	19	80	28	48	43	26	16	6	13	19	180
Winter	67	26	42	39	19	80	27	48	44	26	16	6	12	18	181
Spring	63	25	40	36	19	79	28	47	42	27	15	5	11	16	173
Summer	60	24	39	34	18	81	30	49	42	27	18	6	15	21	180
Average	64	25	41	37	19	80	28	48	43	27	16	6	13	19	179
Prime Situation Comedy															
Fall	57	23	36	32	17	79	30	47	41	27	18	8	21	29	183
Winter	57	22	35	32	18	79	29	46	40	28	18	11	21	32	186
Spring	54	21	33	30	17	76	28	45	38	27	19	17	17	34	183
Summer	53	22	34	29	17	78	30	46	38	28	22	8	23	31	184
Average	55	22	35	31	17	78	29	46	39	28	19	11	21	32	184
Prime Feature Films															
Fall	66	26	43	40	18	81	29	50	45	24	14	5	11	16	177
Winter	71	29	49	45	17	77	29	50	46	21	16	6	14	20	184
Spring	67	26	44	40	18	78	27	47	43	25	16	5	12	17	178
Summer	60	24	41	35	16	83	31	53	46	24	16	4	13	17	176
Average	66	26	44	40	17	80	29	50	45	24	16	5	13	18	179

*Boys and Girls are estimated to split about 50/50.

Source: A.C. Nielsen NAD Reports; Oct., Nov., Dec., 1981; Feb., Mar., Apr., May, July 1982.

AUDIENCE & EFFICIENCY OF TV SPORTS
SPORTS PROGRAM TYPES

| | | | | | | Viewers Per 100 Homes (By Sports Program) | | | | | |
| | | | | HH | | | Men | | | Women | |
	Network	Programs #	Cost $M/30" $	Rating %	CPM $	Total	18-34	18-49	25-54	Total	18-49
Baseball-Reg. Season (Apr-Oct)	A/N	27	40.0	8.8	5.46	74	25	39	35	48	23
Baseball-Playoffs (Oct)	N	9	110.0	14.5	9.11	74	24	39	37	52	26
Baseball-World Series (Oct)	A	6	205.0	30.1	8.18	83	28	50	47	66	35
Pro Basketball Season-Post Season (Apr-June)	C	21	45.0	8.1	6.67	88	45	65	52	42	26
NCAA Basketball-Reg. Season (Dec-Mar)	C/N	40	30.0	6.0	6.00	79	30	48	42	44	24
NCAA Basketball Champ Games (Apr)	C	16	65.0	9.9	7.88	83	36	56	47	46	27
NCAA Football-Reg. Season (Sep-Dec)	A	22	35.0	12.2	3.44	79	26	43	40	40	22
NCAA Football-Post Season (Jan)	A/C/N	7	55.0	16.1	4.10	93	32	57	53	57	30
CBS Football-Reg. Season (Sep-Dec)	C	25	115.0	17.8	7.76	94	38	61	54	47	29
NBC Football-Reg. Season (Sep-Dec)	N	23	100.0	14.5	8.28	90	35	57	52	46	27
ABC Monday Night Football (Sep-Dec)	A	14	165.0	21.9	9.05	92	40	62	54	48	31
Pro Football-Post Season (Dec-Jan)	C/N	6	190.0	32.1	7.11	93	35	60	56	58	37
ABC Wide World of Sports (Jan-Dec)	A	42	28.0	10.3	3.26	77	28	50	43	58	33
CBS Sports Spectacular (Jan-Dec)	C	35	28.0	6.1	5.51	74	26	43	39	54	29
NBC Sportsworld (Jan-Dec)	N	30	27.0	6.5	4.99	81	23	51	47	53	32
American Sportsman (Apr-June)	A	12	25.0	4.0	7.50	78	28	48	47	55	34
Golf Tournaments (Jan-June)	A/C/N	49	31.0	5.0	7.44	78	19	33	35	55	21
Horse Racing (May-June)	A/C	3	100.0	11.1	10.82	74	19	36	35	69	32
Tennis Tournaments (Jan-June)	A/C/N	11	35.0	3.8	11.06	62	18	36	34	60	39
Intl Boxing Champ (Feb-Apr)	A	12	40.0	7.0	6.86	75	28	46	43	54	34

Note: Costs are rate costs and are highly subject to negotiation. Price will vary 15-35% depending on packaging.

Source: Nielsen Sports Report. 1981 and 1982; Grey Estimates

RATING BY HOUSEHOLD CHARACTERISTICS
SPORTS PROGRAM TYPES

| | | | | Household Income | | | | Education Of H Of H | | County Size | | |
	Network	Programs #	HH Rating %	Under $10M %	$10-15M %	$15M-20M %	$20M+ %	1+ Yrs College %	4+ Yrs College %	A %	B %	C&D %
Baseball-Reg. Season (Apr-Oct)	A/N	13	5.7	5.6	5.9	5.7	6.1	5.2	4.9	4.3	5.8	7.4
Baseball Playoffs-(Oct)	N	9	14.5	11.0	14.9	15.6	15.5	14.4	14.6	14.6	13.6	15.3
Baseball World Series (Oct)	A	6	30.1	23.2	29.6	28.5	36.0	29.1	29.0	32.2	28.0	29.1
Pro Basketball-Reg. Season (Oct-Apr)	C	13	5.5	3.7	5.7	5.6	6.4	5.1	5.4	5.3	4.7	6.6
Pro Basketball-Post Season (Apr-June)	C	18	8.7	5.3	8.6	8.0	10.6	9.4	10.1	8.5	8.8	8.8
NCAA Basketball-Reg. Season (Jan-Mar)	N	17	5.6	5.0	6.4	5.9	6.8	6.8	8.0	5.3	5.7	7.9
NCAA Basketball-Champ Games (Mar-Apr)	C	11	10.5	6.7	9.0	9.5	12.9	11.6	12.4	8.2	11.6	12.7
NCAA Football Reg. Season (Sept-Jan)	A	22	12.2	6.8	11.8	14.0	14.8	14.0	15.7	11.0	12.6	13.5
NCAA Football Post Season (Jan)	A/C/N	7	16.1	9.0	15.6	17.5	19.6	18.4	20.7	14.8	15.9	18.4
CBS Football Reg. Season (Sept-Dec)	C	25	17.8	9.5	16.6	18.2	22.4	19.6	21.5	17.4	16.7	19.2
NBC Football-Reg. Season (Sept-Dec)	N	23	14.5	9.1	13.5	15.7	18.3	16.0	17.5	14.9	13.1	15.2
ABC Monday Night Football (Sept-Dec)	A	14	21.9	10.1	17.4	23.7	28.7	24.7	25.3	23.2	19.9	22.1
*Pro Football-Post Season (Dec-Jan)	C/N	6	31.9	20.1	25.5	32.5	39.7	27.8	35.1	31.1	32.5	32.5
ABC Wide World of Sports (Jan-Dec)	A	42	10.3	6.9	7.8	11.6	11.2	7.5	7.3	10.4	9.8	10.6
CBS Sports Spectacular (Jan-Dec)	C	35	6.1	5.3	5.6	6.0	6.3	5.0	4.5	5.7	5.5	7.3
NBC Sportsworld (Jan-Dec)	N	34	6.4	5.1	6.8	7.1	7.2	4.7	4.6	5.8	6.2	7.3
American Sportsman (Apr-July)	A	11	3.6	2.9	2.8	3.8	4.2	3.2	3.2	3.3	3.6	3.9
Golf Tournaments (Jan-Dec)	A/C/N	64	4.9	4.2	3.8	4.4	5.2	5.1	5.5	4.5	5.3	5.2
Horse Racing (May-June)	A/C	3	13.7	8.6	12.2	11.8	15.3	13.2	12.6	14.8	13.4	12.7
Tennis Tournaments (Jan-Sept)	A/C/N	23	4.7	3.4	3.6	4.1	6.0	7.5	8.3	4.1	5.6	4.5
Int l. Boxing Champ (Jan-Apr)	A	9	8.6	7.2	7.5	10.8	8.5	7.2	6.4	8.7	7.8	9.2
Auto Racing (Feb-May)	A/C	5	8.7	4.3	8.0	8.7	11.1	8.0	7.4	7.6	9.0	10.0
Pro Bowlers Tour (Jan-Apr)	A	15	8.4	6.6	7.8	9.5	9.3	7.2	6.8	8.8	8.2	8.2

*Does not include Superbowl
Source: Nielsen Sports 1981; Market Section Audience Report. 1982

AUDIENCE COMPOSITION SPOT DAYPART — VIEWERS PER 100 VIEWING HOMES

	TV HH Rtg %	Men 18+	Men 18-34	Men 18-49	Men 50+	Women 18+	Women 18-34	Women 18-49	Women 50+	Teens 12-17	Children* 2-11	Total 2+
Daytime (M-F 9:00am-4:30pm)												
Fall	4.6	26	9	12	14	84	32	47	37	7	12	129
Winter	4.9	28	10	14	15	85	31	46	38	8	13	134
Spring	4.1	25	9	12	13	86	32	48	38	7	12	130
Summer	4.7	24	9	12	12	77	30	44	33	21	22	144
Average	4.6	26	9	13	14	83	31	46	37	11	15	135
Early Fringe (M-F 4:30pm-6:00pm)												
Fall	6.3	41	15	22	20	66	22	35	31	21	34	162
Winter	6.8	42	15	23	20	66	22	35	30	21	34	163
Spring	5.4	40	14	21	19	67	23	35	32	20	29	156
Summer	5.3	40	16	24	17	67	24	37	30	21	31	159
Average	6.0	41	15	23	19	67	23	36	31	21	32	161
Early Evening (M-F 6:00pm-7:30pm)												
Fall	10.7	61	18	31	31	77	21	36	41	12	17	167
Winter	11.0	62	18	32	31	78	21	37	40	12	17	169
Spring	8.9	59	17	28	31	78	20	35	43	11	13	161
Summer	8.2	59	18	30	30	79	21	36	43	11	13	162
Average	9.7	60	18	30	31	78	21	36	42	12	15	165
Prime Time Access (M-F 7:30pm-8:00pm)												
Fall	11.2	61	21	34	27	79	26	42	37	16	26	182
Winter	11.5	61	21	35	27	80	26	42	38	16	26	183
Spring	9.0	57	19	30	27	80	24	40	40	14	20	171
Summer	8.0	57	20	31	26	81	25	41	40	14	19	171
Average	9.9	59	20	33	27	80	25	41	39	15	23	177
Prime Time (Sun-Sat 8:00pm-11:00pm)**												
Fall	11.9	63	25	40	24	80	30	48	32	17	22	182
Winter	12.0	64	24	38	25	82	30	49	33	18	22	186
Spring	10.3	61	23	38	24	81	29	47	33	17	19	178
Summer	8.6	61	23	37	24	80	29	46	33	19	23	183
Average	10.7	62	24	38	24	81	30	48	33	18	22	183
Late News (M-F 11:00-11:30pm)												
Fall	8.6	66	24	42	28	79	22	42	36	7	4	156
Winter	8.9	66	21	38	28	82	25	44	38	7	4	159
Spring	8.5	65	22	38	27	81	25	44	37	7	4	157
Summer	8.1	64	21	37	28	80	25	43	37	11	6	161
Average	8.5	65	22	39	28	81	24	43	37	8	5	159
Late Fringe (M-F 11:30pm-1:00am)												
Fall	3.5	58	25	38	21	71	27	43	28	7	3	139
Winter	3.7	58	25	37	21	73	27	42	31	7	3	141
Spring	3.5	58	24	38	21	71	26	43	28	7	3	139
Summer	3.6	57	24	39	19	72	27	43	29	15	7	151
Average	3.6	58	25	38	21	72	27	43	29	9	4	143
Saturday Morning (7:00am-12:00pm)												
Fall	3.5	27	14	20	7	30	16	22	7	25	83	165
Winter	3.5	27	15	22	5	30	18	24	5	27	90	174
Spring	3.0	25	13	19	6	31	16	22	9	24	84	164
Summer	2.7	28	16	21	7	31	18	24	7	27	86	172
Average	3.2	27	15	21	6	31	17	23	7	26	86	170

*Boys and Girls are estimated to split about 50/50
**Does not include independents

Source: A.C. Nielsen Special DMA Planners Guide—Nov. 1981, Feb., May, July 1982

SPOT TV AUDIENCE—COST & EFFICIENCY BY MARKET GROUPS*

		Population		TV Households Average DMA Rating			Costs per DMA Rating Points (30)				Average CPM (30)		
		(000)	% U.S.	Day (%)	Fringe (%)	Prime (%)	Day ($)	Fringe ($)	Prime ($)	Day ($)	Fringe ($)	Prime ($)	
Homes													
	Top 10	26.133	31	3.1	4.1	7.7	705	964	2.536	2.72	3.46	9.70	
	Top 20	36.994	44	3.3	4.2	8.3	1.042	1.502	3.735	2.91	3.79	10.10	
	Top 30	44.451	53	3.5	4.3	8.7	1.281	1.879	4.522	2.96	3.92	10.10	
	Top 50	55.532	66	3.8	4.5	9.2	1.583	2.325	5.405	2.95	3.85	9.74	
	Top 100	71.790	86	4.2	4.7	10.1	2.017	2.935	6.647	2.90	3.79	9.06	
Total U.S.		83.739	100	4.6	4.8	10.7	2.596	3.763	8.110	2.99	3.41	8.93	
Women 18-49													
	Top 10	17.412	32	1.9	2.2	5.3	1.150	1.795	3.686	6.97	10.12	22.15	
	Top 20	24.366	45	2.2	2.4	5.9	1.562	2.630	5.253	6.90	10.47	22.44	
	Top 30	29.160	54	2.3	2.4	6.1	1.950	3.367	6.451	7.13	11.14	22.80	
	Top 50	36.415	67	2.6	2.6	6.6	2.314	4.022	7.538	6.85	10.58	21.55	
	Top 100	46.838	86	2.9	2.7	7.3	2.923	5.213	9.194	7.16	10.49	19.96	
Total U.S.		54.471	100	3.3	2.8	7.9	3.621	6.455	10.989	6.64	9.45	20.91	
Men 18-49													
	Top 10	16.633	32	0.7	1.8	4.5	—	2.196	3.686	—	11.81	24.94	
	Top 20	23.415	45	0.7	1.9	5.0	—	3.323	5.253	—	12.72	25.44	
	Top 30	28.069	53	0.7	1.9	5.3	—	4.115	6.451	—	13.52	25.25	
	Top 50	35.018	67	0.8	2.0	5.6	—	5.236	7.538	—	13.23	24.41	
	Top 100	46.838	86	0.9	2.1	6.2	—	6.566	9.194	—	12.98	22.59	
Total U.S		52.579	100	0.9	2.1	6.6	—	8.591	10.989	—	11.97	22.27	

*Network Affiliates and Independents
Source: Nielsen Market Rank By TV Household. January 1983: DMA Planners Guide. Nov. 1981; Feb., May. July 1982; Grey Estimates

MARKET BY MARKET—TOP 25 MARKETS

Rank	Designated Market Area	TV Households (000)	% U.S.	Audience Allocation Sun-Sat Viewing 9am-12m Spill-In* %	Spill-Out** %	July 1982 CABLE DMA HH %
1	New York	6.471	7.73	3	8	29.4
2	Los Angeles. Palm Springs	4.303	5.14	1	6	23.8
3	Chicago	2.980	3.56	2	12	9.8
4	Philadelphia	2.426	2.90	5	9	35.3
5	San Francisco-Oakland	2.010	2.40	6	12	42.4
6	Boston. Manchester. Worcester	1.954	2.33	7	15	24.9
7	Detroit	1.674	2.00	3	9	13.2
8	Washington, D.C.. Hagerstown	1.496	1.79	8	14	17.0
9	Cleveland, Akron	1.418	1.69	5	6	30.7
10	Dallas-Fort Worth	1.402	1.68	3	12	23.7
11	Houston	1.309	1.56	2	4	28.6
12	Pittsburgh	1.213	1.45	13	14	50.1
13	Miami-Fort Lauderdale	1.148	1.37	4	10	27.7
14	Seattle-Tacoma	1.121	1.34	1	4	40.6
15	Atlanta	1.104	1.32	6	8	30.6
16	Minneapolis-St. Paul	1.099	1.31	5	10	9.8
17	Tampa. St. Petersburg, Sarasota	1.072	1.28	4	4	29.2
18	St. Louis	1.044	1.25	3	5	12.9
19	Denver	899	1.07	5	12	18.2
20	Baltimore	852	1.02	15	17	14.4
21	Sacramento-Stockton	850	1.02	14	14	30.7
22	Indianapolis	814	.97	9	10	29.6
23	Portland, OR	812	.97	5	9	25.3
24	Phoenix, Flagstaff	763	.91	3	5	21.5
25	San Diego	725	.87	19	1	56.0
Top 25		40.959	48.93			34.0
Total U.S.		83.739	100.00			

Source: NSI Market Rank by TV Households Sept. 1982. NSI Audience Allocation Report 1981-82. NSI DMA Cable Pent. Est. July 1982
To be read: *"Spill-in" 3% of all viewing in New York is to outside stations.   **"Spill-out" 8% of the audience of New York stations is outside of the New York DMA.

SYNDICATION—AUDIENCE COMPOSITION AND EFFICIENCIES

VIEWERS PER 100 VIEWING HOMES & EFFICIENCIES

Programs Appealing to:	Cost/30 $(M)	Natl HH Rtg	HH CPM	% Cov		18+	Adults 18-49	25-54	50+	Men 18+	18-49	25-54	50+	Women 18+	18-49	25-54	50+	Teens 12-17
Women	6.4	3.6	2.14	76	VPVH	104	54	46	51	20	9	8	11	84	45	38	40	7
					CPM	2.06	4.00	4.67	4.23	10.70	24.04	26.10	19.45	2.54	4.80	5.69	5.42	30.57
Men	12.5	2.3	6.52	60	VPVH	134	80	71	54	87	52	47	35	47	28	24	19	11
					CPM	4.87	8.15	9.18	12.07	7.49	12.54	13.87	18.63	13.87	23.29	27.17	34.32	59.27
Adults— Middle	27.5	8.5	3.88	81	VPVH	125	72	65	53	48	30	29	17	79	42	36	37	14
					CPM	3.10	5.38	5.99	7.33	8.15	12.76	13.33	22.56	4.92	9.30	10.87	10.46	27.13
Adults— Old	23.8	8.3	3.44	80	VPVH	138	48	53	90	60	24	25	36	79	24	28	55	7
					CPM	2.49	7.12	6.52	3.82	5.74	14.16	13.71	9.66	4.38	14.33	12.42	6.31	51.34
Youth	13.6	4.7	3.47	80	VPVH	124	90	64	29	54	40	27	14	70	50	37	20	15
					CPM	2.80	3.84	5.39	11.97	6.38	8.65	12.66	24.27	4.98	6.91	9.38	17.79	23.61

*Based on averages of syndicated programs classified into selected groups.

NOTE: These are broad estimates; actual costs subject to specific buys, etc. For special costs and ratings, consult media personnel.

Source: A.C. Nielsen, Grey estimates

CABLE TV
PAY CABLE PROGRAM NETWORKS

Supplier	Owner	Number of Subscribers (000)	Number of Systems
Bravo	Cablevision Inc./ Daniels & Assoc.	70	41
Cinemax	Time-Life, Inc.	1,500	900
Galavision	Spanish Intl. Ntwk.	100	145
Home Box Office	Time-Life, Inc.	9,500	3,600
HTN Plus	Group W	155	325
Movie Channel	Warner	2,200	2,150
Playboy Channel	Cablevision/ Daniels & Assoc./ Cox Cable	300	75
Showtime	Viacom	3,500	1,800
Regional			
Atlantis Entertainment Network	Atlantis Entertainment Ntwk.	1,140	6
Prism	Spectacore/20 Century-Fox	313	114
Rendezvous	Gill Cable	8	1
Sports Channel	Cablevision Inc.	230	28
Z Channel	Group W	95	10

CABLE TV INDUSTRY

Total Systems Operating	4,781
Total Communities Served	13,078
Franchises Not Yet Operating	2,535
Applications Pending	1,579
Communities With Applications	665
Total No. of Subscribers	27,500,000
Est. Total Subscribers, Jan. 1, 1983	28,339,000

NUMBER OF SYSTEMS & SUBSCRIBERS

Subscribers	Cable Systems	%
10,000+	526	11
5,000-10,000	478	10
1,000- 5,000	1,769	37
Under 1,000	2,008	42
	4,781	100

Source: Individual Program Suppliers, Television Factbook, National Cable Television Association. Grey Estimates

CABLE NETWORKS ACCEPTING ADVERTISING

Supplier	Owner	Number of Subscribers (000)	Number of Systems	Number of Hours Programmed/Day	Type of Programming
Arts	Hearst/ABC	8.000	1.650	3	Cultural
Black Entertainment	Black Entertainment Television	2.000	110	6	Entertainment
Cable Health Network	Viacom	4.600	600	24	Health
Cable News Network	Turner Broadcasting	14.670	2.750	24	News
CNN Headlines	Turner Broadcasting	1.700	249	24	Headline News—Local Inserts
Christian Broadcasting Network	Christian Broadcasting Network	17.100	3.124	24	Religious/Entertainment
Daytime	Hearst/ABC	7.047	484	M-F/4	Women
Electronic Program Guide	United Video	870	60	24	Programming Alpha-Numeric
ESPN	Getty Oil	18.780	4.586	24	Sports
Financial News Network	Financial News Broadcasting Co.	760	27	M-F/7	Financial
Modern Satellite Network	Modern Talking Picture Svc.	5.446	419	M-F/3	Public Service/International
Music Television	Warner-Amex	6.000	700	24	Music
North American Newstime	North American Newstime, Inc.	450	52	24	News; Program Guides
Satellite News Channel 1	Group W, Inc.	3.200	341	24	News
SPN	Satellite Program Network, Inc.	4.851	363	24	Lifestyle Programming
SIN	Spanish International Network	3.028	183	24	Spanish
Telefrance	Telefrance/Gaumont Films	8.500	800	24	Variety (French)
UPI Cablenews Wire	UPI Media News Corp.	3.500	600	24	News, Alpha-Numeric
USA Cable Network	Time, Inc./MCA/Paramount	13.000	2.300	24	General Interest, Sports
The Weather Channel	Landmark Communications	4.723	500	24	Weather

Source: Individual Program Suppliers, National Cable Television Association

CABLE NETWORKS—NON-COMMERCIAL

Supplier	Owner	Number of Subscribers (000)	Number of Systems	Number of Hours Programmed/Day	Type of Programming
A.P. Newscable	Associated Press	1.000	480	24	News & info, alpha-numeric
Appalachian Comm. Serv. Ntwk.	Appalachian Regional Commission	1.700	244	Varies	Education & Community Service
C-Span	Cable Satellite Public Affairs Ntwk.	10.500	1.000	24	House of Representatives Covg.
Dow Jones Cable News	Dow Jones & Company, Inc.	600	55	24	News, Stock Market, alpha-numeric
Eternal Word Television Ntwk.	Eternal Word Television Ntwk., Inc.	589	34	4	Religious
National Christian Ntwk.	National Christian Network	1.069	72	14	Religious
National Jewish Television	National Jewish Television, Inc.	1.700	75	Sun. Only 3	Religious
Nickelodeon	Warner-Amex	8.700	1.700	13	Children & Adolescents
PTL	PTL Satellite Network	6.100	629	24	Religious
Trinity Broadcasting Ntwk.	Trinity Broadcasting Network	2.006	213	24	Religious

Source: National Cable Television Association, Individual Program Suppliers

VIEWING PATTERNS OF CABLE HOMES
SHARE OF VIEWING BY TYPE OF TV HOME TO CHANNEL TYPE

TYPE OF TV HOME	CHANNEL TYPE						Total*
	Off-Air				Cable		
Total Week	Network Affiliates	Independents	Total	Pay	Basic	Total	
Cable							
Pay	50	26	76	21	7	28	104
Basic	70	26	96	—	6	6	102
Total Cable	59	26	85	11	7	18	103
Non-Cable	79	22	101	—	—	—	101
Total U.S.	70	24	94	6	3	9	103
Prime Time							
Cable							
Pay	58	20	78	22	6	28	106
Basic	74	22	96	—	5	5	101
Total Cable	66	21	87	12	6	18	105
Non-Cable	84	17	101	—	—	—	101
Total U.S.	76	19	95	5	2	7	102

How to Read: In Pay Cable TV homes combined network affiliates' share of viewing equaled 50%, Independents 26%, Pay Channels 21%, and Basic Cable Channels 7%.

*Totals add up to more than 100 because of simultaneous viewing

Source: Cable TV: A Status Report—May 1982

DEMOGRAPHIC CHARACTERISTICS OF CABLE AND PAY CABLE HOMES

Demographics	Total Adults	% Pop.	Index to Population		
			Total Cable TV	Basic Cable TV	Pay Cable TV
Age	18-24	17.7	93	76	107
	25-34	22.4	107	89	121
	35-54	30.9	114	99	127
	55+	29.0	84	124	58
Education	Att./Grad. Col.	31.8	113	100	120
	H.S. Grad.	38.4	101	99	103
	Less	29.8	85	97	75
HH Income	$35M+	19.1	120	88	146
	$25M+	38.9	122	102	139
	$15M+	66.6	115	105	123
	$10-$15M	12.9	81	92	72
	Under $10M	20.5	63	92	43
HH Size	1-2	44.4	89	107	74
	3-4	38.8	112	98	123
	5+	16.8	104	87	117

Source: MRI. Spring 1982

DISTRIBUTION OF AUDIENCE BY DAYPART

Monday-Friday	Total Persons 12+	Adults 18+	Teens 12-17	Men 18+	Men 18-34	Men 35-49	Men 50+	Women 18+	Women 18-34	Women 35-49	Women 50+
6am-10am	100	92	8	40	15	10	15	52	17	13	22
10am-3pm	100	94	6	41	17	10	14	53	19	13	21
3pm-7pm	100	87	13	41	18	10	13	46	19	11	16
7pm-Midnight	100	80	20	40	20	8	12	40	17	8	15

SEASONAL TRENDS

	Mon-Sun 6am-Mid %	Index	Mon-Fri 6am-10am %	Index	Persons 12+ Mon-Fri 10am-3pm %	Index	Mon-Fri 3pm-7pm %	Index	Mon-Fri 7pm-Mid %	Index	Teens 12-17 Mon-Sun 6am-Mid %	Index	Teens 12-17 Mon-Fri 10am-3pm %	Index
Average 1/2 Hour Radio Listening Levels														
Jan/Feb	16.5	101	23.8	104	18.8	101	18.1	98	9.0	93	11.9	97	6.7	74
Apr/May	16.6	102	23.5	103	18.3	98	18.4	99	10.0	103	12.1	98	6.1	68
Jul/Aug	16.2	99	20.7	91	19.8	106	18.2	99	10.7	110	13.2	107	17.1	190
Oct/Nov	15.9	98	23.0	101	17.7	95	17.5	95	9.1	94	12.0	98	6.1	68
Average	16.3	100	22.8	100	18.7	100	18.4	100	9.7	100	12.3	100	9.0	100

Source: Blair Radio. Arbitron Radio. Sales Marketing Management & Grey Estimates

PEOPLE USING RADIO

AVERAGE QUARTER-HOUR AUDIENCE

		Women 18+ %	Index	Women 18-49 %	Index	Women 25-54 %	Index	Men 18+ %	Index	Men 18-49 %	Index	Men 25-54 %	Index	Adults 18+ %	Index	Teens 12-17 %	Index
Mon-Fri	6am-10am	25	135	26	130	28	140	23	121	23	115	25	135	24	126	16	100
	10am-3pm	21	114	22	110	22	110	21	114	22	110	22	116	21	114	9	56
	3-7pm	18	97	20	100	20	100	19	100	21	105	20	105	19	100	20	125
	7pm-Mid	10	54	11	55	9	45	11	58	12	60	10	54	10	54	17	106
	Average	19	100	20	100	20	100	19	100	20	100	19	100	19	100	16	100
Saturday	6am-10am	17	106	14	82	17	100	15	100	14	93	16	107	16	100	11	73
	10am-3pm	23	144	24	141	24	141	19	127	20	133	20	133	21	131	19	127
	3-7pm	16	100	18	106	17	100	14	93	16	107	15	100	15	94	16	107
	7pm-Mid	9	56	11	65	9	53	10	67	11	73	10	67	10	63	14	93
	Average	16	100	17	100	17	100	15	100	15	100	15	100	16	100	15	100
Sunday	6am-10am	12	100	10	77	11	85	11	92	9	75	11	92	11	92	9	60
	10am-3pm	17	142	18	138	18	138	15	125	16	133	15	125	16	133	19	127
	3-7pm	13	108	14	108	14	108	12	100	13	108	13	108	13	108	17	113
	7pm-Mid	7	58	8	62	7	54	8	67	9	75	8	67	7	58	14	93
	Average	12	100	13	100	13	100	12	100	12	100	12	100	12	100	15	100

Source: RADAR. Spring 1982. Volume 1

NETWORK RADIO RATING LEVELS BY DAYPART

ABC

		Contemporary					Entertainment				
		Women		Men		Teens	Women		Men		Teens
		18-34	18-49	18-34	18-49	12-17	18-34	18-49	18-34	18-49	12-17
Mon.-Fri.	6am-10am	1.6	1.5	1.4	1.2	1.3	1.3	1.3	0.8	1.2	0.2
	10am-3pm	1.4	1.2	1.4	1.2	0.8	0.8	1.0	0.8	0.9	**
	3pm-7pm	1.3	1.2	1.4	1.3	1.3	0.7	0.8	0.9	1.0	0.5
	7pm-Mid.	0.9	0.7	0.8	0.6	1.3	0.4	0.4	0.4	0.4	0.3
Saturday	6am-10am	0.8	0.7	1.1	0.9	1.5	0.9	1.0	0.6	0.9	**
	10am-3pm	1.3	1.1	1.5	1.4	1.9	0.9	0.8	0.7	0.8	0.6
	3pm-7pm	0.9	0.7	0.7	0.7	1.1	0.7	0.7	0.4	0.7	0.9
	7pm-Mid.	0.8	0.6	0.5	0.3	1.3	0.7	0.6	0.1	0.6	0.4
Sunday	6am-10am	*	*	*	*	*	0.7	0.8	0.6	0.6	0.3
	10am-3pm	1.3	1.1	0.6	1.0	2.1	1.1	1.0	0.6	0.6	0.5
	3pm-7pm	1.2	0.9	0.9	0.8	1.6	0.5	0.6	0.5	0.5	0.4
	7pm-Mid.	0.8	0.6	0.6	0.4	1.5	0.4	0.4	0.4	0.6	**

		FM					Information				
		18-34	18-49	18-34	18-49	12-17	18-34	18-49	18-34	18-49	12-17
Mon.-Fri.	6am-10am	1.1	0.9	1.4	1.0	1.2	1.3	1.3	1.1	1.5	0.5
	10am-3pm	1.3	1.0	1.7	1.2	0.6	0.8	0.9	0.9	1.2	0.2
	3pm-7pm	1.1	1.0	1.4	1.0	1.4	0.5	0.5	0.9	1.1	0.4
	7pm-Mid.	0.7	0.5	1.0	0.7	1.1	0.3	0.3	0.3	0.5	0.3
Saturday	6am-10am	0.4	0.4	0.8	0.5	0.7	0.7	1.0	0.6	1.0	**
	10am-3pm	0.9	0.7	1.2	0.9	1.3	1.0	1.0	0.5	0.8	0.2
	3pm-7pm	0.9	0.8	1.1	0.8	1.1	0.8	0.7	0.6	0.8	0.3
	7pm-Mid.	0.5	0.5	0.8	0.5	1.6	0.4	0.3	0.4	0.5	0.3
Sunday	6am-10am	*	*	*	*	*	0.7	0.9	0.4	0.7	0.8
	10am-3pm	0.9	0.8	1.7	1.2	1.2	0.2	0.6	0.4	0.7	0.3
	3pm-7pm	1.1	0.8	1.5	1.0	1.2	0.2	0.4	0.4	0.5	0.3
	7pm-Mid.	0.4	0.4	1.0	0.7	1.2	0.2	0.2	0.3	0.4	0.2

		NBC					CBS				
		18-34	18-49	18-34	18-49	12-17	18-34	18-49	18-34	18-49	12-17
Mon.-Fri.	6am-10am	1.0	1.5	1.0	1.4	0.5	0.5	1.0	0.8	1.1	0.2
	10am-3pm	1.0	1.1	0.9	1.0	0.2	0.5	0.7	0.6	0.7	**
	3pm-7pm	0.8	0.9	0.7	0.8	0.4	0.4	0.5	0.6	0.8	0.2
	7pm-Mid.	0.4	0.5	0.3	0.5	0.6	0.1	0.2	0.4	0.4	**
Saturday	6am-10am	0.5	0.8	0.5	0.6	0.2	0.3	0.4	0.4	0.7	**
	10am-3pm	0.8	0.9	0.6	0.6	0.5	0.5	0.4	0.5	0.5	0.2
	3pm-7pm	0.8	0.8	0.4	0.5	0.3	0.3	0.3	0.5	0.4	**
	7pm-Mid.	0.6	0.5	0.4	0.4	1.0	0.1	0.2	0.2	0.2	**
Sunday	6am-10am	0.9	0.8	0.7	0.7	**	0.1	0.3	0.2	0.5	**
	10am-3pm	0.9	0.9	0.6	0.6	0.4	**	0.2	0.3	0.4	0.2
	3pm-7pm	0.5	0.6	0.4	0.5	0.5	**	0.2	0.5	0.5	**
	7pm-Mid.	0.2	0.3	0.3	0.3	0.9	**	0.1	0.2	0.3	**

		MBS					Sheridan Radio Network (1)				
		18-34	18-49	18-34	18-49	12-17	18-34	18-49	18-34	18-49	12-17
Mon.-Fri.	6am-10am	0.6	1.1	1.2	1.2	0.4	0.3	0.4	0.3	0.4	0.4
	10am-3pm	0.4	0.8	0.9	1.2	**	0.3	0.3	0.4	0.3	**
	3pm-7pm	0.5	0.7	0.9	1.0	0.4	0.3	0.3	0.4	0.3	0.6
	7pm-Mid.	0.3	0.4	0.4	0.4	0.3	0.2	0.2	0.3	0.2	0.6
Saturday	6am-10am	0.3	0.6	0.9	1.0	0.5	0.1	0.2	0.4	0.3	0.2
	10am-3pm	0.9	1.1	0.6	0.9	0.7	0.2	0.2	0.3	0.3	0.3
	3pm-7pm	0.8	0.7	1.1	1.2	0.7	0.3	0.3	0.2	0.3	0.3
	7pm-Mid.	0.4	0.4	0.5	0.6	**	**	0.1	0.2	0.1	**
Sunday	6am-10am	0.4	0.4	0.6	0.6	0.2	*	*	*	*	*
	10am-3pm	0.5	0.6	0.7	0.7	0.3	0.4	0.3	0.4	0.6	0.6
	3pm-7pm	0.2	0.4	0.5	0.4	0.7	0.3	0.2	0.3	0.4	0.6
	7pm-Mid.	0.2	0.3	0.5	0.4	0.3	*	*	*	*	*

* No network clearance during this time
** Insufficient for reporting
(1) Formerly the Mutual Black Radio Network

Source: Radar, Spring 1982, Volume 2, Box 2X

NETWORK RADIO COSTS

Network	# Of Stations	% 30/60	Monday-Friday 6-10 $	10-3 $	3-7 $	7-M $	:30 Costs Saturday 6-10 $	10-3 $	3-7 $	7-M $	Sunday 6-10 $	10-3 $	3-7 $	7-M $
Wired														
ABC-Contemporary	330	50	3,530	2,535	3,310	2,205	2,535	2,535	2,535	2,535	2,205	2,205	2,205	2,205
-Direction	142	50	1,300	1,000	770	220	550	550	450	450	550	550	450	450
-Entertainment	470	50	2,950	2,350	1,295	705	1,295	1,295	1,295	1,295	825	825	825	825
-FM	132	50	1,785	1,365	2,370	1,470	1,575	1,575	1,575	1,575	1,470	1,470	1,470	1,470
-Information	610	50	2,820	1,880	2,120	590	1,175	1,175	1,175	1,175	825	825	825	825
-Rock	57	50	1,900	1,700	2,600	2,600	2,200	2,300	2,300	2,300	2,200	2,300	2,300	2,300
CBS	391	50	3,765	2,000	2,000	1,295	1,880	1,880	1,410	705	1,790	1,880	1,410	705
NBC-Adult	361	70	2,625	1,840	1,890	525	1,285	1,285	1,285	1,285	1,285	1,285	1,285	1,285
-The Source	170	70	4,000	4,000	4,000	4,000	4,000	4,000	4,000	4,000	4,000	4,000	4,000	4,000
-Talk Net	74	70	850	850	850	850	850	850	850	850	850	850	850	850
MBS	850	50	2,435	2,025	1,710	315	1,020	1,020	1,020	315	655	655	655	315
RKO Radio Network I	203	50	2,055	2,015	1,825	1,050	1,840	1,840	1,840	1,840	1,575	1,575	1,575	1,575
RKO Radio Network II	164	50	890	890	890	890	890	890	890	890	890	890	890	890
Sheridan	190	50	630	630	630	630	630	630	630	630	630	630	630	630
Non-Wired														
Katz	-	82	3,865	3,140	3,500	2,660	3,320	3,320	3,320	3,320	3,320	3,320	3,320	3,320
Blair	-	80	5,250	3,780	4,410	2,730	4,410	4,200	2,835	3,465	3,465	3,465	2,730	2,730
Eastman	-	80	3,290	2,890	3,005	2,495	2,665	2,835	2,835	2,665	2,835	2,835	2,835	2,665
McGavren-Guild	-	80	6,280	6,280	6,280	6,280	6,280	6,280	6,280	6,280	6,280	6,280	6,280	6,280

Source: Networks, Grey Estimates

SPOT RADIO AUDIENCE COST*

Market Group	Radio Markets %	WOMEN 18+ Cost/Pt $	CPM $	18-34 Cost/Pt $	CPM $	18-49 Cost/Pt $	CPM $	25-54 Cost/Pt $	CPM $	MEN 18+ Cost/Pt $	CPM $	18-34 Cost/Pt $	CPM $	18-49 Cost/Pt $	CPM $	25-54 Cost/Pt $	CPM $
Top 5	21	842	5.69	483	6.11	605	4.65	842	7.65	863	6.23	544	6.58	863	6.23	1,089	9.62
Top 10	29	1,338	6.13	772	6.76	977	5.34	1,311	8.51	1,296	6.97	826	7.10	1,296	6.97	1,593	9.98
Top 25	45	2,102	6.01	1,385	10.33	1,752	6.61	2,067	9.27	2,058	7.46	1,310	7.66	2,058	7.46	2,417	10.30
Top 50	58	2,954	6.34	1,896	10.46	2,165	6.38	2,886	10.10	2,792	8.15	1,778	8.14	2,792	8.15	3,311	11.06
Top 75	66	3,389	6.34	2,199	10.56	2,574	6.74	3,336	10.41	3,230	8.34	2,133	8.57	3,230	8.34	3,819	11.42
Top 100	71	3,726	5.64	2,450	9.33	3,219	7.76	3,654	10.54	3,616	8.46	2,332	8.81	3,616	8.46	4,249	11.77

Market Group	Radio Markets %	ADULTS 18+ Cost/Pt $	CPM $	18-34 Cost/Pt $	CPM $	18-49 Cost/Pt $	CPM $	25-54 Cost/Pt $	CPM $	TEENS 12-17 Cost/Pt $	CPM $
Top 5	21	904	2.19	562	3.33	809	3.07	1,051	4.68	378	7.21
Top 10	29	1,404	2.34	870	3.63	1,230	3.32	1,529	5.20	535	7.30
Top 25	45	2,177	2.48	1,425	4.06	2,019	3.70	2,324	5.28	787	7.27
Top 50	58	3,031	2.73	1,170	4.33	2,794	4.02	3,197	5.69	1,078	7.70
Top 75	66	3,508	2.81	2,066	4.55	3,230	3.90	3,736	5.83	1,367	8.51
Top 100	71	3,903	2.88	2,521	4.70	3,562	4.20	4,026	5.70	1,549	8.92

*Costs are based on a 50 Reach and an 8 Frequency over a 4 week period in each market

Source: Blair Radio. Grey Estimates

DEMOGRAPHICS OF STATION TYPES*

Format		U.S. Pop.	Adult Contemporary	AOR/ Progressive	Beautiful Music	Black	Classical	Contemp/ Top 40/ Rock	Country	Disco	Jazz	News	Oldies	Religious & Gospel	Talk	Total Usage**
Age																
18-24	% Comp.	17.7	16.0	53.3	9.2	34.0	12.5	31.0	11.6	35.9	32.0	4.7	26.9	8.4	5.4	24.6
	Index	100	90	301	52	192	71	175	66	203	181	27	152	47	31	139
25-34	% Comp.	22.4	24.2	30.3	15.5	28.6	23.6	29.9	22.3	27.5	28.1	14.3	30.2	29.3	13.4	25.0
	Index	100	108	135	69	128	105	133	100	123	125	64	135	131	60	112
35-49	% Comp.	23.3	24.1	10.5	29.8	19.8	30.2	20.8	33.2	21.1	19.7	26.2	20.6	28.8	23.5	22.2
	Index	100	103	45	128	85	130	89	142	91	85	112	88	124	101	95
50-64	% Comp.	21.2	21.8	4.0	30.9	9.1	24.9	12.8	22.6	9.4	10.2	31.7	13.6	17.2	33.2	17.6
	Index	100	103	19	146	43	117	60	107	44	48	150	64	81	157	83
65+	% Comp.	15.4	13.9	1.9	14.6	8.5	8.8	5.5	10.3	6.1	10.0	23.1	8.7	16.3	24.5	10.6
	Index	100	90	12	95	55	57	36	67	40	65	150	56	106	159	69
Education																
Att./Grad. Col.	% Comp.	31.8	37.2	39.4	41.9	22.5	71.3	36.3	23.9	36.1	44.0	39.0	36.0	32.7	35.9	34.6
	Index	100	117	124	132	71	224	114	75	114	138	123	113	103	113	109
H.S. Grad.	% Comp.	38.4	39.4	42.5	37.9	40.3	22.3	41.2	42.2	40.5	38.7	36.5	36.1	34.0	37.3	40.1
	Index	100	103	111	99	105	58	107	110	105	101	95	94	89	97	104
Less	% Comp.	29.8	23.4	18.1	20.2	37.2	6.4	22.5	33.9	23.4	17.3	24.5	27.9	33.3	26.8	25.3
	Index	100	79	61	68	125	21	76	114	79	58	82	94	112	90	85
HH Income																
$35,000+	% Comp.	19.1	22.4	24.4	27.0	6.4	37.8	20.4	17.1	19.7	19.1	25.9	22.6	17.5	25.9	20.3
	Index	100	117	128	141	34	198	107	90	103	100	136	118	92	136	106
$25,000+	% Comp.	38.9	43.6	47.5	48.8	19.0	57.6	42.1	39.4	40.7	38.0	46.8	43.5	38.8	46.6	41.6
	Index	100	112	122	125	49	148	108	101	105	98	120	112	100	120	107
$15,000+	% Comp.	66.6	72.1	77.2	73.1	43.1	82.4	71.7	69.9	66.7	63.1	71.1	72.3	64.1	71.4	68.7
	Index	100	108	116	110	65	124	108	105	100	95	107	109	96	107	103
$10-15,000	% Comp.	12.9	12.2	10.4	12.1	13.9	8.1	11.1	13.9	12.8	10.0	11.8	11.9	11.8	10.8	11.8
	Index	100	95	81	94	108	63	86	108	99	78	91	92	91	84	91
Under $10,000	% Comp.	20.5	15.7	12.4	14.8	43.0	9.5	17.2	16.2	20.5	26.9	17.1	15.8	24.1	17.8	19.5
	Index	100	77	60	72	210	46	84	79	100	131	83	77	118	87	95

* Data reflects cumes for the average day for the format shown.
** Data reflects the average Mon.-Sun. 6AM-12PM half-hour audience.

Source: MRI, Spring 1982

Media Data
655

CITY MAGAZINES—COST AND CIRCULATION*

Market	Publication	Total Circulation (000)	Cost/Page B&W $(000)	Cost/Page 4C $(000)	Cover Date (on sale days prec. cover date)	Closing Date B&W (Approx. weeks prec. cover date)	Closing Date 4C
New York City	Avenue	41	2.3	3.5	9T/Yr(0)	4	7
	New York Magazine	423	9.3	14.7	50T/Yr(7)	3	3
	The New Yorker	480	10.2	16.2	Wkly(5)	3	6
Los Angeles	California Magazine	252	6.2	9.6	Mo(7)	5	5
	Los Angeles Magazine	166	3.8	5.7	Mo(6-7)	3	4
	Palm Springs Life	69	2.7	3.4	Mo(0)	4	4
	Westways	474	4.3	5.1	Mo(0)	8	8
	Los Angeles Weekly	65	1.1	1.6	Wkly(0)	1	1
Chicago	Chicago	230	4.5	7.3	Mo(7)	5	5
	North Shore	28	1.2	1.7	Mo(5)	5	5
Philadelphia	Philadelphia Magazine	151	3.5	5.4	Mo(3-4)	3	3
San Francisco	San Francisco	48	1.7	2.6	Mo(1-7)	5	5
	San Francisco Focus	137	2.7	3.7	Mo(0)	5	5
	San Francisco Bay Views Magazine	30	1.2	1.7	Mo(0)	2	2
Boston	Boston Magazine	116	2.6	3.7	Mo(0)	4	4
Detroit	Monthly Detroit	43	1.3	1.9	Mo(7)	4	4
Washington, D.C.	The Washington Dossier	41	2.7	3.6	Mo(1-4)	4	4
	The Washingtonian Magazine	127	3.3	5.1	Mo(1-4)	5	5
	Georgetown	45	1.6	2.0	Qtrly(0)	5	5
Cleveland	Cleveland Magazine	56	1.5	2.0	Mo(7)	5	5
	Northern Ohio Live	15	0.9	1.3	Mo(0)	1	1
Dallas/Ft. Worth	D Magazine	74	2.3	3.3	Mo(5-6)	5	5
	Dallas	20	1.3	1.8	Mo(10-11)	5	5
	Dallas-Ft. Worth Home & Garden	66	2.4	3.2	Mo(7)	5	7
	Texas Homes	101	3.2	4.7	12T/Yr(0)	7	7
Houston	Houston City Magazine	63	1.9	2.4	Mo(7)	5	5
	Houston Home & Garden	111	4.1	4.3	Mo(7)	6	7
	Houston Magazine	19	1.0	1.7	Mo(0)	4	7
	Houston Monthly	87	1.4	2.0	Mo(7)	5	5
Pittsburgh	Pittsburgh Magazine	55	1.7	2.6	Mo(7)	5	5
Miami/Ft. Lauderdale	Miami Magazine	22	1.4	1.9	Mo(3-4)	5	5
	Gold Coast of Florida	32	1.5	1.9	Mo(1-7)	5	5
	Miami Mensual	25	1.2	1.6	Mo(7)	8	8
	Palm Beach Life	19	1.1	1.5	Mo(2-3)	5	5
Minneapolis/St. Paul	Minneapolis/St. Paul Magazine	43	1.6	2.1	Mo(2-3)	5	5
	Twin Cities	37	1.5	1.7	Mo(0)	5	5
Atlanta	Atlanta Magazine	54	1.7	2.5	Mo(0)	5	5
St. Louis	St. Louis Magazine	41	1.4	2.0	Mo(0)	4	4
Denver	Denver Magazine	18	1.5	2.1	Mo(5-6)	5	5
Baltimore	Baltimore Magazine	56	1.8	2.7	Mo(0)	5	5
Indianapolis	Indianapolis Monthly	26	0.9	1.5	Mo(7)	6	6
Portland	Oregon Magazine	31	1.1	1.5	Mo(0)	5	5
Phoenix	Phoenix Home & Garden	55	1.4	2.2	Mo(7)	7	7
	Phoenix Magazine	28	1.6	2.4	Mo(1-7)	5	5
Hartford/New Haven	Connecticut Magazine	64	2.2	3.2	Mo(0)	6	6
	Connecticut Today	248	3.4	3.6	Bi/Wk(0)	5	5
Cincinnati	Cincinnati Magazine	24	1.2	1.6	Mo(7)	5	5
San Diego	San Diego Magazine	59	1.9	2.8	Mo(5-6)	4	4
Milwaukee	Milwaukee, The Metropolitan Magazine	18	0.9	1.3	Mo(0)	4	4
	Exclusively Yours, Wisconsin	45	1.6	2.1	15T/Yr(0)	4	4

Only publications with over 15,000 circulation included
*Contact Media Analysis for latest readership estimates

CITY MAGAZINES—COST AND CIRCULATION*

Market	Publication	Total Circulation (000)	Cost/Page B&W $(000)	Cost/Page 4C $(000)	Cover Date (on sale days prec. cover date)	Closing Date Approx. weeks prec. cover date B&W	Closing Date 4C
Nashville	Nashville	26	1.1	1.6	Mo(0)	6	6
	Tennessee Monthly	25	1.8	2.1	Mo(0)	6	6
Buffalo	Buffalo Spree	20	0.6	1.0	Qtrly(0)	6	6
Orlando	Orlando Magazine	26	1.2	1.4	Mo(3-7)	4	4
New Orleans	Louisiana Life	42	1.5	2.1	Bi/Mo(0)	9	9
	New Orleans Magazine	40	2.5	3.8	Mo(5-6)	5	5
Memphis	Memphis	20	1.0	1.2	Mo(0)	5	5
Columbus	Columbus Monthly	38	1.3	1.8	Mo(7)	5	5
	Ohio Magazine	60	1.2	1.9	Mo(4-5)	4	4
Wichita	The Wichitan	15	1.0	1.6	Mo(0)	5	5
Honolulu	Honolulu Magazine	35	1.6	2.1	Mo(7)	4	4
	Aloha	73	2.2	2.8	Bi/Mo(0)	9	9
Austin	Austin Homes & Gardens	19	1.0	1.3	Mo(7)	7	6
	Texas Monthly	291	6.5	10.0	Mo(7)	5	5
Atlantic City	Atlantic City Magazine	50	2.0	2.9	Mo(0)	4	4

Only publications with over 15,000 circulation included
*Contact Media Analysis for latest readership estimates

MAGAZINES—COST AND READERSHIP

Publication	Category	U.S. Circ. (000)	Readers Per Copy Adults	Readers Per Copy 18+ Men	Readers Per Copy Women	Cost/Page B&W $(000)	Cost/Page 4C $(000)	Cover Date (on sale days prec. cover date)	Closing Date Approx. weeks prec. cover date B&W	Closing Date 4C
After Dark	—	60	2.00	1.96	.04	1.1	2.1	Mo (4)	8	8
Air Group One (1)	—	1,000	3.86	2.14	1.72	27.3	34.8	Mo (0)	8	8
American Health	—	405	4.29	1.20	3.09	5.4	7.1	Bi/Mo (1)	4	4
American Legion	—	2,543	1.79	1.34	.45	11.4	15.8	Mo (0)	7	10
Ampersand	—	864	.60	.31	.29	15.1	22.3	Bi/Mo (0)	7	8
Architectural Digest	—	517	4.78	1.87	2.91	12.6	18.9	Mo (0)	8	8
Atlanta	—	54	3.23	1.55	1.68	1.7	2.5	Mo (0)	5	5
Atlantic Monthly	SC	350	3.92	2.36	1.56	6.7	10.1	Mo (1)	6	6
Attenzione	—	169	3.00	1.44	1.56	3.7	4.8	Mo (10)	10	10
Audio	—	130	5.55	4.55	1.00	5.2	6.6	Mo (10)	4	4
Audubon	—	355	3.61	1.74	1.87	6.1	9.5	Bi/Mo (0)	6	6
Avenue	—	41	2.85	.94	1.91	2.3	3.5	9T/Yr. (0)	4	7
Barron's	B	262	4.46	3.11	1.35	8.6	—	Wk (0)	5 days	—
Beauty Digest	—	162	4.88	.98	3.90	2.1	2.8	9T/Yr (0)	10	11
Beauty Handbook	—	800	4.88	.98	3.90	6.3	7.8	Qtly (0)	6	6
Better Homes & Gardens	HM	8,033	4.26	1.13	3.13	65.3	79.0	Mo (15)	10	10
BHG Super Spot	—	1,001	4.26	1.13	3.13	15.8	19.9	Mo (15)	10	10
Big Beautiful Woman	—	300	5.58	.91	4.67	3.4	4.0	Bi/Mo (10)	9	9
Black Enterprise	—	260	4.77	3.21	1.56	8.0	10.3	Mo (21)	8	8
Bon Appetit	—	1,214	3.34	.69	2.65	14.5	20.7	Mo (5)	7	7
Boston	—	116	3.23	1.55	1.68	2.6	3.7	Mo (0)	4	4
Boys' Life	—	1,525	.72	.38	.34	10.5	14.6	Mo (0)	7	8
Bride's	—	367	11.06	1.10	9.96	12.4	15.5	6T/Yr (20-25)	9	9
Business Week	B	770	6.86	4.85	2.01	23.1	35.1	Wk (11)	4	5
California Magazine	SC	252	4.16	2.15	2.01	6.2	9.6	Mo (7)	5	5
Campus Life	—	183	.85	.51	.34	2.5	3.3	Mo (10)	8	8
Car & Driver	A	687	4.92	4.40	.52	16.5	24.2	Mo (10)	8	8
Carcraft	A	373	5.47	4.73	.74	6.4	10.2	Mo (0)	9	9
Carnegie Hall	—	85	1.03	.47	.56	1.5	2.2	Mo (0)	4	5
Changing Times	—	1,520	3.59	2.01	1.58	15.2	22.6	Mo (0)	5	5
Chicago	—	230	3.63	1.83	1.80	4.5	7.3	Mo (7)	5	5
Co-Ed	—	744	1.30	.17	1.13	6.0	8.9	10T/Yr (10-11)	8	8
Colonial Homes	HM	575	4.04	1.37	2.67	9.8	13.6	Bi/Mo (10-11)	10	10
Columbia	—	1,359	1.79	1.04	.75	6.4	7.1	Mo (0)	8	8
Cosmopolitan	W	2,581	4.88	.98	3.90	23.9	32.2	Mo (3-4)	9	9
Country Living	—	690	4.45	1.32	3.13	11.6	15.9	Mo (0)	11	11
Creem	—	139	7.08	4.53	2.55	2.2	3.2	Mo (34-39)	10	10
Cuisine	—	731	4.01	1.16	2.85	10.7	15.2	Mo (6-10)	8	8
Cycle	—	425	8.42	7.13	1.29	12.1	17.6	Mo (10-12)	8	8
Cycle World	A	342	8.42	7.13	1.29	9.2	13.7	Mo (12-13)	10	10

657

Publication	Category	U.S. Circ. (000)	Readers Per Copy Adults	18+ Men	Women	Cost/Page B&W $(000)	4C $(000)	Cover Date (on sale days prec. cover date)	Closing Date Approx. weeks prec. cover date B&W	4C
Decorating & Craft Ideas	W	726	6.75	1.15	5.60	8.7	11.3	10T/Yr (0-4)	9	9
Discover	—	864	3.62	1.95	1.67	15.3	22.2	Mo (14-18)	7	7
Dun's Business Month	B	301	2.71	1.96	.75	9.5	12.8	Mo (0)	4	4
East/West Network (2)	—	1,031	5.49	3.27	2.22	34.9	46.5	Mo (0)	6	6
Ebony	—	1,250	6.22	2.54	3.68	16.2	20.8	Mo (6-11)	9	9
18 Almanac	—	735	For Teenagers Only			17.2	20.6	Annually (0)	8	8
Elan	—	150	5.57	1.57	4.00	3.4	5.0	Bi/Mo (0)	10	10
Elks	—	1,656	1.79	1.04	.75	6.8	10.4	10T/Yr (5-6)	6	7
Esquire	M	667	6.59	3.94	2.65	12.9	19.3	Mo (10-12)	10	10
Essence	W	701	4.18	1.18	3.00	8.7	13.0	Mo (14)	9	9
Family Circle	WS	6,639	4.14	.70	3.44	53.4	64.4	17T/Yr (0-6)	9	9
Family Handyman	—	339	4.16	2.65	1.51	11.7	16.8	Wkly (0)	6	6
Field & Stream	S	2,011	6.96	5.25	1.71	22.4	33.8	Mo (6-7)	7	8
50 Plus	—	273	3.50	1.40	2.10	4.5	6.1	Mo (15-21)	6	6
Financial World	—	124	3.62	1.95	1.67	4.7	6.9	Semi-Mo (0)	3	3
Food & Wine	—	110	4.05	1.70	2.35	5.9	8.8	Mo (1-7)	7	7
For Seniors Only	—	400	For Teenagers Only			2.2	4.2	Semi-Annually (0)	2	2
Forbes	B	740	3.77	2.57	1.20	16.5	25.1	Bi/Wkly (0)	4	5
Fortune	B	620	5.76	3.84	1.92	19.8	30.0	26T/Yr (0)	6	6
Frequent Flyer	—	250	2.00	1.72	.28	6.3	8.4	Mo (0)	6	6
Gallery	M	448	3.38	2.94	.44	3.2	4.8	Mo (1-7)	13	13
Games	—	633	3.24	1.39	1.85	7.1	10.2	Mo (20-24)	9	9
Gentleman's Quarterly	M	519	6.56	4.40	2.16	8.5	12.7	Mo (9-15)	9	9
GEO	—	218	2.70	1.75	.95	6.1	7.5	Mo (0)	7	7
Glamour	F	1,904	4.59	.48	4.11	20.1	28.4	Mo (15-16)	9	9
Golf Digest	S	988	3.37	2.29	1.08	19.2	28.8	Mo (6-11)	7	7
Golf Magazine	S	750	3.86	2.80	1.06	14.0	21.0	Mo (14-21)	8	8
Good Housekeeping	WS	5,066	5.62	1.09	4.53	46.2	58.0	Mo (8-13)	10	10
Gourmet	—	563	4.59	1.37	3.22	8.0	13.6	Mo (0)	7	7
Great Recipes	—	650	3.28	1.24	2.04	5.0	6.5	Mo (9-10)	11	11
Guns & Ammo	S	481	9.77	8.61	1.16	6.3	10.1	Mo (0)	9	9
Harper's Bazaar	F	622	4.56	.52	4.04	11.2	16.2	Mo (0)	8	8
Harper's Magazine	SC	291	4.51	1.83	2.67	2.8	4.3	Mo (1-7)	6	6
Health	W	882	4.29	1.20	3.09	7.9	11.1	Mo (0)	7	7
High Fidelity	—	377	5.30	4.19	1.11	13.2	17.5	Mo (10-11)	7	7
High Technology	—	342	4.40	2.75	1.65	7.5	11.2	Bi/Mo (1-7)	7	7
Highwire	—	100	3.97	.72	3.25	2.7	3.5	Qtly (0)	7	7
Home	—	581	5.40	1.12	4.28	8.2	10.9	Mo (10-11)	9	9
Hot Rod	A	742	6.37	5.46	.91	12.8	20.4	Mo (0)	9	9
House & Garden	HM	965	5.25	1.39	3.86	13.8	20.2	Mo (10-11)	9	9
House Beautiful	HM	859	9.07	1.76	7.31	13.5	19.8	Mo (8-13)	10	10
Inc.	—	471	4.08	2.79	1.29	13.4	20.1	Mo (0)	6	6
Inn America	—	250	3.00	1.80	1.20	7.7	9.6	Bi/Mo (0)	6	6
Inside Sports	S	549	8.93	7.76	1.16	9.1	13.7	Mo (7)	7	7
Interview	—	38	3.40	1.00	2.40	1.8	3.0	Mo (0)	7	7
It's Me	—	200	5.58	.91	4.67	3.0	3.8	Bi/Mo (0)	8	8
Jet	—	674	8.49	4.01	4.48	6.1	9.6	Wk (7)	3	3
Kennedy Center	—	210	1.03	.47	.56	3.6	5.6	Mo (0)	4	6
Kiwanis	—	266	1.79	1.04	.75	2.1	3.4	Mo (1-6)	7	7
Ladies' Home Journal	WS	5,141	3.86	.55	3.31	39.0	48.0	Mo (14)	10	10
LHJ Prime Showcase	—	1,110	3.86	.55	3.31	13.0	17.0	Mo (14)	10	10
Lady's Circle	—	111	4.13	.71	3.42	0.8	1.0	Mo (30)	10	10
Leadership Network (3)	—	583	2.94	2.36	.59	12.6	16.4	Var	Var	Var
Life	SC	1,357	10.89	5.61	5.28	26.2	34.7	Mo (6-11)	8	8
Lincoln Center	—	340	1.03	.47	.56	6.3	9.3	Mo (0)	4	6
Lion	—	669	1.79	1.04	.75	3.9	4.7	Mo (5-6)	6	6
Los Angeles	—	166	5.67	2.23	3.44	3.8	5.7	Mo (6-7)	3	4
MacFadden Women's Group (4)	—	2,379	8.03	1.08	6.95	21.1	27.4	Mo (17-21)	10	10
Mademoiselle	F	1,108	4.27	.41	3.86	12.9	18.7	Mo (15-16)	10	10
McCall's	WS	6,258	3.53	.48	3.05	48.7	59.8	Mo (8-13)	10	10
McCall's VIP	—	1,100	3.53	.48	3.05	12.5	16.7	Mo (8-13)	10	10
Mechanix Illustrated	HO	1,600	4.48	3.52	.96	17.5	24.8	Mo (13-18)	9	9
Metropolitan Home	—	742	1.92	.60	1.32	9.9	14.2	Mo (14)	9	9
Minneapolis/St. Paul	—	.43	3.23	1.55	1.68	1.6	2.1	Mo (2-3)	5	5
Modern Bride	—	351	8.45	.81	7.64	12.4	15.5	Bi/Mo (21-24)	12	12
Modern Maturity	—	7,349	2.50	1.00	1.50	47.6	58.1	Bi/Mo (0)	10	10
Modern Photography	—	677	10.08	6.12	3.96	24.2	32.2	Mo (0)	7	7
Money	B	1,119	5.63	3.22	2.41	16.5	25.7	Mo (5-6)	6	6
Montana	—	97	3.23	1.55	1.68	1.0	1.4	Bi/Mo (0)	5	5
Moose	—	1,324	1.79	1.04	.75	5.3	8.0	Mo (15-16)	5	5
Mother Earth News	—	1,078	4.33	2.34	1.99	12.0	18.0	Bi/Mo (0)	7	7
Motor Trend	A	739	5.22	4.57	.65	14.8	23.7	Mo (0)	9	9
Ms.	W	482	4.47	.73	3.74	7.3	9.8	Mo (7-14)	9	9
National Enquirer	—	4,654	4.40	1.57	2.83	21.0	26.5	Wk (1-7)	10	10
National Geographic	SC	7,478	3.41	1.80	1.61	73.5	95.6	Mo (7-14)	8	8

MAGAZINES—COST AND READERSHIP (Cont'd)

Publication	Category	U.S. Circ. (000)	Adults	18+ Men	Women	B&W $(000)	4C $(000)	Cover Date (on sale days prec. cover date)	Closing Date B&W	Closing Date 4C
			Readers Per Copy			Cost/Page			Approx. weeks prec. cover date	
National Lampoon	—	411	7.89	6.21	1.68	6.7	9.9	Mo (15-16)	10	10
National Review	—	107	2.94	2.35	.59	2.2	3.2	Bi-Wk (10)	4	4
Nation's Business	—	1,042	1.69	1.20	.49	16.3	23.8	Mo (0)	4	4
Natural History	SC	464	3.47	1.71	1.76	7.2	10.7	Mo (5-6)	6	6
New Jersey Monthly	—	106	3.23	1.55	1.68	2.7	3.6	Mo (7)	5	5
New Orleans	—	40	3.23	1.55	1.68	2.5	3.8	Mo (5-6)	5	5
New Republic	—	95	2.94	2.35	.59	2.1	3.3	Wk (0)	3	4
Newsweek	NW	2,993	7.27	4.15	3.12	40.9	63.9	Wk (6)	5	7
Newsweek Exec.	—	675	3.94	2.02	1.92	15.0	23.5	Bi-Wk (7)	5	7
Newsweek Woman	W	561	3.64	1.72	1.92	7.0	11.0	Mo (7)	5	7
New Woman	W	1,015	2.90	.26	2.64	11.1	14.8	Bi-Mo (7)	8	8
New York Magazine	—	480	2.82	1.27	1.55	9.3	14.7	50T/Yr (7)	3	3
New Yorker	—	481	5.02	2.72	2.30	10.2	16.2	Wk (4)	3	6
Nuestro	—	150	3.00	1.44	1.56	3.6	6.0	10T/Yr (0)	6	6
Nutshell	—	1,203	.60	.31	.29	27.0	33.6	Spr/Fall (0)	8	8
Omni	—	580	8.55	5.88	2.67	12.2	18.4	Mo (0)	7	7
1001 Home Ideas	HM	1,161	4.05	1.09	2.96	13.4	16.9	Mo (9-11)	12	12
Opera News	—	93	3.40	1.00	2.40	1.9	2.7	17T/Yr (20)	7	7
Oui	M	498	5.32	4.53	.79	5.5	8.6	Mo (1-6)	11	11
Outdoor Life	S	1,477	5.66	4.36	1.30	16.5	24.0	Mo (4-6)	7	8
Outside	—	187	4.33	2.34	1.99	5.4	8.1	8T/Yr (10-15)	8	8
Ovation	—	112	2.66	1.24	1.42	2.5	3.7	Mo (0)	7	7
Parents' Magazine	WS	1,665	4.97	1.05	3.92	24.8	31.7	Mo (0)	11	11
Penthouse	M	3,272	3.08	2.54	.54	24.9	37.0	Mo (24-31)	11	11
People	—	2,342	10.38	3.93	6.45	33.3	43.0	Wk (7)	3	7
Performing Arts	—	580	1.03	.47	.56	7.7	10.4	Mo (0)	3	3
Petersen Action Group (5)	HO	3,661	7.27	6.18	1.09	62.9	100.6	See individual magazines		
Philadelphia	—	151	3.23	1.55	1.68	3.5	5.4	Mo (3-4)	3	3
Pickup Van & 4WD	A	232	8.20	7.56	.64	3.5	5.6	Mo (12-15)	10	10
Playbill (6)	—	1,990	1.03	.47	.56	29.0	40.0	Mo (0)	4	5
Playboy	M	4.412	4.10	3.13	.97	43.8	61.3	Mo (25-31)	16	16
Playgirl	W	578	5.80	1.81	3.99	5.4	7.2	Mo (19-21)	11	11
Popular Hot Rodding	A	235	8.96	7.68	1.28	3.7	5.8	Mo (25-31)	10	10
Popular Mechanics	HO	1,561	6.84	5.50	1.34	19.0	26.9	Mo (15-21)	8	8
Popular Science	HO	1,635	4.65	3.67	.98	18.9	26.8	Mo (0)	8	9
Prevention	—	2,395	3.05	.94	2.11	17.7	26.6	Mo (12-15)	7	7
Psychology Today	SC	1,154	4.79	1.83	2.96	14.2	20.5	Mo (9-11)	6	6
Reader's Digest	—	18,443	2.97	1.30	1.67	86.2	103.6	Mo (5-6)	8	8
Redbook	WS	4,280	3.62	.56	3.06	32.3	42.7	Mo (0)	9	9
Redbook Be Beautiful	—	400	4.88	.98	3.90	5.2	6.5	2T/Yr (0)	8	8
Road & Track	—	582	5.98	5.35	.63	13.8	21.7	Mo (11-12)	10	10
Rolling Stone	—	732	708	4.53	2.55	12.8	19.2	25T/Yr (16-18)	6	7
Rotarian	—	394	1.79	1.04	.75	3.9	5.5	Mo (11-14)	6	6
The Runner	—	199	6.65	3.75	2.90	5.8	8.7	Mo (8-11)	8	8
Runner's World	—	373	6.65	3.75	2.90	7.1	10.0	13T/Yr (0)	8	8
Sail	—	165	5.76	3.84	1.92	5.7	8.1	Mo (0)	6	6
San Francisco	—	48	3.23	1.55	1.68	1.7	2.6	Mo (1-7)	5	5
Saturday Evening Post	SC	662	8.17	4.41	3.76	7.9	11.8	9T/Yr (7-21)	10	10
Savvy	—	261	4.59	.35	4.24	5.3	7.9	Mo (1-7)	8	8
Scholastic Group	—	2,586	—	—	—	16.2	22.3	Bi/Wk	7	7
Science Digest	—	467	6.29	3.76	2.53	9.9	13.2	Mo (0)	10	10
Science '83	—	766	2.91	1.57	1.34	10.8	15.4	Mo (15-21)	8	8
Scientific American	SC	639	5.18	3.55	1.63	14.0	21.0	Mo (6-7)	6	7
Self	W	1,056	2.99	.40	2.59	12.0	17.9	Mo (0)	8	8
Seventeen	—	1,381	3.97	.72	3.25	14.5	20.9	Mo (0)	9	9
Shape	—	247	4.15	.58	3.57	2.0	2.8	Mo (28-31)	12	12
Signature	—	620	3.34	1.63	1.71	9.2	11.2	Mo (0)	7	7
Sixteen	—	161	.40	.05	.35	1.4	2.1	Mo (40-44)	13	14
Ski	S	391	6.39	3.65	2.74	11.0	15.1	7T/Yr (11-15)	9	9
Skiing	—	389	6.39	3.65	2.74	12.1	16.5	7T/Yr (5-15)	8	8
Slimmer	—	251	4.88	.98	3.90	1.9	2.4	Bi/Mo (60)	16	16
Smithsonian	SC	1,981	3.75	1.76	1.99	21.2	31.8	Mo (0)	6	6
Soap Opera Digest	—	560	8.67	1.18	7.49	5.3	6.1	26T/Yr (14-17)	12	12
Southern Living	HM	2,130	3.86	1.20	2.66	24.0	33.8	Mo (14-16)	8	8
Sport	S	910	5.94	4.96	.98	12.9	18.8	Mo (10-12)	9	9
Sporting News	S	484	5.38	4.35	1.03	7.4	9.3	Wk (0)	3	3
Sports Afield	S	537	13.80	11.70	2.10	8.9	12.8	Mo (4-8)	8	8
Sports Illustrated	NW/S	2.506	6.51	4.85	1.66	35.7	55.7	Wk (6)	3	7
Sports Illustrated Select	—	718	6.51	4.85	1.66	15.1	23.6	Bi/Mo (6)	7	7
Spring	—	400	4.15	.58	3.57	5.5	7.6	9T/Yr (21-30)	Varies	
Stagebill-Chicago	—	385	1.03	.47	.56	5.1	7.5	Mo (0)	4	5
Stereo Review	—	527	5.30	4.19	1.11	18.9	26.5	Mo (8-11)	8	8
Sterling Women's Group (7)	—	1,125	6.25	.81	5.44	3.8	4.5	Mo (31-37)	14	16
Sunset	HM	1,411	3.59	1.35	2.24	17.0	23.6	Mo (9-12)	7	7
Technology Illustrated	—	390	4.40	4.05	.35	6.6	9.9	Bi/Mo (7)	8	8

659

| Publication | Category | U.S. Circ. (000) | Readers Per Copy | | | Cost/Page | | Cover Date (on sale days prec. cover date) | Closing Date Approx. weeks prec. cover date | |
			Adults	18+ Men	Women	B&W $(000)	4C $(000)		B&W	4C
Teen	—	1.023	1.35	.21	1.14	9.0	13.5	Mo (17-19)	10	10
Tennis Magazine	S	451	3.32	1.97	1.35	9.2	13.8	Mo (6-11)	6	6
Texas Monthly	—	301	4.48	2.36	2.12	6.5	10.0	Mo (7)	5	5
The Dial	—	1.015	2.66	1.24	1.42	14.7	22.7	Mo (0)	6	6
The Star	—	3.514	3.00	1.05	1.95	17.4	21.4	Mo (1-7)	5	5
Tiger Beat	—	153	.40	.05	.35	1.7	2.2	Mo (12-24)	11	11
Tiger Beat Star	—	107	.40	.05	.35	.9	1.1	Mo (35-37)	11	11
Time	NW	4.645	5.32	2.89	2.43	55.0	85.9	Wk (7)	3	7
Time B	—	1.584	3.06	1.56	1.50	29.9	46.6	Wk (7)	5	7
Time-Big Time	—	2.828	5.32	2.89	2.43	38.3	59.7	Wk (7)	5	7
Town & Country	SC	306	6.78	2.25	4.53	8.5	10.9	Mo (0)	7	7
Travel/Holiday	—	792	2.32	1.14	1.18	8.0	11.0	Mo (10-12)	8	8
Travel & Leisure	SC	917	3.34	1.63	1.71	14.8	19.9	Mo (8-9)	7	7
True Story	—	1.464	3.83	.45	3.38	12.3	16.1	Mo (18-22)	10	10
TV Guide	—	17.703	2.66	1.24	1.42	65.6	77.4	Wk (3)	7	7
Us Magazine	—	1.022	4.53	1.75	2.78	13.0	16.8	Bi/Wk (13-15)	7	7
U.S. News & World Report	NW	2.116	4.71	2.93	1.81	26.9	42.5	Wk (7)	3	6
U.S. News Blue Chip	—	450	2.61	1.58	1.03	10.5	16.6	Bi/Mo (0)	5	6
Venture	—	220	4.08	2.79	1.29	5.9	8.9	Mo (0)	6	6
Village Voice	—	156	7.08	4.53	2.55	4.0	5.5	Wk (0)	1	1
Vogue	F	1.106	6.36	.84	5.52	14.0	20.0	Mo (0)	7	8
Vogue Beauty & Health	—	450	4.88	98	3.90	6.0	8.8	1T/Yr	11	11
"W"	—	198	2.44	.44	2.00	8.3	10.6	Bi/Wk (0)	2	2
Wall St. Journal	B	2.002	2.36	1.52	.84	56.1	—	Dly (0)	Varies	—
Washingtonian	—	127	3.23	1.55	1.68	3.3	5.1	Mo (1-4)	4	4
Weight Watchers	W	710	5.58	.91	4.67	9.8	13.7	Mo (10-12)	10	10
Woman's Day	WS	6.636	3.89	.45	3.44	52.0	62.2	15T/Yr (6-17)	10	10
Women's Sports	—	135	5.45	1.36	4.09	1.9	2.9	Mo (0)	8	8
Workbench	—	762	4.57	3.60	.97	5.9	8.3	Bi/Mo (14-16)	5	5
Working Mother	—	380	4.80	.86	3.94	6.4	8.5	Mo (9-12)	10	10
Working Woman	W	517	4.59	.35	4.24	9.5	13.1	Mo (5-7)	8	8
World Tennis	S	359	2.89	1.80	1.09	8.8	13.2	Mo (5-7)	7	7
Yachting	—	128	5.76	3.84	1.92	5.2	7.9	Mo (0)	6	6
Young Miss	—	627	4.40	.05	.35	5.9	9.1	10T/Yr (10-16)	10	10
Ziff/Davis Group (8)	HO	3.539	5.46	4.19	1.27	58.7	88.8	See individual magazines		

Categories Listed: A—Automotive   F—Fashion   HO—Hobbies   NW—Newsweeklies   SC—Selective Class   WS—Women's Service
B—Business   HM—Home   M—Male   S—Sports   W—Women

These costs and circulations represent national availability. For regions. combination buys. and earned discounts. consult media personnel.

Sources: MRI, Fall 1982; SRDS. 9/82; ABC 6/82; and Grey estimates.

DESCRIPTION OF MAGAZINE GROUPS

1. Air Group One	— American Way, Delta Sky. Frontier. Northwest Passages. TWA Ambassador.
2. East-West Network	— Amtrak Express, Continental Extra. Eastern Review. Ozark. PSA Magazine. Republic Scene. Texas Flyer. United Mainliner. US Air Magazine. Western's World.
3. Leadership Network	— Columbia Journalism Review. Commentary. Foreign Affairs. National Review. New Republic. N.Y. Review of Books. Technological Review, The Wharton Magazine.
4. MacFadden Women's Group	— Modern Romances. Secrets. True Confessions. True Experience. True Love. True Romance. True Story.
5. Petersen Action Group	— Carcraft, 4 Wheel & Off-Road, Guns & Ammo. Hot Rod. Hunting. Motorcyclist. Motor Trend. Petersen Marine Group. Photographic. Pickup Van & 4WD, Skin Diver.
6. Playbill Group	— Covers Theatres In: Boston. Florida, New York City. Philadelphia/Baltimore.
7. Sterling Women's Group	— Daytime TV. Modern Screen. Movie Mirror. Photo Screen. Soap Opera Stars. TV & Movie Screen. TV Picture Life.
8. Ziff-Davis Group	— Boating. Car & Driver. Cycle. Flying. Popular Photography. Skiing. Stereo Review.

MAGAZINE EFFICIENCIES BY MAGAZINE TYPE (PAGE 4-COLOR COSTS)

	Sel. Class	News	Male	Business	Sports	Hobbies	Home	Women's Service	Women	Fashion	Automotive
# of Publications in Group	12	4	6	7	13	5	7	7	10	4	7
Demographics											
Adult Men											
18+	$ 7.60	$ 5.70	$ 4.60	$ 12.10	$ 4.60	$ 4.60	$10.44	$ 15.86	$ 16.97	$ 31.80	$ 5.66
18-24	38.43	24.04	15.72	60.00	19.08	15.10	82.75	128.80	83.67	111.83	13.86
18-34	16.83	11.56	7.02	26.09	8.63	7.87	25.83	41.04	30.73	53.03	8.13
35-49	30.74	22.96	21.01	47.54	19.25	19.53	39.61	57.40	75.20	138.67	28.76
50+	24.92	22.13	37.28	43.09	20.15	25.40	31.38	46.68	78.34	178.27	53.36
HH Inc. Under $10M	59.55	44.69	34.73	134.69	35.56	38.73	90.54	125.06	131.22	343.13	39.65
HH Inc. $15M+	9.91	7.39	6.18	14.05	6.24	6.08	13.51	21.09	23.12	40.23	7.94
HH Inc. $25M+	16.47	12.40	10.65	18.37	11.00	10.67	21.48	36.33	38.50	63.10	14.21
College Educated	13.62	10.12	9.71	16.49	11.11	11.52	21.09	35.02	34.77	50.71	16.71
H.S. Graduate	28.51	19.08	12.85	57.72	11.50	11.50	31.36	46.51	56.26	134.87	13.60
Adult Women											
18+	7.80	8.80	14.80	22.80	15.60	19.51	3.93	2.95	4.08	4.02	38.44
18-24	45.33	47.70	48.59	127.05	69.48	72.56	25.50	17.05	14.58	11.53	117.82
18-34	18.08	20.35	21.92	50.96	33.61	36.60	9.50	6.94	6.92	6.53	63.49
35-49	31.48	34.53	74.67	90.22	55.07	79.40	16.02	12.25	12.86	19.25	137.93
50+	24.06	28.06	117.67	74.60	61.83	88.81	11.52	8.86	9.30	22.90	333.16
HH Inc. Under $10M	43.07	51.03	61.64	161.60	89.49	98.86	20.03	14.06	14.75	21.15	191.22
HH Inc. $15M	11.22	12.77	23.29	30.16	22.50	28.72	6.01	4.65	4.88	6.11	57.38
HH Inc. $25M+	19.89	21.36	42.42	43.44	44.35	53.19	7.90	8.93	9.37	10.92	116.67
College Educated	15.90	17.54	37.88	38.70	46.14	51.88	10.57	8.82	9.25	8.33	131.06
H.S. Graduate	21.70	24.53	32.39	72.40	34.98	46.49	9.49	6.60	6.92	9.85	82.18

Source: SRDS. ABC. MRI. Grey Estimates

SUPPLEMENTS & COMICS*—COST AND READERSHIP

Publication	U.S. Circ. (000)	Readers Per Copy 18+ Adults	18+ Men	18+ Women	Cost/Page B&W $(000)	4C $(000)	Mkts. #	Papers #	Closing Date Approx. Wks. Prec. Cover Date B&W	4C
Dawn	900	2.05	.96	1.09	12	17	43	43	5	7
Family Weekly	12,400	2.05	.96	1.09	93	106	362	362	6	6
Metro. Comics (Total Ntwk)	24,000	1.21	.60	.61	—	256	93	96	—	8
New York Times Magazine	1,462	2.63	1.29	1.34	14	21	1	1	4	7
Parade (Nat'l Ntwk)	22,163	1.98	.95	1.03	168	206	136	136	5	5
Puck Comics (Nat'l Ntwk)	13,324	1.21	.58	.63	—	177	67	67	—	8
(American Ntwk)	4,600	1.21	.58	.63	—	58	74	74	—	8
Sunday (Full Ntwk)	22,723	2.11	1.03	1.08	199	243	49	57	4	5

*Sunday Supplements and Comics represent nat'l buys noted. In most cases optional papers or regionals are available.
For details consult media personnel.
Source: SRDS 1982

MAGAZINE COST CONVERSION FORMULA

Type	Page	Horizontal ½ Pg	⅓ Pg	⅔ Pg	Vertical ½ Pg	⅓ Pg	2nd	Covers 3rd	4th	Digest Size Page
4-Color	100	61	46	75	61	46	116	110	137	62
Black & White	78	41	29	55	41	29				

To be read: If full-page 4-color cost is 100% a ½ page 4-color cost is approximately 61% of full-page 4-color cost.
Source: SRDS, 1982

DAILY NEWSPAPERS
COST AND CIRCULATION

Newspapers Required For 60% Coverage of Metro Markets

Metro Markets	Metro Area Households (MM)	Total U.S. Households %	Papers #	Total Circ. (MM)	Metro Circ. (MM)	1000 Line Ad Open Rate $M	CPM Circ.* (M)
Top 5	12.4	15	22	9.1	7.2	91.4	10.04
Top 10	18.5	22	35	12.8	10.3	129.2	10.09
Top 20	26.3	31	56	17.8	15.3	180.3	10.13
Top 30	32.1	38	73	22.2	19.0	224.2	10.10
Top 50	39.5	47	103	27.6	23.8	280.5	10.16
Top 75	45.6	54	139	31.9	27.7	331.4	10.39
Top 100	49.9	59	179	34.8	30.4	368.2	10.58
Top 150	55.8	66	246	39.4	34.2	428.4	10.87
Top 200	59.6	70	310	42.1	36.5	471.5	11.20

Newspapers Required For 60% Coverage of TV Markets

TV Markets	DMA Households (MM)	Total U.S. Households %	Papers #	Total Circ. (MM)	DMA Circ. (MM)	1000 Line Ad Open Rate $M	CPM Circ.* (M)
Top 5	18.2	22	78	12.0	11.2	127.6	10.63
Top 10	26.1	31	97	16.1	15.5	173.2	10.76
Top 20	37.0	44	148	22.6	21.5	247.9	10.97
Top 30	44.5	53	192	27.4	26.0	309.5	11.30
Top 50	55.5	66	311	34.0	32.4	378.9	11.14
Top 75	65.3	78	445	39.5	37.8	460.8	11.67
Top 100	71.8	86	542	43.0	41.3	510.7	11.88
Top 150	80.2	96	730	47.7	45.9	585.7	12.28
Top 200	83.7	100	846	49.0	47.8	632.6	12.91

*Contact Media Personnel for latest cost data.
Source: SRDS Aug. 1982: Newspaper Advertising Bureau: Grey Estimates

NEWSPAPER READERSHIP

Newspapers	Page Openings Adults %	Men %	Women %
All Pages	62	61	62
General News	94	93	95
Editorial	80	77	81
Business. Finance	77	78	75
Sports	81	88	74
Entertainment	82	78	85
Classified	77	76	77

Newspapers	Page Openings Adults %	Men %	Women %
Radio-TV	79	75	81
Food. Cooking	79	70	86
Comics	77	77	76
Home Furnishings. Improvement	77	71	82
Only Read Certain Sections	38	39	38

TRENDS IN NEWSPAPER REVENUE*

Year	Total ($MM)	National ($MM)	%	Local ($MM)	%
1974	8.001	1.194	14.9	6.807	85.1
1975	8.442	1.221	14.5	7.221	85.5
1976	9.901	1.502	15.2	8.408	84.8
1977	11.132	1.677	15.1	9.455	84.9
1978	12.707	1.787	14.1	10.920	85.9
1979	14.493	2.085	14.3	12.408	85.6
1980	15.541	2.353	15.1	13.188	84.9
1981	17.420	2.729	15.7	14.691	84.3
1982 Est.	19.043	3.059	16.1	15.984	83.9

NEWSPAPER COLOR CONVERSION (Average All Newspapers)

	1-Color & Black %	2-Color & Black %	3-Color & Black %	Hi Fi & Black %	Spectacolor & Black %
1000 Lines	35	51	65	NA	NA
Full Page	17	25	31	100	100

To Be Read: Add 35% to 1000 Line ROP costs for addition of Color and Black.
Contact Media Personnel for specifics on Spectacolor and Hi Fi.

RATING POINT CONVERSION FACTORS

	18+	18-34	35-54	55+	Inc. $15M+	Col. Educ.
Men	100	90	102	114	144	123
Women	100	88	109	107	161	124

ESTIMATED NEWSPAPER READERS PER COPY

Men 18+	Women 18+	Adults 18+
1.0	1.1	2.1

*Including Production Costs
Source: Newspaper Advertising Bureau—Audits & Surveys National Study of Newspaper Reading

BILLBOARD COST BY MARKET GROUP

	Metro County Area Population (000)	#25 Showing			30 Sheet Posters* #50 Showing			#100 Showing		
		Reg. #	Ill. #	Cost Per Month ($)	Reg. #	Ill. #	Cost Per Month ($)	Reg. #	Ill. #	Cost Per Month ($)
Top 10	52.008.5	213	631	274.638	359	1.243	531.471	658	2.369	1.000.371
Top 20	74.972.5	425	898	405.095	686	1.769	772.554	1.254	3.421	1.471.948
Top 30	92.980.1	543	1.142	505.701	858	2.225	955.040	1.558	4.299	1.821.462
Top 50	112.183.2	858	1.429	638.518	1.311	2.770	1.184.901	2.365	5.371	2.262.861
Top 100	134.422.0	1.333	1.748	793.985	2.011	3.376	1.449.156	3.603	6.557	2.756.803

*Same costs apply to 24-Sheet Posters

Definition: #100 Showing: Represents the equivalent of 100% of the adult population covered daily. including duplicated exposures. Since some people will pass by one or more panels several times daily while others are not "exposed" at all, the actual daily reach of such a schedule would be substantially lower.

Source: Out of Home Media Services

KING-SIZE POSTERS—30" X 144"
#100 Showing

Markets	Cost 1 Mo. Rate* ($M)	CPM ($)	Impressions (M)	Reach (%)	Frequency (X)
Top 5	228.5	.67	336.602	88	18
Top 10	345.6	.72	477.824	85	16
Top 15	450.5	.74	611.228	85	21
Top 20	517.2	.73	709.427	89	27
Top 25	545.0	.73	739.026	84	17

*Minimum 12-Month Contract
Source: TDI; Winston Network. Inc.

BILLBOARD AUDIENCE & EFFICIENCY

	% Audience	CPM		% Audience	CPM
Total Adults	100	$0.76	**Household Income**		
			$40.000+	14	5.43
Sex			$25.000+	42	1.81
Male	53	1.43	$15.000-$25.000	24	3.17
Female	47	1.62	$10.000-$15.000	20	3.80
			−$10.000	14	5.43
Age					
18-34	50	1.52	**Marital Status**		
35-44	16	4.75	Single	22	3.46
45-54	12	6.33	Married	63	1.21
55+	22	3.46	Divorced, Separated, Widowed	15	5.07
Education			**Locality Type**		
Attended/Graduated College	37	2.05	Metropolitan Central City	28	2.71
Graduated High School	40	1.90	Metropolitan Suburban	46	1.65
Did not Graduate H.S.	23	3.30	Non-Metropolitan	26	2.92
Individual Employment Income					
$20.000+	21	3.62			
$15.000-$20.000	11	6.91			
$10.000-$15.000	19	4.00			
−$10.000	18	4.22			

Source: Institute of Outdoor Advertising. Grey Estimates

YELLOW PAGES USAGE BY DEMOGRAPHIC CHARACTERISTICS

	% Using	Average No. of References Per User —Yearly	Personal Use %	Business Use %
Sex				
Men	84	80	74	51
Women	83	77	69	44
Age				
18-24	84	79	75	44
25-34	89	88	77	55
35-44	89	90	76	57
45-54	86	81	72	52
55-64	82	67	68	41
65+	68	50	54	30
Household Income				
$40.000+	91	95	81	61
$30.000-$39.999	91	88	80	58
$25.000-$29.999	91	86	80	57
$20.000-$24.999	90	70	79	50
$15.000-$19.999	85	74	75	44
$10.000-$14.999	78	74	64	42
Under $10.000	69	73	53	34
Household Size				
1 Person	74	76	61	42
2 People	83	73	70	46
3 or 4 People	86	81	74	49
5 or More People	86	84	73	49

Source: National Yellow Pages Service Association

NATIONAL YELLOW PAGES SERVICE—Cost by Market Size/Directories Used

Population— Directory Area (000)	Total Directories #	Trademark Heading $	Bold Face Listing $	1/4 Page Display Ad $
1-9	1,631	171,845	52,177	942,656
10-49	2,299	350.403	98,009	1,990,646
50-99	777	160,459	40,453	885,986
100-249	554	147,007	34,280	846,440
250-499	170	56,289	12,273	345,165
500-999	74	32,391	6,055	206,389
1000	80	49,143	8,205	284,581

Source: National Yellow Pages Service Association

BLACK MEDIA AVAILABILITY IN MAJOR BLACK MARKETS

Top Black Markets	Black Population (1)			Radio (2)		Newspapers (3)	
	(M)	% SMSA	% U.S.	Radio Stations (#)	Avg. Cost Per Spot* ($)	Papers (#)	Avg. Open Line Rate ($)
New York	1,925	21	7.1	4	108	6	1.21
Chicago	1.432	20	5.3	5	122	9	.78
Los Angeles	963	13	3.6	5	58	6	.68
Philadelphia	879	19	3.2	3	90	7	.74
Detroit	879	20	3.2	4	70	3	.65
Top 5	6.078	19	22.4	21	448	31	4.06
Washington, D.C.	848	28	3.1	3	57	3	.81
Baltimore	561	26	2.1	3	36	1	1.60
Houston	558	18	2.1	2	50	1	.90
Atlanta	510	24	1.9	2	52	3	.47
Dallas-Ft. Worth	433	14	1.6	4	73	5	.41
Top 10	8.988	19	33.2	35	716	44	8.25
Newark, N.J.	417	21	1.5	—	—	2	.49
St. Louis	403	17	1.5	4	35	4	.65
San Francisco-Oakland	395	12	1.5	3	98	4	1.16
New Orleans	391	32	1.4	4	40	2	.61
Memphis	370	40	1.4	1	72	2	.50
Top 15	10,964	20	40.5	47	961	58	11.66
Top 50	16.387	18	60.5	98	2.148	113	36.98
Total Black U.S.	27.092	12	100.0	—	—	—	—

*Costs reflect early/late drivetime 60's 12 X rate

Source: (1) 1982 Survey of Buying Power; (2) SRDS Aug 1982 and station reps; (3) Black Media Inc. 1982

SPANISH MEDIA AVAILABILITY IN MAJOR SPANISH MARKETS

TV MARKET	Population (1) (M)	% Mkt	% U.S.	Television (1) Stations #	Avg. Cost Per 30" Spot* ($)	Radio (2) Stations #	Avg. Cost Per Spot** ($)	Newspapers (3)*** Papers #	Circ. (M)	Avg. Open Line Rate ($)
Los Angeles	3.047	26	22	2	781	5	76	1	47	.67
New York	2.278	13	16	2	530	3	97	1	95	1.50
Miami	773	26	5	1	515	4	82	1	62	1.20
Chicago	695	9	5	1	241	3	43	-	-	-
San Antonio	694	46	5	1	268	4	61	-	-	-
Top 5	7.487	19	53	7	2.335	19	359	3	204	3.37
San Francisco	671	13	5	1	311	5	40	-	-	-
Houston	531	16	4	-	-	3	69	-	-	-
El Paso	379	61	3	1	100	5	34	3	64	.98
Albuquerque	350	36	2	-	-	1	48	-	-	-
Fresno	321	30	2	1	148	2	17	-	-	-
Top 10	9.739	19	69	10	2.894	35	567	6	268	4.35
San Diego	296	17	2	1	200	3	32	-	-	-
Dallas	288	8	2	-	-	2	45	-	-	-
Phoenix	287	14	2	1	160	2	42	-	-	-
Sacramento-Stockton	272	12	2	1	128	2	19	-	-	-
Corpus Christi	257	53	2	1	101	3	22	-	-	-
Top 15	11.139	18	79	14	3.483	47	727	6	268	4.35
Total U.S.	14.128	7	100							

* Cost reflects average prime-time 30" spot M-S 8:00-11:00pm
** Cost reflects early/late drivetime 60's 12 x rate
*** Daily papers only

Source: 1) Spanish International Network; 2) SRDS. July 1982: 3) SRDS. July 1982

BLACK & SPANISH POPULATION CHARACTERISTICS

	U.S. Pop. %	Black %	Spanish %	Spanish Mexican %	Cuban %	Puerto Rican %	Other %
Age							
18-24	17.5	22.2	24.2	26.6	15.6	23.7	20.1
25-34	23.4	25.2	28.1	30.2	15.8	31.5	22.3
35-44	17.1	16.2	18.9	17.4	24.0	19.3	19.6
45-54	13.1	13.2	13.4	12.5	20.0	12.7	14.9
55+	28.9	23.2	15.3	13.5	24.7	12.9	23.2
Education							
Less than H.S. Grad.	30.0	22.3	28.4	60.9	NA	62.2	40.7*
H.S. Grad.	38.4	51.3	45.3	25.1	NA	25.2	30.4*
Any College	16.9	20.0	18.4	10.2	NA	8.6	16.5*
College Grad.	14.7	6.4	7.9	3.8	NA	4.0	12.4*
HH Income**							
Under $10,000	17.2	40.4	31.7	29.2	23.3	50.5	28.1
$10,000-$14,999	11.1	16.8	19.8	20.1	18.7	17.8	20.7
$15.000-$24,999	26.5	23.0	27.9	31.1	28.1	18.4	25.5
$25,000 & Over	45.2	19.8	20.7	19.6	29.8	13.3	25.8
Type of Residence							
Metro Areas	66.8	77.3	83.5	79.3	96.7	94.5	82.2
Central Cities	26.5	56.0	48.2	43.4	39.5	74.7	46.0
Suburbs	40.3	21.3	35.2	35.8	57.2	19.8	36.2
Non-Metro Areas	33.2	22.7	16.5	20.7	3.3	5.5	17.8

*Includes Cubans.
**1979 Household Income.

Source: U.S. Dept. of Commerce, Bureau of Census; Population Characteristics; Series P-20, No. 361 and 363; May and June 1981 for Black and Spanish Population. Total U.S. Population—Series P-25, No. 917

MARKET DATA BY TV AREA
TV DMA AREA GROUPING

	TV Homes (MM)	% U.S.	Effec. Buying Income $(MMM)	% U.S.	Retail Sales $(MMM)	% U.S.	Food Store Sales $(MMM)	% U.S.	Automotive Sales $(MMM)	% U.S.	Drug Store Sales $(MMM)	% U.S.
Top 5	18.5	22	476.2	24	214.1	20	50.8	21	35.6	20	7.6	22
Top 10	26.1	31	703.7	35	331.3	31	75.5	31	54.4	30	11.6	34
Top 15	32.0	38	846.8	42	405.4	38	92.5	38	62.6	34	13.9	41
Top 25	41.0	49	1.084.6	54	529.8	50	1231.4	50	84.9	46	17.6	52
Top 50	55.5	66	1.412.8	70	705.6	67	161.8	67	121.4	66	23.3	68
Top 75	65.3	78	1.646.4	82	828.4	78	191.1	79	142.3	78	27.3	80
Top 100	71.8	86	1.783.7	89	905.4	86	208.7	86	155.7	85	29.6	87
Top 150	80.2	96	1.966.9	98	1.010.4	96	233.1	96	174.3	95	32.9	97
Total U.S.	83.7	100	2.012.1	100	1.056.1	100	242.8	100	182.8	100	34.1	100

Source: Sales Management 1982 Survey of Buying Power; A.C. Nielsen—U.S. Television Household Estimates. Sept. 1982

665

USAGE PATTERNS—SELECTED DEMOGRAPHICS
AVERAGE MINUTE AUDIENCE LEVELS; DAY AND WEEK REACH MAXIMUMS

Television Daypart	Television Households			Total Women			Women 25-54			Women 55+		
	Avg. Aud. %	Reach Day %	Week %	Avg. Aud. %	Reach Day %	Week %	Avg. Aud. %	Reach Day %	Week %	Avg. Aud. %	Reach Day %	Week %
Daytime (M-F 10:00am-4:30pm)	29	59	76	22	48	65	20	45	64	28	56	70
Early Fringe (M-F 4:30-6:00pm)	44	56	76	28	38	60	25	34	58	35	47	66
Early Evening News (M-F 6:00-7:00pm)	58	64	84	42	48	71	37	44	70	57	62	79
Prime Time Access (M-F 7:30-8:00pm)	64	64	86	49	50	76	45	46	75	63	63	83
Prime Time (Sun-Sat 8:00-11:00pm)	64	79	94	51	68	89	51	69	92	57	73	89
Late News (M-F 11:00-11:30pm)	48	51	53	36	38	63	37	39	67	38	41	60
Late Fringe (M-F 11:30pm-1:00am)	28	40	61	19	29	48	19	30	51	18	28	44
Saturday Morning (8:00am-1:00pm)	25	49	49	11	27	27	10	26	26	9	26	26

Television Daypart	Total Men			Men 25-54			Men 55+			Teens			Children 2-11		
	Avg. Aud. %	Reach Day %	Week %	Avg. Aud. %	Reach Day %	Week %	Avg. Aud. %	Reach Day %	Week %	Avg. Aud. %	Reach Day %	Week %	Avg. Aud. %	Reach Day %	Week %
Daytime (M-F 10:00am-4:30pm)	9	-	-	6	-	-	16	-	-	5	-	-	10	-	-
Early Fringe (M-F 4:30-6:00pm)	20	29	49	16	24	44	30	42	60	27	38	65	43	56	81
Early Evening News (M-F 6:00-7:00pm)	36	42	65	32	37	64	53	59	76	27	32	59	37	45	71
Prime Time Access (M-F 7:30-8:00pm)	43	44	71	40	42	71	59	59	79	32	33	62	47	49	77
Prime Time (Sun-Sat 8:00-11:00pm)	46	63	86	46	64	89	54	71	88	35	54	84	34	59	87
Late News (M-F 11:00-11:30pm)	34	35	59	34	37	62	37	39	61	14	17	42	4	5	14
Late Fringe (M-F 11:30pm-1:00am)	19	29	49	20	30	50	17	28	46	9	14	34	2	3	8
Saturday Morning (8:00am-1:00pm)	10	27	27	10	26	26	10	25	25	17	41	41	44	72	72

Source: NTI People Using Television, Feb. 1982

TELEVISION REACH AND GRP FOR EXTENDED SCHEDULES
TV DAYPART

	Weekly HH GRP Level	4 Weeks			8 Weeks			13 Weeks			19 Weeks			26 Weeks		
		GRP	Reach	Freq.	GRP	Reach	Freq.	GRP	Reach	Freq.	GRP	Reach	Freq.	GRP	Reach	Freq.
Day Network	10	40	23	1.7	80	36	2.2	130	47	2.8	190	56	3.4	260	61	14.3
	15	60	29	2.1	120	42	2.9	195	52	3.8	285	60	4.8	390	65	6.0
	25	100	42	2.4	200	54	3.7	325	63	5.2	475	70	6.8	650	74	8.8
	50	200	54	3.7	400	65	6.2	650	73	8.9	950	79	12.0	1,300	82	15.9
	75	300	62	4.8	600	72	8.3	975	78	12.5	1,425	83	17.2	1,950	86	22.7
Prime Network	10	40	30	1.3	80	46	1.7	130	57	2.3	190	66	2.9	260	71	3.7
	15	60	38	1.6	120	54	2.2	195	65	3.0	285	72	4.0	390	77	5.1
	25	100	59	1.7	200	77	2.6	325	86	3.8	475	91	5.2	650	94	6.9
	50	200	76	2.6	400	90	4.4	650	97	6.7	950	98	9.7	1,300	98	13.3
	75	300	81	3.7	600	93	6.5	975	98	9.9	1,425	98	4.3	1,950	98	19.9
Early Evening Network News	10	40	28	1.4	80	42	1.9	130	53	2.5	190	61	3.1	260	66	3.9
	15	60	32	1.9	120	45	2.7	195	56	3.5	285	64	4.5	390	69	5.7
	25	100	50	2.0	200	64	3.1	325	73	4.5	475	79	6.0	650	82	7.9
	50	200	63	3.2	400	75	5.3	650	82	7.9	950	87	10.9	1,300	90	14.4
	75	300	69	4.3	600	79	7.6	975	83	11.7	1,425	89	16.0	1,950	91	21.4
Late Night Network	10	40	25	1.6	80	37	2.2	130	48	2.7	190	57	3.3	260	63	4.1
	15	60	30	2.0	120	42	2.9	195	52	3.8	285	61	4.7	390	66	5.9
	25	100	43	2.3	200	54	3.7	325	64	5.1	475	72	6.6	650	76	8.6
	50	200	54	3.7	400	65	6.2	650	74	8.8	950	79	12.0	1,300	83	15.7
	75	300	57	5.3	600	69	8.7	975	76	12.8	1,425	81	17.6	1,950	84	23.2
Early/Late Fringe spot	10	40	26	1.5	80	38	2.1	130	49	2.7	190	58	3.3	260	63	4.1
	15	60	34	1.8	120	46	2.6	195	56	3.5	285	65	4.4	390	69	5.7
	25	100	46	2.2	200	57	3.5	325	67	4.9	475	74	6.4	650	78	8.3
	50	200	66	3.0	400	77	5.2	650	85	7.6	950	90	10.6	1,300	92	14.1
	75	300	74	4.1	600	85	7.1	975	92	10.6	1,425	95	15.0	1,950	96	20.3

Source: Grey Estimates

FOUR-WEEK REACH AND FREQUENCY ESTIMATES—RADIO

4-WEEK GRP	ADULTS REACHED BY NUMBER OF NETWORKS						
	1 NETWORK %	2 NETWORKS %	3 NETWORKS %	4 NETWORKS %	5 NETWORKS %	6 NETWORKS %	7 NETWORKS %
20	8	12					
40	12	15					
60	13	19	20	22			
80	14	23	22	25	27	35	35
90	14	23	25	28	30	35	40
100	15	23	30	31	34	35	40
150	17	26	32	37	41	43	44
200	18	28	34	40	47	50	52
250	19	29	36	43	47	54	56
300	20	31	39	45	50	54	59
350		31	41	45	50	57	59
400		33	43	48	53	57	62
450		33	43	50	53	60	62
500		34	43	50	56	60	62
600		36	45	53	58	62	65
700			47	53	61	65	68
800			47	55	61	65	70

Source: RADAR, Grey Estimates

FOUR-WEEK REACH AND FREQUENCY ESTIMATES
MAGAZINES

Number of Publications	Men 18+*			Men 25-54*			Women 18+**			Women 25-54**		
	GRP	Reach	Freq	GRP	Reach	Freq	GRP	Reach	Freq	GRP	Reach	Freq
2	39	33	1.2	45	37	1.2	62	46	1.3	70	51	1.4
3	55	38	1.4	63	43	1.5	94	54	1.7	99	53	1.9
4	71	43	1.7	80	48	1.7	122	56	2.2	135	61	2.2
5	86	49	1.8	98	54	1.8	146	60	2.4	160	64	2.5
6	99	52	1.9	113	56	2.0	169	62	2.7	184	67	2.7
7	111	53	2.1	127	59	2.2	188	66	2.8	205	70	2.9
8	119	54	2.2	137	59	2.3	205	67	3.1	225	72	3.1
9	127	54	2.4	148	61	2.4	221	70	3.2	241	75	3.2
10	137	55	2.5	157	61	2.6	234	71	3.3	255	76	3.4
11	145	56	2.6	167	62	2.7	244	72	3.4	265	77	3.6
12	154	57	2.7	176	62	2.8	252	73	3.5	275	77	3.7
13	162	58	2.8	186	63	3.0	259	74	3.5	287	77	3.9
14	168	58	2.9	193	64	3.0	268	74	3.6	295	78	3.8
15	174	59	2.9	202	64	3.2	275	74	3.7	301	79	3.8
16	179	59	3.0	207	65	3.2	282	75	3.8	309	79	3.8

* Men/News Publications Only
** Women/Women's Service Publications Only
Source: ABC, MRI

NEWSPAPERS—DMA GRP, REACH AND FREQUENCY
ADULT—NUMBER OF INSERTIONS

SMSA Gross Circulation Coverage	GRP	1 Reach	Freq.	GRP	2 Reach	Freq.	GRP	4 Reach	Freq.	GRP	6 Reach	Freq.	GRP	8 Reach	Freq.	GRP	10 Reach	Freq.
30	26	26	1.0	52	33	1.6	104	40	2.6	156	43	3.6	208	45	4.6	260	47	5.5
35	30	30	1.0	60	37	1.6	120	44	2.7	180	47	3.8	240	49	4.9	300	50	6.0
40	34	33	1.0	68	41	1.7	136	48	2.8	204	51	4.0	272	52	5.2	340	54	6.3
45	38	37	1.0	76	44	1.7	152	51	3.0	228	55	4.1	304	56	5.4	380	57	6.7
50	41	40	1.0	82	47	1.7	164	54	3.0	246	59	4.2	328	60	5.5	410	61	6.7
55	44	43	1.0	88	51	1.7	176	58	3.0	264	62	4.3	352	64	5.5	440	65	6.8
60	50	46	1.1	100	55	1.8	200	62	3.2	300	65	4.6	400	66	6.1	500	66	7.6
65	55	50	1.1	110	59	1.9	220	66	3.3	330	69	4.8	440	70	6.3	550	71	7.7
70	60	53	1.1	120	62	1.9	240	70	3.4	360	73	4.9	480	74	6.5	600	75	8.0

Source: Audit Bureau of Circulations, Grey Estimates

OUTDOOR REACH AND FREQUENCY BY SELECTED DEMOGRAPHICS

	#25 Showing GRP	Reach	Freq.	#50 Showing GRP	Reach	Freq.	#75 Showing GRP	Reach	Freq.	#100 Showing GRP	Reach	Freq.
Adults	518	73	7.1	1,029	81	12.7	1,556	85	18.3	2,071	87	23.8
Men	576	72	8.0	1,168	80	14.6	1,735	83	20.9	2,321	85	27.3
Women	466	74	6.3	921	83	11.1	1,401	87	16.1	1,851	89	20.8
Adults by Age												
18-24	632	78	8.1	1,256	86	14.6	1,887	89	21.2	2,475	91	27.2
25-34	656	80	8.2	1,305	87	15.0	1,962	90	21.8	2,603	91	28.6
35-44	525	74	7.1	1,045	81	12.9	1,562	84	18.6	2,073	86	24.1
45-54	449	68	6.6	889	76	11.7	1,337	81	16.5	1,785	83	21.5
55-64	374	68	5.5	755	77	9.8	1,118	81	13.8	1,494	83	18.0
65+	376	66	5.7	737	76	9.7	1,112	80	13.9	1,468	82	17.9
Adults by Household Income												
$25,000+	592	76	7.8	1,179	83	14.2	1,640	86	20.5	2,358	88	26.8
$20,000-$24,999	462	71	6.5	916	79	11.6	1,378	83	16.6	1,828	85	21.5
$15,000-$19,999	524	76	6.9	1,050	84	12.5	1,557	87	17.9	2,074	89	23.3
$10,000-$14,999	533	74	7.2	1,053	81	13.0	1,581	85	18.6	1,944	87	24.3
$ 5,000-$ 9,999	429	66	6.5	844	76	11.1	1,272	80	15.9	1,693	83	20.4
Under $5,000	340	68	5.0	679	78	8.7	1,025	82	12.5	1,360	85	16.0

Source: Institute for Outdoor Advertising, Grey Estimates

ENDNOTE

[1] *1983 Media Modules,* Grey Advertising Inc. I am indebted to Grey Advertising Inc. for permission to use this material.

Glossary

Account executive (or account manager). Advertising agency person who provides liaison between agency and advertiser (client or account) and supervises agency personnel working on the account.

Advertising. Any paid form of nonpersonal presentation and promotion of ideas, goods, or services by an identified sponsor.

Advertising agency. Organization that assists advertisers in promotional planning and strategy and is generally responsible for creating advertisements and planning and buying advertising media time and space.

Advertising Council, The. Nonprofit organization supported by the major advertising associations, agencies, advertisers, and media and through which public service advertising campaigns are planned, created, and run.

Advertising Research Foundation (ARF). Organization of advertisers, agencies, and media that conducts research of industrywide importance, establishes standards and improves methods of research, and helps members to obtain accurate and trustworthy information.

Advertising specialties. Useful items imprinted with the name of the advertiser and given free to prospects with no obligation. Items include inexpensive *specialties, calendars,* and more expensive *executive gifts.*

Advocacy advertising. Corporate or other organization advertising to present views on a controversial issue. Compare *public service advertising.*

Agate line. Unit of measurement of advertising space, one-fourteenth-inch deep by the column width.

Agency networks. A number of noncompetitive advertising agencies located in different parts of the country. They provide members with an interchange of services, information, and resources.

Agency of record. The advertising agency appointed by an advertiser using several agencies to coordinate the total time and space buying for all products so as to effect the greatest quantity discounts.

Agricultural Publishers Association (APA). Organization of farm publications.

Aided recall. Copy testing technique in which respondents are aided by having the advertisement shown to them.

American Academy of Advertising (AAA). Organization of teachers and practitioners interested in the advancement of advertising education.

American Advertising Federation (AAF). National association of local advertising clubs, agencies, media, and related organizations.

American Association of Advertising Agencies (AAAA or 4As). Organization of leading U.S. advertising agencies.

American Business Press (ABP). Organization of trade, industrial, and professional publications.

American Marketing Association (AMA). Organization of teachers and practitioners of marketing to advance the science of marketing.

Animatics. Techniques for filming stills of television commercial scenes with sound to more nearly approximate the finished commercial effect.

Animation. In television, a "cartoon" technique using drawings instead of real people or animals and filming changing drawings, one frame per drawing, so as to achieve the effect of movement.

Answer print. Film of television commercial combining audio, video, and opticals.

Arbitron. A firm that collects information on local television and radio audiences, primarily by means of diaries in which families log viewing habits.

Area of dominant influence (ADI). Concept developed by Arbitron to define television and radio markets by grouping all counties in which the home market stations receive a preponderance of viewing or listening. Also used by media planners for other media.

Association of National Advertisers (ANA). Organization of leading advertisers in the United States.

Audience. In advertising, the total number of people reached by an advertisement or a medium.

Audio. In television, the sound portion of the transmission. Compare *video*.

Audit Bureau of Circulations (ABC). Organization sponsored by publishers, agencies, and advertisers to verify circulation claims of newspapers, magazines, and business publications.

Availability. In broadcasting, time periods available to advertisers for commercials.

Back-to-back. In broadcast advertising, two commercials presented one following the other.

Balance. In advertising layout, artistically combining the various sizes and shapes that make up an advertisement. Takes two basic forms—*formal* and *informal*.

Benday. Photoengraving process in which continual tonal values are added to specific areas of line drawings to give body to the art.

Better Business Bureau (BBB). Local business-sponsored organizations that police advertising and other business practices.

Bipolar scale. The basic scale used in attitude research. Respondents are asked to choose between two extremes on the scale. See *semantic differential*.

Bleed. Printed matter that runs beyond the trim mark of a page or the margin of an outdoor board, thereby leaving no margin.

Body copy (or text). Main blocks of type in an advertisement. Compare *display type* or *headlines*.

Boldface (b.f.). In typography, a heavier version of a typeface.

Boutique. In advertising, a form of limited advertising service organization that provides creative services to advertisers.

Brand. A name, term, symbol, or design, or some combination that identifies the goods or services of a firm.

Brand name. The oral form of branding. Compare *trademark*.

Business Publications Audit of Circulation (BPA). Organization sponsored by publishers, agencies, and advertisers to verify circulation claims of business publications with both *paid* and *qualified* (free) circulations.

Cable television. A system that picks up programming of television stations and delivers the programming to subscribers' receivers by coaxial cable, thus providing better-quality reception.

Campaign. In advertising, a series of advertisements and/or commercials that are variations on a single theme or build in stages toward a specific planned end.

Cash discount. In media buying, a discount given by many media for payment within a specific time period.

Circulation. The number of copies of a newspaper or a periodical delivered, the number of homes tuned to a broadcast station, the number of cars passing outdoor posters, or the number of riders carried in transit company vehicles.

City zone. Newspaper circulation within the city limits. Compare *trading zone*.

Classified advertising. Advertisements in newspapers and magazines presented according to subject and usually limited in terms of type size and illustration.

Client. In advertising, the advertiser or account served by the advertising agency.

Closing date. The deadline date for submitting an advertisment or commercial to a medium.

Collateral. In advertising, work done by advertising agencies for clients for which there is no media commission paid.

Column inch. Unit of measurement of advertising space, one inch deep by the column width.

Combination offer. In sales promotion, combining two or more products in one selling unit at a price below that of the individual items if purchased separately. Used to introduce new products or increase acceptance of slow-moving products.

Commercial. In advertising, the term used to describe advertisements for radio and television.

Commission. In media, money paid by a medium to an advertising agency for time or space bought for a client. Usually 15 percent of the charge. A major source of agency compensation.

Comparative advertising. Advertisements that make direct reference to the competition.

Composition. In typography, setting type characters into words, as in advertisement headlines and body copy. May be done in metal by hand or by machine, or on sensitized paper or film by photography or electronically.

Comprehensive. In advertising, a layout of an advertisement executed very tightly so as to come as close as possible to the finished advertisement.

Contest. In sales promotion, a competition for prizes awarded on the basis of skill in the performance of a stated service. Compare *sweepstakes*.

Cooperative advertising. (1) *Dealer* or *vertical* cooperative advertising involves sharing of advertising expense between manufacturer and distributor for the advertising of the manufacturer's product in the retailer's advertisement (2) *Association* or *horizontal* cooperative advertising is that done by manufacturers or retailers in an industry to stimulate primary demand for the generic product.

Copy. (1) Any or all of the elements (headlines, text, artwork) that are part of an advertisement. (2) The body copy or text.

Copy testing. Pretesting or posttesting the communications effect of advertising.

Copywriter. Person responsible for the words of an advertisement and, as part of the creative team with the art director, for the visualization of the advertisement idea.

Corporate advertising. Designed to sell ideas instead of goods or services. May be used for patronage, public relations, or public service. Used extensively by noncommercial as well as commercial advertisers, and then referred to as *institutional advertising*.

Corrective advertising. Punitive action taken by the Federal Trade Commission to correct deceptive advertising. The advertiser must state the correction as part of the new advertising for a specified period of time.

Cost per thousand (CPM). Formula for determining cost of reaching 1,000 circulation or audience in a particular medium. May also be used as CPM prospects.

Coverage. (1) Geographic area in which a broadcasting station's signal can be heard by people who want to listen. (2) Circulation of a newspaper divided by the number of households in the metropolitan area. (3) Percentage of a demographic market reached by a magazine. (4) Percentage of adults exposed to a fixed number of outdoor posters in a 30-day period.

Creativity. In advertising, the activity directly concerned with developing ideas and producing advertisements and commercials: copywriting, art direction, and production.

Cumulative audience (cume). In broadcasting, the reach or unduplicated audience.

Cut. (1) A printing term for an engraving. (2) A band on a recording. (3) To reduce copy length by deletion.

Dailies. The total footage of film during a day's shooting of a commercial. Also called *rushes.*

Dayparts. In broadcasting, various time segments of the day that carry different rates.

Demarketing. Efforts by firms whose products are in short supply to reduce consumption. Advertising is frequently used in demarketing.

Demographics. In marketing, the vital statistics (age, sex, education, occupation, etc.) that describe the characteristics of a market.

Depth interview. Technique of qualitative research using unstructured approach and permitting respondents to speak freely about the subject under investigation.

Designated Market Area (DMA). A.C. Nielsen Company designation of broadcast markets. See *area of dominant influence.*

Diary. Research technique in which respondents record purchase and use habits or broadcast viewing or listening habits.

Direct mail advertising. Printed or otherwise reproduced communications that are mailed or otherwise distributed to prospects, as compared to advertising through mass communications media.

Direct Mail/Marketing Association (DMMA). Organization of the direct mail and direct marketing industry.

Direct marketing. Marketing efforts to sell goods and services directly, such as mail-order selling. Direct marketers are major users of direct mail advertising, but they also make use of all other forms of advertising. Also referred to as *direct response marketing.*

Directory advertising. Advertising in listings of people, professions, institutions, or the like. Includes Yellow Pages telephone directories.

Direct premium. Premium given at the time of purchase at no additional charge.

Display advertisement. Advertisement that makes use of illustrations and/or large display-type headlines. Compare *classified advertising.*

Display type. Usually, type set in 18-point size or larger and used in advertisements for headlines and subheads.

Double-page spread. Advertisement occupying two facing pages. Called *center spread* when appearing in the center of a publication.

Drive time. Term used to designate radio advertising rates for time periods in which most car-radio listeners are going to and from work.

Editorial matter. The nonadvertising art of publications and broadcasts; articles or programs as distinguished from advertisements or commercials.

Em. In printing, a unit of linear measure of equal height and width specified by the height size of the type in points. A 12-point em is 12 points high and 12 points wide and is known as a *pica em.*

Engraving. In printing, an etched printing plate made by the photoengraving process. Also called a *cut.*

Envelope stuffer. Direct mail advertisement included with billing statements or other mailings.

Exhibit. Promotional technique involving a display, usually at industrial or professional conventions and trade shows.

Eye-movement camera. In evaluating the communications effect of advertising a device that measures the movement of the eye as it goes through an advertisement and the time spent at each point.

Fact sheet. Statement of major selling points supplied to radio personalities, permitting them to deliver the commercials in their own words and style.

Federal Communications Commission (FCC). Agency of the federal government that licenses broadcasting stations and regulates them "in the public interest."

Federal Trade Commission (FTC). Agency of the federal government that regulates interstate commerce; the major government agency that regulates advertising.

Field intensity. In broadcasting, station coverage measurement of signal strength at various distances, used to draw station coverage maps.

Finished layout. A layout worked in sufficient detail to suggest the style of the illustrations and headline type. Used as a guide for artists and typographers, it is generally the layout submitted to the client for approval.

Flat rate. Advertising rate that does not allow for frequency of volume discounts.

Flights. Advertising schedule concentrated in short time periods broken by time periods without advertising. Also called *waves*. Compare *pulsing*.

Focus group interview. Qualitative research technique that uses depth interviewing with a group rather than individual respondents.

Font. Assortment of particular typeface and size, including letters, numerals, punctuation, etc.

Food and Drug Administration (FDA). Agency of the federal government that enforces provisions of the Food, Drug, and Cosmetic Act and other laws as they pertain to these products and their labeling.

Four-color process. In printing, the process that creates the full spectrum of color by printing with four plates using yellow, red, blue, and black.

Frequency. In media planning, the number of times the advertiser reaches the same person. Compare *reach*.

Frequency discount. In media, a rate reduction based on the number of advertisements used during a specified time period.

Full-service agency. An advertising agency offering the full range of advertising services to clients (compare *boutique, media buying services,* and the like). Full-service agencies may be used for only limited services by a client.

General advertising. National (nonlocal) advertising by manufacturers.

Generic name. Technical or common name used to describe a particular kind of product. Compare *brand name*.

Grade A coverage. In television, the station's primary coverage area.

Grade B coverage. In television, the station's secondary coverage area.

Gravure. A printing process in which ink is transferred to paper from depressions in the printing plate. Also called *intaglio*. Most popular form for advertising is *rotogravure*.

Gross rating point (GRP). In television, a GRP is equal to 1 percent of television homes in a market. Similar for radio. In outdoor, a GRP is equal to 1 percent of the population in a market. Sometimes used for other media.

Halftone. A photograph (or wash drawing) that is rephotographed through a screen so that the tones are broken up into a series of dots of varying size, which when printed appear to the eye as if there were lighter and darker areas.

Headlines. Lines of copy set in *display type* size in advertisements. They are used to gain attention and sometimes contain the theme of an advertising campaign. Compare *body copy*.

Heaviside layer. A layer of the ionosphere that can reflect radio waves.

Hi-Fi color. Preprinted color advertisements for newspapers printed on better-quality paper and shipped in rolls so that the newspaper can print other material in black and white on the back side. Advertisements must be so designed that there is neither top nor bottom in order to permit a continuous-feed roll to be cut at any point when being collated with the rest of the newspaper.

Horizontal publications. Business periodicals reaching people at some functional level of business and cutting across industry lines. Compare *vertical publications.*

Households using television (HUT). Percentage of homes whose television sets are turned on.

I.D. (1) In broadcasting, the break-away time used for identifying the local station. (2) The eight-second commercial presented during station identification time.

Idea service. Advertising service company that supplies proofs of complete retail advertisements and components from which advertisers can prepare advertisements, especially for newspapers. These companies used to be called *mat services.*

Industrial advertising. Business advertising directed at industrial producers. Compare *trade advertising* and *professional advertising.*

In-house agency. Advertiser department or subsidiary that either functions in all advertising service areas or carries on only limited services and buys other services from outside sources.

Inquiry test. A method of testing the communications effect of advertisements by counting the number of inquiries received as a result of an offer made in the advertisement.

Institute of Outdoor Advertising (IOA). The marketing arm of the Outdoor Advertising Association of America.

Institutional advertising. See *corporate advertising.*

Intaglio. See *gravure.*

Jingle. In broadcasting, a singing commercial; either a part of or the whole commercial set to music.

Justified type. Type set so that all lines are equal in length.

Lanham Act. The federal law that governs the registration of trademarks; enacted in 1946.

Layout. The format in which the various elements of the advertisement are combined. The physical visualization of a creative idea.

Leading. (Rhymes with *heading*) In typography, spacing between lines of type to improve legibility and aesthetics.

Letterpress. A printing process in which ink is transferred to paper from raised portions of the printing plate. Also called *relief* printing.

Lightface. In typography, a lighter version of a particular typeface.

Linage. Total number of agate lines, as in an advertisement or space contracted for a campaign, etc.

Line. Used to refer to agate lines or a line of type.

Line drawing. A pen-and-ink drawing that when printed gives no gradations of tone.

Line plate. Plate for reproduction that contains art and typography, having no tonal values. In contrast to *halftones,* no screen is used.

Linotype. Machine for casting type from molten metal in one-piece lines called *slugs.*

List broker. In direct mail, an agent who arranges to rent mailing lists of names to advertisers.

Lithography. A printing process in which ink is transferred to paper from a flat-surfaced printing plate through chemical treatment that allows rollers to deposit ink only where printing is to appear. Also known as *planographic* printing. Most popular is *offset* lithography, in which ink is transferred from plate to *rubber blanket* and then to paper.

Local advertising. Advertising placed by a retailer, in contrast to general or national advertising by a manufacturer.

Logotype (logo). The *signature* or standard design for identifying the name or brand of the advertiser.

Lower case (lc). In typography, the small letters of the alphabet as compared to the capitals (*caps*).

Magazine Publishers Association (MPA). Organization of consumer magazine publishers. The *Marketing Division* operates as its advertising promotional arm.

Market. Group of people who have certain common characteristics identifiable geographically, demographically, or psychographically.

Marketing. All those activities that occur from the point of production to the point of consumption.

Marketing concept. Philosophy that looks to the consumer for the direction of the firm.

Marketing mix. The proper combination of the various marketing elements, such as brand, price, channels of distribution, packaging, and promotion.

Marketing plan. A written document, prepared annually, that contains the basic objectives and strategies for a brand for the coming year.

Market segmentation. Division of all people into individual market units whose characteristics are similar.

Market share. Percentage of total sales of a generic product held by any one firm.

Mechanical. A working layout or "blueprint" for production indicating the exact position of the various elements and appropriate instructions for typographers, engravers, and printers. In offset lithography, it is the copy from which the plate is made and is called a *keyline* or *pasteup*.

Media buying services. Independent firms that specialize in planning and buying media for advertisers and that claim to be more economical than advertising agencies.

Media representative (media rep). Person or firm acting as a sales agent for a number of noncompetitive media selling advertising time or space.

Medium (plural is media). A vehicle for carrying the advertising message, such as newspapers, television, outdoor, direct mail, etc.

Merchandising. (1) See *sales promotion*. (2) Promotion of an advertiser's consumer campaign to the trade—*merchandising the advertising*.

Milline rate. Unit for measuring the cost of newspaper advertising for comparison purposes. Less frequently used today in favor of *cost per thousand,* which permits comparisons with other types of media.

Motivation research (MR). Qualitative research technique that makes use of various projective methods borrowed from psychology in order to better explain consumer behavior.

National advertising. See *general advertising*.

National Advertising Review Board (NARB). Industry-sponsored organization that, through self-regulation, controls national advertising by reviewing complaints and persuading users of questionable advertising to refrain from continuing such practices.

National Association of Broadcasters (NAB). Organization of individual radio and television stations and networks.

National brand. A manufacturer's brand as compared to a *private label* of a retailer or wholesaler.

Near-pack premium. A premium separate from the merchandise, with premium near the product and frequently accompanied by a point-of-purchase display.

Network. In broadcasting, a series of connected stations transmitting the same programming.

Newspaper Advertising Bureau. Organization of publishers of daily newspapers to promote the medium to advertisers.

Nielsen (A.C.) Company. Firm engaged in syndicated research in broadcast ratings and store inventory movement.

Offset. See *lithography*.

On-pack premium. Premium attached to the package of the product. Also called *banded premium*.

Open rate. Basic advertising rate from which discounts are offered for volume and/or frequency.

Opticals. Special visual effects added to film for commercials when making the *answer print.*

Outdoor. Advertising signs of standardized nature, called *poster panels* and *painted bulletins.*

Outdoor Advertising Association of America (OAAA). Organization of outdoor advertising plant owners.

Out-of-home media. Nondelivered media, as outdoor posters and transit car cards, which are placed in nonhome locations.

Painted bulletin. Outdoor advertisement painted on a panel instead of on a poster. Also called *painted display.*

Participation. In broadcasting, a commercial scheduled to be played during a program. Compare *spot announcement.*

Photoengraving. See *engraving.*

Photoscript. Stills taken from frames of a television commercial film and arranged on a page with the audio printed beneath it to approximate a finished version of the storyboard. Used for publicity, merchandising the advertising, and easy reference to the film content.

Phototypography. The major typesetting method used in advertising today, it uses no metal but reproduces type photographically and electronically.

Pica. Most frequently used printer's measure of width. One pica is equal to 12 points and to one-sixth of an inch.

Planography. See *lithography.*

Plans board. In an advertising agency, a group of executives who review the advertising strategy before presenting it to the client.

Plant. The individual outdoor advertising company in a specific geographic area.

Plate. The various printing surfaces used in the different printing processes.

Point (pt.). Printer's basic unit of measure of the height of type. One point is equal to $1/72$ inch. Most popular body copy type sizes are 6, 8, 10, 12, and 14 points. Display type sizes usually start with 18 point.

Point-of-purchase advertising (P-O-P). A manufacturer's advertising display material that is placed in a retail store.

Point-of-Purchase Advertising Institute (POPAI). Organization of the P-O-P industry.

Position. In media, the location of the advertisement.

Positioning. Developing and marketing a product to appeal to the values of a specific market segment.

Poster. An outdoor advertising sign that is printed on paper and mounted on a standardized panel.

Preemption. In broadcast advertising, a station's right to run a commercial other than the one scheduled. Can be avoided by payment of higher rates for nonpreemptible commercials.

Preferred position. Premium rated location of an advertisement.

Premium. An article of merchandise offered as an incentive to buy or examine other goods or services.

Price packs. Manufacturer-initiated price reduction specified on the package.

Primary coverage. In radio, the area of the station's signal where reception is good virtually all the time. Compare *secondary coverage.*

Primary demand. Demand facing the industry; demand for the generic product as compared with demand for a specific brand.

Prime time. In broadcasting, the daypart with the heaviest viewing or listening and hence the highest advertising rates.

Private label. Goods that bear the brand of the retailer or wholesaler, as compared with national brands. Also called *private brand*.

Production. In advertising, all those activities involved in taking a layout or storyboard and developing it into the finished advertisement or commercial.

Product manager. In consumer packaged goods and other producer organizations, the person responsible for the profitability of a product or product line, including decisions regarding advertising strategy. Also called *brand manager*.

Professional advertising. Business advertising directed at professionals, such as doctors, lawyers, accountants, professors, etc. Compare *industrial advertising* and *trade advertising*.

Progressive proofs (progs). A series of proofs in the four-color process showing a proof for each color plate separately and combined.

Projective techniques. In research, a variety of methods of motivation research in which the respondents project their own behavior into situations involving others.

Promotion. The broad term that encompasses all selling activities—advertising, personal selling, public relations, and sales promotion. The way these elements are combined by a firm is referred to as the *promotional mix*.

Psychogalvanometer. Instrument psychologists use to measure people's emotions and reactions to psychological stimuli. In advertising, the *electropsychograph* is a supersensitive version that measures sweat-gland activity.

Psychographics. Behavioral research technique providing a statistical analysis of the market in terms of activities, interests, and opinions; a quantitative measure of lifestyle.

Publicity. Information about a company and its products prepared at the firm's instigation and distributed to media for their dissemination; an activity of public relations.

Public relations. Activities designed to favorably direct the opinions of others toward the disseminator. Frequently makes use of advertising to communicate.

Public service advertising. A kind of institutional advertising used to promote noncontroversial causes in the interest of the public.

Puffery. Exaggeration made by advertisers that is held to be reasonable, hence legal.

Pulsing. A scheduling technique that uses continuous advertising but alternates periods of high intensity with periods of low intensity. Compare *flights*.

Pupilometer. An instrument that is used to elevate the communications effect of advertising by measuring the dilation of the pupil of the eye.

Qualified circulation. Term used to describe the practice of many business publications that distribute some or all of their copies free of charge to qualified readers. Previously called *controlled circulation*.

Qualitative research. Techniques involving small samples in an attempt to get impressionistic rather than definitive data. Frequently exploratory or diagnostic in nature.

Radio Advertising Bureau (RAB). Organization that serves as the sales development arm of the medium.

Rate card. Folder published by media for advertisers giving rates, circulation data, mechanical requirements, etc. Separate rate cards are usually available for national or general and local or retail rates.

Rating. In broadcasting, the percentage of homes in a sample tuned to a specific station at a specific time period.

Reach. In media planning, the total number of people actually covered by an advertiser. Compare *frequency*.

Readership. Estimated number of people who read a particular publication. See *circulation*.

Rebate. Payment by the medium to the advertiser whose volume or frequency of advertising earns a lower rate than the one contracted.

Recall test. A method of evaluating the communications effect of advertising by evaluating what a consumer remembers after being exposed to the advertisement. See *aided recall.*

Recognition test. A method of evaluating the communications effect of advertising by reviewing advertisements in periodicals and having the respondents note advertisements previously seen and read.

Relief printing. See *letterpress.*

Retail advertising. Advertising by retailers. Usually local advertising, but may also be national in scope. Compare *national advertising* or *general advertising.*

Roman type. Face distinguished by thick and thin strokes ending with serifs.

Rotogravure. See *gravure.*

Rough. A preliminary layout of an advertisement.

Rough cut. In television, the rough form of edited film of a commercial.

Run. Unit of sale for carcards in transit advertising.

Run-of-paper (ROP). Advertisement placed in a publication at the discretion of the publisher. Compare *preferred position.*

Rushes. See *dailies.*

Sales promotion. All special activities between manufacturers and dealers or consumers for the purpose of stimulating demand. Also sometimes used as synonymous with *promotion.*

Sampling. (1) In research, a representative portion of the universe. (2) In sales promotion, providing free trials of the product to induce purchase.

Sans serif. Typeface without serifs (end finishing marks); generally, all strokes are of the same thickness.

Schedule. In media planning, media listed by insertion dates and size.

Scratchboard. Art technique using stylus to scratch out white lines from a black-ink-coated drawing board.

Screen. Glass plate or film on which are drawn a series of lines at right angles to one another and through which copy is photographed in making halftone plates.

Script. In broadcasting, the typewritten audio together with instructions for action. In television, the script frequently precedes the storyboard.

Secondary coverage. In radio, the area of the station's signal where reception is good only most of the time. Compare *primary coverage.*

Selective demand. Demand facing the firm; demand for a specific brand as compared with demand for the generic product.

Self-liquidating premium. Premium whose cost to the firm is recouped through a charge to the consumer.

Semantic differential. In research, a method of measuring attitudes toward concepts using *bipolar scales* that usually have seven intervals.

Serifs. The end finishing marks appearing in roman typefaces.

Share of audience (share). In broadcasting, the percentage of homes with sets turned on reached by a station during a specific time period.

Short rate. The penalty or higher rate that an advertiser must pay a medium if the advertiser has not met the quantity requirements of the contract.

Showing. The basis on which transit advertising exterior displays are sold. Also used as the basis for selling outdoor posters, but now referred to as *gross rating points.*

Signature. See *logotype.*

Silk screen. A printing method in which a stenciled design is applied to a screen. The ink is squeezed through the mesh of the screen onto the surface below.

Simmons Market Research Bureau (SMRB). Firm engaged in syndicated research on product usage and demographics of media audiences.

Slice-of-life. In commercials, a dramatic technique involving an episode designed to simulate real-life experiences.

Spectacolor. Similar to *Hi-Fi color*, except that in spectacolor, the advertisement can be centered on the page.

Spectacular. Large permanent signs that make use of elaborate lighting and action effects.

Split run. In larger-circulation publications in which more than one set of presses is used, the running of two different advertisements in the alternate presses. This permits evaluating the communications effect of the advertisements, usually by inviting inquiries to determine which advertisement pulled better.

Spot announcement. Term for a commercial presented between programs or as participations during programs, as compared to those presented during programs sponsored by the advertiser. (This latter practice is little used today.)

Spot broadcasting. Placing commercials with individual stations instead of buying network time.

Standard Metropolitan Statistical Area (SMSA). Market areas surrounding large cities and bounded by county lines as established by the federal government.

Standard Rate & Data Service (SRDS). Firm that publishes catalogs of advertising media rates and other data.

Station break. In broadcasting, the time between programs for local station identification.

Stop motion. Photographic technique that makes inanimate objects appear animate.

Storyboard. A "layout" for television commercials consisting of a series of sketches of key scenes, together with typewritten audio and video instructions.

Supplements. Magazine-like sections of Sunday newspapers.

Sweepstakes. In sales promotion, a competition for prizes awarded on a chance drawing. Compare *contest*.

Syndication. In television, independent firms that sell to individual stations reruns of television shows or newly originated shows that are non-network-affiliated.

Tabloid. A small-format newspaper measuring approximately five columns wide by fourteen inches deep.

Tag. In broadcasting, a local retailer's add-on to a national advertiser's commercial. The tag usually identifies the retail source of supply.

Take-ones. Brochures or coupons attached to interior transit advertisements.

Target market. That segment of the market that the advertiser identifies as the people to whom the marketing and advertising efforts will be directed.

Tear sheet. Copy of an advertisement torn from a publication and sent to the advertiser for purposes of verification.

Test market. Evaluation of products or advertising in the field by marketing and advertising the product in a small area where the results of the marketing effort can be measured by means of various research techniques.

Thirty-sheet (30-sheet). The most popular size outdoor poster today. The 24-sheet poster used to be the most popular.

Three-sheet. A small, standardized poster usually placed on panels mounted on the sides of retail establishments.

Thumbnail sketch. A quickly executed rough layout done in miniature, used to examine alternative possibilities, one or more of which will then be reworked in the same size as the advertisement in *rough* or *finished* layout form.

Trade advertising. A kind of business advertising directed at the various types of middlemen. Compare *industrial advertising* and *professional advertising*.

Trade character. A person, animal, or animated object used to identify a brand and provide personality to the promotional effort.

Trademark. The pictorial form of branding, as distinguished from *brand name*. Also used as synonym with *brand* in a legal frame of reference.

Trade name. The name of a company, not the brand; however, it is possible for a trade name and a brand name to be the same.

Trading zone. Newspaper circulation outside the city limits but within the retail trading area. Compare *city zone*.

Traffic Audit Bureau (TAB). Organization that audits circulation (traffic) claims of outdoor plants.

Traffic count. The number of pedestrians and vehicles exposed to an outdoor panel in a specific time period.

Traffic department. In an advertising agency, the department responsible for keeping advertising jobs flowing through the various departments so as to meet schedules.

Transit advertising. Out-of-home medium using facilities of public transportation for interior and exterior advertising displays.

Transit Advertising Association (TAA). The trade association of the transit advertising industry.

Type family. A group of typefaces that are variations on one design, such as *light, regular, bold, italics, extended,* and *condensed*.

Vehicle. An individual advertising medium.

Verified Audit Circulation Company (VAC). A private firm that audits both paid and qualified circulation.

Vertical publications. Business periodicals reaching people at all the different levels within one industry. Compare *horizontal publications*.

Video. In television, the picture portion of the transmission. Compare *audio*.

Videotape. In television, an electromagnetic tape capable of recording pictures and sound. Increasingly used for producing commercials.

Visualization. Seeing in the mind's eye the form of an advertising idea as it will appear in an advertisement or commercial.

Voice-over. Audio portion of television commercial carrying an off-camera voice.

Wash drawing. An advertising art technique of painting with ink and water to achieve tonal values.

D

Bibliography

F ollowing is a list of suggested readings on advertising. In some cases, a book may cover areas other than the one under which it is listed. Additional references may be found in the endnotes throughout the book.

GENERAL

Aaker, David A., and John G. Myers, *Advertising Management,* 2nd ed., Englewood Cliffs, N.J.: Prentice-Hall, Inc., 1978.

DeLozier, M. Wayne, *The Marketing Communications Process.* New York: McGraw-Hill Book Company, 1976.

Evans, W. A., *Advertising Today and Tomorrow.* George Allen & Unwin, Ltd., 1974.

Groome, Harry C., Jr., *This Is Advertising.* Philadelphia: Ayer Press, 1975.

Patti, Charles H., and John H. Murphy, *Advertising Management.* New York: John Wiley & Sons, 1978.

Rogers, Edward J., *Getting Hired.* Englewood Cliffs, N.J.: Prentice-Hall, Inc., 1982.

Roman, Kenneth, and Jane Maas, *How to Advertise.* New York: St. Martin's Press, 1976.

Sargent, Hugh, ed., *Frontiers of Advertising Theory and Research.* Palo Alto, Calif.: Pacific Books, Publishers, 1972.

Seiden, Hank, *Advertising Pure and Simple.* New York: AMACOM Division of American Management Association, 1976.

HISTORY

Atwan, Robert, Donald McQuade, and John W. Wright, *Edsels, Luckies, and Frigidaires: Advertising the American Way.* New York: Dell Publishing Co., Inc., 1979.

Bartels, Robert, *The History of Marketing Thought.* Columbus, Ohio: Grid, Inc., 1976.

Darwin, Bernard, ed., *The Dickens Advertiser.* London: Elkin Matthews and Marrot, 1930.

Foster, G. Allen, *Advertising: Ancient Marketplace to Television.* New York: Criterion Books, 1967.

Gunther, John, *Taken at the Flood: The Story of Albert D. Lasker.* New York: Harper & Row, Publishers, 1960.

Holme, Brian, *Advertising: Reflections of a Century.* New York: Viking Press, 1982.

Hopkins, Claude C., *My Life in Advertising.* New York: Harper & Brothers Publishers, 1936.

Hotchkiss, George Burton, *Milestones of Marketing.* New York: The Macmillan Company, 1938.

Hower, Ralph M., *The History of an Advertising Agency*, rev. ed. Cambridge Mass.: Harvard University Press, 1949.

Jones, Edgar Robert, *Those Were the Good Old Days: A Happy Look at American Advertising, 1880–1930.* New York: Simon & Schuster, 1959.

Larwood, Jacob, and John Camden Hotten, *English Inn Signs.* London: Chatto & Windus, 1951.

Lewis, Lawrence, *The Advertisements of the Spectator.* Boston: Houghton Mifflin Company, 1909.

Nevett, T. R., *Advertising in Britain: A History.* North Pomfret, Vt.: David & Charles, Inc., 1982.

Pope, Daniel, *The Marketing of Modern Advertising.* New York: Basic Books, Inc., 1983.

Presbrey, Frank, *The History and Development of Advertising.* Garden City, N.Y.: Doubleday & Company, Inc., 1929.

Sackheim, Maxwell, *My First Sixty Years in Advertising,* Englewood Cliffs, N.J.: Prentice-Hall, Inc., 1970.

Sampson, Henry, *A History of Advertising.* London: Chatto & Windus, 1875.

Turner, Ernest Sackville, *The Shocking History of Advertising.* New York: E. P. Dutton & Co., Inc., 1953.

Wood, James Playsted, *The Story of Advertising.* New York: The Ronald Press Company, 1958.

ECONOMIC, SOCIAL, AND LEGAL ASPECTS

Albion Mark S., and Paul W. Farris, *The Advertising Controversy.* Boston: Auburn House Publishing Company, 1981.

Backman, Jules, *Advertising and Competition.* New York: New York University Press, 1967.

Bartos, Rena, and Theodore F. Dunn, *Advertising and Consumers: New Perspectives.* New York: American Association of Advertising Agencies, 1977.

Berman, Ronald, *Advertising and Social Change.* Beverly Hills, Calif.: Sage Publications, 1981.

Bloom, Paul N., *Advertising, Competition, and Public Policy: A Simulation Study.* Cambridge, Mass.: Ballinger Publishing Company, 1976.

Borden, Neil H., *The Economic Effects of Advertising.* Homewood, Ill.: Richard D. Irwin, 1942.

Brozen, Yale, ed., *Advertising and Society.* New York: New York University Press, 1974.

Comanor, William S., and Thomas A. Wilson, *Advertising and Mass Market Power.* Cambridge, Mass.: Harvard University Press, 1974.

Courtney, Alice, and Thomas Whipple, *Sex Stereotyping in Advertising.* Lexington, Mass.: Lexington Books, 1983.

Cowling, Keith, John Cable, Michael Kelly, and Tony McGuinness, *Advertising and Economic Behaviour.* London: The Macmillan Press Ltd., 1975.

Divita, S. F., ed., *Advertising and the Public Interest.* Chicago: American Marketing Association, 1974.

Ferguson, James M., *Advertising and Competition: Theory, Measurement, Fact.* Cambridge, Mass.: Ballinger Publishing Company, 1974.

Fletcher, Alan D., *Advertising and Society.* Columbus, Ohio: Grid Publishing Inc., 1983.

Francois, William E., *Mass Media Law and Regulation,* 3rd ed. Columbus, Ohio: Grid Publishing Inc., 1982.

Fritschler, A. Lee, *Smoking and Politics,* 2nd ed. Englewood Cliffs, N.J.: Prentice-Hall, Inc., 1975.

Howard, John A., and James Hulbert, *Advertising and the Public Interest.* Chicago: Crain Books, 1977.

Hyman, Allen, and M. Bruce Johnson, eds., *Advertising and Free Speech.* Lexington, Mass.: D.C. Heath and Company, 1977.

Lambin, Jean Jacques, *Advertising, Competition and Market Conduct in Oligopoly over Time.* Amsterdam: North-Holland Publishing Company, 1976.

Nelson, Harold L., and Dwight L. Teeter, Jr., *Law of Mass Communications,* 3rd ed. Mineola, N.Y.: The Foundation Press, Inc., 1978.

Nicosia, Francesco M., *Advertising, Management, and Society.* New York: McGraw-Hill Book Company, 1974.

Ornstein, Stanley I., *Industrial Concentration and Advertising Intensity.* Washington, D.C.: American Enterprise Institute for Public Policy Research, 1977.

Pearce, Michael, Scott M. Cunningham, and Avon Miller, *Appraising the Economic and Social Effects of Advertising.* Cambridge, Mass.: Marketing Science Institute, 1971.

Pember, Don R., *Mass Media Law.* Dubuque, Iowa: Wm. C. Brown Company Publishers, 1977.

Preston, Ivan L., *The Great American Blow-Up.* Madison, Wis.: The University of Wisconsin Press, 1975.

Rosden, George, and Peter Rosden, *The Law of Advertising.* New York: Matthew Bender and Company, 1978.

Schmalensee, Richard, *The Economics of Advertising.* Amsterdam: North-Holland Publishing Company, 1972.

Schrank, Jeffrey, *Deception Detection.* Boston: Beacon Press, 1975.

Simon, Julian L., *Issues in the Economics of Advertising.* Urbana, Ill.: University of Illinois Press, 1970.

Stridsberg, Albert B., *Progress in Effective Advertising Self-Regulation.* New York: International Advertising Association, 1976.

Tuercke, David G., ed., *Issues in Advertising.* Washington, D.C.: American Enterprise Institute, 1978.

——, *The Political Economy of Advertising.* Washington, D.C.: American Enterprise Institute for Public Policy Research, 1978.

Worcester, Dean, A., Jr., *Welfare Gains from Advertising.* Washington, D.C.: American Enterprise Institute for Public Policy Research, 1978.

ADVERTISER AND AGENCY ORGANIZATION

Association of National Advertisers, *Advertising Services: Full Service Agency, a la Carte, or In-House.* New York: Association of National Advertisers, Inc., 1979.

——, *Agency Compensation.* New York: Association of National Advertisers, Inc., 1979.

——, *Current Advertiser Practices in Compensating Their Advertising Agencies.* New York: Association of National Advertisers, Inc., 1976.

——, *Evaluating Agency Performance.* New York: Association of National Advertisers, Inc., 1979.

Brower, Charlie, *Me and Other Advertising Geniuses.* Garden City, N.Y.: Doubleday & Company, Inc., 1974.

Buell, Victor P., *Organizing for Marketing/Advertising Success.* New York: Association of National Advertisers, Inc., 1982.

Buxton, Ed., *Growth Tactics for Advertising Agencies and Communications Firms.* New York: Executive Communication, 1977.

Buxton, Edward, *Promise Them Anything.* New York: Stein & Day, 1972.

Claggett, William M., *Current Advertising Management Practices.* New York: Association of National Advertisers, Inc., 1974.

Daniels, Draper, *Giants, Pigmies, and Other Advertising People.* Chicago: Crain Books, 1974.

Della Femina, Jerry, *From Those Wonderful Folks Who Gave You Pearl Harbor.* New York: Simon & Schuster, 1970.

Gardner, Herbert S., Jr., *The Advertising Agency Business.* Chicago: Crain Books, 1977.

Miller, Donald B., Richard C. Christian, Arthur W. Schultz, and Stuart B. Upson, *Next Generation of Agency Management.* New York: American Association of Advertising Agencies, 1976.

Morgan, Eric A. G., *Choosing and Using Advertising Agencies.* London: Business Books, 1974.

O'Toole, John, *The Trouble with Advertising.* . . . New York: Chelsea House, 1981.

Polykoff, Shirley, *Does She or Doesn't She—And How She Did It.* Garden City, N.Y.: Doubleday & Company, Inc., 1975.

Vaupen, Burton, Robert F. Lyman, and Thomas R. Vohs, *Agency Compensation and Fee Arrangements.* New York: American Association of Advertising Agencies, 1976.

Weilbacher, William M., *Choosing an Advertising Agency.* Chicago: Crain Books, 1983.

MARKETING MANAGEMENT

Ennis, F. Beaven, *Effective Marketing Management.* New York: Association of National Advertisers, Inc., 1973.

Garfunkle, Stanley, *Developing the Advertising Plan.* New York: Random House, 1980.

Hughes, G. David, *Marketing Management.* Reading, Mass.: Addison-Wesley Publishing Company, 1978.

Luck, David J., and Ferrell, O. C., *Marketing Strategy and Plans.* Englewood Cliffs, N.J.: Prentice-Hall, Inc., 1979.

Mandell, Maurice I., and Larry J. Rosenberg, *Marketing,* 2nd ed. Englewood Cliffs, N.J.: Prentice-Hall, Inc., 1981.

Marsteller, William A., *Creative Management.* Chicago: Crain Books, 1981.

Schultz, Don E., *Essentials of Advertising Strategy.* Chicago: Crain Books, 1981.

——, and Dennis G. Martin, *Strategic Advertising Campaigns.* Chicago: Crain Books, 1979.

Simon, Julian L., *The Management of Advertising.* Englewood Cliffs, N.J.: Prentice-Hall, Inc., 1971.

Stapleton, John, *How to Prepare a Marketing Plan.* London: Gower Press, 1971.

MARKETING MIX INGREDIENTS

Cummins, Edward C., *A Management Guide to Cooperative Advertising.* New York: Association of National Advertisers, Inc., 1970.

Dakin, Tony, ed., *Sales Promotion Handbook.* London: Gower Press, 1974.

Diamond, Sidney A., *Trademark Problems and How to Avoid Them.* Chicago: Crain Books, 1974.

Dichter, Ernest, *Packaging: The Sixth Sense?* Boston: Cahners Books, 1975.

Hise, Richard T., *Product/Service Strategy.* New York: Petrocelli/Charter, 1977.

Neubauer, Robert G., *Packaging.* New York: Van Nostrand Reinhold Company, 1973.

Sachs, William S., and George Benson, *Product Planning and Management.* Tulsa, Okla.: PennWell Books, 1981.

Schultz, Don E., and William A. Robinson, *Sales Promotion Essentials.* Chicago: Crain Books, 1982.

Spitz, A. Edward, ed., *Product Planning,* 2nd ed. New York: Petrocelli/Charter, 1977.

Stauff, James A. R., *How to Plan and Develop New Products That Sell.* Chicago: The Dartnell Corporation, 1974.

Stone, Merlin, *Product Planning.* New York: John Wiley & Sons, 1976.

Werkman, Casper J., *Trademarks.* New York: Barnes & Noble, 1974.

Young, Robert F., and Stephen A. Greyser, *Managing Cooperative Advertising.* Lexington, Mass.: Lexington Books, 1983.

BUDGETING

Hurwood, David L., and James K. Brown, *Some Guidelines for Advertising Budgeting*. New York: The Conference Board, 1972.

Kelly, Richard J., *The Advertising Budget*. New York: Association of National Advertisers, Inc., 1967.

McNiven, Malcolm A., *How Much to Spend for Advertising*? New York: Association of National Advertisers, Inc., 1969.

Riso, Ovid, *Advertising Cost Control Handbook*. New York: Van Nostrand Reinhold Company, 1973.

BEHAVIOR, RESEARCH, AND EVALUATION

Assael, Henry, *Consumer Behavior and Marketing Action*. Boston: Kent Publishing Company, 1981.

Barker, Raymond F., *Marketing Research*. Reston, Va.: Reston Publishing Company, Inc., 1983.

Bellenger, Danny N., Kenneth L. Bernhardt, and Jac L. Goldstucker, *Qualitative Research in Marketing*. Chicago: American Marketing Association, 1976.

Block, Carl E., and Kenneth J. Roering, *Essentials of Consumer Behavior*, 2nd ed. Hinsdale, Ill.: The Dryden Press, 1979.

Boyd, Harper W., Jr., Ralph L. Westfall, and Stanley F. Stasch, *Marketing Research*. Homewood, Ill.: Richard D. Irwin, 1977.

Engel, James F., Roger D. Blackwell, and David T. Kollat, *Consumer Behavior*, 3rd ed. New York: Holt, Rinehart and Winston, 1978.

Fletcher, Alan D., and Thomas A. Bowers, *Fundamentals of Advertising Research*, 2nd ed. Columbus, Ohio: Grid Publishing Inc., 1983.

Holbert, Neil, *Advertising Research*. Chicago: American Marketing Association, 1975.

Lovell, Mark, and Jack Potter. *Assessing the Effectiveness of Advertising*. London: Business Books, 1975.

Luck, David J., Hugh G. Wales, Donald A. Taylor, and Ronald S. Rubin, *Marketing Research*, 5th ed. Englewood Cliffs, N.J.: Prentice-Hall, Inc., 1978.

Percy, Larry, and Arch G. Woodside. *Advertising and Consumer Psychology*. Lexington, Mass.: Lexington Books, 1983.

Ramond, Charles, *Advertising Research: The State of the Art*. New York: Association of National Advertisers, Inc., 1976.

Reynolds, Fred D., and William D. Wells, *Consumer Behavior*. New York: McGraw-Hill Book Company, 1977.

Schiffman, Leon G., and Leslie Lazar Kanuk, *Consumer Behavior*. Englewood Cliffs, N.J.: Prentice-Hall, Inc., 1978.

Tolley, B. Stuart, *Advertising & Marketing Research*. Chicago: Nelson-Hall, 1977.

Wells, William D., ed., *Life Style and Psychographics*. Chicago: American Marketing Association, 1974.

Wheatley, John J., ed., *Measuring Advertising Effectiveness*. Homewood, Ill.: Richard D. Irwin, Inc., 1969.

MEDIA

Barban, Arnold M., Stephen Cristol, and Frank J. Kopek, *Essentials of Media Planning*. Chicago: Crain Books, 1976.

Brann, Christian, *Direct Mail and Direct Response Promotion*. London: Kogan Page Ltd., 1971.

Broadbent, Simon, *Spending Advertising Money*, 3d ed. London: Business Books Limited, 1979.

Gensch, Dennis H., *Advertising Planning: Mathematical Models in Advertising Media Planning.* Amsterdam: Elsevier Scientific Publishing Company, 1973.

Harrington, Ken, ed., *Principles and Practices of Classified Advertising.* 3rd ed. Danville, Ill.: Association of Newspaper Classified Advertising Managers, Inc., 1975.

Herpel, George L., and Richard A. Collins, *Specialty Advertising in Marketing.* Homewood, Ill.: Dow Dones—Irwin, Inc., 1972.

Jugenheimer, Donald W., and Peter B. Turk, *Advertising Media.* Columbus, Ohio: Grid Publishing Inc., 1980.

McGann, Anthony F., and J. Thomas Russell, *Advertising Media.* Homewood, Ill.: Richard D. Irwin, Inc., 1981.

Sissors, Jack Z., and E. Reynold Petray, *Advertising Media Planning*, 2nd ed. Chicago: Crain Books, 1982.

Surmanek, Jim, *Media Planning.* Chicago: Crain Books, 1980.

CREATIVITY

Arlen, Michael J., *Thirty Seconds.* New York: Penguin Books, 1981.

Baker, Stephen, *Systematic Approach to Advertising Creativity.* New York: McGraw-Hill Book Company, 1979.

Bellaire, Arthur, *Controlling Your TV Commercial Costs.* Chicago: Crain Books, 1976.

Bockus, William H., Jr., *Advertising Graphics*, 3rd ed. New York: Macmillan Publishing Co., Inc., 1979.

Boddewyn, J.J., and Katherin Marton, *Comparison Advertising.* New York: Hastings House, Publishers, 1978.

Burton, Philip Ward, *Advertising Copywriting*, 5th ed. Columbus, Ohio: Grid Publishing Inc., 1983.

Buxton, Edward, *Creative People at Work.* New York: Executive Communications, Inc., 1975.

Caples, John, *Tested Advertising Methods*, 4th ed. Englewood Cliffs, N.J.: Prentice-Hall, Inc., 1974.

Donahue, Bud, *The Language of Layout*, Englewood Cliffs, N.J.: Prentice-Hall, Inc., 1978.

Hafer, W. Keith, and Gordon E. White, *Advertising Copywriting*, 2nd ed. St. Paul, Minn.: West Publishing Company, 1982.

Heighton, Elizabeth, and Don R. Cunningham, *Advertising in the Broadcast Media.* Belmont, Calif.: Wadsworth Publishing Company, 1976.

International Paper Company, *Pocket Pal*, 12th ed. New York: International Paper Company, 1979.

Jewler, A. Jerome, *Creative Strategy in Advertising.* Belmont, Calif.: Wadsworth Publishing Company, 1981.

Latimer, Henry C., *Preparing Art and Camera Copy for Printing.* New York: McGraw-Hill Book Company, 1977.

Malickson, David L., and John W. Nelson, *Advertising—How to Write The Kind That Works.* New York: Charles Scribner's Sons, 1977.

McMahan, Harry Wayne, *How to Evaluate Your Own TV Commercial.* East Greenwich, R.I.: Weaver Publishing Co., Inc., 1973.

Nelson, Roy Paul, *The Design of Advertising*, 4th ed. Dubuque, Iowa: Wm. C. Brown Company Publishers, 1981.

Paetro, Maxine, *How to Put Your Book Together and Get a Job in Advertising.* New York: Executive Communications, Inc., 1979.

Peck, William A., *Anatomy of Local Radio—TV Copy*, 4th ed. Summit, Penn.: TAB Books, 1976.

Schlemmer, Richard M., *Handbook of Advertising Art Production*, 2nd ed. Englewood Cliffs, N.J.: Prentice-Hall, Inc., 1976.

Teixeira, Antonio, *Music to Sell By: The Craft of Jingle Writing*. Boston: Berklee Press Publications. 1974.

White, Hooper, *How to Produce an Effective TV Commercial*. Chicago: Crain Books, 1981.

OTHER VIEWS

Corey, E. Raymond, ed., *Industrial Marketing*, 2nd ed. Englewood Cliffs, N.J.: Prentice-Hall, Inc., 1976.

Dunn, S. Watson, and E. S. Lorimor, *International Advertising and Marketing*. Columbus, Ohio: Grid Publishing Inc., 1979.

Edwards, Charles M., Jr., and Carl F. Lebowitz, *Retail Advertising and Sales Promotion*, 4th ed. Englewood Cliffs, N.J.: Prentice-Hall, Inc., 1981.

Garbett, Thomas F., *Corporate Advertising*. New York: McGraw-Hill Book Company, 1981.

Haight, William, *Retail Advertising*. Morristown, N.J.: General Learning Press, 1976.

Hart, Norman A., *Industrial Advertising and Publicity*. New York: John Wiley & Sons, 1978.

Roth, Robert F., *Handbook of International Marketing Communications*. Chicago: Crain Books, 1982.

Spitzer, Harry, and Richard F. Schwartz, *Inside Retail Sales Promotion and Advertising*. New York: Harper Row, 1982.

PERIODICALS

The following periodicals include articles on advertising:

Advertising Age	*Journal of Advertising*
Ad Day	*Journal of Advertising Research*
Adweek	*Journal of Marketing*
Broadcasting	*Journal of Marketing Research*
Direct Marketing	*Madison Avenue*
Gallagher Report	*Marketing & Media Decisions*
Incentive Marketing	*Marketing Communications*

SUBJECT AND NAME INDEX

ADVERTISEMENT INDEX